Selected Antitrust Cases

LANDMARK DECISIONS

Selected Antitrust Cases

LANDMARK DECISIONS

IRWIN M. STELZER

President
National Economic Research Associates, Inc.
New York City

with the assistance of

HOWARD P. KITT

Economic Analyst
National Economic Research Associates, Inc.

FOURTH EDITION · 1972

Richard D. Irwin, Inc.   *Homewood, Illinois   60430*
IRWIN-DORSEY INTERNATIONAL   *London, England   WC2H 9NJ*
IRWIN-DORSEY LIMITED   *Georgetown, Ontario   L7G 4B3*

Fourth Edition

First Printing, May 1972
Second Printing, September 1973

Library of Congress Catalog Card No. 70–185439
Printed in the United States of America

To A. S.

PREFACE

The purpose of this book is to provide students of economics, government, and business administration with an opportunity to obtain an understanding of the manner in which economic theory is reflected in antitrust policy. Teachers in these fields are almost uniform in their agreement that there is no substitute for an actual reading of the case materials, in order to facilitate an understanding of the legal and economic issues raised by our antitrust laws, and to provide the student with interesting concrete problems. Students can rarely be required, however, to read lengthy court opinions in addition to a standard text. Consequently, I have compiled a list of the leading decisions in this area and edited them to manageable proportions, taking care, at the same time, to preserve all that is of lasting significance in the opinions. In every instance, the original language of the court has been retained; the deletions made were not permitted to interfere with the smooth flow of thought and language of these judicial opinions. Any footnotes added by the author are initialed.

A word about the selection of cases is, I believe, in order. Only those which represent truly landmark opinions have been included. An attempt has been made to select cases so that the student will have both an understanding of the law as it now stands, and a knowledge of the historical development of the attitude of the courts on the various legal-economic issues.

Although each section of the book is self-contained in the sense that it covers an issue or problem in its entirety, the various chapters are definitely interrelated. Thus, for example, Chapter 1 treats court attitudes toward overwhelming market power, while Chapter 2 deals with the legal and economic issues raised by direct price-fixing agreements. The cases in these portions of the book were also selected so that the student might easily *compare* court attitudes toward price-fixing agreements, on the one hand, and monopoly power on the other.

This book has now been revised three times since its initial appearance over 15 years ago. This current revision was, in a way, the most difficult, since so many new cases had to be added to reflect developments since 1966. Our desire to keep costs at a level which would encourage continued use of this book as a supplementary text had to be balanced against the need to up-date sections and to add new ones. Thirty-two new cases were added, bringing the total number to 71 (as compared with 44 in the previous edition). Entire new sections on reciprocity (Chapter 7) and franchising (Chapter 12) were needed, and the materials relating to the application of antitrust principles to regulated industries (Chapter 13) required considerable expansion.

In addition, greater space has been devoted to dissenting opinions, so that students can better understand the inherent complexities of the economic issues faced by the courts.

Finally, a brief introduction, designed to summarize and integrate the case materials, has been included.

Although final responsibility for selection of materials remains mine, I am indebted to others for their advice. Alfred E. Kahn, Dean of the College of Arts and Sciences at Cornell University, continued his policy of constant availability; without his assistance throughout my professional career I doubt very much whether I would have found the field as rewarding and stimulating as it has been. John Shenefield graciously took time from his antitrust practice at Hunton, Williams, Gay & Gibson to provide detailed suggestions concerning materials to be included. Joel B. Dirlam, of the University of Rhode Island, was, as usual, extremely helpful. Howard P. Kitt, a young economist with our firm, alone edited several cases in this edition and made important contributions to the reorganization of the book. Ms. Deanna Donovan and Ms. Barbara Rochman carefully proofread each selection against the official published decisions—a tedious but (by virtue of this preface) no longer thankless chore.

Any published work by a consulting economist can be prepared only in hours which should properly have been devoted to his family. My wife Agnes' patience and encouragement, in the late hours of the evening and on weekends, ultimately produced this revision.

April 1972   IRWIN M. STELZER

CONTENTS

Introduction   1

PART I
OVERWHELMING MONOPOLY POWER AND DIRECT CONSPIRACY

Chapter 1   Overwhelming Monopoly Power   9
             Standard Oil of New Jersey and the Adoption of the Rule of
             Reason. Application of the Rule in *United States Steel*. *Alcoa*
             and the "New Sherman Act." A Modified Rule of Reason—The
             Shoe Machinery Case. Economic Performance and the Law—
             The *Cellophane* Case. *Grinnell* and the Reaffirmation of *Alcoa*.

Chapter 2   Direct Price-Fixing Agreements   63
             The "Reasonableness" of Price-Fixing Agreements—*Addyston
             Pipe* and *Trenton Potteries*. Market Power, Distress Conditions,
             and the Law—*Appalachian Coals* and *Socony-Vacuum*. Price-
             Fixing and the Exchange of Information—*Container Corporation
             of America*.

PART II
INDIRECT CONSPIRACIES AND OLIGOPOLY

Chapter 3   Trade Association Activities   87
             The *Cement* Case—the Multiple Basing Point System as an Un-
             fair Method of Competition. Permissible Activities—*Tag Manu-
             facturers*. *Automobile Manufacturers*—Benefits of Joint R&D vs.
             Maintenance of Competition.

Chapter 4   Oligopoly   103
             Rational Oligopoly Behavior and the Sherman Act—*American
             Tobacco*. Conscious Parallelism Defined—*Triangle Conduit*.
             Conscious Parallelism Distinguished—*Theatre Enterprises*. Con-
             scious Parallelism and Conspiracy Re-examined—*Chas. Pfizer*.

PART III
MERGERS AND THE PROBLEMS THEY POSE

Chapter 5   Mergers and Market Power   127
             Thatcher Manufacturing Company and the Emasculation of
             Section 7 of the Clayton Act. Revival of Antimerger Policy—

11595

Brown Shoe and the Amended Clayton Act; *Continental Can* and the Sharpening of Economic Tools. *Von's Grocery* and the Doctrine of Incipiency.

Chapter 6   Mergers and Product Extension   168

Deep Pockets and Potential Competition—*Procter and Gamble*. *Bendix* and the Toehold Acquisition.

Chapter 7   Mergers and Reciprocity   193

The Issue Defined—*Consolidated Foods*. A Per Se Approach to Reciprocity Potential—*Allis-Chalmers*. The *ITT-Grinnell* Case —Towards a Rule of Reason. *Ling-Temco-Vought* and the Prevention of Reciprocity.

Chapter 8   Joint Ventures—A Form of Merger   226

The Issue of Equal Access—*Terminal Railroad*. Joint Ventures and Potential Competition—*Penn-Olin*.

PART IV
TRADE PRACTICES

Chapter 9   Price Discrimination   247

Quantity Discounts and the Reasonable Possibility of Competitive Injury—*Morton Salt*. Price Discrimination in Good Faith —*Standard of Indiana* and *Standard of Indiana* Revisited. *Borden* and the Issue of "Like Grade and Quality." *Utah Pie* and Predatory Competition.

Chapter 10   Tying Devices   276

American Can and the Use of Monopoly "Leverage." Tied Sales in the Presence of "Sufficient" but Not Monopolistic Economic Power—*Northern Pacific* and *Fortner*. The "New Business" Justification—*Jerrold*. *Loew's* and Block Booking.

Chapter 11   Exclusive Dealing Arrangements   318

Standard Fashion—Exclusive Dealing and the Incipiency of the Threat to Competition. *Standard Stations* and the Substantiality of the Commerce Affected. The Permissible Area of Exclusive Dealing—*Tampa Electric*.

Chapter 12   Other Customer Restrictions   332

Carvel and the Rights of the Franchisor. Customer Resale Restrictions: *General Motors* and the Issue of Conspiracy; *Schwinn* and the Doctrine of Alienation; *Tripoli* and the Question of Overriding Public Interest. Franchising and the Suppression of Competition—*Chicken Delight*.

PART V
ANTITRUST AND REGULATION

Chapter 13   Does Regulation Make a Difference?   369

Application of Antitrust in the Presence of Regulation—*Parker* and *Seaboard*. Clayton Act Principles Applied to Prevent Mergers Approved by Regulatory Agencies in Banking—*Philadelphia National Bank*; and in Natural Gas Pipelines—*El Paso*. *Thill Securities*—Statutory Self-Regulation and Antitrust Policy.

PART VI
LEGAL MONOPOLIES AND ANTITRUST

Chapter 14   Patents—The Right and Its Limits   405

General Electric and the Rights of the Patent Licensor. Patent Pools, Cross Licensing and the Problem of Adequate Remedy—*Hartford-Empire*. Tied Sales and the Patent Right—*International Salt*. *Lear* and the Rights of the Patent Licensee.

Index of Cases   423

INTRODUCTION

Perhaps the most interesting single conclusion which a reading of these cases permits is that the approaches followed by the courts and commissions over the past 80 years have generally reflected the state of contemporary economic theory. Thus, where economic theory has spoken out strongly and consistently, the courts have appeared to do likewise; alternatively, where economists have been more hesitant about passing judgment upon a particular structural or behavioral form, the courts have followed a less certain path.

The cases selected for inclusion in this edition are particularly illustrative of these developments. They contrast, for example, the purposefulness with which the courts have attacked direct price-fixing, a practice without defenders in the economic profession, with the relative ambivalence displayed toward the relationship of antitrust to government regulatory policy. Accordingly, a brief description of the organization of the parts and chapters of this new edition may help to bring this out more clearly.

Parts I and II, and the four chapters they contain, are closely related. Part I incorporates cases in which the fundamental issues might be described as *relatively* simple. Chapter 1 presents cases in which the issue of overwhelming monopoly power was considered. The "reasonableness" of such power, and the methods by which it was obtained, has to be considered. But we have in Chapter 1 cases in which the defendant possessed not just some market power, but an overwhelming power—and did not have that power thrust upon it: the 90 percent market share of Standard Oil, obtained by a series of clearly unfair practices; Alcoa's 90 percent share of the ingot market, of which it was not a "passive beneficiary" and which it retained by methods the Court held to be exclusionary in character; United Shoe's 85 percent of its market, retained not solely by efficiency, but by erecting "barriers to competition." So the courts, after solving the question of how to define the market, found power which economists would certainly label as "monopoly," and behavior which could not be rationalized as mere business response to such underlying economic forces as scale economies. The finding of illegality would certainly find parallel support in economic theory. Monopoly, so obtained, can have only undesirable effects.

1

Chapter 2 deals with direct price-fixing conspiracies, held (with the exception of *Appalachian Coals*) to be undesirable by economists and unlawful by the courts. There is, after all, little to be said in favor of such conspiracies—so the fact question becomes one of finding whether or not they indeed existed. Even in this area, however, matters often are not as simple as they at first seem. In the *Container Corporation* case, newly included, the Court's majority found that the exchange of price information among competitors had a "chilling" effect on the vigor of price competition, while two dissenters found that the exchange of price information led to more "complete market knowledge" and "was actually employed for the purpose of engaging in active price competition."

Part II contains somewhat more complex versions of the problems addressed in Part I. Chapter 3 deals with price-fixing which may result from, be associated with, or be masked by otherwise desirable activities. Here we have instances in which the courts had to decide whether compilation and dissemination of price statistics by a trade association had the same effect as the direct conspiracies dealt with in Chapter 2—not quite as simple a chore as detecting direct price-fixing conspiracies and dealing with them.

Chapter 4 deals with instances in which something short of the overwhelming market power discussed in Chapter 1 was found to exist. Here we have instances of oligopoly—a handful of sellers whose individual market shares are not overwhelming, but who in total account for such a dominant share. The problem of dealing with these situations—of determining, for example, when advertising stops being a legitimate business expense and becomes a warning to potential entrants that their capital requirements may escalate suddenly—is, as the cases reveal, a difficult one. Jurists again find themselves in a situation similar to that of economists—they can effectively and relatively easily decide monopoly cases, but find oligopoly situations less susceptible to generalization.

Part III includes, in its Chapters 5 through 8, cases in which mergers and the problems associated with them have been considered. The most familiar of these is the competitive impact of the merger—is there a probability (possibility? certainty?) that the effect of the acquisition, in the words of amended Section 7 of the Clayton Act, "may be substantially to lessen competition, or to tend to create a monopoly in any line of commerce in any section of the country." The cases included in Chapter 5 show how difficult a question this often is; how necessary to its resolution is a wealth of information about the economic and business facts of the industry being studied; and how reasonable men can differently interpret masses of economic data (see, in this connection, the dissent in *Von's*).

Chapter 6 covers cases in which the mergers involved no addition to a firm's share of the market for a product. Rather, they deal with attempts by firms with leading positions in some product market(s) to acquire producers of still other products. Almost by definition, then, these cases do not involve increases in market concentration as conventionally defined. But fear persists that they may nevertheless result in a substantial lessening of competition. The cases presented in this chapter deal with the questions of whether (1) entry-via-merger might not be a substitute for *de novo* entry, and hence diminish otherwise attainable levels of competition; (2) entry of financially powerful firms might not create greater barriers to entry by independents; and (3) whether such powerful newcomers might not give the acquired firm an undue competitive "edge" over its rivals.

Chapter 7 deals with the much discussed and misunderstood question of reciprocity as it is raised in merger situations. It is important to note that we are not here concerned with the casual and obviously unpreventable practice of doing business with "friends." Reciprocity of the sort considered in these cases involves systematic record keeping by the sales department, transmission of those records to the purchasing department, and firm executive pronouncements to assure that good customers are given preference by purchasing agents. In large companies implementation of a program of reciprocity often involves establishing an entire division to gather data and see that the policy is implemented. A reading of the *LTV* decree provides some understanding of the apparatus required to maintain a reciprocity program, and the nonquixotic nature of the campaign to eliminate it.

It is perhaps worth pointing out that Chapter 7 best exemplifies the problem confronted by anyone attempting to place complex antitrust issues into neat categories. The *ITT* case, included in this chapter because of its extended analysis of the conditions which are required if the threat of reciprocity is to be raised above a remote possibility, also contains a valuable discussion of the "superconcentration" issue. The government, concerned that assets are becoming increasingly concentrated in the hands of a few conglomerates, and unable to show substantial lessening of competition in any specific line of commerce, sought to have the merger stricken down because of the effect it and others like it might have on the overall level of concentration of economic power. This, Judge Timbers refused to do.

Chapter 8 deals with a form of merger—joint ventures. In addition to typical questions in merger cases, these raise the further questions of: (1) who shall be permitted to participate in the joint venture—the reasonableness of the standards of admission to the group; and (2) the terms on which nonmembers shall be granted access to the facilities of the joint ventures. Again, the necessary categorization of cases in this book should not be permitted to obscure the relationship between the access issue raised in *Terminal Railroad* and that raised in connection with the New York Stock Exchange in a series of cases including *Thill* (see Chapter 13).

In Part IV (Chapters 9 through 12) we deal with the problems posed by particular trade practices. Many of these are covered by specific sections of the Clayton Act; as such, they have been found to run afoul of its proscriptions whenever the courts have found that ". . . the effect . . . may be to substantially lessen competition. . . ."

Chapter 9 covers the area of price discrimination. The Robinson-Patman amendment to Section 2 of the Clayton Act has long been a favorite target for economists and lawyers who believe that the effect of the act has been to impede rather than promote competition. Indeed, it has been said by many that the courts have too often equated injury to competitors with injury to competition. We have therefore selected cases which present a broad view of the economic issues involved, in order to demonstrate the complexity of dealing with a subject for which the underlying economic theory is by no means well settled.

Chapter 10 is concerned with tying devices, where sales of one product are conditioned upon the sale of another or others. Economists long have recognized that for the most part tying contracts serve hardly any purpose other than the suppression of competition; that they involve the use of economic power in one market to achieve dominance in other markets; and that where the interests of both the buyer and the seller are truly in accord (as has been argued in several cases), the same result generally could be achieved with a less restrictive alternative.

Reflecting the overall soundness of this view, the courts have moved vigorously against tying devices; indeed, there are many who argue that such devices have become illegal per se, whenever the courts find that a "not insubstantial" amount of commerce is involved (see the *Fortner* case, for example). Only where the courts have determined that less restrictive measures were in fact not economically feasible have they displayed a measure of flexibility. As stated in the *Jerrold* case, ". . . [W]hile the *per se* rule should be followed in almost all cases, the court must always be conscious of the fact that a case might arise in which the facts indicate that an injustice would be done by blindly accepting the *per se* rule."

Exclusive dealing, the subject of Chapter 11, is in principle treated under Section 3 of the Clayton Act, the same section used in the adjudication of tying devices. This is not inappropriate, since both practices involve the attachment of terms and conditions to the purchase of a given product. In contrast to their approach to tying devices, however, the courts have adopted a much more flexible position toward exclusive dealing arrangements, in response to the theory that while the former seldom have any purpose other than the suppression of competition, the latter may often possess some redeeming virtue. This is amply demonstrated in the cases included in this chapter, particularly the *Tampa Electric* decision.

In Chapter 12, we treat issues in relation to which, at the present time, much of the law has yet to be written. Included herein are cases involving the delineation of the restrictions upon producers in controlling the distribution of their products (the *General Motors, Schwinn,* and *Tripoli* cases providing examples of the problems faced in this area), and the *Carvel* and *Chicken Delight* decisions, which come to grips with the questions posed by the practice of franchising. In each case the courts have faced two distinct issues. First, there is the task of balancing the rights of the seller (franchiser) with those of the buyer (franchisee). This is essentially a problem of equity. Second, there are the economic problems, which involve the reconciliation of potentially divergent goals. On the one hand, excessive circumscription of the freedom of the seller (franchiser) may frustrate the encouragement of innovation in the fields of marketing and distribution, which in the past has often increased the vigor of competition. On the other hand, restrictions upon the rights of customers (franchisees) to deal with (say) suppliers of their own choosing may foreclose important markets to the affected suppliers and heighten significantly the barriers facing potential entrants. Because of these conflicting considerations, the courts have thus far shied away from the imposition of per se rules.

In Part V we examine some of the problems arising from efforts to reconcile the conflicting means used by antitrust enforcement agencies and by regulators to reach the common objective of efficient resource allocation. Antitrust policy rests on the assumption that free competition will promote optimal economic performance. In regulated industries, due to the existence of special structural characteristics, government supervision has replaced competition as a regulator of economic activity. Nowhere is the pervasiveness of regulation more apparent than in the electric utility industry, where the assumption of natural monopoly has led to the development of state and federal commission regulation and the delineation of exclusive service areas.

Recently, emphasis has been placed on the desirability of expanding the role of competition within the regulated industries. Underlying this development is the feeling that regulation often doesn't work, that "shortly following the establishment of administrative procedures the regulatory agency usually becomes dominated by the industry which it was created to regulate." (See the *Thill* case.) On the other hand, there is an apparent disinclination to permit antitrust considerations to override *effective* regulation (see *Parker* v. *Brown*).

The final section of the book, Part VI (Chapters 14 and 15), presents a series of cases which involve the application of the antitrust laws to legal monopolies that result from the issuance of patents. As in Part V, we find in this area a developing tendency to favor competition; this in turn has resulted in a steady erosion of the rights and privileges accorded patent and/or copyright holders. (See especially the *Hartford-Empire* and *Lear* decisions.) As in many of the aforementioned areas, the policy has both its defenders and detractors. According to the latter, abrogation of the protections afforded to patent holders will seriously impair the incentives to invent and innovate; this in turn must necessarily result in a reduced rate of technological progressiveness. In the view of those who favor the present policy, the purpose is simply to strike a more equitable balance between the rights of the individual creator and the public interest, which heretofore has been much too heavily weighted in the direction of the former.

PART I

Overwhelming Monopoly Power
and Direct Conspiracy

OVERWHELMING
MONOPOLY POWER

Since the enactment of the antitrust laws, enforcement officials and the courts have traditionally been called upon to apply them to two types of combines—the so-called close-knit combinations, formed by trust, holding company, merger or consolidation, and the loose-knit confederation to be discussed in Chapter 2. The cases presented below trace the development of court attitudes from the adoption of the "rule of reason" in the *Standard Oil* decision of 1911. This doctrine, which required the courts to examine the circumstances surrounding the formation of a combination as well as the pattern of its business behavior in an attempt to discover an intent to monopolize, gave rise to the corollary statement in the *United States Steel* case that the law does not make mere size an offense. Critics of the rule of reason professed to see the emergence of a "New Sherman Act" from the *Alcoa* case, and received further encouragement from the *American Tobacco* decision. (See Chapter 4.) Whether these decisions did in fact mark the gutting of the rule of reason, or merely its intelligent application, it is generally agreed that these two cases greatly increased the effectiveness of antitrust policy. The *Shoe Machinery* case represents an attempt to apply a rule of reason modified to account for the *Alcoa* decision. The *Cellophane* case represents an attempt by the judiciary to wrestle with the economist's concept of workable or effective competition as it relates to antitrust problems. Finally, the *Grinnell* case represents a reaffirmation of the holding of *Alcoa*—that overwhelming monopoly power, consciously acquired, necessarily runs afoul of the Sherman Act.

Standard Oil Company of New Jersey v. *United States*

221 U.S. 1 (1911)

Note: Mr. Chief Justice White delivered the opinion of the Court, the legal reasoning of which is abstracted below. The findings of fact, too lengthy to be set forth in detail here, were essentially as follows: Standard of Ohio, organized by John D. and William Rockefeller in 1870, had by

1872 acquired all but 3 or 4 of the 35 to 45 refineries in Cleveland. By obtaining preferential rates and large rebates from the railroads the combination was able to force competitors to join it or be driven out of business. As a result, the combine obtained control of 90 percent of the petroleum industry, a dominance which enabled it to fix the price of both crude and refined petroleum. In 1899 Standard Oil of New Jersey was established as a holding company to replace the Ohio trust. The new organization continued to obtain preferential treatment from railroads, engaged in several unfair practices against competing pipelines so as to obtain control of that means of transportation as well, engaged in local price cutting to suppress competition, set up bogus independents, engaged in industrial espionage, and earned enormous profits. The Court continued:

. . . The text of the [Sherman A]ct and its meaning.

. . . The debates . . . conclusively show . . . that the main cause which led to the legislation was the thought that it was required by the economic condition of the times; that is, the vast accumulation of wealth in the hands of corporations and individuals, the enormous development of corporate organization, the facility for combination which such organizations afforded, the fact that the facility was being used, and that combinations known as trusts were being multiplied, and the widespread impression that their power had been and would be exerted to oppress individuals and injure the public generally. . . .

There can be no doubt that the sole subject with which the first section deals is restraint of trade as therein contemplated, and that the attempt to monopolize and monopolization is the subject with which the second section is concerned. It is certain that those terms, at least in their rudimentary meaning, took their origin in the common law, and were also familiar in the law of this country prior to and at the time of the adoption of the act in question.

We shall endeavor then, first to seek their meaning . . . by making a very brief reference to the elementary and indisputable conceptions of both the English and American law on the subject prior to the passage of the Anti-trust Act. . . .

Without going into detail, and but very briefly surveying the whole field, it may be with accuracy said that the dread of enhancement of prices and of other wrongs which it was thought would flow from the undue limitation on competitive conditions caused by contracts or other acts of individuals or corporations, led, as a matter of public policy, to the prohibition or treating as illegal all contracts or acts which were unreasonably restrictive of competitive conditions, either from the nature or character of the contract or act or where the surrounding circumstances were such as to justify the conclusion that they had not been entered into or performed with the legitimate purpose of reasonably forwarding personal interest and developing trade, but on the contrary were of such a character as to give rise to the inference or presumption that they had been entered into or done with the intent to do wrong to the general public and to limit the right of individuals, thus restraining the free flow of commerce and tending to bring about the evils, such as enhancement of prices, which were considered to be against public policy. It is equally true to say that the survey of the legislation in this country on this subject from the beginning will show, depending as it did, upon the economic conceptions which obtained at the time when the legislation was adopted or judicial decision was rendered, that contracts or acts were at one time deemed to be of such a character as to justify the inference of wrongful intent which were at another period thought not to be of that character. But this again, as we have seen, simply followed the line of development of the law of England.

Let us consider the language of the 1st and 2d sections, guided by the principle that where words are employed in a statute which had at the time a well-known meaning at common law or in the law of this country, they are presumed to have been used in that sense unless the context compels to the contrary.

As to the 1st section. . . . [A]s the contracts or acts embraced in the provision were not expressly defined, since the enumeration addressed itself simply to classes of acts, those classes being broad enough to embrace every conceivable contract or combination which could be made concerning trade or commerce or the subjects of such commerce, and thus caused any act done by any of the enumerated methods anywhere in the whole field of human activity to be illegal if in restraint of trade, it inevitably follows that the provision necessarily called for the exercise of judgment which required that some standard should be resorted to for the purpose of determining whether the prohibitions contained in the statute had or had not in any given case been violated. Thus not specifying but indubitably contemplating and requiring a standard, it follows that it was intended that the standard of reason which had been applied at the common law in this country in dealing with subjects of the character embraced by the statute, was intended to be the measure used for the purpose of determining whether in a given case a particular act had or had not brought about the wrong against which the statute provided.

And a consideration of the text of the 2d section serves to establish that it was intended to supplement the 1st, and to make sure that by no possible guise could the public policy embodied in the 1st section be frustrated or evaded. . . .

. . . In other words, having by the 1st section forbidden all means of monopolizing trade, that is, unduly restraining it by means of every contract, combination, etc., the 2d section seeks, if possible, to make the prohibitions of the act all the more complete and perfect by embracing all attempts to reach the end prohibited by the 1st section, that is, restraints of trade, by any attempt to monopolize, or monopolization thereof, even although the acts by which such results are attempted to be brought about or are brought about be not embraced within the general enumeration of the 1st section. And, of course, when the 2d section is thus harmonized with and made as it was intended to be the complement of the 1st, it becomes obvious that the criteria to be resorted to in any given case for the purpose of ascertaining whether violations of the section have been committed, is the rule of reason guided by the established law and by the plain duty to enforce the prohibitions of the act, and thus the public policy which its restrictions were obviously enacted to subserve. And it is worthy of observation, as we have previously remarked concerning the common law, that although the statute, by the comprehensiveness of the enumerations embodied in both the 1st and 2d sections, makes it certain that its purpose was to prevent undue restraints of every kind or nature, nevertheless by the omission of any direct prohibition against monopoly in the concrete it indicates a consciousness that the freedom of the individual right to contract when not unduly or improperly exercised was the most efficient means for the prevention of monopoly, since the operation of the centrifugal and centripetal forces resulting from the right to freely contract was the means by which monopoly would be inevitably prevented if no extraneous or sovereign power imposed it and no right to make unlawful contracts having a monopolistic tendency were permitted. In other words that freedom to contract was the essence of freedom from undue restraint on the right to contract. . . .

. . . The contentions of the parties as to the meaning of the statute and the decisions of this court relied upon concerning those contentions.

In substance, the propositions urged by the Government are reducible to this: That the language of the statute embraces every contract, combination, etc., in restraint of trade, and hence its text leaves no room for the exercise of judgment, but simply imposes the plain duty of applying its prohibitions to every case within its literal language. The error involved lies in assuming the matter to be decided. This is true because as the acts which may come under the classes stated in the 1st section and the restraint of trade to which that section applies are not specifically enumerated or defined, it is obvious that judgment must in every case be called into play in order to determine whether a particular act is embraced within the statutory classes, and whether if the act is within such classes its nature or effect causes it to be a restraint of trade within the intendment of the act. To hold to the contrary would require the conclusion either that every contract, act, or combination of any kind or nature, whether it operated a restraint on trade or not, was within the statute, and thus the statute would be destructive of all right to contract or agree or combine in any respect whatever as to subjects embraced in interstate trade or commerce, or if this conclusion were not reached, then the contention would require it to be held that as the statute did not define the things to which it related and excluded resort to the only means by which the acts to which it relates could be ascertained—the light of reason—the enforcement of the statute was impossible because of its uncertainty. The merely generic enumeration which the statute makes of the acts to which it refers and the absence of any definition of restraint of trade as used in the statute leaves room for but one conclusion, which is, that it was expressly designed not to unduly limit the application of the act by precise definition, but while clearly fixing a standard, that is, by defining the ulterior boundaries which could not be transgressed with impunity, to leave it to be determined by the light of reason, guided by the principles of law and the duty to apply and enforce the public policy embodied in the statute, in every given case whether any particular act or contract was within the contemplation of the statute.

But, it is said, persuasive as these views may be, they may not be here applied, because the previous decisions of this court have given to the statute a meaning which expressly excludes the construction which must result from the reasoning stated. The cases are *United States* v. [*Trans-Missouri*] *Freight Association* . . . and *United States* v. *Joint Traffic Association.* . . . Both the cases involved the legality of combinations or associations of railroads engaged in interstate commerce for the purpose of controlling the conduct of the parties to the association or combination in many particulars. The association or combination was assailed in each case as being in violation of the statute. It was held that they were. It is undoubted that in the opinion in each case general language was made use of, which, when separated from its context, would justify the conclusion that it was decided that reason could not be resorted to for the purpose of determining whether the acts complained of were within the statute. It is, however, also true that the nature and character of the contract or agreement in each case was fully referred to and suggestions as to their unreasonableness pointed out in order to indicate that they were within the prohibitions of the statute. As the cases cannot by any possible conception be treated as authoritative without the certitude that reason was resorted to for the purpose of deciding them, it follows as a matter of course that it must have been held by the light of reason, since the conclusion could not have been otherwise reached, that the assailed contracts or agreements were within the general enumeration of the statute, and that their operation and effect brought about the restraint of trade which the statute prohibited. This being inevitable, the deduction can in reason only be this: That in the cases relied upon it having been found that the acts complained of were within the statute and operated to produce the injuries which the statute forbade, that resort to reason was not permissible in order to allow that to be done which the statute prohibited. This being true, the rulings in the case relied upon when rightly appreciated were therefore this and nothing more: That as considering the contracts or agreements, their necessary effect and the character of the parties by whom they were made, they were clearly restraints of trade within the purview of the statute, they could not be taken out of that category by indulging in general reasoning as to the expediency or non-expediency of having made the contracts or the wisdom or want of wisdom of the statute which prohibited their being made. That is to say, the cases but decided that the nature and character of the contracts, creating as they did, a conclusive presumption which brought them within the statute, such result was not to be disregarded by the substitution of a judicial appreciation of what the law ought to be for the plain judicial duty of enforcing the law as it was made.

But aside from reasoning it is true to say that the cases relied upon do not when rightly construed sustain the doctrine contended for, is established by all of the numerous decisions of this court which have applied and enforced the Anti-trust Act, since they all in the very nature of things, rest upon the premise that reason was the guide by which the provisions of the act were in every case interpreted. . . .

And in order not in the slightest degree to be wanting in frankness, we say that in so far, however, as by separating the general language used in the opinions in the *Freight Association* and *Joint Traffic cases* from the context and the subject and parties with which the cases were concerned, it may be conceived that the language referred to conflicts with the construction which we give the statute, they are necessarily now limited and qualified. . . .

. . . *The facts and the application of the statute to them.*

. . . Giving to the facts . . . the weight which it was deemed they were entitled to, in the light afforded by the proof of other cognate facts and circumstances, the court below held that the acts and dealings established by the proof operated to destroy the "potentiality of competition" which otherwise would have existed to such an extent as to cause the transfers of stock which were made to the New Jersey corporation and the control which resulted over the many and various subsidiary corporations to be a combination or conspiracy in restraint of trade in violation of the 1st section of the act, but also to be an attempt to monopolize and a monopolization bringing about a perennial violation of the 2d section.

We see no cause to doubt the correctness of these conclusions . . .

a. Because the unification of power and control over petroleum and its products which was the inevitable result of the combining in the New Jersey corporation by the increase of its stock and the transfer to it of the stocks of so many other corporations, aggregating so vast a capital, gives rise, in and of itself, in the absence of countervailing circumstances, to say the least, to the *prima facie* presumption of intent and purpose to maintain the dominancy over the oil industry, not as a result of normal methods of industrial development, but by new means of combination which were resorted to in order that greater power might be added than would otherwise have arisen had normal methods been followed, the whole with the purpose of excluding others from the trade and thus centralizing in the combination a perpetual control of the movements of petroleum and its products in the channels of interstate commerce.

b. Because the *prima facie* presumption of intent to restrain trade, to monopolize and to bring about monopolization . . . is made conclusive by considering, *1*, the conduct of the persons . . . instrumental in bringing about the extension of power . . . ; , 2, . . . the proof as to what was done under those [trust] agreements . . . as well as by weighing the modes in which the power vested . . . has been exerted and the results which have arisen from it.

. . . [W]e think no disinterested mind can survey the period in question without being irresistibly driven to the conclusion that the very genius for commercial development and organization which it would seem was manifested from the beginning soon begot an intent and purpose to exclude others which was frequently manifested by acts and dealings wholly inconsistent with the theory that they were made with the single conception of advancing the development of business power by usual methods, but which on the contrary necessarily involved the intent to drive others from the field and to exclude them from their right to trade and thus accomplish the mastery which was the end in view. . . . The exercise of the power which resulted from that organization fortifies the foregoing conclusions, since the development which came, the acquisition here and there which ensued of every efficient means by which competition could have been asserted, the slow but resistless methods which followed by which means of transportation were absorbed and brought under control, the system of marketing which was adopted by which the country was divided into districts and the trade in each district in oil was turned over to a designated corporation within the combination and all others were excluded, all lead the mind up to a conviction of a purpose and intent which we think is so certain as practically to cause the subject not to be within the domain of reasonable contention. . . .

. . . *The remedy to be administered.*

It may be conceded that ordinarily where it was found that acts had been done in violation of the statute, adequate measure of relief would result from restraining the doing of such acts in the future. . . . But in a case like this, where the condition which has been brought about in violation of the statute, in and of itself, is not only a continued attempt to monopolize, but also a monopolization, the duty to enforce the statute requires the application of broader and more controlling remedies. . . .

In applying remedies for this purpose, however, the fact must not be overlooked that injury to the public by the prevention of an undue restraint on, or the monopolization of trade or commerce is the foundation upon which the prohibitions of the statute rest, and moreover that one of the fundamental purposes of the statute is to protect, not to destroy, rights of property. . . .

So far as the decree held that the ownership of the stock of the New Jersey corporation constituted a combination in violation of the 1st section and an attempt to create a monopoly or to monopolize under the 2d section and commanded the dissolution of the combination, the decree was clearly appropriate. . . .

Our conclusion is that the decree below was right and should be affirmed, except as to the minor matters concerning which we have indicated the decree should be modified. Our order will therefore be one of affirmance with directions, however, to modify the decree in accordance with this opinion. The court below to retain jurisdiction to the extent necessary to compel compliance in every respect with its decree.

And it is so ordered.

[Mr. Justice Harlan concurred in part and dissented in part.]

United States v. United States Steel Corporation

251 U.S. 417 (1920)

Mr. Justice McKenna delivered the opinion of the Court.

Suit against the Steel Corporation and certain other companies which it directs and controls by reason of the ownership of their stock, it and they being separately and collectively charged as violators of the Sherman Anti-trust Act.

It is prayed that it and they be dissolved because engaged in illegal restraint of trade and the exercise of monopoly.

Special charges of illegality and monopoly are made and special redresses and remedies are prayed, among others, that there be a prohibition of stock ownership and exercise of rights under such ownership, and that there shall be such orders and distribution of the stock and other properties as shall be in accordance with equity and good conscience and "shall effectuate the purpose of the Anti-trust Act." General relief is also prayed.

The Steel Corporation is a holding company only; the other companies are the operating ones, manufacturers in the iron and steel industry, 12 in number. There are, besides, other corporations and individuals more or less connected with the activities of the other defendants, that are alleged to be instruments or accomplices in their activities and offendings; and that these activities and offendings (speaking in general terms) extend from 1901 to 1911, when the bill was filed. . . .

The case was heard in the District Court by four judges. They agreed that the bill should be dismissed; they disagreed as to the reasons for it. . . . One opinion (written by Judge Buffington and concurred in by Judge McPherson) expressed the view that the Steel Corporation was not formed with the intention or purpose to monopolize or restrain trade, and did not have the motive or effect "to prejudice the public interest by unduly restricting competition or unduly obstructing the course of trade." The corporation, in the view of the opinion, was an evolution, a natural consummation of the tendencies of the industry on account of changing conditions. . . . And the concentration of powers (we are still representing the opinion) was only such as was deemed necessary, and immediately manifested itself in improved methods and products and in an increase of domestic and foreign trade. . . .

Not monopoly, therefore, was the purpose of the organization of the corporation but concentration of efforts with resultant economies and benefits. . . .

All considerations deemed pertinent were expressed and their influence was attempted to be assigned and, while conceding that the Steel Corporation after its formation in times of financial disturbance, entered into informal agreements or understandings with its competitors to maintain prices, they terminated with their occasions, and, as they had ceased to exist, the court was not justified in dissolving the corporation.

The other opinion (by Judge Woolley and concurred in by Judge Hunt . . .) was in some particulars, in antithesis to Judge Buffington's. The view was expressed that neither the Steel Corporation nor the preceding combinations, which were in a sense its antetypes, had the justification of industrial conditions, nor were they or it impelled by the necessity for integration, or compelled to unite in comprehensive enterprise because such had become a condition of success under the new order of things. On the contrary, that the organizers of the corporation and the preceding companies had illegal purpose from the very beginning, and the corporation became "a combination of combinations, by which, directly or indirectly, approximately 180 independent concerns were brought under one business control," which, measured by the amount of production, extended to 80 percent or 90 percent of the entire output of the country, and that its purpose was to secure great profits which were thought possible in the light of the history of its constituent combinations, and to accomplish permanently what those combinations had demonstrated could be accomplished temporarily, and thereby monopolize and restrain trade.

The organizers, however (we are still representing the opinion), underestimated the opposing conditions and at the very beginning the Corporation instead of relying upon its own power sought and obtained the assistance and the cooperation of its competitors (the independent companies). In other words, the view was expressed that the testimony did "not show that the corporation in and of itself ever possessed or exerted sufficient power when acting alone to control prices of the products of the industry." Its power was efficient only when in cooperation with its competitors, and hence it concerted with them in the expedients of pools, associations, trade meetings, and finally in a system of dinners inaugurated in 1907 by the president of the company, E. H. Gary, and called "the Gary Dinners."

The dinners were congregations of producers and "were nothing but trade meetings," successors of the other means of associated action and control through such action. They were instituted first in "stress of panic," but, their potency being demonstrated, they were afterwards called to control prices "in periods of industrial calm." "They were pools without penalties" and more efficient in stabilizing prices. But it was the further declaration that "when joint action was either refused or withdrawn the Corporation's prices were controlled by competition."

The Corporation, it was said, did not at any time abuse the power or ascendency it possessed. It resorted to none of the brutalities or tyrannies that the cases illustrate of other combinations. . . . It combined its power with that of its competitors. It did not have power in and of itself, and the control it exerted was only in and by association with its competitors. Its offense, therefore, such as it was, was not different from theirs and was distinguished from theirs "only in the leadership it assumed in promulgating and perfecting the policy." This leadership it gave up and it had ceased to offend against the law before this suit was brought. It was hence concluded that it should be distinguished from its organizers and that their intent and unsuccessful attempt should not be attributed to it, that it "in and of itself is not now and has never been a monopoly or a combination in restraint of trade," and a decree of dissolution should not be entered against it.

This summary of the opinions . . . indicates that the evidence admits of different deductions as to the genesis of the Corporation and the purpose of its organizers, but only of a single deduction as to the power it attained and could exercise. Both opinions were clear and confident that the power of the Corporation never did and does not now reach to monopoly, and their review of the evidence, and our independent examination of it, enables us to elect between their respective estimates of it, and we concur in the main with that of Judges Woolley and Hunt. And we add no comment except, it may be, that they underestimated the influence of the tendency and movement to integration, the appreciation of the necessity or value of the continuity of manufacture from the ore to the finished product. . . .

. . . In other words, our consideration should be of not what the Corporation had power to do or did, but what it has now power to do and is doing, and what judgment shall be now pronounced—whether its dissolution, as the Government prays, or the dismissal of the suit, as the Corporation insists?

The alternatives are perplexing—involve conflicting considerations, which, regarded in isolation, have diverse tendencies. . . . Monopoly . . . was not achieved, and competitors had to be persuaded by pools, associations, trade meetings, and through the social form of dinners, all of them, it may be, violations of the law, but transient in their purpose and effect. They were scattered through the years from 1901 (the year of the formation of the Corporation), until 1911, but, after instances of success and failure, were abandoned nine months before this suit was brought. There is no evidence that the abandonment was in prophecy of or dread of suit; and the illegal practices have not been resumed, nor is there any evidence of an intention to resume them, and certainly no "dangerous probability" of their resumption. . . .

What, then can now be urged against the Corporation? Can comparisons in other regards be made with its competitors and by such comparisons guilty or innocent existence be assigned it? It is greater in size and productive power than any of its competitors, equal or nearly equal to them all, but its power over prices was not and is not commensurate with its power to produce.

It is true there is some testimony tending to show that the Corporation had such power, but there was also testimony and a course of action tending strongly to the contrary. The conflict was by the judges of the District Court unanimously resolved against the existence of that power, and in doing so they but gave effect to the greater weight of the evidence. It is certain that no such power was exerted. On the contrary, the only attempt at a fixation of prices was, as already said, through an appeal to and confederation with competitors, and the record shows besides that when competition occurred it was not in pretense, and the Corporation, declined in productive powers—the competitors growing either against or in consequence of the competition. If against the competition we have an instance of movement against what the Government insists was an irresistible force; if in consequence of competition, we have an illustration of the adage that "competition is the life of trade" and is not easily repressed. The power of monopoly in the Corporation under either illustration is an untenable accusation. . . .

. . . [C]ompetitors, dealers, and customers of the Corporation testify in multitude that no adventitious interference was employed to either fix or maintain prices and that they were constant or varied according to natural conditions. Can this testimony be minimized or dismissed by inferring that, as intimated, it is an evidence of power not of weakness; and power exerted not only to suppress competition but to compel testimony, is the necessary inference, shading into perjury to deny its exertion? The situation is indeed singular, and we may wonder at it, wonder that the despotism of the Corporation, so baneful to the world in the representation of the Government, did not produce protesting victims.

But there are other paradoxes. . . . In one competitors (the independents) are represented as oppressed by the superior power of the Corporation; in the other they are represented as ascending to opulence by imitating that power's prices, which they could not do if at disadvantage from the other conditions of competition; and yet confederated action is not asserted. If it were this suit would take on another cast. The competitors would cease to be the victims of the Corporation, and would become its accomplices. And there is no other alternative. The suggestion that lurks in the Government's contention that the acceptance of the Corporation's prices is the submission of impotence to irresistible power is, in view of the testimony of the competitors, untenable. They, as we have seen, deny restraint in any measure or illegal influence of any kind. The Government, therefore, is reduced to the assertion that the size of the Corporation, the power it may have, not the exertion of the power, is an abhorrence to the law, or, as the Government says, "the combination embodied in the Corporation unduly restrains competition by its *necessary effect* . . . , and therefore is unlawful regardless of purpose." . . . To assent to that, to what extremes should we be led? . . .

We have pointed out that there are several of the Government's contentions which are difficult to represent or measure, and, the one we are now considering, that is, the power is "unlawful regardless of purpose," is another of them. It seems to us that it has for its ultimate principle and justification that strength in any producer or seller is a menace to the public interest and illegal because there is potency in it for mischief. The regression is extreme, but short of it the government cannot stop. The fallacy it conveys is manifest. . . .

. . . The Corporation is undoubtedly of impressive size, and it takes an effort of resolution not to be affected by it or to exaggerate its influence. But we must adhere to the law and the law does not make mere size an offense or the existence of unexerted power in offense. It, we repeat, requires overt acts, and trusts to its prohibition of them and its power to repress or punish them. It does not compel competition, nor require all that is possible. . . .

. . . We have seen whatever there was of wrong intent could not be executed; whatever there was of evil effect, was discontinued before this suit was brought, and this, we think, determines the decree. We say this in full realization of the requirements of the law. It is clear in its denunciation of monopolies and equally clear in its direction that the courts of the Nation shall prevent and restrain them (its language is "to prevent and restrain violations of" the act), but the command is necessarily submissive to the conditions which may exist and the usual powers of a court of equity to adapt its remedies to those conditions. In other words, it is not expected to enforce abstractions and do injury thereby, it may be, to the purpose of the law. It is this flexibility of discretion—indeed essential function— that makes it value in our jurisprudence—value in this case as in others. We do not mean to say that the law is not its own measure, and that it can be disregarded, but only that the appropriate relief in each instance is remitted to a court of equity to determine, not, and let us be explicit in this, to advance a policy contrary to that of the law, but in submission to the law and its policy, and in execution of both. And it is certainly a matter for consideration that there was no legal attack on the Corporation until 1911, 10 years after its formation and the commencement of its career.

We do not, however speak of the delay simply as to its time—that there is estoppel in it because of its time—but on account of what was done during that time—the many millions of dollars spent, the development made, and the enterprises undertaken, the investments by the public that have been invited and are not to be ignored. And what of the foreign trade that has been developed and exists? . . .

The Government, however, tentatively presents a proposition which has some tangibility. It submits that certain of the subsidiary companies are so mechanically equipped and so officially directed as to be released and remitted to independent action and individual interests and the competition to which such interests prompt, without any disturbance to business. . . . They are fully integrated, it is said, possess their own supplies, facilities of transportation and distribution. They are subject to the Steel Corporation is, in effect, the declaration, in nothing but its control of their prices. We may say parenthetically that they are defendants in the suit and charged as offenders, and we have the strange circumstance of violators of the law being urged to be used as expedients of the law.

But let us see what guide to a procedure of dissolution of the corporation and the dispersion as well of its subsidiary companies, for they are asserted to be illegal combinations, is prayed. And the fact must not be overlooked or underestimated. The prayer of the Government calls for not only a disruption of present conditions, but the restoration of the conditions of 20 years ago, if not literally, substantially. . . .

In conclusion we are unable to see that the public interest will be served by yielding to the contention of the Government respecting the dissolution of the Company or the separation from it of some of its subsidiaries; and we do see in a contrary conclusion a risk of injury to the public interest, including a material disturbance of, and, it may be serious detriment to, the foreign trade. And in submission to the policy of the law and its fortifying prohibitions the public interest is of paramount regard.

We think, therefore, that the decree of the District Court should be affirmed.

So ordered.

MR. JUSTICE MCREYNOLDS and MR. JUSTICE BRANDEIS took no part in the consideration or decision of the case.

MR. JUSTICE DAY, dissenting.

This record seems to me to leave no fair room for a doubt that the defendants, in the United States Steel Corporation and the several subsidiary corporations which make up that organization, were formed in violation of the Sherman Act. I am unable to accept the conclusion which directs a dismissal of the bill instead of following the well-settled practice, sanctioned by previous decisions of this court, requiring the dissolution of combinations made in direct violation of the law.

It appears to be thoroughly established that the formation of the corporations, here under consideration, constituted combinations between competitors, in violation of law, and intended to remove competition and to directly restrain trade. I agree with the conclusions of Judges Woolley and Hunt, expressed in the court below . . . that the combinations were not submissions to business conditions but were designed to control them for illegal purposes, regardless of other consequences, and "were made upon a scale that was huge and in a manner that was wild," and "properties were assembled and combined with less regard to their importance as integral parts of an integrated whole than to the advantages expected from the elimination of the competition which theretofore existed between them." Those judges found that the constituent companies of the United States Steel Corporation, nine in number, were themselves combinations of steel manufacturers, and the effect of the organization of these combinations was to give a control over the industry at least equal to that theretofore possessed by the constituent companies and their subsidiaries; that the Steel Corporation was a combination of combinations by which directly or indirectly 180 independent concerns were brought under one control. . . .

The enormous overcapitalization of companies and the appropriation of $100,000,000 in stock to promotion expenses were represented in the stock issues of the new organizations thus formed, and were the basis upon which large dividends have been declared from the profits of the business. This record shows that the power obtained by the corporation brought under its control large competing companies which were of themselves illegal combinations, and succeeded to their power; that some of the organizers of the Steel Corporation were parties to the preceding combinations, participated in their illegality, and by uniting them under a common direction intended to augment and perpetuate their power. It is the irresistible conclusion from these premises that great profits to be derived from unified control were the object of these organizations.

The contention must be rejected that the combination was an inevitable evolution of industrial tendencies compelling union of endeavor. . . .

For many years, as the record discloses, this unlawful organization exerted its power to control and maintain prices by pools, associations, trade meetings, and as the result of discussion and agreements at the so-called "Gary Dinners," where the assembled trade opponents secured cooperation and joint action through the machinery of special committees of competing concerns, and by prudent prevision took into account the possibility of defection, and the means of controlling and perpetuating that industrial harmony which arose from the control and maintenance of prices.

It inevitably follows that the corporation violated the law in its formation and by its immediate practices. The power, thus obtained from the combination of resources almost unlimited in the aggregation of competing organizations, had within its control the domination of the trade, and the ability to fix prices and restrain the free flow of commerce upon a scale heretofore unapproached in the history of corporate organization in this country.

These facts established, as it seems to me they are by the record, it follows that, if the Sherman Act is to be given efficacy, there must be a decree undoing so far as is possible that which has been achieved in open, notorious, and continued violation of its provisions.

I agree that the act offers no objection to the mere size of a corporation, nor to the continued exertion of its lawful power, when that size and power have been obtained by lawful means and developed by natural growth, although its resources, capital and strength may give to such corporation a dominating place in the business and industry with which it is concerned. It is entitled to maintain its size and the power that legitimately goes with it, provided no law has been transgressed in obtaining it. But I understand the reiterated decisions of this court construing the Sherman Act to hold that this power may not legally be derived from conspiracies, combinations, or contracts in restraint of trade. To permit this would be to practically annul the Sherman Law by judicial decree. This principle has been so often declared by the decisions that it is only necessary to refer to some of them. It is the scope of such combinations, and their power to suppress and stifle competition and create or tend to create monopolies, which, as we have declared so often as to make its reiteration monotonous, it was the purpose of the Sherman Act to condemn, including all combinations and conspiracies to restrain the free and natural flow of trade in the channels of interstate commerce. . . .

As I understand the conclusions of the court, affirming the decree directing dismissal of the bill, they amount to this: that these combinations, both the holding company and the subsidiaries which comprise it, although organized in plain violation and bold defiance of the provisions of the act, nevertheless are immune from a decree effectually ending the combinations and putting it out of their power to attain the unlawful purposes sought, because of some reasons of public policy requiring such conclusion. I know of no public policy which sanctions a violation of the law, nor of any inconvenience to trade, domestic or foreign, which should have the effect of placing combinations, which have been able thus to organize one of the greatest industries of the country in defiance of law, in an impregnable position above the control of the law forbidding such combinations. Such a conclusion does violence to the policy which the law was intended to enforce, runs counter to the decisions of the court, and necessarily results in a practical nullification of the act itself. . . .

Nor can I yield assent to the proposition that this combination has not acquired a dominant position in the trade which enables it to control prices and production when it sees fit to exert its power. Its total assets on December 31, 1913, were in excess of $1,800,000,000; its outstanding capital stock was $868,583,600; its surplus $151,798,428. Its cash on hand ordinarily was $75,000,000; this sum alone exceeded the total capitalization of any of its competitors, and with a single exception, the total capitalization and surplus of any one of them. That such an organization thus fortified and equipped could if it saw fit dominate the trade and control competition would seem to be a business proposition too plain to require extended argument to support it. Its resources, strength and comprehensive ownership of the means of production enable it to adopt measures to do again as it has done in the past, that is, to effectually dominate and control the steel business of the country. From the earliest decisions of this court it has been declared that it was the effective power of such organizations to control and restrain competition and the freedom of trade that Congress intended to limit and control. That the exercise of the power may be withheld, or exerted with forbearing benevolence, does not place such combinations beyond the authority of the statute which was intended to prohibit their formation, and when formed to deprive them of the power unlawfully attained.

It is said that a complete monopolization of the steel business was never attained by the offending combinations. To insist upon such result would be beyond the requirements of the statute and in most cases practicably impossible. . . .

It is affirmed that to grant the Government's request for a remand to the District Court for a decree of dissolution would not result in a change in the conditions of the steel trade. Such is not the theory of the Sherman Act. That act was framed in the belief that attempted or accomplished monopolization, or combinations which suppress free competition, were hurtful to the public interest, and that a restoration of competitive conditions would benefit the public. We have here a combination in control of one-half of the steel business of the country. If the plan were followed, as in the *American Tobacco Case*, of remanding the case to the District Court, a decree might be framed restoring competitive conditions as far as practicable. . . . In my judgment the principles there laid down if followed now would make a very material difference in the steel industry. Instead of one dominating corporation, with scattered competitors, there would be competitive conditions throughout the whole trade which would carry into effect the policy of the law.

It seems to me that if this act is to be given effect, the bill, under the findings of fact made by the court, should not be dismissed, and the cause should be remanded to the District Court, where a plan of effective and final dissolution of the corporations should be enforced by a decree framed for that purpose.

Mr. Justice Pitney and Mr. Justice Clarke concur in this dissent.

United States v. *Aluminum Company of America*[1]

148 F.2d 416 (2d Cir. 1945)

Before L. Hand, Swan, and Augustus N. Hand, Circuit Judges.

L. Hand, Circuit Judge.

. . . For convenience we have divided our discussion into four parts: (1) whether "Alcoa" monopolized the market in "virgin" aluminum ingot; (2) whether "Alcoa" was guilty of various unlawful practices, ancillary to the establishment of its monopoly; (3) whether [Aluminum] "Limited" and "Alcoa" were in an unlawful conspiracy; and whether, if not, "Limited" was guilty of a conspiracy with foreign producers; (4) what remedies are appropriate in the case of each defendant who may be found to have violated the Act.

I. "Alcoa's" Monopoly of "Virgin" Ingot.

There are various ways of computing "Alcoa's" control of the aluminum market—as distinct from its production—depending upon what one regards as competing in that market. The judge [in the District Court] figured its share—during the years 1929–1938, inclusive—as only about thirty-three percent; to do so he included "secondary," and excluded that part of "Alcoa's" own production which it fabricated and did not therefore sell as ingot. If, on the other hand, "Alcoa's" total production, fabricated and sold, be included, and balanced against the sum of imported "virgin" and "secondary," its share of the market was in the neighborhood of sixty-four percent for that period. The percentage we have already mentioned—over ninety—results only if we both include all "Alcoa's" production and exclude "secondary." That percentage is enough to constitute a monopoly; it is doubtful whether sixty or sixty-four percent would be enough; and certainly thirty-three percent is not. Hence it is necessary to settle what we shall treat as competing in the ingot market. That part of its production which "Alcoa" itself fabricates, does not of course ever reach the market as ingot; and we recognize that it is only when a restriction of production either inevitably affects prices, or is intended to do so, that it violates Section 1 of the Act. . . . However, even though we were to assume that a monopoly is unlawful under Section 2 only in case it controls prices, the ingot fabricated by "Alcoa," necessarily had a direct effect upon the ingot market. All ingot—with trifling exceptions—is used to fabricate inter-

---

[1] Because the Supreme Court was unable to obtain a quorum to review the District Court's opinion in this case, it was sent to the Circuit Court of Appeals for final decision. IMS.

mediate, or end, products; and therefore all intermediate, or end, products which "Alcoa" fabricates and sells, pro tanto reduce the demand for ingot itself.... We cannot therefore agree that the computation of the percentage of "Alcoa's" control over the ingot market should not include the whole of its ingot production.

As to "secondary," . . . we can say nothing more definite than that, although "secondary" does not compete at all in some uses, (whether because of "sales resistance" only, or because of actual metallurgical inferiority), for most purposes it competes upon a substantial equality with "virgin." On these facts the judge found that "every pound of secondary or scrap aluminum which is sold in commerce displaces a pound of virgin aluminum which otherwise would, or might have been, sold." We agree: so far as "secondary" supplies the demand of such fabricators as will accept it, it increases the amount of "virgin" which must seek sale elsewhere; and it therefore results that the supply of that part of the demand which will accept only "virgin" becomes greater in proportion as "secondary" drives away "virgin" from the demand which will accept "secondary." (This is indeed the same argument which we used a moment ago to include in the supply that part of "virgin" which "Alcoa" fabricates; it is not apparent to us why the judge did not think it applicable to that item as well.) At any given moment therefore "secondary" competes with "virgin" in the ingot market; further, it can, and probably does, set a limit or "ceiling" beyond which the price of "virgin" cannot go, for the cost of its production will in the end depend only upon the expense of scavenging and reconditioning. It might seem for this reason that in estimating "Alcoa's" control over the ingot market, we ought to include the supply of "secondary," as the judge did. Indeed, it may be thought a paradox to say that anyone has the monopoly of a market in which at all times he must meet a competition that limits his price. We shall show that it is not.

In the case of a monopoly of any commodity which does not disappear in use and which can be salvaged, the supply seeking sale at any moment will be made up of two components: (1) the part which the putative monopolist can immediately produce and sell; and (2) the part which has been, or can be, reclaimed out of what he has produced and sold in the past. By hypothesis he presently controls the first of these components; the second he has controlled in the past, although he no longer does. During the period when he did control the second, if he was aware of his interest, he was guided, not alone by its effect at that time upon the market, but by his knowledge that some part of it was likely to be reclaimed and seek the future market. That consideration will to some extent always affect his production until he decides to abandon the business, or for some other reason ceases to be concerned with the future market. Thus, in the case at bar "Alcoa" always knew that the future supply of ingot would be made up in part of what it produced at

the time, and, if it was as far-sighted as it proclaims itself, that consideration must have had its share in determining how much to produce. How
accurately it could forecast the effect of present production upon the
future market is another matter. Experience, no doubt, would help; but
it makes no difference that it had to guess; it is enough that it had an
inducement to make the best guess it could, and that it would regulate
that part of the future supply, so far as it should turn out to have guessed
right. The competition of "secondary" must therefore be disregarded, as
soon as we consider the position of "Alcoa" over a period of years; it
was as much within "Alcoa's" control as was the production of the "virgin" from which it had been derived. . . .

We conclude therefore that "Alcoa's" control over the ingot market
must be reckoned at over ninety percent; that being the proportion which
its production bears to imported "virgin" ingot. . . .

. . . Was this a monopoly within the meaning of Section 2? The judge
found that, over the whole half century of its existence, "Alcoa's" profits
upon capital invested, after payment of income taxes, had been only about
ten percent, and, although the plaintiff puts this figure a little higher, the
difference is negligible. . . . This assumed, it would be hard to say that
"Alcoa" had made exorbitant profits on ingot, if it is proper to allocate
the profit upon the whole business proportionately among all its products—
ingot, and fabrications from ingot. A profit of ten percent in such an
industry, dependent, in part at any rate, upon continued tariff protection,
and subject to the vicissitudes of new demands, to the obsolescence of plant
and process—which can never be accurately gauged in advance—to the
chance that substitutes may at any moment be discovered which will
reduce the demand, and to the other hazards which attend all industry; a
profit of ten percent, so conditioned, could hardly be considered
extortionate.

There are however, two answers to any such excuse; and the first is
that the profit on ingot was not necessarily the same as the profit of the
business as a whole, and that we have no means of allocating its proper
share to ingot. . . . But the whole issue is irrelevant anyway, for it is
no excuse for "monopolizing" a market that the monopoly has not been
used to extract from the consumer more than a "fair" profit. The Act has
wider purposes. Indeed, even though we disregarded all but economic
considerations, it would by no means follow that such concentration of
producing power is to be desired, when it has not been used extortion-
ately. Many people believe that possession of unchallenged economic
power deadens initiative, discourages thrift and depresses energy; that
immunity from competition is a narcotic, and rivalry is a stimulant, to
industrial progress; that the spur of constant stress is necessary to counter-
act an inevitable disposition to let well enough alone. Such people believe
that competitors, versed in the craft as no consumer can be, will be quick
to detect opportunities for saving and new shifts in production, and be

eager to profit by them. In any event the mere fact that a producer, having command of the domestic market, has not been able to make more than a "fair" profit, is no evidence that a "fair" profit could not have been made at lower prices. . . . True, it might have been thought adequate to condemn only those monopolies which could not show that they had exercised the highest possible ingenuity, had adopted every possible economy, had anticipated every conceivable improvement, stimulated every possible demand. No doubt, that would be one way of dealing with the matter, although it would imply constant scrutiny and constant supervision, such as courts are unable to provide. Be that as it may, that was not the way that Congress chose; it did not condone "good trusts" and condemn "bad" ones; it forbade all. Moreover, in so doing it was not necessarily actuated by economic motives alone. It is possible, because of its indirect social or moral effect, to prefer a system of small producers, each dependent for his success upon his own skill and character, to one in which the great mass of those engaged must accept the direction of a few. These considerations, which we have suggested only as possible purposes of the Act, we think the decisions prove to have been in fact its purposes.

It is settled, at least as to Section 1, that there are some contracts restricting competition which are unlawful, no matter how beneficent they may be; no industrial exigency will justify them; they are absolutely forbidden. . . . Starting, however, with the authoritative premise that all contracts fixing prices are unconditionally prohibited, the only possible difference between them and a monopoly is that while a monopoly necessarily involves an equal, or even greater, power to fix prices, its mere existence might be thought not to constitute an exercise of that power. That distinction is nevertheless purely formal; it would be valid only so long as the monopoly remained wholly inert; it would disappear as soon as the monopoly began to operate; for, when it did—that is, as soon as it began to sell at all—it must sell at some price and the only price at which it could sell is a price which it itself fixed. Thereafter the power and its exercise must needs coalesce. Indeed it would be absurd to condemn such contracts unconditionally, and not to extend the condemnation to monopolies; for the contracts are only steps toward that entire control which monopoly confers: they are really partial monopolies.

But we are not left to deductive reasoning. Although in many settings it may be proper to weigh the extent and effect of restrictions in a contract against its industrial or commercial advantages, this is never to be done when the contract is made with intent to set up a monopoly. . . . Perhaps, it has been idle to labor the point at length; there can be no doubt that the vice of restrictive contracts and of monopoly is really one, it is the denial to commerce of the supposed protection of competition. To repeat, if the earlier stages are proscribed, when they are parts of a plan, the mere projecting of which condemns them unconditionally, the realization of the plan itself must also be proscribed.

We have been speaking only of the economic reasons which forbid monopoloy; but, as we have already implied, there are others, based upon the belief that great industrial consolidations are inherently undesirable, regardless of their economic results. . . . Throughout the history of these [antitrust] statutes it has been constantly assumed that one of their purposes was to perpetuate and preserve, for its own sake and in spite of possible cost, an organization of industry in small units which can effectively compete with each other. We hold that "Alcoa's" monopoly of ingot was of the kind covered by Section 2.

It does not follow because "Alcoa" had such a monopoly, that it "monopolized" the ingot market: it may not have achieved monopoly; monopoly may have been thrust upon it. If it had been a combination of existing smelters which united the whole industry and controlled the production of all aluminum ingot, it would certainly have "monopolized" the market. . . . We may start therefore with the premise that to have combined ninety percent of the producers of ingot would have been to "monopolize" the ingot market; and, so far as concerns the public interest, it can make no difference whether an existing competition is put an end to, or whether prospective competition is prevented. . . . Nevertheless, it is unquestionably true that from the very outset the courts have at least kept in reserve the possibility that the origin of a monopoly may be critical in determining its legality. . . . This notion has usually been expressed by saying that size does not determine guilt; that there must be some "exclusion" of competitors; that the growth must be something else than "natural" or "normal"; that there must be a "wrongful intent," or some other specific intent; or that some "unduly" coercive means must be used. At times there has been emphasis upon the use of the active verb, "monopolize," as the judge noted in the case at bar. . . . What engendered these compunctions is reasonably plain; persons may unwittingly find themselves in possession of a monopoly, automatically so to say: that is, without having intended either to put an end to existing competition, or to prevent competition from arising when none had existed; they may become monopolists by force of accident. . . . A single producer may be the survivor out of a group of active competitors, merely by virtue of his superior skill, foresight and industry. . . . The successful competitor, having been urged to compete, must not be turned upon when he wins. . . .

It would completely misconstrue "Alcoa's" position in 1940 to hold that it was the passive beneficiary of a monopoly, following upon an involuntary elimination of competitors by automatically operative economic forces. . . . This increase and this continued and undisturbed control did not fall undesigned into "Alcoa's" lap; obviously it could not have done so. It could only have resulted, as it did result, from a persistent determination to maintain the control, with which it found itself vested in 1912. There were at least one or two abortive attempts to enter the industry, but "Alcoa" effectively anticipated and forestalled all competition, and succeeded in holding the field alone. True, it stimulated demand and opened new uses for the metal, but not without making sure that it could supply what it had evoked. . . . It was not inevitable that it should always anticipate increases in the demand for ingot and be prepared to supply them. Nothing compelled it to keep doubling and redoubling its capacity before others entered the field. It insists that it never excluded competitors; but we can think of no more effective exclusion than progressively to embrace each new opportunity as it opened, and to face every newcomer with new capacity already geared into a great organization, having the advantage of experience, trade connections and the elite of personnel. Only in case we interpret "exclusion" as limited to manoeuvres not honestly industrial, but actuated solely by a desire to prevent competition, can such a course, indefatigably pursued, be deemed not "exclusionary." So to limit it would in our judgment emasculate the Act; would permit just such consolidations as it was designed to prevent. . . .

We disregard any question of "intent." . . . By far the greatest part of the fabulous record piled up in the case at bar, was concerned with proving such an intent. The plaintiff was seeking to show that many transactions, neutral on their face, were not in fact necessary to the development of "Alcoa's" business, and had no motive except to exclude others and perpetuate its hold upon the ingot market. Upon that effort success depended in case the plaintiff failed to satisfy the court that it was unnecessary under Section 2 to convict "Alcoa" of practices unlawful of themselves. The plaintiff has so satisfied us, and the issue of intent ceases to have any importance. . . . In order to fall within Section 2, the monopolist must have both the power to monopolize, and the intent to monopolize. . . . [N]o monopolist monopolizes unconscious of what he is doing. So here, "Alcoa" meant to keep, and did keep, that complete and exclusive hold upon the ingot market with which it started. That was to "monopolize" that market, however innocently it otherwise proceeded. So far as the judgment held that it was not within Section 2, it must be reversed. . . .

II. "ALCOA'S" UNLAWFUL PRACTICES.

[Since it was found that Alcoa had monopolized the ingot market, the question of its unlawful practices would, according to the Court, be moot. But war-wrought changes in the ingot market made consideration of these charges necessary to the proper framing of a decree.]

. . . In spite of the prolixity of the evidence, the challenged practices can be divided into three classes: . . .

(*a*) *"Pre-emption" of Bauxite and Water-Power.* The plaintiff attempted to prove, and asserts that it did prove, that "Alcoa" bought up bauxite deposits . . . in excess of its needs, and under circumstances which showed that the purchases were not for the purpose of securing an adequate future supply, but only in order to seize upon any available supply and so assure its monopoly. The very statement of this charge shows that it depends upon "Alcoa's" intent, for, if the purchases provided for the future needs of the business, or for what "Alcoa" honestly believed were its future needs, they were innocent. . . . The judge . . . overruled all the plaintiff's contentions . . . [and] we should be unwarranted in declaring these findings "clearly erroneous." . . .

(*b*) *Suppression of Competitors Seeking to Invade the Ingot Market.* [Alcoa's purchases of various potential competitors were treated by the court in the same manner as its purchases of bauxite and water-power sites, i.e., the finding of the lower court that these acquisitions did not evidence an intent to suppress competition was upheld.] . . . .

(*c*) *"Alcoa's" Domination of the Fabricating Fields.* The last of "Alcoa's" supposedly unlawful practices was its infiltration into, and manipulation of, some of the markets for fabricated goods. These were three kinds: (1) buying an interest in the Aluminum Castings Company, and Aluminum Manufactures, Inc.; (2) the "Price Squeeze"; (3) the "Piston Patent Pool." (1) "Castings" were one of the earliest uses of aluminum. . . . Five of these [casting producers] combined in . . . [1909] to form the Aluminum Castings Company, of whose shares "Alcoa" received fifty percent in exchange for advances made. . . .

The Aluminum Goods Manufacturing Company makes cooking and other utensils out of aluminum. . . . At the trial thirty-one percent of the shares were held by "Alcoa" and its officers. . . . [T]here is nothing to support the conclusion that here was a practice or manoeuvre merely to suppress or exclude competitors. . . .

(2) *The "Price Squeeze."* The plaintiff describes as the "Price Squeeze" a practice by which, it says, "Alcoa" intended to put out of business the manufacturers of aluminum "sheet" who were its competitors; for "Alcoa" was itself a large—in fact much the largest—maker of that product. . . .

The plaintiff's theory is that "Alcoa" consistently sold ingot at so high a price that the "sheet rollers," who were forced to buy from it, could not pay the expenses of "rolling" the "sheet."

. . . [W]e think that the plaintiff made out a prima facie case that "Alcoa" had been holding ingot at a price higher than a "fair price," and had reduced the price only because of pressure [resulting from a Department of Justice investigation into the complaints of several "sheet" makers]. If that was not so, it should have rebutted the inference.

In spite of this evidence the judge found that in these years [1925–1932] "Alcoa" had not intended to monopolize the "sheet" market; or to exclude others; or to fix discriminatory prices, or prices of any kind; or to sell below the cost of production, measuring ingot price as part of the cost. . . . That is indeed hard to believe. . . . That it was unlawful to set the price of "sheet" so low and hold the price of ingot so high, seems to us unquestionable, provided, as we have held, that on this record the price of ingot must be regarded as higher than a "fair price." True, this was only a consequence of "Alcoa's" control over the price of ingot, and perhaps it ought not to be considered as a separate wrong; moreover, we do not use it as part of the reasoning by which we conclude that the monopoly was unlawful. But it was at least an unlawful exercise of "Alcoa's" power after it had been put on notice by the "sheet rollers'" complaints; and this is true, even though we assent to the judge's finding that it was not part of an attempt to monopolize the "sheet" market. . . .

(3) *The Piston Patent Situation.* The plaintiff charges "Alcoa" with three kinds of misuses of patents: (1) an unlawful limitation of the production of licensees of its own patents; (2) accepting a license agreement from another patentee that unlawfully limited its own production; (3) using its own patents to force the purchase of ingot upon licensees. [The court held that in two instances the evidence was not sufficient to establish unlawfulness, while in the third, expiration of the patents involved made it unnecessary for the court to pass upon the agreement.]

III.   "Limited."

[In this portion of its decision the court found that cartel arrangements between Limited, a Canadian firm, and Alliance, a Swiss concern, affected imports into the United States and therefore violated the Sherman Act. It was held, however, that "Alcoa" had not participated in the cartel, and therefore could not be held responsible for the import restrictions.]

IV.   The Remedies.

Nearly five years have passed since the evidence was closed; during that time the aluminum industry . . . has been revolutionized by the nation's efforts in a great crisis. That alone would make it impossible to dispose of the action upon the basis of the record as we have it. . . .

. . . [I]t is impossible to say what will be "Alcoa's" position in the industry after the war. . . . Dissolution is not a penalty but a remedy; if the industry will not need it for its protection, it will be a disservice to break up an aggregation which has for so long demonstrated its efficiency. . . .

But there is another, and even more persuasive, reason why we should not now adjudge a dissolution of any kind. The Surplus Property Act of 1944 provides . . . [that the disposal agencies shall dispose of government properties in such a manner as] ". . . to give maximum aid in the reestablishment of a peacetime economy of free independent private enterprise"; [and] ". . . to discourage monopolistic practices and to strengthen and preserve the competitive position of small business concerns in an economy of free enterprise." . . . [If the disposal authorities fail to reestablish competitive conditions, it will then be necessary for the District Court to act.]

[An injunction was then issued against resumption of the "price squeeze," and "Limited" was enjoined from entering into any agreement covering imports into this country.]

Judgment reversed, and cause remanded for further proceedings not inconsistent with the foregoing.

United States v. United Shoe Machinery Corp.

110 F.Supp. 295 (D. Mass. 1953)

WYZANSKI, District Judge.

. . . . .

December 15, 1947 the Government filed a complaint against United Shoe Machinery Corporation under Section 4 of the Sherman Act . . . in order to restrain alleged violations of Sections 1 and 2 of that Act. . . .

Stripped to its essentials, the 52 page complaint charged, *first*, that since 1912 United had been "monopolizing interstate trade and commerce in the shoe machinery industry of the United States." The *second* principal charge laid by the complaint was that United had been (*a*) "monopolizing the distribution in interstate commerce of numerous . . . shoe factory supplies" and (*b*) "attempting to monopolize the distribution in interstate commerce of . . . other such supplies." . . . *Third*, the complaint alleged United was "attempting to monopolize and monopolizing the manufacture and distribution in interstate commerce of tanning machinery used in the manufacture of shoe leather." . . .

In support of this three-pronged attack, directed to shoe machinery, shoe factory supplies, and tanning machinery, the Government set forth detailed allegations with respect to acquisitions, leases, patents, and a host of other aspects of United's business. . . .

After stating its changes, the Government prayed for an adjudication of United's violations of both Section 1 and Section 2 of the Sherman Act; an injunction against future violations; a cancellation of United's shoe machinery leases; a requirement that United offer for sale all machine types "manufactured and commercialized by it and be enjoined from leasing shoe machinery except upon terms . . . approved by the Court"; a requirement that, on such terms as the court may deem appropriate, United make available to all applicants all patents and inventions relating to shoe machinery; an injunction against United manufacturing or distributing shoe factory supplies; a cancellation of exclusive contracts governing shoe factory supplies; and a divestiture of United's ownership of virtually all branches and subsidiaries concerned with shoe factory supplies or tanning machinery.

Defendant answered seasonably, denying all the significant allegations. . . .

A trial of prodigious length followed. . . .

In an anti-trust case a trial court's task is to reduce, as far as fairness permits, a complex record to its essentials, so that the parties, the Supreme Court, other courts, the bar, and the general public may understand the decree, and may recognize the premises on which that judgment rests. It is not the Court's duty to make a precise finding on every detail of four decades of an industry. It is not its duty to approach the issues as an historian, an archaeologist . . . , an economist, or even a master appointed to settle every factual dispute. A trial judge who undertakes such tasks will unnecessarily sacrifice the rights of litigants in other cases clamoring for attention. Moreover, he will encourage just that type of extravagant presentation which has come to plague the field of anti-trust law. Hence this opinion is to be construed as denying on the ground of immateriality every request not granted. . . .

III.

Opinion on Alleged Violations

. . . . .

There are 18 major processes for the manufacturing of shoes by machine. Some machine types are used only in one process, but others are used in several; and the relationship of machine types to one another may be competitive or sequential. The approximately 1460 shoe manufacturers themselves are highly competitive in many respects, including their choice of processes and other technological aspects of production. Their total demand for machine services, apart from those rendered by dry thread sewing machines in the upper-fitting room, constitutes an identifiable market which is a "part of the trade or commerce among the several States." Section 2 of the Sherman Act. . . .

United, the largest source of supply, is a corporation lineally descended from a combination of constituent companies, adjudged lawful by the Supreme Court of the United States in 1918. . . . It now has assets rising slightly over 100 million dollars and employment rolls around 6,000. In recent years it has earned before federal taxes 9 to 13.5 million dollars annually.

Supplying different aspects of that market are at least 10 other American manufacturers and some foreign manufacturers, whose products are admitted to the United States free of tariff duty. Almost all the operations performed in the 18 processes can be carried out without the use of any of United's machines, and (at least in foreign areas, where patents are no obstacle,) a complete shoe factory can be efficiently organized without a United machine.

Nonetheless, United at the present time is supplying over 75%, and probably 85% of the current demand in the American shoe machinery market, as heretofore defined. This is somewhat less than the share it was supplying in 1915. In the meantime, one important competitor, Compo Shoe Machinery Corporation, became the American innovator of the cement process of manufacture. In that sub-market Compo roughly equals United. . . .

United is the only machinery enterprise that produces a long line of machine types, and covers every major process. It is the only concern that has a research laboratory covering all aspects of the needs of shoe manufacturing; though Compo has a laboratory concentrating on the needs of those in the cement process. . . . Through its own research, United has developed inventions many of which are now patented. Roughly 95 % of its 3915 patents are attributable to the ideas of its own employees.

Although at the turn of the century, United's patents covered the fundamentals of shoe machinery manufacture, those fundamental patents have expired. Current patents cover for the most part only minor developments, so that it is possible to "invent around" them, to use the words of United's chief competitor. However, the aggregation of patents does to some extent block potential competition. It furnishes a trading advantage. It leads inventors to offer their ideas to United, on the general principle that new complicated machines embody numerous patents. And it serves as a hedge or insurance for United against unforeseen competitive developments.

In the last decade and a half, United has not acquired any significant patents, inventions, machines, or businesses from any outside source, and has rejected many offers made to it. Before then, while it acquired no going businesses, in a period of two decades it spent roughly $3,500,000 to purchase inventions and machines. Most of these were from moribund companies, though this was not true of the acquisitions underlying the significant Littleway process and the less significant heel seat fitting machines and patents, each of which was from an active enterprise and might have served as a nucleus of important, though, at least initially, not extensive competition.

In supplying its complicated machines to shoe manufacturers, United, like its more important American competitors, has followed the practice of never selling, but only leasing. Leasing has been traditional in the shoe machinery field since the Civil War. So far as this record indicates, there is virtually no expressed dissatisfaction from consumers respecting that system; and Compo, United's principal competitor, endorses and uses it. Under the system, entry into shoe manufacture has been easy. The rates charged for all customers have been uniform. The machines supplied have performed excellently. United has, without separate charge, promptly and efficiently supplied repair service and many kinds of other service useful to shoe manufacturers. These services have been particularly important, because in the shoe manufacturing industry a whole line of production can be adversely affected, and valuable time lost, if some of the important machines go out of function, and because machine breakdowns have serious labor and consumer repercussions. The cost to the average shoe manufacturer of its machines and services supplied to him has been less than 2 % of the wholesale price of his shoes.

However, United's leases, in the context of the present shoe machinery market, have created barriers to the entry by competitors into the shoe machinery field.

First, the complex of obligations and rights accruing under United's leasing system in operation deter a shoe manufacturer from disposing of a United machine and acquiring a competitor's machine. . . . The lessee is now held closely to United by the combined effect of the 10 year term, the requirement that if he has work available he must use the machine to full capacity, and by the return charge which can in practice, through the right of deduction fund, be reduced to insignificance if he keeps this and other United machines to the end of the periods for which he leased them.

Second, when a lessee desires to replace a United machine, United gives him more favorable terms if the replacement is by another United machine than if it is by a competitive machine.

Third, United's practice of offering to repair, without separate charges, its leased machines, has had the effect that there are no independent service organizations to repair complicated machines. In turn, this has had the effect that the manufacturer of a complicated machine must either offer repair service with his machine, or must face the obstacle of marketing his machine to customers who know that repair service will be difficult to provide. . . .

Although maintaining the same nominal terms for each customer, United has followed, as between machine types, a discriminatory pricing policy. . . . [T]hese sharp and relatively durable differentials are traceable, at least in large part, to United's policy of fixing a higher rate of return where competition is of minor significance, and a lower rate of return where competition is of major significance. . . .

On the foregoing facts, the issue of law is whether defendant in its shoe machinery business has violated that provision of Section 2 of the Sherman Act. . . .

Yet, in these recent authorities[1] there are discernible at least three different, but cognate, approaches.

The approach which has the least sweeping implications really antedates the decision in Aluminum. But it deserves restatement. An enterprise has monopolized in violation of Section 2 of the Sherman Act if it has acquired or maintained a power to exclude others as a result of using an unreasonable "restraint of trade" in violation of Section 1 of the Sherman Act. . . .

A more inclusive approach was adopted by Mr. Justice Douglas in *United States v. Griffith.* . . . He stated that to prove a violation of Section 2 it was not always necessary to show a violation of Section 1. . . . And he concluded that an enterprise has monopolized in violation of Section 2 if

---

[1] U.S. *v.* Aluminum Co. of America, 148 F.2d 416 (1945); American Tobacco Co. *v.* U.S., 328 U.S. 781 (1946); U.S. *v.* Griffith, 334 U.S. 100 (1948); Schine Chain Theatres *v.* U.S., 334 U.S. 110 (1948); U.S. *v.* Paramount Theatres, 334 U.S. 131 (1948); U.S. *v.* Columbia Steel Co., 334 U.S. 495 (1948). IMS.

it (*a*) has the power to exclude competition, and (*b*) has exercised it, or has the purpose to exercise it. . . . The least that this conclusion means is that it is a violation of Section 2 for one having effective control of the market to use, or plan to use, any exclusionary practice, even though it is not a technical restraint of trade. But the conclusion may go further.

Indeed the way in which Mr. Justice Douglas used the terms "monopoly power" and "effective market control," . . . and cited Aluminum suggests that he endorses a third and broader approach, which orginated with Judge Hand. It will be recalled that Judge Hand said that one who has acquired an overwhelming share of the market "monopolizes" whenever he does business, . . . apparently even if there is no showing that his business involves any exclusionary practice. But, it will also be recalled that this doctrine is softened by Judge Hand's suggestion that the defendant may escape statutory liability if it bears the burden of proving that it owes its monopoly solely to superior skill. . . .

This Court finds it unnecessary to choose between the second and third approaches. For, taken as a whole, the evidence satisfies the tests laid down in both Griffith and Aluminum. The facts show that (1) defendant has, and exercises, such overwhelming strength in the shoe machinery market that it controls that market, (2) this strength excludes some potential, and limits some actual, competition, and (3) this strength is not attributable solely to defendant's ability, economies of scale, research, natural advantages, and adaptation to inevitable economic laws. . . .

To combat United's market control, a competitor must be prepared with knowledge of shoemaking, engineering skill, capacity to invent around patents, and financial resources sufficient to bear the expense of long developmental and experimental processes. The competitor must be prepared for consumers' resistance founded on their long-term, satisfactory relations with United, and on the cost to them of surrendering United's leases. Also, the competitor must be prepared to give, or point to the source of, repair and other services, and to the source of supplies for machine parts, expendable parts, and the like. Indeed, perhaps a competitor who aims at any large scale success must also be prepared to lease his machines. These considerations would all affect *potential* competition, and have not been without their effect on *actual* competition.

Not only does the evidence show United has control of the market, but also the evidence does not show that the control is due entirely to excusable causes. The three principal sources of United's power have been the original constitution of the company, the superiority of United's products and services, and the leasing system. The first two of these are plainly beyond reproach. . . .

But United's control does not rest solely on its original constitution, its ability, its research, or its economies of scale. There are other barriers to competition, and these barriers were erected by United's own business policies. Much of United's market power is traceable to the magnetic ties inherent in its system of leasing, and not selling, its more important machines. The lease-only system of distributing complicated machines has many "partnership" aspects, and it has exclusionary features such as the 10-year term, the full capacity clause, the return charges, and the failure to segregate service charges from machine charges. Moreover, the leasing system has aided United in maintaining a pricing system which discriminates between machine types.

In addition to the foregoing three principal sources of United's power, brief reference may be made to the fact that United has been somewhat aided in retaining control of the shoe machinery industry by its purchases in the secondhand market, by its acquisitions of patents, and, to a lesser extent, by its activities in selling to shoe factories supplies which United and others manufacture. . . .

. . . [T]hey are not practices which can be properly described as the inevitable consequences of ability, natural forces, or law. They represent something more than the use of accessible resources, the process of invention and innovation, and the employment of those techniques of employment, financing, production, and distribution, which a competitive society must foster. They are contracts, arrangements, and policies which, instead of encouraging competition based on pure merit, further the dominance of a particular firm. In this sense, they are unnatural barriers; they unnecessarily exclude actual and potential competition; they restrict a free market. While the law allows many enterprises to use such practices, the Sherman Act is now construed by superior courts to forbid the continuance of effective market control based in part upon such practices. Those courts hold that market control is inherently evil and constitutes a violation of Section 2 unless economically inevitable, or specifically authorized and regulated by law.

It is only fair to add that . . . United's power does not rest on predatory practices. Probably few monopolies could produce a record so free from any taint of that kind of wrongdoing. The violation with which United is now charged depends not on moral considerations, but on solely economic considerations. United is denied the right to exercise effective control of the market by business policies that are not the inevitable consequences of its capacities or its natural advantages. That those policies are not immoral is irrelevant. . . .

Moreover, . . . United has not proved that monopoly is economically compelled by the thinness of the shoe machinery market. It has not shown that no company could undertake to develop, manufacture, and distribute certain types of machines, unless it alone met the total demand for those types of machines.

Nor has United affirmatively proved that it has achieved spectacular results at amazing rates of speed, nor has it proved that comparable research results and comparable economies of production, distribution, and service could not be achieved as well by, say, three important shoe machinery firms, as by one. Compo with a much smaller organization indicates how much research can be done on a smaller scale. Yet since Compo is limited to the simpler cement process machines, too much reliance should not be placed on this comparison. Nonetheless, one point is worth recalling. Compo's inventors first found practical ways to introduce the cement process which United had considered and rejected. This experience illustrates the familiar truth that one of the dangers of extraordinary experience is that those who have it may fall into grooves created by their own expertness. They refuse to believe that hurdles which they have learned from experience are insurmountable, can in fact be overcome by fresh, independent minds.

So far, nothing in this opinion has been said of defendant's *intent* in regard to its power and practices in the shoe machinery market. This point can be readily disposed of by reference once more to Aluminum. . . . Defendant intended to engage in the leasing practices and pricing policies which maintained its market power. That is all the intent which the law requires when both the complaint and the judgment rest on a charge of "monopolizing," not merely "attempting to monopolize." Defendant having willed the means, has willed the end.

Next, come those issues relating to supplies. . . .

In certain of those supply fields . . . United has control of the market . . . [which] comes principally from United's power over the shoe machinery market. And for that reason the exercise of dominant power in those supply fields is unlawful. An enterprise that by monopolizing one field, secures dominant market power in another field, has monopolized the second field, in violation of Section 2 of the Sherman Act. . . .

IV.

Opinion on Remedy

. . . . .

The Government's proposal that the Court dissolve United into three separate manufacturing companies is unrealistic. United conducts all machine manufacture at one plant in Beverly, with one set of jigs and tools, one foundry, one laboratory for machinery problems, one managerial staff, and one labor force. It takes no Solomon to see that this organism cannot be cut into three equal and viable parts. . . .

A petition for dissolution should reflect greater attention to practical problems and should involve supporting economic data and prophesies such as are presented in corporate reorganization and public utility dissolution cases. Moreover, the petition should involve a more formal commitment by the Attorney General, than is involved in the divergent proposals that his assistants have made in briefs and in oral arguments addressed to the Court.

On the whole, therefore, the suggested remedy of dissolution is rejected.

From the opinion on defendant's violations it follows that some form of relief regarding defendant's leases and leasing practices is proper and necessary. . . .

Although leasing should not now be abolished by judicial decree, the Court agrees with the Government that the leases should be purged of their restrictive features. In the decree filed herewith, the term of the lease is shortened, the full capacity clause is eliminated, the discriminatory commutative charges are removed, and United is required to segregate its charges for machines from its charges for repair service. . . .

The Court also agrees with the Government that if United chooses to continue to lease any machine type, it must offer that type of machine also for sale. . . . Insofar as United's machines are sold rather than leased, they will ultimately, in many cases, reach a second-hand market. From that market, United will face a type of substitute competition which will gradually weaken the prohibited market power which it now exercises. Moreover, from that market, or from United itself, a competitor of United can acquire a United machine in order to study it, to copy its unpatented features, and to experiment with improvements in, or alterations of, the machine. Thus, in another and more direct way, United's market power will be diminished. . . .

One other phase of the decree to which this opinion should expressly advert is the method of handling those subsidiaries and branches which produce supplies in fields which United has monopolized. The clearest examples are nails and tacks, and eyelets for the shoe machinery market. These are large scale monopolizations attributable to the machinery monopoly. And United should be divested of its business of manufacturing and distributing these particular supplies, because this is the kind of dissolution which can be carried out practically, and which will also reduce monopoly power in each of the affected supply fields. . . .

Note: Some ten years after this decision the Government petitioned the District Court to review the efficacy of the remedies it had prescribed. The District Court ruled that its power to modify the original decree was limited to cases involving "(1) a clear showing of (2) grievous wrong (3) evoked by new and unforeseen circumstances." On appeal, the Court, Mr. Justice Fortas writing its opinion, reversed, 391 U.S. 244 (1968), holding it to be established that "in a Section 2 case, upon appropriate findings of violation, it is the duty of the court to prescribe relief which will terminate the illegal monopoly, deny to the defendant the fruits of its statutory violation, and ensure that there remain no practices likely to result in monopolization in the future."

The District Court was directed to determine whether the relief it had granted had restored "workable competition in the market" and assured "the complete extirpation of the illegal monopoly."

Judge Wyzanski then accepted a consent decree under which United Shoe Machinery Corp. would divest itself of "particular shoe machine models, which models accounted for $8,500,000 in gross revenues to defendant from lease and sale of shoe machinery." This reduction in revenues, the parties estimated, "would be sufficient to reduce defendant's share of the shoe machinery market during the base year to no more than 33 percent."

In order to facilitate divestiture, the company agreed to assign any patent principally relating to the models divested (and their parts); to provide the purchaser with service for two years; to train the purchaser's personnel in such service; and, for ten years after the sale to provide replacement parts at "a reasonable price." In addition, United agreed to compulsory licensing, for about a decade, under substantially all of its shoe machine and product patents.

United States v. *E. I. duPont de Nemours and Company*

351 U.S. 377 (1956)

Mr. Justice Reed delivered the opinion of the Court.

The United States brought this civil action under Section 4 of the Sherman Act. . . . The complaint, filed December 13, 1947, . . . charged duPont with monopolizing, attempting to monopolize and conspiracy to monopolize interstate commerce in cellophane and cellulosic caps and bands in violation of Section 2 of the Sherman Act. Relief by injunction was sought against defendant and its officers, forbidding monopolizing or attempting to monopolize interstate trade in cellophane. The prayer also sought action to dissipate the effect of the monopolization by divestiture or other steps. . . . [J]udgment was entered for duPont on all issues.[1]

The Government's direct appeal here . . . "attacks only the ruling that duPont has not monopolized trade in cellophane." At issue for determination is only this alleged violation by duPont of Section 2. . . .

During the period that is relevant to this action, duPont produced almost 75% of the cellophane sold in the United States, and cellophane constituted less than 20% of all "flexible packaging material" sales. . . .

The Government contends that, by so dominating cellophane production, duPont monopolized a "part of the trade or commerce" in violation of Section 2. Respondent agrees that cellophane is a product which constitutes "a 'part' of commerce within the meaning of Section 2." . . . But it contends that the prohibition of Section 2 against monopolization is not violated because it does not have the power to control the price of cellophane or to exclude competitors from the market in which cellophane is sold. The court below found that the "relevant market for determining the extent of duPont's market control is the market for flexible

---

[1] *United States* v. *E. I. duPont de Nemours & Co.*, 118 F. Supp. 41. The opinion occupies 192 pages of the volume. The Findings of Fact, 854 in number, cover 140 pages. . . . [Citations to the lower court's findings have been omitted. IMS.]

packaging materials," and that competition from those other materials prevented duPont from possessing monopoly powers in its sales of cellophane. . . .

The Government . . . argues that the market for other wrappings is distinct from the market for cellophane and that the competition afforded cellophane by other wrappings is not strong enough to be considered in determining whether duPont has monopoly powers. Market delimitation is necessary under duPont's theory to determine whether an alleged monopolist violates Section 2. The ultimate consideration in such a determination is whether the defendants control the price and competition in the market for such part of trade or commerce as they are charged with monopolizing. Every manufacturer is the sole producer of the particular commodity it makes but its control in the above sense of the relevant market depends upon the availability of alternative commodities for buyers: *i.e.*, whether there is a cross-elasticity of demand between cellophane and the other wrappings. This interchangeability is largely gauged by the purchase of competing products for similar uses considering the price, characteristics and adaptability of the competing commodities. The court below found that the flexible wrappings afforded such alternatives. This Court must determine whether the trial court erred in its estimate of the competition afforded cellophane by other materials. . . .

Two additional questions were raised in the record and decided by the court below. That court found, that even if duPont did possess monopoly power over sales of cellophane, it was not subject to Sherman Act prosecution, because (1) the acquisition of that power was protected by patents, and (2) that power was acquired solely through duPont's business expertness. It was thrust upon duPont. . . .

Since the Government specifically excludes attempts and conspiracies to monopolize from consideration, a conclusion that duPont has no monopoly power would obviate examination of these last two issues.

I. *Factual Background.* . . . In the early 1900's Jacques Brandenberger, a Swiss chemist, [inadvertently discovered the first "cellophane."] . . . This first "cellophane" was thick, hard, and not perfectly transparent, but Brandenberger apparently foresaw commercial possibilities in his discovery. . . . He obtained patents to cover . . . his process.

. . . [H]owever, . . . the disclosures of these early patents were not sufficient to make possible the manufacture of commercial cellophane. . . .

In 1917 Brandenberger assigned his patents to La Cellophane Societe Anonyme and joined that organization. . . .

In 1923 duPont organized with La Cellophane an American company for the manufacture of plain cellophane. The undisputed findings are that:

. . . La Cellophane . . . granted duPont Cellophane Company the exclusive right to make and sell in North and Central America under La Cellophane's secret processes for cellophane manufacture. DuPont Cellophane Company granted to La Cellophane exclusive rights for the rest of the world under any cellophane patents or processes duPont Cellophane Company might develop. . . .

Subsequently duPont and La Cellophane licensed several foreign companies, allowing them to manufacture and vend cellophane in limited areas. . . . Technical exchange agreements with these companies were entered into at the same time. However, in 1940, duPont notified these foreign companies that sales might be made in any country, and by 1948 all the technical exchange agreements were canceled.

Sylvania, an American affiliate of a Belgian producer of cellophane, not covered by the license agreements above referred to, began the manufacture of cellophane in the United States in 1930. Litigation between the French and Belgian companies resulted in a settlement whereby La Cellophane came to have a stock interest in Sylvania, contrary to the La Cellophane-duPont agreement. This resulted in adjustments as compensation for the intrusion into United States of La Cellophane that extended duPont's limited territory. . . . Since 1934 Sylvania has produced about 25% of United States cellophane.

An important factor in the growth of cellophane . . . was the perfection of moistureproof cellophane, a superior product of duPont research and patented by that company through a 1927 application. . . .

In 1931 Sylvania began the manufacture of moistureproof cellophane under its own patents. After negotiations over patent rights, duPont in 1933 licensed Sylvania to manufacture and sell moistureproof cellophane produced under the duPont patents at a royalty of 2% of sales. These licenses, with the plain cellophane licenses from the Belgian Company, made Sylvania a full cellophane competitor, limited on moistureproof sales by the terms of the licenses to 20% of the combined sales of the two companies of that type by the payment of a prohibitive royalty on the excess. . . . There was never an excess production. The limiting clause was dropped on January 1, 1945, and Sylvania was acquired in 1946 by the American Viscose Corporation with assets of over $200,000,000.

Between 1928 and 1950, duPont's sales of plain cellophane increased from $3,131,608 to $9,330,776. Moistureproof sales increased from $603,-222 to $89,850,416, although prices were continuously reduced. . . . It could not be said that this immense increase in use was solely or even largely attributable to the superior quality of cellophane or to the technique or business acumen of duPont, though doubtless those factors were important. The growth was a part of the expansion of the commodity-packaging habits of business, a by-product of general efficient competitive merchandising to meet modern demands. The profits, which were large, apparently arose from this trend in marketing, the development of the industrial use of chemical research and production of synthetics, rather than from elimination of other producers from the relevant market. . . .

II. *The Sherman Act and the Courts.*—The Sherman Act has received long and careful application by this Court to achieve for the Nation the freedom of enterprise from monopoly or restraint envisaged by the Congress that passed the Act in 1890. Because the Act is couched in broad terms, it is adaptable to the changing types of commercial production and distribution that have evolved since its passage. . . . It was said in *Standard Oil Co.* v. *United States*, . . . that fear of the power of rapid accumulations of individual and corporate wealth from the trade and industry of a developing national economy caused its passage. . . . While the economic picture has changed, large aggregations of private capital, with power attributes, continue. Mergers go forward. Industries such as steel, automobiles, tires, chemicals, have only a few production organizations. A considerable size is often essential for efficient operation. . . .

Judicial construction of antitrust legislation has generally been left unchanged by Congress. This is true of the Rule of Reason. While it is fair to say that the Rule is imprecise, its application in Sherman Act litigation, as directed against enhancement of price or throttling of competition, has given a workable content to antitrust legislation. . . . It was judicially declared a proper interpretation of the Sherman Act in 1911. . . . This Court has not receded from its position on the Rule. There is not, we think, any inconsistency between it and the development of the judicial theory that agreements as to maintenance of prices or division of territory are in themselves a violation of the Sherman Act. It is logical that some agreements and practices are invalid *per se*, while others are illegal only as applied to particular situations. . . .

. . . It is true that Congress has made exceptions to the generality of monopoly prohibitions. . . . But those exceptions express legislative determination of the national economy's need of reasonable limitations on cutthroat competition or prohibition of monopoly. "[W]here exceptions are made, Congress should make them." *United States* v. *Line Material Co.*, 333 U.S. 287, 310. . . . We therefore turn to Section 2 . . . to determine whether duPont has violated that section by its dominance in the manufacture of cellophane in the before-stated circumstances.

III. *The Sherman Act, Section 2—Monopolization.*—The only statutory language of Section 2 pertinent on this review is: "Every person who shall monopolize . . . shall be deemed guilty. . . ." . . . Our cases determine that a party has monopoly power if it has, over "any part of the trade or commerce among the several States," a power of controlling prices or unreasonably restricting competition. . . .

Senator Hoar, in discussing Section 2, pointed out that monopoly involved something more than extraordinary commercial success, "that it involved something like the use of means which made it impossible for other persons to engage in fair competition." This exception to the Sherman Act prohibitions of monopoly power is perhaps the monopoly "thrust upon" one of *United States* v. *Aluminum Co. of America*, 148 F.2d 416, 429. . . .

If cellophane is the "market" that duPont is found to dominate, it may be assumed it does have monopoly power over that "market." Monopoly power is the power to control prices or exclude competition. It seems apparent that duPont's power to set the price of cellophane has only been limited by the competition afforded by other flexible packaging materials. Moreover, it may be practically impossible for anyone to commence manufacturing cellophane without full access to duPont's technique. However, duPont has no power to prevent competition from other wrapping materials. The trial court consequently had to determine whether competition from the other wrappings prevented duPont from possessing monopoly power in violation of Section 2. Price and competition are so intimately entwined that any discussion of theory must treat them as one. It is inconceivable that price could be controlled without power over competition or vice versa. This approach to the determination of monopoly power is strengthened by this Court's conclusion in prior cases that, when an alleged monopolist has power over price and competition, an intention to monopolize in a proper case may be assumed.[2]

If a large number of buyers and sellers deal freely in a standardized product, such as salt or wheat, we have complete or pure competition. Patents, on the other hand, furnish the most familiar type of classic monopoly. As the producers of a standardized product bring about significant differentiations of quality, design, or packaging in the product that permit differences of use, competition becomes to a greater or less degree incomplete and the producer's power over price and competition greater over his article and its use, according to the differentiation he is able to create and maintain. A retail seller may have in one sense a monopoly on certain trade because of location, as an isolated country store or filling station, or because no one else makes a product of just the quality or attractiveness of his product, as for example in cigarettes. Thus one can theorize that we have monopolistic competition in every nonstandardized commodity with each manufacturer having power over the price and production of his own product.[3] However, this power that, let us say, automobile or soft-drink manufacturers have over their trademarked products is not the power that makes an illegal monopoly. Illegal power must be appraised in terms of the competitive market for the product.

Determination of the competitive market for commodities depends on how different from one another are the offered commodities in character or use, how far buyers will go to substitute one commodity for another. For example, one can think of building materials as in commodity competition but one could hardly say that brick competed with steel or wood or

---

[2] Here the Court cited United States *v*. Columbia Steel Co., 334 U.S. 495, 525; United States *v*. Paramount Pictures, 334 U.S. 131, 173; and Apex Hosiery Co. *v* Leader, 310 U.S. 469, 501. IMS.

[3] Here the Court cited Chamberlin, *Theory of Monopolistic Competition*, c. IV. IMS.

cement or stone in the meaning of Sherman Act litigation; the products are too different. This is the interindustry competition emphasized by some economists. . . . On the other hand, there are certain differences in the formulae for soft drinks but one can hardly say that each one is an illegal monopoly. Whatever the market may be, we hold that control of price or competition establishes the existence of monopoly power under Section 2. Section 2 requires the application of a reasonable approach in determining the existence of monopoly power just as surely as did Section 1. This of course does not mean that there can be a reasonable monopoly. . . . Our next step is to determine whether duPont has monopoly power over cellophane: that is, power over its price in relation to or competition with other commodities. The charge was monopolization of cellophane. The defense, that cellophane was merely a part of the relevant market for flexible packaging materials.

IV. *The Relevant Market.*—When a product is controlled by one interest, without substitutes available in the market, there is monopoly power. Because most products have possible substitutes, we cannot, as we said in *Times-Picayune Co.* v. *United States*, 345 U.S. 594, 612, give "that infinite range" to the definition of substitutes. Nor is it a proper interpretation of the Sherman Act to require that products be fungible to be considered in the relevant market.

The Government argues:

> We do not here urge that in *no* circumstances may competition of substitutes negative possession of monopolistic power over trade in a product. The decisions make it clear at the least that the courts will not consider substitutes other than those which are substantially fungible with the monopolized product and sell at substantially the same price.

But where there are market alternatives that buyers may readily use for their purposes, illegal monopoly does not exist merely because the product said to be monopolized differs from others. If it were not so, only physically identical products would be a part of the market. To accept the Government's argument, we would have to conclude that the manufacturers of plain as well as moistureproof cellophane were monopolists, and so with films such as Pliofilm, foil, glassine, polyethylene, and Saran, for each of these wrapping materials is distinguishable. These were all exhibits in the case. New wrappings appear, generally similar to cellophane: is each a monopoly? What is called for is an appraisal of the "cross-elasticity" of demand in the trade. . . . The varying circumstances of each case determine the result. In considering what is the relevant market for determining the control of price and competition, no more definite rule can be declared than that commodities reasonably interchangeable by consumers for the same purposes make up that "part of the trade or commerce," monopolization of which may be illegal. As respects flexible packaging materials, the market . . . is nationwide.

Industrial activities cannot be confined to trim categories. Illegal monopolies under Section 2 may well exist over limited products in narrow fields where competition is eliminated. That does not settle the issue here. In determining the market under the Sherman Act, it is the use or uses to which the commodity is put that control. The selling price between commodities with similar uses and different characteristics may vary, so that the cheaper product can drive out the more expensive. Or, the superior quality of higher priced articles may make dominant the more desirable. Cellophane costs more than many competing products and less than a few. But whatever the price, there are various flexible wrapping materials that are bought by manufacturers for packaging their goods in their own plants or are sold to converters who shape and print them for use in the packaging of the commodities to be wrapped.

Cellophane differs from other flexible packaging materials. From some it differs more than from others. . . . It will adequately illustrate the similarity in characteristics of the various products by noting . . . [that the use of glassine] is almost as extensive as cellophane, . . . and many of its characteristics [are] equally or more satisfactory to users.

It may be admitted that cellophane combines the desirable elements of transparency, strength and cheapness more definitely than any of the others. . . .

But, despite cellophane's advantages, it has to meet competition from other materials in every one of its uses. . . . Food products are the chief outlet, with cigarettes next. The Government makes no challenge to Finding 283 that cellophane furnishes less than 7% of wrappings for bakery products, 25% for candy, 32% for snacks, 35% for meats and poultry, 27% for crackers and biscuits, 47% for fresh produce, and 34% for frozen foods. Seventy-five to eighty percent of cigarettes are wrapped in cellophane. . . . Thus, cellophane shares the packaging market with others. The over-all result is that cellophane accounts for 17.9% of flexible wrapping materials, measured by the wrapping surface. . . .

Moreover a very considerable degree of functional interchangeability exists between these products. . . . It will be noted . . . that except as to permeability to gases, cellophane has no qualities that are not possessed by a number of other materials. . . . Pliofilm is more expensive . . . but its superior physical characteristics apparently offset cellophane's price advantage. While retailers shift continually between the two, the trial court found that Pliofilm is increasing its share of the business. . . .

An element for consideration as to cross-elasticity of demand between products is the responsiveness of the sales of one product to price changes of the other. If a slight decrease in the price of cellophane causes a considerable number of customers of other flexible wrappings to switch to cellophane, it would be an indication that a high cross-elasticity of demand exists between them; that the products compete in the same market. The court below held that the "[g]reat sensitivity of customers in the flexible packaging markets to price or quality changes" prevented duPont from possessing monopoly control over price. . . . The record sustains these findings. . . .

We conclude that cellophane's interchangeability with the other materials mentioned suffices to make it a part of this flexible packaging material market.

The Government stresses the fact that the variation in price between cellophane and other materials demonstrates they are noncompetitive. As these products are all flexible wrapping materials, it seems reasonable to consider, as was done at the trial, their comparative cost to the consumer in terms of square area. . . . Cellophane costs two or three times as much, surface measure, as its chief competitors for the flexible wrapping market, glassine and greaseproof papers. Other forms of cellulose wrappings and those from other chemical or mineral substances, with the exception of aluminum foil, are more expensive. The uses of these materials . . . are largely to wrap small packages for retail distribution. The wrapping is a relatively small proportion of the entire cost of the article. Different producers need different qualities in wrappings and their need may vary from time to time as their products undergo change. But the necessity for flexible wrappings is the central and unchanging demand. We cannot say that these differences in cost gave duPont monopoly power over prices in view of the findings of fact on that subject.

It is the variable characteristics of the different flexible wrappings and the energy and ability with which the manufacturers push their wares that determine choice. A glance at "Modern Packaging," a trade journal, will give, by its various advertisements, examples of the competition among manufacturers for the flexible packaging market. The trial judge visited the 1952 Annual Packaging Show at Atlantic City, with the consent of counsel. He observed exhibits offered by "machinery manufacturers, converters and manufacturers of flexible packaging materials." He states that these personal observations confirmed his estimate of the competition between cellophane and other packaging materials . . . .

The record establishes plain cellophane and moistureproof cellophane are each flexible packaging materials which are functionally interchangeable with other flexible packaging materials and sold at same time to same customers for same purpose at competitive prices; there is no cellophane market distinct and separate from the market for flexible packaging materials; the market for flexible packaging materials is the relevant market for determining nature and extent of duPont's market control; and duPont has at all times competed with other cellophane producers and manufacturers of other flexible packaging materials in all aspects of its cellophane business.

The facts above considered dispose also of any contention that competitors have been excluded by duPont from the packaging material market. That market has many producers and there is no proof duPont ever has possessed power to exclude any of them from the rapidly expanding flexible packaging market. The Government apparently concedes as much, for it states that "lack of power to inhibit entry into this so-called market [*i.e.*, flexible packaging materials], comprising widely disparate products, is no indicium of absence of power to exclude competition in the manufacture and sale of cellophane." The record shows the multiplicity of competitors and the financial strength of some with individual assets running to the hundreds of millions. . . . Indeed, the trial court found that duPont could not exclude competitors even from the manufacture of cellophane, . . . an immaterial matter if the market is flexible packaging material. Nor can we say that duPont's profits, while liberal (according to the Government's 15.9% net after taxes on the 1937–1947 average), demonstrate the existence of a monopoly without proof of lack of comparable profits during those years in other prosperous industries. . . . There is no showing that duPont's rate of return was greater or less than that of other producers of flexible packaging materials. . . .

The "market" which one must study to determine when a producer has monopoly power will vary with the part of commerce under consideration. The tests are constant. That market is composed of products that have reasonable interchangeability for the purposes for which they are produced—price, use and qualities considered. While the application of the tests remains uncertain, it seems to us that duPont should not be found to monopolize cellophane when that product has the competition and interchangeability with other wrappings that this record shows.

On the findings of the District Court, its judgment is *Affirmed*.

MR. JUSTICE CLARK and MR. JUSTICE HARLAN took no part in the consideration or decision of this case.

. . . . .

MR. JUSTICE FRANKFURTER, concurring.

. . . . .

MR. CHIEF JUSTICE WARREN, with whom MR. JUSTICE BLACK and MR. JUSTICE DOUGLAS join, dissenting.

This case, like many under the Sherman Act, turns upon the proper definition of the market. In defining the market in which duPont's economic power is to be measured, the majority virtually emasculate Section 2 of the Sherman Act. They admit that "cellophane combines the desirable elements of transparency, strength and cheapness more definitely than any of" a host of other packaging materials. Yet they hold that all of those materials are so indistinguishable from cellophane as to warrant their inclusion in the market. We cannot agree that cellophane, in the language of *Times-Picayune Publishing Co.* v. *United States* . . . is "the selfsame product" as glassine, greaseproof and vegetable parchment papers, waxed papers, sulphite papers, aluminum foil, cellulose acetate, and Pliofilm and other films.

The majority opinion states that "[I]t will adequately illustrate the similarity in characteristics of the various products by noting here Finding 62 as to glassine." But Finding 62 merely states the respects in which the selected flexible packaging materials are as satisfactory as cellophane; it does not compare all the physical properties of cellophane and other materials. The Table incorporated in Finding 59 does make such a comparison, and enables us to note cellophane's unique combination of qualities lacking among less expensive materials in varying degrees.[4] . . . Indeed, the majority go further than placing cellophane in the same market with such products. They also include the transparent films, which are more expensive than cellophane. These bear even less resemblance to the lower priced packaging materials than does cellophane. . . .

If the conduct of buyers indicated that glassine, waxed and sulphite papers and aluminum foil were actually "the selfsame products" as cellophane, the qualitative differences demonstrated by the comparison of physical properties in Finding 59 would not be conclusive. But the record provides convincing proof that businessmen did not so regard these products. During the period covered by the complaint (1923–1947) cellophane enjoyed phenomenal growth. DuPont's 1924 production was 361,249 pounds, which sold for $1,306,662. Its 1947 production was 133,502,858 pounds, which sold for $55,339,626. Findings 297 and 337. Yet throughout this period the price of cellophane was far greater than that of glassine, waxed paper or sulphite paper. Finding 136 states that in 1929 cellophane's price was even seven times that of glassine; in 1934, four times, and in 1949 still more than twice glassine's price. Reference to DX-994, the graph upon which Finding 136 is based, shows that cellophane had a similar price relation to waxed paper and that sulphite paper sold at even less than glassine and waxed paper. We cannot believe that buyers, practical businessmen, would have bought cellophane in increasing amounts over a quarter of a century if close substitutes were available at from one-seventh to one-half cellophane's price. That they did so is testimony to cellophane's distinctiveness.

The inference yielded by the conduct of cellophane buyers is reinforced by the conduct of sellers other than duPont. Finding 587 states that Sylvania, the only other cellophane producer, absolutely and immediately

---

[4] . . . The majority opinion quotes at length from Stocking and Mueller, "The Cellophane Case," XLV *Amer. Economic Rev.* 29, 48–49, in noting the comparative characteristics of cellophane and other products. Unfortunately, the opinion fails to quote the conclusion reached by these economists. They state: "The [trial] court to the contrary notwithstanding, the market in which cellophane meets the 'competition' of other wrappers is narrower than the market for all flexible packaging materials." *Id.*, at 52. And they conclude that ". . . cellophane is so differentiated from other flexible wrapping materials that its cross elasticity of demand gives duPont significant and continuing monopoly power." *Id.*, at 63.

followed every duPont price change, even dating back its price list to the effective date of duPont's change. Producers of glassine and waxed paper, on the other hand, displayed apparent indifference to duPont's repeated and substantial price cuts. DX-994 shows that from 1924 to 1932 duPont dropped the price of plain cellophane 84%, while the price of glassine remained constant. And during the period 1933–1946 the prices for glassine and waxed paper actually increased in the face of a further 21% decline in the price of cellophane. If "shifts of business" due to "price sensitivity" had been substantial, glassine and waxed paper producers who wanted to stay in business would have been compelled by market forces to meet duPont's price challenge just as Sylvania was. . . . Surely there was more than "a slight decrease in the price of cellophane" during the period covered by the complaint. That producers of glassine and waxed paper remained dominant in the flexible packaging materials market without meeting cellophane's tremendous price cuts convinces us that cellophane was not in effective competition with their products.[5]

Certainly duPont itself shared our view. From the first, duPont recognized that it need not concern itself with competition from other packaging materials. For example, when duPont was contemplating entry into cellophane production, its Development Department reported that glassine "is so inferior that it belongs in an entirely different class and has hardly to be considered as a competitor of cellophane." This was still duPont's view in 1950 when its survey of competitive prospects wholly omitted reference to glassine, waxed paper or sulphite paper and stated that "competition for duPont cellophane will come from competitive cellophane and from non-cellophane films made by us or by others."[6]

DuPont's every action was directed toward maintaining dominance over cellophane. Its 1923 agreements with La Cellophane, the French concern which first produced commercial cellophane, gave duPont exclusive North and Central American rights to cellophane's technology, manufacture and sale, and provided, without any limitation in time, that all existing and future information pertaining to the cellophane process be considered "secret and confidential," and be held in an exclusive common pool. In its subsequent agreements with foreign licensees, duPont was careful to preserve its continental market inviolate. In 1929, while it was still the sole domestic producer of cellophane, duPont won its long struggle to raise the tariff from 25% to 60%, ad valorem, on cellophane imports, substantially foreclosing foreign competition. When Sylvania became the second American cellophane producer the following year and duPont filed suit claiming infringement of its moistureproof patents, they settled the suit by entering into a cross-licensing agreement. . . . If close substitutes

---

[5] See Stocking and Mueller, "The Cellophane Case," XLV *Amer. Economic Rev.* 29, 56.

[6] R. 4070. It is interesting to note that duPont had almost 70% of the market which this report considered relevant.

for cellophane had been commercially available, duPont, an enlightened enterprise, would not have gone to such lengths to control cellophane.

As predicted by its 1923 market analysis, duPont's dominance in cellophane proved enormously profitable from the outset. After only five years of production, when duPont bought out the minority stock interests in its cellophane subsidiary, it had to pay more than fifteen times the original price of the stock. But such success was not limited to the period of innovation, limited sales and complete domestic monopoly. A confidential duPont report shows that during the period 1937–1947, despite great expansion of sales, duPont's "operative return" (before taxes) averaged 31%, while its average "net return" (after deduction of taxes, bonuses, and fundamental research expenditures) was 15.9%. Such profits provide a powerful incentive for the entry of competitors.[7] Yet from 1924 to 1951 only one new firm, Sylvania, was able to begin cellophane production. And Sylvania could not have entered if La Cellophane's secret process had not been stolen.[8] It is significant that for 15 years Olin Industries, a substantial firm, was unsuccessful in its attempt to produce cellophane, finally abandoning the project in 1944 after having spent about $1,000,-000. . . .

The trial court found that

> DuPont has no power to set cellophane prices arbitrarily. If prices for cellophane increase in relation to prices of other flexible packaging materials it will lose business to manufacturers of such materials in varying amounts for each of duPont's cellophane's major end uses.   Finding 712.

This further reveals its misconception of the antitrust laws. A monopolist seeking to maximize profits cannot raise prices "arbitrarily." Higher prices of course mean smaller sales, but they also mean higher per-unit profit. Lower prices will increase sales but reduce per-unit profit. Within these limits a monopolist has a considerable degree of latitude in determining which course to pursue in attempting to maximize profits. The trial judge thought that, if duPont raised its price, the market would "penalize" it with smaller profits as well as lower sales. DuPont proved him wrong. When

---

[7] See Stocking and Mueller, "The Cellophane Case," XLV *Amer. Economic Rev.* 29, 60–63, where the authors compare the domestic economic history of rayon with that of cellophane. The first American rayon producer earned 64.2 percent on its investment in 1920, thereby attracting duPont. After a loss in 1921, duPont's average return for the next four years was roughly 32%. As more firms began rayon production, duPont's and the industry's return on investment began to drop. When 6 new firms entered the industry in 1930, bringing the number of producers to 20, average industry earnings for that year declined to 5% and duPont suffered a net loss. "From the beginning of the depression in 1929 through the succeeding recovery and the 1938 recession duPont averaged 29.6 per cent before taxes on its cellophane investment. On its rayon investment it averaged only 6.3 per cent." *Id.*, at 62–63.

[8] In 1924 two of La Cellophane's principal officials absconded with complete information on the cellophane process. A Belgian concern was then set up to use this process in making cellophane, and it later organized Sylvania as an American affiliate. Findings 615–618.

1947 operating earnings dropped below 26% for the first time in 10 years, it increased cellophane's price 7% and boosted its earnings in 1948. DuPont's division manager then reported that "if an operative return of 31% is considered inadequate then an upward revision in prices will be necessary to improve the return." It is this latitude with respect to price, this broad power of choice, that the antitrust laws forbid. DuPont's independent pricing policy and the great profits consistently yielded by that policy leave no room for doubt that it had power to control the price of cellophane. The findings of fact cited by the majority cannot affect this conclusion. For they merely demonstrate that, during the period covered by the complaint, duPont was a "good monopolist," *i.e.*, that it did not engage in predatory practices and that it chose to maximize profits by lowering price and expanding sales. Proof of enlightened exercise of monopoly power certainly does not refute the existence of that power.

The majority opinion purports to reject the theory of "interindustry competition." Brick, steel, wood, cement and stone, it says, are "too different" to be placed in the same market. But cellophane, glassine, wax papers, sulphite papers, greaseproof and vegetable parchment papers, aluminum foil, cellulose acetate, Pliofilm and other films are not "too different," the opinion concludes. The majority approach would apparently enable a monopolist of motion picture exhibition to avoid Sherman Act consequences by showing that motion pictures compete in substantial measure with legitimate theatre, television, radio, sporting events and other forms of entertainment. Here, too, "shifts of business" undoubtedly accompany fluctuations in price and "there are market alternatives that buyers may readily use for their purposes." . . . [T]he formula of "reasonable interchangeability," as applied by the majority, appears indistinguishable from the theory of "interindustry competition." The danger in it is that, as demonstrated in this case, it is "perfectly compatible with a fully monopolized economy."[9]

The majority hold in effect that, because cellophane meets competition for many end uses, those buyers for other uses who need or want only cellophane are not entitled to the benefits of competition within the cellophane industry. . . . Furthermore, those buyers who have "reasonable alternatives" between cellophane and other products are also entitled to competition within the cellophane industry, for such competition may lead to lower prices and improved quality.

The foregoing analysis of the record shows conclusively that cellophane is the relevant market. Since duPont has the lion's share of that market, it must have monopoly power, as the majority concede. This being so, we think it clear that, in the circumstances of this case, duPont is guilty of "monopolization." The briefest sketch of duPont's business history pre-

[9] Adams, "The 'Rule of Reason': Workable Competition or Workable Monopoly?," 63 *Yale L. J.* 348, 364.

cludes it from falling within the "exception to the Sherman Act prohibitions of monopoly power" (majority opinion, pp. 390–391) by successfully asserting that monopoly was "thrust upon" it. DuPont was not "the passive beneficiary of a monopoly" within the meaning of *United States* v. *Aluminum Co. of America, supra,* at 429–430. It sought and maintained dominance through illegal agreements dividing the world market, concealing and suppressing technological information, and restricting its licensee's production by prohibitive royalties, and through numerous maneuvers which might have been "honestly industrial" but whose necessary effect was nevertheless exclusionary. DuPont cannot bear "the burden of proving that it owes its monopoly *solely* to superior skill. . . ." (Emphasis supplied.) *United States* v. *United Shoe Machinery Corp.* . . .

Nor can duPont rely upon its moistureproof patents as a defense to the charge of monopolization. Once duPont acquired the basic cellophane process as a result of its illegal 1923 agreements with La Cellophane, development of moistureproofing was relatively easy. DuPont's moistureproof patents were fully subject to the exclusive pooling arrangements and territorial restrictions established by those agreements. And they were the subject of the illicit and exclusionary duPont-Sylvania agreement. Hence, these patents became tainted as part and parcel of duPont's illegal monopoly. Cf., *Mercoid Corp.* v. *Mid-Continent Co.,* 320 U.S. 661, 670. Any other result would permit one who monopolizes a market to escape the statutory liability by patenting a simple improvement on his product.

If competition is at the core of the Sherman Act, we cannot agree that it was consistent with that Act for the enormously lucrative cellophane industry to have no more than two sellers from 1924 to 1951. The conduct of duPont and Sylvania illustrates that a few sellers tend to act like one and that an industry which does not have a competitive structure will not have competitive behavior. The public should not be left to rely upon the dispensations of management in order to obtain the benefits which normally accompany competition. Such beneficence is of uncertain tenure. Only actual competition can assure long-run enjoyment of the goals of a free economy.

We would reverse the decision below and remand the cause to the District Court with directions to determine the relief which should be granted against duPont.

United States v. Grinnell Corporation

384 U.S. 563 (1966)

MR. JUSTICE DOUGLAS delivered the opinion of the Court.

This case presents an important question under §2 of the Sherman Act. . . . The District Court held for the Government and entered a decree. All parties appeal, the United States because it deems the relief inadequate

and the defendants both on the merits and on the relief and on the ground
that the District Court denied them a fair trial. . . .

Grinnell manufactures plumbing supplies and fire sprinkler systems.
It also owns 76% of the stock of ADT, 89% of the stock of AFA, and
100% of the stock of Holmes.[1] ADT provides both burglary and fire
protection services; Holmes provides burglary services alone; AFA
supplies only fire protection service. Each offers a central station service
under which hazard-detecting devices installed on the protected premises automatically transmit an electric signal to a central station. The
central station is manned 24 hours a day. Upon receipt of a signal, the central station, where appropriate, dispatches guards to the protected premises
and notifies the police or fire department direct. There are other forms
of protective services. But the record shows that subscribers to accredited
central station service (*i.e.*, that approved by the insurance underwriters)
receive reductions in their insurance premiums that are substantially
greater than the reduction received by the users of other kinds of protection service. In 1961 accredited companies in the central station service
business grossed $65,000,000. ADT, Holmes, and AFA are the three largest
companies in the business in terms of revenue: ADT (with 121 central
stations in 115 cities) has 73% of the business; Holmes (with 12 central
stations in three large cities) has 12.5%; AFA (with three central stations
in three large cities) has 2%. Thus the three companies that Grinnell controls have over 87% of the business. . . .

[The Court here detailed the numerous acquisitions—37 by ADT and
3 by Holmes—and the various geographic and product-line market-sharing
agreements entered into over the years by ADT, Holmes and others.]

ADT over the years reduced its minimum basic rates to meet competition and renewed contracts at substantially increased rates in cities where
it had a monopoly of accredited central station service. ADT threatened
retaliation against firms that contemplated inaugurating central station
service. And the record indicates that, in contemplating opening a new
central station, ADT officials frequently stressed that such action would
deter their competitors from opening a new station in that area.

The District Court found that the defendant companies had committed
per se violations of §1 of the Sherman Act as well as §2 and entered a
decree. . . .

I.

The offense of monopoly under §2 of the Sherman Act has two elements: (1) the possession of monopoly power in the relevant market and
(2) the willful acquisition or maintenance of that power as distinguished
from growth or development as a consequence of a superior product, busi-

---

[1] These are the record figures. Since the time of the trial, Grinnell's holdings have
increased. Counsel for Grinnell has advised this Court that Grinnell now holds 80%
of ADT's stock and 90% of the stock of AFA.

ness acumen, or historic accident. We shall see that this second ingredient presents no major problem here, as what was done in building the empire was done plainly and explicitly for a single purpose. In *United States* v. *du-Pont & Co.*, 351 U.S. 377, 391, we defined monopoly power as "the power to control prices or exclude competition." The existence of such power ordinarily may be inferred from the predominant share of the market. . . . In the present case, 87% of the accredited central station service business leaves no doubt that the congeries of these defendants have monopoly power—power which, as our discussion of the record indicates, they did not hesitate to wield—if that business is the relevant market. The only remaining question therefore is, what is the relevant market?

In case of a product it may be of such a character that substitute products must also be considered, as customers may turn to them if there is a slight increase in the price of the main product. That is the teaching of the *duPont* case . . . , *viz.*, that commodities reasonably interchangeable make up that "part" of trade or commerce which §2 protects against monopoly power.

The District Court treated the entire accredited central station service business as a single market and we think it was justified in so doing. Defendants argue that the different central station services offered are so diverse that they cannot under *duPont* be lumped together to make up the relevant market. For example, burglar alarm services are not interchangeable with fire alarm services. They further urge that *duPont* requires that protective services other than those of the central station variety be included in the market definition.

But there is here a single use, *i.e.*, the protection of property, through a central station that receives signals. It is that service, accredited, that is unique and that competes with all the other forms of property protection. We see no barrier to combining in a single market a number of different products or services where that combination reflects commercial realities. To repeat, there is here a single basic service—the protection of property through use of a central service station—that must be compared with all other forms of property protection.

In §2 cases under the Sherman Act, as in §7 cases under the Clayton Act (*Brown Shoe Co.* v. *United States*, 370 U.S. 294, 325) there may be submarkets that are separate economic entities. We do not pursue that question here. First, we deal with services, not with products; and second, we conclude that the accredited central station is a type of service that makes up a relevant market and that domination or control of it makes out a monopoly of a "part" of trade or commerce within the meaning of §2 of the Sherman Act. The defendants have not made out a case for fragmentizing the types of services into lesser units.

Burglar alarm service is in a sense different from fire alarm service; from waterflow alarms; and so on. But it would be unrealistic on this record to break down the market into the various kinds of central station protective services that are available. Central station companies recognize that to compete effectively, they must offer all or nearly all types of service.[2] The different forms of accredited central station service are provided from a single office and customers utilize different services in combination. We held in *United States* v. *Philadelphia Nat. Bank*, 374 U.S. 321, 356, that "the cluster" of services denoted by the term "commercial banking" is "a distinct line of commerce." There is, in our view, a comparable cluster of services here. That bank case arose under §7 of the Clayton Act where the question was whether the effect of a merger "in any line of commerce" may be "substantially to lessen competition." We see no reason to differentiate between "line" of commerce in the context of the Clayton Act and "part" of commerce for purposes of the Sherman Act. See *United States* v. *First Nat. Bank & Trust Co.*, 376 U.S. 665, 667–668. In the §7 national bank case just mentioned, *services*, not *products* in the mercantile sense, were involved. In our view the lumping together of various kinds of *services* makes for the appropriate market here as it did in the §7 case.

There are, to be sure, substitutes for the accredited central station service. But none of them appears to operate on the same level as the central station service so as to meet the interchangeability test of the *duPont* case. Nonautomatic and automatic local alarm systems appear on this record to have marked differences, not the low degree of differentiation required of substitute services as well as substitute articles.

Watchman service is far more costly and less reliable. Systems that set off an audible alarm at the site of a fire or burglary are cheaper but often less reliable. They may be inoperable without anyone's knowing it. Moreover, there is a risk that the local ringing of an alarm will not attract the needed attention and help. Proprietary systems that a customer purchases and operates are available; but they can be used only by a very large business or by government and are not realistic alternatives for most concerns. There are also protective services connected directly to municipal police or fire departments. But most cities with an accredited central station do not permit direct, connected service for private businesses. These alternate services and devices differ, we are told, in utility, efficiency, reliability, responsiveness, and continuity, and the record sustains that position. And, as noted, insurance companies generally allow a greater reduction in premiums for accredited central station service than for other types of protection.

Defendants earnestly urge that despite these differences, they face

[2] Thus, of the 38 nondefendant firms operating a central service station protective service in the United States in 1961, 24 offered all of the following services: automatic fire alarm; waterflow alarm and sprinkler supervision; watchman's reporting and manual fire alarm; and burglar alarm. Of the other firms, 11 provided no watchman's reporting and manual fire alarm service; six provided no automatic fire alarm service; and two offered no sprinkler supervisory and waterflow alarm service. Moreover, of the 14 firms not providing the full panoply of services, 10 lacked only *one* of the above-described services. Appellant ADT's assertion that "very few accredited central stations furnish the full variety of services" is flatly contradicted by the record.

competition from these other modes of protection. They seem to us seriously to overstate the degree of competition, but we recognize that (as the District Court found) they "do not have unfettered power to control the price of their services . . . due to the fringe competition of other alarm or watchmen services." 236 F. Supp., at 254. What defendants overlook is that the high degree of differentiation between central station protection and the other forms means that for many customers, only central station protection will do. Though some customers may be willing to accept higher insurance rates in favor of cheaper forms of protection, others will not be willing or able to risk serious interruption to their businesses, even though covered by insurance, and will thus be unwilling to consider anything but central station protection.

The accredited, as distinguished from nonaccredited service, is a relevant part of commerce. Virtually the only central station companies in the status of the nonaccredited are those that have not yet been able to meet the standards of the rating bureau. The accredited ones are indeed those that have achieved, in the eyes of underwriters, superiorities that other central stations do not have. The accredited central station is located in a building of approved design, provided with an emergency lighting system and two alternate main power sources, manned constantly by at least a required minimum of operators, provided with a direct line to fire headquarters and, where possible, a direct line to a police station; and equipped with all the devices, circuits, and equipment meeting the requirements of the underwriters. These standards are important as insurance carriers often require accredited central station service as a condition to writing insurance. There is indeed evidence that customers consider the unaccredited service is inferior. . . .

We have said enough about the great hold that the defendants have on this market. The percentage is so high as to justify the finding of monopoly. And, as the facts already related indicate, this monopoly was achieved in large part by unlawful and exclusionary practices. The restrictive agreements that preempted for each company a segment of the market where it was free of competition of the others were one device. Pricing practices that contained competitors were another. The acquisitions by Grinnell of ADT, AFA, and Holmes were still another. . . . By those acquisitions it perfected the monopoly power to exclude competitors and fix prices.[3]

II.

[In this section, the Court considered the scope of the decree imposed

---

[3] Since the record clearly shows that this monopoly power was consciously acquired, we have no reason to reach the further position of the District Court that once monopoly power is shown to exist, the burden is on the defendants to show that their dominance is due to skill, acumen, and the like.

by the District Court. It found the decree to be inadequate in terms of the nature of the divestiture conditions imposed upon Grinnell.]

. . . . .

The judgment below is affirmed except as to the decree. We remand for further hearings on the nature of the relief consistent with the views expressed herein.

It is so ordered.

MR. JUSTICE HARLAN, dissenting.

. . . . .

MR. JUSTICE FORTAS, with whom MR. JUSTICE STEWART joins, dissenting.

I agree that the judgment below should be remanded, but I do not agree that the remand should be limited to reshaping the decree. Because I believe that the definition of the relevant market here cannot be sustained, I would reverse and remand for a new determination of this basic issue, subject to proper standards.

We have here a case under both §1 and §2 of the Sherman Act. . . . The judicial task is not difficult to state: Does the record show a combination in restraint of trade or a monopoly or attempt to monopolize? If so, what are its characteristics, scope, and effect? And, finally, what is the appropriate remedy for a court of equity to decree?

Each of these inquiries depends upon two basic referents: definition of the geographical area of trade or commerce restrained or monopolized, and of the products or services involved. In §1 cases this problem ordinarily presents little difficulty because the combination in restraint of trade itself delineates the "market" with sufficient clarity to support the usual injunctive form of relief in those cases. See, e.g., *United States* v. *Griffith*, 334 U.S. 100. In the present case, however, the essence of the offense is monopolization, achieved or attempted, and the major relief is divestiture. For these purposes, "market" definition is of the essence, just as in §7 cases the kindred definition of the "line of commerce" is fundamental. . . .

In §2 cases, the search for "the relevant market" must be undertaken and pursued with relentless clarity. It is, in essence, an economic task put to the uses of the law. Unless this task is well done, the results will be distorted in terms of the conclusion as to whether the law has been violated and what the decree should contain.

In this case, the relevant geographical and product markets have not been defined on the basis of the economic facts of the industry concerned. They have been tailored precisely to fit defendants' business. The Government proposed and the trial court concluded that the relevant market is not the business of fire protection, or burglary protection, or protection against waterflow, etc., or all of these together. It is not even the business of furnishing these from a central location. It is the business, viewed nationally, of supplying "insurance accredited central station protection services" (CSPS)—that is, fire, burglary and other kinds of protection furnished from a central station which is accredited by insurance companies. The business of defendants fits neatly into the product and geographic market so defined. In fact, it comes close to filling the market so defined. This Court has now approved this Procrustean definition.

The geographical market is defined as nationwide. But the need and the service are intensely local—more local by far, for example, than the market which this Court found to be local in *United States* v. *Philadelphia Nat. Bank*, 374 U.S. 321, 357–362. . . . Protection must be provided on the spot. It must be furnished by local personnel able to bring help to the scene within minutes. Even the central stations can provide service only within a 25-mile radius. Where the tenants of the premises turn to central stations for this service, they must make their contracts locally with the central station and purchase their services from it on the basis of local conditions.

But because these defendants, the trial court found, are connected by stock ownership, interlocking management and some degree of national corporate direction, and because there is some national participation in selling as well as national financing, advertising, purchasing of equipment, and the like,[4] the court concluded that the competitive area to be considered is national. This Court now affirms that conclusion.

This is a non sequitur. It is not permissible to seize upon the nationwide scope of defendants' operation and to bootstrap a geographical definition of the market from this. The purpose of the search for the relevant geographical market is to find the area or areas to which a potential buyer may rationally look for the goods or services that he seeks. The test, as this Court said in *United States* v. *Philadelphia Nat. Bank*, is "the geographic structure of supplier-customer relations," 374 U.S. 321, 357, quoting Kaysen & Turner, Antitrust Policy 102 (1959). And, as MR. JUSTICE CLARK put it in *Tampa Electric Co.* v. *Nashville Coal Co.*, 365 U.S. 320, 327, the definition of the relevant market requires "careful selection of the market area in which the seller operates, and to which the purchaser can practicably turn for supplies."[5] The central issue is where does a potential buyer look for potential suppliers of the service—what is the geographical area in which the buyer has, or, in the absence of monopoly, would have, a real choice as to price and alternative facilities? This depends upon the facts of the market place, taking into account such economic factors as the distance over which supplies and services may be feasibly furnished, consistently with cost and functional efficiency. . . .

---

[4] . . . There is neither finding nor record to support the implication that rates are to any substantial extent fixed on a nationwide basis, or that there are nationwide contracts with multistate businesses in any significant degree, or that insurers inspect or certify central stations on a nationwide basis.

[5] See also *Brown Shoe Co.* v. *United States*, 370 U.S. 294, 336–37.

Here, there can be no doubt that the correct geographic market is local. The services at issue are intensely local: they can be furnished only locally. The business as it is done is local—not nationwide. If, as might well be the case on this record, defendants were found to have violated the Sherman Act in a number of these local areas, a proper decree, directed to those markets, as well as to general corporate features relevant to the condemned practices, could be fashioned. . . . This Court now directs the trial court to require "some [unspecified] divestiture" locally by the alarm companies. This is a recognition of the economic reality that the relevant competitive areas are local. . . .

The trial court's definition of the "product" market even more dramatically demonstrates that its action has been Procrustean—that it has tailored the market to the dimensions of the defendants. It recognizes that a person seeking protective services has many alternative sources. . . . The court relies solely upon its finding that the services offered by accredited central stations are of better quality, and upon its conclusion that the insurance companies tend to give "noticeably larger" discounts to policyholders who use accredited central station protective services. This Court now approves this strange red-haired, bearded, one-eyed man-with-a-limp classification. . . .

Moreover, we are told that the "relevant market" must assume this strange and curious configuration despite evidence in the record and a finding of the trial court that "fringe competition" from such locally available alternatives as watchmen, local alarm systems, proprietary systems, and unaccredited central stations has, in at least 20 cities, forced the defendants to operate at a "loss" even though defendants have a total monopoly in these cities of the "market"—namely, the "accredited central station protective services." And we are led to this odd result even though there is in the record abundant evidence that customers switch from one form of property protection to another, and not always in the direction of accredited central station service.

I believe this approach has no justification in economics, reason or law. . . . As this Court held in *Brown Shoe* . . . , the "reasonable interchangeability of use or the cross-elasticity of demand," determines the boundaries of a product market. 370 U.S., at 325. See also the *Cellophane Case*, 351 U.S., at 380. In plain language, this means that the court should have defined the relevant market here to include all services which, in light of geographical availability, price and use characteristics, are in realistic rivalry for all or some part of the business of furnishing protective services to premises. . . .

I do not suggest that wide disparities in quality, price and customer appeal could never affect the definition of the market. But this follows only where the disparities are so great that they create separate and distinct categories of buyers and sellers. The record here and the findings do not approach this standard. They fall far short of justifying the narrowing of the market as practiced here. I need refer only to the exclusion of non-accredited central stations, which the court seeks to justify by reference to differentials in insurance discounts. These differentials may indeed affect the relative cost to the consumer of the competing modes of protection. But, in the absence of proof that they result in eliminating the competing services from the category of those to which the purchaser "can practicably turn" for supplies,[6] they do not justify such total exclusion. This sort of exclusion of the supposedly not-quite-so-attractive service from the basic definition of the kinds of business and service against which defendants' activity will be measured, is entirely unjustified on this record.[7] . . .

. . . Now, because of this Court's mandate, the market-by-market inquiry must begin for purposes of the decree. But this should have been the foundation of judgment, not its superimposed conclusion. This inquiry should —in my opinion, it must—take into account the *total* economic situation— all of the options available to one seeking protection services. It should not be limited to central stations, and certainly not to "insurance accredited central station protective services" which this Court sanctions as the relevant market. . . .

[6] *Tampa Electric Co.* v. *Nashville Coal Co.*, 365 U.S., at 327.

[7] The example used by the court in its findings is illuminating and disturbing. In explanation of its narrow market definition, the court says that the difference between the accredited central station protective services and all others "could be compared" to the difference between a compact six-cylinder car and a chauffeur-driven sedan. It is probably true that the degree of direct competition between luxury automobiles and compacts is slight. But it is by no means as clear-cut as the trial court seems to suggest. The question would require careful analysis in light of the total facts and issues. For example, if the antitrust problem at hand involved an acquisition of the business of a manufacturer of compacts by a maker of luxury cars, it is by no means inconceivable that sufficient competitive overlap would be found to place both products in the "relevant market."

Chapter 2   DIRECT PRICE-FIXING AGREEMENTS

Cases instituted under Section 1 of the Sherman Act do, in a sense, fall into a simpler and far more consistent pattern than those brought under Section 2. With the exception of the *Appalachian Coals* decision, the Court has steadily refused to consider the "reasonableness" of direct price-fixing agreements, holding instead that these agreements among individual competitors were per se violations of the law. This, combined with the adoption of a Section 2 rule of reason in the *Standard Oil of New Jersey* decision presented above, introduced into the law what has come to be called the "double standard." In other words, while agreements among individual competitors concerning matters such as price policy have been held to be illegal in and of themselves, consolidations which yielded equal or greater market power have been tested for their "reasonableness." Feeling among economists on the double standard is divided. Two otherwise widely divergent groups agree that it is inconsistent to permit a firm to accomplish by consolidation what it is not permitted to do by contract. They part company, however, on the method of eliminating this "inconsistency." Some feel that the double standard can best be eliminated by abolishing the rule of reason used in Section 2 cases and thereby expanding the area of per se violation. Others propose to subject Section 1 as well as Section 2 cases to a test of reasonableness, a proposal which would—if adopted—allow defendants to justify conspiratorial activities by showing that favorable economic results were produced. A third group of economists and lawyers, who might be called "traditionalists," contend that the double standard is necessary if we are to maintain a dynamic, progressive, and noncartelized economy. To accomplish this they feel nothing must be done to penalize business size which may result from successful and fair competition only, while at the same time we must continue to hold any and all attempts to mitigate the force of competition through collusion and conspiracy to be violations of the law.

The cases presented below are intended to show court attitudes toward price-fixing agreements. Although—with the exception of *Appalachian Coals*—price-fixing conspiracies were uniformly condemned, the bases of the opinions vary. Thus, where the *Trenton Potteries* condemnation hinged at least in part on the market power of the conspirators, the later and controlling *Socony-Vacuum* decision held any attempt to influence prices, regardless of the market power of the group, to be illegal. Only in the *Appalachian Coals* case did the Court explicitly attempt to consider the "reasonableness" of price-fixing agreements, and even here one might contend that it was the lack of market power, not the "reasonableness" of the agreement, which prevented condemnation. In any event since *Socony-Vacuum*, the courts have consistently refused to move from the dogmatic position established therein. In the *Container Corporation* case, one of the latest to be decided under that doctrine, Justice Douglas summarily disposed of any consideration of the "reasonableness" of price-fixing arrangements.

Addyston Pipe and Steel Company v. United States

175 U.S. 211 (1899)

Note: This case involved an agreement among the six leading manufacturers of iron pipe to divide the market into several regional monopolies, and to fix prices.

MR. JUSTICE PECKHAM . . . delivered the opinion of the court. . . .

We are thus brought to the question whether the contract or combination proved in this case is one which is either a direct restraint or a regulation of commerce among the several States or with foreign nations contrary to the act of Congress [the Sherman Act]. It is objected on the part of the appellants that even if it affected interstate commerce the contract or combination was only a reasonable restraint upon a ruinous competition among themselves, and was formed only for the purpose of protecting the parties thereto in securing prices for their product that were fair and reasonable to themselves and the public. . . .

. . . [W]e are of opinion that the agreement or combination was not one which simply secured for its members fair and reasonable prices for the article dealt in by them. Even if the objection thus set up would, if well founded in fact, constitute a defense, we agree with the Circuit Court of Appeals in its statement of the special facts upon this branch of the case and with its opinion thereon as set forth by Circuit Judge Taft, as follows:

> The defendants being manufacturers and vendors of cast-iron pipe entered into a combination to raise the prices for pipe . . . [in] considerably more than three-quarters of the territory of the United States, . . . significantly called by the associates 'pay' territory. . . . Within the margin of the freight per ton which Eastern manufacturers would have to pay to deliver pipe in 'pay' territory, the defendants, by controlling two-thirds of the output in 'pay' territory,

were practically able to fix prices. . . . The most cogent evidence that they had this power is the fact everywhere apparent in the record that they exercised it. . . .

The defendants were by their combination therefore able to deprive the public in a large territory of the advantages otherwise accruing to them from the proximity of defendants' pipe factories and, by keeping prices just low enough to prevent competition by Eastern manufacturers, to compel the public to pay an increase over what the price would have been if fixed by competition between defendants, nearly equal to the advantage in freight rates enjoyed by defendants over Eastern competitors. The defendants acquired this power by voluntarily agreeing to sell only at prices fixed by their committee and by allowing the highest bidder at the secret 'auction pool' to become the lowest bidder of them at the public letting. Now, the restraint thus imposed on themselves was only partial. It did not cover the United States. There was not a complete monopoly. It was tempered by the fear of competition and it affected only a part of the price. But this certainly does not take the contract of association out of the annulling effect of the rule against monopolies. . . .

It has been earnestly pressed upon us that the prices at which the cast-iron pipe was sold in 'pay' territory were reasonable. . . . We do not think the issue an important one, because . . . we do not think that at common law there is any question of reasonableness open to the courts with reference to such a contract. Its tendency was certainly to give defendants the power to charge unreasonable prices, had they chosen to do so. But if it were important we should unhesitatingly find that the prices charged in the instances which were in evidence were unreasonable. . . .

The facts thus set forth show conclusively that the effect of the combination was to enhance prices beyond a sum which was reasonable. . . .

The views above expressed lead generally to an affirmance of the judgment of the Court of Appeals. . . . [But to] the extent that the present decree includes in its scope the enjoining of defendants thus situated from combining in regard to contracts for selling pipe in their own State, it is modified, and limited to that portion of the combination or agreement which is interstate in its character. As thus modified, the decree is *Affirmed*.

United States v. Trenton Potteries Co.

273 U.S. 392 (1927)

MR. JUSTICE STONE delivered the opinion of the Court.

Respondents, twenty individuals and twenty-three corporations, were convicted in the district court . . . of violating the Sherman Anti-Trust Law. . . . The indictment was in two counts. The first charged a combination to fix and maintain uniform prices for the sale of sanitary pottery, in restraint of interstate commerce; the second, a combination to restrain interstate commerce by limiting sales of pottery to a special group known to respondents as "legitimate jobbers." On appeal, the court of appeals . . .

reversed the judgment of conviction on both counts on the ground that there were errors in the conduct of the trial. . . . This Court granted certiorari. . . .

Respondents, engaged in the manufacture or distribution of 82 per cent. of the vitreous pottery fixtures produced in the United States for use in bathrooms and lavatories, were members of a trade organization known as the Sanitary Potters' Association. . . .

There is no contention here that the verdict was not supported by sufficient evidence that respondents, controlling some 82 per cent. of the business of manufacturing and distributing in the United States vitreous pottery . . . combined to fix prices and to limit sales in interstate commerce to jobbers.

The issues raised here by the government's specification of errors relate only to the decision of the court of appeals upon its review of certain rulings of the district court made in the course of its trial. It is urged that the court below erred in holding in effect . . . that the trial court should have submitted to the jury the question whether the price agreement complained of constituted an unreasonable restraint of trade. . . .

The trial court charged, in submitting the case to the jury that, if it found the agreements or combination complained of, it might return a verdict of guilty without regard to the reasonableness of the prices fixed, or the good intentions of the combining units, whether prices were actually lowered or raised or whether sales were restricted to the special jobbers, since both agreements of themselves were unreasonable restraints.

. . . The court below held specifically that the trial court erred in refusing to charge as requested and held in effect that the charge as given on this branch of the case was erroneous. . . .

. . . The question therefore to be considered here is whether the trial judge correctly withdrew from the jury the consideration of the reasonableness of the particular restraints charged.

That only those restraints upon interstate commerce which are unreasonable are prohibited by the Sherman Law was the rule laid down by the opinions of this Court in the *Standard Oil* and *Tobacco* cases. But it does not follow that agreements to fix or maintain prices are reasonable restraints and therefore permitted by the statute, merely because the prices themselves are reasonable. Reasonableness is not a concept of definite and unchanging content. Its meaning necessarily varies in the different fields of the law, because it is used as a convenient summary of the dominant considerations which control in the application of legal doctrines. Our view of what is a reasonable restraint of commerce is controlled by the recognized purpose of the Sherman Law itself. Whether this type of restraint is reasonable or not must be judged in part at least in the light of its effect on competition, for whatever difference of opinion there may be among economists as to the social and economic desirability of an unrestrained competitive system, it cannot be doubted that the Sherman Law and the judicial decisions interpreting it are based upon the assumption that the public interest is best protected from the evils of monopoly and price control by the maintenance of competition. . . .

The aim and result of every price-fixing agreement, if effective, is the elimination of one form of competition. The power to fix prices, whether reasonably exercised or not, involves power to control the market and to fix arbitrary and unreasonable prices. The reasonable price fixed today may through economic and business changes become the unreasonable price of tomorrow. Once established, it may be maintained unchanged because of the absence of competition secured by the agreement for a price reasonable when fixed. Agreements which create such potential power may well be held to be in themselves unreasonable or unlawful restraints, without the necessity of minute inquiry whether a particular price is reasonable or unreasonable as fixed and without placing on the government in enforcing the Sherman Law the burden of ascertaining from day to day whether it has become unreasonable through the mere variation of economic conditions. Moreover, in the absence of express legislation requiring it, we should hesitate to adopt a construction making the difference between legal and illegal conduct in the field of business relations depend upon so uncertain a test as whether prices are reasonable —a determination which can be satisfactorily made only after a complete survey of our economic organization and a choice between rival philosophies. . . .

The charge of the trial court, viewed as a whole, fairly submitted to the jury the question whether a price-fixing agreement as described in the first count was entered into by the respondents. Whether the prices actually agreed upon were reasonable or unreasonable was immaterial in the circumstances charged in the indictment and necessarily found by the verdict. The requested charge[1] . . . [was] inapplicable to the case in hand and rightly refused. . . .

MR. JUSTICE VAN DEVANTER, MR. JUSTICE SUTHERLAND and MR. JUSTICE BUTLER dissent.

MR. JUSTICE BRANDEIS took no part in the consideration or decision of this case.

Appalachian Coals, Inc. v. *United States*
288 U.S. 344 (1933)

MR. CHIEF JUSTICE HUGHES delivered the opinion of the Court.

This suit was brought to enjoin a combination alleged to be in restraint of interstate commerce in bituminous coal and in attempted monopoliza-

[1] Defendants had requested that the court charge the following: "The essence of the law is injury to the public. It is not every restraint of competition and not every restraint of trade that works an injury to the public; it is only an undue and unreasonable restraint of trade that has such an effect and is deemed to be unlawful." IMS.

tion of part of that commerce, in violation of Sections 1 and 2 of the Sherman Anti-Trust Act. . . . The District Court, composed of three Circuit Judges, made detailed findings of fact and entered final decree granting the injunction. . . .

Defendants, other than Appalachian Coals, Inc., are 137 producers of bituminous coal in eight districts (called for convenience Appalachian territory). . . . In 1929 (the last year for which complete statistics were available) the total production of bituminous coal east of the Mississippi river was 484,786,000 tons, of which defendants mined 58,011,367 tons, or 11.96 per cent. In the so-called Appalachian territory and the immediately surrounding area, the total production was 107,008,209 tons, of which defendants' production was 54.21 per cent, or 64 per cent if the output of "captive" mines (16,455,001 tons) be deducted. With a further deduction of 12,000,000 tons of coal produced in the immediately surrounding territory, which however, is not essentially different from the particular area described in these proceedings as Appalachian territory, defendants' production in the latter region was found to amount to 74.4 per cent.

The challenged combination lies in the creation by the defendant producers of an exclusive selling agency. This agency is the defendant Appalachian Coals, Inc., which may be designated as the Company. Defendant producers own all its capital stock, their holdings being in proportion to their production. The majority of the common stock, which has exclusive voting right, is held by seventeen defendants. By uniform contracts, separately made, each defendant producer constitutes the Company an exclusive agent for the sale of all coal (with certain exceptions) which the producer mines in Appalachian territory. The Company agrees to establish standard classifications, to sell all the coal of all its principals at the best prices obtainable and, if all cannot be sold, to apportion orders upon a stated basis. . . .

The Government's contention, which the District Court sustained, is that the plan violates the Sherman Anti-Trust Act,—in view that it eliminates competition among the defendants themselves and also gives the selling agency power substantially to affect and control the price of bituminous coal in many interstate markets. . . .

Defendants insist that the primary purpose of the formation of the selling agency was to increase the sale, and thus the production, of Appalachian coal through better methods of distribution, intensive advertising and research; to achieve economies in marketing, and to eliminate abnormal, deceptive and destructive trade practices. . . . Defendants contend that the evidence establishes that the selling agency will not have the power to dominate or fix the price of coal in any consuming market; that the price of coal will continue to be set in an open competitive market; and that their plan by increasing the sale of bituminous coal from Appalachian territory will promote, rather than restrain, interstate commerce.

First. There is no question as to the test to be applied in determining the legality of the defendants' conduct. The purpose of the Sherman Anti-Trust Act is to prevent undue restraints of interstate commerce, to maintain its appropriate freedom in the public interest, to afford protection from the subversive or coercive influences of monopolistic endeavor. . . . Its general phrases, interpreted to attain its fundamental objects, set up the essential standard of reasonableness. They call for vigilance in the detection and frustration of all efforts unduly to restrain the free course of interstate commerce, but they do not seek to establish a mere delusive liberty either by making impossible the normal and fair expansion of that commerce or the adoption of reasonable measures to protect it from injurious and destructive practices and to promote competition upon a sound basis. . . .

In applying this test, a close and objective scrutiny of particular conditions and purposes is necessary in each case. Realities must dominate the judgment. The mere fact that the parties to an agreement eliminate competition between themselves is not enough to condemn it. . . . The question of the application of the statute is one of intent and effect, and is not to be determined by arbitrary assumptions. It is therefore necessary in this instance to consider the economic conditions peculiar to the coal industry, the practices which have obtained, the nature of defendants' plan of making sales, the reasons which led to its adoption, and the probable consequences of the carrying out of that plan in relation to market prices and other matters affecting the public interest in interstate commerce in bituminous coal.

Second. The findings of the District Court, upon abundant evidence, leave no room for doubt as to the economic condition of the coal industry. That condition, as the District Court states, "for many years has been indeed deplorable." . . . And in a graphic summary of the economic situation, the court found that "numerous producing companies have gone into bankruptcy or into the hands of receivers, many mines have been shut down, the number of days of operation per week have been greatly curtailed, wages to labor have been substantially lessened, and the States in which coal producing companies are located have found it increasingly difficult to collect taxes."

Third. The findings also fully disclose the proceedings of the defendants in formulating their plan and the reasons for its adoption. . . . The District Court found that "the evidence tended to show that other selling agencies with a control of at least 70 percent of the production in their respective districts will be organized if the petition in this case is dismissed"; that in that event "there will result an organization in most of the districts whose coal is or may be competitive with Appalachian coal; but the testimony tends to show that there will still be substantial, active competition in the sale of coal in all markets in which Appalachian coal is sold."

Defendants refer to the statement of purposes in their published plan of organization,—that it was intended to bring about "a better and more orderly marketing of the coals from the region to be served by this company. . . ."

. . . . .

No attempt was made to limit production. The producers decided that it could not legally be limited and, in any event, it could not be limited practically. . . .

Fourth. Voluminous evidence was received with respect to the effect of defendants' plan upon market prices. As the plan has not gone into operation, there are no actual results upon which to base conclusions. The question is necessarily one of prediction. The court below found that, as between defendants themselves, competition would be eliminated. . . .

The more serious question relates to the effect of the plan upon competition between defendants and other producers. As already noted, the District Court found that "the great bulk" of the coal produced in Applachian territory is sold "in the highly competitive region east of the Mississippi river and north of the Ohio river under an adverse freight rate." Elaborate statistics were introduced. . . . It would be impossible to make even a condensed statement of this evidence, . . . but an examination of it fails to disclose an adequate basis for the conclusion that the operation of the defendants' plan would produce an injurious effect upon competitive conditions, in view of the vast volume of coal available, the conditions of production, and the network of transportation facilities at immediate command. . . .

Fifth. We think that the evidence requires the following conclusions:

(1) With respect to defendant's purposes, we find no warrant for determining that they were other than those they declared. Good intentions will not save a plan otherwise objectionable, but knowledge of actual intent is an aid in the interpretation of facts and prediction of consequences. . . . The unfortunate state of the industry would not justify any attempt unduly to restrain competition or to monopolize, but the existing situation prompted defendants to make, and the statute did not preclude them from making, an honest effort to remove abuses, to make competition fairer, and thus to promote the essential interests of commerce. The interests of producers and consumers are interlinked. When industry is grievously hurt, when producing concerns fail, when unemployment mounts and communities dependent upon profitable production are prostrated, the wells of commerce go dry. So far as actual purposes are concerned, the conclusion of the court below was amply supported that defendants were engaged in a fair and open endeavor to aid the industry in a measurable recovery from its plight. The inquiry then, must be whether despite this objective the inherent nature of their plan was such as to create an undue restraint upon interstate commerce.

(2) The question thus presented chiefly concerns the effect upon prices.

The evidence as to the conditions of the production and distribution of bituminous coal, the available facilities for its transportation, the extent of developed mining capacity, and the vast potential undeveloped capacity, makes it impossible to conclude that defendants through the operation of their plan will be able to fix the price of coal in the consuming markets. . . . Defendants' coal will continue to be subject to active competition. In addition to the coal actually produced and seeking markets in competition with defendants' coal, enormous additional quantities will be within reach and can readily be turned into the channels of trade if an advance of price invites that course. . . .

The contention is, and the court below found, that while defendants could not fix market prices, the concerted action would "affect" them, that is, that it would have a tendency to stabilize market prices and to raise them to a higher level than would otherwise obtain. But the facts found do not establish, and the evidence fails to show, that any effect will be produced which in the circumstances of this industry will be detrimental to fair competition. . . . The fact that the correction of abuses may tend to stabilize a business, or to produce fairer price levels, does not mean that the abuses should go uncorrected or that cooperative endeavor to correct them necessarily constitutes an unreasonable restraint of trade. The intelligent conduct of commerce through the acquisition of full information of all relevant facts may properly be sought by the cooperation of those engaged in trade, although stabilization of trade and more reasonable prices may be the result. . . .

Decisions cited in support of a contrary view were addressed to very different circumstances from those presented here. They dealt with combinations which on the particular facts were found to impose unreasonable restraints through the suppression of competition, and in actual operation had that effect. . . .

(3) The question remains whether, despite the foregoing conclusions, the fact that the defendants' plan eliminates competition between themselves is alone sufficient to condemn it. Emphasis is placed upon defendants' control of about 73 per cent of the commercial production in Appalachian territory. But only a small percentage of that production is sold in that territory. . . . Defendants insist that . . . no valid objection could have been interposed under the Sherman Act if the defendants had eliminated competition between themselves by a complete integration of their mining properties in a single ownership. . . . We agree that there is no ground for holding defendants' plan illegal merely because they have not integrated their properties and have chosen to maintain their independent plants, seeking not to limit but rather to facilitate production. We know of no public policy, and none is suggested by the terms of the Sherman Act, that, in order to comply with the law, those engaged in industry should be driven to unify their properties and businesses, in order to correct abuses which may be corrected by less drastic measures. Public policy might in-

deed be deemed to point in a different direction. . . . The argument that integration may be considered a normal expansion of business, while a combination of independent producers in a common selling agency should be treated as abnormal—that one is a legitimate enterprise and the other is not—makes but an artificial distinction. The Anti-Trust Act aims at substance. Nothing in theory or experience indicates that the selection of a common selling agency to represent a number of producers should be deemed to be more abnormal than the formation of a huge corporation bringing various independent units into one ownership. Either may be prompted by business exigencies, and the statute gives to neither a special privilege. The question in either case is whether there is an unreasonable restraint of trade or an attempt to monopolize. If there is, the combination cannot escape because it has chosen corporate form; and, if there is not, it is not to be condemned because of the absence of corporate integration. . . .

. . . We recognize . . . that the case has been tried in advance of the operation of defendants' plan . . . . If in actual operation it should prove to be an undue restraint upon interstate commerce, . . . the decision upon the present record should not preclude the Government from seeking the remedy which would be suited to such a state of facts. . . .

The decree will be reversed and . . . the court shall retain jurisdiction of the cause. . . .

Reversed and remanded.

MR. JUSTICE McREYNOLDS thinks that the court below reached the proper conclusion and that its decree should be affirmed.

United States v. Socony-Vacuum Oil Co., Inc.

310 U.S. 150 (1940)

MR. JUSTICE DOUGLAS delivered the opinion of the Court.

Respondents were convicted by a jury . . . under an indictment charging violations of Section 1 of the Sherman Anti-Trust Act. . . . The Circuit Court of Appeals reversed and remanded for a new trial. . . . The case is here on a petition and cross-petition for certiorari, both of which we granted because of the public importance of the issues raised. . . .

The indictment was returned in December 1936 in the United States District Court for the Western District of Wisconsin. It charges that certain major oil companies, selling gasoline in the Mid-Western area . . . , (1) "combined and conspired together for the purpose of artificially raising and fixing the tank car prices of gasoline" in the "spot markets" in the East Texas and Mid-Continent fields; (2) "have artificially raised and fixed said spot market tank car prices of gasoline and have maintained said prices at artificially high and non-competitive levels, and at levels agreed upon among them and have thereby intentionally increased and fixed the tank car prices of gasoline contracted to be sold and sold in interstate commerce as aforesaid in the Mid-Western area"; (3) "have arbitrarily," by reason of the provisions of the prevailing form of jobber contracts which made the price to the jobber dependent on the average spot market price, "exacted large sums of money from thousands of jobbers with whom they have had such contracts in said Mid-Western area"; and (4) "in turn have intentionally raised the general level of retail prices prevailing in said Mid-Western area."

The *manner* and *means* of effectuating such conspiracy are alleged in substance as follows: Defendants, from February 1935 to December 1936 "have knowingly and unlawfully engaged and participated in two concerted gasoline buying programs" for the purchase "from independent refiners in spot transactions of large quantities of gasoline in the East Texas and Mid-Continent fields at uniform, high, and at times progressively increased prices." The East Texas buying program is alleged to have embraced purchases of gasoline in spot transactions from most of the independent refiners in the East Texas field, who were members of the East Texas Refiners' Marketing Association, formed in February 1935 with the knowledge and approval of some of the defendants "for the purpose of selling and facilitating the sale of gasoline to defendant major oil companies." It is alleged that arrangements were made and carried out for allotting orders for gasoline received from defendants among the members of that association; and that such purchases amounted to more than 50% of all gasoline produced by those independent refiners. The Mid-Continent buying program is alleged to have included "large and increased purchases of gasoline" by defendants from independent refiners located in the Mid-Continent fields pursuant to allotments among themselves. Those purchases, it is charged, were made from independent refiners who were assigned to certain of the defendants at monthly meetings of a group representing defendants. It is alleged that the purchases in this buying program amounted to nearly 50% of all gasoline sold by those independents. As respects both the East Texas and the Mid-Continent buying programs, it is alleged that the purchases of gasoline were in excess of the amounts which defendants would have purchased but for those programs; that at the instance of certain defendants these independent refiners curtailed their production of gasoline. . . .

The methods of marketing and selling gasoline in the Mid-Western area are set forth in the indictment in some detail. Since we hereafter develop the facts concerning them, it will suffice at this point to summarize them briefly. Each defendant major oil company owns, operates or leases retail service stations in this area. It supplies those stations, as well as independent retail stations, with gasoline from its bulk storage plants. All but one sell large quantities of gasoline to jobbers in tank car lots under term contracts. In this area these jobbers exceed 4,000 in number and distribute about 50% of all gasoline distributed to retail service stations therein, the bulk of the jobbers' purchases being made from the defendant companies. The price to the jobbers under those contracts with defendant companies is made dependent on the spot market price, pursuant to a formula hereinafter discussed. And the spot market tank car prices of gasoline directly and substantially influence the retail prices in the area. In sum, it is alleged that defendants by raising and fixing the tank car prices of gasoline in these spot markets could and did increase the tank car prices and the retail prices of gasoline sold in the Mid-Western area. The vulnerability of these spot markets to that type of manipulation or stabilization is emphasized by the allegation that spot market prices published in the journals were the result of spot sales made chiefly by independent refiners of a relatively small amount of the gasoline sold in that area—virtually all gasoline sold in tank car quantities in spot market transactions in the Mid-Western area being sold by independent refiners, such sales amounting to less than 5% of all gasoline marketed therein.

So much for the indictment. . . .

The first meeting of the Tank Car Committee[1] was held February 5, 1935, and the second on February 11, 1935. At these meetings the alleged conspiracy was formed, the substance of which, so far as it pertained to the Mid-Continent phase, was as follows:

It was estimated that there would be between 600 and 700 tank cars of distress gasoline produced in the Mid-Continent oil field every month by about 17 independent refiners. These refiners, not having regular outlets for the gasoline, would be unable to dispose of it except at distress prices. Accordingly, it was proposed and decided that certain major companies (including the corporate respondents) would purchase gasoline from these refiners. The Committee would assemble each month information as to the quantity and location of this distress gasoline. Each of the major companies was to select one (or more) of the independent refiners having distress gasoline as its "dancing partner," and would assume responsibility for purchasing its distress supply. In this manner buying power would be co-ordinated, purchases would be effectively placed, and the results would be much superior to the previous haphazard purchasing. There were to be no formal contractual commitments to purchase this gasoline, either between the major companies or between the majors and the independents. Rather it was an informal gentlemen's agreement or understanding whereby each undertook to perform his share of the joint undertaking. Purchases were to be made at the "fair going market price." . . .

. . . Before . . . [the end of March] all companies alleged to have participated in the program (except one or two) made purchases; 757 tank cars were bought from all but three of the independent refiners who were named in the indictment as sellers. . . .

[1] A division of the N.R.A.-sanctioned Petroleum Administrative Board. IMS.

. . . On May 27, 1935, this Court held . . . that the code-making authority conferred by the National Industrial Recovery Act was an unconstitutional delegation of legislative power. Shortly thereafter the Tank Car Stabilization Committee held a meeting to discuss their future course of action. It was decided that the buying program should continue. . . .

In the meetings when the Mid-Continent buying program was being formulated it was recognized that it would be necessary or desirable to take the East Texas surplus gasoline off the market so that it would not be a "disturbing influence in the Standard of Indiana territory." The reason was that weakness in East Texas spot market prices might make East Texas gasoline competitive with Mid-Continent gasoline in the Mid-Western area and thus affect Mid-Continent spot market prices. . . .

Early in 1935 the East Texas Refiners' Marketing Association was formed to dispose of the surplus gasoline manufactured by the East Texas refiners. . . .

. . . And it is clear that this East Texas buying program was, as we have said, supplementary or auxiliary to the Mid-Continent program. . . .

As a result of these buying programs it was hoped and intended that both the tank car and the retail markets would improve. The conclusion is irresistible that defendants' purpose was not merely to raise the spot market prices but, as the real and ultimate end, to raise the price of gasoline in their sales to jobbers and consumers in the Mid-Western area. Their agreement or plan embraced not only buying on the spot markets but also, at least by clear implication, an understanding to maintain such improvements in Mid-Western prices as would result from those purchases of distress gasoline. The latter obviously would be achieved by selling at the increased prices, not by price cutting. Any other understanding would have been wholly inconsistent with and contrary to the philosophy of the broad stabilization efforts which were under way. In essence the raising and maintenance of the spot market prices were but the means adopted for raising and maintaining prices to jobbers and consumers. . . . Certainly there was enough evidence to support a finding by the jury that such were the scope and purpose of the plan. . . .

Respondents do not contend that the buying programs were not a factor in the price rise and in the stabilization of the spot markets during 1935 and 1936. But they do contend that they were relatively minor ones, because of the presence of other economic forces. . . .

In *United States* v. *Trenton Potteries Co.* . . . , this Court sustained a conviction under the Sherman Act where the jury was charged that an agreement on the part of the members of a combination, controlling a substantial part of an industry, upon the prices which the members are to charge for their commodity is in itself an unreasonable restraint of trade without regard to the reasonableness of the prices or the good intentions of the combining units. . . . This Court pointed out that the so-called "rule of reason" announced in *Standard Oil Co.* v. *United States*, 221 U.S.

1, and in *United States* v. *American Tobacco Co.*, 221 U.S. 106, had not affected this view of the illegality of price-fixing agreements. . . .

But respondents claim that other decisions of this Court afford them adequate defenses to the indictment. Among those on which they place reliance are *Appalachian Coals, Inc.* v. *United States*, 288 U.S. 344. . . .

. . . [I]n reality the only essential thing in common between the instant case and the *Appalachian Coals* case is the presence in each of so-called demoralizing or injurious practices. The methods of dealing with them were quite divergent. In the instant case there were buying programs of distress gasoline which had as their direct purpose and aim the raising and maintenance of spot market prices and of prices to jobbers and consumers in the Mid-Western area, by the elimination of distress gasoline as a market factor. The increase in the spot market prices was to be accomplished by a well organized buying program on that market: regular ascertainment of the amounts of surplus gasoline; assignment of sellers among the buyers; regular purchases at prices which would place and keep a floor under the market. Unlike the plan in the instant case, the plan in the *Appalachian Coals* case was not designed to operate *vis-à-vis* the general consuming market and to fix the prices on that market. Furthermore, the effect, if any, of that plan on prices was not only wholly incidental but also highly conjectural. For the plan had not then been put into operation. Hence this Court expressly reserved jurisdiction in the District Court to take further proceedings if, *inter alia*, in "actual operation" the plan proved to be "an undue restraint upon interstate commerce." And as we have seen it would *per se* constitute such a restraint if price-fixing were involved. . . .

Thus for over forty years this Court has consistently and without deviation adhered to the principle that price-fixing agreements are unlawful *per se* under the Sherman Act and that no showing of so-called competitive abuses or evils which those agreements were designed to eliminate or alleviate may be interposed as a defense. . . .

Therefore the sole remaining question on this phase of the case is the applicability of the rule of the *Trenton Potteries* case to these facts.

Respondents seek to distinguish the *Trenton Potteries* case from the instant one. . . .

But we do not deem those distinctions material.

In the first place, there was abundant evidence that the combination had the purpose to raise prices. And likewise, there was ample evidence that the buying programs at least contributed to the price rise and the stability of the spot markets, and to increases in the price of gasoline sold in the Mid-Western area during the indictment period. That other factors also may have contributed to that rise and stability of the markets is immaterial. . . . Proof that there was a conspiracy, that its purpose was to raise prices, and that it caused or contributed to a price rise is proof of the actual consummation or execution of a conspiracy under Section 1 of the Sherman Act.

Secondly, the fact that sales on the spot markets were still governed by some competition is of no consequence. For it is indisputable that that competition was restricted through the removal by respondents of a part of the supply which but for the buying programs would have been a factor in determining the going prices on those markets. . . . Competition was not eliminated from the markets; but it was clearly curtailed, since restriction of the supply of gasoline, the timing and placement of the purchases under the buying programs and the placing of a floor under the spot markets obviously reduced the play of the forces of supply and demand.

The elimination of so-called competitive evils is no legal justification for such buying programs. . . . If the so-called competitive abuses were to be appraised here, the reasonableness of prices would necessarily become an issue in every price-fixing case. In that event the Sherman Act would soon be emasculated; its philosophy would be supplanted by one which is wholly alien to a system of free competition; it would not be the charter of freedom which its framers intended.

. . . Those who controlled the prices. . . . would have it in their power to destroy or drastically impair the competitive system. But the thrust of the rule is deeper and reaches more than monopoly power. Any combination which tampers with price structures is engaged in an unlawful activity. Even though the members of the price-fixing group were in no position to control the market, to the extent that they raised, lowered, or stabilized prices they would be directly interfering with the free play of market forces. The Act places all such schemes beyond the pale and protects that vital part of our economy against any degree of interference. Congress. . . . has not permitted the age-old cry of ruinous competition and competitive evils to be a defense to price-fixing conspiracies. It has no more allowed genuine or fancied competitive abuses as a legal justification for such schemes than it has the good intentions of the members of the combination. If such a shift is to be made, it must be done by the Congress. Certainly Congress has not left us with any such choice. . . .

Nor is it important that the prices paid by the combination were not fixed in the sense that they were uniform and inflexible. Price-fixing as used in the *Trenton Potteries* case has no such limited meaning. . . . Hence, prices are fixed within the meaning of the *Trenton Potteries* case . . . because they are agreed upon. And the fact that, as here, they are fixed at the fair going market price is immaterial. . . .

Under the Sherman Act a combination formed for the purpose and with the effect of raising, depressing, fixing, pegging, or stabilizing the price of a commodity in interstate or foreign commerce is illegal *per se*. . . . Price-fixing agreements may have utility to members of the group though the power possessed or exerted falls far short of domination and control.

Monopoly power . . . is not the only power which the Act strikes down, as we have said. Proof that a combination was formed for the purpose of fixing prices and that it caused them to be fixed or contributed to that result is proof of the completion of a price-fixing conspiracy under Section 1 of the Act. The indictment in this case charged that this combination had that purpose and effect. And there was abundant evidence to support it. Hence the existence of power on the part of members of the combination to fix prices was but a conclusion from the finding that the buying programs caused or contributed to the rise and stability of prices. . . .

The judgment of the Circuit Court of Appeals is reversed and that of the District Court affirmed. . . .

[The Chief Justice and Mr. Justice Murphy did not participate in the consideration or decision of this case. Mr. Justice Roberts, with whom Mr. Justice McReynolds concurred, dissented.]

United States v. Container Corp. of America, et al.

393 U.S. 333 (1969)

MR. JUSTICE DOUGLAS delivered the opinion of the Court.

This is a civil antitrust action charging a price-fixing agreement in violation of §1 of the Sherman Act. . . .

The case as proved is unlike any of other price decisions we have rendered. There was here an exchange of price information but no agreement to adhere to a price schedule as in *Sugar Institute* v. *United States*, 297 U.S. 553, or *United States* v. *Socony-Vacuum Oil Co.*, 310 U.S. 150. There was here an exchange of information concerning specific sales to identified customers, not a statistical report on the average cost to all members, without identifying the parties to specific transactions, as in *Maple Flooring Mfrs. Assn.* v. *United States*, 268 U.S. 563. While there was present here, as in *Cement Mfrs. Protective Assn.* v. *United States*, 268 U.S. 588, an exchange of prices to specific customers, there was absent the controlling circumstance, *viz.*, that cement manufacturers, to protect themselves from delivering to contractors more cement than was needed for a specific job and thus receiving a lower price, exchanged price information as a means of protecting their legal rights from fraudulent inducements to deliver more cement than needed for a specific job.

Here all that was present was a request by each defendant of its competitor for information as to the most recent price charged or quoted, whenever it needed such information and whenever it was not available from another source. Each defendant on receiving that request usually furnished the data with the expectation that it would be furnished reciprocal information when it wanted it. That concerted action is of course sufficient to establish the combination or conspiracy, the initial ingredient of a violation of §1 of the Sherman Act.

There was of course freedom to withdraw from the agreement. But the fact remains that when a defendant requested and received price information, it was affirming its willingness to furnish such information in return.

There was to be sure an infrequency and irregularity of price exchanges between the defendants; and often the data were available from the records of the defendants or from the customers themselves. Yet the essence of the agreement was to furnish price information whenever requested.

Moreover, although the most recent price charged or quoted was sometimes fragmentary, each defendant had the manuals with which it could compute the price charged by a competitor on a specific order to a specific customer.

Further, the price quoted was the current price which a customer would need to pay in order to obtain products from the defendant furnishing the data.

The defendants account for about 90% of the shipment of corrugated containers from plants in the Southeastern United States. While containers vary as to dimensions, weight, color, and so on, they are substantially identical, no matter who produces them, when made to particular specifications. The prices paid depend on price alternatives. Suppliers when seeking new or additional business or keeping old customers, do not exceed a competitor's price. It is common for purchasers to buy from two or more suppliers concurrently. A defendant supplying a customer with containers would usually quote the same price on additional orders, unless costs had changed. Yet where a competitor was charging a particular price, a defendant would normally quote the same price or even a lower price.

The exchange of price information seemed to have the effect of keeping prices within a fairly narrow ambit. Capacity has exceeded the demand from 1955 to 1963, the period covered by the complaint, and the trend of corrugated container prices has been downward. Yet despite this excess capacity and the downward trend of prices, the industry has expanded in the Southeast from 30 manufacturers with 49 plants to 51 manufacturers with 98 plants. An abundance of raw materials and machinery makes entry into the industry easy with an investment of $50,000 to $75,000.

The result of this reciprocal exchange of prices was to stabilize prices though at a downward level. Knowledge of a competitor's price usually meant matching that price. The continuation of some price competition is not fatal to the Government's case. The limitation or reduction of price competition brings the case within the ban, for as we held in *United States* v. *Socony-Vacuum Oil Co., supra*, at 224, n. 59, interference with the setting of price by free market forces is unlawful *per se*. Price information exchanged in some markets may have no effect on a truly competitive price.

But the corrugated container industry is dominated by relatively few sellers. The product is fungible and the competition for sales is price. The demand is inelastic, as buyers place orders only for immediate, short-run needs. The exchange of price data tends toward price uniformity. For a lower price does not mean a larger share of the available business but a sharing of the existing business at a lower return. Stabilizing prices as well as raising them is within the ban of §1 of the Sherman Act. . . . The inferences are irresistible that the exchange of price information has had an anticompetitive effect in the industry, chilling the vigor of price competition. . . .

Price is too critical, too sensitive a control to allow it to be used even in an informal manner to restrain competition.[1]

Reversed.

Mr. Justice Fortas, concurring.

I join in the judgment and opinion of the Court. I do not understand the Court's opinion to hold that the exchange of specific information among sellers as to prices charged to individual customers, pursuant to mutual arrangement, is a *per se* violation of the Sherman Act.

Absent *per se* violation, proof is essential that the practice resulted in an unreasonable restraint of trade. There is no single test to determine when the record adequately shows an "unreasonable restraint of trade"; but a practice such as that here involved, which is adopted for the purpose of arriving at a determination of prices to be quoted to individual customers, inevitably suggests the probability that it so materially interfered with the operation of the price mechanism of the marketplace as to bring it within the condemnation of this Court's decisions. . . .

Mr. Justice Marshall, with whom Mr. Justice Harlan and Mr. Justice Stewart join, dissenting.

I agree with the Court's holding that there existed an agreement among the defendants to exchange price information whenever requested. However, I cannot agree that the agreement should be condemned, either as illegal *per se* or as having had the purpose or effect of restricting price competition in the corrugated container industry in the Southeastern United States. . . .

---

[1] Thorstein Veblen in *The Theory of Business Enterprise* (1904) makes clear how the overabundance of a commodity creates a business appetite to regulate or control prices or output or both. Measures short of monopoly may have "a salutary effect," as for example a degree of control or supervision over prices not obtainable while the parties "stood on their old footing of severalty." But that relief is apt to be "only transient," for as the costs of production decline and growth of the industry "catches up with the gain in economy," the need for further controls or restraints increases. And so the restless, never-ending search for price control and other types of restraint. . . .

Per se rules always contain a degree of arbitrariness. They are justified on the assumption that the gains from imposition of the rule will far outweigh the losses and that significant administrative advantages will result. In other words, the potential competitive harm plus the administrative costs of determining in what particular situations the practice may be harmful must far outweigh the benefits that may result. If the potential benefits in the aggregate are outweighed to this degree, then they are simply not worth identifying in individual cases.

I do not believe that the agreement in the present case is so devoid of potential benefit or so inherently harmful that we are justified in condemning it without proof that it was entered into for the purpose of restraining price competition or that it actually had that effect. The agreement in this case was to supply, when requested, price data for identified customers. Each defendant supplied the necessary information on the expectation that the favor would be returned. The nature of the exchanged information varied from case to case. In most cases, the price obtained was the price of the last sale to the particular customer; in some cases, the price was a current quotation to the customer. In all cases, the information obtained was sufficient to inform the defendants of the price they would have to beat in order to obtain a particular sale.

Complete market knowledge is certainly not an evil in perfectly competitive markets. This is not, however, such a market, and there is admittedly some danger that price information will be used for anticompetitive purposes, particularly the maintenance of prices at a high level. If the danger that price information will be so used is particularly high in a given situation, then perhaps exchange of information should be condemned.

I do not think the danger is sufficiently high in the present case. Defendants are only 18 of the 51 producers of corrugated containers in the Southeastern United States. Together, they do make up 90% of the market and the six largest defendants do control 60% of the market. But entry is easy; an investment of $50,000 to $75,000 is ordinarily all that is necessary. In fact, the number of sellers has increased from 30 to the present 51 in the eight-year period covered by the complaint. The size of the market has almost doubled because of increased demand for corrugated containers. Nevertheless, some excess capacity is present. The products produced by defendants are undifferentiated. Industry demand is inelastic, so that price changes will not, up to a certain point, affect the total amount purchased. The only effect of price changes will be to reallocate market shares among sellers.

In a competitive situation, each seller will cut his price in order to increase his share of the market, and prices will ultimately stabilize at a competitive level—*i.e.*, price will equal cost, including a reasonable return on capital. Obviously, it would be to a seller's benefit to avoid such price competition and maintain prices at a higher level, with a corresponding increase in profit. In a market with very few sellers, and detailed knowledge of each other's price, such action is possible. However, I do not think it can be concluded that this particular market is sufficiently oligopolistic, especially in light of the ease of entry, to justify the inference that price information will necessarily be used to stabilize prices. Nor do I think that the danger of such a result is sufficiently high to justify imposing a *per se* rule without actual proof.

In this market, we have a few sellers presently controlling a substantial share of the market. We have a large number competing for the remainder of the market, also quite substantial. And total demand is increasing. In such a case, I think it just as logical to assume that the sellers, especially the smaller and newer ones, will desire to capture a larger market share by cutting prices as it is that they will acquiesce in oligopolistic behavior. The likelihood that prices will be cut and that those lower prices will have to be met acts as a deterrent to setting prices at an artificially high level in the first place. Given the uncertainty about the probable effect of an exchange of price information in this context, I would require that the Government prove that the exchange was entered into for the purpose of, or that it had the effect of, restraining price competition. . . .

The Court does not hold that the agreement in the present case was a deliberate attempt to stabilize prices. . . . The weight of the evidence in the present case indicates that the price information was employed by each defendant on an individual basis, and was used by that defendant to set its prices for a specific customer; ultimately each seller wanted to obtain all or part of that customer's business at the expense of a competitor. The District Court found that there was no explicit agreement among defendants to stabilize prices and I do not believe that the desire of a few industry witnesses to use the information to minimize price cuts supports the conclusion that such an agreement was implicit. On the contrary, the evidence establishes that the information was used by defendants as each pleased and was actually employed for the purpose of engaging in active price competition. . . .

The record indicates that defendants have offered voluminous evidence concerning price trends and competitive behavior in the corrugated container market. Their exhibits indicate a downward trend in prices, with substantial price variations among defendants and among their different plants. There was also a great deal of shifting of accounts. The District Court specifically found that the corrugated container market was highly competitive and that each defendant engaged in active price competition. The Government would have us ignore this evidence and these findings, and assume that because we are dealing with an industry with overcapacity and yet continued entry, the new entrants must have been attracted by high profits. The Government then argues that high profits can only result from stabilization of prices at an unduly high level. Yet, the Government did not introduce any evidence about the level of profits in this industry, and no evidence about price levels. . . . The Government admits that the price trend was down, but asks the Court to assume that the trend would have been accelerated with less informed, and hence more vigorous, price competition.[2] In the absence of any proof whatsoever, I cannot make such an assumption. It is just as likely that price competition was furthered by the exchange as it is that it was depressed.

Finally, the Government focuses on the finding of the District Court that in a majority of instances a defendant, when it received what it considered reliable price information, would quote or charge substantially the same price.[3] The Court and my Brother FORTAS also focus on this finding. Such an approach ignores, however, the remainder of the District Court's findings. The trial judge found that price decisions were individual decisions, and that defendants frequently did cut prices in order to obtain a particular order. And, the absence of any price parallelism or price uniformity and the downward trend in the industry undercut the conclusion that price information was used to stabilize prices.[4]

The Government is ultimately forced to fall back on the theoretical argument that prices would have been more unstable and would have fallen faster without price information. As I said earlier, I cannot make this assumption on the basis of the evidence in this record. The findings of the Court below simply do not indicate that the exchange of information had a significant anticompetitive effect; if we rely on these findings, at worst all we can assume is that the exchange was a neutral factor in the market. . . . [T]he record indicates that, while each defendant occasionally received price information from a competitor, that information was used in the same manner as other reliable market information—*i.e.*, to reach an individual price decision based upon all available information. The District Court's findings that this was a competitive industry, lacking any price parallelism or uniformity, effectively refute the Government's assertion that the result of those decisions was to maintain or tend to maintain prices at other than a competitive level. Accordingly, I would affirm the decision of the court below.

---

[2] There was no effort to demonstrate that the price behavior of those manufacturers who did not exchange price information, if any, varied significantly from the price behavior of those who did. In fact, several of the District Court's findings indicate that when certain defendants stopped exchanging price information, their price behavior remained essentially the same, and, in some cases, prices actually increased.

[3] It should be noted that, in most cases, this information was obtained from a customer rather than a competitor, a practice the Government does not condemn.

[4] As mentioned above, no evidence was introduced that would indicate that more than minimal price cuts were economically feasible.

PART II

Indirect Conspiracies And Oligopoly

Chapter 3 TRADE ASSOCIATION ACTIVITIES

The problem of distinguishing between those trade association activities which serve to improve businessmen's knowledge of market conditions and thereby make competition more perfect, and those which have as their purpose the elimination of competition is often a difficult one. The dissemination of trade statistics, for example, may result in greater price uniformity either by providing entrepreneurs with a better grasp of business conditions and thereby enabling them to perform their ecnomic functions more intelligently, or in discouraging competition by insuring that price reductions will become immediately known and met. Although difficult, the problem is not insoluble. The following cases indicate that it is possible to distinguish the legal from the illegal, the economically desirable from the economically undesirable. In *American Column and Lumber Co.* v. *United States*,[1] one of the first such cases to reach the Supreme Court, it was held that minute disclosure of the operations of individual members provided the lumber manufacturers' trade organization with information which was used to convince firms in the industry of the necessity of maintaining a spirit of harmony. This substitution of co-operation for competition was found to have gone so far that the Sherman Act had been violated. The *Cement Institute* case set forth the doctrine that collusive adoption of a delivered price system by members of a trade association was an unfair method of competition within the meaning of the Federal Trade Commission Act. In the *Tag Manufacturers* case the various criteria which have evolved over the years for determining the permissible sphere of trade association activities were applied to exonerate an association whose members accounted for some 95 percent of the industry's capacity. A comparison of the *Tag* case with those preceding it provides a good indication of the extent to which the earlier rulings have led to a modification and refinement of trade association methods, and throws light on what may be a new, broader interpretation of the legality of exchange of certain types of trade information. Of course, as

[1] 257 U.S. 377 (1921).

the consent decree entered into by the Automobile Manufacturers Association illustrates, certain activities will continue to be challenged. In this regard, see also the *Container Corporation* case in Chapter 2 above.

Federal Trade Commission v. Cement Institute

333 U.S. 683 (1948)

MR. JUSTICE BLACK delivered the opinion of the Court.

We granted certiorari to review the decree of the Circuit Court of Appeals which, with one judge dissenting, vacated and set aside a cease and desist order issued by the Federal Trade Commission against the respondents. . . . Those respondents are: The Cement Institute . . . ; the 74 corporate members of the Institute; and 21 individuals who are associated with the Institute. . . .

The proceedings were begun by a Commission complaint of two counts. The first charged that certain alleged conduct set out at length constituted an unfair method of competition in violation of Section 5 of the Federal Trade Commission Act. . . . The core of the charge was that the respondents had restrained and hindered competition in the sale and distribution of cement by means of a combination among themselves made effective through mutual understanding or agreement to employ a multiple basing point system of pricing. It was alleged that this system resulted in the quotation of identical terms of sale and identical prices for cement by the respondents at any given point in the United States. This system had worked so successfully, it was further charged, that for many years prior to the filing of the complaint, all cement buyers throughout the nation, with rare exceptions, had been unable to purchase cement for delivery in any given locality from any one of the respondents at a lower price or on more favorable terms than from any of the other respondents.

The second count of the complaint, resting chiefly on the same allegations of fact set out in Count I, charged that the multiple basing point system of sales resulted in systematic price discriminations between the customers of each respondent. These discriminations were made, it was alleged, with the purpose of destroying competition in price between the various respondents in violation of Section 2 of the Clayton Act, . . . as amended by the Robinson-Patman Act. . . .

Resting upon its findings, the Commission ordered that respondents cease and desist from "carrying out any planned common course of action, understanding, agreement, combination, or conspiracy" to do a number of things . . . , all of which things, the Commission argues, had to be restrained in order effectively to restore individual freedom of action among the separate units in the cement industry. . . .

Jurisdiction. At the very beginning we are met with a challenge to the Commission's jurisdiction. . . . [Respondents'] argument runs this way: Count I in reality charges a combination to restrain trade. Such a combination constitutes an offense under Section 1 of the Sherman Act. . . . Hence, continue respondents, the Commission, whose jurisdiction is limited to "unfair methods of competition," is without power to institute proceedings. . . . Assuming, without deciding, that the conduct charged in each count constitutes a violation of the Sherman Act, we hold that the Commission does have jurisdiction to conclude that such conduct may also be an unfair method of competition and hence constitute a violation of Section 5 of the Federal Trade Commission Act. . . .

The Multiple Basing Point Delivered Price System. Since the multiple basing point delivered price system of fixing prices and terms of cement sales is the nub of this controversy, it will be helpful at this preliminary stage to point out in general what it is and how it works. A brief reference to the distinctive characteristics of "factory" or "mill prices" and "delivered prices" is of importance to an understanding of the basing point delivered price system here involved.

Goods may be sold and delivered to customers at the seller's mill or warehouse door or may be sold free on board (f.o.b.) trucks or railroad cars immediately adjacent to the seller's mill or warehouse. In either event the actual cost of the goods to the purchaser is, broadly speaking, the seller's "mill price" plus the purchaser's cost of transportation. However, if the seller fixes a price at which he undertakes to deliver goods to the purchaser where they are to be used, the cost to the purchaser is the "delivered price." A seller who makes the "mill price" identical for all purchasers of like amount and quality simply delivers his goods at the same place (his mill) and for the same price (price at the mill). He thus receives for all f.o.b. mill sales an identical net amount of money for like goods from all customers. But a "delivered price" system creates complications which may result in a seller's receiving different net returns from the sale of like goods. The cost of transporting 500 miles is almost always more than the cost of transporting 100 miles. Consequently if customers 100 and 500 miles away pay the same "delivered price," the seller's net return is less from the more distant customer. This difference in the producer's net return from sales to customers in different localities under a "delivered price" system is an important element in the charge under Count I of the complaint and is the crux of Count II.

The best known early example of a basing point price system was called "Pittsburgh plus." It related to the price of steel. The Pittsburgh price was the base price, Pittsburgh being therefore called a price basing point. In order for the system to work, sales had to be made only at delivered prices. Under this system the delivered price of steel from anywhere in the United States to a point of delivery anywhere in the United States was in general the Pittsburgh price plus the railroad freight rate from Pittsburgh to the point of delivery. Take Chicago, Illinois, as an illustration of the operation and consequences of the system. A Chicago steel producer was not free to sell his steel at cost plus a reasonable profit. He must sell it at the Pittsburgh price plus the railroad freight rate from Pittsburgh to the point of delivery. Chicago steel customers were by this pricing plan thus arbitrarily required to pay for Chicago produced steel the Pittsburgh base price plus what it would have cost to ship the steel by rail from Pittsburgh to Chicago had it been shipped. The theoretical cost of this fictitious shipment became known as "phantom freight." But had it been economically possible under this plan for a Chicago producer to ship his steel to Pittsburgh, his "delivered price" would have been merely the Pittsburgh price, although he actually would have been required to pay the freight from Chicago to Pittsburgh. Thus the "delivered price" under these latter circumstances required a Chicago (non-basing point) producer to "absorb" freight costs. That is, such a seller's net returns became smaller and smaller as his deliveries approached closer and closer to the basing point.

Several results obviously flow from use of a single basing point system such as "Pittsburgh plus" originally was. One is that the "delivered prices" of all producers in every locality where the deliveries are made are always the same regardless of the producers' different freight costs. Another is that sales made by a non-base mill for delivery at different localities result in net receipts to the seller which vary in amounts equivalent to the "phantom freight" included in, or the "freight absorption" taken from the "delivered price."

As commonly employed by respondents, the basing point system is not single but multiple. That is, instead of one basing point, like that in "Pittsburgh plus," a number of basing point localities are used. In the multiple basing point system, just as in the single basing point system, freight absorption or phantom freight is an element of the delivered price on all sales not governed by a basing point actually located at the seller's mill. And all sellers quote identical delivered prices in any given locality regardless of their different costs of production and their different freight expenses. Thus the multiple and single systems function in the same general manner and produce the same consequences—identity of prices and diversity of net returns.[1] Such differences as there are in matters here pertinent are therefore differences of degree only. . . .

[1] The Commission in its findings explained . . . , "The formula used to make this system operative is that the delivered price at any location shall be the lowest combination of base price plus all-rail freight. Thus, if Mill *A* has a base price of $1.50 per barrel, its delivered price at each location where it sells cement will be $1.50 per barrel plus the all-rail freight from its mill to the point of delivery, except that when a sale is made for delivery at a location at which the combination of the base price plus all-rail freight from another mill is a lower figure, Mill *A* uses this lower combination so that its delivered price at such location will be the same as the delivered price of the other mill. At all locations where the base price of Mill *A* plus freight is the lowest combination, Mill *A* recovers $1.50 net at the mill, and at locations where the combination of base price plus freight of another mill is lower, Mill *A* shrinks its mill net sufficiently to equal that price. Under these conditions it is obvious that the highest mill net which can be recovered by Mill *A* is $1.50 per barrel, and on sales where it has been necessary to shrink its mill net in order to match the delivered price of another mill, its net recovery at the mill is less than $1.50." . . .

Findings and Evidence. It is strongly urged that the Commission failed to find, as charged in both counts of the complaint, that the respondents had by combination, agreements, or understandings among themselves utilized the multiple basing point delivered price system as a restraint to accomplish uniform prices and terms of sale. A subsidiary contention is that assuming the Commission did so find, there is no substantial evidence to support such a finding. We think that adequate findings of combination were made and that the findings have support in the evidence.

The Commission's findings of fact set out at great length and with painstaking detail numerous concerted activities carried on in order to make the multiple basing point system work in such way that competition in quality, price and terms of sale of cement would be non-existent, and that uniform prices, job contracts, discounts, and terms of sale would be continuously maintained. . . . Among the collective methods used to accomplish these purposes, according to the findings, were boycotts; discharge of uncooperative employees; organized opposition to the erection of new cement plants; selling cement in a recalcitrant price cutter's sales territory at a price so low that the recalcitrant was forced to adhere to the established basing point prices; discouraging the shipment of cement by truck or barge; and preparing and distributing freight rate books which provided respondents with similar figures to use as actual or "phantom" freight factors, thus guaranteeing that their delivered prices (base prices plus freight factors) would be identical on all sales whether made to individual purchasers under open bids or to governmental agencies under sealed bids. These are but a few of the many activities of respondents which the Commission found to have been done in combination to reduce or destroy price competition in cement. . . .

Thus we have a complaint which charged collective action by respondents designed to maintain a sales technique that restrained competition, detailed findings of collective activities by groups of respondents to achieve that end, then a general finding that respondents maintained the combination, and finally an order prohibiting the continuance of the combination. It seems impossible to conceive that anyone reading these findings in their entirety could doubt that the Commission found that respondents collectively maintained a multiple basing point delivered price system for the purpose of suppressing competition in cement sales. The findings are sufficient. The contention that they are not is without substance. . . .

Although there is much more evidence to which reference could be made, we think that the following facts shown by evidence in the record, some of which are in dispute, are sufficient to warrant the Commission's finding of concerted action.

When the Commission rendered its decision there were about 80 cement manufacturing companies in the United States operating about 150 mills. Ten companies controlled more than half of the mills and there were substantial corporate affiliations among many of the others. This concentration of productive capacity made concerted action far less difficult than it would otherwise have been. The belief is prevalent in the industry that because of the standardized nature of cement, among other reasons, price competition is wholly unsuited to it. That belief is historic. It has resulted in concerted activities to devise means and measures to do away with competition in the industry. Out of those activities came the multiple basing point delivered price system. Evidence shows it to be a handy instrument to bring about elimination of any kind of price competition. The use of the multiple basing point delivered price system by the cement producers has been coincident with a situation whereby for many years, with rare exceptions, cement has been offered for sale in every given locality at identical prices and terms by all producers. Thousands of secret sealed bids have been received by public agencies which corresponded in prices of cement down to a fractional part of a penny.[2]

Occasionally foreign cement has been imported, and cement dealers have sold it below the delivered price of the domestic product. Dealers who persisted in selling foreign cement were boycotted by the domestic producers. Officers of the Institute took the lead in securing pledges by producers not to permit sales f.o.b. mill to purchasers who furnished their own trucks, a practice regarded as seriously disruptive of the entire delivered price structure of the industry.

During the depression in the 1930's, slow business prompted some producers to deviate from the prices fixed by the delivered price system. Meetings were held by other producers; an effective plan was devised to punish the recalcitrants and bring them into line. The plan was simple but successful. Other producers made the recalcitrant's plant an involuntary base point. The base price was driven down with relatively insignificant losses to the producers who imposed the punitive basing point, but with heavy losses to the recalcitrant who had to make all its sales on this basis. In one instance, where a producer had made a low public bid, a punitive base point price was put on its plant and cement was reduced 10¢ per barrel; further reductions quickly followed until the base price at which this recalcitrant had to sell its cement dropped to 75¢ per barrel, scarcely one-half of its former base price of $1.45. Within six weeks after the base price hit 75¢ capitulation occurred and the recalcitrant joined a portland cement association. Cement in that locality then bounced back to $1.15, later to $1.35, and finally to $1.75.

The foregoing are but illustrations of the practices shown to have been utilized to maintain the basing point price system. Respondents offered testimony that cement is a standardized product, that "cement is cement," that no differences existed in quality or usefulness, and that pur-

[2] A footnote table pointed out that each of eleven companies, bidding for a 6,000 barrel United States Government order in 1936, entered sealed bids of $3.286854 per barrel. IMS.

chasers demanded delivered price quotations because of the high cost of transportation from mill to dealer. There was evidence, however, that the Institute and its members had, in the interest of eliminating competition, suppressed information as to the variations in quality that sometimes exist in different cements. Respondents introduced the testimony of economists to the effect that competition alone could lead to the evolution of a multiple basing point system of uniform delivered prices and terms of sale for an industry with a standardized product and with relatively high freight costs. These economists testified that for the above reasons no inferences of collusion, agreement, or understanding could be drawn from the admitted fact that cement prices of all United States producers had for many years almost invariably been the same in every given locality in the country. There was also considerable testimony by other economic experts that the multiple basing point system of delivered prices as employed by respondents contravened accepted economic principles and could only have been maintained through collusion.

The Commission did not adopt the views of the economists produced by the respondents. It decided that even though competition might tend to drive the price of standardized products to a uniform level, such a tendency alone could not account for the almost perfect identity in prices, discounts, and cement containers which had prevailed for so long a time in the cement industry. The Commission held that the uniformity and absence of competition in the industry were the results of understandings or agreements entered into or carried out by concert of the Institute and the other respondents. It may possibly be true, as respondents' economists testified, that cement producers will, without agreement express or implied and without understanding explicit or tacit, always and at all times (for such has been substantially the case here) charge for their cement precisely, to the fractional part of a penny, the price their competitors charge. Certainly it runs counter to what many people have believed, namely, that without agreement, prices will vary—that the desire to sell will sometimes be so strong that a seller will be willing to lower his prices and take his chances. We therefore hold that the Commission was not compelled to accept the views of respondents' economist-witnesses that active competition was bound to produce uniform cement prices. The Commission was authorized to find understanding, express or implied, from evidence that the industry's Institute actively worked, in cooperation with various of its members, to maintain the multiple basing point delivered price system; that this pricing system is calculated to produce, and has produced, uniform prices and terms of sale throughout the country; and that all of the respondents have sold their cement substantially in accord with the pattern required by the multiple basing point system. . . .

Unfair Methods of Competition. We sustain the Commission's holding that concerted maintenance of the basing point delivered price system is an unfair method of competition prohibited by the Federal Trade Commission Act. . . .

We cannot say that the Commission is wrong in concluding that the delivered-price system as here used provides an effective instrument which, if left free for use of the respondents, would result in complete destruction of competition and the establishment of monopoly in the cement industry. . . . We uphold the Commission's conclusion that the basing point delivered price system employed by respondents is an unfair trade practice which the Trade Commission may suppress.[3]

The Price Discrimination Charge in Count Two. The Commission found that respondents' combination to use the multiple basing point delivered price system had effected systematic price discrimination in violation of Section 2 of the Clayton Act as amended by the Robinson-Patman Act. . . .

The Commission held that the varying mill nets received by respondents on sales between customers in different localities constituted a "discrimination in price between different purchasers" within the prohibition of Section 2(*a*), and that the effect of this discrimination was the substantial lessening of competition between respondents. The Circuit Court of Appeals reversed the Commission on this count. It agreed that respondents' prices were unlawful insofar as they involved the collection of phantom freight, but it held that prices involving only freight absorption came within the "good faith" proviso of Section 2(*b*).

The respondents contend that the differences in their net returns from sales in different localities which result from use of the multiple basing point delivered price system are not price discriminations within the meaning of Section 2(*a*). If held that these net return differences are price discriminations prohibited by Section 2(*a*), they contend that the discriminations were justified under Section 2(*b*) because "made in good faith to meet an equally low price of a competitor." Practically all the arguments presented by respondents in support of their contentions were considered by this Court and rejected in 1945 in *Corn Products Co.* v. *Federal Trade Comm'n* . . . , and in the related case of *Federal Trade Comm'n* v. *Staley Co.* . . . Consequently, we see no reason for again reviewing the questions that were there decided.

In the *Corn Products* case the Court, in holding illegal a single basing point system, specifically reserved decision upon the legality under the Clayton Act of a multiple basing point price system, but only in view of the "good faith" proviso of Section 2(*b*), and referred at that point to the companion *Staley* opinion. . . . The latter case held that a seller could

---

[3] While we hold that the Commission's findings of combination were supported by evidence, that does not mean that existence of a "combination" is an indispensable ingredient of an "unfair method of competition" under the Trade Commission Act. . . .

not justify the adoption of a competitor's basing point price system under Section 2(b) as a good faith attempt to meet the latter's equally low price. Thus the combined effect of the two cases was to forbid the adoption for sales purposes of any basing point pricing system. . . .

Section 2(b) permits a single company to sell one customer at a lower price than it sells to another if the price is "made in good faith to meet an equally low price of a competitor." But this does not mean that Section 2(b) permits a seller to use a sales system which constantly results in his getting more money for like goods from some customers than he does from others. We held to the contrary in the *Staley* case. . . . Each of the respondents, whether all its mills were basing points or not, sold some cement at prices determined by the basing point formula and governed by other base mills. Thus, all respondents to this extent adopted a discriminatory pricing system condemned by Section 2. As this in itself was evidence of the employment of the multiple basing point system by the respondents as a practice rather than as a good faith effort to meet "individual competitive situations," we think the Federal Trade Commission correctly concluded that the use of this cement basing point system violated the Act. Nor can we discern under these circumstances any distinction between the "good faith" proviso as applied to a situation involving only phantom freight and one involving only freight absorption. Neither comes within its terms. . . .

The Order. There are several objections to the Commission's cease and desist order. We consider the objections, having in mind that the language of its prohibitions should be clear and precise in order that they may be understood by those against whom they are directed. . . . But we also have in mind that the Commission has a wide discretion generally in the choice of remedies to cope with trade problems entrusted to it by the Commission Act. . . .

There is a special reason, however, why courts should not lightly modify the Commission's orders made in efforts to safeguard a competitive economy. . . .

In the present proceeding the Commission has exhibited the familiarity with the competitive problems before it which Congress originally anticipated the Commission would achieve from its experience. The order it has prepared is we think clear and comprehensive. At the same time the prohibitions in the order forbid no activities except those which if continued would directly aid in perpetuating the same old unlawful practices. Nor do we find merit to the charges of surplusage in the order's terms.

Most of the objections to the order appear to rest on the premise that its terms will bar an individual cement producer from selling cement at delivered prices such that its net return from one customer will be less than from another, even if the particular sale be made in good faith to meet the lower price of a competitor. The Commission disclaims that the order can possibly be so understood. Nor do we so understand it. As we read the order, all of its separate prohibiting paragraphs and subparagraphs, which need not here be set out, are modified and limited by a preamble. This preamble directs that all of the respondents "do forthwith cease and desist from entering into, continuing, cooperating in, or carrying out any planned common course of action, understanding, agreement, combination, or conspiracy between and among any two or more of said respondents, or between any one or more of said respondents and others not parties hereto, to do or perform any of the following things. . . ." Then follow the prohibitory sentences. It is thus apparent that the order by its terms is directed solely at concerted, not individual activity on the part of the respondents. . . .

The Commission's order should not have been set aside by the Circuit Court of Appeals. Its judgment is reversed and the cause is remanded to that court with directions to enforce the order.

It is so ordered.

MR. JUSTICE DOUGLAS and MR. JUSTICE JACKSON took no part in the consideration or decision of these cases.

[Mr. Justice Burton dissented.]

Tag Manufacturing Institute et al. v. Federal Trade Commission
174 F.2d 452 (1st. Cir. 1949)

Before MAGRUDER, Chief Judge, WOODBURY, Circuit Judge, and PETERS, District Judge.

MAGRUDER, Chief Judge.

Petitioners in this case ask us . . . to review and set aside or modify a cease and desist order of the Federal Trade Commission. . . .

On May 2, 1941, the Commission issued its complaint. . . . The complaint alleged that . . . petitioners "have entered into and carried out an understanding, agreement, combination, and conspiracy to restrict, restrain, suppress and eliminate price competition in the sale and distribution of said tag products" in interstate commerce; that pursuant to said agreement, petitioners "have fixed and maintained, and still fix and maintain, uniform prices, terms and conditions of sale for said tag products"; that the acts and practices of petitioners "have a dangerous tendency to and have actually hindered and prevented price competition" in the sale of tags in interstate commerce, have placed in petitioners the power to control and enhance prices on said products, have unreasonably restrained such commerce "and constitute unfair methods of competition in commerce within the intent and meaning of the Federal Trade Commission Act." . . .

The manufacturing petitioners sell and distribute approximately 95 per cent of the tag products purchased and used in the United States, with

55 per cent of the business of the industry shared by the four largest manufacturers.

Certain standardized tags are made in advance of sale and sold out of stock, such as plain unprinted stock shipping tags. However, over 80 per cent of the business is in made-to-order tags, the varieties of which are almost unlimited, representing as they do selective combinations of materials and processes, or component elements, in various sizes and shapes. The much greater part of the products of the industry, particularly of made-to-order tags, is sold direct to consumers, but there is a considerable volume of sales to distributors and others for resale. To some extent, tag manufacturers buy from other manufacturers, for resale, types of tags which they do not themselves manufacture. Orders for tags are generally small in dollar value, averaging between $20 to $40, and a thousand or more orders for tags are placed with manufacturers each business day.

In such an industry, it would evidently not be practicable for a manufacturer to give a price on each order, based upon an individual cost estimate of that order. Hence, early in the history of the industry, manufacturers began to issue price lists to their salesmen, distributors and customers. The simple stock tags were customarily listed at stated prices for the finished product. With respect to the more elaborate, and infinitely various made-to-order tags, the price lists would enumerate the prices of the various basic components, such as tag stock, strings, wires, punches, eyelets, stapling, gumming, printing, etc.—from which the price for any particular tag, made up from the desired combination of components, might be computed.

. . . The price list does serve to indicate to the trade the scale of prices which the seller hopes and expects to maintain in the generality of future transactions until further notice. . . . In other words, from the nature of things it is reasonably to be expected that off-list sales would be the exception rather than the rule, and that the greater portion of sales would be at the prices stated in the seller's current price list. This is particularly true in an industry such as the tag industry, with its wide variety of products and tremendous number of sales transactions each of small dollar volume on the average.

The issuance of price lists by tag manufacturers had become established as a general practice in the industry prior to the formation of the Institute and prior to the execution of the various Tag Industry Agreements, later to be described, which formed the principal basis of the Commission's complaint against petitioners.

The Institute was organized in 1933, and has operated continuously since that time. All the manufacturing petitioners have become members of the Institute. At all times since its organization, the active management of the Institute has been in the hands of petitioner Frank H. Baxter, its secretary-treasurer and executive director. The Institute has concerned itself with typical trade association activities, and among other things has fostered efforts at more refined standardization of tag products and components thereof.

While the National Industrial Recovery Act . . . was in effect, a Code of Fair Competition for the Tag Industry was promulgated. . . . Under the Code, a so-called "open-price plan of selling" was prescribed, under which each member of the industry was required to file a schedule of his prices and terms of sale. . . . Further, it was provided that no member of the industry "shall sell such product for less than such price or upon terms or conditions more favorable" than stated in his filed price schedule. . . .

After the National Industrial Recovery Act was invalidated . . . members of the industry adopted a succession of four Tag Industry Agreements, so-called, in 1935, 1936, 1937 and 1940. The 1940 agreement was in effect when the Commission's complaint was filed, and was still in effect at the time of the final hearing before the Commission. . . .

. . . [T]he agreements were concerned chiefly with the reporting and dissemination of industry statistics. . . .

Article II of the 1940 agreement requires the Subscribers to report to the Associates (Baxter) the prices, terms and conditions of each sale or contract to sell any tag products covered by the agreement. . . .

A further important provision of Article II is as follows:

. . . Nothing herein shall be construed as a limitation or restriction upon the right of each Subscriber independently to establish such prices, or such terms and conditions of sale, or policies of whatever nature affecting prices or sales, as he may deem expedient. Nothing in any report made to the Associates by any Subscriber hereunder shall be construed as a representation or pledge as to prices, terms, conditions of sale, or policies in current or future transactions.

With reference to the use by Baxter of the foregoing information, it is provided: . . .

All information relating to prices, terms and conditions of sale disseminated to the Subscribers pursuant hereto shall be freely and fully available to public agencies, distributors and consumers of the products, and to any other properly interested persons; and shall be disseminated in the same manner as to Subscribers, to such of them as may apply therefore and arrange for payment of the reasonable cost of such service.

Each Subscriber agrees that he will notify purchasers from him of the availability of this information.

Article III of the 1940 agreement requires each Subscriber throughout the life of the agreement to mail to Baxter "duplicates of every invoice or other memorandum of shipment or delivery of the products and of all credit memoranda applicable thereto. . . ." . . . It is provided that the Associates (Baxter) "shall compile the information submitted to them pursuant to this Article in such a way as not to disclose the information of any one Subscriber or the names of any purchasers. . . ."

Article IV of the 1940 agreement relates to the enforcement of the aforesaid reporting undertakings. It is recited that a breach of Article II or Article III by any Subscriber . . . [shall cause to be imposed on him fines ranging from $5–$25 per day; and for] failure to transmit copies of invoices or memoranda as described in Article III "within ten (10) days after the date of mailing of the original of each such invoice or memorandum," the "liquidated damages" [fines] are stated to be an amount equivalent to 10 per cent of the aggregate value of all the Subscriber's transactions proved to be affected by such failure, up to a maximum of $100 applicable to a single day's billing by one Subscriber. . . .

The final Article in the 1940 agreement, Article V, provides for termination of the entire agreement "by written agreement of a majority of the parties" . . . . It is further provided that any manufacturer of tag products "may become a Subscriber to this Agreement at any time by signing the same and making the payments provided in Article I hereof." . . .

We think the evidence does warrant a finding that during the life of the Tag Industry Agreements there has from time to time been considerable list price uniformity with respect to types of tags constituting a large portion of the industry's business. Such a finding, in conjunction with the unchallenged finding that on the average 75 per cent of the industry's business is done at list, would warrant the inference that during the years in which the Tag Industry Agreements have been in effect there has been a considerable uniformity of actual selling prices. The evidence does not, however, warrant the Commission's finding that the effect of the operation of the Tag Industry Agreements "has resulted in a substantial uniformity of prices for tags and tag products among the respondent members." In the first place, this implies that the instances of departure from uniformity are insignificant and unsubstantial—which certainly cannot be said. In the second place, there is no evidence that such uniformity as has existed is a result of the operation of the Tag Industry Agreements, for it does not appear whether there has been an increase or decrease of uniformity either in list prices or in actual selling prices since the agreements have been in operation. . . .

In support of its conclusion, the Commission refers to the provisions in the Tag Industry Agreements designed to insure compliance with the reporting commitments of the Subscribers. . . . The evidence is uncontradicted that Baxter's only concern with off-list transactions was to find out if they had been reported, after the event, as the agreement required. If the investigation indicated a violation of any reporting obligation of a Subscriber, Baxter would institute proceedings for assessment of "liquidated damages" as specified in the agreement. Total assessments for acts of non-compliance amounted to less than $10,000 for the period 1935–1941. The record contains not a single instance of an assessment for failure to adhere to a list price. . . .

Whether they are "liquidated damages," as they purport to be, or "penalties," as the Commission calls them, is hardly decisive. If the reporting commitments they are designed to buttress are otherwise lawful, the agreement does not become a violation of the anti-trust laws or the Federal Trade

Commission Act merely because the reporting plan is accompanied by a penalty provision which would not be legally enforceable. . . .

There has been some tendency to look askance at reporting agreements between competitors, where the information exchanged is reserved exclusively to themselves and withheld from buyers or the public generally. Presumably this is because such secrecy more readily suggests the inference that the agreement is inspired by some unlawful purpose and precludes the argument that the information thus secretly exchanged serves a function similar to that of market information made available through the activities of commodity exchanges, trade journals, etc. . . .

. . . It is noteworthy that the Commission has failed to produce a single tag buyer to testify that he was unaware of the existence of this information service, or that he sought information from Baxter and could not get it, or that he sought to subscribe to the service and was refused. . . .

We have come to the conclusion that the reporting agreements herein, and the practices of petitioners thereunder, are lawful under the controlling authorities. . . . Once a price list has been issued to the trade it necessarily becomes pretty much public property. There is certainly nothing secret about it. It would be no great feat for a manufacturer to obtain copies of his competitors' price lists. The Tag Industry Agreement merely facilitates the assembling of such data. As to the obligation of Subscribers to report off-list sales and to furnish copies of all invoices, that is no more than the reporting of past transactions. The Commission has endeavored to show that the agreement was something more than this, that it was a price-fixing agreement having the purpose and actual effect of restraining and preventing price competition. We believe that such findings are unsupported by the evidence or by any reasonable inferences to be drawn therefrom. We say this with full recognition of our limited scope of review of findings of fact by the Commission. . . .

Since in our view of the case, the cease and desist order will have to be set aside, it becomes unnecessary for us to consider certain seriously pressed objections by petitioners to the breadth of the order.

A judgment will be entered setting aside the order of the Commission.

United States v. Automobile Mfrs. Assn., Inc.; General Motors Corp.; Ford Motor Co.; Chrysler Corp.; and American Motors Corp.

307 F. Supp. 617 (C. D. Cal. 1969),
1969 Trade Cases ¶72, 907, appeals
dismissed and aff'd, 397 U.S. 248 (1970)

FINAL JUDGMENT

CURTIS, D. J.: The plaintiff, United States of America, having filed its complaint herein on January 10, 1969, and the plaintiff and the defendants by their respective attorneys having severally consented to the entry of this Final Judgment without trial or adjudication of or finding on any issues of fact or law herein and without this Final Judgment constituting evidence or an admission by any of them in respect to any such issue;

Now, Therefore, before any testimony has been taken and without trial or adjudication of or finding on any issue of fact or law herein, and upon consent of the parties as aforesaid, it is hereby

Ordered, Adjudged and Decreed as follows:

. . . . .

II

As used in this Final Judgment:

(A) "Devices" means air pollution emission control designs, devices, equipment, methods, or parts thereof, for motor vehicles.

(B) "Restricted information" means all unpublished information of the type usually classified as company confidential concerning applied as distinguished from basic research in, or concerning the development, innovation, manufacture, use, sale or installation of Devices. It includes trade secrets, unpublished company policy, and other unpublished technical information for developing, making, improving, or lowering the cost of Devices by a motor vehicle manufacturer. . . .

. . . . .

IV

(A) Each defendant is enjoined and restrained from:

(1) Combining or conspiring to prevent, restrain or limit the development, manufacture, installation, distribution or sale of Devices;

(2) Entering into, adhering to, enforcing or claiming any rights under any provisions of any agreement, arrangement, understanding, plan or program (hereinafter "agreement") with any other defendant or manufacturer of motor vehicles or Devices:

(a) to exchange restricted information;

(b) to cross-license patents or patent rights on Devices which cross-license includes patents or patent rights acquired subsequent to the date of any such cross-license;

(c) to delay installation of Devices or otherwise restrain individual decisions as to installation dates;

(d) to restrict publicity of research and development relating to Devices;

(e) to employ joint assessment of the value of patents or patent rights of any third party relating to Devices;

(f) to require that acquisition of patent rights relating to Devices be conditioned upon availability of such rights to others upon a most-favored-purchaser basis;

(g) to file, in the absence of a written authorization for a joint statement by the agency involved, with any governmental regulatory agency in the United States authorized to issue emission standards or regulations for new motor vehicles or Federal motor vehicle safety standards or regulations, any joint statement regarding such standards or regulations except joint statements relating to (i) the authority of the agency involved, (ii) the draftsmanship of or the scientific need for standards or regulations, (iii) test procedures or test data relevant to standards or regulations, or (iv) the general engineering requirements of standards or regulations based upon publicly available information; provided that no joint statement shall be filed which discusses the ability of one or more defendants to comply with a particular standard or regulation or to do so by a particular time, in the absence of a written agency authorization for such a joint statement, and provided also that any defendant joining in a joint statement shall also file a statement individually upon written request by the agency involved; or

(h) not to file individual statements with any governmental regulatory agency in the United States authorized to issue emission standards or regulations for new motor vehicles or Federal motor vehicle safety standards or regulations. . . .

V

(A) Each manufacturing defendant is ordered and directed to exercise its right to withdraw from the AMA cross-licensing agreement of July 1, 1955, as amended, and to take such steps as are necessary to accomplish said withdrawal within one hundred twenty (120) days from the date of entry of this Final Judgment. . . .

(B) Defendant AMA is ordered and directed to relinquish its responsibilities under the AMA cross-licensing agreement of July 1, 1955, as amended, within sixty (60) days from the date of entry of this Final Judgment.

. . . . .

Chapter   OLIGOPOLY
4

Both in cases involving overwhelming market dominance, consciously achieved, by a single firm and in those characterized by direct conspiracy among competitors the government has had a relatively easy time of it. Once evidence of either had been established, the outcome, for all practical purposes, was no longer in doubt. There remained, however, the thorny question of what to do about an industry made up of a small number of firms of intermediate size, whose behavior exhibited all the manifestations of a concerted agreement, yet where none could be found to exist. As we saw in Chapter 2, this issue was first explored (tentatively to be sure), in *U.S. v. U.S. Steel*. In that case, U.S. Steel did not have a large enough market share to come under the doctrine of the *Standard Oil* decision, nor was the government able to establish the existence of a concerted agreement.

As a result of the *Steel* case, the government did not pursue cases of that type for many years. Consequently, the issue remained relatively dormant until 1946, when the *American Tobacco* decision was handed down. For the first time it was established that the existence of an agreement could be inferred from the identity of the behavior of the defendants. This finding was hailed by a number of commentators as an implicit recognition by the Supreme Court of the economic theory of oligopoly—that in an industry characterized by a small number of firms, these firms, purely as a matter of independent self-interest, may refrain from actively competing with one another. Thus it seemed that the bulk of American industry, whose structural characteristics were not unlike those peculiar to oligopoly, was now fair game for the antitrust authorities.

But the courts proceeded to fashion new distinctions. In the *Triangle Conduit & Cable* decision, the concept of conscious parallelism was developed; and the *Theatre Enterprises* case provided the Supreme Court with the opportunity to employ it as a device for distinguishing lawful from unlawful activity. The government, therefore, became reluctant to continue its frontal attack on oligopoly, which after the *American Tobacco* decision had seemed so promising. Indeed, evidence that this reluctance

103

has been justified can be found in the recent affirmation, by an evenly divided Supreme Court, of the Court of Appeals decision in *U.S.* v. *Chas. Pfizer, et al.*, which is apparently consistent with the doctrine enunciated in *Theatre Enterprises.* Thus, at least for the present, it does not appear as though the Supreme Court is prepared to reconsider its earlier position.

American Tobacco Company v. *United States*

328 U.S. 781 (1946)

Mr. Justice Burton delivered the opinion of the Court.

The petitioners are The American Tobacco Company, Liggett & Myers Tobacco Company, R. J. Reynolds Tobacco Company, American Suppliers, Inc., a subsidiary of American, and certain officials of the respective companies who were convicted by a jury, in the District Court of the United States for the Eastern District of Kentucky, of violating §§1 and 2 of the Sherman Anti-trust Act. . . .

Each petitioner was convicted on four counts: (1) conspiracy in restraint of trade, (2) monopolization, (3) attempt to monopolize, and (4) conspiracy to monopolize. Each count related to interstate and foreign trade and commerce in tobacco. No sentence was imposed under the third count as the Court held that count was merged in the second. Each petitioner was fined $5,000 on each of the other counts, making $15,000 for each petitioner and a total of $255,000. . . .

The Circuit Court of Appeals for the Sixth Circuit . . . affirmed each conviction. . . . This opinion is limited to the convictions under §2 of the Sherman Act. . . .

The issue . . . emphasized in the order allowing certiorari and primarily argued by the parties has not been previously decided by this Court. It is raised by the following instructions which were especially applicable to the second count but were related also to the other counts under §2 of the Sherman Act:

Now, the term '*monopolize*' as used in Section 2 of the Sherman Act, as well as in the last three counts of the Information, means the joint acquisition or maintenance by the members of the conspiracy formed for that purpose, of the *power to control and dominate interstate trade and commerce in a commodity to such an extent that they are able, as a group, to exclude actual or potential competitors from the field, accompanied with the intention and purpose to exercise such power.*

The phrase 'attempt to monopolize' means the employment of methods, means and practices which would, if successful, accomplish monopolization, and which, though falling short, nevertheless approach so close as to create a dangerous probability of it, which methods, means and practices are so employed by the members of and pursuant to a combination or conspiracy formed for the purpose of such accomplishment.

It is in no respect a violation of the law that a number of individuals or corporations, each acting for himself or itself, may own or control a large part, or even all of a particular commodity, or all the business in a particular commodity.

An essential element of the illegal monopoly or monopolization charged *in this case is the existence of a combination or conspiracy to acquire and maintain the power to exclude competitors to a substantial extent.*

Thus you will see that *an indispensable ingredient of each of the offenses charged in the Information is a combination or conspiracy.* (Italics supplied [by the Supreme Court].) . . .

. . . The trial court's instructions did not call for proof of an "actual exclusion" of competitors on the part of the petitioners. For the purposes of this opinion, we shall assume, therefore, that an actual exclusion of competitors by the petitioners was not claimed or established by the prosecution. Simply stated the issue is: Do the facts called for by the trial court's definition of monopolization amount to a violation of §2 of the Sherman Act? . . .

. . . To support the verdicts it was not necessary to show power and intent to exclude *all* competitors, or to show a conspiracy to exclude *all* competitors. The requirement stated to the jury and contained in the statute was only that the offenders shall "monopolize any part of the trade or commerce among the several States, or with foreign nations." This particular conspiracy may well have derived special vitality, in the eyes of the jury, from the fact that its existence was established, not through the presentation of a formal written agreement, but through the evidence of widespread and effective conduct on the part of petitioners in relation to their existing or potential competitors. . . .

First of all, the monopoly found by the jury to exist in the present cases appears to have been completely separable from the old American Tobacco Trust which was dissolved in 1911. The conspiracy to monopolize and the monopolization charged here do not depend upon proof relating to the old tobacco trust but upon a dominance and control by petitioners in recent years over purchases of the raw material and over the sale of the finished product in the form of cigarettes. The fact, however, that the purchases of leaf tobacco and the sales of so many products of the tobacco industry have remained largely within the same general group of business organizations for over a generation, inevitably has contributed to the ease with which control over competition within the industry and the mobilization of power to resist new competition can be exercised. . . . The verdicts indicate that practices of an informal and flexible nature were adopted and that the results were so uniformly beneficial to the petitioners in protecting their common interests as against those of competitors that, entirely from circumstantial evidence, the jury found that a combination or conspiracy existed among the petitioners from 1937 to 1940, with power and intent to exclude competitors to such a substantial extent as to violate the Sherman Act as interpreted by the trial court.

The position of the petitioners in the cigarette industry from 1931 to 1939 is clear. . . . [A]lthough American, Liggett and Reynolds gradually dropped in their percentage of the national domestic cigarette production from 90.7% in 1931 to 73.3%, 71% and 68%, respectively, in 1937, 1938 and 1939, they have accounted at all times for more than 68%, and usually for more than 75%, of the national production. The balance of the cigarette production has come from six other companies. No one of those six ever has produced more than 10.6% once reached by Brown & Williamson in 1939. . . . [W]hile the percentage of cigarettes produced by American, Liggett and Reynolds in the United States dropped gradually from 90.7% to 68%, their combined volume of production actually increased. . . .

The further dominance of American, Liggett and Reynolds within their special field of burley blend cigarettes, as compared with the so-called "10 cent cigarettes," is also apparent. In 1939, the 10 cent cigarettes constituted about 14½% of the total domestic cigarette production. Accordingly, the 68% of the total cigarette production enjoyed by American, Liggett and Reynolds amounted to 80% of that production within their special field of cigarettes. . . . In addition . . . they also produced over 63% of the smoking tobacco and over 44% of the chewing tobacco. They never were important factors in the cigar or snuff fields of the tobacco industry.

The foregoing demonstrates the basis of the claim of American, Liggett and Reynolds to the title of the "Big Three." . . . Without adverse criticism of it, comparative size on this great scale inevitably increased the power of these three to dominate all phases of their industry. . . . An intent to use this power to maintain a monopoly was found by the jury in these cases.

The record further shows that . . . [i]n each of the years 1937, 1938 and 1939, American, Liggett and Reynolds expended a total of over $40,000,000 a year for advertising. Such advertising is not here criticized as a business expense. Such advertising may benefit indirectly the entire industry, including the competitors of the advertisers. Such tremendous advertising, however, is also a widely published warning that these companies possess and know how to use a powerful offensive and defensive weapon against new competition. New competition dare not enter such a field, unless it be well supported by comparable national advertising. Large inventories of leaf tobacco, and large sums required for payment of federal taxes in advance of actual sales, further emphasize the effectiveness of a well financed monopoly in this field against potential competitors if there merely exists an intent to exclude such competitors. Prevention of all potential competition is the natural program for maintaining a monopoly here, rather than any program of actual exclusion. "Prevention" is cheaper and more effective than any amount of "cure." . . .

The verdicts show that the jury found that the petitioners conspired to fix prices and to exclude undesired competition against them in the purchase of the domestic type of flue-cured tobacco and of burley tobacco. These are raw materials essential to the production of cigarettes of the grade sold by the petitioners and also, to some extent, of the 10 cent grade of cigarettes which constitutes the only substantial competition to American, Liggett and Reynolds in the cigarette field of the domestic tobacco industry. . . . The petitioners purchased a combined total of between 50% and 80% of the domestic flue-cured tobacco. . . . [and] from 60% to 80% of the annual crop of burley.[1] . . .

The Government introduced evidence showing . . . that petitioners refused to purchase tobacco on these [auction] markets unless the other petitioners were also represented thereon. There were attempts made by others to open new tobacco markets but none of the petitioners would participate in them unless the other petitioners were present. Consequently, such markets were failures due to the absence of buyers. . . . In this way the new tobacco markets and their locations were determined by the unanimous consent of the petitioners and, in arriving at their determination, the petitioners consulted with each other as to whether or not a community deserved a market.

The Government presented evidence to support its claim that, before the markets opened, the petitioners placed limitations and restrictions on the prices which their buyers were permitted to pay for tobacco. None of the buyers exceeded these price ceilings. Grades of tobacco were formulated in such a way as to result in the absence of competition between the petitioners. There was manipulation of the price of lower grade tobaccos in order to restrict competition from manufacturers of the lower priced cigarettes. Methods used included the practice of the petitioners of calling their respective buyers in, prior to the opening of the annual markets, and giving them instructions as to the prices to be paid for leaf tobacco in each of the markets. These instructions were in terms of top prices or price ranges. The price ceilings thus established for the buyers were the same for each of them. . . .

Where one or two of the petitioners secured their percentage of the crop on a certain market or were not interested in the purchase of certain offerings of tobacco, their buyers, nevertheless, would enter the bidding in order to force the other petitioners to bid up to the maximum price. The petitioners were not so much concerned with the prices they paid for the leaf tobacco as that each should pay the same price for the same grade and that none would secure any advantage in purchasing tobacco. . . .

---

[1] Flue-cured, or bright tobacco, takes its name from the fact that it is cured in barns heated by a system of flues. Burley tobacco is produced largely in Kentucky and Tennessee, and is cured by exposing the leaves to the air, without heat. IMS.

At a time when the manufacturers of lower priced cigarettes were beginning to manufacture them in quantity, the petitioners commenced to make large purchases of the cheaper tobacco leaves used for the manufacture of such lower priced cigarettes. No explanation was offered as to how or where this tobacco was used by petitioners. The compositions of their respective brands of cigarettes calling for the use of more expensive tobaccos remained unchanged during this period of controversy and up to the end of the trial. The Government claimed that such purchases of cheaper tobacco evidenced a combination and a purpose among the petitioners to deprive the manufacturers of cheaper cigarettes of the tobacco necessary for their manufacture, as well as to raise the price of such tobacco to such a point that cigarettes made therefrom could not be sold at a sufficiently low price to compete with the petitioners' more highly advertised brands.

The verdicts show also that the jury found that the petitioners conspired to fix prices and to exclude undesired competition in the distribution and sale of their principal products. The petitioners sold and distributed their products to jobbers and to selected dealers who bought at list prices, less discounts. . . . The list prices charged and the discounts allowed by petitioners have been practically identical since 1923 and absolutely identical since 1928. Since the latter date, only seven changes have been made by the three companies and those have been identical in amount. The increases were first announced by Reynolds. American and Liggett thereupon increased their list prices in identical amounts.

The following record of price changes is circumstantial evidence of the existence of a conspiracy and of a power and intent to exclude competition coming from cheaper grade cigarettes. . . . [1931] was one of the worst years of financial and economic depression in the history of the country. On June 23, 1931, Reynolds, without previous notification or warning to the trade or public, raised the list price of Camel cigarettes, constituting its leading cigarette brand, from $6.40 to $6.85 a thousand. The same day, American increased the list price for Lucky Strike cigarettes, its leading brand, and Liggett the price for Chesterfield cigarettes, its leading brand, to the identical price of $6.85 a thousand. No economic justification for this raise was demonstrated. The president of Reynolds stated that it was "to express our own courage for the future and our own confidence in our industry." The president of American gave as his reason for the increase, "the opportunity of making some money." . . . The officials of Liggett claimed that they thought the increase was a mistake . . . but they contended that unless they also raised their list price for Chesterfields, the other companies would have greater resources to spend in advertising and thus would put Chesterfield cigarettes at a competitive disadvantage. This general price increase soon resulted in higher retail prices and in a loss in volume of sales. Yet in 1932, in the midst of the national depression with the sales of the petitioners' cigarettes falling off greatly in number, the petitioners still were making tremendous profits as a result of the price increase. Their net profits in that year amounted to more than $100,000,000. This was one of the three biggest years in their history.

. . . [A]fter the above described increase in list prices of the petitioners in 1931, the 10 cent brands made serious inroads upon the sales of the petitioners. These cheaper brands of cigarettes were sold at a list price of $4.75 a thousand and from 1931 to 1932 the sales of these cigarettes multiplied 30 times, rising from 0.28% of the total cigarette sales of the country in June, 1931, to 22.78% in November, 1932. In response to this threat of competition . . . the petitioners . . . cut the list price of their three leading brands . . . to $5.50 a thousand. The evidence tends to show that this cut was directed at the competition of the 10 cent cigarettes. . . . Following the . . . price cut by petitioners, the sales of the 10 cent brands fell off considerably. . . . When the sale of the 10 cent brands had dropped from 22.78% of the total cigarette sales in November, 1932, to 6.43% in May, 1933, the petitioners, in January, 1934, raised the list price of their leading brands from $5.50 back up to $6.10 a thousand. During the period that the list price of $5.50 a thousand was in effect, Camels and Lucky Strikes were being sold at a loss by Reynolds and American. Liggett at the same time was forced to curtail all of its normal business activities and cut its advertising to the bone in order to sell at this price. [Subsequent increases brought the price to $6.53 by 1940.] . . .

Certain methods used by the petitioners to secure a reduction in the retail prices of their cigarettes were in evidence. Reynolds and Liggett required their retailers to price the 10 cent brands at a differential of not more than 3 cents below Camel and Chesterfield cigarettes. They insisted upon their dealers correcting a greater differential by increasing the retail price of the 10 cent brands to 11 cents with petitioners' brands at 14 cents a package, or by requiring that petitioners' brands be priced at 13 cents with the lower priced cigarettes at 10 cents a package. . . . After the list price reductions were made and at the height of the price war, the petitioners commenced the distribution of posters advertising their brands at 10 cents a package and made attempts to have dealers meet these prices. . . . In addition to the use of . . . inducements, petitioners also used threats and penalties to enforce compliance with their retail price program. . . . There was evidence that when dealers received an announcement of the price increase from one of the petitioners and attempted to purchase some of the leading brands of cigarettes from the other petitioners at their unchanged prices before announcement of a similar change, the latter refused to fill such orders until their prices were also raised, thus bringing about the same result as if the changes had been precisely simultaneous.

It was on the basis of such evidence that the Circuit Court of Appeals found that the verdicts of the jury were sustained by sufficient evidence on each count. The question squarely presented here by the order of this

Court in allowing the writs of certiorari is whether actual exclusion of competitors is necessary to the crime of monopolization in these cases under §2 of the Sherman Act. We agree with the lower courts that such actual exclusion of competitors is not necessary to that crime in these cases and that the instructions given to the jury, and hereinbefore quoted, correctly defined the crime. A correct interpretation of the statute and of the authorities makes it the crime of monopolizing, under §2 of the Sherman Act, for parties, as in these cases, to combine or conspire to acquire or maintain the power to exclude competitors from any part of the trade or commerce among the several states or with foreign nations, provided they also have such a power that they are able, as a group, to exclude actual or potential competition from the field and provided that they have the intent and purpose to exercise that power. See *United States v. Socony-Vacuum Oil Co.* . . . .

It is not the form of the combination or the particular means used but the result to be achieved that the statute condemns. It is not of importance whether the means used to accomplish the unlawful objectives are in themselves lawful or unlawful. Acts done to give effect to the conspiracy may be in themselves wholly innocent acts. Yet, if they are part of the sum of the acts which are relied upon to effectuate the conspiracy which the statute forbids, they come within its prohibition. No formal agreement is necessary to constitute an unlawful conspiracy. Often crimes are a matter of inference deduced from the acts of the person accused and done in pursuance of a criminal purpose. Where the conspiracy is proved, as here, from the evidence of the action taken in concert by the parties to it, it is all the more convincing proof of an intent to exercise the power of exclusion acquired through that conspiracy. The essential combination or conspiracy in violation of the Sherman Act may be found in a course of dealing or other circumstances as well as in an exchange of words. . . . Where the circumstances are such as to warrant a jury in finding that the conspirators had a unity of purpose or a common design and understanding, or a meeting of minds in an unlawful arrangement, the conclusion that a conspiracy is established is justified. Neither proof of exertion of the power to exclude nor proof of actual exclusion of existing or potential competitors is essential to sustain a charge of monopolization under the Sherman Act. . . .

[The Court then took this opportunity to endorse the key portions of Judge Learned Hand's decision in *United States v. Aluminum Company of America*, 148 F.2d 416.]

In the present cases, the petitioners have been found to have conspired to establish a monopoly and also to have the power and intent to establish and maintain the monopoly. To hold that they do not come within the prohibition of the Sherman Act would destroy the force of that Act. Accordingly, the instructions of the trial court under §2 of the Act are approved and the judgment of the Circuit Court of Appeals is *Affirmed*.

MR. JUSTICE FRANKFURTER entirely agrees with the judgment and opinion in these cases. He, however, would have enlarged the scope of the orders allowing the petitions for certiorari so as to permit consideration of the alleged errors in regard to the selection of the jury.

MR. JUSTICE REED and MR. JUSTICE JACKSON took no part in the consideration or decision of these cases.

[MR. JUSTICE RUTLEDGE concurred.]

Triangle Conduit & Cable Co., Inc. v.
Federal Trade Commission
168 F.2d 175 (7th Cir. 1948)[1]

Before SPARKS, KERNER, and MINTON, Circuit Judges.
KERNER, Circuit Judge.

Petitioners, fourteen corporate manufacturers of rigid steel conduit,[2] and five representatives of these corporations ask us to review and set aside a cease and desist order of the Federal Trade Commission, upon a complaint in two counts, charging that petitioners collectively have violated Section 5 of the Federal Trade Commission Act . . . , which declares unlawful "unfair methods of competition in commerce." . . .

In substance the first count alleged the existence and continuance of a conspiracy for the purpose and with the effect of substantially restricting and suppressing actual and potential competition in the distribution and sale of rigid steel conduit in commerce, effectuated by the adoption and use of a basing point method of quoting prices for rigid steel conduit. The second count did not rest upon an agreement or combination. It charged that each corporate petitioner and others violated Section 5 of the Federal Trade Commission Act "through their concurrent use of a formula method of making delivered price quotations with the knowledge that each did likewise, with the result that price competition between and among them was unreasonably restrained." It alleged that nearby customers were deprived of price advantages which they would have naturally enjoyed by reason of their proximity to points of production, and that such course of action created in said conduit sellers a monopolistic control over price in the sale and distribution of rigid steel conduit.

Petitioners answered the complaint. They denied any agreement or

---

[1] On April 25, 1949 the Supreme Court upheld the Federal Trade Commission order—affirmed in this lower court decision—under Count II of the complaint by a four-to-four tie vote. *Clayton Mark et al.* v. *Federal Trade Commission*, 336 U.S. 956 (1949) consists of a 23-word order. Mr. Justice Jackson took no part in the case. IMS.

[2] Rigid steel conduit is a steel pipe, used primarily in the roughing-in stage of building construction where electrical wiring is necessary in order to furnish a container for the wiring. It is a standard commodity made from standard steel pipe. IMS.

combination. After extensive hearings before a trial examiner, the Commission made its findings of fact and conclusions of law therefrom. It found the charges to be fully substantiated by the evidence. . . .

The argument [of defendants] is that there is no direct evidence of any conspiracy; that if the Commission made such a finding, it is based upon a series of inferences; and that the general use of the basing point method of pricing and the uniformity of prices does not justify an inference of conspiracy. We think there was direct proof of the conspiracy, but whether there was or not, in determining if such a finding is supported, it is not necessary that there be direct proof of an agreement. Such an agreement may be shown by circumstantial evidence. . . .

In this case there was evidence showing collective action to eliminate the Evanston basing point, and collective activities in promoting the general use of the formula presently to be noted. The record clearly establishes the fact that conduit manufacturers controlling 93% of the industry use a system under which they quote only delivered prices, which are determined in accordance with a formula consisting of a base price at Pittsburgh or Chicago plus rail freight, depending upon which basing point price controls at any particular destination or in any particular section of the United States; that as a result of using that formula the conduit producers were enabled to match their delivered price quotations, and purchasers everywhere were unable to find price advantages anywhere; and that purchasers at or near a place of production could not buy more cheaply from their nearby producer than from producers located at greater distances, and producers located at great distances from any given purchaser quoted as low a delivered price as that quoted by the nearest producer.

. . . Not only did petitioners match their bids when submitted under seal to agencies of public bodies, but each, with the knowledge of the others, did likewise—used the formula for the purpose of presenting to prospective private purchasers conditions of matched price quotations.

. . . Our study of this record and of applicable law has convinced us that the Commission was justified in drawing the inference that the petitioners acted in concert in a price-fixing conspiracy.

We now turn to consider petitioners' contention that the individual use of the basing point method, with knowledge that other sellers use it, does not constitute an unfair method of competition. This contention embodies the theory of the second count of the complaint. . . .

Briefly, the argument is that individual freight absorption is not illegal per se, and that the Commission's order is a denial of the right to meet competition. More specifically, petitioners say that conduit is a homogeneous product; that no buyer will pay more for the product of one seller than he will for that of another; that the buyer is not interested in the seller's cost of transportation or in any other factor of the seller's cost; that effective competition requires that traders have large freedom of action when conducting their own affairs; that in any particular market, the seller must adjust his own price to meet the market price or retire from that market altogether; that it has always been the custom of merchants to send their goods to distant markets to be sold at the prices there prevailing; that there is no lessening of competition, or injury to competitors, when a seller absorbs freight traffic to meet lawful competition; and that it is for the court to decide as a matter of law what constitutes an unfair method of competition under Section 5 of the Act. . . .

On the other hand, the Commission contends that unfair methods of competition include not only methods that involve deception, bad faith, and fraud, but methods that involve oppression or such as are against public policy because of their dangerous tendency unduly to hinder competition or create monopoly.

As already noted, each conduit seller knows that each of the other sellers is using the basing point formula; each knows that by using it he will be able to quote identical delivered prices and thus present a condition of matched prices under which purchasers are isolated and deprived of choice among sellers so far as price advantage is concerned. Each seller must systematically increase or decrease his mill net price for customers at numerous destinations in order to match the delivered prices of his competitors. Each seller consciously intends not to attempt the exclusion of any competition from his natural freight advantage territory by reducing the price, and in effect invites the others to share the available business at matched prices in his natural market in return for a reciprocal invitation.

In this situation, and indeed all parties to these proceedings agree, the legal question presented is identical with the one the Supreme Court considered in the *Federal Trade Commission* v. *Cement Institute* case. . . .

In the light of that opinion, we cannot say that the Commission was wrong in concluding that the individual use of the basing point method as here used does constitute an unfair method of competition. . . .

The Commission's order is affirmed and an enforcement decree will be entered. It is so ordered.

Theatre Enterprises, Inc. v. *Paramount Film Distributing Corp.*

346 U.S. 537 (1954)

Mr. Justice Clark delivered the opinion of the Court.

Petitioner brought this suit for treble damages and an injunction under §§4 and 16 of the Clayton Act, alleging that respondent motion picture producers and distributors had violated the antitrust laws by conspiring to restrict "first-run"[1] pictures to downtown Baltimore theatres, thus confining its suburban theatre to subsequent runs and unreasonable "clearances."[2] After hearing the evidence a jury returned a general verdict for respondents. The Court of Appeals for the Fourth Circuit affirmed the judgment based on the verdict. . . .

The opinion of the Court of Appeals contains a complete summary of the evidence presented to the jury. We need not recite that evidence again. It is sufficient to note that petitioner owns and operates the Crest Theatre, located in a neighborhood shopping district some six miles from the downtown shopping center in Baltimore, Maryland. The Crest, possessing the most modern improvements and appointments, opened on February 26, 1949. Before and after the opening, petitioner, through its president, repeatedly sought to obtain first-run features for the theatre. Petitioner approached each respondent separately, initially requesting exclusive first-runs, later asking for first-runs on a "day and date" basis.[3] But respondents uniformly rebuffed petitioner's efforts and adhered to an established policy of restricting first-runs in Baltimore to the eight downtown theatres. Admittedly there is no direct evidence of illegal agreement between the respondents and no conspiracy is charged as to the independent exhibitors in Baltimore, who account for 63% of first-run exhibitions. The various respondents advanced much the same reasons for denying petitioner's offers. Among other reasons, they asserted that day-and-date first-runs are normally granted only to noncompeting theatres. Since the Crest is in "substantial competition" with the downtown theatres, a day-and-date arrangement would be economically unfeasible. And even if respondents wished to grant petitioner such a license, no downtown exhibitor would waive his clearance rights over the Crest and agree to a simultaneous showing. As a result, if petitioner were to receive first-runs, the license would have to be an exclusive one. However, an exclusive license would be economically unsound because the Crest is a suburban theatre, located in a small shopping center, and served by limited public transportation facilities; and, with a drawing area of less than one-tenth that of a downtown theatre, it cannot compare with those easily accessible theatres in the power to draw patrons. Hence the downtown theatres offer far greater opportunities for the widespread advertisement and exploitation of newly released features, which is thought necessary to maximize the over-all return from subsequent runs as well as first-runs. The respondents, in the light of these conditions, attacked the guaranteed offers of petitioner, one of

---

[1] "Runs are successive exhibitions of a feature in a given area, first-run being the first exhibition in that area, second-run being the next subsequent, and so on. . . ." *United States* v. *Paramount Pictures, Inc.*, 334 U.S. 131, 144–45, n. 6 (1948).

[2] "A clearance is the period of time, usually stipulated in license contracts, which must elapse between runs of the same feature within a particular area or in specified theatres." *United States* v. *Paramount Pictures, Inc.*, 334 U.S. 131, 144, n. 6 (1948).

[3] A first-run "day and date" means that two theatres exhibit a first-run at the same time. Had petitioner's request for a day-and-date first-run been granted, the Crest and a downtown theatre would have exhibited the same features simultaneously.

which occurred during the trial, as not being made in good faith. Respondents Loew's and Warner refused petitioner an exclusive license because they owned the three downtown theatres receiving their first-run product.

The crucial question is whether respondents' conduct toward petitioner stemmed from independent decision or from an agreement, tacit or express. To be sure, business behavior is admissible circumstantial evidence from which the fact finder may infer agreement. . . . But this Court has never held that proof of parallel business behavior conclusively establishes agreement or, phrased differently, that such behavior itself constitutes a Sherman Act offense. Circumstantial evidence of consciously parallel behavior may have made heavy inroads into the traditional judicial attitude toward conspiracy; but "conscious parallelism" has not yet read conspiracy out of the Sherman Act entirely. Realizing this, petitioner attempts to bolster its argument . . . by urging, that the conscious unanimity of action by respondents should be "measured against the background and findings in the *Paramount* case." In other words, since the same respondents had conspired in the *Paramount* case to impose a uniform system of runs and clearances without adequate explanation to sustain them as reasonable restraints of trade, use of the same device in the present case should be legally equated to conspiracy. But the *Paramount* decrees, even if admissible, were only prima facie evidence of a conspiracy covering the area and existing during the period there involved. Alone or in conjunction with the other proof of the petitioner, they would form no basis for a directed verdict. Here each of the respondents had denied the existence of any collaboration and in addition had introduced evidence of the local conditions surrounding the Crest operation which, they contended, precluded it from being a successful first-run house. They also attacked the good faith of the guaranteed offers of the petitioner for first-run pictures and attributed uniform action to individual business judgment motivated by the desire for maximum revenue. This evidence, together with other testimony of an explanatory nature, raised fact issues requiring the trial judge to submit the issue of conspiracy to the jury. . . .

Affirmed.

United States v. Chas. Pfizer & Co., Inc., American Cyanamid Co. and Bristol-Myers Co.

426 F.2d 32 (2d Cir. 1970),
aff'd, 404 U.S. 548 (1972)

MOORE, Circuit Judge.

Chas. Pfizer & Co., Inc. (Pfizer), American Cyanamid Company (Cyanamid) and Bristol-Myers Company (Bristol) appeal from convictions after a jury trial for violations of the Sherman Act. . . . The indictment contained three counts, (I) "Combination and Conspiracy in Restraint of Trade"; (II) "Combination and Conspiracy to Monopolize"; and (III) "Monopolization." The defendants were found guilty on all three counts.

Two co-conspirators were named in the indictment, Olin Mathieson Chemical Corporation (Squibb) and The Upjohn Company (Upjohn). . . .

The indictment charged a conspiracy by defendants and co-conspirators to restrain trade in the broad spectrum antibiotic drug market. These drugs are enumerated more specifically later. In substance the alleged conspiratorial agreements were that:

(a) The manufacture of tetracycline be confined to Pfizer, Cyanamid and Bristol.

(b) The sale of tetracycline products be confined to Pfizer, Cyanamid, Bristol, Upjohn and Squibb.

(c) The sale of bulk tetracycline be confined to Bristol and bulk tetracycline be sold by Bristol only to Upjohn and Squibb.

(d) The sale of broad spectrum antibiotic products by the defendant companies and the co-conspirator companies be at substantially identical and non-competitive prices.

. . . The alleged illegal acts were (a) in November 1953 "the illegal cross-license and bulk sales arrangement between Pfizer and Cyanamid which initiated the conspiracy in November 1953" . . . ; (b) Pfizer's confining the tetracycline market to Pfizer and Cyanamid in January 1954; (c) an allegedly illegal agreement in November 1955 whereby Bristol deprived Squibb and Upjohn of their right to manufacture tetracycline; and (d) illegal arrangements between Pfizer and Bristol in December 1955 settling the Bristol-Pfizer patent litigation and depriving Squibb and Upjohn of the right to manufacture tetracycline. . . .

The government's case, except for minor details, was constructed in large measure:

(1) upon the testimony of John E. McKeen, President and Chairman of the Board of Directors of Pfizer, Wilbur G. Malcolm, Vice-President (to September 1, 1957), President (to April 25, 1961), and Chairman of the Board of Cyanamid and Frederic N. Schwartz, President of Bristol (and prior to January 1, 1958, President of Bristol Laboratories).

(2) upon written argeements entered into between some or all of the corporate defendants, many of which agreements related to the disposition of the patent controversies which had arisen *inter sese;*

(3) upon a mass of statistical information relating to production costs, gross profits, prices, etc., of the antibiotics here involved, designed to show that the defendants were reaping unusually high profits from their antibiotic drugs; and

(4) upon some eight days of testimony and exhibits related thereto dealing with the obtaining of the Pfizer tetracycline patent.

These officials testified at length as to the business situations which confronted them during the indictment period and the reasons for the actions taken in the exercise of their judgments to meet each situation as it arose and which called for solution in the light of the facts then confronting them.

Thus the government's case, insofar as actual proof is concerned, rests almost entirely upon oral and written statements from defendants themselves. Because of this circumstance, the facts may be said to be virtually undisputed. . . .

The subject matter of the suit was the production and marketing by Pfizer, Cyanamid, and Bristol of a broad spectrum antibiotic drug, tetracycline. Prior to 1952 there were three effective drugs in this field. In September 1949 Cyanamid had obtained a patent on aureomycin which it had first marketed in September 1948. In July 1950 Pfizer had secured a patent on terramycin which it introduced on the market in March 1950. Parke, Davis (a pharmaceutical company not involved in this case either as a defendant or as a co-conspirator) in October 1949 had received a patent for chloromycetin which it had put on the market in January 1949.

In 1952 a new drug, tetracycline, was developed. The activities of the three defendants with respect to this drug create the basis of the indictment's charges. . . .

Aureomycin (Cyanamid) was produced and sold exclusively by Cyanamid, was covered by patents (Duggar and Niedercorn-fermentation process) and was available to the public from December, 1948.

Chloromycetin (Parke, Davis patent) was manufactured and sold to the public from 1949.

Terramycin (Pfizer) was produced and sold by Pfizer from 1950 as the sole manufacturer.

No licenses or cross-licenses were granted by any of these companies to each other or to other drug manufacturers.

Each of these drugs was a prescription drug, namely, available only on a doctor's prescription and although somewhat interchangeable their sales were dependent upon the doctor's views as to their respective effectiveness in the treatment of the particular ailment of the patient. To this extent they were competitive. Each company, taking advantage of its patents and believing in the efficacy of its product but with full knowledge of the similarity in medical usefulness of its competitors' drugs, kept a competitive eye on the prices of the others and refrained from the issuance of licenses. There had been price stability between aureomycin, terramycin and chloromycetin for several years prior to the alleged conspiracy.

Into this somewhat stable situation in the early 1950s came tetracycline, considered by many as superior to the other three. . . .

Pfizer claimed that in June 1952 one of its scientists, Dr. Conover, had discovered tetracycline which was obtainable by subjecting aureomycin (patent held by Cyanamid) to a dechlorination process. Application was made in October 1952 for a patent on product and process claims. As a result of publicity of the Pfizer discovery, Cyanamid in March 1953 applied for a product and process patent for tetracycline. Thus there were two pending applications for patents for the same drug. To resolve the conflict, the Patent Office declared an interference.

Briefly stated Pfizer believed that it had priority (Dr. Conover—June 1952) over Cyanamid (March 1953), but the outcome was uncertain. However, Pfizer, even were it to win, was completely dependent for production, upon Cyanamid's aureomycin, either by purchase or license to manufacture. In an attempt to resolve these business problems, McKeen of Pfizer and Malcolm of Cyanamid met in November 1953. . . .

. . . Two meetings between Pfizer and Cyanamid were held, the first (McKeen and Malcolm) was somewhat preliminary, the second (McKeen, Malcolm, Powers of Pfizer and Martin of Cyanamid) resulted in written agreements (January 11, 1954). . . . The subject matter of the negotiations was the tetracycline patent interference situation. If Pfizer won, its victory could have been hollow because Cyanamid controlled the vital aureomycin, unless it reached an agreement with Cyanamid to obtain it. Cyanamid with its aureomycin risked being blocked from making tetracycline by Pfizer's Conover patent. To protect the respective interests of both companies, agreements were reached which provided in substance (1) that the parties exchange proofs as to priority, the Patent Office being the ultimate arbiter and that the party prevailing should give a non-exclusive license to the other in consideration of a certain royalty, and (2) that Cyanamid would license Pfizer also non-exclusively, to make aureomycin for use in producing tetracycline and to supply certain technical information. Another important item underlying the settlement from Pfizer's point of view was the obtaining of an agreement by Cyanamid to sell Pfizer a large initial quantity of bulk tetracycline to enable Pfizer rapidly to get into the market. Thereafter proofs of priority were exchanged and as a result Cyanamid filed a concession of priority in Pfizer's favor in the Patent Office on February 4, 1954. . . .

Bristol, having learned in February 1954, of the Pfizer-Cyanamid concession of priority whereby it appeared most likely that Pfizer would receive a patent and concerned over a trade paper report that Pfizer would not license any other company than Cyanamid, thus potentially excluding all other competitors, communicated with Pfizer. Pfizer reaffirmed its policy not to license anyone and its intention to bring suit against manufacturers or sellers of tetracycline if in a legal position to do so. Nevertheless, Bristol in mid-1954 agreed to sell to Squibb and Upjohn bulk tetracycline, Bristol being indemnified by them against damages resulting from any infringement suit. Thus, Bristol was subjected to potential patent infringement liability. . . .

On January 11, 1955 Pfizer received its tetracycline patent and on the same day filed infringement suits against Bristol, Squibb and Upjohn. Bristol with its two essential customers, Upjohn and Squibb, at stake was most anxious to settle the patent litigation, particularly since there were some negotiations for a two-party settlement between Pfizer and Upjohn. To forestall this possibility, agreements were entered into between Bristol and Upjohn and Bristol and Squibb (November 1955) whereby Bristol assumed control of the patent litigation, . . . no independent settlements with Pfizer were to be made and, if Bristol settled with Pfizer, licenses limited to purchase, use, and sale of tetracycline were to be obtained for Squibb and Upjohn. . . .

Prior to December 1955 Pfizer had taken an adamant position in refusing to license Bristol. Quite unrelated to tetracycline, the trial of John G. Broady, a lawyer-investigator, had just (November–December 1955) taken place in the New York courts. Broady had been convicted of tapping telephone wires amongst which were those of Bristol and Squibb. Broady apparently had been retained by Pfizer's general counsel. Bristol threatened to use this newly discovered material in the patent litigation. Pfizer was fearful of the adverse publicity if the incident were disclosed. The Broady incident brought about a radical change in Pfizer's attitude and a meeting was quickly arranged between McKeen (Pfizer) and Schwartz (Bristol) to discuss settlement. . . .

Briefly reviewing the situation up to December 15, 1955, Bristol's policy of setting its prices at the same level as Pfizer, Cyanamid and Parke, Davis, its agreements with Squibb and Upjohn, and its limitation to two bulk customers was concededly legal and not pursuant to any conspiracy.

The government does not claim that the agreement of December 14–15, 1955, was illegal *per se;* in fact it concedes the contrary. . . . It further admits that Bristol's actions prior thereto were not illegal. It does stress the absence in the licenses granted of the right to manufacture but . . . concedes that Upjohn never sought this right through its bargaining agent Bristol. . . .

There was no change in Bristol's practices after the December 1955 meetings. Prices remained as stable as in the years preceding the alleged conspiracy. Bristol reduced its costs drastically in 1954 but made no selling price reduction. As a result of developing a sales force and enabling Squibb and Upjohn to market tetracycline products, Bristol's percentage of the market increased substantially with a consequent diminution of Pfizer's and Cyanamid's shares. . . .

Before the openings by counsel, the trial court by way of preliminary instructions had stated to the jury that the conspiracy included "the creation of uniform, non-competitive and unreasonably high prices to the users of broad spectrum antibiotics." In its opening the government had stressed "enormous" profits by comparing factory cost and selling price and gave as an illustration of Cyanamid's 1954 cost a figure of $2.55 production cost for 100 capsules, a 1956 cost of $1.76 and a 1958 cost of $1.59 against a selling price to the druggist of $30.60 and $51.00 to the consumer.

The government conceded that production cost did "not include such items as research, promotion, advertising, executive overhead and things like that" but asked the jury to consider the significance of low production cost in relation to selling prices. The jury was also told that even in the pre-conspiracy, pre-tetracycline days there were "unreasonably high profits involved." . . .

During the early weeks of the trial, the government proceeded to offer a vast amount of testimony and scores of exhibits relating to factory production costs and alleged profits. . . . The government devoted much of its summation to the profits obtained by the respective defendants from their particular drugs (illustrative: "in those seven years Bristol made approximately $57 million in profits"—$69 million, production cost $12 million). In 1954 it cost Cyanamid $2.26, in 1955 it cost them $1.57. That listed for $51.00. The druggist paid $30.60—2,000% mark up * * * I think it is a fair inference from this chart that Cyanamid and Pfizer and Bristol starting in 1956 were making an unreasonably high profit."

I

Amongst other grounds defendants seek reversal because they . . . assert that the court, instead of charging the jury that the conspiracy as alleged must be found within the scope of the indictment and bill of particulars, in fact charged the opposite in instructing that the central requirement of an agreement "does not mean, however, that in order to create an unlawful combination or a conspiracy, the parties must meet together at some time or place or, indeed, that they must meet together at all"; "that proof of a conspiracy does not necessarily require proof of express agreements or proof that the alleged conspirators had any face-to-face meetings at all"; and despite the government's introduction of the written agreements that "This is rarely the way in which criminal conspiracies are formed."

Had the government relied on a general course of conduct throughout the years, these instructions might well have been apposite. But this was not such a case. The vast amount of time taken by the government in stressing high prices and profits and alleged patent frauds, together with the court's charge depreciating the testimony of defendants' officers, may well have succeeded in diverting the jury from the real issues as framed by the indictment and bill of particulars.

Defendants contend that the charge as given cut the government loose from the theory on which it had tried the case and allowed the jury to convict on the basis of conduct during the indictment period without making the essential decision as to whether agreements were actually made at the meetings.

Instead of charging that the government had relied (Bill of Particulars) on specific dates and specified individuals, the court charged that:

. . . . .

This central requirement of an "agreement" does not mean, however, that in order to create an unlawful combination or a conspiracy, the parties must meet together at some time and place or, indeed, that they must meet together at all. Nor does it mean that their undertaking must be embodied in express or formal contractual statements, or express words of any kind.

. . . . . .

Because express agreements are neither necessary nor common in establishing unlawful conspiracies the crime is one which may be shown from circumstantial evidence as to a course of conduct or business dealings. In other words, whether the prosecution has sustained its burden of proving a conspiracy must frequently be judged by what the jury finds the parties actually did rather than from the words they used.

. . . . .

A review of the entire charge leaves the definite impression that although the circumstantial evidence and "unreasonably high profits" aspects of the case were stressed, the key issue as to the formation of the conspiracy as particularized by the government was not given proper attention and the importance of establishing a conspiracy as charged so minimized that there can be no assurance that the jury was not misled [as] to defendants' serious prejudice. . . .

In contrast to concentrating on the conspiracy as alleged, the government in its summation and the court in its charge virtually ignored the allegedly conspiratorial meetings. Instead, the patent situation and high prices were stressed. . . .

Towards the end of the charge, ten pages were expended on the relation of allegedly unreasonably high prices. The court charged that "* * * uniform prices, maintained at a constant level over long periods of time—if such prices are artificial and unrelated to supply and demand or to other variations or changes in the pertinent economic factors—may be considered by you as some evidence from which an agreement or understanding or concerted action to restrain trade may be inferred."

The court read to the jury the last three of the "means and methods" charged in the indictment, namely:

1. Pfizer and Cyanamid maintained substantially identical and unreasonably high prices on Terramycin products and Aureomycin products, respectively.

2. Pfizer, Cyanamid, Bristol, Upjohn and Squibb each introduced its tetracycline products on the market at prices which were substantially identical with each other and which conformed to the prices of Terramycin products and Aureomycin products in effect as of November 1953, and all these companies maintained such substantially identical and unreasonably high prices until at least July 1960.

3. Pfizer, Cyanamid, Bristol, Upjohn and Squibb each introduced its tetracycline products on the market in dosage forms and customer classifications substantially identical with the Terramycin products and Aureomycin product dosage forms and customer classifications in effect as of November 1953, and

have continued to use such substantially identical dosage forms and classifications to date.

Referring to the government's contention "that broad spectrum antibiotic sales comprised a major portion of the business, and a major source of the profits, of the defendant companies in varying proportions," the court charged that these assertions "may be considered as part of the general background and setting in which the events of the case transpired." The court told the jury that they could ask themselves "whether price cuts or price changes of any kind would seem to have been indicated or desirable for any of the companies involved from the viewpoint of their self-interest." The court instructed that "neither the Sherman Act nor any other law that concerns us in this case imposes any limit on the price a company may charge for its commodity" and that the jury should not be influenced "by any notion that drug prices were too high or too low or even just right" and explained its reason for allowing cost and profit data in evidence because thereby the government sought to establish (presumably by inference a conclusion of conspiracy) stability of prices over a long period of time despite a disparity of production costs and market shares amongst the defendants.

Defendants take particular exception to two portions of the charge relating to profits and costs. They say as to profits that the charge that "Unreasonably or extraordinarily high prices or profits charged uniformly by competing sellers over a substantial period of time may be evidence, taken with all the other circumstances of the case, supporting an inference that the parties had an agreement rather than a competitive situation with respect to prices," was not justified and could well have misled the jury.

As to costs the court charged:

> There has been evidence of so-called "production costs" or "factory" or "standard" costs from records kept by the companies and comparisons in these records between such costs and selling prices. Many of these records omit many factors that should be included in costs in order to compute net profits. Such factors, without exhausting them, were research, promotion expenses, and other kinds of costs. You should have these omissions in mind and take them into account when you consider the figures I have just mentioned.

This instruction, defendants argue, permitted the jury, without the benefit of any proof of the "many factors that should be included in costs in order to compute net profits" or the factors which defendants have represented as constituting 90% of true cost, to speculate as to what proper costs would have been. The absence of the factors, which the court stated had been omitted, namely, "research, promotion expenses, and other kinds of costs," gave to the jury they say, without any proof of what the omissions might have been, uncontrolled discretion to keep "these omissions in mind and take them into account when you consider the figures." Defendants contend that with 90% of the material essential to an accurate determination of costs withheld from the jury by exclusion, it was being instructed "to reach its verdict on its own crude lay notions and subjective impressions as to whether prices and profits were 'unusual,' 'artificial,' 'extraordinary' or 'unreasonably high.' "

Probably, of neccesity, the government virtually had to ignore or at least play down the business reasons asserted by the defendants' executives as motivating their agreements and the actions taken by them and to concentrate on the possibly more jury appealing aspects such as abnormally high prices and profits and patent fraud. . . .

Under these circumstances it was highly important that the jury's attention be directed in the charge to the primary issue framed by the government. But as the case was submitted to the jury, this issue was subordinated in government summation and charge to the more inflamatory issues of illegally exorbitant prices charged to a victimized public and patent fraud. But the conspiratorial agreements, as charged, did not emanate from these issues.

A review of the entire record leads to the conclusion that the judgments of conviction against Cyanamid, Pfizer and Bristol must be reversed and that a new trial be had as to them.

HAYS, Circuit Judge (dissenting). . . .

The indictment charged defendants, in three counts, with having combined and conspired in restraint of trade in the broad spectrum antibiotic market, with having combined and conspired to monopolize that market, and with having illegally monopolized it. It was alleged that defendants conspired to exclude competitors and to fix prices and that, having sufficient market power to do so, defendants succeeded in accomplishing the objects of their conspiracy.

The government's evidence establishes that the price of tetracycline, a broad spectrum antibiotic controlled by defendants and having a very large sale, did not change at all from 1953 until 1960. Throughout that whole period each defendant charged exactly the same amount although Pfizer and Cyanamid were consistently producing tetracycline at a cost substantially lower than the production costs of Bristol, Squibb and Upjohn. Pfizer and Cyanamid allowed themselves to lose significant portions of their market to the higher cost producers without ever attempting to regain those portions by cutting prices. Although the production costs of all producers markedly decreased, the resulting savings were not reflected by any price reductions.

The agreement to exclude competitors centers on the 1953 patent settlement between Pfizer and Cyanamid. Pfizer licensed Cyanamid to produce and sell tetracycline while Cyanamid licensed Pfizer to manufacture, though not to sell, aureomycin. Neither Pfizer nor Cyanamid, then, with Parke, Davis, the only producers of broad spectrum antibiotics, had previously licensed any other drug companies to produce or sell their respective broad spectrum antibiotics. The government presented evidence from which the jury could infer an agreement between Pfizer and Cyanamid that Pfizer would not license anyone other than Cyanamid to manufacture tetracycline. Shortly after their meeting at which the parties had the opportunity to discuss such an agreement Pfizer publicly announced that the company policy was not to issue any licenses for tetracycline. That policy was strongly impressed upon Bristol, Squibb and Upjohn, and almost certainly would have resulted in litigation had the Broady wiretap incident not intervened. The point at which the understanding between the parties merged into an agreement is, perhaps, difficult to define with precision, but this constitutes no reason for denying to the jury the power to conclude that such an agreement existed. . . .

The court's instructions on the issues of patent fraud and unreasonably high prices were entirely proper. The evidence introduced on these issues tended to support the charge of conspiracy.

The government did not contend that Pfizer and Cyanamid agreed to defraud the patent office, but only that their conduct was evidence of the underlying conspiracy to exclude competitors. The jury would have been justified in finding that Pfizer's statement to the patent office that the processes of the prior art produced no tetracycline was deliberately false and that it was made in the expectation that Cyanamid would not challenge the statement. Cyanamid's participation in such a course of conduct is readily explainable by its expectation that it would be Pfizer's sole licensee.

The evidence relating to the high price level for broad spectrum antibiotics was equally relevant to the issue of conspiracy. There was evidence that the price for the antibiotics remained the same notwithstanding differences in costs among the defendants, notwithstanding overall decreases in costs through the period of the conspiracy, and notwithstanding changes in the market percentages controlled by each defendant. The jury would be justified in finding that the failure of any defendant at any time over a period of seven years to lower these extremely high prices evidenced a conspiracy. Defendants attempted to convince the jury that the oligopolistic nature of the broad spectrum antibiotics market made the ordinary concept of a competitive market irrelevant. The jury was not compelled to accept defendants' representations, and we are not justified in questioning its refusal to do so. . . .

PART III

Mergers and the Problems They Pose

Chapter   **MERGERS AND**

5   **MARKET POWER**

      Traditionally, corporate mergers have been grouped into one of three categories: horizontal, vertical, or conglomerate. The cases presented in this chapter provide a history of the legislative and court attitudes toward mergers of the first two types, i.e., those involving two or more firms in the same industry and those in which the acquired firm is either a customer or supplier of the acquiring firm. In the *Thatcher* case (which marked what most observers considered the judicial emasculation of the original Section 7 of the Clayton Act) the Court decided that the Federal Trade Commission's power to prevent mergers which might substantially lessen competition extended only to acquisitions of stock. This opened the way to merger via *asset* acquisition and, for all practical purposes, eliminated the Clayton Act as an effective antimerger weapon. Indeed, it was not until 1950 that events finally prompted Congress to enact the Celler-Kefauver Amendment, which brought asset acquisitions under the purview of Section 7 and eliminated the requirement that competition be shown to have been lessened "between the corporation . . . so acquired and the corporation making the acquisition."

      Brown Shoe represents the first comprehensive Supreme Court interpretation of the legal-economic goals of the amended Clayton Act, and provides useful insight into judicial treatment of such economic concepts as the geographic and product scope of a market. These concepts are further refined in *Continental Can*. Finally, in the *Von's* decision, the Court extended the doctrine of reasonable probability of competitive injury to proscribe a horizontal merger where the effect on market concentration did not appear to be significant.

Thatcher Manufacturing Company **v.** *Federal Trade Commission*

272 U.S. 554 (1926)

Mr. Justice McReynolds delivered the opinion of the Court.

. . . . .

      The Commission entered complaint against the petitioner, March 1, 1921, and charged that the latter contrary to Section 7 of the Clayton Act, first acquired the stock of four competing corporations—Lockport Glass Company, Essex Glass Company, Travis Glass Company and Woodbury Glass Company—and thereafter took transfers of all the business and assets of the first three and caused their dissolution. . . . [T]he Commission ruled that the acquisitions of all these stocks were unlawful and ordered the petitioner to cease and desist from ownership, operation, management and control of the assets, properties, rights, etc., of the Lockport, Essex and Travis Glass Companies secured through such stock ownership, and to divest itself of the assets, properties, rights, etc., formerly held by them. Also, that it should divest itself of the stock of the Woodbury Glass Company.

The court below held that the last-named company was not in competition with petitioner within the meaning of the statute and modified the order accordingly. Therein we agree and to that extent affirm its decree.

The court further ruled, in effect, that as the stocks of the remaining three companies were unlawfully obtained and ownership of the assets came through them, the Commission properly ordered the holder so to dispossess itself of the properties as to restore prior lawful conditions. With this we cannot agree. When the Commission institutes a proceeding based upon the holding of stock contrary to Section 7 of the Clayton Act, its power is limited by Section 11 to an order requiring the guilty person to cease and desist from such violation, effectually to divest itself of the stock, and to make no further use of it. The Act has no application to ownership of a competitor's property and business obtained prior to any action by the Commission, even though this was brought about through stock unlawfully held. The purpose of the Act was to prevent continued holding of stock and the peculiar evils incident thereto. If purchase of property has produced an unlawful status a remedy is provided through the courts. . . . The Commission is without authority under such circumstances.

Affirmed in part; reversed in part.

[Mr. Justice Brandeis, with whom the Chief Justice, Mr. Justice Holmes and Mr. Justice Stone joined, dissented in part.]

Brown Shoe Co., Inc. v. U.S.

370 U.S. 294 (1962)

MR. CHIEF JUSTICE WARREN delivered the opinion of the Court.

I.

This suit was initiated in November 1955 when the government filed a civil action in the United States District Court for the Eastern District of Missouri alleging that a contemplated merger between the G. R. Kinney Company, Inc. (Kinney), and the Brown Shoe Company, Inc. (Brown), through an exchange of Kinney for Brown stock, would violate Section 7 of the Clayton Act. . . .

The Industry

The District Court found that although domestic shoe production was scattered among a large number of manufacturers, a small number of large companies occupied a commanding position. Thus, while the 24 largest manufacturers produced about 35% of the Nation's shoes, the top 4— International, Endicott-Johnson, Brown (including Kinney) and General Shoe—alone produced approximately 23% of the Nation's shoes or 65% of the production of the top 24.

In 1955, domestic production of nonrubber shoes was 509.2 million pairs, of which about 103.6 million pairs were men's shoes, about 271 million pairs were women's shoes, and about 134.6 million pairs were children's shoes. The District Court found that men's, women's, and children's shoes are normally produced in separate factories.

The public buys these shoes through about 70,000 retail outlets, only 22,000 of which, however, derive 50% or more of their gross receipts from the sale of shoes and are classified as "shoe stores" by the Census Bureau. These 22,000 shoe stores were found generally to sell (1) men's shoes only, (2) women's shoes only, (3) women's and children's shoes, or (4) men's, women's, and children's shoes.

The District Court found a "definite trend" among shoe manufacturers to acquire retail outlets. . . . Brown, itself, with no retail outlets of its own prior to 1951, had acquired 845 such outlets by 1956. Moreover, between 1950 and 1956 nine independent shoe store chains, operating 1,114 retail shoe stores, were found to have become subsidiaries of these large firms and to have ceased their independent operations.

And once the manufacturers acquired retail outlets, the District Court found there was a "definite trend" for the parent-manufacturers to supply an ever increasing percentage of the retail outlets' needs, thereby foreclosing other manufacturers from effectively competing for the retail accounts. Manufacturer-dominated stores were found to be "drying up" the available outlets for independent producers.

Another "definite trend" found to exist in the shoe industry was a decrease in the number of plants manufacturing shoes. And there appears to have been a concomitant decrease in the number of firms manufacturing shoes. In 1947, there were 1,077 independent manufacturers of shoes, but by 1954 their number had decreased about 10% to 970.[1]

Brown Shoe

Brown Shoe was found not only to have been a participant, but also a moving factor, in these industry trends. Although Brown had experimented several times with operating its own retail outlets, by 1945 it had

---

[1] U.S. Bureau of the Census, 1958 Census of Manufacturers, MC 58(2)–31A–6. By 1958, the number of independent manufacturers had decreased by another 10% to 872. Ibid.

disposed of them all. However, in 1951, Brown again began to seek retail outlets by acquiring the Nation's largest operator of leased shoe departments, Wohl Shoe Company (Wohl), which operated 250 shoe departments in department stores throughout the United States. Between 1952 and 1955 Brown made a number of smaller acquisitions. . . . In 1954, Brown made another major acquisition: Regal Shoe Corporation which, at the time, operated one manufacturing plant producing men's shoes and 110 retail outlets.

The acquisition of these corporations was found to lead to increased sales by Brown to the acquired companies. . . .

During the same period of time, Brown also acquired the stock or assets of seven companies engaged solely in shoe manufacturing. As a result, in 1955, Brown was the fourth largest shoe manufacturer in the country, producing about 25.6 million pairs of shoes or about 4% of the Nation's total footwear production.

Kinney

Kinney is principally engaged in operating the largest family-style shoe store chain in the United States. At the time of trial, Kinney was found to be operating over 400 such stores in more than 270 cities. These stores were found to make about 1.2% of all national retail shoe sales by dollar volume. Moreover, in 1955 the Kinney stores sold approximately 8 million pairs of nonrubber shoes or about 1.6% of the national pairage sales of such shoes. . . .

In addition to this extensive retail activity, Kinney owned and operated four plants which manufactured men's, women's, and children's shoes and whose combined output was 0.5% of the national shoe production in 1955, making Kinney the twelfth largest shoe manufacturer in the United States.

Kinney stores were found to obtain about 20% of their shoes from Kinney's own manufacturing plants. At the time of the merger, Kinney bought no shoes from Brown; however, in line with Brown's conceded reasons[2] for acquiring Kinney, Brown had, by 1957, become the largest outside supplier of Kinney's shoes, supplying 7.9% of all Kinney's needs.

· · · · ·

III.

LEGISLATIVE HISTORY

This case is one of the first to come before us in which the Government's complaint is based upon allegations that the appellant has violated

---

[2] As stated in the testimony of Clark R. Gamble, President of Brown Shoe Company:

"It was our feeling, in addition to getting a distribution into the field of prices which we were not covering, it was also the feeling that as Kinney moved into the shopping centers in these free standing stores, they were going into a higher income neighborhood and they would probably find the necessity of up-grading and adding

Section 7 of the Clayton Act, as that section was amended in 1950. The amendments adopted in 1950 culminated extensive efforts over a number of years, on the parts of both the Federal Trade Commission and some members of Congress, to secure revision of a section of the antitrust laws considered by many observers to be ineffective in its then existing form. . . . In the light of this extensive legislative attention to the measure, and the broad, general language finally selected by Congress for the expression of its will, we think it appropriate to review the history of the amended Act in determining whether the judgment of the court below was consistent with the intent of the legislature. . . .

The dominant theme pervading congressional consideration of the 1950 amendments was a fear of what was considered to be a rising tide of economic concentration in the American economy. Apprehension in this regard was bolstered by the publication in 1948 of the Federal Trade Commission's study on corporate mergers. Statistics from this and other current studies were cited as evidence of the danger to the American economy in unchecked corporate expansions through merger. Other considerations cited in support of the bill were the desirability of retaining "local control" over industry and the protection of small businesses.[3] Throughout the recorded discussion may be found examples of Congress' fear not only of accelerated concentration of economic power on economic grounds, but also of the threat to other values a trend toward concentration was thought to pose.

What were some of the factors, relevant to a judgment as to the validity of a given merger, specifically discussed by Congress in redrafting Section 7?

First, there is no doubt that Congress did wish to "plug the loophole" and to include within the coverage of the Act the acquisition of assets no less than the acquisition of stock.

Second, by the deletion of the "acquiring-acquired" language in the original text, it hoped to make plain that Section 7 applied not only to mergers between actual competitors, but also to vertical and conglomerate mergers whose effect may tend to lessen competition in any line of commerce in any section of the country.[4]

---

additional lines to their very successful operation that they had been doing and it would give us an opportunity we hoped to be able to sell them in that category. Besides that, it was a very successful operation and would give us a good diversified investment to stabilize our earnings." . . .

[3] . . . Cf. *United States* v. *Aluminum Co. of America*, 148 F.2d 416, 429 (C. A. 2d Cir., per Learned Hand, J.): "Throughout the history of these [antitrust] statutes it has been constantly assumed that one of their purposes was to perpetuate and preserve, for its own sake and in spite of possible cost, an organization of industry in small units which can effectively compete with each other."

[4] That Section 7 was intended to apply to all mergers—horizontal, vertical or conglomerate—was specifically reiterated by the House Report on the final bill. H. R. Rep. No. 1191, 81st Cong., 1st Sess. 11. . . .

Third, it is apparent that a keystone in the erection of a barrier to what Congress saw was the rising tide of economic concentration, was its provision of authority for arresting mergers at a time when the trend to a lessening of competition in a line of commerce was still in its incipiency. Congress saw the process of concentration in American business as a dynamic force; it sought to assure the Federal Trade Commission and the courts the power to brake this force at its outset and before it gathered momentum.

Fourth, and closely related to the third, Congress rejected, as inappropriate to the problem it sought to remedy, the application to Section 7 cases of the standards for judging the legality of business combinations adopted by the courts in dealing with cases arising under the Sherman Act, and which may have been applied to some early cases arising under original Section 7.

Fifth, at the same time that it sought to create an effective tool for preventing all mergers having demonstrable anticompetitive effects, Congress recognized the stimulation to competition that might flow from particular mergers. When concern as to the Act's breadth was expressed, supporters of the amendments indicated that it would not impede, for example, a merger between two small companies to enable the combination to compete more effectively with larger corporations dominating the relevant market, nor a merger between a corporation which is financially healthy and a failing one which no longer can be a vital competitive factor in the market. The deletion of the word "community" in the original Act's description of the relevant geographic market is another illustration of Congress' desire to indicate that its concern was with the adverse effects of a given merger on competition only in an economically significant "section" of the country. Taken as a whole, the legislative history illuminates congressional concern with the protection of *competition*, not *competitors*, and its desire to restrain mergers only to the extent that such combinations may tend to lessen competition.

Sixth, Congress neither adopted nor rejected specifically any particular tests for measuring the relevant markets, either as defined in terms of product or in terms of geographic locus of competition, within which the anticompetitive effects of a merger were to be judged. Nor did it adopt a definition of the word "substantially," whether in quantitative terms of sales or assets or market shares or in designated qualitative terms, by which a merger's effects on competition were to be measured.

Seventh, while providing no definite quantitative or qualitative tests by which enforcement agencies could guage the effects of a given merger to determine whether it may "substantially" lessen competition or tend toward monopoly, Congress indicated plainly that a merger had to be functionally viewed, in the context of its particular industry. That is, whether the consolidation was to take place in an industry that was fragmented rather than concentrated, that had seen a recent trend toward domination by a few leaders or had remained fairly consistent in its distribution of market shares among the participating companies, that had experienced easy access to markets by suppliers and easy access to suppliers by buyers or had witnessed foreclosure of business, that had witnessed the ready entry of new competition or the erection of barriers to prospective entrants, all were aspects, varying in importance with the merger under consideration, which would properly be taken into account.[5]

Eighth, Congress used the words *"may be* substantially to lessen competition" (emphasis supplied), to indicate that its concern was with probabilities, not certainties. Statutes existed for dealing with clear-cut menaces to competition; no statute was sought for dealing with ephemeral possibilities. Mergers with a probable anticompetitive effect were to be proscribed by this Act.

It is against this background that we return to the case before us.

IV.

THE VERTICAL ASPECTS OF THE MERGER

Economic arrangements between companies standing in a supplier-customer relationship are characterized as "vertical." The primary vice of a vertical merger or other arrangement tying a customer to a supplier is that, by foreclosing the competitors of either party from a segment of the market otherwise open to them, the arrangement may act as a "clog on competition," *Standard Oil Co. of California* v. *United States*, 337 U.S. 293, 314, which "deprive[s] . . . rivals of a fair opportunity to compete."[6] . . . Every extended vertical arrangement by its very nature, for at least a time, denies to competitors of the supplier the opportunity to compete for part or all of the trade of the customer-party to the vertical arrangement. However, the Clayton Act does not render unlawful all such vertical arrangements, but forbids only those whose effect "may be substantially to lessen competition, or to tend to create a monopoly" "in any line of commerce in any section of the country." . . . The "area of effective competition" must be determined by reference to a product mar-

---

[5] Subsequent to the adoption of the 1950 amendments, both the Federal Trade Commission and the courts have, in the light of Congress' expressed intent, recognized the relevance and importance of economic data that places any given merger under consideration within an industry framework almost inevitably unique in every case. Statistics reflecting the shares of the market controlled by the industry leaders and the parties to the merger are, of course, the primary index of market power; but only a further examination of the particular market—its structure, history and probably future—can provide the appropriate setting for judging the probable anticompetitive effect of the merger. . . .

[6] In addition, a vertical merger may disrupt and injure competition when those independent customers of the supplier who are in competition with the merging customer, are forced either to stop handling the supplier's lines, thereby jeopardizing the goodwill they have developed, or to retain the supplier's lines, thereby forcing them into competition with their own supplier. . . .

ket (the "line of commerce") and a geographic market (the "section of the country").

The Product Market

The outer boundaries of a product market are determined by the reasonable interchangeability of use or the cross-elasticity of demand between the product itself and substitutes for it.[7] However, within this broad market, well-defined submarkets may exist, which, in themselves, constitute product markets for antitrust purposes. *United States v. E. I. duPont de Nemours & Co.*, 353 U.S. 586, 593–595. The boundaries of such a submarket may be determined by examining such practical indicia as industry or public recognition of the submarket as a separate economic entity, the product's peculiar characteristics and uses, unique production facilities, distinct customers, distinct prices, sensitivity to price changes, and specialized vendors. Because Section 7 of the Clayton Act prohibits any merger which may substantially lessen competition "in *any* line of commerce" (emphasis supplied), it is necessary to examine the effects of a merger in each such economically significant submarket to determine if there is a reasonable probability that the merger will substantially lessen competition. If such a probability is found to exist, the merger is proscribed.

Applying these considerations to the present case, we conclude that the record supports the District Court's finding that the relevant lines of commerce are men's, women's, and children's shoes. These product lines are recognized by the public; each line is manufactured in separate plants; each has characteristics peculiar to itself rendering it generally noncompetitive with the others; and each is, of course, directed toward a distinct class of customers.

Appellant, however, contends that the District Court's definitions fail to recognize sufficiently "price/quality" and "age/sex" distinctions in shoes. Brown argues that the predominantly medium-priced shoes which it manufactures occupy a product market different from the predominantly low-priced shoes which Kinney sells. But agreement with that argument would be equivalent to holding that medium-priced shoes do not compete with low-priced shoes. We think the District Court properly found the facts to be otherwise. It would be unrealistic to accept Brown's contention that, for example, men's shoes selling below $8.99 are in a different product market from those selling above $9.00.

This is not to say, however, that "price/quality" differences, where they exist, are unimportant in analyzing a merger; they may be of importance in determining the likely effect of a merger. But the boundaries of the relevant market must be drawn with sufficient breadth to include the competing products of each of the merging companies and to recognize

[7] The cross-elasticity of production facilities may also be an important factor in defining a product market within which a vertical merger is to be viewed. . . .

competition where, in fact, competition exists. Thus we agree with the District Court that in this case a further division of product lines based on "price/quality" differences would be "unrealistic."

Brown's contention that the District Court's product market definitions should have recognized further "age/sex" distinctions raises a different problem. Brown's sharpest criticism is directed at the District Court's finding that children's shoes constituted a single line of commerce. Brown argues, for example, that "a little boy does not wear a little girl's black patent leather pump" and that "[a] male baby cannot wear a growing boy's shoes." Thus Brown argues that "infants' and babies' " shoes, "misses' and children's" shoes and "youths' and boys' " shoes should each have been considered a separate line of commerce. Assuming, *arguendo*, that little boys' shoes, for example, do have sufficient peculiar characteristics to constitute one of the markets to be used in analyzing the effects of this merger, we do not think that in this case the District Court was required to employ finer "age/sex" distinctions than those recognized by its classifications of "men's," "women's," and "children's" shoes. Further division does not aid us in analyzing the effects of this merger. . . .

The Geographic Market

We agree with the parties and the District Court that insofar as the vertical aspect of this merger is concerned, the relevant geographic market is the entire Nation. The relationships of product value, bulk, weight and consumer demand enable manufacturers to distribute their shoes on a nationwide basis, as Brown and Kinney, in fact, do. The anticompetitive effects of the merger are to be measured within this range of distribution.

The Probable Effect of the Merger

Once the area of effective competition affected by a vertical arrangement has been defined, an analysis must be made to determine if the effect of the arrangement "may be substantially to lessen competition, or to tend to create a monopoly" in this market.

Since the diminution of the vigor of competition which may stem from a vertical arrangement results primarily from a foreclosure of a share of the market otherwise open to competitors, an important consideration in determining whether the effect of a vertical arrangement "may be substantially to lessen competition, or to tend to create a monopoly" is the size of the share of the market foreclosed. However, this factor will seldom be determinative. If the share of the market foreclosed is so large that it approaches monopoly proportions, the Clayton Act will, of course, have been violated; but the arrangement will also have run afoul of the Sherman Act. And the legislative history of Section 7 indicates clearly that the tests for measuring the legality of any particular economic arrangement under the Clayton Act are to be less stringent than those used in applying the Sherman Act. On the other hand, foreclosure of a *de minimis* share of the market will not tend "substantially to lessen competition."

Between these extremes, in cases such as the one before us, in which the foreclosure is neither of monopoly nor *de minimis* proportions, the percentage of the market foreclosed by the vertical arrangement cannot itself be decisive. In such cases, it becomes necessary to undertake an examination of various economic and historical factors in order to determine whether the arrangement under review is of the type Congress sought to proscribe.

A most important such factor to examine is the very nature and purpose of the arrangement.[8] Congress not only indicated that "the tests of illegality [under Section 7] are intended to be similar to those which the courts have applied in interpreting the same language as used in other sections of the Clayton Act," but also chose for Section 7 language virtually identical to that of Section 3 of the Clayton Act, 15 U.S.C. Section 14, which had been interpreted by this Court to require an examination of the interdependence of the market share foreclosed by, and the economic purpose of, the vertical arrangement. Thus, for example, if a particular vertical arrangement, considered under Section 3, appears to be a limited term exclusive-dealing contract, the market foreclosure must generally be significantly greater than if the arrangement is a tying contract before the arrangement will be held to have violated the Act. . . . The reason for this is readily discernible. The usual tying contract forces the customer to take a product or brand he does not necessarily want in order to secure one which he does desire. Because such an arrangement is inherently anticompetitive, we have held that its use by an established company is likely "substantially to lessen competition" although only a relatively small amount of commerce is affected. *International Salt Co.* v. *United States*. . . . Thus, unless the tying device is employed by a small company in an attempt to break into a market . . . the use of a tying device can rarely be harmonized with the strictures of the antitrust laws, which are intended primarily to preserve and stimulate competition. . . . On the other hand, requirement contracts are frequently negotiated at the behest of the customer who has chosen the particular supplier and his product upon the basis of competitive merit. . . . Of course, the fact that requirement contracts are not inherently anticompetitive will not save a particular agreement if, in fact, it is likely "substantially to lessen competition, or tend to create a monopoly." . . .

---

[8] Although it is "unnecessary for the Government to speculate as to what is in the 'back of the minds' of those who promote a merger," H.R. Rep. No. 1191, 81st Cong., 1st Sess. 8, evidence indicating the purpose of the merging parties, where available, is an aid in predicting the probable future conduct of the parties and thus the probable effects of the merger. *Swift & Co.* v. *United States*, 196 U.S. 375, 396; *United States* v. *Maryland & Virginia Milk Producers Assn.*, 167 F. Supp. 799, 804 (D. C. D. C.), aff'd, 362 U.S. 458.

Yet a requirement contract may escape censure if only a small share of the market is involved, if the purpose of the agreement is to insure to the customer a sufficient supply of a commodity vital to the customer's trade or to insure to the supplier a market for his output and if there is no trend toward concentration in the industry. . . . Similar considerations are pertinent to a judgment under Section 7 of the Act.

The importance which Congress attached to economic purpose is further demonstrated by the Senate and House Reports on H. R. 2734, which evince an intention to preserve the "failing company" doctrine. . . . Similarly, Congress foresaw that the merger of two large companies or a large and a small company might violate the Clayton Act while the merger of two small companies might not, although the share of the market foreclosed be identical, if the purpose of the small companies is to enable them in combination to compete with larger corporations dominating the market.

The present merger involved neither small companies nor failing companies. In 1955, the date of this merger, Brown was the fourth largest manufacturer in the shoe industry with sales of approximately 25 million pairs of shoes and assets of over $72,000,000 while Kinney had sales of about 8 million pairs of shoes and assets of about $18,000,000. Not only was Brown one of the leading manufacturers of men's, women's, and children's shoes, but Kinney, with over 350 retail outlets, owned and operated the largest independent chain of family shoe stores in the Nation. Thus, in this industry, no merger between a manufacturer and an independent retailer could involve a larger potential market foreclosure. Moreover, it is apparent both from past behavior of Brown and from the testimony of Brown's President, that Brown would use its ownership of Kinney to force Brown shoes into Kinney stores. Thus, in operation this vertical arrangement would be quite analogous to one involving a tying clause.[9]

Another important factor to consider is the trend toward concentration in the industry. It is true, of course, that the statute prohibits a given merger only if the effect of *that* merger may be substantially to lessen competition. But the very wording of Section 7 requires a prognosis of the probable *future* effect of the merger.

The existence of a trend toward vertical integration, which the District Court found, is well substantiated by the record. Moreover, the court found a tendency of the acquiring manufacturers to become increasingly important sources of supply for their acquired outlets. The necessary corollary of these trends is the foreclosure of independent manufacturers from markets otherwise open to them. And because these trends are not the product of accident but are rather the result of deliberate policies of

[9] Moreover, ownership integration is a more permanent and irreversible tie than is contract integration. See Kessler and Stern, "Competition, Contract, and Vertical Integration," 69 *Yale L. J.* 1, 78 (1959).

Brown and other leading shoe manufacturers, account must be taken of these facts in order to predict the probable future consequences of this merger. It is against this background of continuing concentration that the present merger must be viewed.

Brown argues, however, that the shoe industry is at present composed of a large number of manufacturers and retailers, and that the industry is dynamically competitive. But remaining vigor cannot immunize a merger if the trend in that industry is toward oligopoly. . . . It is the probable effect of the merger upon the future as well as the present which the Clayton Act commands the courts and the Commission to examine.

Moreover, as we have remarked above, not only must we consider the probable effects of the merger upon the economics of the particular markets affected but also we must consider its probable effects upon the economic way of life sought to be preserved by Congress. Congress was desirous of preventing the formation of further oligopolies with their attendant adverse effects upon local control of industry and upon small business. Where an industry was composed of numerous independent units, Congress appeared anxious to preserve this structure. . . .

The District Court's findings, and the record facts, many of them set forth in Part I of this opinion, convince us that the shoe industry is being subjected to just such a cumulative series of vertical mergers which, if left unchecked, will be likely "substantially to lessen competition."

We reach this conclusion because the trend toward vertical integration in the shoe industry, when combined with Brown's avowed policy of forcing its own shoes upon its retail subsidiaries, may foreclose competition from a substantial share of the markets for men's, women's, and children's shoes, without producing any countervailing competitive, economic, or social advantages.

V.

THE HORIZONTAL ASPECTS OF THE MERGER

An economic arrangement between companies performing similar functions in the production or sale of comparable goods or services is characterized as "horizontal." The effect on competition of such an arrangement depends, of course, upon its character and scope. Thus, its validity in the face of the antitrust laws will depend upon such factors as: the relative size and number of the parties to the arrangement; whether it allocates shares of the market among the parties; whether it fixes prices at which the parties will sell their product; or whether it absorbs or insulates competitors. Where the arrangement effects a horizontal merger between companies occupying the same product and geographic market, whatever competition previously may have existed in that market between the parties to the merger is eliminated. Section 7 of the Clayton Act, prior to its amendment, focused upon this aspect of horizontal combinations by proscribing acquisitions which might result in a lessening of competition between the acquiring and the acquired companies. The 1950 amendments made plain Congress' intent that the validity of such combinations was to be gauged on a broader scale: their effect on competition generally in an economically significant market.

Thus, again, the proper definition of the market is a "necessary predicate" to an examination of the competition that may be affected by the horizontal aspects of the merger. The acquisition of Kinney by Brown resulted in a horizontal combination at both the manufacturing and retailing levels of their businesses. Although the District Court found that the merger of Brown's and Kinney's *manufacturing* facilities was economically too insignificant to come within the prohibitions of the Clayton Act, the Government has not appealed from this portion of the lower court's decision. Therefore, we no occasion to express our views with respect to that finding. On the other hand, appellant does contest the District Court's finding that the merger of the companies' *retail* outlets may tend substantially to lessen competition.

The Product Market

Shoes are sold in the United States in retail shoe stores and in shoe departments of general stores. These outlets sell: (1) men's shoes, (2) women's shoes, (3) women's or children's shoes, or (4) men's, women's or children's shoes. Prior to the merger, both Brown and Kinney sold their shoes in competition with one another through the enumerated kinds of outlets characteristic of the industry. . . .

The Geographic Market

The criteria to be used in determining the appropriate geographic market are essentially similar to those used to determine the relevant product market. . . . Moreover, just as a product submarket may have Section 7 significance as the proper "line of commerce," so may a geographic submarket be considered the appropriate "section of the country." . . . Congress prescribed a pragmatic, factual approach to the definition of the relevant market and not a formal, legalistic one. The geographic market selected must, therefore, both "correspond to the commercial realities" of the industry and be economically significant. Thus, although the geographic market in some instances may encompass the entire Nation, under other circumstances it may be as small as a single metropolitan area. . . . The fact that two merging firms have competed directly on the horizontal level in but a fraction of the geographic markets in which either has operated, does not, in itself, place their merger outside the scope of Section 7. That section speaks of "any . . . section of the country," and if anticompetitive effects of a merger are probable in "any" significant market, the merger—at least to that extent—is proscribed.

The parties do not dispute the findings of the District Court that the

Nation as a whole is the relevant geographic market for measuring the anticompetitive effects of the merger viewed vertically or of the horizontal merger of Brown's and Kinney's manufacturing facilities. As to the retail level, however, they disagree. . . .

We believe, however, that the record fully supports the District Court's findings that shoe stores in the outskirts of cities compete effectively with stores in central downtown areas, and that while there is undoubtedly some commercial intercourse between smaller communities within a single "standard metropolitan area," the most intense and important competition in retail sales will be confined to stores within the particular communities in such an area and their immediate environs.

We therefore agree that the District Court properly defined the relevant geographic markets in which to analyze this merger as those cities with a population exceeding 10,000 and their environs in which both Brown and Kinney retailed shoes through their own outlets. Such markets are large enough to include the downtown shops and suburban shopping centers in areas contiguous to the city, which are the important competitive factors, and yet are small enough to exclude stores beyond the immediate environs of the city, which are of little competitive significance.

The Probable Effect of the Merger

Having delineated the product and geographic markets within which the effects of this merger are to be measured, we turn to an examination of the District Court's finding that as a result of the merger competition in the retailing of men's, women's and children's shoes may be lessened substantially in those cities in which both Brown and Kinney stores are located. . . .

. . . [W]e believe the record is adequate to support the findings of the District Court. While it is true that the court concentrated its attention on the structure of competition in the city in which it sat and as to which detailed evidence was most readily available, it also heard witnesses from no less than 40 other cities in which the parties to the merger operated. The court was careful to point out that it was on the basis of all the evidence that it reached its conclusions concerning the boundaries of the relevant markets and the merger's effects on competition within them. We recognize that variations of size, climate and wealth as enumerated by Brown exist in the relevant markets. However, we agree with the court below that the markets with respect to which evidence was received provide a fair sampling of all the areas in which the impact of this merger is to be measured. The appellant has not shown how the variables it has mentioned could affect the structure of competition within any particular market so as to require a change in the conclusions drawn by the District Court. Each competitor within a given market is equally affected by these factors, even though the city in which he does business may differ from St. Louis in size, climate or wealth. Thus, we believe the District Court properly reached its conclusions on the basis of the evidence available to it. There is no reason to protract already complex antitrust litigation by detailed analyses of peripheral economic facts, if the basic issues of the case may be determined through study of a fair sample.[10]

In the case before us, not only was a fair sample used to demonstrate the soundness of the District Court's conclusions, but evidence of record fully substantiates those findings as to each relevant market. An analysis of undisputed statistics of sales of shoes in the cities in which both Brown and Kinney sell shoes at retail, separated into the appropriate lines of commerce, provides a persuasive factual foundation upon which the required prognosis of the merger's effects may be built. Although Brown objects to some details in the Government's computations used in drafting these exhibits, appellant cannot deny the correctness of the more general picture they reveal. . . . They show, for example, that during 1955 in 32 separate cities, ranging in size and location from Topeka, Kansas, to Batavia, New York, and Hobbs, New Mexico, the combined share of Brown and Kinney sales of women's shoes (by unit volume) exceeded 20%.[11] In 31 cities—some the same as those used in measuring the effect of the merger in the women's line—the combined share of children's shoes sales exceeded 20%; in 6 cities their share exceeded 40%. In Dodge City, Kansas, their combined share of the market for women's shoes was over 57%; their share of the children's shoe market in that city was 49%. In the 7 cities in which Brown's and Kinney's combined shares of the market for women's shoes were greatest (ranging from 33% to 57%) each of the parties alone, prior to the merger, had captured substantial portions of those markets (ranging from 13% to 34%); the merger intensified this existing concentration. In 118 separate cities the combined shares of the market of Brown and Kinney in the sale of one of the relevant lines of commerce exceeded 5%. In 47 cities, their share exceeded 5% in all three lines.

The market share which companies may control by merging is one of the most important factors to be considered when determining the probable effects of the combination on effective competition in the relevant market.

---

[10] See . . . U.S. Atty. Gen. Nat. Comm. to Study the Antitrust Laws, Report 126 (1955): "While sufficient data to support a conclusion is required, sufficient data to give the enforcement agencies, the courts and business certainty as to competitive consequences would nullify the words 'Where the effect may be' in the Clayton Act and convert them into 'Where the effect is.' " And the Committee of the Judicial Conference of the United States on Procedure in Antitrust and Other Protracted Cases has also emphasized the need for limiting the mass of possibly relevant evidence in cases of this type in order to avoid confusion and its concomitant increased possibility of error. 13 F. R. D. 62, 64.

[11] Although the sum of the parties' pre-existing shares of the market will normally equal their combined share of the immediate post-merger market, we recognize that this share need not remain stable in the future. Nevertheless, such statistics provide a graphic picture of the immediate impact of a merger, and, as such, also provide a meaningful base upon which to build conclusions of the probable future effects of the merger.

In an industry as fragmented as shoe retailing, the control of substantial shares of the trade in a city may have important effects on competition. If a merger achieving 5% control were now approved, we might be required to approve future merger efforts by Brown's competitors seeking similar market shares. The oligopoly Congress sought to avoid would then be futhered and it would be difficult to dissolve the combinations previously approved. Furthermore, in this fragmented industry, even if the combination controls but a small share of a particular market, the fact that this share is held by a large national chain can adversely affect competition. Testimony in the record from numerous independent retailers, based on their actual experience in the market, demonstrates that a strong, national chain of stores can insulate selected outlets from the vagaries of competition in particular locations and that the large chains can set and alter styles in footwear to an extent that renders the independents unable to maintain competitive inventories. A third significant aspect of this merger is that it creates a large national chain which is integrated with a manufacturing operation. The retail outlets of integrated companies, by eliminating wholesalers and by increasing the volume of purchases from the manufacturing division of the enterprise, can market their own brands at prices below those of competing independent retailers. Of course, some of the results of large integrated or chain operations are beneficial to consumers. Their expansion is not rendered unlawful by the mere fact that small independent stores may be adversely affected. It is competition, not competitors, which the Act protects. But we cannot fail to recognize Congress' desire to promote competition through the protection of viable, small, locally owned businesses. Congress appreciated that occasional higher costs and prices might result from the maintenance of fragmented industries and markets. It resolved these competing considerations in favor of decentralization. We must give effect to that decision.

Other factors to be considered in evaluating the probable effects of a merger in the relevant market lend additional support to the District Court's conclusion that this merger may substantially lessen competition. One such factor is the history of tendency toward concentration in the industry.[12] As we have previously pointed out, the shoe industry has, in recent years, been a prime example of such a trend. Most combinations have been between manufacturers and retailers, as each of the larger pro-

[12] . . . A company's history of expansion through mergers presents a different economic picture than a history of expansion through unilateral growth. Internal expansion is more likely to be the result of increased demand for the company's products and is more likely to provide increased investment in plants, more jobs and greater output. Conversely, expansion through merger is more likely to reduce available consumer choice while providing no increase in industry capacity, jobs or output. It was for these reasons, among others, Congress expressed its disapproval of successive acquisitions. Section 7 was enacted to prevent even small mergers that added to concentration in an industry. . . .

ducers has sought to capture an increasing number of assured outlets for its wares. Although these mergers have been primarily vertical in their aim and effect, to the extent that they have brought ever greater numbers of retail outlets within fewer and fewer hands, they have had an additional important impact on the horizontal plane. By the merger in this case, the largest single group of retail stores still independent of one of the large manufacturers was absorbed into an already substantial aggregation of more or less controlled retail outlets. As a result of this merger, Brown moved into second place nationally in terms of retail stores directly owned. Including the stores on its franchise plan, the merger placed under Brown's control almost 1,600 shoe outlets, or about 7.2% of the Nation's retail "shoe stores" as defined by the Census Bureau, and 2.3% of the Nation's total retail shoe outlets.[13] We cannot avoid the mandate of Congress that tendencies toward concentration in industry are to be curbed in their incipiency, particularly when those tendencies are being accelerated through giant steps striding across a hundred cities at a time. In the light of the trends in this industry we agree with the Government and the court below that this is an appropriate place at which to call a halt.

At the same time appellant has presented no mitigating factors, such as the business failure or the inadequate resources of one of the parties that may have prevented it from maintaining its competitive position, nor a demonstrated need for combination to enable small companies to enter into a more meaningful competition with those dominating the relevant markets. On the basis of the record before us, we believe the Government sustained its burden of proof. We hold that the District Court was correct in concluding that this merger may tend to lessen competition substantially in the retail sale of men's, women's, and children's shoes in the overwhelming majority of those cities and their environs in which both Brown and Kinney sell through owned or controlled outlets.

The judgment is *Affirmed*.

United States v. Continental Can Co. et al.

378 U.S. 441 (1964)

MR. JUSTICE WHITE delivered the opinion of the Court.

In 1956, Continental Can Company, the Nation's second largest producer of metal containers, acquired all of the assets, business and good will of Hazel-Atlas Glass Company, the Nation's third largest producer of glass containers, in exchange for 999,140 shares of Continental's common

---

[13] Although statistics concerning the degree of concentration and the rank of Brown-Kinney in terms of controlled retail stores in each of the relevant product and geographic markets would have been more helpful in analyzing the results of this merger, neither side has presented such statistics. The figures in the record, based on national rank, are, nevertheless, useful in depicting the trends in the industry.

stock and the assumption by Continental of all of the liabilities of Hazel-Atlas. The Government brought this action seeking a judgment that the acquisition violated Section 7 of the Clayton Act and requesting an appropriate divestiture order. Trying the case without a jury, the District Court found that the Government had failed to prove reasonable probability of anticompetitive effect in any line of commerce, and accordingly dismissed the complaint at the close of the Government's case. . . . We noted probable jurisdiction to consider the specialized problems incident to the application of Section 7 to interindustry mergers and acquisitions.[1] . . . We reverse the decision of the District Court.

I

The industries with which this case is principally concerned are, as found by the trial court, the metal can industry, the glass container industry and the plastic container industry, each producing one basic type of container made of metal, glass, and plastic, respectively.

Continental Can is a New York corporation organized in 1913 to acquire all the assets of three metal container manufacturers. Since 1913 Continental has acquired 21 domestic metal container companies as well as numerous others engaged in the packaging business, including producers of flexible packaging; a manufacturer of polyethylene bottles and similar plastic containers; 14 producers of paper containers and paperboard; four companies making closures for glass containers; and one—Hazel-Atlas—producing glass containers. In 1955, the year prior to the present merger, Continental, with assets of $382 million, was the second largest company in the metal container field, shipping approximately 33% of all such containers sold in the United States. It and the largest producer, American Can Company, accounted for approximately 71% of all metal container shipments. National Can Company, the third largest, shipped approximately 5%, with the remaining 24% of the market being divided among 75 to 90 other firms. . . .

Hazel-Atlas was a West Virginia corporation which in 1955 had net sales in excess of $79 million and assets of more than $37 million. Prior to the absorption of Hazel-Atlas into Continental the pattern of dominance

---

[1] Both parties and the District Court refer to this as an interindustry merger. The word "industry" is susceptible of more than one meaning. It might be defined in terms of end uses for which various products compete; so defined it would be roughly equivalent to the concept of a "line of commerce." According to this interpretation the glass and metal container businesses, to the extent they compete, are in the same industry. On the other hand, "industry" might also denote an aggregate of enterprises employing similar production and marketing facilities and producing products having markedly similar characteristics. In many instances, the segments of economic endeavor embraced by these two concepts of "industry" will be substantially coextensive, since those who employ the same types of machinery to turn out the same general product often compete in the same market. Since this is not such a case it will be helpful to use the word "industry" as referring to similarity of production facilities and products. So viewed, "interindustry competition" becomes a meaningful concept.

among a few firms in the glass container industry was similar to that which prevailed in the metal container field. Hazel-Atlas, with approximately 9.6% of the glass container shipments in 1955, was third. Owens-Illinois Glass Company had 34.2% and Anchor-Hocking Glass Company 11.6%, with the remaining 44.6% being divided among at least 39 other firms. . . .

II

We deal first with the relevant market. It is not disputed here, and the District Court held, that the geographical market is the entire United States. As for the product market, the court found, as was conceded by the parties, that the can industry and the glass container industry were relevant lines of commerce. Beyond these two product markets, however, the Government urged the recognition of various other lines of commerce, some of them defined in terms of the end uses for which tin and glass containers were in substantial competition. These end-use claims were containers for the beer industry, containers for the soft drink industry, containers for the canning industry, containers for the toiletry and cosmetic industry, containers for the medicine and health industry, and containers for the household and chemical industry. . . .

The court, in dealing with these claims, recognized that there was interindustry competition. . . . Furthermore the court found that:

Hazel-Atlas and Continental were part of this overall industrial pattern, each in a recognized separate industry producing distinct products but engaged in inter-industry competition for the favor of various end users of their products. . . .

The court, nevertheless, with one exception—containers for beer—rejected the Government's claim that existing competition between metal and glass containers had resulted in the end-use product markets urged by the Government: "The fact that there is inter-industry or inter-product competion between metal, glass and plastic containers is not determinative of the metes and bounds of a relevant product market." . . . In the trial court's view, the Government failed to make "appropriate distinctions . . . between inter-industry or overall commodity competition and the type of competition between products with reasonable interchangeability of use and cross-elasticity of demand which has Clayton Act significance." . . . The interindustry competition, concededly present, did not remove this merger from the category of the conglomerate combination, "in which one company in two separate industries combined with another in a third industry for the purpose of establishing a diversified line of products." . . .

We cannot accept this conclusion. The District Court's findings having established the existence of three product markets—metal containers, glass containers and metal and glass beer containers—the disputed issue on which that court erred is whether the admitted competition between metal and glass containers for uses other than packaging beer was of the type and quality deserving of Section 7 protection and therefore the basis for defining a relevant product market. In resolving this issue we are instructed on the one hand that "[f]or every product, substitutes exist. But a relevant market cannot meaningfully encompass that infinite range." *Times-Picayune* v. *United States.* . . . On the other hand it is improper "to require that products be fungible to be considered in the relevant market." *United States* v. *duPont* 351 377, 394. In defining the product market between these terminal extremes, we must recognize meaningful competition where it is found to exist. Though the "outer boundaries of a product market are determined by the reasonable interchangeability of use or the cross-elasticity of demand between the product itself and substitutes for it," there may be "within this broad market, well-defined submarkets . . . which, in themselves, constitute product markets for antitrust purposes." *Brown Shoe Co.* v. *United States.* . . . Concededly these guidelines offer no precise formula for judgment and they necessitate, rather than avoid, careful consideration based upon the entire record.

It is quite true that glass and metal containers have different characteristics which may disqualify one or the other, at least in their present form, from this or that particular use; that the machinery necessary to pack in glass is different from that employed when cans are used; that a particular user of cans or glass may pack in only one or the other container and does not shift back and forth from day to day as price and other factors might make desirable; and that the competition between metal and glass containers is different from the competition between the can companies themselves or between the products of the different glass companies. These are relevant and important considerations but they are not sufficient to obscure the competitive relationships which this record so compellingly reveals.

Baby food was at one time packed entirely in metal cans. Hazel-Atlas played a significant role in inducing the shift to glass as the dominant container by designing "what has become the typical baby food jar." According to Continental's estimate, 80% of the Nation's baby food now moves in glass containers. Continental has not been satisfied with this contemporary dominance by glass, however, and has made intensive efforts to increase its share of the business at the expense of glass. . . .

In the soft drink business, a field which has been, and is, predominantly glass territory, the court recognized that the metal can industry had "[a]fter considerable initial difficulty . . . developed a can strong enough to resist the pressures generated by carbonated beverages" and "made strenuous efforts to promote the use of metal cans for carbonated beverages as against glass bottles." . . . Continental has been a major factor in this rivalry. It studied the results of market tests to determine the extent to which metal cans could "penetrate this tremendous market," and its advertising has centered around the advantages of cans over glass as soft drink containers, emphasizing such features as convenience in stacking and storing, freedom from breakage and lower distribution costs resulting from the lighter weight of cans.

The District Court found that "[a]lthough at one time almost all packaged beer was sold in bottles, in a relatively short period the beer can made great headway and may well have become the dominant beer container." . . . Regardless of which industry may have the upper hand at a given moment, however, an intense competitive battle on behalf of the beer can and the beer bottle is being waged both by the industry trade associations and by individual container manufacturers, one of the principal protagonists being Continental. Technological development has been an important weapon in this battle. A significant factor in the growth of the beer can appears to have been its no-return feature. The glass industry responded with the development of a lighter and cheaper one-way bottle.

In the food canning, toiletry and cosmetic, medicine and health, and household and chemical industries the existence of vigorous competition was also recognized below. In the case of food it was noted that one type of container has supplanted the other in the packaging of some products and that in some instances similar products are packaged in two or more different types of containers. In the other industries "glass container, plastic container and metal container manufacturers are each seeking to promote their lines of containers at the expense of other lines, . . . all are attempting to improve their products or to develop new ones so as to have a wider customer appeal," . . . the result being that "manufacturers from time to time may shift a product from one type of container to another." . . .

In the light of this record and these findings, we think the District Court employed an unduly narrow construction of the "competition" protected by Section 7 and of "reasonable interchangeability of use or the cross-elasticity of demand" in judging the facts of this case. We reject the opinion below insofar as it holds that these terms as used in the statute or in *Brown Shoe* were intended to limit the competition protected by Section 7 to competition between identical products, to the kind of competition which exists, for example, between the metal containers of one company and those of another, or between the several manufacturers of glass containers. Certainly, that the competition here involved may be called "interindustry competition" and is between products with distinctive characteristics does not automatically remove it from the reach of Section 7.

Interchangeability of use and cross-elasticity of demand are not to be used to obscure competition but to "recognize competition where, in fact, competition exists." *Brown Shoe Co.* v. *United States*. . . . In our view there is and has been a rather general confrontation between metal and glass containers and competition between them for the same end uses which is insistent, continuous, effective and quantitywise very substantial. Metal has replaced glass and glass has replaced metal as the leading container for some important uses; both are used for other purposes; each is trying to expand its share of the market at the expense of the other; and each is attempting to preempt for itself every use for which its product is physically suitable, even though some such uses have traditionally been regarded as the exclusive domain of the competing industry.[2] In differing degrees for different end uses manufacturers in each industry take into consideration the price of the containers of the opposing industry in formulating their own pricing policy.[3] Thus, though the interchangeability of use may not be so complete and the cross-elasticity of demand not so immediate as in the case of most intraindustry mergers, there is over the long run the kind of customer response to innovation and other competitive stimuli that brings the competition between these two industries within Section 7's competition-preserving proscriptions.

Moreover, price is only one factor in a user's choice between one container or the other. That there are price differentials between the two products or that the demand for one is not particularly or immediately responsive to changes in the price of the other are relevant matters but not determinative of the product market issue. Whether a packager will use glass or cans may depend not only on the price of the package but also upon other equally important considerations. The consumer, for example, may begin to prefer one type of container over the other and the manufacturer of baby food cans may therefore find that his problem is the housewife rather than the packer or the price of his cans.[4] This may not be price competition but it is nevertheless meaningful competition between interchangeable containers.

We therefore conclude that the area of effective competition between the metal and glass container industry is far broader than that of con-

---

[2] Ford Sammis & Company, a firm of market economists, conducted for the Glass Container Manufacturers Institute market surveys of 28 different product classifications. . . .

"Every consumer product tends to standardize on a single type of container. . . .

"However, no traditional market is ever secure for any type of container. Marketers are apt to try out new containers at any time, in their constant search for ways to increase sales.

"When this happens, the result is a period of container competition. . . ."

[3] The chairman of the board of Owens-Illinois Glass Co. testified that he takes into account the price of metal containers in pricing glass containers for beer, soft drinks, and household and chemical products, and to a lesser degree for toiletries and cosmetics. In assessing the likelihood that it could "penetrate [the] tremendous market" for soft drink containers Continental concluded "[a]ssuming that the merchandising factors are favorable and that the product quality is well received, the upper limit on market acceptance will then be determined by *price*." Continental also stated in an intercompany memorandum that in the fight between the beer can and the one-way bottle "[t]he key factor, in our estimation, is *pricing*," and concluded that a reduction in the price of one-way beer bottles was to "be regarded as a further attempt on the part of the glass manufacturers to maintain their position in the one-way package field."

[4] An official of the Glass Container Manufacturers Institute described that organization's advertising program as three-pronged, directed at the packer, the retailer, and the ultimate consumer.

tainers for beer. It is true that the record in this case does not identify with particularity all end uses for which competition exists and all those for which competition may be non-existent, too remote, or too ephemeral to warrant Section 7 application. Nor does the record furnish the exact quantitative share of the relevant market which is enjoyed by the individual participating can and glass companies. But "[t]he 'market,' as most concepts in law or economics, cannot be measured by metes and bounds. . . . Obviously no magic inheres in numbers." *Times-Picayune* v. *United States* . . . "Industrial activities cannot be confined to trim categories." *United States* v. *duPont*, 351 U.S. 377, 395. The claimed deficiencies in the record cannot sweep aside the existence of a large area of effective competition between the makers of cans and the makers of glass containers. We know enough to conclude that the rivalry between cans and glass containers is pervasive and that the area of competitive overlap between these two product markets is broad enough to make the position of the individual companies within their own industries very relevant to the merger's impact within the broader competitive area that embraces both of the merging firms' respective industries.

Glass and metal containers were recognized to be two separate lines of commerce. But given the area of effective competition between these lines, there is necessarily implied one or more other lines of commerce embracing both industries. Since the purpose of delineating a line of commerce is to provide an adequate basis for measuring the effects of a given acquisition, its contours must, as nearly as possible, conform to competitive reality. Where the area of effective competition cuts across industry lines, so must the relevant line of commerce; otherwise an adequate determination of the merger's true impact cannot be made.

Based on the evidence thus far revealed by this record we hold that the interindustry competition between glass and metal containers is sufficient to warrant treating as a relevant product market the combined glass and metal container industries and all end uses for which they compete. There may be some end uses for which glass and metal do not and could not compete, but complete interindustry competitive overlap need not be shown. We would not be true to the purpose of the Clayton Act's line of commerce concept as a framework within which to measure the effect of mergers on competition were we to hold that the existence of noncompetitive segments within a proposed market area precludes its being treated as a line of commerce. . . .

Nor are we concerned by the suggestion that if the product market is to be defined in these terms it must include plastic, paper, foil and any other materials competing for the same business. That there may be a broader product market made up of metal, glass and other competing containers does not necessarily negative the existence of submarkets of cans, glass, plastic or cans and glass together, for "within this broad market, well-defined submarkets may exist which, in themselves, constitute product markets for antitrust purposes." *Brown Shoe Co.* v. *United States.* . . .

III

We approach the ultimate judgment under Section 7 having in mind the teachings of *Brown Shoe,* supplemented by their application and elaboration in *United States* v. *Philadelphia National Bank* . . . and *United States* v. *El Paso Natural Gas Co.* . . . The issue is whether the merger between Continental and Hazel-Atlas will have probable anticompetitive effect within the relevant line of commerce. Market shares are the primary indicia of market power but a judgment under Section 7 is not to be made by any single qualitative or quantitative test. The merger must be viewed functionally in the context of the particular market involved, its structure, history and probable future. Where a merger is of such a size as to be inherently suspect, elaborate proof of market structure, market behavior and probable anticompetitive effects may be dispensed with in view of Section 7's design to prevent undue concentration. Moreover, the competition with which Section 7 deals includes not only existing competition but that which is sufficiently probable and imminent. See *United States* v. *El Paso Natural Gas Co., supra.*

Continental occupied a dominant position in the metal can industry. It shipped 33% of the metal cans shipped by the industry and together with American shipped about 71% of the industry total. Continental's share amounted to 13 billion metal containers out of a total of 40 billion and its $433 million gross sales of metal containers amounted to 31.4% of the industry's total gross of $1,380,000,000. Continental's total assets were $382 million, its net sales and operating revenues $666 million.

In addition to demonstrating the dominant position of Continental in a highly concentrated industry, the District Court's findings clearly revealed Continental's vigorous efforts all across the competitive front between metal and glass containers. Continental obviously pushed metal containers wherever metal containers could be pushed. Its share of the beer can market ran from 43% in 1955 to 46% in 1957. Its share of both beer can and beer bottle shipments, disregarding the returnable bottle factor, ran from 36% in 1955 to 38% in 1957. Although metal cans have so far occupied a relatively small percentage of the soft drink container field, Continental's share of this can market ranged from 36% in 1955 to 26% in 1957 and its portion of the total shipments of glass and metal soft drink and beverage containers, disregarding the returnable bottle factor, was 7.2% in 1955, approximately 5.4% in 1956 and approximately 6.2% in 1957 (for 1956 and 1957 these figures include Hazel-Atlas' share). In the category covering all nonfood products, Continental's share was approximately 30% of the total shipments of metal containers for such uses.

Continental's major position in the relevant product market—the combined metal and glass container industries—prior to the merger is undeniable. Of the 59 billion containers shipped in 1955 by the metal (39¾ billion) and glass (19⅓ billion) industries, Continental shipped 21.9%, to a great extent dispersed among all of the end uses for which glass and metal compete.[5] Of the six largest firms in the product market it ranked second.

When Continental acquired Hazel-Atlas it added significantly to its position in the relevant line of commerce. Hazel-Atlas was the third largest glass container manufacturer in an industry in which the three top companies controlled 55.4% of the total shipments of glass containers. Hazel-Atlas' share was 9.6%, which amounted to 1,857,000,000 glass containers out of a total of 19⅓ billion industrial total. Its annual sales amounted to $79 million, its assets exceeded $37 million and it had 13 plants variously located in the United States. In terms of total containers shipped, Hazel-Atlas ranked sixth in the relevant line of commerce, its almost 2 billion containers being 3.1% of the product market total.

The evidence so far presented leads us to conclude that the merger between Continental and Hazel-Atlas is in violation of Section 7. The product market embracing the combined metal and glass container industries was dominated by six firms having a total of 70.1% of the business.[6] Continental, with 21.9% of the shipments, ranked second within

[5] Determination of market shares is made somewhat more difficult in this case than in the ordinary intraindustry merger because the indices of total production of the two industries are expressed differently, the metal container industry reporting to the Census Bureau in terms of tinplate consumed in manufacture, and the glass container industry in terms of units of containers. On the basis of figures and data supplied by the Census Bureau and the Can Manufacturers Institute the Government has derived a conversion factor showing the relationship between tinplate consumption and total containers manufactured, thereby permitting a comparison of the relative positions of the firms competing within the glass and metal container line of commerce. It would appear that the District Court relied on figures disclosed by application of this factor, since it found that American and Continental shipped approximately 38% and 33%, respectively, of the metal cans sold in the United States. . . .

Continental objects to the use of this conversion scheme, however, arguing that it ignores such considerations as size of cans and the returnable feature of some types of bottles. We are not persuaded. Since different systems of statistical notation are employed by these industries, a common referential standard is an absolute prerequisite to a comparison of market shares. Consistent with this Court's declarations in other cases concerning the high degree of relevance of market shares to the effect of mergers on competition, we believe that slight variations one way or the other which may inhere in the use of a conversion formula should not blind us to the broad significance of the resulting percentages. In the compilation of statistics "precision in detail is less important than the accuracy of the broad picture presented." *Brown Shoe Co. v. United States.* . . .

[6] The six largest firms, and their respective percentages of the relevant market as of the year prior to the merger are:

American Can Co.	26.8%
Continental Can Co.	21.9%
Owens-Illinois Glass Co.	11.2%
Anchor-Hocking Glass Co.	3.8%
National Can Co.	3.3%
Hazel-Atlas Glass Co.	3.1%
Total	70.1%

this product market, and Hazel-Atlas, with 3.1% ranked sixth. Thus, of this vast market—amounting at the time of the merger to almost $3 billion in annual sales—a large percentage already belonged to Continental before the merger. By the acquisition of Hazel-Atlas stock Continental not only increased its own share more than 14% from 21.9% to 25%, but also reduced from five to four the most significant competitors who might have threatened its dominant position. The resulting percentage of the combined firms approaches that held presumptively bad in *United States* v. *Philadelphia National Bank*. . . . The case falls squarely within the principle that where there has been a "history of tendency toward concentration in the industry" tendencies toward further concentration "are to be curbed in their incipiency." *Brown Shoe Co.* v. *United States*. . . . Where "concentration is already great, the importance of preventing even slight increases in concentration and so preserving the possibility of eventual deconcentration is correspondingly great." *United States* v. *Philadelphia National Bank*. . . .

Continental insists, however, that whatever the nature of interindustry competition in general, the types of containers produced by Continental and Hazel-Atlas at the time of the merger were for the most part not in competition with each other and hence the merger could have no effect on competition. This argument ignores several important matters.

First: The District Court found that both Continental and Hazel-Atlas were engaged in interindustry competition characteristic of the glass and metal can industries. While the position of Hazel-Atlas in the beer and soft drink industries was negligible in 1955, its position was quite different in other fields. Hazel-Atlas made both wide-mouthed glass jars and narrow-necked containers but more of the former than the latter. Both are used in packing food, medicine and health supplies, household and industrial products and toiletries and cosmetics, among others, and Hazel-Atlas' position in supplying the packaging needs of these industries was indeed important. . . . Continental, as we have said, in 1955 shipped 30% of the containers used for these same nonfood purposes. In these industries the District Court found that the glass container and metal container manufacturers were each seeking to promote their lines of containers at the expense of the other lines and that all were attempting to improve their products or to develop new ones so as to have a wider customer appeal. We think it quite clear that Continental and Hazel-Atlas were set off directly against one another in this process and that the merger therefore carries with it the probability of foreclosing actual and potential competition between these two concerns. Hazel-Atlas has been removed as an independent factor in the glass industry and in the line of commerce which includes both metal cans and glass containers. . . .

Second: Continental would view these developments as representing an acceptable effort by it to diversify its product lines and to gain the resulting competitive advantages, thereby strengthening competition which it declared the antitrust laws are designed to promote. But we think the answer is otherwise when a dominant firm in a line of commerce in which market power is already concentrated among a few firms makes an acquisition which enhances its market power and the vigor and effectiveness of its own competitive efforts.

Third: A merger between the second and sixth largest competitors in a gigantic line of commerce is significant not only for its intrinsic effect on competition but also for its tendency to endanger a much broader anticompetitive effect by triggering other mergers by companies seeking the same competitive advantages sought by Continental in this case. As the Court said in *Brown Shoe*, "[i]f a merger achieving 5% control were now approved, we might be required to approve future merger efforts by Brown's competitors seeking similar market shares." . . .

Fourth: It is not at all self-evident that the lack of current competition between Continental and Hazel-Atlas for some important end uses of metal and glass containers significantly diminished the adverse effect of the merger on competition. Continental might have concluded that it could effectively insulate itself from competition by acquiring a major firm not presently directing its market acquisition efforts toward the same end uses as Continental, but possessing the potential to do so. . . . Our view of the record compels us to disagree with the District Court's conclusion that Continental, as a result of the merger, was not "likely to cease being an innovator in either [the glass or metal container] line." . . . It would make little sense for one entity within the Continental empire to be busily engaged in persuading the public of metal's superiority over glass for a given end use, while the other is making plans to increase the Nation's total glass container output for that same end use. Thus, the fact that Continental and Hazel-Atlas were not substantial competitors of each other for certain end uses at the time of the merger may actually enhance the long-run tendency of the merger to lessen competition.

We think our holding is consonant with the purpose of Section 7 to arrest anticompetitive arrangements in their incipiency. Some product lines are offered in both metal and glass containers by the same packer. In such areas the interchangeability of use and immediate interindustry sensitivity to price changes would approach that which exists between products of the same industry. In other lines, as where one packer's products move in one type container while his competitor's move in another, there are inherent deterrents to customer diversion of the same type that might occur between brands of cans or bottles. But the possibility of such transfers over the long run acts as a deterrent against attempts by the dominant members of either industry to reap the possible benefits of their position by raising prices above the competitive level or engaging in other comparable practices. And even though certain lines are today regarded as safely within the domain of one or the other of those industries, this pattern may be altered, as it has in the past. From the point of view not only of the static competitive situation but also the dynamic long-run potential, we think that the Government has discharged its burden of proving prima facie anticompetitive effect. Accordingly the judgment is reversed and the case remanded for further proceedings consistent with this opinion.

Reversed.

MR. JUSTICE GOLDBERG, concurring. . . .

MR. JUSTICE HARLAN, whom MR. JUSTICE STEWART joins, dissenting.

Measured by any antitrust yardsticks with which I am familiar, the Court's conclusions are, to say the least, remarkable. Before the merger which is the subject of this case, Continental Can manufactured metal containers and Hazel-Atlas manufactured glass containers. The District Court found, with ample support in the record, that the Government had wholly failed to prove that the merger of these two companies would adversely affect competition in the metal container industry, in the glass container industry, or between the metal container industry and the glass container industry. Yet this Court manages to strike down the merger under Section 7 of the Clayton Act, because, in the Court's view, it is anticompetitive. With all respect, the Court's conclusion is based on erroneous analysis, which makes an abrupt and unwise departure from established antitrust law. . . .

Recognition that the purpose of Section 7 is not to be thwarted by limiting its protection to intramural competition within strictly defined "industries," does not mean, however, that the concept of a "line of commerce" is no longer serviceable. More precisely, it does not, as the majority seems to think, entail the conclusion that wherever "meaningful competition" exists, a "line of commerce" is to be found. The Court declares the initial question of this case to be "whether the admitted competition between metal and glass containers for uses other than packaging beer was of the type and quality deserving of Section 7 protection and *therefore* the basis for defining a relevant product market." . . . (Emphasis added.) And the Court's answer is similarly phrased: ". . . [W]e hold that *the interindustry competition* between glass and metal containers *is sufficient to warrant treating as a relevant product market* the combined glass and metal container industries and all end uses for which they compete." . . . (Emphasis added.) Quite obviously, such a conclusion simply reads the "line of commerce" element out of Section 7, and destroys its usefulness as an aid to analysis.

The distortions to which this approach leads are evidenced by the Court's application of it in this case. Having found that there is "interindustry competition between glass and metal containers" the Court concludes that "the combined glass and metal container industries" is the relevant line of commerce or "product market" in which anticompetitive effects must be measured. . . . Applying that premise, the Court then notes Continental's "dominant position" in the *metal can industry*, . . . and finds that Continental has a "major position" in the "relevant product market—*the combined metal and glass container industries*," . . . . (Emphasis added.) Hazel-Atlas, being the third largest producer of *glass containers*, is found to rank sixth in the relevant product market—again, the combined metal and glass container industries. . . . This "evidence," coupled with the market shares of Continental and Hazel-Atlas in the combined product market, leads the Court to conclude that the merger violates Section 7.

"The resulting percentage of the combined firms," the Court says, "approaches that held presumptively bad in *United States* v. *Philadelphia National Bank*. . . . *The Philadelphia Bank* case, which involved the merger of two banks plainly engaged in the same line of commerce, is, however, entirely distinct from the present situation, which involves two separate industries. The bizarre result of the Court's approach is that market percentages of a nonexistent market enable the Court to dispense with "elaborate proof of market structure, market behavior and probable anticompetitive effects". . . . As I shall show, the Court has "dispensed with" proof which, given heed, shows how completely fanciful its market-share analysis is.

. . . The truth is that "glass and metal containers" form a distinct line of commerce only in the mind of this Court.

The District Court found, and this Court accepts the finding, that this case "deals with three separate and distinct industries manufacturing separate and distinct types of products": metal, glass, and plastic containers. . . .

Only this Court . . . without support in reason or fact, . . . dips into this network of competition and establishes metal and glass containers as a separate "line of commerce," leaving entirely out of account all other kinds of containers: "plastic, paper, foil and any other materials competing for the same business," . . .[7] *Brown Shoe*, . . . on which the Court relies for this travesty of economics, . . . spoke of "*well-defined* submarkets" within a broader market, and said that "the boundaries of such a submarket" were to be determined by "*practical indicia*," . . . . (Emphasis added.) Since the Court here provides its own definition of a market, unrelated to any market reality whatsoever, *Brown Shoe* must in this case be regarded as a bootstrap. . . .

[7] If the competition between metal and glass containers is sufficient to constitute them collectively a "line of commerce," why does their competition with plastic containers and "other materials competing for the same business" not require that all such containers be included in the same line of commerce? The Court apparently concedes that the competition is multilateral.

If attention is paid to the conclusions of the court below, it is obvious that this Court's analysis has led it to substitute a meaningless figure—the merged companies' share of a nonexistent "market"—for the sound, careful factual findings of the District Court. . . .

Surely this failure of the Court's mock-statistical analysis to reflect the facts as found on the record demonstrates what the Government concedes, and what one would in any event have thought to be obvious: When a merger is attacked on the ground that competition *between* two distinct industries, or lines of commerce, will be affected, the shortcut "market share" approach developed in the *Philadelphia Bank* case, . . . has no place. In such a case, the legality of the merger must surely depend, as it did below, on an inquiry into competitive effects in the actual lines of commerce which are involved. In this case, the result depends—or should depend—on the impact of the merger in the two lines of commerce here involved: the metal container industry and the glass container industry. As the findings of the District Court . . . make plain, reference to these two actual lines of commerce does not preclude protection of inter-industry competition. Indeed, by placing the merged company in the setting of other companies in each of the respective lines of commerce which are also engaged in inter-industry competition, this approach is far more likely than the Court's to give Section 7 full, but not artificial, scope.

The Court's spurious market-share analysis should not obscure the fact that the Court is, in effect, laying down a *"per se"* rule that mergers between two large companies in related industries are presumptively unlawful under Section 7. . . .

In any event, the Court . . . . chooses . . . to invent a line of commerce the existence of which no one, not even the Government, has imagined; for which businessmen and economists will look in vain; a line of commerce which sprang into existence only when the merger took place and will cease to exist when the merger is undone. I have no idea where Section 7 goes from here, nor will businessmen or the antitrust bar. Hitherto, it has been thought that the validity of a merger was to be tested by examining its effect in identifiable, "well-defined" (*Brown Shoe*, . . .) markets. Hereafter, however slight (or even nonexistent) the competitive impact of a merger on any actual market, businessmen must rest uneasy lest the Court create some "market," in which the merger presumptively dampens competition, out of bits and pieces of real ones. No one could say that such a fear is unfounded since the Court's creative powers in this respect are declared to be as extensive as the competitive relationships between industries. This is said to be recognizing "meaningful competition where it is found to exist." It is in fact imagining effects on competition where none has been shown.

I would affirm the judgment of the District Court.

United States v. Von's Grocery Company

384 U.S. 270 (1966)

MR. JUSTICE BLACK delivered the opinion of the Court.

On March 25, 1960, the United States brought this action charging that the acquisition by Von's Grocery Company of its direct competitor Shopping Bag Food Stores, both large retail grocery companies in Los Angeles, California, violated §7 of the Clayton Act . . . as amended in 1950 by the Celler-Kefauver Anti-Merger Act. . . . On March 28, 1960, three days later, the District Court refused to grant the Government's motion for a temporary restraining order and immediately Von's took over all of Shopping Bag's capital stock and assets including 36 grocery stores in the Los Angeles area. After hearing evidence on both sides, the District Court made findings of fact and concluded as a matter of law that there was "not a reasonable probability" that the merger would tend "substantially to lessen competition" or "create a monopoly" in violation of §7. For this reason the District Court entered judgment for the defendants. . . . The Government appealed directly to this Court. . . . The sole question here is whether the District Court properly concluded on the facts before it that the Government had failed to prove a violation of §7.

The record shows the following facts relevant to our decision. The market involved here is the retail grocery market in the Los Angeles area. In 1958 Von's retail sales ranked third in the area and Shopping Bag's ranked sixth. In 1960 their sales together were 7.5% of the total two and one-half billion dollars of retail groceries sold in the Los Angeles market each year. For many years before the merger both companies had enjoyed great success as rapidly growing companies. From 1948 to 1958 the number of Von's stores in the Los Angeles area practically doubled from 14 to 27, while at the same time the number of Shopping Bag's stores jumped from 15 to 34. During that same decade, Von's sales increased fourfold and its share of the market almost doubled while Shopping Bag's sales multiplied seven times and its share of the market tripled. The merger of these two highly successful, expanding and aggressive competitors created the second largest grocery chain in Los Angeles with sales of almost $172,488,000 annually. In addition the findings of the District Court show that the number of owners operating single stores in the Los Angeles retail grocery market decreased from 5,365 in 1950 to 3,818 in 1961. By 1963, three years after the merger, the number of single-store owners had dropped still further to 3,590.[1] During roughly the same period from 1953 to 1962, the number

[1] Despite this steadfast concentration of the Los Angeles grocery business into fewer and fewer hands, the District Court, in Finding of Fact No. 80, concluded as follows:

of chains with two or more grocery stores increased from 96 to 150. While the grocery business was being concentrated into the hands of fewer and fewer owners, the small companies were continually being absorbed by the larger firms through mergers. According to an exhibit prepared by one of the Government's expert witnesses, in the period from 1949 to 1958 nine of the top 20 chains acquired 126 stores from their smaller competitors. . . . Moreover, . . . acquisitions and mergers in the Los Angeles retail grocery market have continued at a rapid rate since the merger. These facts alone are enough to cause us to conclude contrary to the District Court that the Von's-Shopping Bag merger did violate §7. Accordingly, we reverse. . . .

Like the Sherman Act in 1890 and the Clayton Act in 1914, the basic purpose of the 1950 Celler-Kefauver Act was to prevent economic concentration in the American economy by keeping a large number of small competitors in business. . . . As we said in *Brown Shoe Co.* v. *United States*, 370 U.S. 294, 315, "The dominant theme pervading congressional consideration of the 1950 amendments was a fear of what was considered to be a rising tide of economic concentration in the American economy." To arrest this "rising tide" toward concentration into too few hands and to halt the gradual demise of the small businessman, Congress decided to clamp down with vigor on mergers. . . .

The facts of this case present exactly the threatening trend toward concentration which Congress wanted to halt. The number of small grocery companies in the Los Angeles retail grocery market had been declining rapidly before the merger and continued to decline rapidly afterwards. This rapid decline in the number of grocery store owners moved hand in hand with a large number of significant absorptions of the small companies by the larger ones. In the midst of this steadfast trend toward concentration, Von's and Shopping Bag, two of the most successful and largest companies in the area, jointly owning 66 grocery stores merged to become the second largest chain in Los Angeles. This merger cannot be defended on the ground that one of the companies was about to fail or that the two had to merge to save themselves from destruction by some larger and more powerful competitor. What we have on the contrary is simply the case of two already powerful companies merging in a way which makes them even more powerful than they were before. If ever such a merger would not violate §7, certainly it does when it takes place in a market character-

---

"There has been no increase in concentration in the retail grocery business in the Los Angeles Metropolitan Area either in the last decade or since the merger. On the contrary, economic concentration has decreased. . . ."

This conclusion is completely contradicted by Finding No. 23 which makes plain the steady decline in the number of individual grocery store owners referred to above. It is thus apparent that the District Court, in Finding No. 80, used the term "concentration" in some sense other than a total decrease in the number of separate competitors which is the crucial point here.

ized by a long and continuous trend toward fewer and fewer owner-competitors which is exactly the sort of trend which Congress, with power to do so, declared must be arrested.

Appellees' primary argument is that the merger between Von's and Shopping Bag is not prohibited by §7 because the Los Angeles grocery market was competitive before the merger, has been since, and may continue to be in the future. Even so, §7 "requires not merely an appraisal of the immediate impact of the merger upon competition, but a prediction of its impact upon competitive conditions in the future; this is what is meant when it is said that the amended §7 was intended to arrest anticompetitive tendencies in their 'incipiency.'" *U.S.* v. *Philadelphia Nat. Bank*, 374 U.S. 321, 362. It is enough for us that Congress feared that a market marked at the same time by both a continuous decline in the number of small businesses and a large number of mergers would slowly but inevitably gravitate from a market of many small competitors to one dominated by one or a few giants, and competition would thereby be destroyed. Congress passed the Celler-Kefauver Act to prevent such a destruction of competition. Our cases since the passage of that Act have faithfully endeavored to enforce this congressional command. We adhere to them now.

Here again as in *United States* v. *El Paso Gas Co.*, 376 U.S. 651, 662, since appellees "have been on notice of the antitrust charge from almost the beginning . . . we not only reverse the judgment below but direct the District Court to order divestiture without delay." . . .

Reversed and remanded.

[Mr. Justice Fortas took no part in the consideration or decision of this case. Mr. Justice White concurred.]

Mr Justice Stewart, with whom Mr. Justice Harlan joins, dissenting.

We first gave consideration to the 1950 amendment of §7 of the Clayton Act in *Brown Shoe Co.* v. *United States*. . . . The thorough opinion The Chief Justice wrote for the Court in that case made two things plain: First, the standards of §7 require that every corporate acquisition be judged in the light of the contemporary economic context of its industry. Second, the purpose of §7 is to protect competition, not to protect competitors, and every §7 case must be decided in the light of that clear statutory purpose. Today the Court turns its back on these two basic principles and on all the decisions that have followed them.

The Court makes no effort to appraise the competitive effects of this acquisition in terms of the contemporary economy of the retail food industry in the Los Angeles area.[2] Instead, through a simple exercise in sums,

---

[2] This is the first case to reach the Court under the 1950 amendment to §7 that involves a merger between firms engaged solely in retail food distribution. Kaysen

it finds that the number of individual competitors in the market has decreased over the years, and, apparently on the theory that the degree of competition is invariably proportional to the number of competitors, it holds that this historic reduction in the number of competing units is enough under §7 to invalidate a merger within the market, with no need to examine the economic concentration of the market, the level of competition in the market, or the potential adverse effect of the merger on that competition. This startling *per se* rule is contrary not only to our previous decisions, but contrary to the language of §7, contrary to the legislative history of the 1950 amendment, and contrary to economic reality.

Under §7, as amended, a merger can be invalidated if, and only if, "the effect of such acquisition may be substantially to lessen competition, or to tend to create a monopoly." No question is raised here as to the tendency of the present merger to create a monopoly. Our sole concern is with the question whether the effect of the merger may be substantially to lessen competition.

The principal danger against which the 1950 amendment was addressed was the erosion of competition through the cumulative centripetal effect of acquisitions by large corporations, none of which by itself might be sufficient to constitute a violation of the Sherman Act. Congress' immediate fear was that of large corporations buying out small companies. A major aspect of that fear was the perceived trend toward absentee ownership of local business. Another, more generalized, congressional purpose revealed by the legislative history was to protect small businessmen and to stem the rising tide of concentration in the economy.[3] These goals, Congress thought, could be achieved by "arresting mergers at a time when the trend to a lessening of competition in a line of commerce was still in its incipiency." *Brown Shoe Co.* v. *United States, supra,* at 317.

. . . The legislative history leaves no doubt that the applicable standard

---

& Turner, Antitrust Policy 40 (1959), have discussed this industry in the following terms: "As a guess, we can say that the most important distributive trades, especially the food trades, are structurally unconcentrated in the metropolitan areas. . . . [T]he significance of structural oligopoly in terms of policy is far different in [these trades] than in manufacturing and mining. . . . [T]he traditional view that the local-market industries are essentially competitive in character is probably correct. . . ."

3 Much of the fuel for the congressional debates on concentration in the American economy was derived from a contemporary study by the Federal Trade Commission on corporate acquisitions between 1940 and 1947. See Report of the Federal Trade Commission on the Merger Movement: A Summary Report (1948). A critical study of the FTC report, published while the 1950 amendment was pending in Congress, concluded that the effect of the recent merger movement on concentration had been slight. Lintner & Butters, Effect of Mergers on Industrial Concentration, 1940–1947, 32 *Rev. of Econ. & Statistics* 30 (1950). Two economists for the Federal Trade Commission later acquiesced in that conclusion. Blair & Houghton, The Lintner-Butters Analysis of the Effect of Mergers on Industrial Concentration, 1940–1947, 33 *Rev. of Econ. & Statistics 63,* 67, n. 12 (1951).

for measuring the substantiality of the effect of a merger on competition was that of a "reasonable probability" of lessening competition. The standard was thus more stringent than that of a "mere possibility" on the one hand and more lenient than that of a "certainty" on the other.[4] I cannot agree that the retail grocery business in Los Angeles is in an incipient or any other stage of a trend toward a lessening of competition, or that the effective level of concentration in the industry has increased. Moreover, there is no indication that the present merger, or the trend in this industry as a whole, augurs any danger whatsoever for the small businessman. The Court has substituted bare conjecture for the statutory standard of a reasonable probability that competition may be lessened.

The Court rests its conclusion on the "crucial point" that, in the 11-year period between 1950 and 1961, the number of single-store grocery firms in Los Angeles decreased 29% from 5,365 to 3,818.[5] Such a decline should, of course, be no more than a fact calling for further investigation of the competitive trend in the industry. For the Court, however, that decline is made the end, not the beginning, of the analysis. . . .

I believe that even the most superficial analysis of the record makes plain the fallacy of the Court's syllogism that competition is necessarily reduced when the bare number of competitors has declined. In any meaningful sense, the structure of the Los Angeles grocery market remains unthreatened by concentration. Local competition is vigorous to a fault, not only among chain stores themselves but also between chain stores and

---

[4] Although Congress eschewed exclusively mathematical tests for assessing the impact of a merger, it offered several generalizations indicative of the sort of merger that might be proscribed, *e.g.*: Whether the merger eliminated an enterprise that had been a substantial factor in competition; whether the increased size of the acquiring corporation threatened to give it a decisive advantage over competitors; whether an undue number of competing enterprises had been eliminated. H. R. Rep. No. 1191, 81st Cong., 1st Sess., p. 8. See *Brown Shoe Co.* v. *United States*, 370 U.S. 294, 321, n. 36. Only the first of these generalizations is arguably applicable to the present merger; the market-extension aspects of the merger, as well as the evidence of Shopping Bag's declining profit margin and weak price competition, suggest that any conclusion under this test would be equivocal. See *infra*, pp. 295–296; 298, n. 30. Senator Kefauver stated explicitly on the Senate floor that the mere elimination of competition between the merged firms would not make the acquisition illegal; rather, "the merger would have to have the effect of lessening competition generally." 96 Cong. Rec. 16456.

[5] The decline continued at approximately the same rate to 1963, the last year for which data are available, when there were 3,590 single-store grocery firms in the area. The record contains no breakdown of the figures on single-store concerns. In an extensive study of the retail grocery industry on a national scale, the Federal Trade Commission found that between 1939 and 1954 the total number of grocery stores in the United States declined by 109,000, or 28%. The entire decrease was suffered by stores with annual *gross* sales of less than $50,000. During the same period, the number of stores in all higher sales brackets increased. The Commission noted that the census figures, from which its data were taken, included an undetermined number of grocery firms liquidating after 1948 that merely closed their grocery operations and continued their remaining lines of business, such as nongrocery retailing, food wholesaling, food manufacturing, etc. Staff Report to the Federal Trade Commission, Economic Inquiry Into Food Marketing, Part I, Concentration and Integration in Retailing 48, 54 (1960).

single-store operators. The continuing population explosion of the Los Angeles area, which has outrun the expansion plans of even the largest chains, offers a surfeit of business opportunity for stores of all sizes. Affiliated with cooperatives that give the smallest store the buying strength of its largest competitors, new stores have taken full advantage of the remarkable ease of entry into the market. And, most important of all, the record simply cries out that the numerical decline in the number of single-store owners is the result of transcending social and technological changes that positively preclude the inference that competition has suffered because of the attrition of competitors.

Section 7 was never intended by Congress for use by the Court as a charter to roll back the supermarket revolution. Yet the Court's opinion is hardly more than a requiem for the so-called "Mom and Pop" grocery stores—the bakery and butcher shops, the vegetable and fish markets—that are now economically and technoligically obsolete in many parts of the country. No action by this Court can resurrect the old single-line Los Angeles food stores that have been run over by the automobile or obliterated by the freeway. . . . Today's dominant enterprise in food retailing is the supermarket. Accessible to the housewife's automobile from a wide radius, it houses under a single roof the entire food requirements of the family. Only through . . . [a] reactionary philosophy . . . can the Court read into the legislative history of §7 its attempt to make the automobile stand still, to mold the food economy of today into the market pattern of another era.

. . . [T]he record offers abundant evidence of the dramatic history of growth and prosperity of the retail food business in Los Angeles.

. . . Between 1948 and 1958, the market share of Safeway, the leading grocery chain in Los Angeles, declined from 14% to 8%. The combined market shares of the top two chains declined from 21% to 14% over the same period; for the period 1952–1958, the combined shares of the three, four, and five largest firms also declined. It is true that between 1948 and 1958, the combined shares of the top 20 firms in the market increased from 44% to 57%. The crucial fact here, however, is that seven of these top 20 firms in 1958 were not even in existence as chains in 1948. Because of the substantial turnover in the membership of the top 20 firms, the increase in market share of the top 20 as a group is hardly a reliable indicator of any tendency toward market concentration.[6]

In addition, statistics in the record for the period 1953–1962 strongly suggest that the retail grocery industry in Los Angeles is less concentrated today than it was a decade ago. During this period, the number of chain store firms in the area rose from 96 to 150, or 56%. That increase occurred overwhelmingly among chains of the very smallest size, those composed of

[6] See Joskow, Structural Indicia: Rank-Shift Analysis as a Supplement to Concentration Ratios, VI Antitrust Bulletin 9 (1961). In addition, the overall market share of the top 20 firms in fact showed a slight decline between 1958 and 1960. . . .

two or three grocery stores. Between 1953 and 1962, the number of such "chains" increased from 56 to 104, or 86%. Although chains of 10 or more stores increased from 10 to 24 during the period, seven of these 24 chains were not even in existence as chains in Los Angeles in 1953.

Yet even these dramatic statistics do not fully reveal the dynamism and vitality of competition in the retail grocery business in Los Angeles during the period. The record shows that . . . during the period 1953–1962 . . . . 173 new chains made their appearance in the market area, and 119 chains went out of existence as chain stores. The vast majority of this market turbulence represented turnover in chains of two or three stores. . . . [A]lmost without exception, these new chains were the outgrowth of successful one-store operations.[7] There is no indication that comparable turmoil did not equally permeate single-store operations in the area.[8] In fashioning its *per se* rule, based on the net arithmetical decline in the number of single-store operators, the Court completely disregards the obvious procreative vigor of competition in the market as reflected in the turbulent history of entry and exit of competing small chains.

To support its conclusion the Court invokes three sets of data regarding absorption of smaller firms by merger with larger firms. In each of the acquisitions detailed in . . . the Court's opinion, the acquired units were grocery *chains*. Not one of these acquisitions was of a firm operating only a single store.[9] The Court cannot have it both ways. It is only among single-store operators that the decline in the unit number of competitors, so heavily relied upon by the Court, has taken place. Yet the . . . [data] show not a trace of merger activity involving the acquisition of single-store operators. And the number of *chains* in the area has in fact shown a substantial net increase during the period, in spite of the fact that some of the chains have been absorbed by larger firms. How then can the Court rely on these acquisitions as evidence of a tendency toward market concentration in the area? . . .

[7] On the basis of these facts, one witness concluded: ". . . It must be remembered that in 1953, only 10 chains with as many as 10 stores each were operating in the area. These chains are recognized as being among the best managed, most successful and most aggressive supermarket operators in the country. They themselves have engaged in expansion programs of significant proportions since 1953. Yet, 10 years later, instead of having swept aside all competition and being left alone to compete among themselves, these same 10 chains are now faced with the necessity of competing against no less than 14 new chains of 10 or more stores each, a significantly greater number of smaller chains and a host of successful single store operators, of whom many are affiliated with powerful voluntary chains or other cooperative groups. . . ."

[8] Data for 1960, the only year for which such figures are available in the record, reveal a comparable agitation of entry and exit among operators of single stores. Although there was a net loss of 132 single-outlet stores in 1960, 128 new single-outlet stores opened during the year.

[9] As to Table 1 in the Appendix of the Court's opinion, this fact is obvious on the face of the table. As to Table 2 in the Appendix, examination of the record discloses that each of the nine acquisitions listed as involving a single store represented purchases of single stores from chains ranging in size from two to 49 stores.

The Court's reliance on the fact that nine of the top 20 chains acquired 120 stores in the Los Angeles area between 1949 and 1958 does not withstand analysis in light of the complete record. Forty percent of these acquisitions . . . were made by [chains] . . . which ranked 9th, 11th, and 20th, . . . according to 1958 sales in the market. Each of these firms subsequently went into bankruptcy as a result of overexpansion, undercapitalization, or inadequate managerial experience. This substantial post-acquisition demise of relatively large chains hardly comports with the Court's tacit portrayal of the inexorable march of the market toward oligopoly.

Further, the table relied on by the Court to sustain its view that acquisitions have continued in the Los Angeles area at a rapid rate in the three-year period following this merger indiscriminately lumps together horizontal and market-extension mergers. . . . [A]t a time when the number of single-store concerns was well over 3,500, horizontal mergers over a three-year period between going concerns achieved at most only the *de minimis* level of 10 acquisitions involving 20 stores. It cannot seriously be maintained that the effect of the negligible market share foreclosed by these horizontal mergers may be substantially to lessen competition within the meaning of §7. . . .

Moreover, contrary to the assumption on which the Court proceeds, the record establishes that the present merger itself has substantial, even predominant, market-extension overtones. The District Court found that the Von's stores were located in the southern and western portions of the Los Angeles metropolitan area, and that the Shopping Bag stores were located in the northern and eastern portions. In each of the areas in which Von's and Shopping Bag stores competed directly, there were also at least six other chain stores and several smaller stores competing for the patronage of customers. . . . Even among those stores which competed at least partially with one another, the overlap in sales represented only approximately 25% of the combined sales of the two chains in the overall Los Angeles area. The present merger was thus three parts market-extension and only one part horizontal, but the Court nowhere recognizes this market-extension aspect that exists within the local market itself. The actual market share foreclosed by the elimination of Shopping Bag as an independent competitor was thus slightly less than 1% of the total grocery store sales in the area. The share of the market preempted by the present merger was therefore practically identical with the 0.77% market foreclosure accepted as "quite insubstantial" by the Court in *Tampa Electric Co.* v. *Nashville Coal Co.*, 365 U.S. 320, 331–333.

The irony of this case is that the Court invokes its sweeping new construction of §7 to the detriment of a merger between two relatively successful, local, largely family-owned concerns, each of which had less than 5% of the local market and neither of which had any prior history of growth by acquisition.[10] In a sense, the defendants are being punished for the sin of aggressive competition. The Court is inaccurate in its suggestions, *ante*, pp. 277–278, that the merger makes these firms more "powerful" than they were before, and that Shopping Bag was itself a "powerful" competitor at the time of the merger. There is simply no evidence in the record, and the Court makes no attempt to demonstrate, that the increment in market *share* obtained by the combined stores can be equated with an increase in the market *power* of the combined firm. . . .

With regard to the "plight" of the small businessman, the record is unequivocal that his competitive position is strong and secure in the Los Angeles retail grocery industry. The most aggressive competitors against the larger retail chains are frequently the operators of single stores.[11] The vitality of these independents is directly attributable to the recent and spectacular growth in California of three large cooperative buying organizations. . . . The rise of these cooperative organizations has introduced a significant new source of countervailing power against the market power of the chain stores, without in any way sacrificing the advantages of independent operation. In the face of the substantial assistance available to independents through membership in such cooperatives, the Court's implicit equation between the market power and the market share resulting from the present merger seems completely invalid.

Moreover, it is clear that there are no substantial barriers to market entry. The record contains references to numerous highly successful instances of entry with modest initial investments. . . . Enhancing free access to the market is the absence of any such restrictive factors as patented technology, trade secrets, or substantial product differentiation.

Numerous other factors attest to the pugnacious level of grocery competition in Los Angeles, all of them silently ignored by the Court in its emphasis solely on the declining number of single-store competitors

[10] . . . So far as the record reveals, the competitive behavior of these firms was impeccable throughout their expansion, which took place solely by internal growth. In discussing the success of comparable firms *vis-à-vis* the Sherman Act, Judge Learned Hand stated: ". . . The successful competitor, having been urged to compete, must not be turned upon when he wins." *United States* v. *Aluminum Co. of America*, 148 F.2d 416, 430.

[11] One single-store operator, located adjacent to one supermarket and within a mile of two others, testified, "I have often been asked if I could compete successfully against this sort of competition. My answer is and always has been that the question is not whether I can compete against them, but whether they can compete against me."

Another single-store operator testified, "Competition in the grocery business is on a store-by-store basis and any aggressive and able operator like myself can out-compete the store of any of the chains because of personalized service, better labor relations, and being in personal charge of the store and seeing that it is run properly."

A third single-store operator testified, "The chains in this area are good operators, but when they grow too large, they are actually easier to compete with from an independent's viewpoint. If I had a choice, I would rather operate a store near a chain unit than near another independent."

in the market. Three thousand five hundred and ninety single-store firms is a lot of grocery stores. The large number of separate competitors and the frequent price battles between them belie any suggestion that price competition in the area is even remotely threatened by a descent to the sort of consciously interdependent pricing that is characteristic of a market turning the corner toward oligopoly. The birth of dynamic new competitive forces—discount food houses and food departments in department stores, bantams and superettes, deli-liquor stores and drive-in dairies—promises unremitting competition in the future. In the more than four years following the merger, the District Court found not a shred of evidence that competition had been in any way impaired by the merger. . . .

The harsh standard now applied by the Court to horizontal mergers may prejudice irrevocably the already difficult choice faced by numerous successful small and medium-sized businessmen in the myriad smaller markets where the effect of today's decision will be felt, whether to expand by buying or by building additional facilities. And by foreclosing future sale as one attractive avenue of eventual market exit, the Court's decision may over the long run deter new market entry and tend to stifle the very competition it seeks to foster.

In a single sentence and an omnibus footnote at the close of its opinion, the Court pronounces its work consistent with the line of our decisions under §7 since the passage of the 1950 amendment. The sole consistency that I can find is that in litigation under §7, the Government always wins. The only precedent that is even within sight of today's holding is *U.S.* v. *Philadelphia Nat. Bank*, 374 U.S. 321. In that case, in the interest of practical judicial administration, the Court proposed a simplified test of merger illegality: "[W]e think that a merger which produces a firm controlling an undue percentage share of the relevant market, and results in a significant increase in the concentration of firms in that market, is so inherently likely to lessen competition substantially that it must be enjoined in the absence of evidence clearly showing that the merger is not likely to have such anticompetitive effects." *U.S.* v. *Philadelphia Nat. Bank*, *supra*, at 363. The merger between Von's and Shopping Bag produced a firm with 1.4% of the grocery stores and 7.5% of grocery sales in Los Angeles, and resulted in an increase of 1.1% in the market share enjoyed by the two largest firms in the market and 3.3% in the market share of the six largest firms. The former two figures are hardly the "undue percentage" of the market, nor are the latter two figures the "significant increase" in concentration, that would make this merger inherently suspect under the standard of *Philadelphia Nat. Bank*. Instead, the circumstances of the present merger fall far outside the simplified test established by that case for precisely the sort of merger here involved.[12] . . .

---

[12] . . . The Court's opinion is remarkable for its failure to support its conclusion by reference to even a single piece of economic theory. I shall not dwell here on the barometers of competition that have been suggested by the commentators. But it

The emotional impact of a merger between the third and sixth largest competitors in a given market, however fragmented, is understandable, but that impact cannot substitute for the analysis of the effect of the merger on competition that Congress required by the 1950 amendment. Nothing in the present record indicates that there is more than an ephemeral possibility that the effect of this merger may be substantially to lessen competition. Section 7 clearly takes "reasonable probability" as its standard. That standard has not been met here, and I would therefore affirm the judgment of the District Court.

---

seems important to note that the present merger falls either outside, or at the very fringe, of the various mechanical tests that had been proposed. See *e.g.*, Kaysen & Turner, *Antitrust Policy* 133–136 (1959) (horizontal merger with direct competitor is prima facie unlawful where acquiring company accounts for 20% or more of the market, or where merging companies together constitute 20% or more of the market; acquisitions producing less than 20% market control unlawful only where special circumstances are present, such as serious barriers to entry or substantial influence on prices by the acquired company); Stigler, Mergers and Preventive Antitrust Policy, 104 *U. Pa. L. Rev.* 176, 179–182 (1955) (acquisition unlawful if it produces a combined market share of 20% or more; acquisition permitted if the combined share is less than 5–10%); Bok, Section 7 of The Clayton Act and the Merging of Law and Economics, 74 *Harv. L. Rev.* 226, 308–329 (1960) (no merger by the dominant firm in an industry if its market share is increased by more than 2–3%; no merger by other large firms in the industry where the combined market shares of the two-to-eight largest firms after the merger are increased by 7–8% or more over the shares that existed at any time during the preceding 5–10 years; no merger where acquired firm has 5% market share or more). See also Markham, Merger Policy Under the New Section 7: A Six-Year Appraisal, 43 *Va. L. Rev.* 489, 521–522 (1957). The 40% rule promoted by the concurring opinion in the present case seems no more than an ad hoc endeavor to rationalize the holding of the Court.

Chapter 6

MERGERS AND PRODUCT EXTENSION

The third category of mergers—conglomerates—involves those among firms which formerly were neither customers, suppliers nor competitors of one another. As the cases in this chapter demonstrate, however, this is not to say that the prospective partners' lines of commerce are necessarily completely unrelated; rather, it has been recognized that because of common characteristics, certain industries are particularly conducive to entry by firms currently doing business in other sectors. Mergers involving firms in industries such as these have been termed "product-extension" mergers, in the belief that they involve industries and products into which, in the absence of the merger, either or both of the partners might logically be expected to enter independently. As such, the adjudication of these mergers has frequently involved a determination of the importance of the acquiring firm as a potential competitor—would the firm either have entered by itself or would it have remained at the edge of the market, thereby providing a constraint upon the activities of those firms already a part of the industry.

Another aspect which has often been crucial to the outcome of these cases has been the courts' estimate of the power brought to the industry by the acquiring firm. More specifically, will the "deep financial pockets" of the acquiring firm give the newly acquired firm an unfair advantage over its rivals, ultimately lessening competition.

These issues were graphically presented in both the *Procter & Gamble* and *Bendix* cases. The latter is particularly interesting in that it marks the first enunciation of the "toehold" doctrine, whereby product-extension mergers may be permitted by a powerful outsider with an industry's smaller firms, so as to enable the acquiring firm to gain a toehold in the industry.

Federal Trade Commission v. *Procter & Gamble Co.*

386 U.S. 568 (1967)

MR. JUSTICE DOUGLAS delivered the opinion of the Court.

This is a proceeding initiated by the Federal Trade Commission charging that respondent, Procter & Gamble Co., had acquired the assets of Clorox Chemical Co. in violation of §7 of the Clayton Act, . . . as amended by the Celler-Kefauver Act. . . . The charge was that Procter's acquisition of Clorox might substantially lessen competition or tend to create a monopoly in the production and sale of household liquid bleaches. . . .

As indicated by the Commission in its painstaking and illuminating report, it does not particularly aid analysis to talk of this merger in conventional terms, namely, horizontal or vertical or conglomerate. This merger may most appropriately be described as a "product-extension merger," as the Commission stated. . . .

At the time of the merger, in 1957, Clorox was the leading manufacturer in the heavily concentrated household liquid bleach industry. It is agreed that household liquid bleach is the relevant line of commerce. The product is used in the home as a germicide and disinfectant, and, more importantly, as a whitening agent in washing clothes and fabrics. It is a distinctive product with no close substitutes. Liquid bleach is a low-price, high-turnover consumer product sold mainly through grocery stores and supermarkets. The relevant geographical market is the Nation and a series of regional markets. Because of high shipping costs and low sales price, it is not feasible to ship the product more than 300 miles from its point of manufacture. Most manufacturers are limited to competition within a single region since they have but one plant. Clorox is the only firm selling nationally; it has 13 plants distributed throughout the Nation. Purex, Clorox's closest competitor in size, does not distribute its bleach in the northeast or mid-Atlantic States; in 1957, Purex's bleach was available in less than 50% of the national market.

At the time of the acquisition, Clorox was the leading manufacturer of household liquid bleach, with 48.8% of the national sales—annual sales of slightly less than $40,000,000. Its market share had been steadily increasing for the five years prior to the merger. Its nearest rival was Purex, which manufactures a number of products other than household liquid bleaches, including abrasive cleaners, toilet soap, and detergents. Purex accounted for 15.7% of the household liquid bleach market. The industry is highly concentrated; in 1957, Clorox and Purex accounted for almost 65% of the Nation's household liquid bleach sales, and, together with four other firms, for almost 80%. The remaining 20% was divided among over 200 small producers. Clorox had total assets of $12,000,000; only eight producers had assets in excess of $1,000,000 and very few had assets of more than $75,000.

In light of the territorial limitations on distribution, national figures do not give an accurate picture of Clorox's dominance in the various regions. Thus, Clorox's seven principal competitors did no business in New England, the mid-Atlantic States, or metropolitan New York. Clorox's share of the sales in those areas was 56%, 72%, and 64% respectively. Even in regions where its principal competitors were active, Clorox maintained a dominant position. Except in metropolitan Chicago and the west-central States Clorox accounted for at least 39%, and often a much higher percentage, of liquid bleach sales.

Since all liquid bleach is chemically identical, advertising and sales promotion are vital. In 1957 Clorox spent almost $3,700,000 on advertising, imprinting the value of its bleach in the mind of the consumer. In addition, it spent $1,700,000 for other promotional activities. The Commission found that these heavy expenditures went far to explain why Clorox maintained so high a market share despite the fact that its brand, though chemically indistinguishable from rival brands, retailed for a price equal to or, in many instances, higher than its competitors.

Procter is a large, diversified manufacturer of low-price, high-turnover household products sold through grocery, drug, and department stores. Prior to its acquisition of Clorox, it did not produce household liquid bleach. Its 1957 sales were in excess of $1,100,000,000 from which it realized profits of more than $67,000,000; its assets were over $500,000,000. Procter has been marked by rapid growth and diversification. It has successfully developed and introduced a number of new products. Its primary activity is in the general area of soaps, detergents, and cleansers; in 1957, of total domestic sales, more than one-half (over $500,000,000) were in this field. Procter was the dominant factor in this area. It accounted for 54.4% of all packaged detergent sales. The industry is heavily concentrated—Procter and its nearest competitors, Colgate-Palmolive and Lever Brothers, account for 80% of the market.

In the marketing of soaps, detergents, and cleansers, as in the marketing of household liquid bleach, advertising and sales promotion are vital. In 1957, Procter was the Nation's largest advertiser, spending more than $80,000,000 on advertising and an additional $47,000,000 on sales promotion. Due to its tremendous volume, Procter receives substantial discounts from the media. As a multiproduct producer Procter enjoys substantial advantages in advertising and sales promotion. Thus, it can and does feature several products in its promotions, reducing the printing, mailing, and other costs for each product. It also purchases network programs on behalf of several products, enabling it to give each product network exposure at a fraction of the cost per product that a firm with only one product to advertise would incur.

Prior to the acquisition, Procter was in the course of diversifying into product lines related to its basic detergent-soap-cleanser business. Liquid bleach was a distinct possibility since packaged detergents—Procter's primary product line—and liquid bleach are used complementarily in washing clothes and fabrics, and in general household cleaning. As noted by the Commission:

. . . From the consumer's viewpoint, packaged detergents and liquid bleach are closely related products. But the area of relatedness between products of

Procter and of Clorox is wider. Household cleansing agents in general, like household liquid bleach, are low-cost, high-turnover household consumer goods marketed chiefly through grocery stores and pre-sold to the consumer by the manufacturer through mass advertising and sales promotions. Since products of both parties to the merger are sold to the same customers, at the same stores, and by the same merchandising methods, the possibility arises of significant integration at both the marketing and distribution levels. . . .

The decision to acquire Clorox was the result of a study conducted by Procter's promotion department designed to determine the advisability of entering the liquid bleach industry. The initial report noted the ascendancy of liquid bleach in the large and expanding household bleach market, and recommended that Procter purchase Clorox rather than enter independently. Since a large investment would be needed to obtain a satisfactory market share, acquisition of the industry's leading firm was attractive. . . .

The Commission found that the acquisition might substantially lessen competition. . . .

The Court of Appeals said that the Commission's finding of illegality had been based on "treacherous conjecture," mere possibility and suspicion. . . . [It] also heavily relied on post-acquisition "evidence . . . to the effect that the other producers subsequent to the merger were selling more bleach for more money than ever before" (358 F.2d, at 80), and that "[t]here [had] been no significant change in Clorox's market share in the four years subsequent to the merger" (*ibid.*). . . . The Court of Appeals, in our view, misapprehended the standards for its review and the standards applicable in a §7 proceeding.

Section 7 of the Clayton Act was intended to arrest the anticompetitive effects of market power in their incipiency. The core question is whether a merger may substantially lessen competition, and necessarily requires a prediction of the merger's impact on competition, present and future. . . . The section can deal only with probabilities, not with certainties. . . . And there is certainly no requirement that the anticompetitive power manifest itself in anticompetitive action before §7 can be called into play. If the enforcement of §7 turned on the existence of actual anticompetitive practices, the congressional policy of thwarting such practices in their incipiency would be frustrated.

All mergers are within the reach of §7, and all must be tested by the same standard, whether they are classified as horizontal, vertical, conglomerate[1] or other. As noted by the Commission, this merger is neither horizontal, vertical, nor conglomerate. Since the products of the acquired company are complementary to those of the acquiring company and may be produced with similar facilities, marketed through the same channels and in the same manner, and advertised by the same media, the Commission aptly called this acquisition a "product-extension merger". . . .

[1] A pure conglomerate merger is one in which there are no economic relationships between the acquiring and the acquired firm.

The anticompetitive effects with which this product-extension merger is fraught can easily be seen: (1) the substitution of the powerful acquiring firm for the smaller, but already dominant, firm may substantially reduce the competitive structure of the industry by raising entry barriers and by dissuading the smaller firms from aggressively competing; (2) the acquisition eliminates the potential competition of the acquiring firm.

The liquid bleach industry was already oligopolistic before the acquisition, and price competition was certainly not as vigorous as it would have been if the industry were competitive. Clorox enjoyed a dominant position nationally, and its position approached monopoly proportions in certain areas. The existence of some 200 fringe firms certainly does not belie that fact. Nor does the fact, relied upon by the court below, that, after the merger, producers other than Clorox "were selling more bleach for more money than ever before." 358 F.2d, at 80. In the same period, Clorox increased its share from 48.8% to 52%. The interjection of Procter into the market considerably changed the situation. There is every reason to assume that the smaller firms would become more cautious in competing due to their fear of retaliation by Procter. It is probable that Procter would become the price leader and that oligopoly would become more rigid.

The acquisition may also have the tendency of raising the barriers to new entry. The major competitive weapon in the successful marketing of bleach is advertising. Clorox was limited in this area by its relatively small budget and its inability to obtain substantial discounts. By contrast, Procter's budget was much larger; and, although it would not devote its entire budget to advertising Clorox, it could divert a large portion to meet the short-term threat of a new entrant. Procter would be able to use its volume discounts to advantage in advertising Clorox. Thus, a new entrant would be much more reluctant to face the giant Procter than it would have been to face the smaller Clorox.[2]

Possible economies cannot be used as a defense to illegality. Congress was aware that some mergers which lessen competition may also result in economies but it struck the balance in favor of protecting competition. . . .

The Commission also found that the acquisition of Clorox by Procter eliminated Procter as a potential competitor. The Court of Appeals declared that this finding was not supported by evidence because there was no evi-

---

[2] The barriers to entry have been raised both for entry by new firms and for entry into new geographical markets by established firms. The latter aspect is demonstrated by Purex's lesson in Erie, Pennsylvania. In October 1957, Purex selected Erie, Pennsylvania—where it had not sold previously—as an area in which to test the salability, under competitive conditions, of a new bleach. The leading brands in Erie were Clorox, with 52%, and the "101" brand, sold by Gardner Manufacturing Company, with 29% of the market. Purex launched an advertising and promotional campaign to obtain a broad distribution in a short time, and in five months captured 33% of the Erie market. Clorox's share dropped to 35% and 101's to 17%. Clorox responded by offering its bleach at reduced prices, and then added an offer of a $1-value ironing board cover for 50¢ with each purchase of Clorox at the reduced price. It also increased its advertising with television spots. The result was to restore Clorox's lost market share and, indeed, to increase it slightly. Purex's share fell to 7%. . . .

dence that Procter's management had ever intended to enter the industry independently and that Procter had never attempted to enter. The evidence, however, clearly shows that Procter was the most likely entrant. Procter had recently launched a new abrasive cleaner in an industry similar to the liquid bleach industry, and had wrested leadership from a brand that had enjoyed even a larger market share than had Clorox. Procter was engaged in a vigorous program of diversifying into product lines closely related to its basic products. Liquid bleach was a natural avenue of diversification since it is complementary to Procter's products, is sold to the same customers through the same channels, and is advertised and merchandised in the same manner. Procter had substantial advantages in advertising and sales promotion, which, as we have seen, are vital to the success of liquid bleach. No manufacturer had a patent on the product or its manufacture, necessary information relating to manufacturing methods and processes was readily available, there was no shortage of raw material, and the machinery and equipment required for a plant of efficient capacity were available at reasonable costs. Procter's management was experienced in producing and marketing goods similar to liquid bleach. Procter had considered the possibility of independently entering but decided against it because the acquisition of Clorox would enable Procter to capture a more commanding share of the market.

It is clear that the existence of Procter at the edge of the industry exerted considerable influence on the market. First, the market behavior of the liquid bleach industry was influenced by each firm's prediction of the market behavior of its competitors, actual and potential. Second, the barriers to entry by a firm of Procter's size and with its advantages were not significant. There is no indication that the barriers were so high that the price Procter would have to charge would be above the price that would maximize the profits of the existing firms. Third, the number of potential entrants was not so large that the elimination of one would be insignificant. Few firms would have the temerity to challenge a firm as solidly entrenched as Clorox. Fourth, Procter was found by the Commission to be the most likely entrant. These findings of the Commission were amply supported by the evidence.

The judgment of the Court of Appeals is reversed and remanded with instructions to affirm and enforce the Commission's order.

It is so ordered.

MR. JUSTICE STEWART and MR. JUSTICE FORTAS took no part in the consideration or decision of this case.

MR. JUSTICE HARLAN, concurring.

I agree that the Commission's order should be sustained, but. . . . [i]t is regrettable to see this Court as it enters this comparatively new field of economic adjudication starting off with what has almost become a kind of *res ipsa loquitur* approach to antitrust cases.

The type of merger represented by the transaction before us is becoming increasingly important as large corporations seek to diversify their operations . . . and "[c]ompanies looking for new lines of business tend to buy into those fields with which they have at least some degree of familiarity, and where economies and efficiencies from assimilation are at least possible." Turner, Conglomerate Mergers and Section 7 of the Clayton Act, 78 Harv. L. Rev. 1313, 1315. Application of §7 to such mergers has been troubling to the Commission and the lower courts. . . .

I thus believe that it is incumbent upon us to make a careful study of the facts and opinions below in this case, and at least to embark upon the formulation of standards for the application of §7 to mergers which are neither horizontal nor vertical and which previously have not been considered in depth by this Court. . . . My prime difficulty with the Court's opinion is that it makes no effort in this direction at all, and leaves the commission, lawyers, and businessmen at large as to what is to be expected of them in future cases of this kind.

I

The Court's opinion rests on three separate findings of anticompetitive effect. The Court first declares that the market here was "oligopolistic" and that interjection of Procter would make the oligopoly "more rigid" because "[t]here is every reason to assume that the smaller firms would become more cautious in competing due to their fear of retaliation by Procter." The Court, however, does not indicate exactly what reasons lie behind this assumption or by what standard such an effect is deemed "reasonably probable." It could equally be assumed that smaller firms would become more aggressive in competing due to their fear that otherwise Procter might ultimately absorb their markets and that Procter, as a new entrant in the bleach field, was vulnerable to attack.

But assumption is no substitute for reasonable probability as a measure of illegality under §7 . . . and Congress has not mandated the Commission or the courts "to campaign against 'superconcentration' in the absence of any evidence of harm to competition." Turner *supra*, at 1395. . . .

The Court next stresses the increase in barriers to new entry into the liquid bleach field caused primarily, it is thought, by the substitution of the larger advertising capabilities of Procter for those of Clorox. Economic theory would certainly indicate that a heightening of such barriers has taken place. But the Court does not explain why it considers this change to have significance under §7, nor does it indicate when or how entry barriers affect competition in a relevant market. In this case, for example, the difficulties of introducing a new nationally advertised bleach were already so great that even a great company like Procter, which the Court finds the most likely entrant, believed that entry would not "pay out."

Why then does the Court find that a further increase of incalculable proportions in such barriers substantially lessens competition? Such a conclusion at least needs the support of reasoned analysis.[3]

Finally, the Court places much emphasis on the loss to the market of the most likely potential entrant, Procter. Two entirely separate anticompetitive effects might be traced to this loss, and the Court fails to distinguish between them. The first is simply that loss of the most likely entrant increases the operative barriers to entry by decreasing the likelihood that any firm will attempt to surmount them.[4] But this effect merely reinforces the Court's previous entry-barrier argument, which I do not find convincing as presented. The second possible effect is that a reasonably probable entrant has been excluded from the market and a measure of horizontal competition has been lost. Certainly the exclusion of what would promise to be an important independent competitor from the market may be sufficient, in itself, to support a finding of illegality under §7, . . . when the market has few competitors. The Commission, however, expressly refused to find a reasonable probability that Procter would have entered this market on its own, and the Sixth Circuit was in emphatic agreement. . . .

Thus I believe, with all respect, that the Court has failed to make a convincing analysis of the difficult problem presented, and were no more to be said in favor of the Commission's order I would vote to set it aside.

II

The Court, following the Commission, points out that this merger is not a pure "conglomerate" merger but may more aptly be labeled a "product-extension" merger. . . .

At the outset, it seems to me that there is a serious question whether the state of our economic knowledge is sufficiently advanced to enable a sure-footed administrative or judicial determination to be made *a priori* of substantial anticompetitive effect in mergers of this kind. It is clear enough that Congress desired that conglomerate and product-extension mergers be brought under §7 scrutiny, but well versed economists have argued that such scrutiny can never lead to a valid finding of illegality. . . .

---

[3] The need for analysis is even clearer in light of the fact that entry into the market by producers of nonadvertised, locally distributed bleaches was found to be easy. There were no technological barriers to entry, and the capital requirements for entry, with the exception of advertising costs, were small. The Court must at least explain why the threat of such entry and the presence of small competitors in existing regional markets cannot be considered the predominant, and unaffected, form of competition. To establish its point, the Court must either minimize the importance of such competition or show why it would be substantially lessened by the merger.

[4] Bain's pioneering study of barriers to entry, *Barriers to New Competition*, recognized that such barriers could be surmounted at different price levels by different potential entrants. Thus even without change in the nature of the barriers themselves, the market could become more insulated through loss of the most likely entrant simply because the prevailing market price would have to rise to a higher level than before to induce entry.

Lending strength to this position is the fact that such mergers do provide significant economic benefits which argue against excessive controls being imposed on them. The ability to merge brings large firms into the market for capital assets and encourages economic development by holding out the incentive of easy and profitable liquidation to others. Here, for example, the owners of Clorox who had built the business, were able to liquefy their capital on profitable terms without dismantling the enterprise they had created. Also merger allows an active management to move rapidly into new markets bringing with its intervention competitive stimulation and innovation. It permits a large corporation to protect its shareholders from business fluctuation through diversification, and may facilitate the introduction of capital resources, allowing significant economies of scale, into a stagnating market. . . .

At the other end of the spectrum, it has been argued that the entry of a large conglomerate enterprise may have a destructive effect on competition in any market. . . . Thus it is contended that a large conglomerate may underprice in one market, adversely affecting competition, and subsidize the operation by benefits accruing elsewhere.[5] It is also argued that the large company generates psychological pressure which may force smaller ones to follow its pricing policies, and that its very presence in the market may discourage entrants or make lending institutions unwilling to finance them. . . . [t]hese observations do indicate that significant dangers to competition may be presented by some conglomerate and product-extension mergers. Further, congressional concern in enacting §7 extended not only to anticompetitive behavior in particular markets, but also to the possible economic dominance of large companies which had grown through merger. Thus, while fully agreeing that mergers of this kind are not to be regarded as something entirely set apart from scrutiny under §7, I am of the view that when this Court does undertake to establish the standards for judging their legality, it should proceed with utmost circumspection. . . .

III

In adjudicating horizontal and vertical combinations under §7 where the effects on competition are reasonably obvious and substantiality is the key issue, the responsible agencies have moved away from an initial emphasis on comprehensive scrutiny and opted for more precise rules of thumb which provide advantages of administrative convenience and predictability for the business world. . . . A conglomerate case, however, is not only too new to our experience to allow the formulation of simple rules but also involves "concepts of economic power and competitive effect that are still largely unformulated. . . .

---

[5] But see Turner, "Conglomerate Mergers and Section 7 of the Clayton Act," 78 *Harv. L. Rev.* 1313, 1340. "[T]he belief that predatory pricing is a likely consequence of conglomerate size, and hence of conglomerate merger, is wholly unverified by any careful studies. . . ."

Procter . . . has insisted throughout this proceeding that anticompetitive effects must be proved *in fact* from post-merger evidence in order for §7 to be applied. The Court gives little attention to this contention, but I think it must be considered seriously, both because it is arguable and because it was, in a sense, the main source of difference between the Commission and the Sixth Circuit. . . .

If §7 is to serve the purposes Congress intended for it, we must, I think, stand with the Commission on this issue. Only by focusing on market structure can we begin to formulate standards which will allow the responsible agencies to give proper consideration to such mergers and allow businessmen to plan their actions with a fair degree of certainty. . . . The value of post-merger evidence seems more than offset by the difficulties encountered in obtaining it. And the post-merger evidence before us in this proceeding is at best inconclusive.

Deciding that §7 inquiry in conglomerate or product-extension merger cases should be directed toward reasonably probable changes in market structure does not, however, determine how that inquiry should be narrowed and focused. The Commission and the Court isolate two separate structural elements, the degree of concentration in the existing market and the "condition of entry." The interplay of these two factors is said to determine the existence and extent of market power, since the "condition of entry" determines the limits potential competition places on the existing market. It must be noted, however, that economic theory teaches that potential competition will have no effect on the market behavior of existing firms unless present market power is sufficient to drive the market price to the point where entry would become a real possibility. So long as existing competition is sufficient to keep the market price below that point, potential competition is of marginal significance as a market regulator. Thus in a conglomerate or product-extension case, where the effects on market structure which are easiest to discover are generally effects on the "condition of entry," an understanding of the workings of the premerger market cannot be ignored, and, indeed, is critical to a determination whether the visible effects on "condition of entry" have any competitive significance.

The Commission pinned its analysis of the premerger market exclusively on its concentration, the large market share enjoyed by the leading firms. . . . The Sixth Circuit discounted the Commission's analysis because of the presence of some 200 small competitors in the market. The Court bases its agreement with the Commission and its rejection of the Court of Appeals' position on Clorox's alleged domination of the market. But domination is an elusive term, for dominance in terms of percentage of sales is not the equivalent of dominance in terms of control over price or other aspects of market behavior. Just as the total number of sellers in the market is not determinative of its operation, the percentage of sales made by any group of sellers is similarly not conclusive. The determinative issue is, instead, how the sellers interact and establish the pattern of market behavior. The significance of concentration analysis is that it allows measurement of one easily determined variable to serve as an opening key to the pattern of market behavior.

I think that the Commission, on *this* record, was entitled to regard the market as "oligopolistic" and that it could properly ignore the impact of the smaller firms. I hasten to add, however, that there are significant "economic dissents" from oligopoly analysis in general. . . . In adjudicating §7 questions in a conglomerate or product-extension merger context where the pattern of behavior in the existing market is apt to be crucial, I would, therefore, allow the introduction by a defendant of evidence designed to show that the actual operation of the market did not accord with oligopoly theory, or whatever other theory the Commission desires to apply. In other words, I believe that defendants in §7 proceedings are entitled, in the case of conglomerate or product-extension mergers, to build their own economic cases for the proposition that the mergers will not substantially impair competition. . . . But to challenge effectively the presumption which the Commission is entitled to draw from general economic theory, a defendant must present, in my opinion, not only contradictory facts but a more cogent explanation of the pattern of market behavior.

If the proof as a whole establishes that pricing power may be exercised by a firm or firms in the market—that prices may be raised in the long run over competitive prices—then the Commission may legitimately focus on the role of potential competition and the "condition of entry." . . . In so doing, however, a new difficulty is encountered. The threat of potential competition merely affects the range over which price power extends. Potential competition does not compel more vigorous striving in the market, nor advance any other social goal which Congress might be said to have favored in passing §7. Thus it may legitimately be questioned whether even a substantial increase in entry barriers creates a substantial lessening of competition or tendency to monopoly as required by §7.

Two justifications for the use of entry barriers as a determinant under §7 can be given. The first is that an increased range over which pricing power may be exercised is contrary to the mandate of §7 because Congress' use of the word "competition" was a shorthand for the invocation of the benefits of a competitive market, one of which is a price close to average cost. Such an approach leads also to the conclusion that economic efficiencies produced by the merger must be weighed against anticompetitive consequences in the final determination whether the net effect on competition is substantially adverse. . . . The second justification is found in the tendency-to-monopoly clause of §7. Certainly the clearest evil of monopoly is the excessive power the monopolist has over price. Since "antitrust operates to forestall concentrations of economic power which, if allowed to develop unhindered, would call for much more intrusive government supervision of the economy," Blake & Jones, In Defense of Antitrust, 65 Col. L. Rev. 377, 383, increased power over price should be attackable under §7. . . . For these reasons I conclude that the Commission may properly find a conglomerate or product-extension merger illegal under §7 because it substantially increases pricing power in the relevant market.

Given the development of a case against the merger in this area, however, the problem of efficiencies raised above must still be faced. The Court attempts to brush the question aside by asserting that Congress preferred competition to economies, but neglects to determine whether certain economies are inherent in the idea of competition. If it is conceded, as it must be, that Congress had reasons for favoring competition, then more efficient operation must have been among them. It is of course true that a firm's ability to achieve economies enhances its competitive position, but adverse effects on competitors must be distinguished from adverse effects on competition. . . . Economies achieved by one firm may stimulate matching innovation by others, the very essence of competition. They always allow the total output to be delivered to the consumer with an expenditure of fewer resources. Thus when the case against a conglomerate or product-extension merger rests on a market-structure demonstration that the likelihood of anticompetitive consequences has been substantially increased, the responsible agency should then move on to examine and weigh possible efficiencies arising from the merger in order to determine whether, on balance, competition has been substantially lessened. Where detriments to competition are apt to be "highly speculative" it seems wisest to conclude that "possibilities of adverse effects on competitive behavior are worth worrying about only when the merger does not involve substantial economies. . . ." Turner, *supra*, at 1354. . . .

To summarize then, four important guides to the adjudication of conglomerate or product-extension mergers under §7 seem to come forward. First, the decision can rest on analysis of market structure without resort to evidence of post-merger anticompetitive behavior. Second, the operation of the premerger market must be understood as the foundation of successful analysis. The responsible agency may presume that the market operates in accord with generally accepted principles of economic theory, but the presumption must be open to challenge of alternative operational formulations. Third, if it is reasonably probable that there will be a change in market structure which will allow the exercise of substantially greater market power, then a prima facie case has been made out under §7. Fourth, where the case against the merger rests on the probability of increased market power, the merging companies may attempt to prove that there are countervailing economies reasonably probable which should be weighed against the adverse effects.

IV

The Commission's decision did, I think, conform to this analysis. . . . To hold the merger unlawful, the Commission relied on five factors which taken together convinced it that "substantial" anticompetitive consequences could be expected. A "substantial" impact was said to be "significant and real, and discernible not merely to theorists or scholars but to practical, hard-headed businessmen." . . . The relevant factors were (1) the excessive concentration in the industry at the time of the merger and the commanding market position of Clorox, (2) the relative disparity in size and strength between Procter and the firms in the liquid bleach industry, (3) the position of Procter in other markets, (4) the elimination of Procter as a potential competitor, and (5) the nature of the "economies" expected from the merger. The net of these factors was to establish a substantial effect on the market structure variable involved, condition of entry. . . .

. . . The Commission—in my opinion quite correctly—seemed to accept the idea that economies could be used to defend a merger, noting that "[a] merger that results in increased efficiency of production, distribution or marketing may, in certain cases, increase the vigor of competition in the relevant market." . . . But advertising economies were placed in a different classification since they were said "only to increase the barriers to new entry" and to be "offensive to at least the spirit, if not the letter, of the antitrust laws." . . . Advertising was thought to benefit only the sellers by entrenching his market position, and to be of no use to the consumer.

I think the Commission's view overstated and oversimplified. Proper advertising serves a legitimate and important purpose in the market by educating the consumer as to available alternatives. This process contributes to consumer demand being developed to the point at which economies of scale can be realized in production. The advertiser's brand name may also be an assurance of quality, and the value of this benefit is demonstrated by the general willingness of consumers to pay a premium for the advertised brands. Undeniably advertising may sometimes be used to create irrational brand preferences and mislead consumers as to the actual differences between products, but it is very difficult to discover at what point advertising ceases to be an aspect of healthy competition. . . . It is not the Commission's function to decide which lawful elements of the "product" offered the consumer should be considered useful and which should be considered the symptoms of industrial "sickness." It is the consumer who must make that election through the exercise of his purchasing power. In my view, true efficiencies in the use of advertising must be considered in assessing economies in the marketing process, which as has been noted are factors in the sort of §7 proceeding involved here.

I do not think, however, that on the record presented Procter has shown any true efficiencies in advertising. Procter has merely shown that it is able to command equivalent resources at a lower dollar cost than other bleach producers. No peculiarly efficient marketing techniques have been demonstrated, nor does the record show that a smaller net advertising expenditure could be expected. Economies cannot be premised solely on dollar figures, lest accounting controversies dominate §7 proceedings. Economies employed in defense of a merger must be shown in what economists label "real" terms, that is in terms of resources applied to the accomplishment of the objective. For this reason, the Commission, I think, was justified in discounting Procter's efficiency defense.

Federal Trade Commission: The Bendix Corp.

Docket No. 8739 (1970), 1970
Trade Cases ¶19, 288

OPINION OF THE COMMISSION

I. *Introduction*

By *Commissioner Elman:* On June 29, 1967, one day before consummation of a merger between Fram Corporation (Fram) and the Bendix Corporation (Bendix), the Commission issued its complaint herein charging that the merger violated Section 7 of the Clayton Act . . . and Section 5 of the Federal Trade Commission Act. . . . Although the merger was thereafter consummated, Fram has been operated as a separate subsidiary of Bendix by agreement between the parties.

The complaint alleged that the effect of the Bendix-Fram merger "may be substantially to lessen competition, or to tend to create a monopoly" in three lines of commerce involving filters: automotive filters, aerospace filters, and filter water separators. . . .

. . . However, since a finding of legality or illegality as to the major line of filters involved, automotive filters, is dispositive of the complaint and order in this case, we shall concern ourselves only with that line of commerce.

II. *Facts and Background*

. . . . .

A. *The Industry*

Three types of automotive filters—oil, air, and fuel—are used on virtually all kinds of engines, from light truck and passenger car engines to heavy truck and off-highway equipment engines. There are two general markets for these filters: sales to the original equipment manufacturers for installation in the new engine (the OEM market) and sales to firms for replacing worn-out filters (the replacement or after market). . . .

There are over 30 manufacturers of automotive filters, including the giant auto makers, General Motors and Ford. Nevertheless, the market is a relatively concentrated one. In 1966, in the broad overall market, the top three companies accounted for 62.9% of industry sales, and the top six companies accounted for 79.6%. The first ranking company in sales was General Motors Corporation, whose AC Division (GMC-AC) accounted for 32.4% of 1966 sales; the second ranking firm was Purolator Products, Inc. (Purolator), with 18.3% and Fram ranked third with 12.4%. Bendix, with sales of slightly over $1 million, accounted for approximately 0.35% of automotive filter sales in 1966. In the narrower market—passenger car replacement filters—concentration was even higher. The same three firms accounted for 71.3% of total sales as follows: GMC-AC 32.4%; Purolator 21.7%; and Fram 17.2%. However, between 1962 and 1966, the three-firm concentration had declined somewhat: in the total automotive filter market from 69.8% to 62.9%; in the passenger car filter aftermarket from 74.5% to 71.3%.

The manufacture of most automotive filters involves relatively simple, unsophisticated, and well-known technology, and there are no important existing patents. Furthermore, the list prices as well as the discount prices of the leading filter markers [*sic*] do not vary significantly, and the prices of the majors are generally higher than the prices of some smaller companies. Rather, the most important ingredient of success has been a good marketing and merchandising organization. . . .

B. *The Respondents*

1. *Fram* is a leading United States producer of various kinds of filters, including automotive filters, aerospace filters, and filter water separators. . . . Its sales, earnings, and assets in 1966 were the highest in its history, and it was a financially sound, profitable, and growing company. . . .

Approximately 55% of Fram's 1966 sales were in automotive filters. In that field, Fram was not only the third-ranking producer, with 12.4% of the market, but a pioneer in technology and promotion. . . . Although Fram sold filters in all the distributional channels in the industry, about 90% of Fram's filter sales were in the passenger car filter aftermarket, where Fram ranked third in sales with 17.2% of the market.

2. *Bendix* is a diversified manufacturer of components and assemblies for aerospace, automotive, automation, scientific, oceanic, and other uses. . . . In 1966, Bendix was the 69th largest industrial corporation in the United States; by 1967, it had become the 61st largest.

Over half of Bendix's sales are concentrated in sophisticated equipment for aircraft, missiles, and spacecraft—including aerospace filters and filter water separators. Bendix is also heavily dependent upon government and defense contracts.

Bendix has always been significantly involved in the automotive parts industry. . . .

Bendix sells, through eight separate divisions, a wide variety of automotive parts: fuel pumps, starter drives, ignition components, brakes, brake drums, power steerings, universal joints, carburetors, radios, speed controls, temperature controls, and filters. While the predominant portion of these automotive sales is made to automobile manufacturers and other original equipment makers, Bendix makes substantial sales to the automotive aftermarket, both as proprietary and private brands. . . . Indeed, in 1961, Bendix formed an Automotive Services Division to facilitate the distribution of all Bendix automotive parts in the aftermarket. . . .

In the automotive filter industry, Bendix focused upon the production and sale of heavy duty oil and fuel filters for original equipment makers. The Bendix Filter Division was one of the company's smallest and in the early 1960's was losing money. . . . The only filter product manufactured by Bendix specifically for passenger car application was an air filter element made in the late 1950's for Ford and American Motors. After losing money on the venture, Bendix in 1960 began subcontracting these filters, until 1963 when its Ford contract was terminated.

III. *The Legal Issue: Elimination of Potential Competition*

Complaint counsel's principal contentions as to the automotive filter line of commerce are that the examiner erred in failing to find this merger unlawful because it (1) confers upon Fram certain advantages that will be injurious to competition in the automotive filter market; and (2) eliminates substantial potential competition between Bendix and Fram in that market.

A review of the record convinces us that the hearing examiner properly concluded that Bendix did not confer upon Fram any advantages so significant as substantially to lessen competition in the automotive filter market.

Thus, the principal remaining issue in this case is whether the merger may substantially lessen competition by eliminating Bendix as a potential entrant and competitor in the automotive filter market.

With the growing concentration of American markets, and the growing mobility of business investments, the crucial role of "potential competition" as a regulator of economic behavior has been recognized. Not only is actual new entry an essential source of new competition, the potential for which must be preserved, but the mere threat of new entry by firms waiting at the edge of a concentrated, relatively uncompetitive market may be an important support for competition in that market. Thus, Section 7 clearly applies not only to mergers that substantially raise the barriers to new entry . . . but to mergers which, by eliminating potential competitors and entrants, have the likely effect of substantially lessening competition in the relevant market. . . .

IV. *Elimination of Potential Competition: The Facts*

A. *The Relevant Line of Commerce*

The hearing examiner properly concluded that the three types of automotive filters—oil, air, and fuel—may be combined, and that the relevant geographic market is the nation as a whole. The hearing examiner, however, failed to resolve the dispute between the parties as to a further delineation of the line of commerce. Complaint counsel contend that all automotive filters constitute the relevant market. The respondents contend that the market should be limited to passenger car and light truck filters sold for replacement—thus excluding all heavy duty filters and all filters sold for original equipment. The hearing examiner made his findings on the basis of treating both product markets as relevant.

We agree that both markets are relevant here, and that the legality of this merger can be determined on the basis of its effects on competition in either market. The broader overall automotive filter market is clearly proper;[1] and, as the hearing examiner concluded, the passenger car filter aftermarket is "at least an appropriate submarket". . . .

B. *Bendix as a Likely Entrant and Competitor*

The evidence in the record and the hearing examiner's relevant findings overwhelmingly establish that Bendix was likely and able to enter the passenger car filter aftermarket, one way or another. The probability of its entry into this market was clear: the only question was the form that such entry would take.

Bendix was a major participant in the automotive parts business, with 1966 sales well over $200 million. Bendix also made substantial sales in the automotive parts replacement market, with 1966 sales of $40.6 million; and half of these sales were under Bendix's proprietary label. . . .

Furthermore, Bendix was already a minor participant in the automotive filter industry. In 1966, Bendix's automotive filter sales allowed Bendix to control 0.35% of the market—a share equal to or larger than almost one-third of the firms in that market. . . .

In sum, from the objective evidence only one conclusion is possible: the whole logic of Bendix's corporate development, its size, resources, and direct proximity to the passenger car filter aftermarket, and the unambiguous direction of its business growth, all pointed to expansion into the passenger car filter aftermarket.

---

[1] The broader market is particularly appropriate in light of the customer overlap between the narrower and broader markets: the original equipment makers buy filters not only for installation in new engines, but for sale through franchised dealers as replacements. . . .

The record also establishes that this was recognized by Bendix's management. . . .

. . . [I]t . . . was convinced that Bendix should make a substantial entry into the passenger car filter aftermarket, in an attempt to salvage the current Bendix investment in filters, and to bring greater profits and stability to the corporation as a whole.

C. *Form of Bendix Entry*

Despite this overwhelming evidence as to the likelihood of Bendix's entry into the aftermarket, the hearing examiner concluded that complaint counsel had failed to establish that Bendix was a potential entrant.

To the hearing examiner it was dispositive of this case that the evidence showed that Bendix would not enter the passenger car filter aftermarket by internal expansion but only through merger with another firm already in that market. The examiner assumed that, from the standpoint of Section 7, it made no difference whether Bendix merged with Fram, an established market leader, or with a smaller firm which, by combining with Bendix's vast resources and managerial skills, would become a new and substantial competitive force in the market confronting Fram and the other established leading firms.

The examiner's analysis of the potential competition problem—focusing exclusively on the probability of Bendix's entry by internal expansion and neglecting the likelihood of entry by merger other than with Fram—was unduly narrow and must be rejected, because it rests upon a misconception of the basic purpose and policy of Section 7. Various forms of merger entry other than through acquisition of a leading company—for example, a "toehold" acquisition of a small company capable of expansion into a substantial competitive force—may be as economically desirable and beneficial to competition as internal expansion into a relevant market, and must be considered in assessing the potential competition of the acquiring firm which has been eliminated as a result of the challenged merger. . . .

We think it clear that Congress was concerned in Section 7 with the preservation of new and potential competition in any form: that new entry, if beneficial and procompetitive, is to be encouraged regardless of its form, and that a merger with a leading firm, especially in a concentrated industry, which eliminates the likelihood of such desirable entry through a toehold acquisition is embraced within the prohibitions of the statute.

In enacting Section 7, Congress was pursuing both positive and negative objectives. By prohibiting mergers whose effect may be substantially to lessen competition in any line of commerce, the statute channels merger activity in the direction deemed by Congress to be beneficial as a matter of national economic policy. The enforcement of Section 7 was designed to encourage those mergers which are likely to maintain and expand competition. . . . [F]or example, in a highly concentrated, sluggish market, the acquisition of a small industry member by a powerful, innovative firm which, by building upon the base of the smaller firm, can pose a more effective competitive challenge to the industry giants. Such procompetitive mergers are not only not forbidden by Section 7, they are positively encouraged.

Thus, all likely routes for potential entry into the relevant market must be considered in determining the legality of the merger route which was in fact chosen. A potential entrant may enter not only by internal expansion; he may enter the market by acquiring a failing company, or a small company in difficulty, or by making a toehold acquisition of a small member of the industry. These methods of entry, no less than internal expansion, and in some cases perhaps more than entry by internal expansion, may inject a new competitive element of vigor and strength into an otherwise stagnant market. Indeed, where entry into some markets by internal expansion is foreclosed and/or restricted, entry by toehold acquisition may be the most feasible route for developing new competition. Furthermore, in an age of mergers and acquisitions, the threat of a toehold merger by a powerful firm may often serve as a much greater incentive to competitive performance in the affected market than does the prospect of more costly and slower internal, *de novo* expansion.

In short, it is offensive to the merger law to eliminate the potential competition offered by likely entrants at a market's edge that may come into it through a toehold or other procompetitive acquisition, especially where the market is a concentrated one in need of new competition. . . .

D. *Bendix Entry by Toehold Acquisition and Expansion*

The hearing examiner found "that complaint counsel have failed to sustain the burden of establishing that Bendix was a potential entrant into the automotive filter replacement market *by internal development.*" While we have serious doubts as to the evidentiary support for such a finding, we do not deem it necessary to overturn it. For the respondents concede, and the hearing examiner found, that Bendix was a well-recognized and quite capable potential entrant by some form of acquisition. . . . But, more important, we believe that the evidence of record unequivocally shows that Bendix possessed the incentives and capacity, and was likely, to make a toehold acquisition of a small firm in the passenger car filter aftermarket, and to attempt competitively significant expansion of that firm, if acquisition of a market leader like Fram were foreclosed to it by law. The record leaves no doubt that, if Bendix had based its expansion decisions on a correct legal premise, namely, that Section 7 firmly closed the door to entry into the aftermarket by a leading firm acquisition but left the door wide open to a toehold acquisition, Bendix would long ago have entered the market by the latter route.

The evidence as to the likelihood of such an acquisition entry is substantial. . . . [I]n the 1960's, Bendix management decided to diversify into non-government, non-military business. One area seen as not only lucrative but compatible with Bendix's other business was the automotive filter market—particularly the profitable and growing aftermarket.

As a result, between 1961 and 1966, Bendix considered the acquisition of numerous filter makers. . . .

Finally, the evidence indicates a willingness by Bendix to expand any small firm acquired. . . . Bendix clearly contemplated a major move into the submarket, since it already maintained a marginal presence in the broader market. Obviously, putting Section 7 to one side, the quickest and easiest method was to buy a leader. However, Bendix's management did contemplate the small acquisition-plus-expansion route. As one executive was noted as having stated: "If we buy Wix only we must have policy of building via internal development. Must pull all stops." . . .

Not only does subjective evidence show the likelihood of acquisition entry accompanied by expansion, the objective evidence clearly confirms the economic capability of Bendix to accomplish this. Bendix possessed the resources and size necessary to engage in any prolonged battle against the major filter makers, which included the nation's industrial giants—Ford and General Motors. Bendix also had the experience and necessary technology for making filters. This could be advantageous in expanding a small filter maker that might not have the experience in producing a full line of filters.

Bendix also had the 80-man sales force of its Automotive Service Division for distributing and selling in the aftermarket, the know-how for weaving a way through the automotive parts aftermarket distribution system, and an established name in both the automotive parts business and the automotive aftermarket. The Bendix name could be useful in expanding a small manufacturer without the necessary brand identification. Bendix could also bring to a small firm its experience in selling to, and contracts with, original equipment makers, defense contractors, and the government, as well as its existing arrangements with warehouse distributors and jobbers in the aftermarket. While perhaps all of these assets were relatively insignificant in terms of aiding or entrenching Fram, they might be very significant in developing a smaller and less established filter maker acquired by Bendix.

If any barrier to entry by this acquisition route existed for Bendix, it was, as respondents contend, due to the mass marketing and promotional techniques necessary to sell filters in the aftermarket. But this was precisely the barrier that Bendix could have surmounted by a toehold acquisition of a firm with substantial promotional facilities. . . .

The picture that emerges from the record is clear: Bendix was doing everything it possibly could to enter the passenger car filter aftermarket through merger. This was a logical and inevitable way for the company to expand. No firm could be more accurately characterized as a potential entrant into that market, actively exploring every possible means of access to it. From the standpoint of Section 7, and the statutory policy of favoring mergers which may increase competition and prohibiting mergers which may lessen competition, it made a crucial difference whether Bendix merged with Fram or another leading firm, or with [any] one of the various smaller and less established firms with which it unsuccessively negotiated. The outcome of these negotiations was unquestionably affected by Bendix's erroneous assumption that it was as free under Section 7 to merge with Fram as it was to acquire one of the smaller companies. In any event, under any definition of the term, Bendix was a likely potential entrant into the market which could have come into it through a toehold acquisition; and it was such potential entry, and the competition with Fram that would have resulted, which was eliminated when Bendix bought Fram.

V. *Effect of the Instant Merger Upon Competition*

On the basis of the findings of the Commission and the hearing examiner, and the applicable legal principles, we hold that the effect of the present merger may be substantially to lessen competition in the passenger car filter replacement market by eliminating the potential competition of Bendix in that market.

This is not a case in which the elimination of potential competition is a matter of theory or conjecture. What we have here, rather, is a merger between Fram, a leading producer in the relevant market, and Bendix, a firm that already competed in closely related filter and automotive markets, had canvassed the market for all likely acquisition candidates during a five-year period, was committed to entering the market in some fashion, and possessed all the qualities necessary to carry out a successful toehold acquisition followed by expansion.

And if Bendix had been allowed to make such an entry, it would have become an actual competitor of Fram, just as Fram would have become an actual competitor of Bendix. That potential rivalry between a leading firm and a significant, well financed, resourceful, and likely new entrant by toehold acquisition was frustrated and extinguished by Bendix's merger with Fram. In the most fundamental and basic sense, the merger eliminated direct—indeed, one could say horizontal—competition between Fram and Bendix. And this competition is no less substantial and significant for antitrust purposes because it was potential rather than actual.

No real dispute exists as to the imminence, likelihood, or ability of Bendix to have become a real and substantial competitor of Fram in the passenger car filter aftermarket. The only question was the form that new entry would take. Bendix had three choices: (1) to expand internally; (2) to make a toehold acquisition looking toward expansion on that base; and (3) to merge with a leading firm. If Bendix had taken either of the first two routes of entry, it would have become an actual competitor of Fram, and would have provided a beneficial new element in the market. Either of those two routes would have promoted competition; neither violated Section 7; indeed, either was the sort of entry into a new market which Congress intended to encourage. Instead, Bendix chose the third route—acquisition of Fram, a leading firm—and thus the likelihood of substantial competition between these two firms was forever eliminated. By the same token, the competitive input that Bendix could have brought to the entire market, had it entered by a toehold acquisition, was also lost.

The adverse effects on competition resulting from Bendix's merger with Fram are further evidenced by the following factors present in the record.

First, this merger eliminated not merely the competition likely to result from the probable entry of Bendix into the market by another acquisition route, but also the threat of such entry that Bendix was capable of exercising merely by remaining at the market's edge, ready and able to enter at the appropriate moment. The threat of such entry was likely to have a beneficial effect upon the action of competitors in the market, particularly since Bendix's many abilities would give credibility to any threatened entry. This potential competition in the automotive filter market was eliminated by Bendix in acquiring Fram.

Second, evidence in the record and the partial findings of the hearing examiner indicate that competition is quite weak in the passenger car filter aftermarket. Thus, the elimination of any potential competition is likely to have a much greater effect upon overall competition.[2]

Respondents' own evidence indicates that the passenger car filter aftermarket is highly concentrated. In 1966, three firms accounted for 71.3% of aftermarket sales; the top four firms for 80.8%; and the top six firms for 88.6%.[3]

Moreover, as the hearing examiner found, "The automotive filter industry is a highly profitable one" and this "favorable profit trend in the industry has included a number of the smaller companies, as well as the industry's leaders." Apparently not only are the industry leaders content to maintain relatively stable market shares and profits among themselves, they are content to leave the smaller companies with a "living" portion of the remainder.

The competitively lethargic state of the industry is reflected in the stabilized pricing patterns found by the hearing examiner. Whatever competition there is seems to be in terms of promotion, selling and distribution.

[2] ... When a concentrated, relatively uncompetitive market is involved, any merger with an industry member should be closely scrutinized to ensure that it is productive of new competition, not further stabilization of an oligopolistic situation.

[3] ... Concentration had declined slightly since 1962, when three firms held 74.5%, four firms held 84.1% and six firms held 91.5%. This decline, however, occurred when industry sales were increasing significantly—from $121,967,000 in 1962 to $189,352,000 in 1966.

The leader, AC Division of General Motors Corporation, had been increasing its share of the market, as the shares of Purolator and Fram had declined. However, the sales of all three had shown steady growth. Furthermore, the statistics in the record submitted by respondents may exaggerate the dominance of General Motors. These figures appear to include in GMC-AC sales the filters sold by the GMC-AC Division to GMC. ...

Manufacturers build up sales by brand differentiation, advertising, by large numbers of salesmen and promotional men, and by such promotional gimmicks as bonus stamps, coupons, contests, and prizes. All these various forms of nonprice competition seem to have contributed to a continued dominance by the leaders in the industry, and the comfortable profits prevalent among all sellers. . . .

In sum, the record fully supports a finding that competition in the market would be likely to benefit from new entrants, as well as from the presence of potential entrants at the market's edge; and that competition in this market would be likely to suffer from the elimination—by this merger—of a significant potential entrant and competitor such as Bendix.

Third, the record indicates that there are some significant entry barriers to the passenger car filter aftermarket, thus rendering the market even more susceptible to injury from the elimination of Bendix as a potential entrant. These barriers result primarily from (a) the presence in the market of the nation's first and third largest industrial corporations—General Motors and Ford; and (b) the distributional and promotional techniques used in the aftermarket.[4]

The auto companies not only could deter smaller companies from entering by sheer size, . . . but also could discourage new competitors by their control over automotive design and warranty—and thus over the future of the filter market.

As for the sales practices in the market, brand differentiation advertising is heavy for an industry where most of the advertising is aimed at the trade, rather than at ultimate consumers. Manufacturers also utilize various promotional schemes, such as quantity purchase bonus stamps, contests, and prizes. Finally, the industry members employ not merely salesmen, but great numbers of promotional men—termed "missionary men." The three leading filter makers each employed over one hundred such missionary men.

The purposes of these various promotional programs are twofold: first, to build demand, sales, and brand allegiance at the retail level; and second, to thereby build brand allegiance at the warehouse distributor level. The latter goal—obtaining the service and loyalty of the distributor—was particularly crucial. Many warehouse distributors found it more feasible to carry only one major, or full line of filters. The prospect of breaking the brand allegiance of either the retailers or the warehouse distributors, through the necessary volume advertising and large use of missionary men, would not be an inviting one for outsiders. . . .

---

[4] The record also discloses that a certain amount of resources, technological expertise, and capital may be necessary for entering into production of automotive filters, but that such barriers to entry cannot be regarded as very high. . . . And although many direct purchasers required a volume larger than some firms might be able to attain, . . . economies of scale could probably be reached at a fairly low level of output. . . .

The record as to recent entries supports a conclusion that entry barriers are indeed significant for this industry. Despite a substantial growth in the sales and profits, the evidence indicates that from 1962 to the time of the hearings there were only three new entrants—and two of these entered before 1963.

In conclusion, the barriers for entry into this market were substantial enough that the elimination of a potential competitor and entrant was likely to have a significant competitive effect. The number of companies with the size, experience, automotive parts brand name, and other necessary capabilities for entry, was likely to be small, and thus any lessening of that number would be substantial. . . .

Fourth, the record indicates that few, if any, firms were likely to be as imminent or as substantial potential entrants as Bendix. Thus, the disappearance of Bendix from the market's edge was particularly significant. . . .

As to the potential entrants by a toehold merger, it is likely that few firms possessed the various capabilities of Bendix in this regard: Bendix's size and finances; Bendix's contacts in the original equipment, defense, and military business; the prestige and name of Bendix in automotive parts, including the aftermarket; the automotive aftermarket warehouse and jobber connections; an aftermarket sales force, and actual facilities for making filters. . . .

In conclusion, while we do not find nor believe that Bendix was the only potential entrant, internally or by acquisition, or that of all possible entries, that of Bendix would be the most significant, we do conclude that . . . Bendix was among the most likely of a limited number of possible entrants capable of making a significant entry by acquisition and expansion of a smaller firm. Consequently, the elimination of that potential entrant and competitor is even more significant for its effect upon competition.

VI. *Conclusion*

The evidence clearly indicates that the passenger car filter aftermarket is in need of new competition. It is an industry characterized by chronically high concentration, high profits, little real competition, substantial entry barriers, few recent entrants, and relatively few firms at the market's edge ready or able to overcome the entry barriers. The evidence also indicates that Bendix was—by virtue of its size, growth pattern, reputation and experience in automotive parts and filters, and its proximity to the market— a significant potential competitor for the passenger car filter aftermarket. In addition, it was a likely entrant by toehold acquisition: Bendix was virtually committed to some kind of entry into the market; it had considered a small firm merger; and it was quite able and likely to expand a small firm so acquired into a substantial competitor able to hold its own with the industry leaders.

Instead, Bendix chose to enter the passenger car filter aftermarket by merging with a leading firm. While the industry was in need of a more beneficial acquisition, and while Bendix was able and likely to make such an acquisition, Bendix effected a merger with Fram—thus eliminating the competition, which clearly would have been substantial, that Fram and other industry members would have had to meet if Bendix had made, and expanded, a toehold acquisition of a small firm.

The respondents admit—even argue—that integration or other efficiency-promoting methods will not result from the merger between Fram and Bendix. In any event, a toehold merger could surely have realized the potential competition which Bendix was capable of bringing to this market. But the Bendix-Fram merger removed not only the possibility of such a beneficial entry into the market, but also the threat of such entry by one of the few firms at the market's edge able to carry out that threat. . . .

VII. *Relief*

Only complete divestiture can return the two parties to a position which assures the viability of the potential competition forces derived from Bendix's existence at the edge of the passenger car filter replacement market. . . .

We also believe that requiring prior Commission approval for Bendix's acquisitions for the next ten years in the automotive filter industry, as well as the aerospace filter and filter water separator industries is warranted. . . .

MERGERS AND RECIPROCITY

There can be no question that diversification through merger enhances the possibility of reciprocity. A business firm engaged in many areas of activity can demand from suppliers of one division reciprocal business for another. Indeed, in some instances it need make no explicit demand; the matter can be left to its suppliers' imaginations, and what several observers have called the "reciprocity effect" may occur. Whether reciprocity is coercive or voluntary, the result may be a foreclosure of important markets to the detriment both of actual and potential suppliers.

In cases where alleged reciprocity is at issue the courts have been faced with two distinct tasks: (a) detection of the practice itself; and (b) the fashioning of a suitable remedy. Thus, in the *Consolidated Foods* case, evidence was admitted as to the extent to which Consolidated actively sought reciprocity and the effect thereon of its acquisition of Gentry. And in *ITT* the court went to great lengths to determine whether the "profit center" concept, pursuant to which each division of a diversified firm is responsible for its own profit performance, offset any tendency to reciprocity inherent in the Grinnell acquisition.

Federal Trade Commission v. *Consolidated Foods Corp.*

380 U.S. 592 (1965)

MR. JUSTICE DOUGLAS delivered the opinion of the Court.

The question presented involves an important construction and application of Section 7 of the Clayton Act . . . amended. . . . Consolidated Foods Corp.—which owns food processing plants and a network of wholesale and retail food stores—acquired Gentry, Inc., in 1951. Gentry manufactures principally dehydrated onion and garlic. The Federal Trade Commission held that the acquisition violated Section 7 because it gave respondent the advantage of a mixed threat and lure of reciprocal buying in its competition for business and "the power to foreclose competition from a substantial share of the markets for dehydrated onion and garlic." It concluded, in other words, that the effect of the acquisition "may be substantially to lessen competition" within the meaning of Section 7, and it ordered divestiture and gave other relief. . . . The Court of Appeals, relying mainly on 10 years of post-acquisition experience, held that the Commission had failed to show a probability that the acquisition would substantially lessen competition. . . . The case is here on certiorari. . . .

We hold at the outset that the "reciprocity" made possible by such an acquisition is one of the congeries of anticompetitive practices at which the antitrust laws are aimed. The practice results in "an irrelevant and alien factor," . . . intruding into the choice among competing products, creating at the least "a priority on the business at equal prices." *International Salt Co.* v. *United States.* . . ; *Northern Pac. R. Co.* v. *United States.* . . . Reciprocal trading may ensue not from bludgeoning or coercion but from more subtle arrangements. A threatened withdrawal of orders if products of an affiliate cease being bought, as well as a conditioning of future purchases on the receipt of orders for products of that affiliate, is an anticompetitive practice. Section 7 of the Clayton Act is concerned "with probabilities, not certainties." *Brown Shoe Co.* v. *United States* . . . ; *United States* v. *Philadelphia Nat. Bank.* . . . Reciprocity in trading as a result of an acquisition violates Section 7, if the probability of a lessening of competition is shown. We turn then to that, the principal, aspect of the present case.

Consolidated is a substantial purchaser of the products of food processors who in turn purchase dehydrated onion and garlic for use in preparing and packaging their food. Gentry, which as noted is principally engaged in the manufacture of dehydrated onion and garlic, had in 1950, immediately prior to its acquisition by Consolidated, about 32% of the total sales of the dehydrated garlic and onion industry and, together with its principal competitor, Basic Vegetable Products, Inc., accounted for almost 90% of the total industry sales. The remaining 10% was divided between two other firms. By 1958 the total industry output of both products had doubled, Gentry's share rising to 35% and the combined share of Gentry and Basic remaining at about 90%.

After the acquisition Consolidated (though later disclaiming adherence to any policy of reciprocity) did undertake to assist Gentry in selling. An official of Consolidated wrote as follows to its distributing divisions:

Oftentimes, it is a great advantage to know when you are calling on a prospect, whether or not that prospect is a supplier of someone within your own organization. Everyone believes in reciprocity providing all things are equal.

Attached is a list of prospects for our Gentry products. We would like to have you indicate on the list whether or not you are purchasing any of your supplies from them. If so, indicate whether your purchases are relatively large, small or insignificant. . . .

Food processors who sold to Consolidated stated they would give their onion and garlic business to Gentry for reciprocity reasons if it could meet the price and quality of its competitors' products. . . .

Some suppliers responded and gave reciprocal orders. Some who first gave generous orders later reduced them or abandoned the practice. It is impossible to recreate the precise anatomy of the market arrangements following the acquisition, though respondent offers a factual brief seeking to prove that "reciprocity" either failed or was not a major factor in the post-acquisition history.

The Commission found, however, that "merely as a result of its connection with Consolidated, and without any action on the latter's part, Gentry would have an unfair advantage over competitors enabling it to make sales that otherwise might not have been made." . . .

The Court of Appeals, on the other hand, gave post-acquisition evidence almost conclusive weight. It pointed out that, while Gentry's share of the dehydrated onion market increased by some 7%, its share of the dehydrated garlic market decreased 12%. . . . It also relied on apparently unsuccessful attempts at reciprocal buying. . . . The Court of Appeals concluded that "Probability can best be gauged by what the past has taught." . . .

The Court of Appeals was not in error in considering the post-acquisition evidence in this case. . . . But we think it gave too much weight to it. . . . No group acquiring a company with reciprocal buying opportunities is entitled to a "free trial" period. To give it such would be to distort the scheme of Section 7. . . . Probability of the proscribed evil is required, as we have noted. If the post-acquisition evidence were given conclusive weight or allowed to override all probabilities, then acquisitions would go forward willy-nilly, the parties biding their time until reciprocity was allowed fully to bloom. It is, of course, true that post-acquisition conduct may amount to a violation of Section 7 even though there is no evidence to establish probability *in limine*. . . . But the force of Section 7 is still in probabilities, not in what later transpired. That must necessarily be the case, for once the two companies are united no one knows what the fate of the acquired company and its competitors would have been but for the merger.

Moreover, the post-acquisition evidence here tends to confirm, rather than cast doubt upon, the probable anticompetitive effect which the Commission found the merger would have. The Commission found that Basic's product was superior to Gentry's—as Gentry's president freely and repeatedly admitted. Yet Gentry, in a rapidly expanding market, was able to increase its share of onion sales by 7% and to hold its losses in garlic to a 12% decrease. . . .

We do not go so far as to say that any acquisition, no matter how small, violates Section 7 if there is a probability of reciprocal buying. Some situations may amount only to *de minimis*. But where, as here, the acquisition is of a company that commands a substantial share of a market, a finding of probability of reciprocal buying by the Commission, whose expertise the Congress trusts, should be honored, if there is substantial evidence to support it.

The evidence is in our view plainly substantial. Reciprocity was tried over and again and it sometimes worked. The industry structure was peculiar, Basic being the leader with Gentry closing the gap. Moreover there is evidence, as the Commission found, "that many buyers have determined that their source of supply may best be protected by a policy of buying from two suppliers." When reciprocal buying—or the inducement of it—is added, the Commission observed:

> Buyers are likely to lean toward Basic on the ground of quality, but, in seeking a second, protective supply channel, to purchase from Gentry in the belief that this will further their sales to Consolidated. Not only does Gentry thus obtain sales that might otherwise go to Basic or Puccinelli, but the two-firm oligopoly structure of the industry is strengthened and solidified and new entry by others is discouraged. . . .

We conclude that there is substantial evidence to sustain that conclusion and that the order of the Commission should not have been denied enforcement. The judgment of the Court of Appeals is accordingly

Reversed.

[Mr. Justice Harlan, concurred.]

MR. JUSTICE STEWART, concurring in the judgment.

. . . While I agree with the result that the Court has reached, I am persuaded to file this separate statement of my views regarding the issues involved.

Clearly the opportunity for reciprocity is not alone enough to invalidate a merger under Section 7. The Clayton Act was not passed to outlaw diversification. Yet large scale diversity of industrial interests almost always presents the possibility of some reciprocal relationships. Often the purpose of diversification is to acquire companies whose present management can benefit from the technical skills and sales acumen of the acquiring corporation. Without more, Section 7 of the Clayton Act does not prohibit mergers whose sole effect is to introduce into an arena of "soft" competition the experience and skills of a more aggressive organization.

It obviously requires more than this kind of bare potential for reciprocal buying to bring a merger within the ban of Section 7. Before a merger may be properly outlawed under Section 7 on the basis solely of reciprocal buying potentials, the law requires a more closely textured economic analysis. . . .

. . . Certainly the mere effort at reciprocity cannot be the basis for finding the probability of a significant alteration in the market structure. Section 7 does not punish intent. No matter how bent on reciprocity Consolidated might have been, if its activities would not have the requisite probable impact on competition, it cannot be held to have violated this law. And, I think, it is not enough to say that the merger is illegal merely because the reciprocity attempts "sometimes worked." If the opportunity for reciprocity itself is not a violation of the Act when the merger occurs, then some standard must be established for determining how effective reciprocity must be before the merger is subject to invalidation. Nor do I think that illegality of this merger can be rested upon the fact that "[t]he industry structure was peculiar, Basic being the leader with Gentry closing the gap." There is evidence that in the years following 1951, when the merger took place, increased emphasis was placed on solving technical problems which had prevented some processors from relying on dehydrated, rather than raw, onions. The 1950's were a time of flux for the industry. Basic was sometimes the innovator of technological change leading to increased sales; sometimes Gentry had the upper hand. It is possible that this shift to more intensive competition was connected with the merger. Faced with a new competitive situation, Basic may have determined to solve quality control problems which had long been dormant. Indeed, the evidence seems to show that, after the acquisition, the industry reflected the salutary qualities normally associated with free competition. Overall, both Basic and Gentry were furnishing a better product at the end of this period than at the beginning. It is true that the industry had oligopolistic features, but there is no evidence to indicate that barriers to entry were particularly severe.[1] And Gentry, while it was "closing the gap" with regard to dehydrated onions, was falling even farther behind Basic in the sales of dehydrated garlic. Finally, I can attach no significance to the fact that processors, seeking a second source of supply, normally relied on Gentry rather than Puccinelli. That fact can rest on so many alternative hypotheses that it is persuasive as to none.

The touchstone of Section 7 is the probability that competition will be lessened. But before a court takes the drastic step of ordering divestiture, the evidence must be clear that such a probability exists. . . .

To determine that probability, the courts and the Commission should rely on the best information available, whether it is an examination of the market structure before the merger has taken place, or facts concerning the changes in the market after the merger has been consummated. For that reason, I differ with the Court in its assessment of the weight to be accorded post-acquisition evidence. That evidence is the best evidence available to determine whether the merger will distort market forces in the dehydrated onion and garlic industry. The Court of Appeals, in my view,

---

[1] Indeed, by the time of the Commission's decision an additional firm, Gilroy Foods, Inc., had entered this market.

was not wrong because it "gave too much weight" to the post-acquisition evidence. It erred because of the gloss it placed on the statistics and testimony adduced before the hearing examiner and the Commission. . . .

Allis-Chalmers Manufacturing Company v. White Consolidated Industries, Inc.

414 F.2d 506 (3d Cir. 1969), cert. denied, 396 U.S. 1009 (1970)

OPINION OF THE COURT

STAHL, Circuit Judge.

This appeal by Allis-Chalmers Manufacturing Company, appellant . . . is from an order of the district court denying Allis-Chalmers' application for preliminary relief against allegedly threatened violations of the antitrust laws.

In December 1968, White Consolidated Industries, Inc., appellee, "a diversified manufacturer, specializing in a wide variety of machinery and equipment, household appliances, and industrial supplies," 294 F.Supp. at 1265, purchased 31.2% of the outstanding stock of Allis-Chalmers from Gulf and Western Industries. The avowed purpose underlying White's stock purchase is the acquisition of Allis-Chalmers, and to that end White proposes to make a tender offer to Allis-Chalmers stockholders in order to increase substantially its share of ownership.

I. *Proceedings in District Court*

Alleging that White's acquisition of a substantial part of its stock and the proposed acquisition of additional stock constitute a violation of §7 of the Clayton Act, . . . appellant Allis-Chalmers instituted the present action seeking a preliminary injunction to restrain White from acquiring any additional stock and from exercising its present share of ownership in any manner that would accomplish its takeover purpose. . . .

On the basis of affidavits, exhibits and legal arguments advanced by counsel, the district court concluded that appellant Allis-Chalmers had failed to demonstrate a reasonable probability of success on a final trial of the antitrust issues and hence denied preliminary injunctive relief.

For the reasons hereafter set forth, I believe a preliminary injunction should have been granted.

. . . . .

c. Status of the Parties. Allis-Chalmers is a large manufacturing company with annual sales of $821,000,000 during 1967. With 18 plants and more than 30,000 employees, Allis is a major manufacturer of diverse capital goods and equipment for numerous industries, and is also a major manufacturer of construction and agricultural machinery and electrical generation, transmission, distribution and utilization equipment.

White is also a highly diversified manufacturer, with total sales of approximately $825,000,000 in 1968. White's tremendous growth in recent years has resulted in large part from a series of acquisitions,[1] one of the most recent being the 1968 acquisition of Blaw-Knox Company. Blaw-Knox is a major producer of foundry and mill machinery products, finishing and processing lines for the steel and non-ferrous metal industries, steel castings, material handling equipment and construction equipment. In addition, a significant part of Blaw-Knox's net sales are derived from the design and construction of chemical plants. Blaw-Knox's sales volume approximates $200,000,000 per year.

Allis-Chalmers alleges that its acquisition by White would have unlawful anticompetitive effects in some 20 separate lines of commerce. While the proposed acquisition might best be characterized as a conglomerate one, Allis maintains that there are also economically significant and adverse horizontal and vertical effects. (The proposed combination here has some of the attributes of what Professor Turner has called a "mixed conglomerate,"—"the acquisition of a company manufacturing a different product which is nevertheless related to a product or products of the acquiring firm because it can be produced with much the same facilities, sold through the same distribution channels, or made a part of the same research and development efforts." Turner, Conglomerate Mergers and Section 7 of the Clayton Act, 78 Harv. L. Rev. 1313, 1315 (1965))....

II.　*Reversal by This Court*

On the question of whether there has been a showing of reasonable probability of success on final trial of the §7 issue, I am compelled to disagree with the district court....

Product Extension.　As previously noted, Blaw-Knox is one of the major manufacturers of metal rolling mills. The record indicates that the manufacture of such mills is a distinct line of commerce and that the industry is a highly concentrated one. According to Allis the four major manufacturers of rolling mill machinery account for more than 80% of the market, Blaw-Knox being the third largest supplier of such mills, with a market share of approximating 20%.

The electrical drives and controls which run rolling mills represent a significant part of the cost of a completed mill, comprising approximately one-third of the cost of a fully-installed mill. Other equipment and machinery in·the mill account for another third of the total cost, the remaining

---

[1] ... Originally a manufacturer and seller of sewing machines, since 1950 White has expanded and diversified through 32 acquisitions to its present rank as approximately 100th among the nation's largest industrial corporations. Its major acquisitions were made between 1965, when its annual sales were still only $54.7 million, and 1968, when its annual sales reached $825 million....

third going for design, construction and buildings. Industry-wide shipments of rolling mill equipment and machinery, including electrical components, exceed $300,000,000 annually.

The major mill manufacturers do not manufacture the electrical drive and control systems which form an integral part of the mill. The industry practice is for the mill purchaser to acquire the control components separately or through the mill manufacturer, with the latter acting as the purchaser's agent. The major suppliers of the electrical control systems are General Electric, Westinghouse and Allis-Chalmers, and those three companies account for approximately 90% of the electrical equipment supplied for metal rolling mills. In terms of percentage figures, General Electric and Westinghouse account for over 80% of the sales, with Allis-Chalmers a distant third.

While the two leaders are presently Blaw-Knox's primary suppliers of electric drives for its rolling mills, over the past five years Allis has supplied approximately a half million dollars worth of such equipment to Blaw-Knox annually. . . .

In addition to its major position in the rolling mill industry, Blaw-Knox also utilizes its significant engineering construction capability for designing and building complete industrial plants.

The probable anticompetitive effects of an Allis-Chalmers-Blaw-Knox (i.e., White) combination are significant. Blaw-Knox's design and construction capabilities and its position as a leading manufacturer of rolling mills, when coupled with Allis' position as the third largest supplier of the electrical drive components for such mills, would result in Blaw-Knox becoming the only company capable of designing, producing and installing a complete metal rolling mill. The emergence of a company offering such a complete product would raise higher the already significant barriers to the entry of others into the various segments of the metal rolling mill market. . . . The potential entrenchment of the market power of a merged Allis-Chalmers-White industrial complex as a "full-line manufacturer" in the field of metal rolling mill machinery is an example of "product extension" consequences which may be anticompetitive and violative of Section 7, as held in *FTC v. Procter & Gamble Co.*, 386 U.S. 568. . . .

Reciprocity. The major purchasers of rolling mills are steel companies. In the past few years Allis-Chalmers has purchased an average of $30,000,000 worth of steel annually from the ten steel companies which are Blaw-Knox's principal customers for its rolling mills. . . . Allis' total annual purchases of steel mill products appear to be approximately $44,000,000. When coupled with White's annual purchases of steel mill products, about $42,000,000 in value, a White-Allis combination would buy a far larger amount of steel than any of Blaw-Knox's competitors in the rolling mill market. The danger to competition inherent to that market situation is not difficult to perceive.

An acquisition which creates a market structure conducive to reciprocal dealing presents the acquiring company with an advantage over competitors, an advantage which by its very nature is anticompetitive. . . . And the reciprocal trading made possible by such an acquisition need not ensue "from bludgeoning or coercion." [*FTC* v. *Consolidated Foods Corp.*, 380 U.S. at 594.] . . .

The tremendous purchasing power of a White-Allis combine, coupled with Blaw-Knox's enhanced position in the rolling mill market, may foreclose White's competitors in the sale of rolling mill machinery to the steel industry.

Market Share. We must not forget that the Clayton Act comes into play where the effect of an acquisition "*may be* substantially to lessen competition, . . ." (emphasis added; . . .). As the Supreme Court has said, the concern of Congress was with *probabilities*, not certainties. *Brown Shoe Co.* v. *United States*, 370 U.S. 294, 323. . . .

I do not mean to imply that §7 prohibits diversification per se. But at this date there can be no doubt that §7 was designed to arrest the rising tide of economic concentration and to curb, in its incipiency, a lessening of competition made probable by the possession of market power acquired via corporate acquisitions within the scope of §7. . . .

I have not dealt expressly with the matter if each party's share of the market in the lines of commerce under consideration as I do not believe the question of market shares is dispositive in the present preliminary stage of the proceedings, particularly in a conglomerate merger situation. In Turner, Conglomerate Mergers and Section 7 of the Clayton Act, 78 Harv. L. Rev. 1313, 1315–1316 (1965), the author has stated:

> . . . The rules developed for determining the validity of horizontal and vertical mergers clearly will not do for conglomerate acquisitions generally. In the familiar types of horizontal and vertical merger cases, the Supreme Court has come to place important if not decisive weight on the share of the relevant markers controlled by the acquiring and acquired company. . . . But whatever significance can be attached to market shares in these cases, quite clearly the significance becomes less with conglomerate mergers, and indeed may completely vanish. . . .

. . . . .

My concern here is primarily with the anticompetitive effects made probable by the entrenchment of already significant market power. The metal rolling mill and some of the other product markets involved in this case appear to be oligopolistic in structure, with either White or Allis being one of a small number of sellers who account for a significant share of the market. In light of such market structures, I think it proper to be less concerned, e.g., with the asserted small percentage of total steel purchases, nationwide, which a White-Allis combine would account for than with a comparison of the dollar volume of steel purchases by such a combine vis-a-vis the dollar volume of steel purchases by White's competitors in the manufacture and sale of rolling mills. . . .

IV. *Department of Justice Guidelines*

In presenting its case concerning the probable anticompetitive effects of a White takeover, Allis-Chalmers has relied upon and sought support from the Justice Department's 1968 Merger Guidelines . . . and has argued that a White-Allis combination is clearly violative of the portions of the guidelines dealing with mergers involving potential entrants, mergers creating a danger of reciprocal buying and mergers which entrench market power. I recognize that the primary purpose of the guidelines is to indicate the standards being applied by the Department of Justice in determining whether to challenge corporate acquisitions and mergers under §7, (subject to reevaluation of the standards by the present head of the Department's Antitrust Division. . . .), and that the standards do not purport to be a concise statement of the present status of the law which the courts are bound to follow. But because the Justice Department is obviously one of the principal government agencies charged with the duty of enforcing the antitrust laws, I think its position is entitled to some consideration, particularly when elements of the Guidelines find support in the developing case law. . . .

In light of the clear purpose of §7 to preserve and promote meaningful competition, and because the structure of a particular market has a significant effect on competition in that market, the department's merger policy focuses chiefly upon market structure. In dealing with conglomerate mergers, the Justice Department regards mergers involving potential entrants and mergers creating a significant danger of reciprocal buying as having sufficiently identifiable anticompetitive effects as to be the subject of relatively specific structural guides. The Guidelines are also concerned with conglomerate mergers involving acquisitions of a leading firm in a relatively concentrated or rapidly concentrating market where the acquisition may serve to entrench or increase the market power of that firm or raise barriers to entry in the firm's market. . . .

Basically, what is at stake in the instant appeal is the life or death of Allis, a viable independent company, eager to continue as such, pitted against White, an aggressive, fast-moving acquirer of many diverse businesses, particularly in the past few years. White's motives may be of the highest as designed to promote one concept of the American free enterprise system, but I am of the firm view that the proposed takeover is very likely to have anticompetitive effects in violation of §7 of the Clayton Act. To deny preliminary relief could very well mean the end of the road for appellant as an independent economic entity.

In summary the proposed acquisition of Allis by White poses the probability of a violation of the antitrust laws because the acquisition threatens to:

(a) eliminate potential competition in the metal rolling mill industry and other relevant markets;

(b) diminish potential independent competition in other diversified markets; and

(c) enhance the power of a White-Allis combination to engage in reciprocal dealing.[2]

. . . . .

The order of the district court denying a preliminary injunction will be reversed and the case will be remanded to the district court for further proceedings consistent with this opinion.

[SEITZ, Circuit Judge, concurred.]

ALDISERT, Circuit Judge (dissenting).

I must respectfully dissent from the action taken by the majority. . . .

One question of law will turn this case: whether there was a showing by Allis-Chalmers of a reasonable probability of success on final hearing. The trial judge found that plaintiff had not met its burden; the majority would reverse, and say that the burden was met. . . .

In concert, the majority suggests that there is a distinct anti-competitive danger of unlawful reciprocal dealing in the rolling mill-steel industries. My brother Stahl finds an equally anti-competitive effect on the potential entry of Allis-Chalmers into the metal rolling mill market and the potential product extension ramifications of White's acquisition of Allis' present capabilities in the field of rolling mill electrical components.

I disagree. . . .

I. *Elimination of Potential Competition*

In the many points of disagreement between appellant and appellee in the proceedings below, there was one matter about which there was no dispute: it was agreed that Allis could not make out a case of actual competition between the merging companies. Instead, it had to proceed on a theory of "potential competition," a newly emerging theory which in recent times has been embraced by the courts as a legitimate concern in antitrust considerations.[3]

---

[2] While each case, of course, must stand on its own feet, we should not be oblivious to the current trends in our economy and to the possible impact of this case on the movement toward further economic concentration by merger. . . .

[3] See Davidow, "Conglomerate Concentration and Section Seven: The Limitations of the Anti-Merger Act," 68 *Colum. L. Rev.* 1231, 1241–49 (1968).

Potential, as distinguished from actual, competition must manifest itself in precise forms to come within the scrutiny of those who would enforce the spirit of the Clayton Act. . . .

It becomes obvious therefore that the literal meaning of the word "potential" is not to be applied to the doctrine of potential competition in anti-trust law. He who would urge a case based on this doctrine must perforce prove more than a naked possibility of competition, or that a possible entrant into a market is capable of developing into an actual competitor. It would seem that to forestall a merger because the proposed combination would eliminate potential competition in the anti-trust sense, it is necessary to show first, a market so concentrated that potential competition provides one of the few checks on oligopolistic pricing and then: (1) that the acquired firm must be a significant factor in that market; and (2) one of the firms, in terms of its objective capabilities must appear to be a likely competitor of the other at some time in the future; or (3) as suggested by some commentators, the potential entrant must appear to be preeminent among the possible likely entrants, or that there are very few others in a similar position.[4]

It is only with these principles in mind that we may appropriately examine the theory of the potential entry of Allis-Chalmers into a new market, potential product extension and potential reciprocity consequences.

This has been done in the discussion hereinafter set forth at length. And having done so, there is no basic area where I find myself in agreement with my brothers. I find the theories advanced on potential entry, product extension, and reciprocity to be devoid of precedental support or endorsement by any recognized commentator. Indeed, I view this approach to be an uncharted excursion into a sensitive area of the American economic community, embracing a truly radical concept of the doctrine of potential competition in antitrust law; a theory which seems to hold that so long as there exists a mere possibility of entry in a market, or a mere possibility of product extension, or a mere possibility of reciprocity, then the proposed merger must be enjoined. I cannot accept this hypothesis; nor, as previously observed, has any previous court decision or commentator suggested it. . . .

---

[4] Davidow, 68 *Colum. L. Rev.* at 1244. This standard was suggested by Donald F. Turner, former head of the Justice Department's Antitrust Division. See Turner, "Conglomerate Mergers and Section 7 of the Clayton Act," 78 *Harv. L. Rev.* 1313, 1363 (1965). It is to be noted that the instant case is atypical in that the alleged potential entrant is not the acquiring company, as in the usual case, but the acquired company. This presents a more difficult burden of proof problem: the motivation to prove a future intention to enter and thereby block the merger via the anti-trust laws becomes obvious. Because of this, it is of even greater importance that the alleged potential entrant be judged in terms of its *objective capabilities* as suggested by Mr. Davidow. It is one thing for Allis-Chalmers to allege its intention to enter any of a given number of market areas presently occupied by White or one of its subsidiaries, in order to prevent the takeover, but it is quite another to present objective evidence of this intention, and to demonstrate the capability to do so.

II. *Reciprocity*

Although I agree with the majority's statement of the law governing anti-competitive effects of reciprocity. I find the present record devoid of sufficient facts to support a preliminary injunction of the White-Allis acquisition.

From the barest of facts, the majority have conjured vivid overtones of reciprocity in the rolling mill-steel industries. The only statistic capable of being gleaned from the record is that Allis-Chalmers purchases approximately $30,000,000 of steel annually. To this my brother Stahl adds a figure, not in the record below, of the annual steel purchase of Blaw-Knox; and then a conclusion is proffered, without factual support, that "A White-Allis combination would buy a far larger amount of steel than any of Blaw-Knox's competitors in the rolling mill market."

Even if this were true, which, I emphasize, cannot be determined on the present state of the record, I fail to see how a conclusion of anti-competitive reciprocity follows. Nearly every acquisition has, to some extent, elements of reciprocity. This is especially true where, as here, the industries involved are consumers of the basic component steel.

But the vice of reciprocity, *i.e.*, the ability to transform substantial buying power into a weapon against competitors less favorably situated, can only be determined in the context of the market involved. Otherwise, all that is portrayed is the "potential for reciprocity." Cf. [*FTC* v.] *Consolidated Foods* [Corp., 380 U.S. 592 (1965)]. . . .

The trial record on this point is anything but clear and convincing; it suffers from factual anemia and an examination discloses that it is symptomatic of only a bare suspicion of possible reciprocity. As the Supreme Court has stated, we are concerned with "probabilities, not certainties." The test is exactly that: probabilities of reciprocity, not possibilities. . . .

III. *Potential Entry Into the Rolling Mill Market*

Based on its review of the evidence, the district court determined:

. . . Aside from the fact that Allis-Chalmers now manufacturers and constructs paper-making machinery, . . . there is nothing in the record to confirm that Allis-Chalmers has the technological capacity to enter this market. Nor is there evidence to confirm financial capacity to enter, the ability of the market to support an additional competitor, or Allis-Chalmers' serious consideration of entry. Finally, the record does not indicate that Allis-Chalmers, by the nature of its present business, stands close enough to the edge of the metal rolling market to exert a competitive influence on others in that industry.

My brother Stahl concludes, however, that "further inquiry into Allis' status as a potential entrant into this industry" is warranted. The form of this further inquiry is a discussion of what is described as an "uncontroverted affidavit [that] Allis manufactured components and sub-assemblies for *complete* metal rolling mills." An examination of this affidavit, however, reveals only "some information concerning components and subassemblies." And an examination of the source cited in the affidavit, Exhibit QQ, demonstrates that the supportive data itself contradicts the opinion expressed in the affidavit. . . .

IV. *Product Extension*

Stripped of explanatory materials, my brother Stahl's analysis of "product extension" and "entrenchment" is nothing more than a conclusion that a mere possibility of product extension will probably generate anti-competitive effects outlawed by §7 of the Clayton Act. It becomes necessary to put this problem in its proper perspective. In the context of anti-trust considerations, product extension is not . . . a factor which has significance in and of itself. It assumes importance only when, by reason of the conduct of the acquired or acquiring party, there occurs such a shift in market power as to produce anti-competitive effects. The law usually is not concerned with ordinary transfers of market power. It is only when the transfer occurs in a market structure so concentrated as to pose a serious threat of creating or enhancing a present monopolistic or oligopolistic market position that it becomes circumspect; and it becomes so because of the probability that competition could be substantially lessened.

Product extension becomes important in the context of anti-trust considerations only when it becomes a means whereby the proposed merger might enhance market power to the point where it becomes "entrenched." It is not difficult to predict the probable anti-competitive effect of a take-over by a larger firm of a smaller firm whose product is in a market already concentrated or oligopolistic. Such a merger could increase the existing concentration in the market of the acquired firm by strengthening the position of the smaller, acquired firm. Thus, the typical entrenchment case arises in an acquisition of a dominant firm in a relatively small industry by a much larger firm. The market position of the smaller firm may become "entrenched" through predatory pricing, so-called "deep pocket practices" of the parent,[5] through various promotional advantages not available to the smaller competitors in the market of the acquired company, or because of the advantage gained through "product extension"— *i.e.*, the ability of the combined companies "to offer a complete line of equipment to its consumers and to further enhance its position and dominance in the market. . . ."[6]

[5] *Reynolds Metal Co.* v. *F.T.C.*, 309 F.2d, . . . at p. 229. The essence of this theory is a presumption that the "rich parent" has the financial wherewithal to sell at prices approximating cost or below, and thus to "undercut and ravage the less affluent competition." Again, this argument obviously has much more forcefulness if the acquiring company fulfills the "rich parent" characterization.

[6] The best example is probably our own case of *United States* v. *Ingersoll-Rand*, 320 F.2d 509, 524 (3 Cir. 1963).

In the case at bar we do not have the typical case of a smaller dominant company being acquired by a larger outside company. The record indicates variously that Blaw-Knox controls between 11 and 20 per cent of the metal rolling mills market. Allis-Chalmers, the acquired company, has none of this market. It is not in the metal rolling mill business. Although it does supply electrical equipment to this market, it is not even a prominent supplier. Suppliers of electrical equipment, with their respective shares of the market, are: General Electric, 45%; Westinghouse, 40%; Allis-Chalmers, 6%; Reliance Electric, 5%; Cuttler-Hammer, 3%; and Clark Controller (A. O. Smith), 1%....

Nonetheless, the conclusion is proffered that in the area of product extension, "the probable anti-competitive effects of an Allis-Chalmers-Blaw-Knox (i.e., White) combination are significant." This conclusion is based substantially on the interpretation and application of three decisions: *FTC* v. *Procter & Gamble Co.*, 386 U.S. 568 ... (1967); *General Foods Corp.* v. *FTC*, 386 F.2d 936 (3 Cir. 1967), cert. den. 391 U.S. 919 ... (1968), and *United States* v. *Wilson Sporting Goods Co.*, 288 F.Supp. 543 (N.D. Ill. 1968)....

I do not consider the facts in *Clorox, General Foods* or *Wilson Sporting* comparable to the case at bar. In all of these cases, the corporations involved, both the acquiring firm and the acquired, were dominant in their respective industries....

In contrast to the giants represented in these cases, the present appeal involves midgets. If Blaw-Knox controls between 11 to 20 per cent of the rolling mill market, it is by no means the industry's dominant figure. Allis-Chalmers has none of it. And even if we are to consider Allis' share of the market for electrical equipment for rolling mills, its share is only 6 per cent, a feeble percentage when compared to the 45 per cent and 40 per cent share commanded by General Electric and Westinghouse. Nevertheless, from these meager facts, the majority conclude that the probable "anti-competitive effects . . . are significant."

Upon this emaciated skeleton of facts, the cloak of anti-competitive effects just does not fit. There is no takeover by a larger firm of a smaller one whose product is in a market already oligopolistic; there is no evidence that the market position of the combined firm may become entrenched by predatory pricing or promotional advantages not available to other competitors of the acquired company....

V. *The Significance of Market Share and Concentration Data*

. . . . .

Conceding that the same quantum of proof was not required at the preliminary injunction stage as would be at the trial on the merits, I suggest that the appellant was obliged to present at least some evidence of relevant facts, figures and statistics describing the affected markets and the shares of these markets commanded by the companies involved. . . .

. . . [Instead,] [l]acking adequate factual support for its thesis of anti-competitive oligopoly, Allis-Chalmers attempted to bottom its case upon a theory of economics, asserting this hypothesis: because White Consolidated is a large corporate conglomerate, its size, without more, will produce anti-competitive effects in affected markets.

This hypothesis is nothing more than a restatement of a "Brandeisian bias in favor of human sized institutions," a nostalgic attempt to equate bigness with badness. But Congress has not written this theory into its anti-trust legislation; nor should any court attempt to legislate such a doctrine into it. So long as the legislative proscription of anti-trust activities turns on factors beyond the mere "possibilities" of anti-competitive effects, the courts must be diligent not to substitute the Brandeisian bias for sound analysis.

The characterization of a company as a "large conglomerate" should not impose a presumption of anti-competitive guilt. Section 7 of the Clayton Act nowhere so provides. It is the company's activities—not its form and size—which the Congress has sought to regulate. And judicial enforcement of this regulation should only be had upon a factual determination that the activity "may be substantially to lessen competition, or to tend to create a monopoly." 15 U.S.C.A. §18. . . .

But one other aspect of the majority's action causes me no little concern. . . . [S]ome of the language expressed by my brother Stahl is so sweeping and conclusatory that I fear little remains for an objective determination of the basic issues at the trial still to be had. . . . This is amply demonstrated by the following statement contained in the majority opinion:

Basically, what is at stake in the instant appeal is the life or death of Allis, a viable independent company eager to continue as such, pitted against White, an aggressive, fast-moving acquirer of many diverse businesses, particularly in the past few years.

First, I question the validity of this conclusion, reached without a trial, that Allis-Chalmers cannot survive as an ongoing business if acquired by White. Moreover, I reject the assumption underlying this statement that the judicial branch has been entrusted with the task of policing the economy, preserving the "viability" of the corporate structure. Such a role cannot be justified within the framework of existing anti-trust legislation. It is only where the "life or death" of a corporate entity has anti-competitive effects that judicial intervention is proper.

The district court concluded that Allis-Chalmers failed to establish a probability of anti-competitive effects. On the basis of the law and the evidence, I do not find that conclusion clearly erroneous.

I would affirm the judgment of the lower court for the reasons set forth in the opinion of the learned trial judge.

Accordingly, I dissent.

United States v. International Telephone and Telegraph Corporation

324 F.Supp. 19 (D. Conn. 1970)

MEMORANDUM OF DECISION AFTER TRIAL ON THE MERITS[1]

TIMBERS, Chief Judge:

QUESTION PRESENTED

In this action brought by the United States (government), . . . to enjoin the acquisition by International Telephone and Telegraph Corporation (ITT) of the stock of Grinnell Corporation (Grinnell) as an alleged violation of Section 7 of the Clayton Act, . . . the essential question for determination by the Court after trial on the merits is whether, upon the entire record, the government has sustained its burden of establishing that "in any line of commerce in any section of the country, the effect of such acquisition may be substantially to lessen competition."

For the reasons stated below, the Court holds that the government has not sustained its burden upon the essential issue set forth above. Defendant accordingly is entitled to judgment dismissing the complaint. . . .

. . . [ITT] employs approximately 353,000 persons; during 1969, it had consolidated sales and revenues of slightly less than $5,500,000,000, consolidated net income of $234,000,000 and consolidated assets of approximately $5,200,000,000, at the end of that year; it is the ninth largest industrial corporation in the United States according to Fortune Magazine; approximately 40%–45% of its consolidated sales and revenues and income are from operations outside the United States and Canada; during the period 1955 through 1969, its total consolidated sales and revenues increased from $448,000,000 to almost $5,500,000,000; during the decade 1960–1969, it acquired 85 domestic corporations; and at the end of 1969, it had in excess of 200 subsidiaries worldwide engaged in a wide variety of enterprises. . . .

I

CLAIM THAT GRINNELL IS THE DOMINANT
COMPETITOR IN CERTAIN LINES OF COMMERCE
AND IN CERTAIN SECTIONS OF THE COUNTRY

The law is well settled that when a company which is the dominant competitor in a relatively oligopolistic market is acquired by a much larger company, such acquisition violates Section 7 of the Clayton Act

---

[1] In an earlier opinion the Court had denied the government's motion for a preliminary injunction to enjoin the proposed acquisition, but had ordered ITT to maintain Grinnell "as a separate and viable company pending final decision in this case." *United States* v. *International Telephone and Telegraph Corporation,* 306 F.Suppl. 766 (D. Conn. 1969). The instant opinion consisted of 62 mimeographed pages and 270 footnotes. IMS.

if the acquired company gains marketing and promotional competitive advantages from the merger which will further entrench its position of dominance by raising barriers to entry to the relevant markets and by discouraging smaller competitors from aggressively competing. The effect of such a merger will be substantially to lessen competition. . . .

The Court turns directly, therefore, to the question whether the evidence establishes that Grinnell is the dominant competitor in the relevant product and geographic markets, i.e., "in any line of commerce in any section of the country."

A. *Lines of Commerce*

For the purpose of determining whether Grinnell is the dominant competitor in the lines of commerce here involved, the Court finds that the following are the relevant product markets or lines of commerce:

(1) *Automatic Sprinkler Devices* . . . , the component parts necessary to construct automatic sprinkler systems . . . . (2) *Automatic Sprinkler Systems* . . . complete installations . . . composed of pipe, pipe fittings, pipe hangers, valves and sprinkler devices. (3) *Power Piping* . . . used in utility power generating plants and in segments of the process industries . . . . (4) Pipe Hangers . . . support devices from which piping is suspended. . . .

B. *Sections of the Country*

(1) *Entire United States: For All Lines of Commerce.* There is no dispute between the parties that the relevant geographic market for each line of commerce is the national market. The entire United States therefore is the "section of the country" within which the effects of ITT's acquisition of Grinnell upon the relevant lines of commerce are to be measured.

(2) *Regional Areas: For Installation of Automatic Sprinkler Systems.* The government further claims that, with respect to the installation of automatic sprinkler systems, there are four regional areas, each of which should be regarded as a "section of the country" for the purpose of measuring the impact of this acquisition upon competition in the installation of automatic sprinkler systems. . . .

[Judge Timbers then indicated his agreement that New England, the State of Utah and the Pacific Northwest constituted relevant markets for purposes of this case. However, he declined to accept the government's contention that an area designated as "the Inland Empire" (the Pacific Northwest minus Alaska, Oregon and that part of Washington west of the Cascade Mountains) should be so considered, on the grounds that the evidence did not show it to be "an area of effective competition." Based upon these findings he ultimately concluded that in none of the separate markets defined above was Grinnell a "dominant" competitor within the meaning of Section 7 of the Clayton Act.]

II

CLAIM THAT MERGER WILL CONFER
MARKETING AND PROMOTIONAL COMPETITIVE
ADVANTAGES UPON GRINNELL

[REGARDING AUTOMATIC SPRINKLER DEVICES
AND AUTOMATIC SPRINKLER SYSTEMS MARKETS]

The Court having concluded, upon the entire record, that the evidence does not support the government's claim that Grinnell is the dominant competitor in any of the relevant markets, that should end the case. A bolder Court would enter judgment for defendant and proceed no further.

In view of the likelihood of appellate review and having regard for the enormous expenditure of time and effort on the part of all concerned with respect to the remaining issues in the case, it does appear prudent for the Court to decide such issues and to make appropriate findings and conclusions thereon.

Before doing so, however, the Court believes that it would be remiss if it did not state unequivocally that, in its opinion, this is not even a close case on the issue of Grinnell's dominance. It is not merely a case where the government has failed to sustain its burden of proof on that issue; it is a case where the overwhelming preponderance of the credible evidence clearly establishes that Grinnell is *not* the dominant competitor in *any* relevant market. . . .

Despite that conviction, however, the Court will assume arguendo in this section of the opinion that Grinnell is a dominant competitor in the automatic sprinkler devices and installation markets, and will proceed to consider the government's claim that Grinnell as such will gain marketing and promotional competitive advantages from the merger in the following specific respects:[2]

    A. Package or System Selling
    B. Affiliation with Hartford
    C. Access to ITT's Financial Resources and Advertising
    D. Foreign Expansion
    E. Vertical Foreclosure
    F. Central Stations
    G. Reciprocal Dealing

A. *Package or System Selling*

The government claims that the merger will give Grinnell a competitive marketing advantage by creating an opportunity for Grinnell to include additional products in its automatic sprinkler line and to engage in pack-

---

[2] The government does not contend that any *one* of these marketing and promotional competitive advantages will result in a substantial lessening of competition; it contends that their cumulative effect will have anticompetitive consequences. . . .

age or system selling. In short, the government contends that this is a mixed or product extension conglomerate merger. . . .

It is undisputed that Grinnell has not in fact engaged in package or system selling during the period of more than a year since the merger was consummated. Nor does the government claim to have adduced evidence that this competitive practice is planned or that it is imminent. . . .

The government's primary claim at trial was that a single mechanical contracting company bidding sprinkler work together with plumbing, heating and air conditioning installations would have an advantage over a specialized sprinkler contractor bidding sprinkler work only. . . .

An understanding of the specialized character of sprinkler installation work is necessary properly to evaluate the government's claim in this respect. The majority of significant sprinkler companies throughout the country specialize in sprinkler work only, and do not engage in plumbing, heating or air conditioning work. Most sprinkler work is awarded on the basis of bids that are confined to sprinkler installations. Most general contractors invite and receive separate sprinkler bids, rather than requiring that sprinkler work be bid to mechanical contractors for inclusion in a package bid. Such preference as general contractors may have for dealing with mechanical contractors able to offer a package including sprinklers stems from a desire for installation coordination—a preference which does not require a sprinkler contractor to be a mechanical contractor as well in order to avail himself of it. The advantage, therefore, to a mechanical contractor of being engaged in the sprinkler business, is of doubtful significance, if any. Accordingly, even if there were evidence (and there is none) that ITT or Grinnell as a result of the merger were to engage in mechanical contracting work, the Court would be unable to find that Grinnell thereby would gain a substantial competitive advantage in its sprinkler business.

A further radiation of the government's package or system selling claim at trial was that Grinnell would be able to offer to mechanical contractors or others a package consisting of an *installed* sprinkler system together with *uninstalled* plumbing, heating and air conditioning products, having in mind that other ITT companies manufacture such products. The Court finds the government's claim that Grinnell would gain an advantage over its competitors from such a package to be wholly unsupported by the evidence. Prior to its acquisition by ITT, Grinnell sold hundreds of products to the construction industry but never packaged them with sprinklers —a course it was not inhibited from pursuing had it been thought to be advantageous. No witness at trial, including some with experience in both mechanical contracting and sprinkler installation, testified that he would be interested in or concerned about such a package. Such witnesses did make it clear that packaging requires products with a functional relationship to one another. Mechanical contractors would have no interest in purchasing such a package; nor would the ability of ITT–Grinnell to offer such a package (assuming evidence not adduced) give them any competitive concern. . . . Grinnell's sprinkler device manufacturer competitors have seen no advantage in packaging with sprinklers other products they manufacture. An experienced manufacturer of mechanical hardware believes such a package would not be feasible to offer.

In short, the government has failed to show that there is any likelihood that there will be a "significant integration in the production, distribution or marketing" of automatic sprinkler systems with other ITT companies. *General Foods Corp. v. FTC, supra,* at 944. . . .

The Court holds that the government has not sustained its burden of establishing that Grinnell will gain any competitive advantage from the merger in the form of opportunities for package or system selling.

B. *Affiliation with Hartford*

The government also claims that Grinnell will gain competitive marketing advantages from the ITT–Grinnell merger through its affiliation with Hartford . . . by receiving leads for sprinkler business from Hartford and from Hartford agents, and by becoming the beneficiary of recommendations to potential sprinkler customers from such sources. . . .

The consensus of those witnesses who testified on the subject of insurance leads, and particularly those who struck the Court as being worthy of belief, was that insurance leads and recommendations actually play an insignificant role in the sprinkler industry. Such leads usually relate to existing buildings rather than to new structures; and sprinkler work on existing buildings is a minor part of sprinkler contracting, believed by sprinkler contractors to be relatively undesirable work.

The significance of insurance leads furthermore must be evaluated in light of the highly competitive nature of the sprinkler business; and that applies to sprinkler work originating from insurance sources. Sprinkler contracts are awarded for the most part on the basis of competitive bids. Recommendations of an insurance company or its agents accordingly have little or no effect. The controlling factor is the bid rather than a recommendation. . . .

In the light of the foregoing evidence with respect to the relationship generally in the industry between insurance leads and sprinkler work, the Court turns to the evidence specifically regarding Hartford and Grinnell in connection with this marketing practice. All of Hartford's fire insurance is written through some 13,228 independent agents and 942 brokers. They typically act for a number of different insurance companies. Characteristically they value their independence and they want their clients to understand that they are acting in their clients' best interests. Despite the availability of some 14,170 Hartford agents and brokers, the government was not able to adduce testimony from any of them to the effect that they would favor Grinnell as a result of its affiliation with Hartford. Nor was there any evidence that any Hartford agent or broker had reason to believe he would be favored by Hartford in return for his favoring Grinnell; and there was evidence just to the contrary.

Some indication of the actual effect of an affiliation between a property and casualty insurance company and a large manufacturer of automatic sprinkler devices may be gleaned from the results of the acquisition of Star Sprinkler Corporation by the INA Corporation in 1968. . . .

The chief executive of Star testified that when Star became affiliated with INA he decided that it would not be in the best interests of Star to draw upon its relationship with INA to promote the sale of Star sprinklers or otherwise to rely upon the identification of Star with INA. This is substantially the same view held by the head of Grinnell's sprinkler operations, namely, that if Grinnell were to receive favored treatment from Hartford this would result in a negative reaction from the rest of the insurance industry, to Grinnell's detriment.

This leads to the evidence which strikes the Court as having the most probative force of all upon the issue of whether Grinnell will gain a substantial competitive advantage from its affiliation with Hartford, namely, that it simply would not be in Grinnell's business interests to attempt to exploit in any way its relationship with Hartford. In short, the evidence overwhelmingly demonstrates that Grinnell would stand to lose far more than it could gain from any exploitation of the Hartford affiliation.

The evidence on this is concise but convincing. While Hartford is a large insurance company, its total share of the domestic fire insurance market is only 4.4% and its total share of the sprinklered risk market is approximately 2.4%. . . . The evidence shows that too close an alliance between Hartford and Grinnell would cause other insurance interests to be less friendly with Grinnell and less inclined to furnish leads to, or to make recommendations of, Grinnell; testimony by witnesses called by both sides established beyond any question that the result of any such relationship would be to deter non-Hartford agents from recommending Grinnell sprinklers, although under other circumstances they might have made such a recommendation.

. . . Nor does the record even remotely support the government's claim that the ITT–Hartford merger may spark other insurance-sprinkler combinations and foster a trend toward concentration; and much less does the record support the government's claim that such a supposititious trend would tend to lessen competition in the sprinkler industry.

The Court holds that the government has not sustained its burden of proving that Grinnell will gain competitive marketing advantages from the ITT–Grinnell merger through its affiliation with Hartford.

C. *Access to ITT's Financial Resources and Advertising*

The government further claims that Grinnell will gain a competitive marketing advantage through access to ITT's financial resources and comprehensive advertising program; more particularly, it is claimed that through ITT's finance companies Grinnell will be able to finance the purchase and leasing of sprinkler systems on a larger scale than it now does, and that through access to ITT's advertising expertise and experience Grinnell will be able to expand its advertising and sales promotion programs.

The question naturally arises, in light of this claim, whether Grinnell *needs* such financing and advertising help. The answer provided by the trial record in this case is unequivocally in the negative. . . .

With respect to advertising, the Court finds that it simply is not a significant factor in the sprinkler industry. Witnesses from various sprinkler companies, including Grinnell, testified that advertising is unimportant in the award of sprinkler work; that it is not worthwhile; and, even if they were in a position to invest more in advertising, that they would not do so. . . .

Upon this record the Court finds that Grinnell's access to ITT's financial resources and more comprehensive advertising program cannot be viewed realistically as a competitive advantage since Grinnell is fully capable itself of providing financing, leasing and advertising to the extent business judgment dictates, even absent the ITT–Grinnell merger. . . .

The Court holds that the government has not sustained its burden of proving that the merger will confer upon Grinnell a competitive marketing advantage through access to ITT's financial resources and advertising program.

D.   *Foreign Expansion*

The government also claims that the ITT–Grinnell merger will give Grinnell a competitive advantage in the form of ITT assistance to Grinnell in its overseas expansion, thus leading to foreclosure of Grinnell's competitors from foreign markets and, since profits earned abroad may be used to compete domestically, further resulting in lessening of competition in the domestic market.

The record clearly shows that prior to the merger Grinnell had already expanded into Europe; and that it had done so without the type of assistance ITT might be in a position to provide, such as local contacts, staff support and labor relations. . . .

In any event, in view of the evidence that the automatic sprinkler market in the United States is just coming into its own and is likely to grow dramatically in the future, the Court finds that any substantial expansion of Grinnell in foreign countries, with or without ITT assistance, would probably benefit all United States sprinkler companies. In short, far from foreclosing competitors, such expansion would create a larger market to be shared by all.

The Court holds that the government has not sustained its burden of establishing that the merger will foreclose Grinnell's competitors from foreign markets and thus result in a lessening of competition in the domestic market.

E. *Vertical Foreclosure*

The government also claims that the ITT–Grinnell merger will have some of the characteristics of a vertical merger in that it will foreclose Grinnell's competitors from the ITT market for sprinkler systems. . . .

By common definition, a vertical merger is the acquisition of one company which buys the product sold by the acquiring company or which sells the product bought by the acquiring company. The government's vertical foreclosure claim here is based on the second clause of the foregoing definition.

The short and conclusive answer to the government's vertical foreclosure claim is that ITT's purchases of sprinklers represents a *de minimis* part of the market. While the government points out that 55 sprinkler systems were installed in ITT facilities during the past five years and that ITT contemplates installing approximately 22 new sprinkler systems during the next year, the stark fact is that ITT's planned expenditures in amount of $731,635 for sprinkler systems during the 1970–1972 period represents less than 1/10 of 1% of the total prospective sprinkler system business for those years. When, as here, the size of the market share foreclosed to competition as the result of the vertical integration aspects of a merger is *de minimis*, there can be no Section 7 violation because in such a situation competition can not be said to have been substantially lessened. *Brown Shoe Co.* v. *United States, supra,* at 329.

Furthermore, the uncontroverted evidence shows that since ITT's acquisition of Grinnell the latter has been given no favoritism in the award of sprinkler business from other ITT subsidiaries, having lost as well as won such business. The "profit center" concept around which ITT is organized is not conducive to vertical foreclosure. The individual profit centers purchase on the basis of price, quality and delivery; one profit center in attempting to sell to another must earn its way; in purchasing products normally the subject of competitive bidding, such bidding is done without favoritism between profit centers, as well as with outside companies; and in some instances it is more difficult for an ITT company to sell to another ITT company than to sell to an outsider.

The Court holds that the government has not sustained its burden of establishing its vertical foreclosure claim.

F. *Central Stations*

The government also claims that the ITT–Grinnell merger will give Grinnell a competitive marketing advantage in that ITT will assist Grinnell in reentering the central station alarm business by giving it access to an ITT product known as "Digitor", and that such entry into the central station business in turn will give Grinnell substantial competitive advantages in the installation of automatic sprinkler systems. . . .

The evidence at the trial of the instant case, from witnesses with experience in the installation of sprinkler systems and central station equipment, established overwhelmingly that, even if ITT were to assist Grinnell in reentering the central station business, Grinnell would not thereby gain a significant competitive advantage in the sale and installation of automatic sprinkler systems. Central station companies are not a significant source of leads for sprinkler companies. Most sprinkler witnesses testified they never had received a lead from a central station source. Despite the suggestion of one witness that central station companies might hear about sprinkler work as a result of their periodic inspections of customers' properties, this would not be the case with a company using Digitor, for, as the government concedes in its brief, "[a]dmittedly, the 'Digitor', because of its advanced automated technology, cuts down on the number of personal contacts a central station company need have with its customers. . . ."

Finally, the Court finds nothing in the record to explain why, if installation of central station equipment and automatic sprinklers at the same time were desirable, that could not be accomplished readily by sprinkler and central station companies coordinating their installation work without the necessity of affiliation between them.

The Court holds that the government has not sustained its burden of proving that the merger will give Grinnell an advantage in reentering the central station business or, assuming such reentry, that Grinnell thereby will gain an advantage in the sale and installation of sprinklers.

G. *Reciprocal Dealing*

The major marketing and promotional competitive advantage which the government claims Grinnell will gain from the ITT–Grinnell merger is an enhancement of Grinnell's market position through reciprocal dealing caused by ITT's large purchasing power. More particularly, the government asserts that the merger will give rise to "reciprocity", referring to a seller's practice of utilizing the volume or potential volume of its purchases to induce others to buy its goods or services; and to "reciprocity effect", referring to the tendency of a company selling or desiring to sell to another company to channel its purchases to that company. . . .

There are two essential factual requisites of the government's reciprocal dealing claim, in the light of which the evidence must be analyzed. First, whether the merger will create an opportunity for reciprocal dealing through a market structure conducive to such dealing. Second, whether such reciprocal dealing in fact is likely to occur, even if the merger were to create an opportunity for it. The Court turns directly to an analysis of the evidence to determine whether these essential requisites have been established.

It is common ground that the question of whether a merger will create a market structure conducive to reciprocal dealing is exceedingly complex. The answer depends upon a careful analysis of many variables. Among the factors believed to be relevant to the merger here under consideration are the extent to which ITT suppliers are actual or potential purchasers of sprinklers; whether sprinklers have product characteristics which lend themselves to reciprocal dealing; the scope of the market, represented by ITT, for products sold by ITT suppliers; the size and diversification of other companies to which ITT suppliers sell their products; and the degree to which the markets within which ITT suppliers operate are competitively structured. . . . With the exception of the first two factors mentioned, there is little or no evidence in the present record; and with respect to the remaining critical factors the Court is unable to make appropriate findings one way or the other. . . .

There is no dispute that ITT is a substantial purchaser of goods and services from numerous domestic suppliers, including some of the nation's leading industrial concerns. The government's evidence shows that ITT purchased in excess of $840,000,000 of goods and services in 1968; and that it made purchases in excess of $100,000 from industries which accounted for 71% of total new plant and equipment expenditures by manufacturing industries in 1966. Defendant's evidence shows, however, that in most of the industries just referred to ITT actually purchased from only a small fraction of the companies in the industry. The government's evidence itself indicates that ITT's purchases represent but an infinitesimal percentage of the sales of its suppliers.

In view of the Court's observations above regarding the paucity of evidence with respect to certain factors critical to a determination of whether the merger will create a market structure conducive to reciprocal dealing, it should be noted that there is no evidence from which the Court may determine the percentage of new plant and equipment expenditures made by companies from which ITT in fact purchases. And yet it is abundantly clear, and the Court finds, that the *number of companies from which ITT in fact purchases* is a more reliable measure of the maximum reciprocity and reciprocity effect potential of the ITT-Grinnell merger than the total *number of companies in those industries from which ITT purchases.* This is especially so in view of the absence of any evidence whatever of alleged reciprocity in the sprinkler industry involving a merely *potential* as opposed to an *actual* supplier in the sprinkler industry.

Indeed, the Court is persuaded by a preponderance of the evidence that reciprocity and reciprocity effect are not significant factors in the sprinkler installation industry. The government's witnesses, representing substantial experience in the sprinkler business, with few exceptions testified to no instances of actual or suspected reciprocity involving their companies or any other companies. And other witnesses with long experience in the sprinkler industry, including present and former employees of Grinnell, testified in convincing fashion that they had never encountered a single instance of actual or suspected reciprocity. The Court attributes considerable weight to this evidence in view of the thousands of sprinkler contracts per year entered into by Grinnell which has approximately 20% of the national sprinkler instllation market.

From the standpoint of the market structure of the sprinkler industry, there are significant factors which militate against reciprocity practices. A substantial and increasing proportion of sprinkler work is done for non-industrial customers—such as educational institutions, hospitals and retail establishments—which are not actual or potential ITT suppliers. Most sprinkler work, for all classes of customers, is awarded on a competitive bidding basis, thus minimizing reciprocity and reciprocity effect potential. While it is true that, even with competitive bidding, favoritism may be shown by giving one bidder an opportunity to match the lowest bid, this practice is contrary to the ethical standards of general contractors; and it is self-defeating in that it has the undesirable effect of discouraging others from bidding in the future. Finally, a large proportion of sprinkler work is done in connection with new construction where sprinkler installers bid largely to general and mechanical contractors rather than to owners, thus minimizing the likelihood of significant ITT purchases from industrial sources. . . .

The evidence upon which the government relies to show reciprocity in the sprinkler industry relates for the most part to a period of time more than five years ago and involves alleged reciprocity between Grinnell and certain steel companies. As to the latter, five of the companies which allegedly had reciprocity interest in Grinnell and, in one case, in an ITT subsidiary, have entered into antireciprocity consent decrees designed to assure against future reciprocity or reciprocity effect in their business conduct. Moreover, as indicated below, the consensus of those in the best position to know is that the focus upon the illegality of reciprocity practices in recent years has brought about a substantial decline in the incidence of such practices—a trend which the record in the instant case indicates is more likely to continue than to abate. . . .

Turning from the sprinkler industry and from Grinnell, the Court now directs its attention to the other party to the merger, ITT, to ascertain whether the evidence demonstrates that reciprocal dealing in fact is likely to occur. There are several aspects of ITT's organization and practices which are directly relevant. First, ITT is organized into a series of "profit centers", each managed and staffed by personnel whose business careers, advancement, financial rewards and reputations depend upon the success of the specific profit center with which the men are identified, rather than upon the performance of ITT as a whole. . . . [T]he imposition of reciprocity considerations in the purchasing of supplies . . . would strip the profit center of its essential purpose, namely, to show the maximum profit.

Second, ITT does not collect purchasing and sales data necessary to identify reciprocal purchasing opportunities. ITT in the regular course of its business makes no overall compilation of its purchases by suppliers;

nor is there any communication between ITT's headquarters marketing and purchasing departments, nor between ITT's different profit centers, such as to identify suppliers. . . . Absent such compilations of purchases and communications between profit centers regarding purchases, ITT simply is in no position to respond to any supplier or potential supplier who may have purchased Grinnell sprinklers in the hope of selling goods or services to some other ITT profit center.

Third, ITT has had a written policy against the practice of reciprocity since 1966. This policy has been widely disseminated among ITT's purchasing and sales personnel on a continuing basis. Witnesses with extensive ITT experience testified that they never have encountered any instance of reciprocity or reciprocity effect. And the government has adduced no evidence that any ITT unit has ever obtained business as a result of reciprocity or reciprocity effect.

In view of the foregoing, it is understandable that considerations of prospective reciprocity opportunities played no part in bringing about the ITT–Grinnell merger. . . .

Upon the entire record, the Court holds that the government has not sustained its burden of establishing either that the merger will create an opportunity for reciprocal dealing through a market structure conducive to such dealing, or that reciprocal dealing in fact is likely to occur even if the merger were to create an opportunity for it. . . .

III

CLAIM REGARDING POWER PIPING

Although the Court has held that Grinnell is not the dominant competitor in the power piping industry, it nevertheless will rule upon the government's claims that the ITT–Grinnell merger will confer marketing and promotional advantages upon Grinnell in the power piping market, chiefly in the following respects: package or system selling; access to ITT's financial resources; foreign expansion; and reciprocal dealing. . . .

[The Court disposed of the government's contentions regarding power piping in much the same terms as it had treated claims regarding automatic sprinkler devices and systems.]

The Court holds that the government has not sustained its burden of establishing that in the power piping market the merger may have the effect of substantially lessening competition by giving Grinnell marketing and promotional competitive advantages in the respects claimed, namely, package or system selling, access to ITT's financial resources, foreign expansion or reciprocal dealing—whether viewed separately or cumulatively.

IV

CLAIM REGARDING PIPE HANGERS

The government's position with respect to the alleged anticompetitive effects of the merger in the pipe hanger market . . . is that, since pipe hangers are necessary components of automatic sprinkler systems and power piping systems, Grinnell, by gaining anticompetitive advantages in the installation of sprinkler systems and in the power piping market, will also gain similar advantages in the sale of pipe hangers.

The Court has held that Grinnell is not the dominant competitor in the pipe hanger industry. And, as with the power piping market, concededly the record contains no market or industry statistics by which any company's share of the pipe hanger market can be determined accurately. While there is no evidence as to the number or value of pipe hangers used in connection with sprinkler systems or power piping systems, the record does indicate that hangers represent a very small proportion of the value of such systems.

The Court holds that the government has not sustained its burden of establishing that the merger may have the effect of substantially lessening competition in the pipe hanger market.

. . . . .

VI

CLAIM OF ECONOMIC CONCENTRATION

At the preliminary injunction hearing in this case the government raised, and the Court ruled upon, a claim of economic concentration. . . . At the trial on the merits the government, through its offer of the proposed written testimony of Dr. Willard F. Mueller, again raised the same issue but with a different and somewhat ingenious twist.

The new twist to the government's economic concentration claim is that in the wake of a "trend among large diversified industrial firms to acquire other large corporations", it can be established that "anticompetitive consequences will appear in numerous though *undesignated individual 'lines of commerce'*." (Emphasis added)

The Court's short answer to this claim—and the ground for its ruling sustaining defendant's objection to the Mueller testimony for lack of relevance—is that the legislative history, the statute itself and the controlling decisional law all make it clear beyond a peradventure of a doubt that in a Section 7 case the alleged anticompetitive effects of a merger must be examined in the context of *specific product and geographic markets;* and the determination of such markets is a necessary predicate to a determination of whether there has been a substantial lessening of competition within an area of effective competition. To ask the Court to rule with respect to alleged anticompetitive consequences in *undesignated lines of commerce* is tantamount to asking the Court to engage in judicial legislation. This the Court most emphatically refuses to do. . . .

Recognition of the trend toward economic concentration in American industry, including extensive conglomerate merger activity in recent years, is not exactly new. The government points out that the trend during the last two decades toward concentration of assets in the hands

of fewer and larger corporate entities, together with an increasing diversification of those firms which primarily control the assets, has resulted in
certain anticompetitive effects, among which are increased opportunities
for business reciprocity and reciprocity effect, citing *FTC* v. *Consolidated
Foods Corp.*, 380 U.S. 592 (1965). Then, referring to certain of the
theories expressed in Professor Mueller's proposed testimony, the government contends that the most important anticompetitive effect of the trend
toward conglomeration by merger is "conglomerate interdependence and
forebearance", meaning "a system in which competitors respond to each
other and to their own needs rather than to the impersonal disciplining
forces of the market in general." From this the government concludes
that " '[t]rade engaged in by large diversified industrial firms' describes
a combination of many 'lines of commerce'."

   The legislative history of the 1950 amendments to Section 7 of the
Clayton Act . . . reflects a concern on the part of Congress about the
rising tide of economic concentration in American industry caused by all
types of mergers, including conglomerate mergers. . . . But the legislative
history also indicates that Section 7 as amended was not intended to
proscribe all mergers which result in economic concentration. The House
Report recommending passage of amended Section 7 concluded that:

the purpose of the bill [H.R. 2734] is to protect competition *in each line of commerce* in each section of the country. (Emphasis added)

Similarly, the Senate Report stated that:

It is intended that acquisitions which substantially lessen competition, as well as
those which tend to create a monopoly, will be unlawful *if they have the
specified effect in any line of commerce,* whether or not that line of commerce
is a large part of the business of any of the corporations involved in the
acquisition. (Emphasis added)

   Despite the legislative history, the statute itself and the controlling
decisional law, the government urges the Court to adopt an "expansive"
reading of the statutory language "in any line of commerce" so as to read
into the statute an interdiction of all mergers where the effect may be
a substantial lessening of competition "anywhere, in the purchase or sale
of anything" and thus to receive "proof of a merger or series of mergers
which could be demonstrated to have a broad, anticompetitive effect upon
'markets' in general"—in short, to disregard the statutory requirement
that alleged anticompetitive effects of a merger be examined with relation
to a specific "line of commerce" and instead to conduct a roving expedi-
tion to determine whether "anticompetitive consequences will appear in
numerous though *undesignated individual 'lines of commerce.'* " (Emphasis added)

   In response to the Court's inquiry of government trial counsel as to
"whether there is authority, legislative or judicial authority, to support

that claimed line of commerce", government counsel replied, "The Government unfortunately cannot point to a particular case where the Court held that this was a line of commerce."

The Court declines the government's invitation to indulge in an expanded reading of the statutory language and holds that the statute means just what it says. It proscribes only those mergers the effect of which "may be substantially to lessen competition"; it commands that the alleged anticompetitive effects be examined in the context of specific product and geographic markets; and it does not proscribe those mergers the effect of which may be substantially to increase economic concentration. . . .

Whatever may be the merits of the arguments as a matter of social and economic policy in favor of, or opposed to, a standard for measuring the legality of a merger under the antitrust laws by the degree to which it may increase economic concentration rather than by the degree to which it may lessen competition, that is beyond the competence of the Court to adjudicate. As the Court attempted to make clear in its preliminary injunction opinion, 306 F.Supp. at 796–97, if that standard is to be changed, it is fundamental under our system of government that any decision to change the standard be made by the Congress and not by the courts.

Conclusions

Upon the facts found and for the reasons stated above, the Court concludes . . . [t]hat defendant is entitled to judgment dismissing the complaint on the merits. . . .

Note: On September 24, 1971, Judge Joseph Blumenfeld of the U.S. District Court for Connecticut approved a consent decree whereby ITT agreed to divest itself of the Fire Protection Division of Grinnell Corporation in return for the Justice Department's withdrawal of its complaint.

United States v. *Ling-Temco-Vought, Inc.*

1970 Trade Cases ¶73,105 (W. D. Pa. 1970)

Final Judgment

Rosenberg, D. J. . . . upon consent of the parties aforementioned, it is hereby

Ordered, Adjudged and Decreed as follows: . . .

LTV is ordered and directed to divest, by three (3) years from the date of entry of this Final Judgment, all of its interest, direct and indirect, in Braniff and Okonite, or, in the alternative, all of its interest, direct and indirect, in J&L. . . .

Until the divestiture required by this Final Judgment is accomplished, neither LTV nor J&L shall take any action which knowingly impairs the viability of any of the businesses to be divested or LTV's ability to accomplish such divestiture. . . .

Each defendant and each person who submits to the jurisdiction of this Court for the purpose of being bound by the provisions of this Final Judgment (each such person also being referred to in this Section VII as a "defendant") is enjoined and restrained from:

(A) Purchasing, or entering into or adhering to any contract, agreement or understanding to purchase products, goods or services from any actual or potential supplier on the condition or understanding that purchases by such defendant from such supplier will be based on or conditioned upon such supplier's purchases from such defendant;

(B) Selling, or entering into or adhering to any contract, agreement or understanding to sell products, goods or services to any actual or potential customer on the condition or understanding that such defendant's purchases of products, goods or services from such customer will be based on or conditioned upon such customer's or potential customer's purchases from such defendant;

(C) Communicating to such defendant's actual or potential suppliers or contractors that:

(1) In purchasing products, goods or services, defendant will give preference to any supplier or contractor based on or conditioned upon such supplier's or contractor's purchases from such defendant or the dollar value of contracts awarded by such supplier or contractor to such defendant;

(2) In compiling bidder lists or in awarding contracts for projects involving capital expenditures by such defendant, preference will be given to any contractor or supplier based on or conditioned upon such contractor's or supplier's purchases from such defendant or the dollar value of contracts awarded by such supplier or contractor to such defendant;

(3) Such defendant is entitled to receive contracts or orders for products or goods sold or services from such supplier or contractor based on or conditioned upon such defendant's purchases from such supplier or the dollar value of contracts awarded by defendant to such contractor;

(4) In awarding contracts for materials or services, such defendant has or will give preference to any contractor or supplier based upon such supplier's purchases from such defendant or the dollar value of contracts awarded by such supplier or contractor to such defendant;

(D) Comparing or exchanging statistical data with any supplier or contractor to ascertain, facilitate or further any relationship between purchases by such defendant from such supplier or contractor and sales by such defendant to such supplier or contractor;

(E) Engaging in the practice of discussing with any supplier or contractor the relationship between purchases or contract awards by such defendant involving such supplier or contractor, and sales by such defendant to such supplier or contractor;

(F) Preparing or maintaining statistical compilations for any supplier or contractor or any class or grouping of suppliers or contractors which compare purchases by such defendant from suppliers or the dollar value of contracts awarded by defendant to contractors with purchases by such suppliers from such defendant or the dollar value of contracts awarded to such defendant by such contractor;

(G) Issuing, to personnel having responsibilities for purchasing or responsibilities for awarding contracts, lists which identify customers and the magnitude of their purchases from such defendant or which identify companies and the dollar value of contracts they have awarded to such defendant or which specify or recommend that purchases be made from any such customers or that contracts be awarded to such companies;

(H) Referring compilations of bids received for contracts for projects involving capital expenditures by such defendant to any department or unit having sales responsibilities for decision or recommendation by such department or unit as to the identity of the firm or firms to whom contracts for such projects should be awarded. . . .

This Final Judgment shall remain in full force and effect for ten (10) years, and no longer, from the date of entry hereof except as to any provision herein for which a shorter term is specified therein.

<table>
<tr>
<td>

Chapter

8

</td>
<td>

JOINT VENTURES—
A FORM OF MERGER

</td>
</tr>
</table>

Joint ventures can be defined as the creation of a jointly owned business enterprise by two or more corporations. They provide especially formidable problems for students of antitrust because of their potential for both good and evil. On the one hand, they provide a means by which resources can be pooled and risks shared; this often makes possible the completion of projects which, but for the joint venture, would not have been undertaken. On the other hand, the fact that potential competitors are brought into such close contact with one another raises distinct anticompetitive possibilities. The courts, in apparent recognition of the potentiality of joint ventures for increasing or diminishing competition, depending upon the specific circumstances, have adopted a relatively flexible position toward them. In the *Terminal Railroad* decision, the Supreme Court recognized the value of the venture itself, yet sought to mitigate its anticompetitive consequences through the requirement of fair and equal access. In the *Penn-Olin* case the Court sought to extend and refine its analysis of joint ventures, particularly as it related to the question of potential competition.[1]

United States v. Terminal Railroad Association of St. Louis

224 U.S. 383 (1912)

MR. JUSTICE LURTON delivered the opinion of the Court.

The United States filed this bill to enforce the provisions of the Sherman Act of July 2, 1890 . . . against thirty-eight corporate and individual defendants . . . as a combination in restraint of interstate commerce and as a monopoly forbidden by that law. . . .

The principal defendant is the Terminal Railroad Association of St. Louis, hereinafter designated as the Terminal Company. It is a corporation of the State of Missouri, and was organized under an agreement made in

---

[1] In this regard see especially Section 8 of the decision, wherein Justice Clark attempts to define a series of rules for evaluating the consequences of joint ventures.

1889 between Mr. Jay Gould and a number of the defendant railroad companies for the express purpose of acquiring the properties of several independent terminal companies at St. Louis with a view to combining and operating them as a unitary system.

. . . These properties included the great union station, the only existing railroad bridge—the Eads or St. Louis Bridge—and every connecting or terminal company by means of which that bridge could be used by railroads terminating on either side of the river. . . .

. . . [F]or a time, there existed three independent methods by which connection was maintained between railroads terminating on either side of the river at St. Louis: first, the original Wiggins Ferry Company, and its railway terminal connections; second, The Eads Railroad Bridge and the several terminal companies by means of which railroads terminating at St. Louis were able to use that bridge and connect with one another, constituting the system controlled by the Terminal Company, and, third, The Merchants' Bridge and terminal facilities owned and operated by companies in connection therewith.

This resulted in some cases in an unnecessary duplication of facilities, but it at least gave to carriers and shippers some choice, a condition which, if it does not lead to competition in charges, does insure competition in service. Important as were the considerations mentioned, their independence of one another served to keep open the means for the entrance of new lines to the city, and was an obstacle to united opposition from existing lines. The importance of this will be more clearly seen when we come to consider the topographical conditions of the situation.

That the promoters of the Terminal Company designed to obtain the control of every feasible means of railroad access to St. Louis, or means of connecting the lines of railway entering on opposite sides of the river, is manifested by the declarations of the original agreement, as well as by the successive steps which followed. . . .

We come, then, to the question upon which the case must turn: Has the unification of substantially every terminal facility by which the traffic of St. Louis is served resulted in a combination which is in restraint of trade within the meaning and purpose of the Anti-trust Act?

It is not contended that the unification of the terminal facilities of a great city where many railroad systems center is, under all circumstances and conditions, a combination in restraint of trade or commerce. Whether it is a facility in aid of interstate commerce or an unreasonable restraint forbidden by the act of Congress . . . will depend upon the intent to be inferred from the extent of the control thereby secured over instrumentalities which such commerce is under compulsion to use, the method by which such control has been brought about and the manner in which that control has been exerted.

The consequence to interstate commerce of this combination cannot be appreciated without a consideration of natural conditions greatly affecting the railroad situation at St. Louis. Though twenty-four lines of railway converge at St. Louis, not one of them passes through. About one-half of these lines have their termini on the Illinois side of the river. The others, coming from the west and north, have their termini either in the city or on its northern edge. . . . The cost of construction and maintenance of railroad bridges over so great a river makes it impractical for every road desiring to enter or pass through the city to have its own bridge. The obvious solution is the maintenance of toll bridges open to the use of any and all lines upon identical terms. . . . The first bridge, called the Eads Bridge, was, and is, a toll bridge. Any carrier may use it on equal terms. But to use it there must be access over rails connecting the bridge and the railway. On the St. Louis side the bridge terminates at the foot of the great hills upon which the city is built; on the Illinois side it ends in the low and wide valley of the Mississippi. This condition resulted in the organization of independent companies which undertook to connect the bridge on each side with the various railroad termini. . . . Thus, though the bridge might be used by all upon equal terms, it was accessible only by means of the several terminal companies operating lines connecting it with the railroad termini.

This brought about a condition which led to the construction of the second bridge, the Merchants' Bridge. This, too, was, and is, a toll bridge, and may be used by all upon equal terms. . . . But this Merchants' Bridge, like the Eads Bridge, had no rail connections with any of the existing railroad systems, and these facilities, as in the case of the Eads Bridge, were supplied by a number of independent railway companies who undertook to fill in the gaps between the bridge ends and the termini of railroads on both sides of the river. . . . Now, it is evident that these lines connecting railroad termini with the railroad bridges dominated the situation. They stood, as it were, just outside the gateway, and none could enter, though the gate stood open, who did not comply with their terms. . . .

The result of the geographical and topographical situation is that it is, as a practical matter, impossible for any railroad company to pass through, or even enter St. Louis, so as to be within reach of its industries or commerce, without using the facilities entirely controlled by the Terminal Company. . . . Nor is this effect denied, for the learned counsel representing the proprietary companies, as well as the Terminal Company, say in their filed brief: "There indeed is compulsion, but it is inherent in the situation. The other companies use the terminal properties because it is not possible to acquire adequate facilities for themselves. The cost to any one company is prohibitive." Obviously, this was not true before the consolidation of the systems of the Wiggins Ferry Company and the Merchants' Bridge Company with the system theretofore controlled by the Terminal Company. That the non-proprietary companies might have been compelled to use the instrumentalities of one or the other of the three systems then available, and that the advantages secured might not have been so great as those offered by the unified system now operated by the Terminal Company, must be admitted. But that there existed before the three terminal systems were combined a considerable measure of competition for the business of the other companies, and a larger power of competition, is undeniable. . . . The independent existence of these three terminal systems was, therefore, a menace to complete domination as keeping open the way for greater competition. Only by their absorption or some equivalent arrangement was it possible to exclude from independent entrance . . . any . . . company which might desire its own terminals. . . .

The physical conditions which compel the use of the combined system by every road which desires to cross the river, either to serve the commerce of the city or to connect with lines separated by the river, is the factor which gives greatest color to the unlawfulness of the combination as now controlled and operated. If the Terminal Company was in law and fact the agent of all, the mere unification which has occurred would take on quite a different aspect. It becomes, therefore, of the utmost importance to know the character and purpose of the corporation. . . . The fact that the Terminal Company is not an independent corporation at all is of the utmost significance. There are twenty-four railroads converging at St. Louis. The relation of the Terminal Company is not one of impartiality to each of them. It was organized in 1889, at the instance of six of these railroad companies, for the purpose of acquiring all existing terminal instrumentalities for the benefit of the combination, and such other companies as they might thereafter admit to joint ownership by unanimous consent, and upon a consideration to be agreed upon. . . .

That these facilities were not to be acquired for the benefit of any railroad company which might desire a joint use thereof was made plain by a provision in the contract [of 1889] . . . which stipulated that other railroad companies not named therein as proprietary companies might only be admitted "to joint use of said terminal system on unanimous consent, but not otherwise, of the directors of the first party, and on payment of such a consideration as they may determine, and on signing this agreement," etc. Inasmuch as the directors of the Terminal Company consisted of one representative of each of the proprietary companies, selected by itself, it is plain that each of said companies had and still has a veto upon any joint use or control of terminals by any non-proprietary company. . . .

We fail to find . . . any provision abrogating the requirement of unanimous consent to the admission of other companies to the ownership of the Terminal Company, though counsel say that no such company will now find itself excluded from joint use or ownership upon application. . . .

By still another clause in the agreement the proprietary companies obligate themselves to forever use the facilities of the Terminal Company for all business destined to cross the river. This would seem to guarantee against any competitive system, since the companies to the agreement now control about one-third of the railroad mileage of the United States. . . .

That through their ownership and exclusive control they are in possession of advantages in respect to the enormous traffic which must use the St. Louis gateway, is undeniable. That the proprietary companies have not availed themselves of the full measure of their power to impede free competition of outside companies, may be true. Aside from their power under all of the conditions to exclude independent entrance to the city by any outside company, their control has resulted in certain methods which are not consistent with freedom of competition. . . .

We are not unmindful of the essential difference between terminal systems properly so described and railroad transportation companies. The first are but instrumentalities which assist the latter in the transfer of traffic between different lines, and in the collection and distribution of traffic. They are a modern evolution in the doing of railroad business, and are of the greatest public utility. They, under proper conditions, do not restrain, but promote commerce. . . .

While, therefore, the mere combining of several independent terminal systems into one may not operate as a restraint upon the interstate commerce which must use them, yet there may be conditions which will bring such a combination under the prohibition of the Sherman Act. . . .

It cannot be controverted that, in ordinary circumstances, a number of independent companies might combine for the purpose of controlling or acquiring terminals for their common but exclusive use. In such cases other companies might be admitted upon terms or excluded altogether. If such terms were too onerous, there would ordinarily remain the right and power to construct their own terminals. But the situation at St. Louis is most extraordinary, and we base our conclusion in this case, in a large measure, upon that fact. The "physical or topographical condition peculiar to the locality," which is advanced as a prime justification for a unified system of terminals, constitutes a most obvious reason why such a unified system is an obstacle, a hindrance and a restriction upon interstate commerce, unless it is the impartial agent of all who, owing to conditions, are under such compulsion, as here exists, to use its facilities. The witness upon whom the defendants chiefly rely to uphold the advantages of the unified system which has been constructed, Mr. Albert L. Perkins, gives this as his unqualified judgment. . . . The witness, however, points out that such a terminal company should be the agent of every company and, furthermore, that its service should not be for profit or gain. In short, that every railroad using the service should be a joint owner and equally interested in the control and management. . . .

The terminal properties in question are not so controlled and managed, in view of the inherent local conditions, as to escape condemnation as a restraint upon commerce. They are not under a common control and ownership. Nor can this be brought about unless the prohibition against the admission of other companies to such control is stricken out and provision made for the admission of any company to an equal control and management upon an equal basis with the present proprietary companies. . . .

We come now to the remedy . . . . If, as we have already said, the combination of two or more mere terminal companies into a single system does not violate the prohibition of the statute against contracts and combinations in restraint of interstate commerce, it is because such a combination may be of the greatest public utility. But when, as here, the inherent conditions are such as to prohibit any other reasonable means of entering the city, the combination of every such facility under the exclusive ownership and control of less than all of the companies under compulsion to use them violates both the first and second sections of the act, in that it constitutes a contract or combination in restraint of commerce among the States and an attempt to monopolize commerce among the States which must pass through the gateway of St. Louis. . . .

Plainly the combination which has occurred would not be an illegal restraint under the terms of the statute if it were what is claimed for it, a proper terminal association acting as the impartial agent of every line which is under compulsion to use its instrumentalities. If, as we have pointed out, the violation of the statute, in view of the inherent physical conditions, grows out of administrative conditions which may be eliminated and the obvious advantages of unification preserved, such a modification of the agreement between the Terminal Company and the proprietary companies as shall constitute the former the *bona fide* agent and servant of every railroad line which shall use its facilities, and an inhibition of certain methods of administration to which we have referred, will amply vindicate the wise purpose of the statute, and will preserve to the public a system of great public advantage.

These considerations lead to a reversal of the decree dismissing the bill. This is accordingly adjudged and the case is remanded to the District Court, with directions that a decree be there entered directing the parties to submit to the court, within ninety days after receipt of mandate, a plan for the reorganization of the contract between the fourteen defendant railroad companies and the Terminal Company, which we have pointed out as bringing the combination within the inhibition of the statute.

First. By providing for the admission of any existing or future railroad to joint ownership and control of the combined terminal properties, upon such just and reasonable terms as shall place such applying company upon a plane of equality in respect of benefits and burdens with the present proprietary companies.

Second. Such plan of reorganization must also provide definitely for the use of the terminal facilities by any other railroad not electing to become a joint owner, upon such just and reasonable terms and regulations as will, in respect of use, character and cost of service, place every such company upon as nearly an equal plane as may be with respect to expenses and charges as that occupied by the proprietary companies. . . .

Reversed and remanded accordingly.

United States v. Penn-Olin Chemical Co.

378 U.S. 158 (1964)

MR. JUSTICE CLARK delivered the opinion of the Court.

Pennsalt Chemicals Corporation and Olin Mathieson Chemical Corporation jointly formed Penn-Olin Chemical Company to produce and sell sodium chlorate in the southeastern United States. The Government seeks to dissolve this joint venture as violative of both Section 7 of the Clayton Act and Section 1 of the Sherman Act. This direct appeal . . . from the United States District Court for the District of Delaware, raises two questions. First, whether Section 7 of the Clayton Act is applicable where two corporations form a third to engage in a new enterprise; and, second, if this question is answered in the affirmative, whether there is a violation of Section 1 or Section 7 under the facts of this case. The trial court found that the joint venture, on this record, violated neither of these sections and found it unnecessary to reach the first question. . . . In view of the importance of each of these questions in the administration of the antitrust laws, we noted probable jurisdiction. . . . We have concluded that a joint venture as organized here would be subject to the regulation of Section 7 of the Clayton Act and, reaching the merits, we hold that while on the present record there is no violation of Section 1 of the Sherman Act, the District Court erred in dismissing the complaint as to Section 7 of the Clayton Act. Accordingly, the judgment is vacated and remanded for further consideration.

1. LINE OF COMMERCE, RELEVANT MARKET, ETC.

At the outset it is well to note that some of the troublesome questions ordinarily found in antitrust cases have been eliminated by the parties. First, the line of commerce is a chemical known as sodium chlorate. . . . All sodium chlorate of like purity is usable interchangeably and is used primarily in the pulp and paper industry to bleach the pulp, making for a brighter and higher quality paper. . . . The pulp and paper industry consumes about 64% of total production of sodium chlorate. The chemical is also employed in the production of herbicides, agricultural chemicals and in certain derivatives, such as ammonium perchlorate. Next, the relevant market is not disputed. It is the southeastern part of the United States. Nor is the fact that Olin has never engaged in the commercial production of sodium chlorate contested. It has purchased and does purchase amounts of the chemical for internal consumption and has acted as sales agent for Pennsalt in the southeastern territory under contracts dated in December 1957 and February 1958. Olin also owns a patented process for bleaching pulp with chlorine dioxide. This process requires sodium chlorate and has been widely used by paper manufacturers under royalty-free licenses. . . .

2. The Companies Involved

Pennsalt is engaged solely in the production and sale of chemicals and chemical products throughout the United States. Its assets are around a hundred million dollars and its sales are about the same amount. Its sodium chlorate production is located at Portland, Oregon, with a capacity of some 15,000 tons as of 1959. It occupied 57.8% of the market west of the Rocky Mountains. It has marketed sodium chlorate in the southeastern United States to some extent since 1957. Its shipments into that territory in 1960 were 4,186 tons of which Olin sold 3,202 tons on its sales agency contract.

Olin is a large diversified corporation, the result of a merger of Olin Industries, Inc., and Mathieson Chemical Corporation in 1954. One of its seven divisions operates plants in 15 States and produces a wide range of chemicals and chemical products accounting for about 30% of Olin's revenues. Olin's sales in 1960 grossed some $690,000,000 and its total assets were $860,000,000.

Penn-Olin was organized in 1960 as a joint venture of Olin and Pennsalt. Each owns 50% of its stock and the officers and directors are divided equally between the parents. Its plant at Calvert City, Kentucky, was built by equal contribution of the two parents and cost $6,500,000. It has a capacity to produce 26,500 tons of sodium chlorate annually and began operations in 1961. Pennsalt operates the plant and Olin handles the sales. Penn-Olin deals in no other chemicals.

3. Background and Statistics of the Industry

Prior to 1961 the sodium chlorate industry in the United States was made up of three producing companies. The largest producer, Hooker Chemical Corporation, entered the industry in 1956 when it acquired Oldbury Electro Chemical Company, which had been producing sodium chlorate for over half a century. Hooker now has two plants, one in the relevant marketing area at Columbus, Mississippi, which originally had a capacity of 16,000 tons but which was doubled in 1962. The other plant is at Niagara Falls, New York, with a capacity of 18,000 tons. Hooker has assets of almost $200,000,000. American Potash & Chemical Corporation entered the industry in 1955 by the acquisition of Western Electro Chemical Company. American Potash also has two plants, one located at Henderson, Nevada, with a 27,000-ton capacity and the other at Aberdeen, Mississippi (built in 1957), the capacity of which was 15,000 tons.

Its assets are almost $100,000,000. The trial court found that these two corporations "had a virtual monopoly" in the relevant southeast market, holding over 90% of the market.

A third company in the industry was Pennsalt which had a 15,392-ton plant at Portland, Oregon. It entered seriously into the relevant marketing area through a sales arrangement with Olin dated December 1957 and finalized in 1958, which was aimed at testing the availability of the southeastern market. Olin as an exclusive seller was to undertake the sale of 2,000 tons of sodium chlorate per year to pulp and paper mills in the southeast (except for Buckeye Cellulose Co., at Foley, Florida, which Pennsalt reserved to serve directly). In 1960, 4,186 tons of sodium chlorate were marketed in the relevant market with the aid of this agreement. This accounted for 8.9% of the sales in that market.

During the previous decade no new firms had entered the sodium chlorate industry, and little effort had been made by existing companies to expand their facilities prior to 1957. In 1953 Olin had made available to Pennsalt its Mathieson patented process for bleaching pulp with chlorine dioxide and the latter had installed it 100% in all of the western paper mills. This process uses sodium chlorate. At about the same time the process was likewise made available, royalty free, to the entire pulp and paper industry. By 1960 most of the chlorine dioxide generated by paper manufacturers was being produced under the Olin controlled process. This created an expanding demand for sodium chlorate and by 1960 the heaviest concentration of purchasers was located in the relevant southeastern territory. By 1957 Hooker began increasing the capacity of its Columbus plant and by 1960 it had been almost doubled. American Potash sensed the need of a plant in Mississippi to compete with Hooker and began its Aberdeen plant in 1957. It was completed to a 15,000-ton capacity in 1959, and this capacity was expanded 50% by 1961.

The sales arrangement between Pennsalt and Olin, previously mentioned, was superseded by the joint venture agreement on February 11, 1960, and the Penn-Olin plant operations at Calvert City, Kentucky, began in 1961. In the same year Pittsburgh Plate Glass Company announced that it would build a plant at Lake Charles, Louisiana, with a capacity of 15,000 tons. Pittsburgh Plate Glass had operated a sodium chlorate plant in Canada.

As a result of these expansions and new entries into the southeastern market, the projected production of sodium chlorate there more than doubled. . . . Penn-Olin's share of the expanded relevant market was about 27.6%. . . .

4. The Setting from Which the Joint Venture Emerged

As early as 1951 Pennsalt had considered building a plant at Calvert City and starting in 1955 it initiated several cost and market studies for a sodium chlorate plant in the southeast. Three different proposals from within its own organization were rejected prior to 1957, apparently because the rate of return was so unattractive that "the expense of refining these figures further would be unwarranted." When Hooker announced in December 1956 that it was going to increase the capacity of its Columbus plant, the interest of Pennsalt management was reactivated. It appointed a "task force" to evaluate the company's future in the eastern market; it retained management consultants to study that market and its chief engineer prepared cost estimates. However, in December 1957 the management decided that the estimated rate of return was unattractive and considered it "unlikely" that Pennsalt would go it alone. It was suggested that Olin would be a "logical partner" in a joint venture and might in the interim be interested in distributing in the East 2,000 tons of the Portland sodium chlorate production. The sales agreement with Olin, heretofore mentioned, was eventually made. In the final draft the parties agreed that "neither . . . should move in the chlorate or perchlorate field without keeping the other party informed . . ." and that one would "bring to the attention of the other any unusual aspects of this business which might make it desirable to proceed further with production plans." Pennsalt claims that it finally decided, prior to this agreement, that it should not build a plant itself and that this decision was never reconsidered or changed. But the District Court found to the contrary.

During this same period—beginning slightly earlier—Olin began investigating the possibility of entering the sodium chlorate industry. It had never produced sodium chlorate commercially, although its predecessor had done so years before. However, the electrolytic process used in making sodium chlorate is intimately related to other operations of Olin and required the same general knowledge. Olin also possessed extensive experience in the technical aspects of bleaching pulp and paper and was intimate with the pulp and paper mills of the southeast. In April 1958 Olin's chemical division wrote and circulated to the management a "Whither Report" which stated in part:

We have an unparalleled opportunity to move sodium chlorate into the paper industry as the result of our work on the installation of chlorine dioxide generators. We have a captive consumption for sodium chlorate.

And Olin's engineering supervisor concluded that entry into sodium chlorate production was "an attractive venture" since it "represents a logical expansion of the product line of the Industrial Chemicals Division . . ." with respect to "one of the major markets, pulp and paper bleaching, [with which] we have a favorable marketing position, particularly in the southeast."

The staff, however, did not agree with the engineering supervisor or the "Whither Report." . . . But, as the trial court found, the testimony indicated that Olin's decision to enter the joint venture was made without determining that Olin could not or would not be an independent competitor. That question, the president of Penn-Olin testified, "never reached the point of final decision."

This led the District Court to find that "[t]he possibility of individual entry into the southeastern market had not been completely rejected by either Pennsalt or Olin before they decided upon the joint venture." . . .

5. SECTION 7 OF THE CLAYTON ACT APPLIES TO "JOINT VENTURES"

Appellees argue that Section 7 applies only where the acquired company is "engaged" in commerce and that it would not apply to a newly formed corporation, such as Penn-Olin. The test, they say, is whether the enterprise to be acquired is engaged in commerce—not whether a corporation formed as the instrumentality for the acquisition is itself engaged in commerce at the moment of its formation. We believe that this logic fails in the light of the wording of the section and its legislative background. The test of the section is the effect of the acquisition. Certainly the formation of a joint venture and purchase by the organizers of its stock would substantially lessen competition—indeed foreclose it—as between them, both being engaged in commerce. This would be true whether they were in actual or potential competition with each other and even though the new corporation was formed to create a wholly new enterprise. Realistically, the parents would not compete with their progeny. Moreover, in this case the progeny was organized to further the business of its parents, already in commerce, and the fact that it was organized specifically to engage in commerce should bring it within the coverage of Section 7. In addition, long prior to trial Penn-Olin was actually engaged in commerce. To hold that it was not "would be illogical and disrespectful of the plain congressional purpose in amending Section 7 . . . [for] it would create a large loophole in a statute designed to close a loophole." *United States* v. *Philadelphia National Bank* . . . (1963). In any event, Penn-Olin was engaged in commerce at the time of suit and the economic effects of an acquisition are to be measured at that point rather than at the time of acquisition. *United States* v. *E. I. duPont de Nemours & Co.* . . . (1957). The technicality could, therefore, be averted by merely refiling an amended complaint at the time of trial. This would be a useless requirement.

6. THE APPLICATION OF THE MERGER DOCTRINE

This is the first case reaching this Court and on which we have written that directly involves the validity under Section 7 of the joint participation of two corporations in the creation of a third as a new domestic producing organization.[1] We are, therefore, plowing new ground. If it is

[1] For a discussion of the problem, see Kaysen & Turner, *Antitrust Policy*, 136–141 (1959).

true, however, that some aspects of the problem might be found in *United States* v. *Terminal R. Assn.*, 224 U.S. 383 (1912), and *Associated Press* v. *United States*, 326 U.S. 1 (1945), where joint ventures with great market power were subjected to control, even prior to the amendment to Section 7.

. . . Their [joint ventures] economic significance has grown tremendously in the last score of years, having been spurred on by the need for speed and size in fashioning a war machine during the early forties. Postwar use of joint subsidiaries and joint projects led to the spawning of thousands of such ventures in an effort to perform the commercial tasks confronting an expanding economy.

The joint venture, like the "merger" and the "conglomeration," often creates anticompetitive dangers. It is the chosen competitive instrument of two or more corporations previously acting independently and usually competitively with one another. The result is "a triumvirate of associated corporations."[2] If the parent companies are in competition, or might compete absent the joint venture, it may be assumed that neither will compete with the progeny in its line of commerce. Inevitably, the operations of the joint venture will be frozen to those lines of commerce which will not bring it into competition with the parents, and the latter, by the same token will be foreclosed from the joint venture's market.

This is not to say that the joint venture is controlled by the same criteria as the merger or conglomeration. The merger eliminates one of the participating corporations from the market while a joint venture creates a new competitive force therein. . . .

Overall, the same considerations apply to joint ventures as to mergers, for in each instance we are but expounding a national policy enunciated by the Congress to preserve and promote a free competitive economy. In furtherance of that policy, now entering upon its 75th year, this Court has formulated appropriate criteria, first under the Sherman Act and now, also, under the Clayton Act and other antitrust legislation. The Celler-Kefauver Amendment to Section 7, with which we now deal, was the answer of the Congress to a loophole found to exist in the original enactment. . . . The grand design of the original Section 7, as to stock acquisitions, as well as the Celler-Kefauver Amendment, as to the acquisition of assets, was to arrest incipient threats to competition which the Sherman Act did not ordinarily reach. It follows that actual restraints need not be proved. The requirements of the amendment are satisfied when a "tendency" toward monopoly or the "reasonable likelihood" of a substantial lessening of competition in the relevant market is shown. Congress made it plain that the validity of such arrangements was to be gauged on a broader scale by using the words "may be substantially to lessen com-

[2] See Note, "Applicability of Section 7 to a Joint Venture," 11 *U. C. L. A. L. Rev.* 393, 396.

petition" which "indicate that its concern was with probabilities, not certainties." . . .

7. THE CRITERIA GOVERNING
SECTION 7 CASES

We apply the light of these considerations in the merger cases to the problem confronting us here. The District Court found that "Pennsalt and Olin each possessed the resources and general capability needed to build its own plant in the southeast and to compete with Hooker and [American Potash] in that market. Each could have done so if it had wished." . . .[3] In addition, the District Court found that, contrary to the position of the management of Olin and Pennsalt, "the forecasts of each company indicated that a plant could be operated with profit." . . .

The District Court held, however, that these considerations had no controlling significance, except "as a factor in determining whether as a matter of probability *both* companies would have entered the market as individual competitors if Penn-Olin had not been formed. Only in this event would potential competition between the two companies have been foreclosed by the joint venture." . . . In this regard the court found it "impossible to conclude that as a matter of reasonable probability *both* Pennsalt and Olin would have built plants in the southeast if Penn-Olin had not been created." . . . The court made no decision concerning the probability that one would have built "while the other continued to ponder." It found that this "hypothesized situation affords no basis for concluding that Penn-Olin had the effect of substantially lessening competition." . . . That would depend, the court said, "upon the competitive impact which Penn-Olin will have as against that which might have resulted if Pennsalt or Olin had been an individual market entrant." . . . The court found that this impact could not be determined from the record in this case. "Solely as a matter of theory," it said, ". . . no reason exists to suppose that Penn-Olin will be a less effective competitor than Pennsalt or Olin would have been. The contrary conclusion is the more reasonable." . . .

We believe that the court erred in this regard. Certainly the sole test would not be the probability that *both* companies would have entered the

[3] The court explained further: "At the time when the joint venture was agreed upon Pennsalt and Olin each had an extensive background in sodium chlorate. Pennsalt had years of experience in manufacturing and selling it. Although Olin had never been a commercial manufacturer, it possessed a substantially developed manufacturing technique of its own, and also had available to it a process developed by Vickers-Krebs with whom it had been negotiating to construct a plant. Olin had contracts among the southeastern pulp and paper mills which Pennsalt lacked, but Pennsalt's own estimates indicate that in a reasonable time it would develop adequate business to support a plant if it decided to build. A suitable location for a plant was available to each company—Calvert City, Kentucky for Pennsalt, and the TVA area around Chattanooga, Tennessee for Olin. The financing required would not have been a problem for either company." . . .

market. Nor would the consideration be limited to the probability that one entered alone. There still remained for consideration the fact that Penn-Olin eliminated the potential competition of the corporation that might have remained at the edge of the market, continually threatening to enter. Just as a merger eliminates actual competition, this joint venture may well foreclose any prospect of competition between Olin and Penn-salt in the relevant sodium chlorate market. The difference, of course, is that the merger's foreclosure is present while the joint venture's is prospective. Nevertheless, "[p]otential competition . . . as a substitute for . . . [actual competition] may restrain producers from overcharging those to whom they sell or underpaying those from whom they buy. . . . Potential competition, insofar as the threat survives [as it would have here in the absence of Penn-Olin], may compensate in part for the imperfection characteristic of actual competition in the great majority of competitive markets." Wilcox, *Competition and Monopoly in American Industry*, TNEC Monograph No. 21 (1940) 7–8. Potential competition cannot be put to a subjective test. It is not "susceptible of a ready and precise answer." . . . The existence of an aggressive, well equipped and well financed corporation engaged in the same or related lines of commerce waiting anxiously to enter an oligopolistic market would be a substantial incentive to competition which cannot be underestimated. Witness the expansion undertaken by Hooker and American Potash as soon as they heard of the interest of Olin Mathieson and of Pennsalt in southeast territory. This same situation might well have come about had either Olin or Pennsalt entered the relevant market alone and the other remained aloof watching developments.

8. THE PROBLEM OF PROOF

Here the evidence shows beyond question that the industry was rapidly expanding; the relevant southeast market was requiring about one-half of the national production of sodium chlorate; few corporations had the inclination, resources and know-how to enter this market; both parent corporations of Penn-Olin had great resources; each had long been identified with the industry, one owning valuable patent rights while the other had engaged in sodium chlorate production for years; each had other chemicals, the production of which required the use of sodium chlorate; right up to the creation of Penn-Olin, each had evidenced a long-sustained and strong interest in entering the relevant market area; each enjoyed good reputation and business connections with the major consumers of sodium chlorate in the relevant market, *i.e.*, the pulp and paper mills; and finally, each had the know-how and the capacity to enter that market and could have done so individually at a reasonable profit. Moreover, each company had compelling reasons for entering the southeast market. Pennsalt needed to expand its sales to the southeast, which it could not do economically without a plant in that area. Olin was motivated by "the fact that [it was] already buying and using a fair quantity [of sodium chlorate] for the production of sodium chlorite and that [it was] promoting the Mathieson process of the generation of chlorine dioxide which uses sodium chlorate." Unless we are going to require subjective evidence, this array of probability certainly reaches the prima facie stage. As we have indicated, to require more would be to read the statutory requirement of reasonable probability into a requirement of certainty. This we will not do.

However, despite these strong circumstances, we are not disposed to disturb the court's finding that there was not a reasonable probability that both Pennsalt and Olin would have built a plant in the relevant market area. But we have concluded that a finding should have been made as to the reasonable probability that either one of the corporations would have entered the market by building a plant, while the other would have remained a significant potential competitor. The trial court said that this question "need not be decided." . . . [W]e prefer that the trial court pass upon this question and we venture no opinion thereon. Since the trial court might have been concerned over whether there was evidence on this point,[4] we reiterate that it is impossible to demonstrate the *precise* competitive effects of the elimination of either Pennsalt or Olin as a potential competitor. . . . There being no proof of specific intent to use Penn-Olin as a vehicle to eliminate competition, nor evidence of collateral restrictive agreements between the joint venturers, we put those situations to one side. We note generally the following criteria which the trial court might take into account in assessing the probability of a substantial lessening of competition: the number and power of the competitors in the relevant market; the background of their growth; the power of the joint venturers; the relationship of their lines of commerce; the competition existing between them and the power of each in dealing with the competitors of the other; the setting in which the joint venture was created; the reasons and necessities for its existence; the joint venture's line of commerce and the relationship thereof to that of its parents; the adaptability of its line of commerce to noncompetitive practices; the potential power of the joint venture in the relevant market; an appraisal of what the competition in the relevant market would have been if one of the joint venturers had entered it alone instead of through Penn-Olin; the effect, in the event of this occurrence, of the other joint venturer's potential competition; and such other factors as might indicate potential risk to competition in the relevant market. In weighing these factors the court should remember that the mandate of the Congress is in terms of the probability of a lessening of substantial competition, not in terms of tangible present restraint.

---

[4] In this regard, the court should, of course, open the record for further testimony if the parties so desire.

The judgment is therefore vacated and the case is remanded for further proceedings in conformity with this opinion.

Vacated and remanded.

MR. JUSTICE WHITE dissents.

MR. JUSTICE DOUGLAS, with whom MR. JUSTICE BLACK agrees, dissenting.

Agreements among competitors to divide markets are *per se* violations of the Sherman Act.[5] The most detailed, grandiose scheme of that kind is disclosed in *Addyston Pipe & Steel Co.* v. *United States*, 175 U.S. 211, where industrialists, acting like commissars in modern communist countries, determined what tonnage should be produced by each company and what territory was "free" and what was "bonus." . . .

In *United States* v. *National Lead Co.* . . . a Sherman Act violation resulted from a division of world markets for titanium pigments, the key being allocation of territories through patent license agreements. A similar arrangement was struck down in *Timken Co.* v. *United States* . . . where world trade territories were allocated among an American, a British, and a French company through intercorporate arrangements called a "joint venture." *Nationwide Trailer Rental System, Inc.* v. *United States*, 355 U.S. 10 (affirming 156 F. Supp 800), held violative of the antitrust laws an agreement establishing exclusive territories for each member of an organization set up to regulate the one-way trailer rental industry and empowering a member to prevent any other operator from becoming a member in his area.

In the late 1950's the only producers of sodium chlorate in the United States were Pennsalt, one of the appellees in this case, Hooker Chemical Corporation, and American Potash and Chemical Corporation. No new firms had entered the industry for a decade. Prices seemed to be stable and little effort had been made to expand existing uses or to develop new ones. But during the 1950's the sodium chlorate market began to grow, chiefly on account of the adoption of chlorine dioxide bleaching in the pulp industry. Domestic production more than quadrupled between 1950 and 1960. The growth was the most pronounced in the southeast. By 1960 the southeast had the heaviest concentration of sodium chlorate buyers, the largest being the pulp and paper mills; and nearly half the national sodium chlorate productive capacity. In 1960 the southeast market was divided among the three producers as follows: Hooker, 49.5%, American Potash, 41.6%, Pennsalt, 8.9%.

Pennsalt, whose only sodium chlorate plant was at Portland, Oregon,

[5] See Oppenheim, "Antitrust Booms and Boomerangs," 59 *Nw. U. L. Rev.* 33, 35 (1964).

became interested in establishing a plant in the rapidly growing southeast sodium chlorate market. It made cost studies as early as 1951 for such a project; and from 1955 on it gave the matter almost continuous consideration. . . .

In the early 1950's Olin too was investigating the possibilities of entering the southeast industry. It took various steps looking toward establishment of a production plant in the southeastern United States. . . .

During the years when Pennsalt and Olin were considering independent entry into the southeast market, they were also discussing joint entry. In order to test the southeast market the two agreed in December of 1957 that Pennsalt would make available to Olin, as exclusive seller, 2,000 tons of sodium chlorate per year for two or three years, Olin agreeing to sell the chemical only to pulp and paper companies in the southeast, except for one company which Pennsalt reserved the right to serve directly. Another agreement entered into in February 1958 provided that neither of the two companies would "move in the chlorate or perchlorate field without keeping the other party informed." And each by the agreement bound itself "to bring to the attention of the other any unusual aspects of this business which might make it desirable to proceed further with production plans." The purpose of this latter agreement, it was found, was to assure that each party would advise the other of any plans independently to enter the market before it would take any definite action on its own.

So what we have in substance is two major companies who on the eve of competitive projects in the southeastern market join forces. In principle the case is no different from one where Pennsalt and Olin decide to divide the southeastern market as was done in *Addyston Pipe* and in the other division-of-markets cases already summarized. Through the "joint venture" they do indeed divide it fifty-fifty. That division through the device of the "joint venture" is as plain and precise as though made in more formal agreements. As we saw in the *Timken* case, "agreements between legally separate persons and companies to suppress competition among themselves and others" cannot be justified "by labeling the project a 'joint venture.' " . . . And we added, "Perhaps every agreement and combination to restrain trade could be so labeled." . . . What may not be done by two companies who decide to divide a market surely cannot be done by the convenient creation of a legal umbrella—whether joint venture or common ownership and control . . . —under which they achieve the same objective by moving in unison.

An actual division of the market through the device of "joint venture" has, I think, the effect "substantially to lessen competition" within the meaning of Section 7 of the Clayton Act. . . .

We do not, of course, know for certain what would have happened if the "joint venture" had not materialized. But we do know that Section 7 deals only with probabilities, not certainties. We know that the interest of each company in the project was lively, that one if not both of them would probably have entered that market, and that even if only one had entered at the beginning the presence of the other on the periphery would in all likelihood have been a potent competitive factor. Cf. *United States v. El Paso Natural Gas Co.* . . . We also know that as between Pennsalt and Olin the "joint venture" foreclosed all future competition by dividing the market fifty-fifty. That could not have been done consistently with our decisions had the "joint venture" been created after Pennsalt and Olin had entered the market or after either had done so. To allow the joint venture to obtain antitrust immunity because it was launched at the very threshold of the entry of two potential competitors into a territory is to let Section 7 be avoided by sophisticated devices.

There is no need to remand this case for a finding "as to the reasonable probability that either one of the corporations would have entered the market by building a plant, while the other would have remained a significant potential competitor." . . . This case—now almost three years in litigation—has already produced a trial extending over a 23-day period, the introduction of approximately 450 exhibits, and a 1,600 page record. We should not require the investment of additional time, money, and effort where, as here, a case turns on one crucial finding and the record is sufficient to enable this Court—which is as competent in this regard as the District Court—to supply it.

MR. JUSTICE HARLAN, dissenting.

I can see no purpose to be served by this remand except to give the Government an opportunity to retreive an antitrust case which it has lost, and properly so. Believing that this Court should not lend itself to such a course, I would affirm the judgment of the District Court.

Note: On remand, the District Court found no reasonable probability that either company would have entered unilaterally [246 F. Supp. 917 (D. Del. 1965)]. This was ultimately affirmed by an equally divided Supreme Court [389 U.S. 308 (1967)].

PART IV

Trade Practices

| Chapter | PRICE DISCRIMINATION |
| 9 | |

Few issues in antitrust enforcement have engendered as much controversy as have efforts to enforce the Robinson-Patman Act. Underlying much of this controversy is the feeling by many economists and lawyers that the Act was designed to protect competitors rather than competition. Clearly, price discrimination may have the effect of promoting competition (e.g., by increasing the ability of new firms to break into established markets), or it may lessen competition by permitting a powerful competitor to "sharp-shoot" against more localized rivals. As a consequence, it is often difficult to determine the purpose or probable effect of discriminatory pricing.

This fundamental perplexity is compounded by several subordinate issues. First, there is the question, discussed in the *Morton Salt* and *Utah Pie* decisions, of the extent to which the Federal Trade Commission must go to prove that a given discrimination "may" injure competition. The second, and perhaps more complex issue concerns the so-called "good faith defense," and is discussed in the *Standard of Indiana* case. In that proceeding the Federal Trade Commission challenged the absolute character of the good faith defense, arguing that a showing of competitive injury removes the need to consider whether or not a seller met competition. In its 1951 decision the Court expressed a contrary view, holding the good faith defense to be absolute; it then upheld, some years later, the adequacy of the evidence of good faith offered by the company.

Finally, the *Borden* case illustrates the problems that emerge in trying to lend economic content to legal phraseology, in this case, in determining whether two products are "of like grade and quality" within the meaning of the Robinson-Patman Act.

Federal Trade Commission v. *Morton Salt Company*

334 U.S. 37 (1948)

MR. JUSTICE BLACK delivered the opinion of the Court.

The Federal Trade Commission, after a hearing, found that the respondent, which manufactures and sells table salt in interstate commerce, had discriminated in price between different purchasers of like grades and qualities, and concluded that such discriminations were in violation of Section 2 of the Clayton Act . . . as amended by the Robinson-Patman Act. . . . It accordingly issued a cease and desist order. . . . Upon petition of the respondent the Circuit Court of Appeals, with one judge dissenting, set aside the Commission's findings and order, directed the Commission to dismiss its complaint against respondent, and denied a cross petition of the Commission for enforcement of its order. 162 F.2d 949. The Court's judgment rested on its construction of the Act, its holding that crucial findings of the Commission were either not supported by evidence or were contrary to the evidence, and its conclusion that the Commission's order was too broad. Since questions of importance in the construction and administration of the Act were presented, we granted certiorari. . . .

Respondent manufactures several different brands of table salt and sells them directly to (1) wholesalers or jobbers, who in turn resell to the retail trade, and (2) large retailers, including chain store retailers. Respondent sells its finest brand of table salt, known as Blue Label, on what it terms a standard quantity discount system available to all customers. Under this system the purchasers pay a delivered price and the cost to both wholesale and retail purchasers of this brand differs according to the quantities bought. These prices are as follows, after making allowance for rebates and discounts:

	Per Case
Less-than-carload purchases	$1.60
Carload purchases	1.50
5,000-case purchases in any consecutive 12 months	1.40
50,000-case purchases in any consecutive 12 months	1.35

Only five companies have ever bought sufficient quantities of respondent's salt to obtain the $1.35 per case price. These companies could buy in such quantities because they operate large chains of retail stores in various parts of the country. As a result of this low price these five companies have been able to sell Blue Label salt at retail cheaper than wholesale purchasers from respondent could reasonably sell the same brand of salt to independently operated retail stores, many of whom competed with the local outlets of the five chain stores. . . .

In addition to these standard quantity discounts, special allowances were granted certain favored customers who competed with other customers to whom they were denied.

First. Respondent's basic contention, which it argues this case hinges upon, is that its "standard quantity discounts, available to all on equal terms, as contrasted, for example, to hidden or special rebates, allowances, prices or discounts, are not discriminatory within the meaning of the Robinson-Patman Act." Theoretically, these discounts are equally available to all, but functionally they are not. For as the record indicates (if reference to it on this point were necessary) no single independent retail grocery store, and probably no single wholesaler, bought as many as 50,-000 cases or as much as $50,000 worth of table salt in one year. Furthermore, the record shows that, while certain purchasers were enjoying one or more of respondent's standard quantity discounts, some of their competitors made purchases in such small quantities that they could not qualify for any of respondent's discounts, even those based on carload shipments. The legislative history of the Robinson-Patman Act makes it abundantly clear that Congress considered it to be an evil that a large buyer could secure a competitive advantage over a small buyer solely because of the large buyer's quantity purchasing ability. The Robinson-Patman Act was passed to deprive a large buyer of such advantages except to the extent that a lower price could be justified by reason of a seller's diminished costs due to quantity manufacture, delivery or sale, or by reason of the seller's good faith effort to meet a competitor's equally low price.

Section 2 of the original Clayton Act had included a proviso that nothing contained in it should prevent "discrimination in price . . . on account of differences in the grade, quality, or quantity of the commodity sold, or that makes only due allowance for difference in the cost of selling or transportation. . . ." That section has been construed as permitting quantity discounts, such as those here, without regard to the amount of the seller's actual savings in cost attributable to quantity sales or quantity deliveries. . . . The House Committee Report on the Robinson-Patman Act considered that the Clayton Act's proviso allowing quantity discounts so weakened Section 2 "as to render it inadequate, if not almost a nullity." . . . And it was . . . to protect competition from all price differentials except those based in full on cost savings that Section 2(a) of the amendment provided "That nothing herein contained shall prevent differentials which make only due allowance for differences in the cost of manufacture, sale, or delivery resulting from the differing methods or quantities in which such commodities are to such purchasers sold or delivered."

The foregoing references, without regard to others which could be mentioned, establish that respondent's standard quantity discounts are discriminatory within the meaning of the Act, and are prohibited by it whenever they have the defined effect on competition. . . .

Second. The Government interprets the opinion of the Circuit Court of Appeals as having held that in order to establish "discrimination in price" under the Act the burden rested on the Commission to prove that respondent's quantity discount differentials were not justified by its cost savings. Respondent does not so understand the Court of Appeals decision, and furthermore admits that no such burden rests on the Commission. We agree that it does not. . . . [S]ection 2(b) of the Act specifically imposes the burden of showing justification upon one who is shown to have discriminated in prices. . . .

Third. It is argued that the findings fail to show that respondent's discriminatory discounts had in fact caused injury to competition. There are specific findings that such injuries had resulted from respondent's discounts, although the statute does not require the Commission to find that injury has actually resulted. The statute requires no more than that the effect of the prohibited price discriminations "may be substantially to lessen competition . . . or to injure, destroy, or prevent competition." After a careful consideration of this provision of the Robinson-Patman Act, we have said that "the statute does not require that the discriminations must in fact have harmed competition, but only that there is a reasonable possibility that they 'may' have such an effect." *Corn Products Co.* v. *Federal Trade Comm'n,* 324 U.S. 726, 742. Here the Commission found what would appear to be obvious, that the competitive opportunities of certain merchants were injured when they had to pay respondent substantially more for their goods than their competitors had to pay. The findings are adequate.

Fourth. It is urged that the evidence is inadequate to support the Commission's findings of injury to competition. As we have pointed out, however, the Commission is authorized by the Act to bar discriminatory prices upon the "reasonable possibility" that different prices for like goods to competing purchasers may have the defined effect on competition. That respondent's quantity discounts did result in price differentials between competing purchasers sufficient in amount to influence their resale prices of salt was shown by evidence. This showing in itself is adequate to support the Commission's appropriate findings that the effect of such price discriminations "may be substantially to lessen competition . . . and to injure, destroy, and prevent competition."

The adequacy of the evidence to support the Commission's findings of reasonably possible injury to competition from respondent's price differentials between competing carload and less-than-carload purchasers is singled out for special attacks here. . . . The argument is that there is an obvious saving to a seller who delivers goods in carload lots. Assuming this to be true, that fact would not tend to disprove injury to the merchant compelled to pay the less-than-carload price. For a ten-cent carload price differential against a merchant would injure him competitively just as much as a ten-cent differential under any other name. However relevant the separate carload argument might be to the question of justifying a differential by cost savings, it has no relevancy in determining whether the differential works an injury to a competitor. Since Congress has not seen fit to give carload discounts any favored classification we cannot do so. Such discounts, like all others, can be justified by a seller who proves that the full amount of the discount is based on his actual savings in cost. The trouble with this phase of respondent's case is that it has thus far failed to make such proof.

It is also argued that respondent's less-than-carload sales are very small in comparison with the total volume of its business and for that reason we should reject the Commission's finding that the effect of the carload discrimination may substantially lessen competition and may injure competition between purchasers who are granted and those who are denied this discriminatory discount. To support this argument, reference is made to the fact that salt is a small item in most wholesale and retail businesses and in consumers' budgets. For several reasons we cannot accept this contention.

There are many articles in a grocery store that, considered separately, are comparatively small parts of a merchant's stock. Congress intended to protect a merchant from competitive injury attributable to discriminatory prices on any or all goods sold in interstate commerce, whether the particular goods constituted a major or minor portion of his stock. Since a grocery store consists of many comparatively small articles, there is no possible way effectively to protect a grocer from discriminatory prices except by applying the prohibitions of the Act to each individual article in the store.

Furthermore, in enacting the Robinson-Patman Act, Congress was especially concerned with protecting small businesses which were unable to buy in quantities, such as the merchants here who purchased in less-than-carload lots. To this end it undertook to strengthen this very phase of the old Clayton Act. . . . Since there was evidence sufficient to show that the less-than-carload purchasers might have been handicapped in competing with the more favored carload purchasers by the differential in price established by respondent, the Commission was justified in finding that competition might have thereby been substantially lessened or have been injured within the meaning of the Act.

Apprehension is expressed in this Court that enforcement of the Commission's order against respondent's continued violations of the Robinson-Patman Act might lead respondent to raise table salt prices to its carload purchasers. Such a conceivable, though, we think, highly improbable, contingency, could afford us no reason for upsetting the Commission's findings and declining to direct compliance with a statute passed by Congress.

The Commission here went much further in receiving evidence than the statute requires. It heard testimony from many witnesses in various parts of the country to show that they had suffered actual financial losses on account of respondent's discriminatory prices. Experts were offered to prove the tendency of injury from such prices. The evidence covers about two thousand pages, largely devoted to this single issue—injury to competition. It would greatly handicap effective enforcement of the Act to require testimony to show that which we believe to be self-evident, namely, that there is a "reasonable possibility" that competition may be adversely affected by a practice under which manufacturers and producers sell their goods to some customers substantially cheaper than they sell like goods to the competitors of these customers. This showing in itself is sufficient to justify our conclusion that the Commission's findings of injury to competition were adequately supported by evidence.

Fifth. The Circuit Court of Appeals held, and respondent here contends, that the order was too sweeping. . . .

. . . True, the Commission did not merely prohibit future discounts, rebates, and allowances in the exact mathematical percentages previously utilized by respondent. Had the order done no more than that, respondent could have continued substantially the same unlawful practices despite the order by simply altering the discount percentages and the quantities of salt to which the percentages applied. . . .

The judgment of the Circuit Court of Appeals is reversed and the proceedings are remanded to that court to be disposed of in conformity with this opinion.

Reversed.

[Mr. Justice Jackson with whom Mr. Justice Frankfurter joined, dissented in part.]

Standard Oil Company (of Indiana) v. *Federal Trade Commission*
340 U.S. 231 (1951)

MR. JUSTICE BURTON delivered the opinion of the Court.

In this case the Federal Trade Commission challenged the right of the Standard Oil Company, under the Robinson-Patman Act, to sell gasoline to four comparatively large "jobber" customers in Detroit at a less price per gallon than it sold like gasoline to many comparatively small service station customers in the same area. The Company's defenses were that (1) the sales involved were not in interstate commerce and (2) its lower price to the jobbers was justified because made to retain them as customers and in good faith to meet an equally low price of a competitor. The Commission, with one member dissenting, ordered the company to cease and desist from making such a price differential. 43 F.T.C. 56. The Court of Appeals slightly modified the order and required its enforcement as modified. 173 F.2d 210. We granted certiorari on petition of the company because the case presents an important issue under the Robinson-Patman Act which has not been settled by this Court. . . .

For the reasons hereinafter stated, we agree with the court below that the sales were made in interstate commerce but we agree with petitioner that, under the Act, the lower price to the jobbers was justified if it was made to retain each of them as a customer and in good faith to meet an equally low price of a competitor.

. . . [T]he material facts are summarized here on the basis of the Commission's findings. The sales described are those of Red Crown gasoline because those sales raise all of the material issues and constitute about 90% of petitioner's sales in the Detroit area.

Since the effective date of the Robinson-Patman Act, June 19, 1936, petitioner has sold its Red Crown gasoline to its "jobber" customers at its tank-car prices. Those prices have been 1½¢ per gallon less than its tank-wagon prices to service station customers for identical gasoline in the same area. In practice, the service stations have resold the gasoline at the prevailing retail service station prices. Each of petitioner's so-called "jobber" customers has been free to resell its gasoline at retail or wholesale. Each, at some time, has resold some of it at retail. One now resells it only at retail. The others now resell it largely at wholesale. As to resale prices, two of the "jobbers" have resold their gasoline only at the prevailing wholesale or retail rates. The other two, however, have reflected, in varying degrees, petitioner's reductions in the cost of the gasoline to them by reducing their resale prices of that gasoline below the prevailing rates. The effect of these reductions has thus reached competing retail service stations in part through retail stations operated by the "jobbers" and in part through retail stations which purchased gasoline from the "jobbers" at less than the prevailing tank-wagon prices. The Commission found that such reduced resale prices "have resulted in injuring, destroying, and preventing competition between said favored dealers and retail dealers in respondent's [petitioner's] gasoline and other major brands of gasoline. . . ."

. . . The distinctive characteristics of these "jobbers" are that each (1) maintains sufficient bulk storage to take delivery of gasoline in tank-car quantities (of 8,000 to 12,000 gallons) rather than in tank-wagon quantities (or 700 to 800 gallons) as is customary for service stations; (2) owns and operates tank wagons and other facilities for delivery of gasoline to service stations; (3) has an established business sufficient to insure purchases of from one to two million gallons a year; and (4) has adequate credit responsibility. While the cost of petitioner's sales and deliveries of gasoline to each of these four "jobbers" is no doubt less, per gallon, than the cost of its sales and deliveries of like gasoline to its service station customers in the same area, there is no finding that such difference accounts for the entire reduction in price made by petitioner to these "jobbers," and we proceed on the assumption that it does not entirely account for that difference.

Petitioner placed its reliance upon evidence offered to show that its lower price to each jobber was made in order to retain that jobber as a customer and in good faith to meet an equally low price offered by one or more competitors. The Commission, however, treated such evidence as not relevant. . . .

[The Commission stated:]

. . . [E]ven though the lower prices in question may have been made by respondent in good faith to meet the lower prices of competitors, this does not constitute a defense in the face of affirmative proof that the effect of the discrimination was to injure, destroy and prevent competition with the retail stations operated by the said named dealers and with stations operated by their retailer-customers. . . .

... In its opinion in the instant case, the Commission recognizes that it is an absolute defense to a charge of price discrimination for a seller to prove, under Section 2(*a*) that its price differential makes only due allowances for differences in cost or for price changes made in response to changing market conditions. 41 F.T.C. at 283. Each of these three defenses is introduced by the same phrase "nothing ... shall prevent," and all are embraced in the same word "justification" in the first sentence of Section 2(*b*). It is natural, therefore, to conclude that each of these defenses is entitled to the same effect, without regard to whether there also appears an affirmative showing of actual or potential injury to competition at the same or a lower level traceable to the price differential made by the seller. The Commission says, however, that the proviso in Section 2(*b*) as to a seller meeting in good faith a lower competitive price is not an absolute defense if an injury to competition may result from such price reduction. We find no basis for such a distinction between the defense in Section 2(*a*) and (*b*).

The defense in subsection (*b*), now before us, is limited to a price reduction made to meet in good faith an equally low price of a competitor. ... [But] the actual core of the defense ... still consists of the provision that wherever a lawful lower price of a competitor threatens to deprive a seller of a customer, the seller, to retain that customer, may in good faith meet that lower price. Actual competition, at least in this elemental form, is thus preserved. ...

This right of a seller, under Section 2(*b*), to meet in good faith an equally low price of a competitor has been considered here before. Both in *Corn Products Refining Co.* v. *Federal Trade Comm'n*, 324 U.S. 726, and in *Federal Trade Comm'n* v. *Staley Mfg. Co.*, 324 U.S. 746, evidence in support of this defense was reviewed at length. There would have been no occasion thus to review it under the theory now contended for by the Commission. While this Court did not sustain the seller's defense in either case, it did unquestionably recognize the relevance of the evidence in support of that defense. The decision in each case was based upon the insufficiency of the seller's evidence to establish its defense, not upon the inadequacy of its defense as a matter of law. ...

In the Staley case ... most of the Court's opinion is devoted to the consideration of the evidence introduced in support of the seller's defense under Section 2(*b*). The discussion proceeds upon the assumption, applicable here, that if a competitor's "lower price" is a lawful individual price offered to any of the seller's customers, then the seller is protected, under Section 2(*b*), in making a counteroffer provided the seller proves that its counteroffer is made to meet in good faith its competitor's equally low price. ...

... All that petitioner asks in the instant case is that its evidence be considered and that findings be made by the Commission as to the sufficiency of that evidence to support petitioner's defense under Section 2(*b*).

In addition, there has been widespread understanding that, under the Robinson-Patman Act, it is a complete defense to a charge of price discrimination for the seller to show that its price differential has been made in good faith to meet a lawful and equally low price of a competitor. This understanding is reflected in actions and statements of members and counsel of the Federal Trade Commission. Representatives of the Department of Justice have testified to the effectiveness and value of the defense under the Robinson-Patman Act. We see no reason to depart now from that interpretation.

The heart of our national economic policy long has been faith in the value of competition. In the Sherman and Clayton Acts, as well as in the Robinson-Patman Act, "Congress was dealing with competition, which it sought to protect, and monopoly, which it sought to prevent." . . . We need not now reconcile, in its entirety, the economic theory which underlies the Robinson-Patman Act with that of the Sherman and Clayton Acts. It is enough to say that Congress did not seek by the Robinson-Patman Act either to abolish competition or so radically to curtail it that a seller would have no substantial right of self-defense against a price raid by a competitor. . . . There is . . . plain language and established practice which permits a seller, through Section 2(b), to retain a customer by realistically meeting in good faith the price offered to that customer, without necessarily changing the seller's price to its other customers.

In a case where a seller sustains the burden of proof placed upon it to establish its defense under Section 2(b), we find no reason to destroy that defense indirectly, merely because it also appears that the beneficiaries of the seller's price reductions may derive a competitive advantage from them or may, in a natural course of events, reduce their own resale prices to their customers. It must have been obvious to Congress that any price reduction to any dealer may always affect competition at that dealer's level as well as at the dealer's resale level, whether or not the reduction to the dealer is discriminatory. Likewise, it must have been obvious to Congress that any price reductions initiated by a seller's competitor would, if not met by the seller, affect competition at the beneficiary's level or among the beneficiary's customers just as much as if those reductions had been met by the seller. The proviso in Section 2(b), as interpreted by the Commission, would not be available when there was or might be an injury to competition at a resale level. So interpreted, the proviso would have such little, if any, applicability as to be practically meaningless. We may, therefore, conclude that Congress meant to permit the natural consequences to follow the seller's action in meeting in good faith a lawful and equally low price of its competitor.

In its argument here, the Commission suggests that there may be some situations in which it might recognize the proviso in Section 2(b) as a complete defense, even though the seller's differential in price did injure competition. In support of this, the Commission indicates that in each case it must weigh the potentially injurious effect of a seller's price reduction upon competition at all lower levels against its beneficial effect in permitting the seller to meet competition at its own level. In the absence of more explicit requirements and more specific standards of comparison than we have here, it is difficult to see how an injury to competition at a level below that of the seller can thus be balanced fairly against a justification for meeting the competition at the seller's level. We hesitate to accept Section 2(*b*) as establishing such a dubious defense. . . .

The judgment of the Court of Appeals, accordingly, is reversed and the case is remanded to that court with instructions to remand it to the Federal Trade Commission to make finding in conformity with this opinion.

It is so ordered.

[Mr. Justice Minton took no part in the consideration or decision of this case. Mr. Justice Reed, joined by The Chief Justice and Mr. Justice Black, dissented.]

Note: In the proceedings following the remand, the Commission held that Standard did *not* act in good faith because its reduced prices were made pursuant to a price *system* rather than being "the result of departures from a nondiscriminatory price scale." 49 F. T. C. 923,954. The Court of Appeals found no basis in the 8 volume, 5,500 page record for such a conclusion, and reversed. 233 F. 2d 649. The Supreme Court, in this decision next abstracted, affirmed the lower court view.

Federal Trade Commission v. *Standard Oil Company {of Indiana}*

355 U.S. 396 (1958)

MR. JUSTICE CLARK delivered the opinion of the Court.

This case is a sequel to *Standard Oil Co.* v. *Federal Trade Comm'n,* 340 U.S. 231 (1951), wherein the Court held that Section 2(b) of the Clayton Act . . . as amended by the Robinson-Patman Act . . . afforded a seller a complete defense to a charge of price discrimination if its lower price was "made in good faith to meet a lawful and equally low price of a competitor." . . . We remanded the case with instructions that the Federal Trade Commission make findings on Standard's contention that its discriminatory prices were so made. The subsequent findings are not altogether clear. The Commission, acting on the same record, seemingly does not contest the fact that Standard's deductions were made to meet the equally low prices of its competitors. However, Standard was held not to have acted in good faith, and the Section 2(b) defense precluded, because of the Commission's determination that Standard's reduced prices were made pursuant to a price system rather than being "the result of departures from a nondiscriminatory price scale." . . . The Court of Appeals found no basis in the record for such a finding and vacated the order of the Commission, holding that Standard's " 'good faith' defense was firmly established." . . . In view of our former opinion and the importance of bringing an end to this protracted litigation, we granted certiorari. . . . Having concluded that the case turns on a factual issue, decided by the Court of Appeals upon a fair assessment of the record, we affirm the decision below.

The long history of this 17-year-old case may be found both in the original opinion of the Court of Appeals . . . and in the original opinion of this Court, *supra*. . . .

The Commission urges us to examine its 8-volume record of over 5,500 pages and determine if its finding that Standard reduced prices to four "jobbers" pursuant to a pricing system was erroneous, as held by the Court of Appeals. The Commission contends that a Section 2(b) defense is precluded if the reductions were so made. If wrong in this, it maintains that the "good faith" element of a Section 2(b) defense is not made out by showing that competitors employ such a pricing system, and in any event is negatived by Standard's failure to make a bona fide effort to review its pricing system upon passage of the Robinson-Patman Act.

On the present posture of the case we believe that further review of the evidence is unwarranted. . . . [I]t now appears that "[p]roper decision of the controversy depends upon a question of fact," and therefore "we adhere to the usual rule of non-interference where conclusions of Circuit Courts of Appeals depend on appreciation of circumstances which admit of different interpretations." . . . We do no more on the issue of insubstantiality than decide that the Court of Appeals has made a "fair assessment" of the record. That conclusion is strengthened by the fact that the finding made by the Court of Appeals accords with that of the trial examiner, two dissenting members of the Commission, and another panel of the Court of Appeals when the case was first before that court in 1949, all of them being agreed that the prices were reduced in good faith to meet offers of competitors.

Both parties acknowledge that discrimination pursuant to a price system would preclude a finding of "good faith." *Federal Trade Comm'n v. A. E. Staley Mfg. Co.* . . . ; *Federal Trade Comm'n v. Cement Institute* . . . ; *Federal Trade Comm'n v. National Lead Co.* . . . The sole question then is one of fact: were Standard's reduced prices to four "jobber" buyers—Citrin-Kolb, Stikeman, Wayne, and Ned's—made pursuant to a pricing system rather than to meet individual competitive situations? . . .

It appears to us that the crucial inquiry is not why reduced prices were first granted to Citrin-Kolb, Stikeman, and Wayne, but rather why the reduced price was continued subsequent to passage of the Act in 1936. The findings show that both major and local suppliers made numerous attempts in the 1936–1941 period to lure these "jobbers" away from Standard with cut-rate prices, oftentimes much lower than the one-and-one-half-cent reduction Standard was giving them.[1] It is uncontradicted, as pointed out in one of the Commission dissents, that Standard lost three of its seven "jobbers" by not meeting competitors' pirating offers in 1933–1934. All of this occurred in the context of a major gasoline price war in the Detroit area, created by an extreme overabundance of supply— a setting most unlikely to lend itself to general pricing policies. . . .

The findings as to Ned's, the only one of the "jobbers" initially to receive the tank-car price *post* Robinson-Patman, are highly significant. After a prolonged period of haggling, during which Ned's pressured Standard with information as to numerous more attractive price offers made by other suppliers, Standard responded to an ultimatum from Ned's in 1936 with a half-cent-per-gallon reduction from the tank-wagon price. The Commission concedes that this first reduction occurred at a time when Ned's did not meet the criteria normally insisted upon by Standard before giving any reduction. Two years later, after a still further period of haggling[2] and another Ned's ultimatum, Standard gave a second reduction of still another cent.

In determining that Standard's prices to these four "jobbers" were reduced as a response to individual competitive situations rather than pursuant to a pricing system, the Court of Appeals considered the factors just mentioned, all of which weigh heavily against the Commission's position. The Commission's own findings thus afford ample witness that a "fair assessment" of the record has been made. Standard's use here of two prices, the lower of which could be obtained under the spur of threats to switch to pirating competitors, is a competitive deterrent far short of the discriminatory pricing of *Staley, Cement,* and *National Lead, supra,* and one which we believe within the sanction of Section 2(b) of the Robinson-Patman Act.

Affirmed.

MR. JUSTICE DOUGLAS, with whom THE CHIEF JUSTICE, MR. JUSTICE BLACK and MR. JUSTICE BRENNAN concur, dissenting.

The Court today cripples the enforcement of the Robinson-Patman Act . . . in an important area. . . .

---

[1] The Commission places great importance on the fact that only one of these offers was a standing offer. This is not a situation involving only one or two competitive raids, however; continuation of reductions once granted is warranted by Section 2(b) when competitors' reduced price offers are recurring again and again in a cutthroat market.

[2] The findings indicate that similar haggling over an extended period of time occurred before each of the other "jobbers" obtained a reduced price. The great time consumed in the haggling process tends to negate any idea that the participants were only deciding whether a given purchaser met Standard's four well-defined "jobber" criteria—annual volume of one to two million gallons, own delivery facilities, bulk storage capable of taking tank-car delivery, and responsible credit rating.

First. Standard admitted that it gave reduced prices to some retailers and refused those reduced prices to other retailers. Before granting these retailers the reduced prices Standard classified them as "jobbers." Standard's definition of a "jobber" took into account the volume of sales of the "jobber," his bulk storage facilities, his delivery equipment, and his credit rating. If Standard's tests were met, the "retailer" became a "jobber" even though he continued to sell at retail. Moreover, Standard's test of who was a "jobber" did not take into account the cost to Standard of making these sales. So Standard's definition of "jobber" was arbitrary, both as respects the matter of *costs* and the matter of *function*. It comes down to this: a big retailer gets one price; a small retailer gets another price. And this occurs at the *ipse dixit* of Standard, not because the cost of serving the big retailer is less nor because the big retailer, as respects the sales in question, performs a function different from any other retailer. . . .

Second. It is argued, however, that the discrimination in favor of the big retailers and against the small ones is justified on the ground that Standard did no more than meet competition. . . .

If a seller offers a reduced price for no other reason than to meet the lawful low price of a competitor, then the seller's otherwise unlawful price falls within the protection of Section 2(b). But where, as here, a seller establishes a discriminatory pricing *system*, this system does not acquire the protection of Section 2(b) simply because in fact use of the system holds a customer against a competitive offer. In other words, a discriminatory pricing system which in fact meets competition is not a good-faith meeting of competition within the meaning of the Act. The effectiveness of the system does not demonstrate the good faith of its initiator.

Third. The mere fact that a competitor offered the lower price does not mean that Standard can lawfully meet it. Standard's system of price discrimination, shown not to be in "good faith," cannot be justified by showing that competitors were using the same system. "This startling conclusion is admissible only upon the assumption that the statute permits a seller to maintain an otherwise unlawful system of discriminatory prices, merely because he had adopted it in its entirety, as a means of securing the benefits of a like unlawful system maintained by his competitors." *Federal Trade Comm'n* v. *Staley Co., supra.* . . . See also *Federal Trade Comm'n* v. *Cement Institute, supra.* . . .

. . . It is only a *lawful* lower price that may be met. Were it otherwise then the law to govern is not the Robinson-Patman Act but the law of the jungle. . . .

When we let Standard classify a "retailer" as a "jobber" and grant a discriminatory price pursuant to arbitrary requirements merely because a competitor employs the same system, we make this provision of the Robinson-Patman Act ineffective. We should read the Act in a more hospitable way and allow Standard to maintain its discriminatory price schedule for retailers if and only if it can show

(a) that that price was justified on the basis of costs or function, or

(b) that it was in good faith meeting the *lawful* offer of a competitor, rather than merely matching a predatory price system, or meeting a competitor's "pirating" offers, to use the Court's word, with a "pirating" system of its own.

I would reverse this judgment and direct enforcement of the Commission's order.

Federal Trade Commission v. *Borden Company*

383 U.S. 637 (1966)

MR. JUSTICE WHITE delivered the opinion of the Court.

The Borden Company, respondent here, produces and sells evaporated milk under the Borden name, a nationally advertised brand. At the same time Borden packs and markets evaporated milk under various private brands owned by its customers. This milk is physically and chemically identical with the milk it distributes under its own brand but is sold at both the wholesale and retail level at prices regularly below those obtained for the Borden brand milk. The Federal Trade Commission found the milk sold under the Borden and the private labels to be of like grade and quality as required for the applicability of §2(a) of the Robinson-Patman Act, held the price differential to be discriminatory within the meaning of the section, ascertained the requisite adverse effect on commerce, rejected Borden's claim of cost justification and consequently issued a cease-and-desist order. The Court of Appeals set aside the Commission's order on the sole ground that as a matter of law, the customer label milk was not of the same grade and quality as the milk sold under the Borden brand. . . . We now reverse the decision of the Court of Appeals and remand the case to that court for the determination of the remaining issues raised by respondent Borden in that court. . . .

The position of Borden and of the Court of Appeals is that the determination of like grade and quality, which is a threshold finding essential to the applicability of §2(a), may not be based solely on the physical properties of the products without regard to the brand names they bear and the relative public acceptance these brands enjoy—"consideration should be given to all commercially significant distinctions which affect market value, whether they be physical or promotional." 339 F. 2d, at 137. Here, because the milk bearing the Borden brand regularly sold at a higher price than did the milk with a buyer's label, the court considered the products to be "commercially" different and hence of different "grade" for the purposes of §2(a), even though they were physically identical and of equal quality. Although a mere difference in brand would not in itself demonstrate a difference in grade, decided consumer preference for one brand over another, reflected in the willingness to pay a higher price for the well-known brand, was, in the view of the Court of Appeals, sufficient to differentiate chemically identical products and to place the price differential beyond the reach of §2(a).

We reject this construction of §2(a), as did both the examiner and the Commission in this case. The Commission's view is that labels do not differentiate products for the purpose of determining grade or quality, even though the one label may have more customer appeal and command a higher price in the marketplace from a substantial segment of the public. That this is the Commission's long-standing interpretation of the present Act, as well as of §2 of the Clayton Act before its amendment by the Robinson-Patman Act,[1] may be gathered from the Commission's decisions dating back to 1936. . . . These views of the agency are entitled to respect . . . and represent a more reasonable construction of the statute than that offered by the Court of Appeals.

Obviously there is nothing in the language of the statute indicating that grade, as distinguished from quality, is not to be determined by the characteristics of the product itself, but by consumer preferences, brand acceptability or what customers think of it and are willing to pay for it. Moreover, what legislative history there is concerning this question supports the Commission's construction of the statute rather than that of the Court of Appeals.

[For example:] During the 1936 hearings on the proposed amendments to Section 2 of the Clayton Act, the attention of the Congress was specifically called to the question of the applicability of §2 to the practice of a manufacturer selling his product under his nationally advertised brand at a different price than he charged when the product was sold under a private label. Because it was feared that the Act would require the elimination of such price differentials . . . and because private brands "would [thus] be put out of business by the nationally advertised brands," it was suggested that the proposed §2(a) be amended so as to apply only to sales of commodities of "like grade, quality and *brand*." (Emphasis added.) *Id.*, at 421. There was strong objection to the amendment and it was not adopted by the Committee. . . .

The Commission's construction of the statute also appears to us to further the purpose and policy of the Robinson-Patman Act. Subject to specified exceptions and defenses, §2(a) proscribes unequal treatment of different customers in comparable transactions, but only if there is the requisite effect upon competition, actual or potential. But if the transactions are deemed to involve goods of disparate grade or quality,

---

[1] A proviso to §2 of the original Clayton Act expected price discrimination "on account of differences in the grade, quality, or quantity of the commodity sold. . . ." 38 Stat. 730 (1914).

the section has no application at all and the Commission never reaches either the issue of discrimination or that of anticompetitive impact. We doubt that Congress intended to foreclose these inquiries in situations where a single seller markets the identical product under several different brands, whether his own, his customers' or both. Such transactions are too laden with potential discrimination and adverse competitive effect to be excluded from the reach of §2(a) by permitting a difference in grade to be established by the label alone or by the label and its consumer appeal.[2]

If two products, physically identical but differently branded, are to be deemed of different grade because the seller regularly and successfully markets some quantity of both at different prices, the seller could, as far as §2(a) is concerned, make either product available to some customers and deny it to others, however discriminatory this might be and however damaging to competition. Those who were offered only one of the two products would be barred from competing for those customers who want or might buy the other. The retailer who was permitted to buy and sell only the more expensive brand would have no chance to sell to those who always buy the cheaper product or to convince others, by experience or otherwise, of the fact which he and all other dealers already know—that the cheaper product is actually identical with that carrying the more expensive label.

The seller, to escape the Act, would have only to succeed in selling some unspecified amount of each product to some unspecified portion of his customers, however large or small the price differential might be. The seller's pricing and branding policy, by being successful, would apparently validate itself by creating a difference in "grade" and thus taking itself beyond the purview of the Act.[3]

Our holding neither ignores the economic realities of the marketplace

---

[2] Borden argues that it spends large sums to insure the high quality of its Borden brand milk on customers' shelves, inferring that there really is a difference between its own milk and the milk sold under private labels, at least by the time it reaches the consumer. Of course, if Borden could prove this difference, it is unlikely that the case would be here. The findings are to the contrary in this case and we write on the premise that the two products are physically the same at the time of consumer purchase. Borden's extra expenses in connection with its own milk are more relevant to the cost justification issue than to the question we have before us.

[3] The market acceptability test would hardly stop with insulating from inquiry the price differential between proprietary and private label sales. That test would also immunize from the Act sales at different prices of the same product under two different producer-owned labels, the one being less advertised and having less market acceptability than the other. And if it is "consumer preferences," . . . which create the difference in grade or quality, why should not Borden be able to discriminate between two purchasers of private label milk, as long as one label commands a higher price from consumers than the other and hence is of a different grade and quality? In this context perhaps the market acceptability test would be refined to preclude this differential on the grounds that Borden's customer, as distinguished from the consumer, will not pay more than his competitor for private label milk and therefore the milk sold by Borden under one private brand is really of the same grade and quality as the milk sold under the other brand even though ultimate consumers will pay more for one

nor denies that some labels will command a higher price than others, at least from some portion of the public. But it does mean that "the economic factors inherent in brand names and national advertising should not be considered in the jurisdictional inquiry under the statutory 'like grade and quality' tests." Report of The Attorney General's National Committee to Study the Antitrust Laws 158 (1955). And it does mean that transactions like those involved in this case may be examined by the Commission under §2(a). The Commission will determine, subject to judicial review, whether the differential under attack is discriminatory within the meaning of the Act, whether competition may be injured, and whether the differential is cost-justified or is defensible as a good-faith effort to meet the price of a competitor. "[T]angible consumer preferences as between branded and unbranded commodities should receive due legal recognition in the more flexible 'injury' and 'cost justification' provisions of the statute." *Id.,* at 159. This, we think, is precisely what Congress intended. The arguments for exempting private brand selling from §2(a) are, therefore, more appropriately addressed to the Congress than to this Court. . . .

. . . The judgment of the Court of Appeals is reversed and the case is remanded for further proceedings consistent with this opinion.

It is so ordered.

Mr. Justice Stewart, with whom Mr. Justice Harlan joins, dissenting.

I cannot agree that mere physical or chemical identity between premium and private label brands is, without more, a sufficient basis for a finding of "like grade and quality" within the meaning of §2(a) of the Robinson-Patman Act. The conclusion that a product that travels at a premium in the marketplace is of "like grade and quality" with products of inferior commercial value is not required by the language of the Robinson-Patman Act, by its logic, or by its legislative history.

---

than the other. Taking this approach, if Borden packed for one wholesale customer under two private labels, one having more consumer appeal than the other because of the customer's own advertising program, Borden must sell both brands at the same price it charges other private label customers because all such milk is of the same grade and quality. At the same time, the customer buying from Borden under two labels could himself sell one label at a reduced price without inquiry under §2(a) because the milk in one container is no longer of the same grade and quality as that in the other, although both the milk and the containers came from Borden. Such an approach would obviously focus not on consumer preference as determinative of grade and quality but on who spent the advertising money that created the preference —Borden's customer, not Borden, created the preference and hence the milk is of the same grade and quality in Borden's hands but not in its customer's. The dissent would exempt the effective advertiser from the Act. We think Congress intended to remit him to his defenses under the Act, including that of cost justification.

It is undisputed that the physical attributes and chemical constituents of Borden's premium and private label brands of evaporated milk are identical. It is also undisputed that the premium and private label brands are not competitive at the same price, and that if the private label milk is to be sold at all, it must be sold at prices substantially below the price commanded by Borden's premium brand. This simple market fact no more than reflects the obvious economic reality that consumer preferences can and do create significant commercial distinctions between otherwise similar products. By pursuing product comparison only so far as the result of laboratory analysis, the Court ignores a most relevant aspect of the inquiry into the question of "like grade and quality" under §2(a): Whether the products are different in the eyes of the consumer.[4]

There is nothing intrinsic to the concepts of grade and quality that requires exclusion of the commercial attributes of a product from their definition. The product purchased by a consumer includes not only the chemical components that any competent laboratory can itemize, but also a host of commercial intangibles that distinguish the product in the market place.[5] The premium paid for Borden brand milk reflects the consumer's awareness, promoted through advertising, that these commercial attributes are part and parcel of the premium product he is purchasing. The record in the present case indicates that wholesale purchasers of Borden's private label brands continued to purchase the premium brand in undiminished quantities. The record also indicates that retail purchasers who bought the premium brand did so with the specific expectation of acquiring a product of premium quality. Contrary to the Court's suggestion . . . this consumer expectation cannot accurately be characterized as a misapprehension. Borden took extensive precautions to insure that a

----

[4] No suggestion is made that any of the private label brands involved in this case show significant commercial differentiation from one another. It is possible, of course, that by extensive promotion private label brands could achieve consumer acceptance equivalent to that of a premium brand. In that situation, the products would still be economically different under the market test of §2(a) elucidated in this opinion, since the relevant comparison would exclude promotional efforts by persons other than the producer of the premium brand. Thus, promotional activities by customers of Borden in the present case could not affect the determination of "like grade and quality" with regard to sales by Borden. . . .

[5] Cf. Chamberlain, "The Theory of Monopolistic Competition," 56 (8th ed. 1962):

"A general class of product is differentiated if any significant basis exists for distinguishing the goods (or services) of one seller from those of another. Such a basis may be real or fancied, so long as it is of any importance whatever to buyers, and leads to a preference for one variety of the product over another. Where such differentiation exists, even though it be slight, buyers will be paired with sellers, not by chance and at random (as under pure competition), but according to their preferences.

"Differentiation may be based upon certain characteristics of the product itself, such as exclusive patented features; trade-marks; trade names; peculiarities of the package or container, if any; or singularity in quality, design, color, or style. . . . In so far as these and other intangible factors vary from seller to seller, the 'product' in each case is different, for buyers take them into account, more or less, and may be regarded as purchasing them along with the commodity itself." . . .

flawed product did not reach the consumer.[6] None of these precautions was taken for the private brand milk packed by Borden.[7] An important ingredient of the premium brand inheres in the consumer's belief, measured by past satisfaction and the market reputation established by Borden for its products, that tomorrow's can will contain the same premium product as that purchased today. To say, as the Court does, that these and other intangibles, which comprise an important part of the commercial value of a product, are not sufficient to confer on Borden's premium brand a "grade" or "quality" different from that of private label brands is to ignore the obvious market acceptance of that difference. . . .

The spare legislative history of the Robinson-Patman Act is in no way inconsistent with a construction of §2(a) that includes market acceptance in the test of "like grade and quality." That history establishes no more than that mere differences in brand or design, unaccompanied by any genuine physical, chemical, or market distinction, are insufficient to negate a finding of "like grade and quality" under §2(a).[8] Nothing that I have found in the legislative history speaks with precision to the sole issue before us here, the application of §2(a) to physically or chemically identical products that are in fact differentiated by substantial market factors.[9]

[6] Borden's Food Products Division maintained a staff of field representatives who inspected code-datings on cans of Borden brand milk in retail stores, in order to insure that older milk was sold first off the retailer's shelves. A witness for Borden testified that the principal dangers of long storage were discoloration of the milk, precipitation of calcium and other minerals, and separation and hardening of fat from the milk. As a further precaution against sales of defective milk, Borden dispatched its milk to wholesalers and retailers under a first-packed, first-shipped rotation plan that occasionally involved high-cost shipments from distant plants or warehouses. In addition, before shipment from a cold storage warehouse, Borden "tempered" its premium brand milk in order to prevent condensation on the cans, which might have resulted in rust to the cans and damage to the labels.

[7] As counsel for the respondent candidly stated on oral argument to the Court, "The difference as to the private label brand packed by Borden is that, as to that product, the Borden Company washes its hands of it at the factory door."

[8] The Court's suggestion, *ante*, p. 644, that a difference in label alone would exclude the reach of §2(a) if a market test were accepted for "like grade and quality" is no part of the present case and has never been offered as a serious interpretation of §2(a). Nor is there any issue raised here as to whether, under a market test of §2(a), a dubious pricing and branding policy adopted by a seller could "validate itself" and escape the Act by creating precarious distinctions in grade or quality. The price differential between Borden's premium and private label brands is concededly grounded upon a legitimate and stable market preference for the premium product. . . .

[9] Certain general language in the congressional reports may be taken, however, as supporting the interpretation that market factors are relevant in the construction of §2(a). The Report of the House Committee on the Judiciary stated that the general object of the bill was "to amend section 2 of the Clayton Act so as to suppress more effectually discriminations between customers of the same seller *not supported by sound economic differences in their business positions.* . . ." H.R. Rep. No. 2287, 74th Cong., 2d Sess., p. 7. (Emphasis added.) The Report of the Senate Committee on the Judiciary is phrased in substantially the same language. S.R. Rep. No. 1502, 74th Cong., 2d Sess., p. 3.

[By rejecting] . . . the proposal to add "and brands" to the "like grade and quality" provision in the bill . . . it can be inferred only that Congress contemplated "no *blanket* exemption . . . for 'like' products which differed *only* in brand . . . , leaving open the application of the Act to differentiated products reflecting more than a nominal or superficial variation." Rowe, *Price Discrimination under the Robinson-Patman Act*, 65 (1962). . . .

The other administrative precedents relied on by the Court also fail to establish any consistently settled interpretation by the Federal Trade Commission that physical identity is the sole touchstone of "like grade and quality." Those decisions singularly fail to focus on the significance of consumer preference as a relevant factor in the test of grade and quality. Moreover, the Commission has itself explicitly resorted to consumer preference or marketability to resolve the issue of "like grade and quality" in cases where minor physical variations accompany a difference in product brand. The caprice of the Commission's present distinction thus invites Borden to incorporate slight tangible variations in its private label products, in order to bring itself within the Commission's current practice of considering market preferences in such cases.

The Commission's determination of "like grade and quality" under §2(a) in this case is seriously inconsistent with the position it has taken under §2(b) in cases where a seller has presented the defense that he is in good faith meeting the equally low price of a competitor. The Commission decisions are clear that the "meeting competition" defense is not available to a seller who reduces the price of his premium product to the level of nonpremium products sold by his competitors. The Commission decisions under §2(b) emphasize that market preference must be considered in determining whether a competitor is "meeting" rather than "beating" competition. In *Standard Oil Co.*, 49 F.T.C. 923, 952, the Commission put it baldly:

> [I]n the retail distribution of gasoline public acceptance rather than chemical analysis of the product is the important competitive factor.[10]

. . . . .

The Court gives no substantial economic justification for its construction of §2(a). The principal rationale of the restriction of that section to commodities of "like grade and quality" is simply that it is not feasible to measure discrimination and injury to competition where different products are involved. That rationale is as valid for economic as for

---

[10] See also . . . *Callaway Mills Co., sub nom. Bigelow-Sanford Carpet Co.*, CCH Trade Reg. Rep. Transfer Binder, 1963–1965, ¶16,800, at p. 21755 (F.T.C. Dkt. 7634, Feb. 10, 1964): "Both the courts and the Commission have consistently denied the shelter of the [meeting competition] defense to sellers whose product, because of . . . intense public demand, normally commands a price higher than that usually received by sellers of competitive goods". . . .

physical variation between products. Once a substantial economic difference between products is found, therefore, the inquiry of the Commission should be ended, just as it is ended when a substantial physical difference is found. . . .

The potential economic impact of Borden's distribution of private label brands on secondary line competition is . . . ambiguous. It is true that a market test of "like grade and quality" would enable Borden, so far as §2(a) is concerned, to make private label brands selectively available to customers of its premium brand. Not all wholesale and retail dealers who carry Borden's premium brand would be able, as of right, to take advantage of Borden's private label production. . . .

[It is also true that under] the Court's view of §2(a), Borden must now make private label milk available to all customers of its premium brand.[11] But that interpretation of §2(a) is hardly calculated to speed private label brands to the shelves of retailers. To avoid supplying a private label brand to a premium brand customer, Borden need only forego further sales of its premium brand to that customer. It is, therefore, not unlikely that the Court's decision will foster a discrimination greater than that which it purports to eliminate, since retailers previously able to obtain the premium Borden brand but not a private label brand, may now find their access to the premium brand foreclosed as well.

In *Automatic Canteen Co.* v. *FTC*, 346 U.S. 61, 63, this Court cautioned against construction of the Robinson-Patman Act in a manner that might "give rise to a price uniformity and rigidity in open conflict with the purposes of other antitrust legislation." Today that warning goes unheeded. In the guise of protecting producers and purchasers from discriminatory price competition, the Court ignores legitimate market preferences and endows the Federal Trade Commission with authority to disrupt price relationships between products whose identity has been measured in the laboratory but rejected in the market place. I do not believe that any such power was conferred upon the Commission by Congress, and I would, therefore, affirm the judgment of the Court of Appeals.

Utah Pie Co. v. Continental Baking Co.

386 U.S. 685 (1967)

Mr. Justice White delivered the opinion of the Court.

This suit for treble damages and injunction under §§4 and 16 of the Clayton Act . . . was brought by petitioner, Utah Pie Company, against respondents, Continental Baking Company, Carnation Company and Pet Milk Company. The complaint charged a conspiracy under §§1

---

[11] The Commission concedes that there is no evidence in the record that Borden refused to sell private label milk to any customer who specifically requested it. . . .

and 2 of the Sherman Act . . . and violations by each respondent of §2(a) of the Clayton Act as amended by the Robinson-Patman Act. . . . The jury found for respondents on the conspiracy charge and for petitioner on the price discrimination charge. . . . The Court of Appeals reversed, addressing itself to the single issue of whether the evidence against each of the respondents was sufficient to support a finding of probable injury to competition within the meaning of §2(a) and holding that it was not. 349 F. 2d 122. We granted certiorari. . . . We reverse.

The product involved is frozen dessert pies—apple, cherry, boysenberry, peach, pumpkin, and mince. The period covered by the suit comprised the years 1958, 1959, and 1960 and the first eight months of 1961. Petitioner is a Utah corporation which for 30 years has been baking pies in its plant in Salt Lake City and selling them in Utah and surrounding States. It entered the frozen pie business in late 1957. It was immediately successful with its new line and built a new plant in Salt Lake City in 1958. The frozen pie market was a rapidly expanding one: 57,060 dozen frozen pies were sold in the Salt Lake City market in 1958, 111,729 dozen in 1959, 184,569 dozen in 1960, and 266,908 dozen in 1961. Utah Pie's share of this market in those years was 66.5%, 34.3%, 45.5%, and 45.3% respectively, its sales volume steadily increasing over the four years. Its financial position also improved. Petitioner is not, however, a large company. . . .

Each of the respondents is a large company and each of them is a major factor in the frozen pie market in one or more regions of the country. Each entered the Salt Lake City frozen pie market before petitioner began freezing dessert pies. None of them had a plant in Utah. . . . The Salt Lake City market was supplied by respondents chiefly from their California operations. They sold primarily on a delivered price basis.

The "Utah" label was petitioner's proprietary brand. Beginning in 1960, it also sold pies of like grade and quality under the controlled label "Frost 'N' Flame" to Associated Grocers and in 1961 it began selling to American Food Stores under the "Mayfresh" label. It also, on a seasonal basis, sold pumpkin and mince frozen pies to Safeway under Safeway's own "Bel-air" label.

The major competitive weapon in the Utah market was price. The location of petitioner's plant gave it natural advantages in the Salt Lake City marketing area and it entered the market at a price below the then going prices for respondents' comparable pies. For most of the period involved here its prices were the lowest in the Salt Lake City market. It was, however, challenged by each of the respondents at one time or another and for varying periods. There was ample evidence to show that each of the respondents contributed to what proved to be a deteriorating price structure over the period covered by this suit, and each of the respondents in the course of the ongoing price competition sold frozen pies in the Salt Lake market at prices lower than it sold pies of like grade and quality in other markets considerably closer to its plants. Utah Pie, which entered the market at a price of $4.15 per dozen at the beginning of the relevant period, was selling "Utah" and "Frost 'N' Flame" pies for $2.75 per dozen when the instant suit was filed some 44 months later. Pet, which was offering pies at $4.92 per dozen in February 1958, was offering "Pet-Ritz" and "Bel-air" pies at $3.56 and $3.46 per dozen respectively in March and April 1961. Carnation's price in early 1958 was $4.82 per dozen but it was selling at $3.46 per dozen at the conclusion of the period, meanwhile having been down as low as $3.30 per dozen. The price range experienced by Continental during the period covered by this suit ran from a 1958 high of over $5 per dozen to a 1961 low of $2.85 per dozen.

I

We deal first with petitioner's case against the Pet Milk Company. . . . Pet's initial emphasis was on quality, but in the face of competition from regional and local companies and in an expanding market where price proved to be a crucial factor, Pet was forced to take steps to reduce the price of its pies to the ultimate consumer. These developments had consequences in the Salt Lake City market which are the substance of petitioner's case against Pet.

First, Pet successfully concluded an arrangement with Safeway, which is one of the three largest customers for frozen pies in the Salt Lake market, whereby it would sell frozen pies to Safeway under the latter's own "Bel-air" label at a price significantly lower than it was selling its comparable "Pet-Ritz" brand in the same Salt Lake market and elsewhere. . . .

Second, it introduced a 20-ounce economy pie under the "Swiss Miss" label and began selling the new pie in the Salt Lake market in August 1960 at prices ranging from $3.25 to $3.30 for the remainder of the period. This pie was at times sold at a lower price in the Salt Lake City market than it was sold in other markets.

Third, Pet became more competitive with respect to the prices for its "Pet-Ritz" proprietary label. . . . According to the Court of Appeals, in seven of the 44 months Pet's prices in Salt Lake were lower than prices charged in the California markets. This was true although selling in Salt Lake involved a 30- to 35-cent freight cost.

The Court of Appeals first concluded that Pet's price differential on sales to Safeway must be put aside in considering injury to competition because in its view of the evidence the differential had been completely cost justified and because Utah would not in any event have been able to enjoy the Safeway custom. Second, it concluded that the remaining discriminations on "Pet-Ritz" and "Swiss Miss" pies were an insufficient predicate on which the jury could have found a reasonably possible injury either to Utah Pie as a competitive force or to competition generally.

We disagree with the Court of Appeals in several respects. First, there was evidence from which the jury could have found considerably more price discrimination by Pet with respect to "Pet-Ritz" and "Swiss Miss" pies than was considered by the Court of Appeals. In addition to the seven months during which Pet's prices in Salt Lake were lower than prices in the California markets, there was evidence from which the jury could reasonably have found that in 10 additional months the Salt Lake City prices for "Pet-Ritz" pies were discriminatory as compared with sales in western markets other than California. Likewise, with respect to "Swiss Miss" pies, there was evidence in the record from which the jury could have found that in five of the 13 months during which the "Swiss Miss" pies were sold prior to the filing of this suit, prices in Salt Lake City were lower than those charged by Pet in either California or some other western market.

Second, with respect to Pet's Safeway business, the burden of proving cost justification was on Pet and, in our view, reasonable men could have found that Pet's lower priced, "Bel-air" sales to Safeway were not cost justified in their entirety. Pet introduced cost data for 1961 indicating a cost saving on the Safeway business greater than the price advantage extended to that customer. These statistics were not particularized for the Salt Lake market, but assuming that they were adequate to justify the 1961 sales, they related to only 24% of the Safeway sales over the relevant period. The evidence concerning the remaining 76% was at best incomplete and inferential. It was insufficient to take the defense of cost justification from the jury, which reasonably could have found a greater incidence of unjustified price discrimination than that allowed by the Court of Appeals' view of the evidence.[1]

With respect to whether Utah would have enjoyed Safeway's business absent the Pet contract with Safeway, it seems clear that whatever the fact is in this regard, it is not determinative of the impact of that contract on competitors other than Utah and on competition generally. There were other companies seeking the Safeway business, including Continental and Carnation, whose pies may have been excluded from the Safeway shelves by what the jury could have found to be discriminatory sales to Safeway. What is more, Pet's evidence that Utah's unwillingness to install quality control equipment prevented Utah from enjoying Safeway's private label business is not the only evidence in the record relevant to that question. There was other evidence to the contrary. The jury would not have

---

[1] . . . Pet admitted that its cost-justification figures were drawn from past performance, so even crediting the data accompanying the 1960 contract regarding cost differences, Pet's additional evidence would bring under the justification umbrella only the 1959 sales. Thus, at the least, the jury was free to consider the 1960 Safeway sales as inadequately cost justified. Those sales accounted for 12.3% of the entire Salt Lake City market in that year. In the context of this case, the sales to Safeway are particularly relevant since there was evidence that private label sales influenced the general market, in this case depressing overall market prices.

been compelled to find that Utah Pie could not have gained more of the Safeway business.

Third, the Court of Appeals almost entirely ignored other evidence which provides material support for the jury's conclusion that Pet's behavior satisfied the statutory test regarding competitive injury. This evidence bore on the issue of Pet's predatory intent to injure Utah Pie.[2] As an initial matter, the jury could have concluded that Pet's discriminatory pricing was aimed at Utah Pie; Pet's own management, as early as 1959, identified Utah Pie as an "unfavorable factor," one which "d[u]g holes in our operation" and posed a constant "check" on Pet's performance in the Salt Lake City market. Moreover, Pet candidly admitted that during the period when it was establishing its relationship with Safeway, it sent into Utah Pie's plant an industrial spy to seek information that would be of use to Pet in convincing Safeway that Utah Pie was not worthy of its custom. . . . Finally, Pet does not deny that the evidence showed it suffered substantial losses on its frozen pie sales during the greater part of the time involved in this suit, and there was evidence from which the jury could have concluded that the losses Pet sustained in Salt Lake City were greater than those incurred elsewhere. It would not have been an irrational step if the jury concluded that there was a relationship between price and the losses.

It seems clear to us that the jury heard adequate evidence from which it could have concluded that Pet had engaged in predatory tactics in waging competitive warfare in the Salt Lake City market. Coupled with the incidence of price discrimination attributable to Pet, the evidence as a whole established, rather than negated, the reasonable possibility that Pet's behavior produced a lessening of competition proscribed by the Act.

II

Petitioner's case against Continental is not complicated. Continental was a substantial factor in the market in 1957. But its sales of frozen 22-ounce dessert pies, sold under the "Morton" brand, amounted to only 1.3% of the market in 1958, 2.9% in 1959, and 1.8% in 1960. Its problems were primarily that of cost and in turn that of price, the controlling factor in the market. In late 1960 it worked out a co-packing arrangement in California by which fruit would be processed directly from the trees into the finished pies without large intermediate packing, storing, and shipping

---

[2] . . . [In] *Anheuser-Busch, Inc.* v. *F.T.C.*, 289 F. 2d 835 . . . the court went so far as to suggest that: "If . . . the projection [to ascertain the future effect of price discrimination] is based upon predatoriness or buccaneering, it can reasonably be forecast that an adverse effect on competition *may* occur. In that event, the discriminations in their incipiency are such that they *may* have the prescribed effect to establish a violation of §2(a). If one engages in the latter type of pricing activity, a reasonable probability may be inferred that its willful misconduct may substantially lessen, injure, destroy or prevent competition." 289 F. 2d, at 843. . . .

expenses. Having improved its position, it attempted to increase its share of the Salt Lake City market by utilizing a local broker and offering short-term price concessions in varying amounts. Its efforts for seven months were not spectacularly successful. Then in June 1961, it took the steps which are the heart of petitioner's complaint against it. Effective for the last two weeks of June it offered its 22-ounce frozen apple pies in the Utah area at $2.85 per dozen. It was then selling the same pies at substantially higher prices in other markets. The Salt Lake City price was less than its direct cost plus an allocation for overhead. . . . Utah's response was immediate. It reduced its price on all of its apple pies to $2.75 per dozen. . . . Continental's total sales of frozen pies increased from 3,350 dozen in 1960 to 18,800 dozen in 1961. Its market share increased from 1.8% in 1960 to 8.3% in 1961. The Court of Appeals concluded that Continental's conduct had had only minimal effect, that it had not injured or weakened Utah Pie as a competitor, that it had not substantially lessened competition and that there was no reasonable possibility that it would do so in the future.

We again differ with the Court of Appeals. Its opinion that Utah was not damaged as a competitive force apparently rested on the fact that Utah's sales volume continued to climb in 1961 and on the court's own factual conclusion that Utah was not deprived of any pie business which it otherwise might have had. But this retrospective assessment fails to note that Continental's discriminatory below-cost price caused Utah Pie to reduce its price to $2.75. The jury was entitled to consider the potential impact of Continental's price reduction absent any responsive price cut by Utah Pie. Price was a major factor in the Salt Lake City market. Safeway, which had been buying Utah brand pies, immediately reacted and purchased a five-week supply of frozen pies from Continental, thereby temporarily foreclosing the proprietary brands of Utah and other firms from the Salt Lake City Safeway market. The jury could rationally have concluded that had Utah not lowered its price, Continental, which repeated its offer once, would have continued it, that Safeway would have continued to buy from Continental and that other buyers, large as well as small, would have followed suit. It could also have resonably concluded that a competitor who is forced to reduce his price to a new all-time low in a market of declining prices will in time feel the financial pinch and will be a less effective competitive force.

Even if the impact on Utah Pie as a competitor was negligible, there remain the consequences to others in the market who had to compete not only with Continental's 22-ounce pie at $2.85 but with Utah's even lower price of $2.75 per dozen for both its proprietary and controlled labels. . . . The evidence was that there were nine other sellers in 1960 who sold 23,473 dozen pies, 12.7% of the total market. In 1961 there were eight other sellers who sold less than the year before—18,565 dozen or 8.2% of the total—although the total market had expanded from 184,569 dozen to 226,908 dozen. We think there was sufficient evidence from which the jury could find a violation of §2(a) by Continental.

III

The Carnation Company entered the frozen dessert pie business in 1955 through the acquisition of "Mrs. Lee's Pies" which was then engaged in manufacturing and selling frozen pies in Utah and elsewhere under the "Simple Simon" label. Carnation also quickly found the market extremely sensitive to price. Carnation decided, however, not to enter an economy product in the market, and during the period covered by this suit it offered only its quality "Simple Simon" brand. Its primary method of meeting competition in its markets was to offer a variety of discounts and other reductions, and the technique was not unsuccessful. . . .

. . . After Carnation's temporary setback in 1959 it instituted a new pricing policy to regain business in the Salt Lake City market. The new policy involved a slash in price of 60¢ per dozen pies, which brought Carnation's price to a level admittedly well below its costs, and well below the other prices prevailing in the market. The impact of the move was felt immediately, and the two other major sellers in the market reduced their prices. Carnation's banner year, 1960, in the end involved eight months during which the prices in Salt Lake City were lower than prices charged in other markets. The trend continued during the eight months in 1961 that preceded the filing of the complaint in this case. In each of those months the Salt Lake City prices charged by Carnation were well below prices charged in other markets, and in all but August 1961 the Salt Lake City delivered price was 20¢ to 50¢ lower than the prices charged in distant San Francisco. The Court of Appeals held that only the early 1960 prices could be found to have been below cost. That holding, however, simply overlooks evidence from which the jury could have concluded that throughout 1961 Carnation maintained a below-cost price structure and that Carnation's discriminatory pricing, no less than that of Pet and Continental, had an important effect on the Salt Lake City market. We cannot say that the evidence precluded the jury from finding it reasonably possible that Carnation's conduct would injure competition.

IV

Section 2(a) does not forbid price competition which will probably injure or lessen competition by eliminating competitors, discouraging entry into the market or enhancing the market shares of the dominant sellers. But Congress has established some ground rules for the game. Sellers may not sell like goods to different purchasers at different prices if the result may be to injure competition in either the sellers' or the buyers' market unless such discriminations are justified as permitted by the Act. This case concerns the sellers' market. In this context, the Court of Appeals placed heavy emphasis on the fact that Utah Pie constantly increased its sales volume and continued to make a profit. But we disagree with its apparent view that there is no reasonably possible injury to competition as long as the volume of sales in a particular market is expanding and at least some of the competitors in the market continue to operate at a profit. Nor do we think that the Act only comes into play to regulate the conduct of price discriminators when their discriminatory prices consistently undercut other competitors. . . . In this case there was some evidence of predatory intent with respect to each of these respondents.[3] There was also other evidence upon which the jury could rationally find the requisite injury to competition. The frozen pie market in Salt Lake City was highly competitive. At times Utah Pie was a leader in moving the general level of prices down, and at other times each of the respondents also bore responsibility for the downward pressure on the price structure. We believe that the Act reaches price discrimination that erodes competition as much as it does price discrimination that is intended to have immediate destructive impact. In this case, the evidence shows a drastically declining price structure which the jury could rationally attribute to continued or sporadic price discrimination. The jury was entitled to conclude that "the effect of such discrimination," by each of these respondents, "may be substantially to lessen competition . . . or to injure, destroy, or prevent competition with any person who either grants or knowingly receives the benefit of such discrimination. . . ." The statutory test is one that necessarily looks forward on the basis of proven conduct in the past. Proper application of that standard here requires reversal of the judgment of the Court of Appeals.[4]

. . . Without intimating any views on the other grounds presented to the Court of Appeals, we reverse its judgment and remand the case to that court for further proceedings.

It is so ordered.

[3] It might be argued that the respondents' conduct displayed only fierce competitive instincts. Actual intent to injure another competitor does not, however, fall into that category, and neither, when viewed in the context of the Robinson-Patman Act, do persistent sales below cost and radical price cuts themselves discriminatory. Nor does the fact that a local competitor has a major share of the market make him fair game for discriminatory price cutting free of Robinson-Patman Act proscriptions. . . .

[4] Each respondent argues here that prior price discrimination cases in the courts and before the Federal Trade Commission, in which no primary line injury to competition was found, establish a standard which compels affirmance of the Court of Appeals' holding. But the cases upon which the respondents rely are readily distinguishable. In *Anheuser-Busch, Inc.* v. *F.T.C.*, 289 F. 2d 835, 839, there was no general decline in price structure attributable to the defendant's price discriminations, nor was there any evidence that the price discriminations were "a single lethal weapon aimed at a victim for a predatory purpose." *Id.*, at 842. In *Borden Co.* v. *F.T.C.*, 339 F. 2d 953, the court reversed the Commission's decision on price discrimination in one market for want of sufficient interstate connection, and the Commission's charge regarding the other market failed to show any lasting impact upon prices caused by the single, isolated incident of price discrimination proved. . . .

THE CHIEF JUSTICE took no part in the decision of this case.

MR. JUSTICE STEWART, with whom MR. JUSTICE HARLAN joins, dissenting.

I would affirm the judgment, agreeing substantially with the reasoning of the Court of Appeals as expressed in the thorough and conscientious opinion of Judge Phillips.

There is only one issue on this case in its present posture: . . . [D]id the respondents' actions have the anticompetitive effect required by the statute as an element of a cause of action?

The Court's own description of the Salt Lake City frozen pie market from 1958 through 1961, shows that the answer to that question must be no. In 1958 Utah Pie had a quasi-monopolistic 66.5% of the market. In 1961—after the alleged predations of the respondents—Utah Pie still had a commanding 45.3%, Pet had 29.4%, and the remainder of the market was divided almost equally between Continental, Carnation, and other, small local bakers. Unless we disregard the lessons so laboriously learned in scores of Sherman and Clayton Act cases, the 1961 situation has to be considered more competitive than that of 1958. Thus, if we assume that the price discrimination proven against the respondents had any effect on competition, that effect must have been beneficial.

That the Court has fallen into the error of reading the Robinson-Patman Act as protecting competitors, instead of competition, can be seen from its unsuccessful attempt to distinguish cases relied upon by the respondents. Those cases are said to be inapposite because they involved "no general decline in price structure," and no "lasting impact upon prices." But lower prices are the hallmark of intensified competition. . . .

I cannot hold that Utah Pie's monopolistic position was protected by the federal antitrust laws from effective price competition, and I therefore respectfully dissent.

Chapter 10   TYING DEVICES

As the Supreme Court noted in the *Standard Stations* case (see Chapter 11), "Tying agreements serve hardly any purpose beyond the suppression of competition." Yet, because of the possibility that such agreements might occasionally be economically justified and legally unexceptionable, the courts have hesitated to declare them to be unlawful per se. Once again, it becomes necessary to examine a trade practice—in this instance tying devices—on a case-by-case basis. The selections presented below indicate that the crucial test in these cases is whether the tie-in involves one product or service in which the company enjoys substantial market power. In other words, the courts attempt to discover whether the tie-in represents an attempt by a firm to exert leverage so that its monopoly power in one area may be extended into another. In the *American Can* case the court concluded that the tying arrangement was being used by American to extend its dominance of can-closing machinery into canmaking. This, combined with American's other trade practices, led the court to find violations of Sections 1 and 2 of the Sherman Act as well as Section 3 of the Clayton Act. In the *Jerrold* case, on the other hand, the courts recognized that under certain conditions tying contracts may result in positive economic benefits. Thus, they refused to strike down an arrangement whereby Jerrold sold electronic equipment to community antenna television companies only on a full system basis and in conjunction with a service contract.

But the *Northern Pacific, Loew's* and *Fortner* cases indicate that, by and large, the Supreme Court still takes a dim view of tying devices. These opinions might profitably be read in connection with the *International Salt* case presented in Chapter 14.

United States v. American Can Company

87 F. Supp. 18 (N.D. Cal. 1949)

Harris, District Judge.

This action was instituted by the government under the Sherman Act, Sections 1 and 2 . . . and the Clayton Act, Section 3 . . . . seeking to enjoin the American Can Company from unlawful practices, allegedly in violation of both acts. The primary question for determination is whether defendant's requirements contracts and closing machine leases are illegal in the particulars specified. . . .

The facts are not in serious dispute save with respect to a conspiracy charged against American Can Company and Continental Can Company. . . .

Plaintiff attacks defendant's contracts under which it sells its metal and fiber containers; plaintiff also challenges the legality of defendant's closing machine leases under which it lets its can closing machines which complete the metal and fiber containers. Plaintiff contends that the can contracts and closing machine leases constitute unreasonable restraints of trade and commerce and, in addition, that such contracts and leases, together with certain specified devices, means, methods which will be discussed below, constitute a violation of Section 3 of the Clayton Act. Plaintiff further contends that defendant's contracts and closing machine leases constitute a mode of operation which gives rise to an attempt to monopolize trade and commerce and has effectuated such a monopoly in certain parts of the trade and commerce in canning, in violation of Sections 1 and 2 of the Sherman Act. . . .

The ultimate remedy sought by the Government is sweeping: it asks for elimination of requirements contracts and complete divestiture of the closing machine phase of the business. In connection with the requirements contracts, American contends that, if the relief sought is granted, the user-customers will be relegated to an uncertain mode of supply and demand not based upon contracts giving rise to enforceable obligations. . . .

Incorporated in New Jersey in 1902, defendant has long been foremost in the can manufacturing business of the United States. At its inception . . . defendant acquired sufficient plants to enable it to make 90 percent of the cans used in the country.

At the time of the [company's first] trial in 1913, American then consumed approximately one-third of the total tin plate used for domestic consumption in the can manufacturing business in the United States. It will be seen . . . that defendant has more than maintained its position in the industry. . . . On the basis of tin plate consumed [in 1946], American's percentage of the whole was somewhat in excess of 40 percent.

Viewed from the standpoint of competitive sales as against total output of cans, American's percentage is even more impressive. Some canning concerns manufacture their own cans and are thus not in the buying market. Among the can manufacturers who sell on a competitive basis, the total received for cans in 1946 was $433,621,729. American's percentage of the total was 46.4 percent.

What does the evidence disclose as to the business conducted by American's competitors? It shows that of not more than 125 manufacturers of cans, up to 25 make tin containers for their own use; of the competitive can companies only five manufacture what are known as packers' and general line cans. . . .

By graphical representation and statistical supporting data, the trial record is convincing, clear, and complete, that the defendant's domination of the industry has grown over the intervening years; that Continental and American manufacture about 80 percent of all cans made for sale; that there are six companies in the United States, making both packers' and general line cans, and they manufacture 93.6 percent of all cans made for sale. . . .

From the above recital of facts, it is clear that from a national standpoint, defendant is the leader in the manufacture of cans, although it has competition in its business and is not in a position of complete monopoly. From a regional standpoint, the story of control is different. Thus, in such an area as Utah, defendant has the only plant which serves the needs of the packers in that state. A similar monopoly exists in Hawaii, while in Alaska defendant has 80 percent of the can business. As might be expected American is the dominant influence in specific sections of the United States.

Viewed from another standpoint—type of container manufactured— defendant far outdistances its competitors in several lines. . . .

The foregoing should suffice to indicate the dominant position of American in the industry.

With respect to closing machines: Since the canning industry progressed from the hole and cap cans, which were used at the turn of the century, to the sanitary or packers' cans which are closed by machines, American has moved into leadership in the manufacture and leasing of closing machines. Today it makes and leases to its customers substantially all of their closing machines. The leasing practice by American is followed by its competitors, with Continental also making its own closing machines for this purpose. The number of independent concerns engaged in the manufacture of closing machines is limited to two—Max Ams Machine Company and The Angelus.

In terms of closing machines leased to canners, American controls 54 percent of all such machines. . . . Continental [controls] . . . approximately 36 percent of the total machines on lease. The independent can-closing machine makers are thus limited in their sales to a market of 12 percent of the closing machine business.

It is the fixed and uniform policy of American to lease rather than sell its closing machines. The only exceptions to this policy arise in the few instances in which American sells machines abroad or sells a few single spindle semi-automatic machines in the Ozarks. Other canmaking concerns follow American's policy. Therefore, the two independent can-closing machine makers, Angelus and Max Ams, have a market limited to the small canmakers, for the ordinary canner will not purchase a can-closing machine as long as he can lease it from his can supplier. An important factor which induces canners to lease their machines has been the low rentals charged for such machines. The defendant admits that low rentals provide an effective "sales tool."

. . . [P]resent rentals are insufficient to cover the complete cost of furnishing and servicing the machines. Other canmakers, on a competitive basis have followed American's policy of imposing low or nominal rentals on their closing machines. Rental figures appear to have been purely arbitrary, depending upon the exigencies and the desirability of the customers' business.

The present case is not directed toward American in its capacity as manufacturer of closing machines. However, it should be noted that the practice of defendant in leasing at below cost figures has tended to restrict the market for closing machine manufacturers and has limited the number of concerns engaged in this business. The record disclosed that others would engage in the manufacture of closing machines if there were a free market in which sellers might compete on an equal basis with the canmakers who now lease their machines. . . .

With respect to the requirements contracts: The Government contends that defendant's contracts are the major tool by which it is able to exclude or limit competition in the canning business and, hence, is able to maintain its dominant position. American now has a standard form of contract which the plaintiff chooses to call "total requirements contract." . . . Over the years defendant has handled only minute portions of its sales on an open order basis. . . .

Throughout its business life American has entered into requirements contracts of varied duration. These have ranged from three to twenty years. Recently, defendant prepared a standardized contract of uniform length of five years. For various reasons, defendant believes that a contract of such duration best serves the interest of both canner and canmaker.

American offers an attractive discount on quantity purchases. The scale serves as an inducement for canners to purchase all of their needs from a single manufacturer. . . . [R]equirements contract customers enjoy a price differential in discounts which are not granted to open order customers. . . .

The defendant's degree of market control: The statistical data in this case is voluminous. So that we may appreciate the impact of "bigness" as it relates to the canning industry, we must advert to the earlier [1916] remarks of Judge Rose in *United States* v. *American Can Company*, 230 F. at page 902. . . . The jurist said that American, although conceived in sin was leading a rather unblemished life and that the earlier transgression should be forgiven and forgotten as a result of its benign attitude. . . .

A decree of dissolution was not ordered. . . .

[From the defendant's history] . . . [i]t is clear an attempt was made both to restrain and monopolize the interstate trade in tin cans.

The closing machine Leases executed by customers with the defendant are violative of Section 3 of the Clayton Act: In the light of *Standard Oil Company* v. *United States*, 337 U.S. 293, . . . this phase of the case is reduced to comparative simplicity. In reaching the conclusion that the leasing practices must be proscribed, we must trace briefly the practices of American since the "tying provision" was admittedly removed from the lease contracts covering closing machines.

In May 1917, in the course of an investigation of American by the Federal Trade Commission, the defendant agreed to eliminate from its forms of contract and lease . . . the offending "tying clause." . . .

The Government contends that the provision, although eliminated from the lease forms, has been kept alive and in effect as a result of the practices engaged in by American of a "subtle and refined" character. The practices, in substance, are as follows:

Defendant leases closing machines only to customers who purchase their cans from it, and closing machine leases run for terms concurrent with the can contracts. Sales policies, as contained in memoranda and directives from the executive officers, bear out the Government's contentions that the "tying provision" for all practical purposes has remained in the contract negotiations. The evidence introduced by the Government in this connection abundantly supports this contention. . . .

That the closing machines represent a most valuable sales tool becomes increasingly manifest when it is considered that defendant has in excess of 9,000 machines on lease of an approximate value of 12 million dollars, many of which have been rented at nominal or low rental values in order to foreclose competition. The evidence herein discloses that American owns and controls more closing machines than the rest of the industry together, and demonstrates that defendant effectively ties the leasing of such machines to the sales of its cans. Defendant owns approximately 54 percent of all closing machines available for lease to the industry.

It may be noted that the closing machines manufactured by American, with slight adjustment, may be used to close the cans of the other can manufacturers; that there are no basic patent rights involved as was the case in the International Salt controversy. . . .

It is manifest to this Court from the record herein that abundant proof has been supplied by the Government, and the Court accordingly finds that the leasing practices of can closing machines violate the said Act for they affect injuriously a sizable part of interstate commerce, i.e., an appreciable segment of interstate commerce.

The devices, means and methods used by defendant in accomplishing the monopoly: Much of the trial, which consumed approximately 117 days and embraced more than 7,000 pages of testimony, concerned the Government's charge that for years American has, by various devices, means and methods, persuaded and induced canners to enter into the requirements contracts. Defendant describes this conduct in many instances as "commercial massage"; the Government counsel refers to the same as "commercial bribery" and other inelegant terms of comparable import.

Suffice it to say, that no useful purpose could be served by recounting herein the details of all the transactions spread over a period of years from 1930. They represent a saga of American business—so-called "big business." Taken alone, or disassociated from the general configuration or picture, many of the transactions would appear to be without probative value. However, as a composite they set a pattern of operations evidencing the extremes defendant saw fit to go in perpetuating the contractual relationship between defendant and the customer-user. The devices took many forms: defendant provided discounts in ancillary contracts; defendant paid large sums of money to obtain business of its customers; defendant furnished equipment, in addition to closing machines, at nominal rentals; defendant paid large claims when it appeared propitious and good policy; defendant purchased canmaking equipment from its customers for inflated values in order to obtain can business. The foregoing represent only part of the claims set up by the Government under the "inducements" phase of the case. . . .

Certain practices, as defendant claims, represent no more nor less than "ordinary business practices . . . in which competitors are seeking to serve the needs of their customers and keep their good will."

The incidents, when examined realistically and not as mere abstractions, are deeper than the typical run-of-the-mill, day-to-day business transactions. They represent a studied, methodical and effective method of retaining and acquiring by refined, gentlemanly and suave means, plus an occasional "commercial massage," the dominant position which American has had and maintained for at least a generation on and over the canning industry. A detailed analysis of this phase of the Government's case convinces that there is little room left in a competitive sense, for the independent small business man. As a competitive influence, he has slowly and sadly been relegated into the limbo of American enterprise.

The evidence establishes violations of Sections 1 and 2 of the Sherman Act: The proof in this case compels the conclusion that the five year requirements contracts and closing machine leases unreasonably restrain trade in violation of the Sherman Act. The evidence discloses that competitors have been foreclosed from a substantial market by the contracts and leases. . . .

With the premise established that American is in a dominant role and a position of preeminent power in the industry, we may then examine the record to determine whether: (*a*) competition has been foreclosed; (*b*) from any substantial market. . . .

Apart from the inevitable conclusion reached that the requirements contracts and closing machine leases, backgrounded by the configuration of the devices and practices, offend against the Sherman Act, Sections 1 and 2 thereof, there is the problem of the user-consumer which must be approached not as a legal abstraction, but realistically. He should not be left without a source of supply. The canners are subject in many instances to the whims of nature over which they have no control. They are, therefore, required to have available a supply of tin containers, fluid in amount, and appropriate from the technological and marketing viewpoints. . . .

In finding the five year requirements contract illegal, we are not thereby compelled to declare void any and all requirements contracts. We *cannot* ignore the testimony of countless witnesses who indicated the vital necessity of some sort of supply contact. . . .

Mindful that requirements contracts are not *per se* unlawful, and that one of the elements which should be considered is the length thereof, it is only fair to conclude after a careful review of the evidence, that a contract for a period of one year would permit competitive influences to operate at the expiration of said period of time, and the vice which is now present in the five year requirements contracts, would be removed. Under a contract limited to one year, the user-consumer would be guaranteed an assured supply and protected by a definite obligation on the part of American to meet the totality of needs of the canner, while he, in turn, would have a fixed obligation to purchase his seasonal needs from American, thus making for mutuality of contract and obligation. . . .

The Government contends that the requirements contracts also offend against Section 3 of the Clayton Act. From a review of the record, the Court perceived that these contracts properly fall within the proscription of Sections 1 and 2 of the Sherman Act and that their provisions must be dealt with accordingly. Defendant's requirements contracts do not come within either the language or the intent of Section 3 of the Clayton Act.

The agreement to fix prices between American and Continental: . . .

It becomes unnecessary, under the issues as framed in this case, to make any finding with respect to a so-called conspiracy or to otherwise allude thereto. The conspiracy, or its absence, cannot serve as a premise in any logical reasoning leading to a conclusion with respect to the practices that are at issue. However, we do find that American and Continental, through their officers, agents, and servants, did directly agree to fix prices. This is manifest from the evidence, as well as the pattern of the price lists which appeared in the exhibits. . . .

The remedies sought by the Government: . . .

The Court's conclusion being that there has been a violation of the Sherman Act as well as the Clayton Act, the final question is one of determining the equitable relief to be had. . . .

. . . With respect to the ultimate remedies or relief, ruling will be deferred until further hearing and upon notice.

Northern Pacific Railway Company v. United States

356 U.S. 1 (1958)

Mr. Justice Black delivered the opinion of the Court.

In 1864 and 1870 Congress granted the predecessor of the Northern Pacific Railway Company approximately forty million acres of land in several Northwestern States and Territories to facilitate its construction of a railroad line from Lake Superior to Puget Sound. In general terms, this grant consisted of every alternate section of land in a belt 20 miles wide on each side of the track through States and 40 miles wide through Territories. The granted lands were of various kinds; some contained great stands of timber, some iron ore or other valuable mineral deposits, some oil or natural gas, while still other sections were useful for agriculture, grazing or industrial purposes. By 1949 the Railroad had sold about 37,000,000 acres of its holdings, but had reserved mineral rights in 6,500,000 of those acres. Most of the unsold land was leased for one purpose or another. In a large number of its sales contracts and most of its lease agreements the Railroad had inserted "preferential routing" clauses which compelled the grantee or lessee to ship over its lines all commodities produced or manufactured on the land, provided that its rates (and in some instances its service) were equal to those of competing carriers. Since many of the goods produced on the lands subject to these "preferential routing" provisions are shipped from one State to another the actual and potential amount of interstate commerce affected is substantial. Alternative means of transportation exist for a large portion of these shipments including the facilities of two other major railroad systems.

In 1949 the Government filed suit under Section 4 of the Sherman Act seeking a declaration that the defendant's "preferential routing" agreements were unlawful as unreasonable restraints of trade under Section 1 of that Act. After various pretrial proceedings the Government moved for summary judgment contending that on the undisputed facts it was entitled, as a matter of law, to the relief demanded. The district judge made numerous findings, as set forth in substance in the preceding paragraph, based on the voluminous pleadings, stipulations, depositions and answers to interrogatories filed in the case, and then granted the Government's motion (with an exception not relevant here). 142 F. Supp. 679. He issued an order enjoining the defendant from enforcing the existing "preferential routing" clauses or from entering into any future agreements containing them. The defendant took a direct appeal to this Court. . . .

The Sherman Act was designed to be a comprehensive charter of economic liberty aimed at preserving free and unfettered competition as the rule of trade. It rests on the premise that the unrestrained interaction of competitive forces will yield the best allocation of our economic resources, the lowest prices, the highest quality and the greatest material progress, while at the same time providing an environment conducive to the preservation of our democratic political and social institutions. But even were that premise open to question, the policy unequivocally laid down by the Act is competition. And to this end it prohibits "Every contract, combination . . . or conspiracy, in restraint of trade or commerce among the several States." Although this prohibition is literally all-encompassing, the courts have construed it as precluding only those contracts or combinations which "unreasonably" restrain competition . . . .

However, there are certain agreements or practices which because of their pernicious effect on competition and lack of any redeeming virtue are conclusively presumed to be unreasonable and therefore illegal without elaborate inquiry as to the precise harm they have caused or the business excuse for their use. This principle of *per se* unreasonableness not only makes the type of restraints which are proscribed by the Sherman Act more certain to the benefit of everyone concerned, but it also avoids the necessity for an incredibly complicated and prolonged economic investigation into the entire history of the industry involved, as well as related industries, in an effort to determine at large whether a particular restraint has been unreasonable—an inquiry so often wholly fruitless when undertaken. Among the practices which the courts have heretofore deemed to be unlawful in and of themselves are price fixing, *United States* v. *Socony-Vacuum Oil Co. . . .*; division of markets, *United States* v. *Addyston Pipe & Steel Co. . . .*; group boycotts, *Fashion Originators' Guild* v. *Federal Trade Comm'n . . .*; and tying arrangements, *International Salt Co.* v. *United States. . . .*

For our purposes a tying arrangement may be defined as an agreement by a party to sell one product but only on the condition that the buyer also purchases a different (or tied) product, or at least agrees that he will not purchase that product from any other supplier. Where such conditions are successfully exacted competition on the merits with respect to the tied product is inevitably curbed. Indeed "tying agreements serve hardly any purpose beyond the suppression of competition." *Standard Oil Co. of California* v. *United States. . . .* They deny competitors free access to the market for the tied product, not because the party imposing the tying requirements has a better product or a lower price but because of his power or leverage in another market. At the same time buyers are forced to forego their free choice between competing products. For these reasons "tying agreements fare harshly under the laws forbidding restraints of trade." *Times-Picayune Publishing Co.* v. *United States. . . .* They are unreasonable in and of themselves whenever a party has sufficient economic power with respect to the tying product to appreciably restrain free competition in the market for the tied product and a "not insubstantial" amount of interstate commerce is affected. *International Salt Co.* v. *United States. . . .* Cf. *United States* v. *Paramount Pictures. . . .* Of course where the seller has no control or dominance over the tying product so that it does not represent an effectual weapon to pressure buyers into taking the tied item any restraint of trade attributable to such tying arrangements would obviously be insignificant at most. . . .

In this case we believe the district judge was clearly correct in entering summary judgment declaring the defendant's "preferential routing" clauses unlawful restraints of trade. We wholly agree that the undisputed facts established beyond any genuine question that the defendant possessed substantial economic power by virtue of its extensive landholdings which it used as leverage to induce large numbers of purchasers and lessees to give it preference, to the exclusion of its competitors, in carrying goods or produce from the land transferred to them. Nor can there be any real doubt that a "not insubstantial" amount of interstate commerce was and is affected by these restrictive provisions.

As pointed out before, the defendant was initially granted large acreages by Congress in the several northwestern states through which its lines now run. This land was strategically located in checkerboard fashion amid private holdings and within economic distance of transportation facilities. Not only the testimony of various witnesses but common sense makes it evident that this particular land was often prized by those who purchased or leased it and was frequently essential to their business activities. In disposing of its holdings the defendant entered into contracts of sale or lease covering at least several million acres of land which included "preferential routing" clauses. The very existence of this host of tying arrangements is itself compelling evidence of the defendant's great power, at least where, as here, no other explanation has been offered for the existence of these restraints. The "preferential routing" clauses conferred no benefit on the purchasers or lessees. While they got the land they wanted by yielding their freedom to deal with competing carriers, the defendant makes no claim that it came any cheaper than if the restrictive clauses had been omitted. In fact any such price reduction in return for rail shipments would have quite plainly constituted an unlawful rebate to the shipper. So far as the Railroad was concerned its purpose obviously was to fence out competitors, to stifle competition. While this may have been exceedingly beneficial to its business, it is the very type of thing the Sherman Act condemns. In short, we are convinced that the essential prerequisites for treating the defendant's tying arrangements as unreasonable *"per se"* were conclusively established below and that the defendant has offered to prove nothing there or here which would alter this conclusion.

In our view *International Salt Co.* v. *United States, . . .* which has been unqualifiedly approved by subsequent decisions, is ample authority for affirming the judgment below. . . .

The defendant attempts to evade the force of *International Salt* on the ground that the tying product there was patented while here it is not. But we do not believe this distinction has, or should have, any significance. In arriving at its decision in *International Salt* the Court placed no reliance on the fact that a patent was involved nor did it give the slightest intimation that the outcome would have been any different if that had not been the case. If anything, the Court held the challenged tying arrangements unlawful *despite* the fact that the tying item was patented, not because of it. . . .

The defendant argues that the holding in *International Salt* was limited by the decision in *Times-Picayune Publishing Co.* v. *United States. . . .* There the Court held that a unit system of advertising in two local newspapers did not violate Section 1 of the Sherman Act. . . . But the Court was extremely careful to confine its decision to the narrow record before it. . . .

While there is some language in the *Times-Picayune* opinion which speaks of "monopoly power" or "dominance" over the tying product as a necessary precondition for application of the rule of *per se* unreasonableness to tying arrangements, we do not construe this general language as requiring anything more than sufficient economic power to impose an appreciable restraint on free competition in the tied product (assuming all the time, of course, that a "not insubstantial" amount of interstate commerce is affected). . . . *Times-Picayune* . . . makes clear . . . that the vice of tying arrangements lies in the use of economic power in one market to restrict competition on the merits in another, regardless of the source from which the power is derived and whether the power takes the form of a monopoly or not.

The defendant contends that its "preferential routing" clauses are subject to so many exceptions and have been administered so leniently that they do not significantly restrain competition. . . . [I]f these restrictive provisions are merely harmless sieves with no tendency to restrain competition, as the defendant's argument seems to imply, it is hard to understand why it has expended so much effort in obtaining them in vast numbers and upholding their validity, or how they are of any benefit to anyone, even the defendant. But however that may be, the essential fact remains that these agreements are binding obligations held over the heads of vendees which deny defendant's competitors access to the fenced-off market on the same terms as the defendant. . . . All of this is only aggravated, of course, here in the regulated transportation industry where there is frequently no real rate competition at all and such effective competition as actually thrives takes other forms.

Affirmed.

[Mr. Justice Clark took no part in the consideration or decision of this case. Mr. Justice Harlan, whom Mr. Justice Frankfurter and Mr. Justice Whittaker joined, dissented.]

United States v. Jerrold Electronics Corporation

187 F.Supp. 545 (E.D. Pa. 1960),
affirmed per curiam 365 U.S. 567 (1961)

VAN DUSEN, District Judge.

This action was commenced with the filing of a complaint on February 15, 1957, charging Jerrold Electronics Corporation, its president, Milton Jerrold Shapp, and five of its corporate subsidiaries with being parties to a conspiracy and contracts in unreasonable restraint of trade and commerce in community television antenna equipment in violation of Section 1 of the Sherman Act . . . ; with being parties to a conspiracy and attempting to monopolize trade and commerce in community television antenna equipment in violation of Section 2 of the Sherman Act . . . ; and with contracting to sell and making sales upon unlawful conditions in violation of Section 3 of the Clayton Act. . . .

. . . . .

II. *Background*

Jerrold Electronics Corporation (hereinafter "Jerrold") was incorporated under the laws of Pennsylvania in March 1948 by Milton Shapp to engage in the sale of a television booster developed by one of his friends. This device was designed to improve television reception in fringe areas by amplifying the weak signals available there. At Shapp's request, his friend began working on the development of master antenna equipment. The purpose of this equipment was to enable a single antenna to serve a number of television receivers. . . .

Jerrold installed the first operational master antenna system for Montgomery Ward in Baltimore during the summer of 1949. The success of this system resulted in a number of orders from other dealers. At first, this master antenna equipment was sold through the distributors who were handling Jerrold's booster. This proved unsatisfactory, however, because these distributors and their customers lacked the technical training and experience with respect to master antenna systems which was necessary to install and maintain them properly. . . .

In October 1950, Shapp was approached by a group of men from Lansford, Pennsylvania, who were interested in bringing television into their community. The people of Lansford were unable to receive any television signals through the use of conventional equipment because of the town's location. It was possible to receive a signal on a hilltop approximately a mile outside of town, however. They wanted to set up an antenna at this site and hook it up with receivers in the town. Subscribers to their service would pay a connection fee and monthly service charge. . . . It was . . . apparent to . . . [Shapp] that this was a natural and promising area for Jerrold to enter, since there were many communities which, because of distance or topographical features, were in the same predicament as Lansford and had no immediate hope of obtaining television from any other source because of the freeze on the licensing of new television stations in effect at that time.

Shapp and the Lansford group finally worked out a mutually satisfactory arrangement. Jerrold was to install a system using its standard equipment, which the Lansford people would purchase. Jerrold was to use the system as an on-the-spot laboratory to work on the problems it anticipated, discover new problems, and develop the equipment necessary to eliminate them. . . . A few days later, a similar arrangement was made with a group from Mahanoy City, Pennsylvania. . . .

The Lansford system was "turned on" in mid-December 1950 and the Mahanoy City system went into operation in January 1951. . . . The initial results were deemed successful and the systems received considerable publicity, including articles in the *Wall Street Journal* and *Newsweek* magazine, since they were the first significant operational systems of this kind. As a result of the publicity, Shapp was approached by people from hundreds of communities interested in community antenna systems, both as a means of bringing television into their homes and as a profitable investment. These people came from all walks of life. Many of them had little or no technical background or knowledge. Furthermore, the system that went into operation in Lansford in December 1950 was only connected to a few showrooms. With the extension and continual operation of the system, the anticipated problems began to arise. They were of such a magnitude that Shapp's organization was completely tied up analyzing them and designing new equipment to cope with them. Also, there were several instances in which aspiring community system operators had obtained Jerrold's standard equipment through its distributors and attempted to install systems with unsatisfactory results. Under these circumstances, it was decided that no Jerrold equipment would be sold for community purposes until gear adequate to the task had been developed.

Some acquaintance with the technical aspects of a community television antenna system is essential to a full understanding of the contentions of both parties in this matter. This seems to be the most appropriate point to digress from the narrative to describe the nature of such a system and some of the particular problems which faced Jerrold and other companies which entered this field.

There are four parts to a community television antenna system. The first is the antenna site, referred to in the trade as the "head end." The second is the apparatus which carries the signal from the antenna into the community, known as the "run to town." The third is the "skeleton system" that is constructed through the town to carry the television signals to the extremities of the area to be covered. Finally, there is the "tap-off" from the skeleton system which carries the signal to the home of each subscriber to the service. . . .

The installation of a successful community television antenna system involves more than simply purchasing certain items of equipment and hooking them together. Each system presents different problems giving rise to different equipment needs because of variations in the frequency, quantity and quality of the signals available at the antenna site, the length of the run to town, and the layout of the town itself. Proper planning is necessary to keep equipment costs at a minimum and, at the same time, produce a saleable picture in town. In the first place, the best antenna site must be determined considering the signals present and the distance from town. The run to town must be set up keeping in mind future maintenance problems. Similarly, the most efficient routing of the lines in town must be determined. In this connection, there arises a special problem of negotiating with the utility companies for the use of their poles. This aspect is important, both in terms of costs and acceptability to the community, since there may be an adverse reaction to the erection of additional poles and wires. Then there is the problem of selecting equipment of the proper specifications, including antennas and cable, as well as electronic gear. Finally, it is essential that the equipment be properly spaced along the line so that the input signal is at a proper level.

III. *Tie-in Sales*

By the spring of 1951, the Jerrold people felt they were prepared to start selling equipment for community television antenna purposes. As a result of their work in Lansford and Mahanoy City, they had developed a new line of equipment for community antenna systems designated "W" equipment. After consulting with his engineers and several of Jerrold's commission salesmen who dealt with the distributors, Shapp decided that the W equipment should only be sold with engineering services to insure that the system would function properly. A general policy, therefore, was established of selling electronic equipment to community antenna companies only on a full system basis and in conjunction with a service contract which provided for technical services with respect to the layout, installation and operation of the system.

The first of the service contracts employed by Jerrold in executing this policy was designated Form 103. . . . Paragraph 8 . . . provided:

8. That in the event Antenna Company desires to receive and distribute the signals of any television stations other than those being received and distributed at the time of the initial installation of the System, Antenna Company agrees to purchase, at the then prevailing prices, whatever additional Jerrold Equipment may be necessary to receive and distribute the desired signals throughout the System, and it is understood that a maximum of three (3) television channels can be so received and distributed in the presently designed System.

Paragraph 12 of the contract provided:

12. That Antenna Company agrees that it will not install, as part of the System, any Equipment or attachments which in the opinion of Jerrold will impair the operation of the System or impair the quality of television reception and signal distribution capabilities of the System, or that might cause damage to or impair the efficiency of any of the Equipment comprising the System.

. . . . .

In October 1953, the Form 103A and 103B service contracts were replaced by the WK–1 Form. . . . The new contract was generally the same as its predecessors. A few changes were made in some of the provisions relevant to the case at bar. The provision contained in paragraph 8 of the earlier contracts was eliminated. Also, the language formerly appearing in paragraph 12 now appeared in paragraph 8 and was revised to read as follows:

VIII. Since the parties acknowledge that Jerrold cannot reasonably be required to perform its obligations hereunder if the System comprises electronic equipment other than that manufactured by Jerrold Electronics Corporation, Antenna Company agrees that it will not install, as a part of the System any equipment or attachments which, in the opinion of Jerrold, will impair the quality of television reception and signal distribution capabilities of the System, or which might cause damage to, or impair the efficiency of, any of the Equipment comprising the System.

Finally, the duration of the contract was reduced from five to two and one-half years.

On March 16, 1954, Jerrold offered its customers two more service contracts designated SP–1 . . . and SP–2. . . . The period of their use overlapped that of the WK–1 contract. The SP–1 contract was designed to accompany the sale of new systems and was of six months' duration. The SP–2 contract was designed to make Jerrold service available to existing systems and was of one year's duration. Each of these contracts contained the following provision, similar to those in the earlier contracts:

Since we cannot reasonably be required to perform our obligations as enumerated in this letter if the system contains electronic equipment other than that manufactured by Jerrold Electronics Corporation, you agree not to install, as part of the system, any equipment or attachments which, in our opinion, will impair the quality of television reception and signal distribution capabilities of the system, or which might cause damage to, or impair the efficiency of, any of the equipment comprising the System.

The Government contends that Jerrold's policy and practice of selling on a system basis only and of making sales only in conjunction with a service contract constituted unlawful tie-ins in violation of Section 1 of the Sherman Act . . . and Section 3 of the Clayton Act. . . . It also asserts that the provision in the 103 series contracts for the exclusive use of Jerrold equipment for the addition of extra channels to the system, and the provision in all of the contracts not to install unapproved, non-Jerrold equipment, violated these sections of the anti-trust laws.

III-A. *Service Contracts*

. . . . .

The Government concedes that Section 3 of the Clayton Act does not apply to . . . tie-ins involving services. The government asserts, however, that sales upon the condition that the purchaser subscribe to the services of the vendor constitute an unreasonable restraint of trade in violation of Section 1 of the Sherman Act. The defendants claim that this requirement was reasonable and offered evidence on this point, which was received over the objection of the Government which maintained that the contracts were unreasonable *per se* under the decision in *Northern Pacific Railway Co.* v. *United States.* . . .

It is clear from the amount of service rendered by Jerrold under its compulsory service contracts that a "not insubstantial" amount of interstate commerce was affected, particularly in view of the relatively limited market. . . .

A more difficult question is presented by the second requirement that Jerrold be shown to have sufficient economic power with respect to its equipment to appreciably restrain free competition in the market for the services it rendered. The minimum amount of economic power required is by no means clear. Fortunately, the facts of this case obviate the necessity of ascertaining that standard. In resolving this matter, the first task is to determine the relevant market in which to measure Jerrold's power. Since in this aspect of the case we are only concerned with power which will appreciably restrain competition in the market for the services of installing, maintaining and operating community antenna systems, we are necessarily only interested in power over equipment used in community systems. Jerrold admits that, as to the sale of complete community television antenna systems, it was an undoubted leader up until mid-1954, and more than a majority of the new systems from 1950 to mid-1954 were purchased from it. Indeed, Jerrold consistently advertised throughout this period that at least 75% of the community systems in the United States were "Jerrold systems." Economic power over a product can be inferred from sales leadership. . . . The Supreme Court also stated in the *Northern Pacific* case that the requisite economic power can be inferred from the very existence of the tying clauses where no other explanation for their use is offered. The majority of the court appears to feel that this explanation must include a showing of some benefit conferred upon the purchasers in return for their sacrifice of a free choice of alternatives, but also considered the seller's motive. This is an extremely difficult burden to meet and, in the opinion of this court, it has not been satisfied by the evidence offered by the defendants in the case at bar. Another fact from which economic power can be inferred is the desirability of the tying product to the purchaser. *Northern Pacific Railway Co.* v. *United States, supra*. . . (dissent). Mr. Shapp has stated that Jerrold's highly specialized head end equipment was the only equipment available which was designed to meet all of the varying problems arising at the antenna site. It was thus in great demand by system operators. This placed Jerrold in a strategic position and gave it the leverage necessary to persuade customers to agree to its service contracts. This leverage constitutes "economic power" sufficient to invoke the doctrine of *per se* unreasonableness.

While the trial judge is of the opinion that the Government has established both of the prerequisites necessary for treating Jerrold's policy and practice of selling its community equipment only in conjunction with a service contract as unreasonable, *per se*, under the *Northern Pacific* decision, he does not believe that the inquiry must end there in view of the rather unique circumstances involved in this particular case. Any judicially, as opposed to legislatively, declared *per se* rule is not conclusively binding on this court as to any set of facts not basically the same as those in the cases in which the rule was applied. In laying down such a rule, a court would be, in effect, stating that in all the possible situations it can think of, it is unable to see any redeeming virtue in tying arrangements which would make them reasonable. The Supreme Court of the United States did not purport in the *Northern Pacific* case to anticipate all of the possible circumstances under which a tying arrangement might be used. Therefore, while the *per se* rule should be followed in almost all cases, the court must always be conscious of the fact that a case might arise in which the facts indicate that an injustice would be done by blindly accepting the *per se* rule. In this case, the court felt that the facts asserted by the defendants in their pre-trial statement and trial brief warranted hearing their testimony and argument on the issue of reasonableness. It was partly influenced in this decision by the fact that the history of the industry was brief, and the position of the defendants did not seem to require a prolonged economic investigation—factors which the Supreme Court felt justified the *per se* rule.

When Jerrold was ready to place its W equipment on the market in May 1950, it was confronted with a rather unique situation. In the first place, while it was convinced that its equipment would work, Jerrold recognized that it was sensitive and unstable. Consequently, modifications were still being made. . . . Secondly, as has already been noted, there were hundreds of people anxious to set up community antenna systems. Most of these people had no technical background at all. None of them had any experience with community systems since, at that time, there was only one other operating system in the country besides the Jerrold systems in Lansford and Mahanoy City.[1] In addition, many of these people did not have solid or extensive financing to back their proposed venture. Finally, Jerrold had directed most of its resources towards the development of its community equipment. It was of utmost importance to it that its investment prove successful.

Shapp, his engineers and salesmen, envisioned widespread chaos if Jerrold simply sold its community equipment to anyone who wanted it. This fear was based on more than mere speculation. . . . The amount of capital necessary to start a system was substantial. Interest would wane rapidly if the systems installed did not consistently produce satisfactory results. Not only Jerrold's reputation but the growth of the entire industry was at stake

[1] This was an experimental system of R.C.A.'s in Pottsville, Pa.

during the development period. In addition to its reputation, Jerrold was also dependent upon successful system operation for payment. Many operators were not in a position to pay cash for the necessary equipment and the risks were such that outside financing could not be obtained. Therefore, payment was often contingent on the success of the system. It appeared that it was cheaper and more practical to insure that a system was properly installed in the first place than to attempt to get it operating once it was strung up. Furthermore, as has already been noted, use of existing utility poles was an important cost and public relations factor. The utility companies were reluctant to have men of unknown ability working on their poles. Therefore, it was desirable that the system be installed under the supervision of men whose ability was known to the utility companies through other dealings. For these reasons, it was decided that community equipment should be sold with engineering services in order to foster the orderly growth of the industry on which the future of Jerrold depended.

The Government does not dispute the reasonableness of the contracts for services but objects to the fact that they were compulsory. The crucial question, therefore, is whether Jerrold could have accomplished the ends it sought without requiring the contracts. It has been suggested that Jerrold could have accomplished the same results by addressing the persuasive argument it made to this court to its customers and leaving use of the contracts on a voluntary basis. . . . This argument assumes that Jerrold and the industry could survive the "transitory disloyalties" this approach would entail. Jerrold's service was costly and many operators, because of their limited finances, preferred to do-it-themselves and save the expense. . . . If Jerrold's equipment was available without a contract, many impatient operators probably would have attempted to install their systems without assistance. . . . Jerrold's supply of equipment was limited. Unrestricted sales would have resulted in much of this equipment going into systems where prospects of success were at best extremely doubtful. Jerrold's short and long-term well-being depended on the success of these first systems. It could not afford to permit some of its limited equipment to be used in such a way that it would work against its interests. A wave of system failures at the start would have greatly retarded, if not destroyed, this new industry and would have been disastrous for Jerrold, who, unlike others experimenting in this field such as R.C.A. and Philco, did not have a diversified business to fall back on but had put most of its eggs in one precarious basket in an all out effort to open up this new field. . . . For these reasons, this court concludes that Jerrold's policy and practice of selling its community equipment only in conjunction with a service contract was reasonable and not in violation of Section 1 of the Sherman Act at the time of its inception. . . .

The court's conclusion is based primarily on the fact that the tie-in was instituted in the launching of a new business with a highly uncertain future. As the industry took root and grew, the reasons for the blanket insistence on a service contract disappeared. The development of the community antenna industry throughout the country was not uniform. It advanced and became established most rapidly in the East, particularly in Pennsylvania. Progress was slower in the Northwest and Southwest. Thus, when the reasons for this policy ceased to exist in the East, there were still good reasons for its continuance in other areas. Oral reports of successful systems 3,000 miles away are not as convincing as a number of failures nearby. Jerrold recognized this fact and abandoned its policy gradually. In March 1954, it dropped the policy as a general rule and thereafter applied it on an area-by-area and case-by-case basis.[2] Mr. Shapp candidly admits that he can "not make the assertion that in each stage of this evolution our timing has been exactly correct." . . . [W]hile Jerrold has satisfied this court that its policy was reasonable at its inception, it has failed to satisfy us that it remained reasonable throughout the period of its use,[3] even allowing it a reasonable time to recognize and adjust its policies to changing conditions. Accordingly, the court concludes that the defendants' refusal to sell Jerrold equipment except in conjunction with a service contract violated Section 1 of the Sherman Act during part of the time this policy was in effect.

III-B. *Full System Sales*

Jerrold also admits that it was its policy and practice from May 1951 to March 1954 not to sell its various items of equipment designed for community antenna systems separately, but only to sell them as components of a complete system. As a result of this program, individual pieces of Jerrold equipment were unavailable for both new systems and existing non-Jerrold systems. The government contends that this too constitutes an unlawful tie-in because Jerrold is driving competitors from the field by using its market power with respect to some of its equipment to induce the purchase of other equipment it manufactures.

Since this aspect of Jerrold's activity involves the tying of goods to goods, Section 3 of the Clayton Act, as well as Section 1 of the Sherman Act, is applicable. . . . The court's determination of the relevant market and finding as to Jerrold's position in that market when considering the engineering service contract requirement are equally applicable to this

---

[2] The Government contends that Jerrold abandoned this policy because of the threat of Government antitrust action. The court finds to the contrary. It is clear that Jerrold persisted in this policy in some areas of the country after it was aware of the Government's interest in the matter. It would, therefore, seem that the Government's activity was not a motivating factor.

[3] In addition to changes in the condition of the industry, it is also noted that there is some indication in the record that in some areas of the country Jerrold was unable to give the service it felt was necessary to install a successful system. Nevertheless, a contract was required. While this court feels that Jerrold was hopeful that the service would be adequate, it feels that it was unreasonable to make sales on this condition when it could not meet its obligations. The proper course would have been to make sales free of any contract requirement or refuse to make any sales at all, as it had done between January and May 1951.

aspect of the case. The record also makes it clear that a not insubstantial amount of commerce was affected.

[Judge Van Deusen then rejected Jerrold's contention that its antenna system was a single product, and hence concluded that its method of selling did constitute a tying arrangement.]

Balancing these considerations only, the defendants' position would seem to be highly questionable. . . . There is a further factor, however, which, in the court's opinion, makes Jerrold's decision to sell only full systems reasonable. There was a sound business reason for Jerrold to adopt this policy. Jerrold's decision was intimately associated with its belief that a service contract was essential. This court has already determined that, in view of the condition of Jerrold, the equipment, and the potential customers, the defendants' policy of insisting on a service contract was reasonable at its inception. Jerrold could not render the service it promised and deemed necessary if the customer could purchase any kind of equipment he desired. The limited knowledge and instability of equipment made specifications an impractical, if not impossible, alternative. Furthermore, Jerrold's policy could not have been carried out if separate items of its equipment were made available to existing systems or any other customer because the demand was so great that this equipment would find its way to a new system.[4] Thus, the court concludes that Jerrold's policy of full system sales was a necessary adjunct to its policy of compulsory service and was reasonably regarded as a product as long as the conditions which dictated the use of the service contract continued to exist.[5] As the circumstances changed and the need for compulsory service contracts disappeared, the economic reasons for exclusively selling complete systems were eliminated. Absent these economic reasons, the court feels that a full system was not an appropriate sales unit. . . .

The defendants also assert a further justification for its policy insofar as it applied to systems using a large quantity of non-Jerrold equipment. Jerrold spent considerable time and effort in developing its head end equipment. As a result, its equipment was considered the best available and an asset to any system, since it affected the quality of the initial signal which would be transmitted through the rest of the system. The head end equipment, while intricate, did not represent a large portion of the investment in a system because only a few items were involved. The real profit in a system came from the sale of the amplifiers, since a large number were involved. Jerrold felt that other companies who had not invested time and money into the development of satisfactory head-end equipment sought to take advantage of it by competing with it as to the amplifiers, but relying

---

[4] There are numerous references in the record to cases where Jerrold's equipment was discovered in non-Jerrold systems which was procured from system operators as second-hand and excess equipment and from Jerrold distributors in violation of their authority from Jerrold.

[5] Jerrold's argument that it was selling a legitimate single product and that no tying was involved would also apply to the installation aspect of the service contracts, since this covers the assembly of the components into the marketed product.

on Jerrold's head end equipment to make the system successful. Shapp resented these other companies "picking our brains" and competing for the real source of profit. Jerrold, therefore, felt justified in recovering its substantial investment in the development of superior head end equipment by using it to preserve for itself a share of the more lucrative market for amplifiers. While the court is sympathetic with Jerrold's predicament, it does not feel that it provides sufficient justification for the use of a tying arrangement. If the demand for Jerrold's equipment was so great, it could recover its investment by raising its prices. Admittedly, the return would not be as great, but it provides sufficient protection to serve as a more reasonable and less restrictive alternative to a tying arrangement.

The court concludes that the defendants' policy of selling full systems only was lawful at its inception but constituted a violation of Section 1 of the Sherman Act and Section 3 of the Clayton Act during part of the time it was in effect.

III-C.   *The Veto Provisions*

In addition to initially selling its equipment only on a full system basis, Jerrold also imposed certain limitations on the equipment that could be added to the system in the future by means of certain provisions in its service contracts. One of these is the provision appearing in all of the contracts to the effect that the operator shall not install any unapproved, non-Jerrold equipment. The Government contends that these clauses prohibit the use of competitive equipment. It is apparent that these clauses do not absolutely require the use of Jerrold equipment. . . . Equipment approved by Jerrold was also permitted. . . .

. . . An examination of the record discloses uncontradicted testimony concerning numerous systems which used non-Jerrold equipment without objection, although this fact was known to the defendants. On the other hand, no instances were brought to the court's attention in which it is clear that an operator considered himself unable to obtain non-Jerrold equipment because of the veto clause. The court finds that these provisions were not intended, and were not used, to prevent the use of competitive equipment in systems covered by a service contract.

The veto provisions were necessary to protect Jerrold in view of its maintenance obligations under the contracts and its financial interest in the success of the systems. Reasonable restraints are permissible for such purposes. *International Salt Co., Inc.* v. *United States, supra.* The restraint imposed by the requirement that Jerrold approve all equipment other than that it manufactured its reasonable in view of the meaning given to this provision as evidenced by Jerrold's conduct with respect to it. It must also be noted that, because of the instability of the equipment and rapid growth of the industry, the use of pre-determined specifications, rather than the more flexible approval approach, would probably have been more restrictive if Jerrold was to be afforded the protection to which it was entitled.

III-D. *The Additional Channels Provision*

The Government also challenges the provision appearing in the 103 series contracts which requires operators to purchase from Jerrold the equipment necessary to receive any stations in addition to those received at the time of the initial installation. . . . The defendants argue that this provision was justified because "it would be a business folly to try to fit someone else's equipment into the actual spaces provided for additional channels." They also urge that these provisions are consistent with its policy of full system sales.

The court agrees with the Government that these provisions constitute unlawful tie-ins in violation of Section 1 of the Sherman Act and Section 3 of the Clayton Act, regardless of the defendants' actual motives. It can discover no reasons which justify this absolute restriction on the operator's choice of equipment which are not served by the "veto provision." . . .

IV. *Corporate Acquisitions*

[In a lengthy section of its decision the court found that the effect of a series of acquisitions by Jerrold of CATV systems "is to foreclose competitors . . . from a share of the market in community television antenna system equipment." Additional acquisitions were barred for three years.]

V. *Conspiracy and Attempt to Monopolize*

· · · ·

The trial judge finds that Jerrold's policy of selling its equipment exclusively on a full system basis and in conjunction with a service contract, while not shown to be reasonable at all times in which it was in effect, was never intended by the defendants to drive competitors from the business of supplying equipment for community television antenna systems and to achieve a monopoly in this field for Jerrold. Among other things, it must be kept in mind that this policy was evolved and put into effect when Jerrold first marketed community antenna equipment. At that time, both R.C.A. and Philco were entering the business. Furthermore, the future of this brand new field was quite uncertain. It is highly unlikely that the most ambitious businessman would enter this business from the beginning with a policy intended to force such formidable competitors as these from the field and acquire the power to control prices or foreclose access to this market. . . .

· · · ·

FINAL JUDGMENT.

· · · ·

The defendants are enjoined and restrained from, directly or indirectly:

(A) Selling or offering to sell equipment on the condition or understanding that the purchaser thereof purchase services from the defendants;

(B) Furnishing or offering to furnish services on the condition or understanding that the recipient thereof purchase any Jerrold equipment;

(C) Selling or offering to sell any item of Jerrold equipment on the condition or understanding that the purchaser thereof buy or use any other Jerrold equipment;

(D) Selling or offering to sell any equipment on the condition or understanding that the purchaser thereof will not purchase or use equipment manufactured or sold by any other person; provided, however, this subsection (D) shall not prohibit defendants from electing to sell or offer for sale Jerrold equipment upon the condition or understanding that defendants will not guarantee, warrant or, in any manner, be responsible for, the operation or efficiency of such equipment, or the system in which the same may be installed or used, if the purchaser thereof installs, as a part of such system, any equipment or attachments manufactured by any other person which, in defendants' opinion, might either (a) impair the quality of television reception or signal distribution capability of the system, or (b) cause damage to, or impair the operation or efficiency of, any of the Jerrold equipment sold or offered for sale. . . .

United States v. Loew's Incorporated

371 U.S. 38 (1962)

MR. JUSTICE GOLDBERG delivered the opinion of the Court.

These consolidated appeals present as a key question the validity under Section 1 of the Sherman Act of block booking of copyrighted feature motion pictures for television exhibition. We hold that the tying agreements here are illegal and in violation of the Act.

The United States brought separate civil antitrust actions in the Southern District of New York in 1957 against six major distributors of pre-1948 copyrighted motion picture feature films for television exhibition, alleging that each defendant had engaged in block booking in violation of Section 1 of the Sherman Act. The complaints asserted that the defendants had, in selling to television stations, conditioned the license or sale of one or more feature films upon the acceptance by the station of a package or block containing one or more unwanted or inferior films. No combination or conspiracy among the distributors was alleged; nor was any monopolization or attempt to monopolize under Section 2 of the Sherman Act averred. The sole claim of illegality rested on the manner in which each defendant had marketed its product. The successful pressure applied to television station customers to accept inferior films along with desirable pictures was the gravamen of the complaint.

After a lengthy consolidated trial, the district judge filed exhaustive findings of fact, conclusions of law, and a carefully reasoned opinion, 189

F. Supp. 373, in which he found that the actions of the defendants constituted violations of Section 1 of the Sherman Act. . . .

The judge recognized that there was keen competition between the defendant distributors, and therefore rested his conclusion solely on the individual behavior of each in engaging in block booking. In reaching his decision he carefully considered the evidence relating to each of the 68 licensing agreements that the Government had contended involved block booking. He concluded that only 25 of the contracts were illegally entered into. Nine of these belonged to defendant C & C Super Corp., which had an admitted policy of insisting on block booking that it sought to justify on special grounds.

Of the others, defendent Loew's, Incorporated, had in two negotiations that resulted in licensing agreements declined to furnish stations KWTV of Oklahoma City and WBRE of Wilkes-Barre with individual film prices and had refused their requests for permission to select among the films in the groups. Loew's exacted from KWTV a contract for the entire Loew's library of 723 films, involving payments of $314,725.20. The WBRE agreement was for a block of 100 films, payments to total $15,000.

Defendant Screen Gems, Inc., was also found to have block booked two contracts, both with WTOP of Washington, D.C., one calling for a package of 26 films and payments of $20,800 and the other for 52 films and payments of $40,000. The judge accepted the testimony of station officials that they had requested the right to select films and that their requests were refused.

Associated Artists Productions, Inc., negotiated four contracts that were found to be block booked. Station WTOP was to pay $118,800 for the license of 99 pictures, which were divided into three groups of 33 films, based on differences in quality. To get "Treasure of the Sierra Madre," "Casablanca," "Johnny Belinda," "Sergeant York," and "The Man Who Came to Dinner," among others, WTOP also had to take such films as "Nancy Drew Troubleshooter," "Tugboat Annie Sails Again," "Kid Nightingale," "Gorilla Man," and "Tear Gas Squad." A similar contract for 100 pictures, involving a license fee of $140,000, was entered into by WMAR of Baltimore. Triangle Publications, owner and operator of five stations, was refused the right to select among Associated's packages, and ultimately purchased the entire library of 754 films for a price of $2,262,000 plus 10% of gross receipts. Station WJAR of Providence, which licensed a package of 58 features for a fee of $25,230, had asked first if certain films it considered undesirable could be dropped from the offered packages and was told that the packages could not be split.

Defendant National Telefilm Associates was found to have entered into five block booked contracts. . . .

The judge found that defendant United Artists Corporation had in three consummated negotiations conditioned the sale of films on the purchase of an entire package. . . .

Since defendant C & C was found to have had an overall policy of block booking, the court did not analyze the particular circumstances of the nine negotiations which had resulted in the licensing of packages of films. C & C's policies resulted in at least one station having to take a package in which "certain of the films were unplayable since they had a foreign language sound track." 189 F. Supp., at 389.

The court entered separate final judgments against the defendants, wherein each was enjoined from

(A) Conditioning or tying, or attempting to condition or tie, the purchase or license of the right to exhibit any feature film over any television station upon the purchase or license of any other film;

(B) Conditioning the purchase or license of the right to exhibit any feature film over any television station upon the purchase or license for exhibition over any other television station of that feature film, or any other film;

(C) Entering into any agreement to sell or license the right to exhibit any feature film over any television station in which the differential between the price or fee for such feature film when sold or licensed alone and the price or fee for the same film when sold or licensed with one or more other film [*sic*] has the effect of conditioning the sale or license of such film upon the sale or license of one or more other films.

All of the defendants except National Telefilm appeal from the decree. The appeals of defendants Loew's, Screen Gems, Associated Artists, and United Artists raise identical issues and are consolidated as No. 43. The appeal of defendant C & C raises additional issues, and is therefore separately numbered as No. 44. The Government, although it won on the merits below, asserts in a cross-appeal (No. 42) that the scope and specificity of the decree entered by the District Court were inadequate to prevent the continued attainment of illegal objectives. It seeks to have the decree broadened in a number of ways. All of the defendants below oppose these modifications. . . . We shall consider No. 43 first, since appellants there raise the fundamental question whether their activities were in violation of the antitrust laws. We shall thereafter consider No. 44, the special arguments of appellant C & C, and finally No. 42, the Government's request for broadening the decree.

I

This case raises the recurring question of whether specific tying arrangements violate Section 1 of the Sherman Act.[1] This Court has recognized that "[t]ying agreements serve hardly any purpose beyond the suppression of competition," *Standard Oil Co. of California* v. *United States*, 337 U.S. 293, 305–306. They are an object of antitrust concern for two reasons—

---

[1] See *International Salt Co.* v. *United States*, 332 U.S. 392; *United States* v. *Paramount Pictures, Inc.*, 334 U.S. 131; *Times-Picayune Pub. Co.* v. *United States*, 345 U.S. 594; *Northern Pacific R. Co.* v. *United States*, 356 U.S. 1.

they may force buyers into giving up the purchase of substitutes for the tied product, see *Times-Picayune Pub. Co.* v. *United States,* 345 U.S. 594, 605, and they may destroy the free access of competing suppliers of the tied product to the consuming market, see *International Salt Co.* v. *United States,* 332 U.S. 392, 396. A tie-in contract may have one or both of these undesirable effects when the seller, by virtue of his position in the market for the tying product, has economic leverage sufficient to induce his customers to take the tied product along with the tying item. The standard of illegality is that the seller must have "sufficient economic power with respect to the tying product to appreciably restrain free competition in the market for the tied product...." *Northern Pacific R. Co.* v. *United States,* 356 U.S. 1, 6. Market dominance—some power to control price and to exclude competition—is by no means the only test of whether the seller has the requisite economic power. Even absent a showing of market dominance, the crucial economic power may be inferred from the tying product's desirability to consumers or from uniqueness in its attributes.[2]

The requisite economic power is presumed when the tying product is patented or copyrighted, *International Salt Co.* v. *United States,* 332 U.S. 392; *United States* v. *Paramount Pictures, Inc.,* 334 U.S. 131. . . . These [and other cited] cases reflect a hostility to use of the statutorily granted patent monopoly to extend the patentee's economic control to unpatented products. The patentee is protected as to his invention, but may not use his patent rights to exact tribute for other articles.

Since one of the objectives of the patent laws is to reward uniqueness, the principle of these cases was carried over into antitrust law on the theory that the existence of a valid patent on the tying product, without more, establishes a distinctiveness sufficient to conclude that any tying arrangement involving the patented product would have anticompetitive consequences. *E.g., International Salt Co.* v. *United States,* 332 U.S. 392. In *United States* v. *Paramount Pictures, Inc.,* 334 U.S. 131, 156–159, the principle of the patent cases was applied to copyrighted feature films which had been block booked into movie theaters. The Court reasoned that

The copyright law, like the patent statutes, makes reward to the owner a secondary consideration. In *Fox Film Corp.* v. *Doyal,* 286 U.S. 123, 127, Chief Justice Hughes spoke as follows respecting the copyright monopoly granted by Congress, The sole interest of the United States and the primary object in

---

[2] Since the requisite economic power may be found on the basis of either uniqueness or consumer appeal, and since market dominance in the present context does not necessitate a demonstration of market power in the sense of Section 2 of the Sherman Act, it should seldom be necessary in a tie-in sale case to embark upon a full-scale factual inquiry into the scope of the relevant market for the tying product and into the corollary problem of the seller's percentage share in that market. This is even more obviously true when the tying product is patented or copyrighted, in which case . . . sufficiency of economic power is presumed. Appellants' reliance on *United States* v. *E. I. duPont de Nemours & Co.,* 351 U.S. 377, is therefore misplaced.

conferring the monopoly lie in the general benefits derived by the public from the labors of authors. It is said that reward to the author or artist serves to induce release to the public of the products of his creative genius. But the reward does not serve its public purpose if it is not related to the quality of the copyright. Where a high quality film greatly desired is licensed only if an inferior one is taken, the latter borrows quality from the former and strengthens its monopoly by drawing on the other. The practice tends to equalize rather than differentiate the reward for the individual copyrights. Even where all the films included in the package are of equal quality, the requirement that all be taken if one is desired increases the market for some. Each stands not on its own footing but in whole or in part on the appeal which another film may have. As the District Court said, the result is to add to the monopoly of the copyright in violation of the principle of the patent cases involving tying clauses. 334 U.S., at 158.

Appellants attempt to distinguish the *Paramount* decision in its relation to the present facts: the block booked sale of copyrighted feature films to exhibitors in a new medium—television. Not challenging the District Court's finding that they did engage in block booking, they contend that the uniqueness attributable to a copyrighted feature film, though relevant in the movie-theater context, is lost when the film is being sold for television use. Feature films, they point out, constitute less than 8% of televion programming, and they assert that films are "reasonably interchangeable" with other types of programming material and with other feature films as well. Thus they argue that their behavior is not to be judged by the principle of the patent cases, as applied to copyrighted materials in *Paramount Pictures*, but by the general principles which govern the validity of tying arrangements of nonpatented products, *e.g.*, *Northern Pacific R. Co. v. United States*, 356 U.S. 1, 6, 11. They say that the Government's proof did not establish their "sufficient economic power" in the sense contemplated for nonpatented products.[3]

Appellants cannot escape the applicability of *Paramount Pictures*. A copyrighted feature film does not lose its legal or economic uniqueness because it is shown on a television rather than a movie screen.

The district judge found that each copyrighted film block booked by appellants for television use "was in itself a unique product"; that feature films "varied in theme, in artistic performance, in stars, in audience appeal, etc.," and were not fungible; and that since each defendant by reason of its copyright had a "monopolistic" position as to each tying product, "sufficient economic power" to impose an appreciable restraint on free competition in the tied product was present, as demanded by the *Northern*

[3] Appellants' framing of their argument in terms of each of them not having dominance in the market for television exhibition of feature films misconceives the applicable legal standard. As noted, *supra*, . . . "sufficient economic powers" as contemplated by the *Northern Pacific* case is a term more inclusive in scope than "market dominance."

Pacific decision. 189 F.Supp., at 381.[4] We agree. These findings of the district judge, supported by the record, confirm the presumption of uniqueness resulting from the existence of the copyright itself.

Moreover, there can be no question in this case of the adverse effects on free competition resulting from appellants' illegal block booking contracts. Television stations forced by appellants to take unwanted films were denied access to films marketed by other distributors who, in turn, were foreclosed from selling to the stations. Nor can there be any question as to the substantiality of the commerce involved. . . . These anticompetitive consequences are an apt illustration of the reasons underlying our recognition that the mere presence of competing substitutes for the tying product, here taking the form of other programming material as well as other feature films, is insufficient to destroy the legal, and indeed the economic, distinctiveness of the copyrighted product. *Standard Oil Co. of California* v. *United States*, 337 U.S. 293, 307; *Times-Picayune Pub. Co.* v. *United States*, 345 U.S. 594, 611 and n. 30. By the same token, the distinctiveness of the copyrighted tied product is not inconsistent with the fact of competition, in the form of other programming material and other films, which is suppressed by the tying arrangements.

It is therefore clear that the tying arrangements here both by their "inherent nature" and by their "effect" injuriously restrained trade. *United States* v. *American Tobacco Co.*, 221 U.S. 106, 179. Accommodation between the statutorily dispensed monopoly in the combination of contents in the patented or copyrighted product and the statutory principles of free competition demands that extension of the patent or copyright monopoly by the use of tying agreements be strictly confined. There may be rare circumstances in which the doctrine we have enunciated under Section 1 of the Sherman Act prohibiting tying arrangements involving patented or copyrighted tying products is inapplicable. However, we find it difficult to conceive of such a case, and the present case is clearly not one. . . .

II

Appellant C & C in its separate appeal raises certain arguments which amount to an attempted business justification for its admitted block booking policy. C & C purchased the telecasting rights in some 742 films known as the "RKO Library." It did so with a bank loan for the total purchase price, and to get the bank loan it needed a guarantor, which it found in the International Latex Corporation. Latex, however, demanded and secured an agreement from C & C that films would not be sold without ob-

---

[4] To use the trial court's apt example, forcing a television station which wants "Gone With The Wind" to take "Getting Gertie's Garter" as well is taking undue advantage of the fact that to television as well as motion picture viewers there is but one "Gone With The Wind."

taining in return a commitment from television stations to show a minimum number of Latex spot advertisements in conjunction with the films. Thus, since stations could not feasibly telecast the minimum number of spots without buying a large number of films to spread them over, C & C by requiring the minimum number of advertisements effectively forced block booking on those stations which purchased its films. C & C contends the block booking was merely the by-product of two legitimate business motives—Latex's desire for a saturation advertising campaign, and C & C's wish to buy a large film library. However, the obvious answer to this contention is that the thrust of the antitrust laws cannot be avoided merely by claiming that the otherwise illegal conduct is compelled by contractual obligations. Were it otherwise, the antitrust laws could be nullified. Contractual obligations cannot thus supersede statutory imperatives. Hence, tying arrangements, once found to exist in a context of sufficient economic power, are illegal "without elaborate inquiry as to . . . the business excuse for their use," *Northern Pacific R. Co.* v. *United States,* 356 U.S. 1, 5.

In Nos. 43 and 44, therefore, we agree with the merits of the District Court's decision. It correctly found that the conditioning of the sale of one or more copyrighted feature films to television stations upon the purchase of one or more other films is illegal. The antitrust laws do not permit a compounding of the statutorily conferred monopoly.

III

. . . . .

The United States contends that the relief afforded by the final judgments is inadequate and that to be adequate it must also: (1) require the defendants to price the films individually and offer them on a picture-by-picture basis; (2) prohibit noncost-justified differentials in price between a film when sold individually and when sold as part of a package; (3) proscribe "temporary" refusals by a distributor to deal on less than a block basis while he is negotiating with a competing television station for a package sale.

Some of the practices which the Government seeks to have enjoined with its requested modifications are acts which may be entirely proper when viewed alone. To ensure, however, that relief is effectual, otherwise permissible practices connected with the acts found to be illegal must sometimes be enjoined. . . .

A. *Initial Offer of Individual Films, Individually Priced*

Under the final judgments entered by the court, a distributor would be free to offer films in a package initially, without stating individual prices. If, however, he delayed at all in producing individual prices upon request, he would subject himself to a possible contempt sanction. The Government's first request would prevent this "first bite" possibility, forcing the offer of the films on an individual basis at the outset (but, as we view it, not precluding a simultaneous package offer, *United States* v. *Paramount Pictures, Inc., supra,* 334 U.S., at 159).

This is a necessary addition to the decrees, in view of the evidence appearing in the record. Television stations which asked for the individual prices of some of the better pictures "couldn't get any sort of a firm kind of an answer," according to one station official. He stated that they received a "certain form of equivocation, like the price for the better pictures that we wanted was so high that it wouldn't be worth our while to discuss the matter, . . . the implication being that it wouldn't happen." A Screen Gems intracompany memorandum about a Baton Rouge station's price request stated that "I told him that I would be happy to talk to him about it, figuring we could start the old round robin that worked so well in Houston & San Antonio." Without the proposed amendment to the decree, distributors might surreptitiously violate it by allowing or directing their salesmen to be reluctant to produce the individual price list on request. This subtler form of sales pressure, though not accompanied by any observable delay over time, might well result in some television stations buying the block rather than trying to talk the seller into negotiating on an individual basis. Requiring the production of the individual list on first approach will obviate this danger.

B. *Prohibition of Noncost-justified Price Differentials*

The final judgments as entered only prohibit a price differential between a film offered individually and as part of a package which "has the effect of conditioning the sale or license of such film upon the sale or license of one or more other films." The Government contends that this provision appearing by itself is too vague and will lead to unnecessary litigation. Differentials unjustified by cost savings may already be prohibited under the decree as it now appears. Nevertheless the addition of a specific provision to prevent such differentials will prevent uncertainty in the operation of the decree. To ensure that litigation over the scope and application of the decrees is not left until a contempt proceeding is brought, the second requested modification should be added. The Government, however, seeks to make distribution costs the only saving which can legitimately be the basis of a discount. We would not so limit the relevant cost justifications. To prevent definitional arguments, and to ensure that all proper bases of quantity discount may be used, the modification should be worded in terms of allowing all legitimate cost justifications.

C. *Prohibition of "Temporary" Refusals to Deal*

The Government's third request is, like the first, designed to prevent distributors from subjecting prospective purchasers to a "run-around" on the purchase of individual films. No doubt temporary refusal to sell in broken lots to one customer while negotiating to sell the entire block to another is a proper business practice, viewed *in vacuo*, but we think that if permitted here it may tend to force some stations into buying pre-set packages to forestall a competitor's getting the entire group. In recognition of this the Government seeks a blanket prohibition against all temporary refusals to deal. We agree in the main. . . . We therefore grant the Government's request, but modify it only to the limited degree necessary to permit a seller briefly to defer licensing or selling to a customer pending the expeditious conclusion of bona fide negotiations already being conducted with a competing station on a proposal wherein the distributor has simultaneously offered to license or sell films either individually or in a package.

The modifications we have specified will bring about a greater precision in the operation of the decrees. We have concluded that they will properly protect the interest of the Government in guarding against violations and the interests of the defendants in seeking in good faith to comply.

The judgments are vacated and the causes are remanded to the District Court for further proceedings in conformity with this opinion.

Vacated and remanded.

[Mr. Justice Harlan, with whom Mr. Justice Stewart joined, concurred in part and dissented in part.]

Fortner Enterprises, Inc. v. *United States Steel Corp.*

394 U.S. 495 (1969)

MR. JUSTICE BLACK delivered the opinion of the Court [on a motion for summary judgment].

. . . Petitioner, Fortner Enterprises, Inc., filed this suit seeking treble damages and an injunction against alleged violations of §§1 and 2 of the Sherman Act. . . . The complaint charged that respondents, United States Steel Corp. and its wholly owned subsidiary, the United States Steel Homes Credit Corp., had engaged in a contract, combination, and conspiracy to restrain trade and to monopolize trade in the sale of prefabricated houses. It alleged that there was a continuing agreement between respondents "to force corporations and individuals, including the plaintiff, as a condition to availing themselves of the services of United States Steel Homes Credit Corporation, to purchase at artificially high prices only United States Steel Homes. . . ." Specifically, petitioner claimed that in order to obtain loans totaling over $2,000,000 from the Credit Corp. for the purchase and development of certain land in the Louisville, Kentucky, area, it had been required to agree, as a condition of the loans, to erect a prefabricated house manufactured by U.S. Steel on each of the lots purchased with the loan proceeds. Petitioner claimed that the prefabricated materials were then supplied by U.S. Steel at unreasonably high prices and proved to be defective and unusable, thus requiring the expenditure of additional sums and delaying the completion date for the development. Petitioner sought treble damages for the profits thus lost, along with a decree enjoining respondents from enforcing the requirement of the loan agreement that petitioner use only houses manufactured by U.S. Steel.

. . . Noting that the agreement involved here was essentially a tying arrangement, under which the purchaser was required to take a tied product—here prefabricated homes—as a condition of being allowed to purchase the tying product—here credit, the District Judge held that petitioner had failed to establish the prerequisites of illegality under our tying cases, namely sufficient market power over the tying product and foreclosure of a substantial volume of commerce in the tied product. . . . Since we find no basis for sustaining this summary judgment, we reverse and order that the case proceed to trial.

We agree with the District Court that the conduct challenged here primarily involves a tying arrangement of the traditional kind. The Credit Corp. sold its credit only on the condition that petitioner purchase a certain number of prefabricated houses from the Homes Division of U.S. Steel. Our cases have made clear that, at least when certain prerequisites are met, arrangements of this kind are illegal in and of themselves, and no specific showing of unreasonable competitive effect is required. The discussion in *Northern Pacific R. Co.* v. *United States* . . . is dispositive of this question:

> . . . They are unreasonable in and of themselves whenever a party has sufficient economic power with respect to the tying product to appreciably restrain free competition in the market for the tied product and a 'not insubstantial' amount of interstate commerce is affected. *International Salt Co.* v. *United States.* . . .

Despite its recognition of this strict standard, the District Court held that petitioner had not even made out a case for the jury. The court held that respondents did not have "sufficient economic power" over credit, the tying product here, because although the Credit Corp.'s terms evidently made the loans uniquely attractive to petitioner, petitioner had not proved that the Credit Corp. enjoyed the same unique attractiveness or economic control with respect to buyers generally. The court also held that the amount of interstate commerce affected was "insubstantial because only a very small percentage of the land available for development in the area was foreclosed to competing sellers of prefabricated houses by the contract with petitioner. We think it plain that the District Court misunderstood the two controlling standards and misconceived the extent of its authority to evaluate the evidence in ruling on this motion for summary judgment. . . .

. . . [I]t is clear that petitioner raised questions of fact which, if proved at trial, would bring this tying arrangement within the scope of the *per se* doctrine. The requirement that a "not insubstantial" amount of commerce be involved makes no reference to the scope of any particular market or to the share of that market foreclosed by the tie, and hence we could not approve of the trial judge's conclusions on this issue even if we agreed that his definition of the relevant market was the proper one.[1] An analysis of market shares might become relevant if it were alleged that an apparently small dollar-volume of business actually represented a substantial part of the sales for which competitors were bidding. But normally the controlling consideration is simply whether a total amount of business, substantial enough in terms of dollar-volume so as not to be merely *de minimis*, is foreclosed to competitors by the tie, for as we said in *International Salt*, it is "unreasonable, *per se*, to foreclose competitors from any substantial market" by a tying arrangement. . . .

The complaint and affidavits filed here leave no room for doubt that the volume of commerce allegedly foreclosed was substantial. . . . [W]e cannot agree with respondents that a sum of almost $200,000 is paltry or "insubstantial." . . . For purposes of determining whether the amount of commerce foreclosed is too insubstantial to warrant prohibition of the practice, therefore, the relevant figure is the total volume of sales tied by the sales policy under challenge, not the portion of this total accounted for by the particular plaintiff who brings suit. . . . In the present case, the annual sales allegedly foreclosed by respondents' tying arrangements throughout the country totaled almost $4,000,000 in 1960, more than $2,-800,000 in 1961, and almost $2,300,000 in 1962. These amounts could scarcely be regarded as insubstantial.

The standard of "sufficient economic power" does not, as the District Court held, require that the defendant have a monopoly or even a dominant position throughout the market for the tying product. Our tie-in cases have made unmistakably clear that the economic power over the tying product can be sufficient even though the power falls far short of dominance and even though the power exists only with respect to some of the buyers in the market. . . .

These decisions rejecting the need for proof of truly dominant power over the tying product have all been based on a recognition that because

---

[1] Since the loan agreements obligated petitioner to erect houses manufactured by U.S. Steel on the land acquired, the trial judge thought the relevant foreclosure was the percentage of the undeveloped land in the county that was no longer open for sites on which homes made by competing producers could be built. This apparently was an insignificant .00032%. But of course the availability of numerous vacant lots on which houses might legally be erected would be small consolation to competing producers once the economic demand for houses had been pre-empted by respondents. It seems plain that the most significant percentage figure with reference to the tied product is the percentage of annual sales of houses, or prefabricated houses, in the area that was foreclosed to other competitors by the tying arrangement.

tying arrangements generally serve no legitimate business purpose that cannot be achieved in some less restrictive way, the presence of any appreciable restraint on competition provides a sufficient reason for invalidating the tie. Such appreciable restraint results whenever the seller can exert some power over some of the buyers in the market, even if his power is not complete over them and over all other buyers in the market. In fact, complete dominance throughout the market, the concept that the District Court apparently had in mind, would never exist even under a pure monopoly. Market power is usually stated to be the ability of a single seller to raise price and restrict output, for reduced output is the almost inevitable result of higher prices. Even a complete monopolist can seldom raise his price without losing some sales; many buyers will cease to buy the product, or buy less, as the price rises. Market power is therefore a source of serious concern for essentially the same reason, regardless of whether the seller has the greatest economic power possible or merely some lesser degree of appreciable economic power. In both instances, despite the freedom of some or many buyers from the seller's power, other buyers— whether few or many, whether scattered throughout the market or part of some group within the market—can be forced to accept the higher price because of their stronger preferences for the product, and the seller could therefore choose instead to force them to accept a tying arrangement that would prevent free competition for their patronage in the market for the tied product. Accordingly, the proper focus of concern is whether the seller has the power to raise prices, or impose other burdensome terms such as a tie-in, with respect to any appreciable number of buyers within the market.

The affidavits put forward by petitioner clearly entitle it to its day in court under this standard. A construction company president stated that competitors of U.S. Steel sold prefabricated houses and built conventional homes for at least $400 less than U.S. Steel's price for comparable models. Since in a freely competitive situation buyers would not accept a tying arrangement obligating them to buy a tied product at a price higher than the going market rate, this substantial price differential with respect to the tied product (prefabricated houses) in itself may suggest that respondents had some special economic power in the credit market. In addition, petitioner's president, A. B. Fortner, stated that he accepted the tying condition on respondents' loan solely because the offer to provide 100% financing, lending an amount equal to the full purchase price of the land to be acquired, was unusually and uniquely advantageous to him. He found that no such financing was available to his corporation on any such cheap terms from any other source during the 1959–1962 period. . . .

We do not mean to accept petitioner's apparent argument that market power can be inferred simply because the kind of financing terms offered by a lending company are "unique and unusual." We do mean, however, that uniquely and unusually advantageous terms can reflect a creditor's unique economic advantages over his competitors.[2] Since summary judgment in antitrust cases is disfavored, *Poller, supra,* the claims of uniqueness in this case should be read in the light most favorable to petitioner. They could well mean that U.S. Steel's subsidiary Credit Corp. had a unique economic ability to provide 100% financing at cheap rates . . . because of economies resulting from the nationwide character of its operations. In addition, potential competitors such as banks and savings and loan associations may have been prohibited from offering 100% financing by state or federal law. . . .

Brief consideration should also also be given to respondents' additional argument that even if their unique kind of financing reflected economic power in the credit market, and even if a substantial volume of commerce was affected, the arrangement involving credit should not be held illegal under normal tie-in principles. In support of this, respondents suggest that every sale on credit in effect involves a tie. They argue that the offering of favorable credit terms is simply a form of price competition equivalent to the offering of a comparable reduction in the cash price of the tied product. Consumers should not, they say, be deprived of such advantageous services, and they suffer no harm because they can buy the tangible product with credit obtained elsewhere if the combined price of the seller's credit-product package is less favorable than the cost of purchasing the components separately.

All of respondents' arguments amount essentially to the same claim— namely, that this opinion will somehow prevent those who manufacture goods from ever selling them on credit. But our holding in this case will have no such effect. There is, at the outset of every tie-in case, including the familiar cases involving physical goods, the problem of determining whether two separate products are in fact involved. In the usual sale on credit the seller, a single individual or corporation, simply makes an agreement determining when and how much he will be paid for his product. In such a sale the credit may constitute such an inseparable part of the purchase price for the item that the entire transaction could be considered to involve only a single product. It will be time enough to pass on the issue of credit sales when a case involving it actually arises. Sales such as that are a far cry from the arrangement involved here, where the credit is provided by one corporation on condition that a product be purchased from a separate corporation, and where the borrower contracts to obtain

[2] Uniqueness confers economic power only when other competitors are in some way prevented from offering the distinctive product themselves. Such barriers may be legal, as in the case of patented and copyrighted products, *e.g., International Salt; Loew's,* or physical, as when the product is land, *e.g., Northern Pacific.* It is true that the barriers may also be economic, as when competitors are simply unable to produce the distinctive product profitably, but the uniqueness test in such situations is somewhat confusing since the real source of economic power is not the product itself but rather the seller's cost advantage in producing it.

a large sum of money over and above that needed to pay the seller for the physical products purchased. Whatever the standards for determining exactly when a transaction involves only a "single product," we cannot see how an arrangement such as that present in this case could ever be said to involve only a single product.

Nor does anything in respondents' arguments serve to distinguish credit from other kinds of goods and services, all of which may, when used as tying products, extend the seller's economic power to new markets and foreclose competition in the tied product. The asserted business justifications for a tie of credit are not essentially different from the justifications that can be advanced when the tying product is some other service or commodity. Although advantageous credit terms may be viewed as a form of price competition in the tied product, so is the offer of any other tying product on advantageous terms. In both instances, the seller can achieve his alleged purpose, without extending his economic power, by simply reducing the price of the tied product itself.[3]

The potential harm is also essentially the same when the tying product is credit. The buyer may have the choice of buying the tangible commodity separately, but as in other cases the seller can use his power over the tying product to win customers that would otherwise have constituted a market available to competing producers of the tied product. "[C]ompetition on the merits with respect to the tied product is inevitably curbed." *Northern Pacific*, 356 U.S., at 6. Nor can it be assumed that because the product involved is money needed to finance a purchase, the buyer would not have been able to purchase from anyone else without the seller's attractive credit. A buyer might have a strong preference for a seller's credit because it would eliminate the need for him to lay out personal funds, borrow from relatives, put up additional collateral, or obtain guarantors, but any of these expedients might have been chosen to finance a purchase from a competing producer if the seller had not captured the sale by means of his tying arrangement.

In addition, barriers to entry in the market for the tied product are raised since, in order to sell to certain buyers, a new company not only must be able to manufacture the tied product but also must have sufficient financial strength to offer credit comparable to that provided by larger competitors under tying arrangements. If the larger companies have achieved economies of scale in their credit operations, they can of course exploit these economies legitimately by lowering their credit charges to consumers who purchase credit only, but economies in financing should not, any more than economies in other lines of business, be used to exert economic power over other products that the company produces no more efficiently than its competitors.

---

[3] Where price reductions on the tied product are made difficult in practice by the structure of that market, the seller can still achieve his alleged objective by offering other kinds of fringe benefits over which he has no economic power.

For all these reasons we can find no basis for treating credit differently in principle from other goods and services. Although money is a fungible commodity—like wheat or, for that matter, unfinished steel—credit markets, like other markets, are often imperfect, and it is easy to see how a big company with vast sums of money in its treasury could wield very substantial power in a credit market. Where this is true, tie-ins involving credit can cause all the evils that the antitrust laws have always been intended to prevent, crippling other companies that are equally, if not more, efficient in producing their own products. Therefore, the same inquiries must be made as to economic power over the tying product and substantial effect in the tied market, but where these factors are present no special treatment can be justified solely because credit, rather than some other product, is the source of the tying leverage used to restrain competition.

The judgment of the Court of Appeals is reversed, and the case is remanded with directions to let this suit proceed to trial.

Reversed and remanded.

Mr. Justice White, with whom Mr. Justice Harlan joins, dissenting.

The Court does not purport to abandon the general rule that some market power in the tying product is essential to a § 1 violation. But it applies the rule to permit proscription of a seller's extension of favorable credit terms conditioned on the purchase of an agreed quantity of the seller's product without any offer of proof that the seller has any market power in the credit market itself. . . . Proscription of the sale of goods on easy credit terms as an illegal tie without proof of market power in credit not only departs from established doctrine but also in my view should not be outlawed as *per se* illegal under the Sherman Act. Provision of favorable credit terms may be nothing more or less than vigorous competition in the tied product, on a basis very nearly approaching the price competition which it has always been the policy of the Sherman Act to encourage. Moreover, it is far from clear that, absent power in the credit market, credit financing of purchases should be regarded as a tie of two distinct products any more than a commodity should be viewed as tied to its own price. Since provision of credit by sellers may facilitate competition, since it may provide essential risk or working capital to entrepreneurs or businessmen, and since the logic of the majority's opinion does away in practice with the requirement of showing market power in the tying product while retaining that requirement in form, the majority's *per se* rule is inappropriate. I dissent.

In this case there is no offer to prove monopoly or dominance in the tying product—money. And in no sense is the money provided to petitioner unique, even though the terms on which it was furnished and was to be repaid may have been advantageous, and indeed the money itself available from no other source on equally good terms. United States Steel was principally interested in the sale of houses, and petitioner in the economical development of its housing project. Before concluding that the financing arrangements on which U.S. Steel sold its houses amounted to anything more than a price reduction on the houses, or that easy financing terms show that their provider has market power in the money market, the Court should have in mind the rationale on which the illegality of tying arrangements is based.

There is general agreement in the cases and among commentators[4] that the fundamental restraint against which the tying proscription is meant to guard is the use of power over one product to attain power over another, or otherwise to distort freedom of trade and competition in the second product. This distortion injures the buyers of the second product, who because of their preference for the seller's brand of the first are artificially forced to make a less than optimal choice in the second. And even if the customer is indifferent among brands of the second product and therefore loses nothing by agreeing to use the seller's brand of the second in order to get his brand of the first,[5] such tying agreements may work significant restraints on competition in the tied product. The tying seller may be working toward a monopoly position in the tied product[6] and, even if he is not, the practice of tying forecloses other sellers of the tied product and makes it more difficult for new firms to enter that market. They must be prepared not only to match existing sellers of the tied product in price and quality, but to offset the attraction of the tying product itself. Even if this is possible through simultaneous entry into production of the tying product, entry into both markets is significantly

---

[4] *E.g.*, Report of the Attorney General's National Committee to Study the Antitrust Laws 145 (1955); Austin, "The Tying Arrangement: A Critique and Some New Thoughts," 1967 *Wis. L. Rev.* 88; Bowman, "Tying Arrangements and the Leverage Problem," 67 *Yale L. J.* 19 (1957); Day, "Exclusive Dealing, Tying and Reciprocity—A Reappraisal," 29 *Ohio St. L. J.* 539, 540–541 (1968); Turner, "The Validity of Tying Arrangements Under the Antitrust Laws," 72 *Harv. L. Rev.* 50, 60–61 (1958).

[5] Theoretically, the tie may do the tier little good unless the buyer is in that position. Even if the seller has a complete monopoly in the tying product, this is the case. The monopolist can exact the maximum price which people are willing to pay for his product. By definition, if his price went up he would lose customers. If he then refuses to sell the tying product without the tied product, and raises the price of the tied product above market, he will also lose customers. The tying link works no magic. However, difficulty in extracting the full monopoly profit without the tie, Burstein, A Theory of Full-Line Forcing, 55 *Nw. U. L. Rev.* 62 (1960), or the marginal advantage of a guaranteed first refusal from otherwise indifferent customers of the tied product, or other advantages mentioned in the text, may make the tie beneficial to its originator.

[6] If the monopolist uses his monopoly profits in the first market to underwrite sales below market price in the second, his monopoly business becomes less profitable. There remains an incentive to do so nonetheless when he thinks he can obtain a monopoly in the tied product as well, permitting him later to raise prices without fear of entry to recoup the monopoly profit he has forgone. But just as the firm whose deep pocket stems from monopoly profits in the tying product may make this takeover, so may anyone else with a deep pocket, from whatever source.

more expensive than simple entry into the tied market, and shifting buying habits in the tied product is considerably more cumbersome and less responsive to variations in competitive offers.[7] In addition to these anticompetitive effects in the tied product, tying arrangements may be used to evade price control in the tying product through clandestine transfer of the profit to the tied product; they may be used as a counting device to effect price discrimination; and they may be used to force a full line of products on the customer so as to extract more easily from him a monopoly return on one unique product in the line.[8]

All of these distortions depend upon the existence of some market power in the tying product quite apart from any relationship which it might bear to the tied product. In this case, what proof of any market power in the tying product has been alleged? Only that the tying product —money—was not available elsewhere on equally good terms, and perhaps not at all. Let us consider these possibilities in turn.

First, if enough money to proceed was available elsewhere and U.S. Steel was simply offering credit at a lower price, in terms of risk of loss, repayment terms, and interest rate, surely this does not establish that U.S. Steel had market power by any measure in the money market. There was nothing unique about U.S. Steel's money except its low cost to petitioner. A low price on a product is ordinarily no reflection of market power. It proves neither the existence of such power nor its absence, although absence of power may be the more reasonable inference. One who has such power benefits from it precisely because it allows him to raise prices, not lower them, and ordinarily he does so.

A low price in the tying product—money, the most fungible item of trade since it is by definition an economic counter—is especially poor proof of market power when untied credit is available elsewhere. In that case, the low price of credit is functionally equivalent to a reduction in the price of the houses sold. Since the buyer has untied credit available elsewhere, he can compare the houses-credit package of U.S. Steel as

---

[7] Even when the terms of the tie allow a competitor to obtain the business in the tied product simply by offering a price lower than, rather than equal to, the tier's the Court has found sufficient restriction in the tied product, as in the *Northern Pacific* case.

[8] Tie-ins may also at times be beneficial to the economy. Apart from the justifications discussed in the text are the following. They may facilitate new entry into fields where established sellers have wedded their customers to them by ties of habit and custom. . . . They may permit clandestine price cutting in products which otherwise would have no price competition at all because of fear of retaliation from the few other producers dealing in the market. They may protect the reputation of the tying product if failure to use the tied product in conjunction with it may cause it to misfunction. . . . And, if the tied and tying products are functionally related, they may reduce costs through economies of joint production and distribution. These benefits which may flow from tie-ins, though perhaps in some cases a potential basis for an affirmative defense, were not sufficient to avoid the imposition of a *per se* proscription, once market power has been demonstrated. But in determining whether even the market-power requirement should be eliminated, as the logic of the majority opinion would do, extending the *per se* rule to absolute dimensions, the fact that tie-ins are not entirely unmitigated evils should be borne in mind.

competitive with the price of the untied credit plus the cost of houses from another source. By cutting the price of his houses, a competitor of U.S. Steel can compete with U.S. Steel houses on equal terms since U.S. Steel's money is no more desirable to the purchaser than money from another source except in point of price. The same money which U.S. Steel is willing to risk or forgo by providing better credit terms it could sacrifice by cutting the price of houses. There is no good reason why U.S. Steel should always be required to make the price cut in one form rather than another, which its purchaser prefers.

Provision of credit financing by the seller of a commodity to its buyer is a very common event in the American economy. Often the seller is not willing to supply credit generally for the business and personal needs of the public at large, but restricts his credit to the purchasers of the commodity which he is principally in the business of selling. In all such cases, the commodity may be viewed as tied to the credit. In all such cases, the money itself is no more desirable from one source than from another. But in all such cases, under the majority opinion, the mere fact that the credit is offered on uniquely advantageous terms makes the transaction a *per se* violation of §1 of the Sherman Act. And so long as the buyer has chosen to accept the seller's credit terms over any others available to him, the buyer, like petitioner here, must have viewed them as uniquely advantageous to him. The logic of the majority opinion, then, casts great doubt on credit financing by sellers. . . .

Second, adopting the other assumption, that sufficient credit to go forward with the enterprise was simply unavailable to petitioner from any other source at all, the result in this case is even worse. Were it not for the credit extended by U.S. Steel, petitioner would have been unable to carry out its development. U.S. Steel would not have foreclosed anyone from selling houses to petitioner since no one would have sold any houses to petitioner. A seller who is willing to take credit risks which no one else finds acceptable is simply engaging in the hard and risky competition which it is the policy of the Sherman Act to encourage. And if he may not do so, then those businesses and entrepreneurs who depend for their survival and growth or for the initiation of new enterprises on the availability of credit financing from sellers may well fail for lack of credit availability from other sources. Of course, if the credit was unavailable elsewhere because U.S. Steel was a monopolist of credit in a relevant market— which petitioner does not assert—the tie would be illegal. But here it was evidently unavailable elsewhere simply because others were not willing to match U.S. Steel's relatively low price for acceptance of high risk.

. . . Where the seller exercises no market power in the tying item but buyers prefer the tie-in because the seller offers the tying product on favorable terms—where the price is unusually low or where the seller gives the product away conditioned on buying other merchandise—the seller in effect is merely competing in the tied product market. Buyers are not burdened. They may buy both tied and tying products elsewhere on normal terms. Nor are the seller's competitors restrained. The economic advantage of the tie-in to buyers can be matched by other sellers of the tied product by offering lower prices on that product. Promotional tie-ins effected by underpricing the tying product do not themselves prove there is any market power to exercise in that product market, unless the economic resources to withstand lower profit margins and the willingness to compete in this manner are themselves suspect. . . .

The principal evil at which the proscription of tying aims is the use of power in one market to acquire power in, or otherwise distort, a second market. This evil simply does not exist if there is no power in the first market. The first market here is money, a completely fungible item. I would not apply a *per se* rule here without independent proof of market power. Cutting prices in the credit market is more likely to reflect a competitive attempt to offset the market power of others in the tied product than it is to reflect existing market power in the credit market. Those with real power do not offer uniquely advantageous deals to their customers; they raise prices.

. . . I do not consider petitioner's allegations that U.S. Steel lowered its price of credit sufficient to establish market power in credit and I can find no offer by petitioner of the necessary supplementary proof.

MR. JUSTICE FORTAS, with whom MR. JUSTICE STEWART joins, dissenting.

I share my Brother WHITE's inability to agree with the majority in this case, and, in general, I subscribe to his opinion. I add this separate statement of the reasons for my dissent.

The facts of this case are materially different from any tying case that this Court has heretofore decided. The tying doctrine originated in situations where the seller of product A offers it for sale only on the condition that the buyer also agree to buy product B from the seller. . . .

. . . But, here, U.S. Steel is not selling or leasing land subject to an agreement that its prefabricated houses be used thereon. If these were the facts, and if U.S. Steel controlled enough land within an economically demarcated area or "market," however defined, the case might well be governed by *Northern Pacific*. But, here, U.S. Steel is not selling or providing land. It is selling prefabricated steel houses to be erected in a subdivision and it is providing financing for the land acquisition, improvement, development, and erection costs. Most of the financing is related not to the land cost but to the purchase and installation of the houses.

U.S. Steel neither owned nor controlled any of the land involved in the venture. On the contrary, the building lots constituting the subdivision on which the houses were to be built were owned by another company of which the principal owner was Mr. Fortner, who owned the petitioner. Nor is U.S. Steel selling credit in any general sense. The financing which it agrees to provide is solely and entirely ancillary to its sale of houses. . . .

. . . This is a sale of a single product with the incidental provision of financing. It is not a sale of one product on condition that the buyer will not deal with competitors for another product or will buy the other product exclusively from the seller.

As my Brother WHITE shows, to treat the financing of the housing development as a "tying" product for the houses is to distort the doctrine and to depart from the reason for its existence. Such an extension of the tying doctrine entirely departs from the factual pattern which is described in §3 of the Clayton Act and which has been the basis of this Court's extension of the doctrine to the Sherman Act and its development of the rule that such tying arrangements are illegal on a *per se* basis—*i.e.*, without any showing that they constitute an unreasonable restraint of trade or tend to create a monopoly. The Court has established this rule because the kind of tying arrangement at issue in prior cases involved the use of a leverage position in the tying product—the patented machine, the copyrighted film, the unique land—to force the buyer to purchase the tied product. To apply this rule to a situation where the only "leverage" is a lower price for the article sold or more advantageous financing or credit terms for the article sold and for ancillary costs connected with the sale is to distort the doctrine, and indeed, to convert it into an instrument which penalizes price competition for the article that is sold. . . .

The effect of this novel extension—this distortion, as I view it—of the tying doctrine may be vast and destructive. It is common in our economy for a seller to extend financing to a distributor or franchisee to enable him to purchase and handle the seller's goods at retail, to rent retail facilities, to acquire fixtures or machinery for service to customers in connection with distribution of the seller's goods, or, as here, to prepare the land for and to acquire and erect the seller's houses for sale to the public. . . . Arrangements of this sort run throughout the economy. They frequently, and perhaps characteristically, represent an indispensable method of financing distributive and service trades, and not until today has it been held that they are tying arrangements and therefore *per se* unlawful. . . .

. . . Almost all modern selling involves providing some ancillary services in connection with making the sale—delivery, installation, supplying fixtures, servicing, training of the customer's personnel in use of the material sold, furnishing display material and sales aids, extension of credit. Customarily—indeed almost invariably—the seller offers these ancillary services only in connection with the sale of his own products, and they are often offered without cost or at bargain rates. It is possible that in some situations, such arrangements could be used to restrain competition or might have that effect, but to condemn them out-of-hand under the "tying" rubric, is, I suggest, to use the antitrust laws themselves as an instrument in restraint of competition.

For these reasons, I dissent.

Chapter	EXCLUSIVE DEALING
11	ARRANGEMENTS

The problems involved in exclusive dealing cases are several. First and foremost is that of separating those arrangements which improve the workability of competition from those which foreclose competitors from a substantial market. Subsidiary to this is the problem of determining just what constitutes a "substantial" market. It may safely be said that what the Court attempts to do in these cases is to strike down exclusive arrangements which, resulting from the exercise of appreciable market power, tend to exclude competitors from a substantial market, while sanctioning those exclusive dealing arrangements which were freely entered into by both parties to serve a legitimate economic need.

The *Standard Fashion* case sets forth the Court's view that the qualifying clause of Sections 2 and 3 of the Clayton Act ("where the effect . . . may be to substantially lessen competition or tend to . . . create a monopoly . . .") is satisfied when it is shown that a contract would *probably* lessen competition. To this was added the *Standard Stations* decision, in which the Court explicitly refused to consider the possible economic justifications of California Standard's exclusive dealing and full requirements contracts. That the Court did not outlaw all exclusive dealing, however, is shown by the later *Tampa Electric* decision—in which Nashville Coal's contract was upheld as necessary business arrangements which had not produced demonstrably deleterious effects on competition.

A fuller understanding of these cases will follow from reading them in conjunction with those presented in Chapters 10 and 12.

Standard Fashion Company v. *Magrane-Houston Company*
258 U.S. 346 (1922)
MR. JUSTICE DAY delivered the opinion of the Court.

. . . . .

Petitioner is a New York corporation engaged in the manufacture and distribution of patterns. Respondent conducted a retail dry goods business

. . . in the City of Boston. On November 25, 1914, the parties entered into a contract by which the petitioner granted to the respondent an agency for the sale of Standard patterns at respondent's store, for a term of two years from the date of the contract, and from term to term thereafter until the agreement should be terminated as thereinafter provided. Petitioner agreed to sell to respondent Standard Patterns at a discount of 50 percent from retail prices, with advertising matter and publications upon terms stated. . . . Respondent agreed not to assign or transfer the agency, or to remove it from its original location without the written consent of the petitioner, and not to sell or permit to be sold on its premises during the term of the contract any other make of patterns, and not to sell Standard Patterns except at label prices. . . .

The principal question in the case, and the one upon which the writ of certiorari was granted involves the construction of Section 3 of the Clayton Act. . . .

. . . The real question is: Does the contract of sale come within the third section of the Clayton Act, because the [effect of the] covenant not to sell the patterns of others "may be to substantially lessen competition or tend to create a monopoly."

The Clayton Act, as its title and the history of its enactment disclose, was intended to supplement the purpose and effect of other anti-trust legislation, principally the Sherman Act of 1890. . . .

The Clayton Act sought to reach the agreements embraced within its sphere in their incipiency, and in the section under consideration to determine their legality by specific tests of its own which declared illegal contracts of sale made upon the agreement or understanding that the purchaser shall not deal in the goods of a competitor or competitors of the seller, which may "substantially lessen competition or tend to create a monopoly." . . .

Section 3 condemns sales or agreements where the effect of such sale or contract of sale "may" be to substantially lessen competition or tend to create a monopoly. It thus deals with consequences to follow the making of the restrictive covenant limiting the right of the purchaser to deal in the goods of the seller only. But we do not think that the purpose in using the word "may" was to prohibit the mere possibility of the consequences described. It was intended to prevent such agreements as would under the circumstances disclosed probably lessen competition, or create an actual tendency to monopoly. That it was not intended to reach every remote lessening of competition is shown in the requirement that such lessening must be substantial.

Both courts below found that the contract interpreted in the light of the circumstances surrounding the making of it was within the provisions of the Clayton Act as one which substantially lessened competition and tended to create monopoly. These courts put special stress upon the fact found that, of 52,000 so-called pattern agencies in the entire country, the petitioner, or a holding company controlling it and two other pattern companies, approximately controlled two-fifths of such agencies. As the Circuit Court of Appeals summarizing the matter, pertinently observed:

The restriction of each merchant to one pattern manufacturer must in hundreds, perhaps in thousands, of small communities amount to giving such single pattern manufacturer a monopoly of the business in such community. Even in the larger cities, to limit to a single pattern maker the pattern business of dealers most resorted to by customers whose purchases tend to give fashions their vogue, may tend to facilitate further combinations; so that the plaintiff, or some other aggressive concern, instead of controlling two-fifths, will shortly have almost, if not quite, all the pattern business.

We agree with these conclusions, and have no doubt that the contract, properly interpreted, with restrictive covenant, brings it fairly within the section of the Clayton Act under consideration.

Affirmed.

Standard Oil Company of California {and Standard Stations, Inc.} v. United States

337 U.S. 293 (1949)

MR. JUSTICE FRANKFURTER delivered the opinion of the Court.

This is an appeal to review a decree enjoining the Standard Oil Company of California and its wholly-owned subsidiary, Standard Stations, Inc., from enforcing or entering into exclusive supply contracts with any independent dealer in petroleum products and automobile accessories. . . . The use of such contracts was successfully assailed by the United States as violative of Section 1 of the Sherman Act and Section 3 of the Clayton Act.

The Standard Oil Company of California . . . owns petroleum-producing resources and refining plants in California and sells petroleum products in what has been termed in these proceedings the "Western area". . . . It sells through its own service stations, to the operators of independent service stations, and to industrial users. It is the largest seller of gasoline in the area. In 1946 its combined sales amounted to 23% of the total taxable gallonage sold there in that year: sales by company-owned service stations constituted 6.8% of the total, sales under exclusive dealing contracts with independent service stations, 6.7% of the total; the remainder were sales to industrial users. Retail service-station sales by Standard's six leading competitors absorbed 42.5% of the total taxable gallonage; the remaining retail sales were divided between more than seventy small companies. It is undisputed that Standard's major competitors employ similar exclusive dealing arrangements. In 1948 only 1.6% of retail outlets were what is known as "split-pump" stations, that is, sold the gasoline of more than one supplier.

Exclusive supply contracts with Standard had been entered into, as of March 12, 1947, by the operators of 5,937 independent stations, or 16% of the retail gasoline outlets in the Western area, which purchased from Standard in 1947, $57,646,233 worth of gasoline and $8,200,089.21 worth of other products. Some outlets are covered by more than one contract so that in all about 8,000 exclusive supply contracts are here in issue. These are of several types, but a feature common to each is the dealer's undertaking to purchase from Standard all his requirements of one or more products. Two types, covering 2,777 outlets, bind the dealer to purchase of Standard all his requirements of gasoline and other petroleum products as well as tires, tubes, and batteries. The remaining written agreements, 4,368 in number, bind the dealer to purchase of Standard all his requirements of petroleum products only. It was also found that independent dealers had entered 742 oral contracts by which they agreed to sell only Standard's gasoline. . . .

Between 1936 and 1946 Standard's sales of gasoline through independent dealers remained at a practically constant proportion of the area's total sales; its sales of lubricating oil declined slightly during that period from 6.2% to 5% of the total. Its proportionate sales of tires and batteries for 1946 were slightly higher than they were in 1936, though somewhat lower than for some intervening years; they have never, as to either of these products, exceeded 2% of the total sales in the Western area.

Since Section 3 of the Clayton Act was directed to prohibiting specific practices even though not covered by the broad terms of the Sherman Act, it is appropriate to consider first whether the enjoined contracts fall within the prohibition of the narrower Act. . . .

The District Court held that the requirement of showing an actual or potential lessening of competition or a tendency to establish monopoly was adequately met by proof that the contracts covered "a substantial number of outlets and a substantial amount of products, whether considered comparatively or not." . . . Given such quantitative substantiality, the substantial lessening of competition—so the court reasoned—is an automatic result, for the very existence of such contracts denies dealers opportunity to deal in the products of competing suppliers and excludes suppliers from access to the outlets controlled by those dealers. . . .

The issue before us, therefore, is whether the requirement of showing that the effect of the agreements "may be to substantially lessen competition" may be met simply by proof that a substantial portion of commerce is affected or whether it must also be demonstrated that competitive activity has actually diminished or probably will diminish. . . .

It is . . . apparent that none of these [earlier] cases[1] controls the dis-

---

[1] The Court had summarized its opinions in the five earlier cases in which it had found violations of Section 3. These were: *United Shoe Machinery Corp.* v. *United States*, 258 U.S. 451; *International Business Machines Corp.* v. *United States*, 298 U.S. 131; *International Salt Company* v. *United States*, 332 U.S. 392; *Standard Fashion Co.* v. *Magrane-Houston Co.*, 258 U.S. 364; and *Fashion Originators' Guild* v. *Federal Trade Commission*, 312 U.S. 457. IMS.

position of the present appeal, for Standard's share of the retail market for gasoline, even including sales through company-owned stations, is hardly large enough to conclude as a matter of law that it occupies a dominant position, nor did the trial court so find. The cases do indicate, however, that some sort of showing as to the actual or probable economic consequences of the agreements, if only the inferences to be drawn from the fact of dominant power, is important, and to that extent they tend to support appellant's position.

Two of the three cases decided by this Court which have held Section 3 inapplicable also lend support to the view that such a showing is necessary. These are, *Federal Trade Comm'n* v. *Sinclair Co.*, 261 U.S. 463, and *Pick Mfg. Co.* v. *General Motors Corp.*, 299 U.S. 3. The third . . . is of no present relevance. . . .

But then came *International Salt Co.* v. *United States*, 332 U.S. 392. That decision, at least as to contracts tying the sale of a nonpatented to a patented product, rejected the necessity of demonstrating economic consequences once it has been established that "the volume of business affected" is not "insignificant or insubstantial" and that the effect of the contracts is to "foreclose competitors from [a] substantial market." . . . Upon that basis we affirmed a summary judgment granting an injunction against the leasing of machines for the utilization of salt products on the condition that the lessee use in them only salt supplied by defendant. . . . It is clear, therefore, that unless a distinction is to be drawn for purposes of the applicability of Section 3 between requirements contracts and contracts tying the sale of a nonpatented to a patented product, the showing that Standard's requirements contracts affected a gross business of $58,-000,000 comprising 6.7% of the total in the area goes far toward supporting the inference that competition has been or probably will be substantially lessened.

In favor of confining the standard laid down by the *International Salt* case to tying agreements, important economic differences may be noted. Tying agreements serve hardly any purpose beyond the suppression of competition. The justification most often advanced in their defense—the protection of the good will of the manufacturer of the tying device—fails in the usual situation because specification of the type and quality of the product to be used in connection with the tying device is protection enough. If the manufacturer's brand of the tied product is in fact superior to that of competitors, the buyer will presumably choose it anyway. The only situation, indeed, in which the protection of good will may necessitate the use of tying clauses is where specifications for a substitute would be so detailed that they could not practicably be supplied. In the usual case only the prospect of reducing competition would persuade a seller to adopt such a contract and only his control of the supply of the tying device, whether conferred by patent monopoly or otherwise obtained, could induce a buyer to enter one. . . . The existence of market control of the tying device, therefore, affords a strong foundation for the presumption that it has been or probably will be used to limit competition in the tied product also.

Requirements contracts, on the other hand, may well be of economic advantage to buyers as well as to sellers, and thus indirectly of advantage to the consuming public. In the case of the buyer, they may assure supply, afford protection against rises in price, enable long-term planning on the basis of known costs, and obviate the expense and risk of storage in the quantity necessary for a commodity having a fluctuating demand. From the seller's point of view, requirements contracts may make possible the substantial reduction of selling expenses, give protection against price fluctuations, and—of particular advantage to a newcomer to the field to whom it is important to know what capital expenditures are justified— offer the possibility of a predictable market. . . . They may be useful, moreover, to a seller trying to establish a foothold against the counterattacks of entrenched competitors. . . . Since these advantages of requirements contracts may often be sufficient to account for their use, the coverage by such contracts of a substantial amount of business affords a weaker basis for the inference that competition may be lessened than would similar coverage by tying clauses, especially where use of the latter is combined with market control of the tying device. A patent, moreover, although in fact there may be many competing substitutes for the patented article, is at least *prima facie* evidence of such control. And so we could not dispose of this case merely by citing *International Salt Co. v. United States.* . . .

Thus, even though the qualifying clause of Section 3 is appended without distinction of terms equally to the prohibition of tying clauses and of requirements contracts, pertinent considerations support, certainly as a matter of economic reasoning, varying standards as to each for the proof necessary to fulfill the conditions of that clause. If this distinction were accepted, various tests of the economic usefulness or restrictive effect of requirements contracts would become relevant. Among them would be evidence that competition has flourished despite use of the contracts, and under this test much of the evidence tendered by appellant in this case would be important. . . . Likewise bearing on whether or not the contracts were being used to suppress competition, would be the conformity of the length of their term to the reasonable requirements of the field of commerce in which they were used. . . . Still another test would be the status of the defendant as a struggling newcomer or an established competitor. Perhaps most important, however, would be the defendant's degree of market control, for the greater the dominance of his position, the stronger the inference that an important factor in attaining and maintaining that position had been the use of requirements contracts to stifle competition rather than to serve legitimate economic needs. . . .

Yet serious difficulties would attend the attempt to apply these tests.

We may assume, as did the court below, that no improvement of Standard's competitive position has coincided with the period during which the requirements-contract system of distribution has been in effect. We may assume further that the duration of the contracts is not excessive and that Standard does not by itself dominate the market. But Standard was a major competitor when the present system was adopted, and it is possible that its position would have deteriorated but for the adoption of that system. When it is remembered that all the other major suppliers have also been using requirements contracts, and when it is noted that the relative share of the business which fell to each has remained about the same during the period of their use, it would not be farfetched to infer that their effect has been to enable the established suppliers individually to maintain their own standing and at the same time collectively, even though not collusively, to prevent a late arrival from wresting away more than an insignificant portion of the market. If, indeed, this were a result of the system, it would seem unimportant that a short-run by-product of stability may have been greater efficiency and lower costs, for it is the theory of the antitrust laws that the long-run advantage of the community depends upon the removal of restraints upon competition. . . .

Moreover, to demand that bare inference be supported by evidence as to what would have happened but for the adoption of the practice that was in fact adopted or to require firm prediction of an increase of competition as a probable result of ordering the abandonment of the practice, would be a standard of proof, if not virtually impossible to meet, at least most ill-suited for ascertainment by courts. . . .

. . . Though it may be that such an alternative to the present system as buying out independent dealers and making them dependent employees of Standard Stations, Inc., would be a greater detriment to the public interest than perpetuation of the system, this is an issue, like the choice between greater efficiency and freer competition, that has not been submitted to our decision. We are faced, not with a broadly phrased expression of general policy, but merely a broadly phrased qualification of an otherwise narrowly directed statutory provision. . . .

We conclude, therefore, that the qualifying clause of Section 3 is satisfied by proof that competition has been foreclosed in a substantial share of the line of commerce affected. It cannot be gainsaid that observance by a dealer of his requirements contract with Standard does effectively foreclose whatever opportunity there might be for competing suppliers to attract his patronage, and it is clear that the affected proportion of retail sales of petroleum products is substantial. In view of the widespread adoption of such contracts by Standard's competitors and the availability of alternative ways of obtaining an assured market, evidence that competitive activity has not actually declined is inconclusive. Standard's use of the contracts creates just such a potential clog on competition as it was the purpose of Section 3 to remove wherever, were it to become actual, it would impede a substantial amount of competitive activity.

Since the decree below is sustained by our interpretation of Section 3 of the Clayton Act, we need not go on to consider whether it might also be sustained by Section 1 of the Sherman Act. . . .

The judgment below is Affirmed.

[Mr. Justice Jackson, with whom The Chief Justice and Mr. Justice Burton joined, dissented. Mr. Justice Douglas separately dissented.]

Tampa Electric Co. v. *Nashville Coal Co.*

365 U.S. 320 (1961)

Mr. Justice Clark delivered the opinion of the Court.

We granted certiorari to review a declaratory judgment holding illegal under Section 3 of the Clayton Act a requirements contract between the parties providing for the purchase by petitioner of all the coal it would require as boiler fuel at its Gannon Station in Tampa, Florida, over a 20-year period. . . . Both the District Court . . . and the Court of Appeals, . . . Judge Weick dissenting, agreed with respondents that the contract fell within the proscription of Section 3 and therefore was illegal and unenforceable. We cannot agree that the contract suffers the claimed antitrust illegality[1] and, therefore, do not find it necessary to consider respondents' additional argument that such illegality is a defense to the action and a bar to enforceability.

The Facts

Petitioner Tampa Electric Company is a public utility located in Tampa, Florida. It produces and sells electric energy to a service area, including the city, extending from Tampa Bay eastward 60 miles to the center of the State, and some 30 miles in width. As of 1954 petitioner operated two electrical generating plants comprising a total of 11 individual generating units, all of which consumed oil in their burners. In 1955 Tampa Electric decided to expand its facilities by the construction of an additional generating plant to be comprised ultimately of six generating units, and to be known as the "Francis J. Gannon Station." Although every electrical generating plant in peninsular Florida burned oil at that time, Tampa Electric decided to try coal as boiler fuel in the first two units constructed at the Gannon Station. Accordingly, it contracted with the respondents[2] to furnish the expected coal requirements for the units. The agreement, dated May 23, 1955, embraced Tampa Electric's "total requirements of fuel . . . for the operation of its first two units to

---

[1] In addition to their claim under Section 3 of the Clayton Act, respondents argue the contract is illegal under the Sherman Act, 15 U.S.C. §§1-2.

[2] The original contract was with Potter Towing Company, and by subsequent agreements with Tampa Electric responsibility thereunder was assumed by respondent West Kentucky Coal Company.

be installed at the Gannon Station . . . not less than 225,000 tons of coal per unit per year," for a period of 20 years. The contract further provided that "if during the first 10 years of the term . . . the Buyer constructs additional units [at Gannon] in which coal is used as the fuel, it shall give the Seller notice thereof two years prior to the completion of such unit or units and upon completion of same the fuel requirements thereof shall be added to this contract." It was understood and agreed, however, that "the Buyer has the option to be exercised two years prior to completion of said unit or units of determining whether coal or some other fuel shall be used in same." Tampa Electric had the further option of reducing, up to 15%, the amount of its coal purchases covered by the contract after giving six months' notice of an intention to use as fuel a by-product of any of its local customers. The minimum price was set at $6.40 per ton delivered, subject to an escalation clause based on labor cost and other factors. Deliveries were originally expected to begin in March 1957, for the first unit, and for the second unit at the completion of its construction.

In April 1957, soon before the first coal was actually to be delivered and after Tampa Electric, in order to equip its first two Gannon units for the use of coal, had expended some $3,000,000 more than the cost of constructing oil-burning units, and after respondents had expended approximately $7,500,000 readying themselves to perform the contract, the latter advised petitioner that the contract was illegal under the antitrust laws, would therefore not be performed, and no coal would be delivered. This turn of events required Tampa Electric to look elsewhere for its coal requirements. The first unit at Gannon began operating August 1, 1957, using coal purchased on a temporary basis, but on December 23, 1957, a purchase order contract for the total coal requirements of the Gannon Station was made with Love and Amos Coal Company. It was for an indefinite period cancellable on 12 months' notice by either party, or immediately upon tender of performance by respondents under the contract sued upon here. The maximum price was $8.80 per ton, depending upon the freight rate. In its purchase order to the Love and Amos Company, Tampa estimated that its requirements at the Gannon Station would be 350,000 tons in 1958; 700,000 tons in 1959 and 1960; 1,000,000 tons in 1961; and would increase thereafter, as required, to "about 2,250,000 tons per year." The second unit at Gannon Station commenced operation 14 months after the first, *i.e.*, October 1958. Construction of a third unit, the coal for which was to have been provided under the original contract, was also begun.

The record indicates that the total consumption of coal in peninsular Florida, as of 1958, aside from Gannon Station, was approximately 700,-000 tons annually. It further shows that there were some 700 coal suppliers in the producing area where respondents operated, and that Tampa Electric's anticipated maximum requirements at Gannon Station, *i.e.*, 2,250,000 tons annually, would approximate 1% of the total coal of the same type produced and marketed from respondents' producing area.

Petitioner brought this suit in the District Court pursuant to 28 U.S.C. Section 2201, for a declaration that its contract with respondents was valid, and for enforcement according to its terms. In addition to its Clayton Act defense, respondents contended that the contract violated both Sections 1 and 2 of the Sherman Act which, it claimed, likewise precluded its enforcement. The District Court, however, granted respondents' motion for summary judgment on the sole ground that the undisputed facts, recited above showed the contract to be a violation of Section 3 of the Clayton Act. The Court of Appeals agreed. Neither court found it necessary to consider the applicability of the Sherman Act.

Decisions of District Court and Court of Appeals

Both courts admitted that the contract "does not expressly contain the 'condition' " that Tampa Electric would not use or deal in the coal of respondents' competitors. Nonetheless, they reasoned, the "total requirements" provision had the same practical effect, for it prevented Tampa Electric for a period of 20 years from buying coal from any other source for use at that station. Each court cast aside as "irrelevant" arguments citing the use of oil as boiler fuel by Tampa Electric at its other stations, and by other utilities in peninsular Florida, because oil was not in fact used at Gannon Station, and the possibility of exercise by Tampa Electric of the option reserved to it to build oil-burning units at Gannon was too remote. Found to be equally remote was the possibility of Tampa's conversion of existing oil-burning units at its other stations to the use of coal which would not be covered by the contract with respondents. It followed, both courts found, that the "line of commerce" on which the restraint was to be tested was coal—not boiler fuels. Both courts compared the estimated coal tonnage as to which the contract pre-empted competition for 20 years, namely 1,000,000 tons a year by 1961, with the previous annual consumption of peninsular Florida, 700,000 tons. Emphasizing that fact as well as the contract value of the coal covered by the 20-year term, *i.e.*, $128,000,000, they held that such volume was not "insignificant or insubstantial" and that the effect of the contract would "be to substantially lessen competition," in violation of the Act. Both courts were of the opinion that in view of the executory nature of the contract, judicial enforcement of any portion of it could not be granted without directing a violation of the Act itself, and enforcement was, therefore, denied.

Application of Section 3 of the Clayton Act

In the almost half century since Congress adopted the Clayton Act, this Court has been called upon 10 times, including the present, to pass upon questions arising under Section 3.[3] . . .

---

[3] A detailed discussion of the *Standard Fashion, United Shoe, International Salt* and *Standard Oil of California* cases followed. IMS.

In practical application, even though a contract is found to be an exclusive-dealing arrangement, it does not violate the section unless the court believes it probable that performance of the contract will foreclose competition in a substantial share of the line of commerce affected. Following the guidelines of earlier decisions, certain considerations must be taken. *First*, the line of commerce, *i.e.*, the type of goods, wares, or merchandise, etc., involved must be determined, where it is in controversy, on the basis of the facts peculiar to the case. *Second*, the area of effective competition in the known line of commerce must be charted by careful selection of the market area in which the seller operates, and to which the purchaser can practicably turn for supplies. In short, the threatened foreclosure of competition must be in relation to the market affected. . . .

Third, and last, the competition foreclosed by the contract must be found to constitute a substantial share of the relevant market. That is to say, the opportunities for other traders to enter into or remain in that market must be significantly limited. . . .

To determine substantiality in a given case, it is necessary to weigh the probable effect of the contract on the relevant area of effective competition, taking into account the relative strength of the parties, the proportionate volume of commerce involved in relation to the total volume of commerce in the relevant market area, and the probable immediate and future effects which pre-emption of that share of the market might have on effective competition therein. It follows that a mere showing that the contract itself involves a substantial number of dollars is ordinarily of little consequence.

The Application of Section 3 Here

In applying these considerations to the facts of the case before us, it appears clear that both the Court of Appeals and the District Court have not given the required effect to a controlling factor in the case—the relevant competitive market area. This omission, by itself, requires reversal, for, as we have pointed out, the relevant market is the prime factor in relation to which the ultimate question, whether the contract forecloses competition in a substantial share of the line of commerce involved, must be decided. For the purposes of this case, therefore, we need not decide two threshold questions pressed by Tampa Electric. They are whether the contract in fact satisfies the initial requirement of Section 3, *i.e.*, whether it is truly an exclusive-dealing one, and, secondly, whether the line of commerce is boiler fuels, including coal, oil and gas, rather than coal alone.[4] We, therefore, for the purposes of this case, as-

---

[4] In support of these contentions petitioner urges us to consider that it remains free to convert existing oil-burning units at its other plants to coal-burning units, the fuel for which it would be free to purchase from any seller in the market; also that just as it is permitted to use oil at its other plants, so, too it may construct all future

sume, but do not decide, that the contract is an exclusive-dealing arrangement within the compass of Section 3, and that the line of commerce is bituminous coal.

Relevant Market of Effective Competition

Neither the Court of Appeals nor the District Court considered in detail the question of the relevant market. They do seem, however, to have been satisfied with inquiring only as to competition within "Peninsular Florida." It was noted that the total consumption of peninsular Florida was 700,000 tons of coal per year, about equal to the estimated 1959 requirements of Tampa Electric. It was also pointed out that coal accounted for less than 6% of the fuel consumed in the entire State.[5] The District Court concluded that though the respondents were only one of 700 coal producers who could serve the same market, peninsular Florida, the contract for a period of 20 years excluded competitors from a substantial amount of trade. Respondents contend that the coal tonnage covered by the contract must be weighed against either the total consumption of coal in peninsular Florida, or all of Florida, or the Bituminous Coal Act area comprising peninsular Florida and the Georgia "finger," or, at most, all of Florida and Georgia. If the latter area were considered the relevant market, Tampa Electric's proposed requirements would be 18% of the tonnage sold therein. Tampa Electric says that both courts and respondents are in error, because the "700 coal producers who could serve" it, as recognized by the trial court and admitted by respondents, operated in the Appalachian coal area and that its contract requirements were less than 1% of the total marketed production of these producers; that the relevant effective area of competition was the area in which these producers operated, and in which they were willing to compete for the consumer potential.

We are persuaded that on the record in this case, neither peninsular Florida, nor the entire State of Florida, nor Florida and Georgia combined constituted the relevant market of effective competition. We do not believe that the pie will slice so thinly. By far the bulk of the overwhelming tonnage marketed from the same producing area as serves Tampa is sold outside of Georgia and Florida, and the producers were "eager" to sell more coal in those States.[6] While the relevant competitive market is not ordinarily susceptible to a "metes and bounds" definition,

---

Gannon units as oil burners; and that in any event it is free to draw a maximum of 15% of its Gannon fuel requirements from by-products of local customers. Petitioner further argues that its novel reliance upon coal in fact created new fuel competition in an area that theretofore relied almost exclusively upon oil and, to a lesser extent, upon natural gas.

[5] Oil and, to a lesser extent, natural gas are the primary fuels consumed in Florida.

[6] Peabody Coal Company offered to supply petitioner with coal from its mines in western Kentucky, for use in the units at another of its Florida stations, and that offer prompted a renegotiation of the price petitioner was paying for the oil then being consumed at that station.

cf. *Times-Picayune Pub. Co.* v. *United States*, 345 U.S. 594, 611, it is of course the area in which respondents and the other 700 producers effectively compete. . . . The record shows that, like the respondents, they sold bituminous coal "suitable for [Tampa's] requirements, "mined in parts of Pennsylvania, Virginia, West Virginia, Kentucky, Tennessee, Alabama, Ohio and Illinois. We take notice of the fact that the approximate total bituminous coal (and lignite) product in the year 1954 from the districts in which these 700 producers are located was 359,289,000 tons, of which some 290,567,000 tons were sold on the open market. Of the latter amount some 78,716,000 tons were sold to electric utilities. We also note that in 1954 Florida and Georgia combined consumed at least 2,304,000 tons, 1,100,000 of which were used by electric utilities, and the sources of which were mines located in no less than seven States. We take further notice that the production and marketing of bituminous coal (and lignite) from the same districts, and assumedly equally available to Tampa on a commercially feasible basis, is currently on a par with prior years. In point of statistical fact, coal consumption in the combined Florida-Georgia area has increased significantly since 1954. In 1959 more than 3,775,000 tons were there consumed, 2,913,000 being used by electric utilities including, presumably, the coal used by the petitioner. The coal continued to come from at least seven States. From these statistics it clearly appears that the proportionate volume of the total relevant coal product as to which the challenged contract pre-empted competition, less than 1%, is, conservatively speaking, quite insubstantial. A more accurate figure, even assuming pre-emption to the extent of the maximum anticipated total requirements, 2,250,000 tons a year, would be .77%.

Effect on Competition in the Relevant Market

It may well be that in the context of antitrust legislation protracted requirements contracts are suspect, but they have not been declared illegal *per se*. Even though a single contract between single traders may fall within the initial broad proscription of the section, it must also suffer the qualifying disability, tendency to work a substantial—not remote—lessening of competition in the relevant competitive market. It is urged that the present contract pre-empts competition to the extent of purchases worth perhaps $128,000,000 and that this "is, of course, not insignificant or insubstantial." While $128,000,000 is a considerable sum of money, even in these days, the dollar volume, by itself, is not the test, as we have already pointed out.

The remaining determination, therefore, is whether the pre-emption of competition to the extent of the tonnage involved tends to substantially foreclose competition in the relevant coal market. We think not. That market sees an annual trade in excess of 250,000,000 tons of coal and over a billion dollars—multiplied by 20 years it runs into astronomical figures. There is here neither a seller with a dominant position in the market as in

Standard Fashions, supra; nor myriad outlets with substantial sales volume, coupled with an industry-wide practice of relying upon exclusive contracts, as in *Standard Oil, supra;* nor a plainly restrictive tying arrangement as in *International Salt, supra.* On the contrary, we seem to have only that type of contract which "may well be of economic advantage to buyers as well as to sellers." *Standard Oil Co.* v. *United States, supra.* . . . In the case of the buyer it "may assure supply," while on the part of the seller it "may make possible the substantial reduction of selling expenses, give protection against price fluctuations, and . . . offer the possibility of a predictable market." *Id.* . . . The 20-year period of the contract is singled out as the principal vice, but at least in the case of public utilities the assurance of a steady and ample supply of fuel is necessary in the public interest. Otherwise consumers are left unprotected against service failures owing to shutdowns; and increasingly unjustified costs might result in more burdensome rate structures eventually to be reflected in the consumer's bill. The compelling validity of such considerations has been recognized fully in the natural gas public utility field. This is not to say that utilities are immunized from Clayton Act proscriptions, but merely that, in judging the term of a requirements contract in relation to the substantiality of the foreclosure of competition, particularized considerations of the parties' operations are not irrelevant. In weighing the various factors, we have decided that in the competitive bituminous coal marketing area involved here the contract sued upon does not tend to foreclose a substantial volume of competition.

We need not discuss the respondents' further contention that the contract also violates Section 1 and Section 2 of the Sherman Act, for if it does not fall within the broader proscription of Section 3 of the Clayton Act it follows that it is not forbidden by those of the former. *Times-Picayune Pub. Co.* v. *United States.* . . .

The judgment is reversed and the case remanded to the District Court for further proceedings not inconsistent with this opinion.

It is so ordered.

Mr. Justice Black and Mr. Justice Douglas are of the opinion that the District Court and the Court of Appeals correctly decided this case and would therefore affirm their judgments.

Chapter

12

OTHER CUSTOMER

RESTRICTIONS

As the chapter's title implies, the cases included herein have involved practices whose effects cannot neatly be categorized. In the *General Motors, Schwinn* and *Tripoli* cases, the courts have sought to define the limits which buyers can impose upon their customers. In the former, the Supreme Court held that once title to the product has passed from the hands of the seller to the buyer, the law takes a very dim view of the imposition of restrictions on the buyer's freedom to dispose of the product as he sees fit. *Tripoli*, however, can be seen as a move to a somewhat less dogmatic position.

The *Carvel* and *Chicken Delight* cases typify the current controversy surrounding the practice of franchising. Again, the courts appear to be seeking a means by which to strike a balance between the right of the franchisor to protect the economic integrity of his franchise, and the freedom of the franchisee to operate in his own best interests.

Bernard Susser v. Carvel Corporation

332 F. 2d 505 (2d Cir. 1964)
cert. dismissed, 381 U.S. 125 (1965)

LUMBARD, Chief Judge (writing for the majority in part and dissenting in part).

The plaintiffs in nine actions which were tried together in the Southern District of New York appeal from the dismissal of their complaints which alleged violations of the antitrust laws and sought treble damages from the Carvel Corporation, a New York corporation which manufactures dairy and primarily soft ice cream products, its subsidiary organizations, certain of its individual officers and attorneys, and a number of its suppliers. . . .

. . . The plaintiffs alleged that Carvel had unlawfully fixed the prices of the retail products sold at the franchise stores and that the franchise agreements embodied tying and exclusive dealing arrangements violative of the Sherman and Clayton acts. The complaints also charged that the contracts between Carvel and the supplier defendants embodied concerted

332

refusals to deal with the plaintiffs violative of the antitrust laws. In a pretrial order the plaintiffs stipulated that they would rely solely upon "per se" violations of the antitrust laws as shown in certain written agreements and other documents. From a judgment which, with one exception,[1] dismissed the complaints against all the defendants on the ground that the plaintiffs had failed to prove violations of the antitrust laws, 206 F.Supp. 636 (S.D. N.Y. 1963), the plaintiffs appeal.

The Carvel Franchise System

Although the franchise operators conduct their stores as independent businessmen, through provisions in the franchise agreement Carvel is able to maintain a chain of 400 stores uniform in appearance as well as in operation. The dealer is obligated to conduct his business in accordance with a Standard Operating Procedure Manual (Manual) which governs in great detail the general operation of the store, including the types of products which may be offered for sale, the recipes for their preparation, the nature and placement of advertising displays in the store, the color of the employees' uniforms, and the hours when the store lights must be turned on. The stores are identical in design, each featuring the Carvel crown and cone trademark on a flat slanting roof, glass walls at its front, and the name "Carvel" on its sides in neon lights. This distinctive design is protected by a design patent. The ice cream, which is processed from a mix prepared from a secret formula, is dispensed from a patented machine which bears the Carvel name or trademark. The paper containers, ice cream cones, and spoons all bear the Carvel name and in some instances are unique in design. . . .

Special counsel retained by Carvel in 1955 for that purpose drafted a new form of the franchise agreement. The new agreement effected two important changes. First, whereas under the earlier agreement the franchise dealer was obligated to sell Carvel products at prices fixed by the parent organization, the new agreement explicitly provides that the dealer has the right to fix his own prices. Second, under the earlier agreement the dealer was obliged to purchase his entire requirements of supplies, machinery, equipment, and paper goods from Carvel or Carvel approved sources. The new agreement requires the purchase from Carvel or Carvel approved sources only of those supplies which are a part of the end product sold to the public and permits the dealer to purchase machinery, equipment, and paper goods from independent sources so long as his store is maintained in accordance with the Manual specifications.

Price-Fixing

It is undisputed that the pre-1955 Manual established "standard selling prices" to which the dealers were obligated to adhere. The pre-1955 franchise required the dealers "To maintain prices on products designated in,

---

[1] Judge Dawson held invalid the pricing provisions of the pre-1955 franchise agreement.

and as per Carvel Standard Operating Procedure and not to conduct any reduced price sales of these items without written consent from Carvel." Judge Dawson held that these price-fixing provisions were illegal. . . . No appeal was taken from this aspect of the judgment below.

The revised franchise provides: "The dealer shall have the right to sell Carvel's Frozen Dairy Product and/or other items authorized for sale by him under the terms of this agreement at any price that the dealer determines. Wherever Carvel recommends a retail price, such recommendation is based upon Carvel's experience concerning all factors that enter into a proper price, but such recommendation is in no manner binding upon the dealer." The appellants contend that notwithstanding this provision Carvel effectively continued to fix prices at which Carvel products were sold to the public and that Judge Dawson's finding to the contrary is clearly erroneous.

Even in the absence of express contractual provisions which evidence an unlawful scheme, a charge of unlawful price-fixing may be substantiated by proof of a course of conduct by which the seller or licensor effectively maintains control of the ultimate retail price at which a product is sold. . . . The appellants direct our attention to the fact that six pages of the revised Manual continued to refer to "Standard selling price"; that in letters to several dealers Carvel emphasized that only 10¢ and 20¢ cones were prescribed by the Manual and that the minimum portions prescribed by the Manual were mandatory; that Carvel sought to have dealers report to it any deviation by other dealers from the requirements of the Manual; and that Carvel suggested that dealers seek its permission before conducting a sale at prices other than those established in the Manual. Moreover, the appellants emphasize the existence of a board of governors consisting of various dealers appointed by Carvel, the function of which is to make recommendations concerning the suggested retail selling price of Carvel products.

As Judge Dawson noted, the mere existence of a means whereby retail price levels are recommended is not sufficient to establish a violation of the Sherman Act, unless there is a showing of an attempt to enforce a price structure upon the retail tradesmen. . . . Here, the franchise provisions explicitly reserved to the individual dealer the right to set whatever price he desired. And, by contrast with the letters to which the appellants referred, Carvel introduced in evidence bulletins circulated to all the dealers as well as letters sent to several emphasizing that Carvel had changed its prior pricing policy and that each dealer now had the right to set his own prices, although Carvel did indicate that its suggested retail prices were based upon its own broad experience in customer sales. . . .

In short, the evidence was contradictory on the question whether Carvel attempted to impose a binding price structure on the retail dealers. . . . There is much evidence to support Judge Dawson's finding of fact that Carvel did not engage in an unlawful price-fixing scheme, and we cannot say that Judge Dawson's conclusion was clearly erroneous.

EXCLUSIVE DEALING AND TYING ARRANGEMENTS

The appellants maintain that the franchise agreements embody violations of the Sherman and Clayton acts insofar as they require the dealer to refrain from selling any non-Carvel product and insofar as they obligate the dealer to purchase directly from Carvel or from a source approved by Carvel his supply not only of the basic Carvel ice cream mix, prepared under a secret formula, but also certain other products used in either the preparation or sale of the end product offered to the public. . . .

As noted above, the pre-1955 franchise obligated the dealer to "purchase and use only standard Carvel approved printed paper goods, napkins, cones, extracts, spoons, and all other Carvel products at standard market prices." The post-1955 franchise requires the dealer to purchase from Carvel or approved sources his entire requirements of all items sold as a part of the retail product but permits the dealer to purchase machinery, equipment, and paper goods from sources other than Carvel so long as the operation is maintained in accordance with the Manual specifications.[2]

The Tying Arrangements. Tying arrangements have been given short shrift under the antitrust laws. . . . Yet it seems clear that in compelling circumstances the protection of goodwill, as embodied for example in a valuable trademark, may justify an otherwise invalid tying arrangement. But "[t]he only situation, indeed, in which the protection of good will may necessitate the use of tying clauses is where specifications for a substitute [for the tied product] would be so detailed that they could not practicably be supplied." *Standard Oil Co. of Cal.* v. *United States,* 337 U.S. 293, 306 . . . (1949). The threshold question is thus whether the Carvel franchise embodies a tying arrangement and, if so, whether that arrangement can be justified as necessary for the protection of Carvel's goodwill.

A tying arrangement may be defined as an agreement under which the vendor will sell one product only if the purchaser agrees to buy another independent product as well. Two types of economic injury characteristically arise from such an arrangement: first, foreclosure to the vendee of alternate sources of supply for the second, or tied, product; and second, foreclosure of possible market outlets to other competing suppliers of the tied product. The source of this injury—and the fundamental element which requires that such arrangements be deemed illegal—lies in the vendor's "sufficient economic power with respect to the tying product to appreciably restrain free competition in the market for the tied product." *Northern Pacific Railway Co.* v. *United States,* . . . 356 U.S. at p. 6. . . . Such power may be found either in the vendor's dominance of the market in the tying product or in its uniqueness or particular appeal to the consumer. *United States* v. *Loew's Inc.,* . . . 371 U.S. at p. 45. . . .

---

[2] The post-1955 agreement provides that "[i]n the event that the Dealer desires to purchase his printed goods from sources other than Carvel, Carvel shall license manufacturers of such products to print the Carvel name thereon in connection with sales to the Dealer, with products made in accordance with Carvel standards."

My brothers would affirm the judgment of the district court in all respects. With regard to the allegations of unlawful tying arrangements, they reason that the plaintiffs limited themselves by pre-trial stipulation to reliance solely on "per se" violations of the antitrust laws and since they failed to establish Carvel's market dominance and that a substantial amount of commerce is affected they have failed as well to make out a *per se* violation of the antitrust laws. I cannot agree.

. . . The only question is whether the plaintiffs in fact introduced sufficient evidence to make out an antitrust violation by the Carvel defendants. I think they did. . . .

The court's focus must be entirely on the state of the record. The crucial question is whether the record satisfies the requirements of proof of an antitrust violation. Each element of a tying arrangement must be considered in turn.

Does Carvel possess the requisite economic leverage? Despite the absence in the record of substantial economic data, in the light of the Supreme Court's decision in *United States* v. *Loew's, Inc.*, supra, I believe that such power may be presumed from the use of the Carvel trademark as the principal feature of the Carvel franchise system. In *Loew's*, the Court declared that "when the tying product is patented or copyrighted * * sufficiency of economic power is presumed." 371 U.S. at 45. . . . I can find little reason to distinguish, in determining the legality of an allegedly unlawful tying arrangement, between the economic power generated by a patent or copyright on the one hand and that generated by a trademark on the other. In all three cases, the Congress has granted a statutory monopoly which places in the hands of the owner the right, within the limitations of federal law, to do as he will with the protected product. The value of the patent, copyright or trademark is, of course, directly proportionate to the consumer desirability of the protected product.

I can find no reason not to extend this presumption of economic power to trademarks.[3] In any event, the claims which Carvel itself proffers lend added weight to the presumption, for Carvel's claim of economic justification is founded upon the substantial value of its trademark and the necessity for contractual restraints upon its dealers to protect that value. . . .

The essential element in the Carvel franchise is the trademark license agreement which permits the dealer to display, label and sell its retail products as "Carvel" products. To reinforce its basic trademark Carvel also possesses some nine design patents covering its building structure, advertising displays, freezers and other apparatus, three patents covering machinery and some twenty trademarks in varying forms for use with the

---

[3] The protection given to trademarks is in some respects even more extensive than that given either patents or copyrights. The duration of a trademark, for example, may, during continued use, be extended beyond 20 years without limit of time, . . . whereas a patent expires after 17 years, . . . and a copyright after 28 years, subject to a renewal period of 28 years. . . .

wide variety of products which are merchandised at the franchise stores. It is the lease or license of the trademark itself, buttressed by this array of patents and subsidiary trademarks, to which are tied the other products.

Having concluded that the Carvel trademark presumptively generates sufficient economic power, we must consider two arguments advanced to support the proposition that the Carvel franchise in any event does not embody an unlawful tying arrangement within the provisions of the Clayton Act. First, it is contended that section 3 of that act condemns only agreements which obligate the purchaser not to "use or deal in the goods . . . of a competitor or competitors of the lessor or seller," and that since Carvel does not compete with suppliers of cones, toppings, extracts, ice cream mix and so forth there has been no improper foreclosure of competition. Generally, Carvel's suppliers accept orders directly from the dealers, bill the dealers and deliver directly to them rather than to Carvel. However, the transaction is cast in the form of a sale directly to Carvel which in turn resells the items to the individual dealers, the suppliers acting as Carvel's agents for payment and delivery. Carvel sets the prices at which these items are sold to the dealers. From the point of view of the legal form adopted, then, it is clear that Carvel does compete with other suppliers of these products. Moreover, there is little difference in economic impact between Carvel's purchasing and reselling these supplies and Carvel's production of these items in the first instance.

With regard to the foreclosure to other suppliers of the Carvel franchise stores as possible market outlets, it must be conceded that vigorous competition would probably exist among such suppliers to secure the initial contract with the Carvel organization. Nevertheless, the nature of this competition must be substantially different from that which would otherwise prevail. In view of the leverage which the Carvel corporation wields in supervising the supplying of some 400 retail outlets, competition will most likely take the form of substantial price concessions and the concomitant inability of smaller suppliers effectively to compete with larger producers who are capable of meeting Carvel's price and service demands.

Of equal significance is the economic impact of the prevailing arrangement in terms of foreclosure to the individual franchise stores of the opportunity to deal with individual suppliers. While under the franchise the dealer may enjoy lower prices on some items, Carvel undoubtedly reaps some economic benefit from its status as an intermediary. There is no indication whether or not the dealers, either individually or in combination, could secure lower prices and better service from local producers of the same products. In short, in order to secure the benefits of employing the Carvel name on his retail products, the dealer has been forced to surrender his right to negotiate with suppliers of his own choice on matters such as price, delivery and other aspects of a contract of sale. Where such a surrender may be traced to the economic leverage of the other party, arising from its trademark, the elements of an unlawful tying arrangement have been established. Certainly the amount of commerce here involved is not insubstantial, in light of Carvel's sales to the franchise dealers in 1960 alone of $3,965,923 in ingredients and other supplies.

The second argument advanced in support of the proposition that the Carvel franchise does not embody a tying arrangement is that we are dealing not with a series of individual products tied together for purposes of sales, but rather with one unified product, that is the Carvel product which is ultimately consumed by the public. I do not agree. Carvel sells supplies as distinct items in large quantities—for example, ten gallons of mix, ten gallons of chocolate syrup, and so forth. Carvel itself purchases these supplies as distinct items from a wide variety of suppliers who in turn make individual deliveries to the franchise outlets. By their very nature it seems clear that there is no reason to treat these separate products as one unified product although to the ultimate consumer of an ice cream cone or a sundae they would seem to be one.

The plaintiffs having proved the essentials of a tying arrangement proscribed by the Clayton Act, the burden fell upon Carvel to justify the arrangement as reasonably necessary to protect its trademark. While it is clear that some quality control is essential for the protection of Carvel's goodwill—if not required by law for a proper trademark licensing agreement . . .—the justification for this control requires proof that the specifications for products to substitute for those offered by Carvel would be so complex and detailed as to make it impracticable for Carvel to establish such specifications. . . .

I find the record with respect to justification of Carvel's control to be unsatisfactory and inconclusive. The evidence before Judge Dawson was for the most part documentary. With the exception of the self-serving statement in the franchise agreement that the dealer's obligation to purchase only from Carvel those items which are part of the end product is necessary "[i]n order to safeguard the integrity of Carvel's trademarks," the documents are of little value on the issue of trademark justification. . . .

In light of this sparse showing, I am unable to find sufficient support for Judge Dawson's conclusion that the tying arrangement was justified by the necessity for Carvel to establish quality controls to protect its trademark. My brothers suggest the difficulty of "controlling something so insusceptible of precise verbalization as the desired texture and taste of an ice cream cone or sundae." Yet, since Carvel itself manufactures none of the ingredients sold to the dealers, it has itself apparently surmounted the difficulty of verbalizing the recipes for the proper preparation of its ingredients. . . .

. . . [Consequently] I would think it best to remand the cause to the district court for a further hearing limited to the issue of justification. If Carvel could establish its claim the result ultimately would be the same.

If Carvel were unable to do so the plaintiffs would have sufficiently established all the elements of an unlawful tying arrangement.

The Exclusive Dealing Arrangements

. . . [O]ur application of the stricter standard of legality established by the Supreme Court to the tying aspects of the Carvel franchise does not preclude us from applying the more flexible standard established by the Court for exclusive dealing arrangements to the requirement in the franchise that the dealer sell at retail only Carvel or Carvel approved products. The plaintiffs maintain that this provision erects an unlawful exclusive dealership violative of the antitrust laws. We do not agree.

In *Tampa Electric Co. v. Nashville Co.*, 365 U. S. 320, . . . (1961), the Supreme Court . . . [a]fter discussing the necessity of delineating the relevant line of commerce and the geographical market, . . . noted that requirements contracts "have not been declared illegal *per se*" and stated that in determining whether or not the contract in issue would substantially lessen competition the courts must take into account "the relative strength of the parties, the proportionate volume of commerce involved in relation to the total volume of commerce in the relevant market area, and the probable immediate and future effects which pre-emption of that share of the market might have on effective competition therein." 365 U.S. at 329. . . . The Court further emphasized the significance of the possible economic justification for the accused arrangement, in light of the legitimate reasons for employing such a device.

. . . [The appellants,] . . . [i]nstead of introducing evidence to establish the economic effects of the Carvel franchise structure, . . . merely protest that anti-competitive effects may be inferred solely from the existence of such a network of exclusive dealerships. But the whole tenor of Tampa Electric does not permit adherence to such a stringent standard of legality.

In any event, we need not rely solely upon the appellants' failure to adduce concrete evidence concerning the relevant line of commerce and geographical market and the probable anti-competitive effects of the Carvel arrangement. For in terms of at least one factor which the Supreme Court deemed significant in Tampa Electric—that of economic justification—the Carvel exclusive dealership arrangement withstands any attacks on its legality.

As Judge Dawson found, "the cornerstone of a franchise system must be the trademark or trade name of a product." The fundamental device in the Carvel franchise agreement itself is the licensing to the individual dealer of the right to employ the Carvel name in his advertising displays, on the products he sells, and on the store itself. . . . The requirement that only Carvel products be sold at Carvel outlets derives from the desirability that the public identify each Carvel outlet as one of a chain which offers identical products at a uniform standard of quality. The antitrust laws certainly do not require that the licenser of a trademark permit his licensees to associate with that trademark other products unrelated to those customarily sold under the mark. It is in the public interest that products sold under one particular trademark should be subject to the control of the trademark owner. . . .

Nor do the antitrust laws proscribe a trademark owner from establishing a chain of outlets uniform in appearance and operation. Trademark licensing agreements requiring the sole use of the trademarked item have withstood attack under the antitrust laws where deemed reasonably necessary to protect the goodwill interest of the trademark owner . . . and such agreements certainly are not unlawful *per se* under the antitrust laws. . . . Judge Dawson was fully warranted in concluding that in the context of the entire Carvel franchise system the requirement that no non-Carvel products be sold at the retail level is reasonably necessary for the protection of Carvel's goodwill.

THE SUPPLIER CONTRACTS

The appellants maintain that the agreements between Carvel and its various suppliers of ice cream mix, cones, and paper products are violative of the antitrust laws insofar as they obligate the suppliers not to deal directly with the individual dealers but solely with Carvel and not to sell to the dealers any merchandise other than that approved by Carvel. We disagree.

With regard to Carvel's contracts with Hood and Rakestraw, which produced Carvel ice cream mix in accordance with a secret formula which they pledged not to divulge, it seems perfectly clear that as the possessor of a secret formula for its ice cream mix Carvel enjoyed the right to sell it to whomever it chose, and this right was not diluted by its agreement with Hood and Rakestraw to produce the mix. Carvel was free to insist that Hood and Rakestraw produce the mix solely for Carvel and subject to Carvel's wishes as to its disposition.

As for the provision in the contracts between Carvel and Hood, Rakestraw, Eagle, a cone manufacturer, and Mohawk, a manufacturer of paper products, that the suppliers would not sell non-Carvel products to the individual dealers, we find no merit in the plaintiffs' claims. Carvel cannot be considered in competition with these suppliers from whom it purchases Carvel supplies, and such an agreement not to deal, even if established, when effected by non-competing enterprises is not illegal. . . . Moreover, the plaintiffs failed to prove that they were foreclosed from alternate sources of supply or indeed that the supplier defendants themselves had been requested to make sales to the dealers and had refused.

Accordingly, the judgments of the district court are affirmed.

FRIENDLY, Circuit Judge, with whom MEDINA, Circuit Judge, joins.

Concurring with most of Chief Judge Lumbard's opinion, Judge Medina and I do not consider that a remand as to the claim with respect to the "tied" purchases of flavoring, toppings and cones is either required or warranted in the light of the pre-trial order to which plaintiffs agreed. . . .

In agreeing to the pre-trial order, plaintiffs may have been relying on the inclusion of tying arrangements in the list of *per se* violations in *Northern Pacific Ry.* v. *United States*, 356 U.S. 1, 5, . . . (1958). But, as that opinion makes clear, not every tying arrangement is illegal *per se*. Tying arrangements "are unreasonable in and of themselves whenever a party has sufficient economic power with respect to the tying product to appreciably restrain free competition in the market for the tied product and a 'not insubstantial' amount of interstate commerce is affected." 356 U.S. at 6 . . .

Here the facts to which plaintiffs were limited by the pre-trial order showed neither that Carvel had "sufficient economic power with respect to the tying product to appreciably restrain free competition in the market for the tied product" nor that "a not insubstantial amount of commerce is affected." Indeed, such figures as exist would prove the contrary. In 1960 there were in New York, Connecticut and Massachusetts, 250 Carvel dealers out of a total of 125,000 outlets where ice cream cones could be purchased—amounting to one-fifth of one per cent of the outlets and apparently doing about one per cent of the business. . . . These dealers competed not only with similar chains—Dairy Queen, Tastee Freez, Dari-Delite, King Kone, Dari-Isle, and others, but also with chains and independents utilizing mobile units, with chain stores and operations such as Howard Johnson, and with the ubiquitous corner drug-store. Although Carvel's aggregate sales are "not insubstantial," the totals shed no light on the amount of the "tied" sales here complained of, which common sense tells us must be a minor part. . . . Not only was the amount of commerce in these not consequential, but any damage to the plaintiffs was even less so. Eagle Cone's billings to Carvel averaged $460 per dealer per year, and Carvel's mark-up was slightly over 5% or about $25 per dealer; whether the dealers suffered even that much damage is questionable since the price Carvel charged them was less than they could have obtained if they bought in smaller quantities than Carvel. . . . And, of course, it remained open to competing suppliers to bid for the Carvel business by soliciting that company—in itself an important contrast with cases where the tied item is produced by the seller.

Our brother Lumbard thinks the first of the deficiencies in proof as to economic power was remedied by Carvel's license of a package of trademarks, design patents relating to the shape of the building, etc., and a patented freezing and dispensing machine. We cannot agree. In the first place, the patented items cannot realistically be considered the "tying product" or the focus of the arrangement. Whatever has been said about the evils of "ties" to patented or copyrighted items is meaningful only in the situation where the desirability of the patented item is what motivates the purchaser to make further commitments or to give up some liberty of choice as to other products. . . . In this case, the patented items appear to have been virtually without motivating significance in bringing about the agreement. The true tying item was rather the Carvel trade-mark, whose growing repute was intended to help the little band of Carvel dealers swim a bit faster than their numerous rivals up the highly competitive stream. There may, of course, be cases where a trade-mark has acquired such prominence that the coupling of some further item to its license would constitute a *per se* violation; but . . . [t]he figures show that Carvel is not such a mark.

Tying arrangements differ from other *per se* violations, such as price-fixing . . . in that they can be justified on occasion, as by proof that "the protection of goodwill may necessitate" their use "where specifications for a substitute would be so detailed that they could not practicably be supplied," *Standard Oil Co. of Calif. and Standard Stations* v. *United States*, 337 U.S. 293, 306 . . . (1949). Since the value of a trade-mark depends solely on the public image it conveys, its holder must exercise controls to assure himself that the mark is not shown in a derogatory light. The record affords no sufficient basis for upsetting the finding of the District Judge that "To require Carvel to limit itself to advance specifications of standards for all the various types of accessory products used in connection with the mix would impose an impractical and unreasonable burden of formulation * * *" Although instances of impossibility of control through specification may indeed be rare in cases involving the proper functioning of mechanical elements of a machine . . . such cases are scarcely relevant to the problem of controlling something so insusceptible of precise verbalization as the desired texture and taste of an ice cream cone or sundae. . . .

Even were we to consider the patented machines and design patents to be a relevant part of the tying arrangement, the Northern Pacific opinion ruled out the idea, thought by some to have been implicit in earlier opinions, that proof of the license of a patented device sufficed . . . to show the market dominance required to render a tying arrangement a *per se* violation.[4] In doing so it appropriately recognized the facts of business life. The society of patents is not egalitarian. As had been well said three years earlier, although with some dissent, in the Report of the Attorney General's Committee to Study the Antitrust Laws (1955), 238:

The patent may be broad and basic, in which event the economic power incident to the patent makes the tying clause illegal. On the other hand, the patent may be narrow and unimportant, in which event it may confer virtually no real market power. Accordingly, where the tying product is patented, the patentee should be permitted to show that in the entire factual setting, including the scope of the patent in relation to other patented or unpatented products,

---

4 "In arriving at its decision in *International Salt* the Court placed no reliance on the fact that a patent was involved nor did it give the slightest intimation that the outcome would have been any different if that had not been the case. If anything, the Court held the challenged tying arrangements unlawful *despite* the fact that the tying item was patented, not because of it." 356 U.S. at 9. . . .

the patent does not create the market power requisite to illegality of the tying clause.

. . . Although there is language in *United States* v. *Loew's Inc., supra,* 371 U.S. at 44–48, . . . which lends support to a theory that the mere existence of a patent of any description is not merely *prima facie* but irrebutable [*sic*] evidence of market control, we find it hard to believe that the Court would thus have obliquely reversed the position taken in Northern Pacific. . . ; the language rather must be read in the context of the Court's previous proscription of block-booking of motion picture films in *United States* v. *Paramount Pictures, Inc.,* 334 U.S. 131, 156–159. . . .

United States v. General Motors Corporation

384 U.S. 127 (1966)

Mr. Justice Fortas delivered the opinion of the Court.

This is a civil action brought by the United States to enjoin the appellees from participating in an alleged conspiracy to restrain trade in violation of §1 of the Sherman Act. The United States District Court for the Southern District of California concluded that the proof failed to establish the alleged violation, and entered judgment for the defendants. . . . We reverse.

I

The appellees are the General Motors Corporation, which manufactures, among other things, the Chevrolet line of cars and trucks, and three associations of Chevrolet dealers in and around Los Angeles, California. All of the Chevrolet dealers in the area belong to one or more of the appellee associations.

Chevrolets are ordinarily distributed by dealers operating under a franchise from General Motors. The dealers purchase the cars from the manufacturer, and then retail them to the public. The relationship between manufacturer and dealer is incorporated in a comprehensive uniform Dealer Selling Agreement. This agreement does not restrict or define those to whom the dealer may sell. Nor are there limitations as to the territory within which the dealer may sell. Compare *White Motor Co.* v. *United States,* 372 U.S. 253. The franchise agreement does, however, contain a clause (hereinafter referred to as the "location clause") which prohibits a dealer from moving to or establishing "a new or different location, branch sales office, branch service station, or place of business including any used car lot or location without the prior written approval of Chevrolet."

Beginning in the late 1950's, "discount houses" engaged in retailing consumer goods in the Los Angeles area and "referral services" began offering to sell new cars to the public at allegedly bargain prices. Their sources of supply were the franchised dealers. By 1960 a number of individual Chevrolet dealers, without authorization from General Motors, had developed working relationships with these establishments. A customer would enter one of these establishments and examine the literature and price lists for automobiles produced by several manufacturers. In some instances, floor models were available for inspection. Some of the establishments negotiated with the customer for a trade-in of his old car, and provided financing for his new-car purchase.

The relationship with the franchised dealer took various forms. One arrangement was for the discounter to refer the customer to the dealer. The car would then be offered to him by the dealer at a price previously agreed upon between the dealer and the discounter. In 1960, a typical referral agreement concerning Chevrolets provided that the price to the customer was not to exceed $250 over the dealer's invoiced cost. For its part in supplying the customer, the discounter received $50 per sale.

Another common arrangement was for the discounter itself to negotiate the sale, the dealer's role being to furnish the car and to transfer title to the customer at the direction of the discounter. One dealer furnished Chevrolets under such an arrangement, charging the discounter $85 over its invoiced cost, with the discounter getting the best price it could from its customer.

These were the principal forms of trading involved in this case, although within each there were variations, and there were schemes which fit neither pattern.[1] By 1960 these methods for retailing new cars had reached considerable dimensions. Of the 100,000 new Chevrolets sold in the Los Angeles area in that year, some 2,000 represented discount house or referral sales. One Chevrolet dealer attributed as much as 25% of its annual sales to participation in these arrangements, while another accounted for between 400 and 525 referral sales in a single year.

Approximately a dozen of the 85 Chevrolet dealers in the Los Angeles area were furnishing cars to discounters in 1960. As the volume of these sales grew, the nonparticipating Chevrolet dealers located near one or more of the discount outlets began to feel the pinch. Dealers lost sales because potential customers received, or thought they would receive,[2] a more attractive deal from a discounter who obtained its Chevrolets from

---

[1] At least one discount house actually purchased its cars from cooperative dealers, then resold them to its customers. In this situation, which in the trade is referred to as "bootlegging," the customer does not receive a new-car warranty. General Motors, while disapproving of the practice, does not assert that it violates the "location clause." In those arrangements against which General Motors and the associations did direct their efforts, title to the new car passed directly from dealer to retail customer, who thus obtained a new-car warranty and service agreement.

There must also be distinguished the ubiquitous practice of using "bird dogs"— informal sources who steer occasional customers toward a particular dealer, in return for relatively small fees—often a bottle of liquor. This practice is not only deemed by General Motors not to violate the "location clause," but has the corporation's endorsement as a desirable sales device.

[2] There is evidence in the record that discount sales undercut the prices at which franchised dealers were able to, or chose to compete. . . . Moreover, the discounters advertised and actually provided auto loans at interest rates substantially lower than those offered by G.M.A.C., General Motors' financing subsidiary. . . .

a distant dealer. The discounters vigorously advertised Chevrolets for sale, with alluring statements as to price savings. The discounters also advertised that all Chevrolet dealers were obligated to honor the new-car warranty and to provide the free services contemplated therein; and General Motors does indeed require Chevrolet dealers to service Chevrolet cars, wherever purchased, pursuant to the new-car warranty and service agreement. Accordingly, nonparticipating dealers were increasingly called upon to service, without compensation, Chevrolets purchased through discounters. Perhaps what grated most was the demand that they "precondition" cars so purchased—make the hopefully minor adjustments and do the body and paint work necessary to render a factory-fresh car both customer-and road-worthy.

On June 28, 1960, at a regular meeting of the appellee Losor Chevrolet Dealers Association, member dealers discussed the problem and resolved to bring it to the attention of the Chevrolet Division's Los Angeles zone manager, Robert O'Connor. . . . O'Connor promised he would speak to the offending dealers. When no help was forthcoming . . . [t]he member dealers . . . agreed . . . to flood General Motors and the Chevrolet Division with letters and telegrams asking for help. Salesmen, too, were to write.

Hundreds of letters and wires descended upon Detroit—with telling effect. Within a week Chevrolet's O'Connor was directed to furnish his superiors in Detroit with "a detailed report of the discount house operations . . . as well as what action we in the Zone are taking to curb such sales."

By mid-December General Motors had formulated its response. . . .

General Motors personnel proceeded to telephone all area dealers, both to identify those associated with the discounters and to advise nonparticipants that General Motors had entered the lists. The principal offenders were treated to unprecedented individual confrontations with [Roy] Cash, the regional manager [of the Chevrolet Division]. These brief meetings were wholly successful in obtaining from each dealer his agreement to abandon the practices in question. Some capitulated during the course of the four- or five-minute meeting, or immediately thereafter. One dealer, who met not with Cash but with the city sales manager for Chevrolet, put off decision for a week "to make sure that the other dealers, or most of them, had stopped their business dealings with the discount houses."[3]

[3] According to Francis Bruder, a dealer who had been doing business with the discounters since 1957, "Cash told me that he felt certain that the other dealers would discontinue dealing with discount houses and referral services as well. I left this meeting with the impression that every dealer who had been doing business with a discount house or referral service would soon quit."

This was precisely the impression General Motors had intended to implant. As was explained in an inter-office memorandum to the general sales manager of General Motors' Chevrolet Division, "[All dealers were talked to] in order that every dealer with whom the subject was discussed would know that a similar discussion was being held with all other dealers so that, if certain dealers should elect to discontinue their cooperation with a discount house, we might be able to discourage some other dealer who might be solicited from starting the practice."

There is evidence that unanimity was not obtained without reference to the ultimate power of General Motors. . . .

By mid-January General Motors had elicited from each dealer a promise not to do business with the discounters. But such agreements would require policing—a fact which had been anticipated. General Motors earlier had initiated contacts with firms capable of performing such a function. This plan, unilaterally to police the agreements, was displaced, however, in favor of a joint effort between General Motors, the three appellee associations, and a number of individual dealers.

. . . Early in 1961, the three associations agreed jointly to finance the "shopping" of the discounters to assure that no Chevrolet dealer continued to supply them with cars. Each of the associations contributed $5,000, and a professional investigator was hired. He was instructed to try to purchase new Chevrolets from the proscribed outlets, to tape-record the transactions, if any, and to gather all the necessary documentary evidence— which the associations would then lay "at the doorstep of Chevrolet." These joint associational activities were both preceded and supplemented by similar "shopping" activities by individual dealers and by appellee Losor Chevrolet Dealers Association.

General Motors collaborated with these policing activities. There is evidence that zone manager O'Connor and a subordinate, Jere Faust, actively solicited the help of individual dealers in uncovering violations. . . .

By the spring of 1961, the campaign to eliminate the discounters from commerce in new Chevrolet cars was a success. Sales through the discount outlets seem to have come to a halt. Not until a federal grand jury commenced an inquiry into the matters which we have sketched does it appear that any Chevrolet dealer resumed its business association with the discounters.

II

On these basic facts, the Government first proceeded criminally. A federal grand jury in the Southern District of California returned an indictment. After trial, the defendants were found not guilty. The present civil action, filed shortly after return of the indictment, was then brought to trial.

Both the government and the appellees urge the importance, for purposes of decision, of the "location clause" in the Dealer Selling Agreement which prohibits a franchised dealer from moving to or establishing "a new or different location, branch sales office, branch service station, or place of business . . . without the prior written approval of Chevrolet." . . .

We need not reach . . . questions concerning the meaning, effect, or validity of the "location clause" or of any other provision in the Dealer Selling Agreement, and we do not. We do not decide whether the "location clause" may be construed to prohibit a dealer, party to it, from selling through discounters, or whether General Motors could by unilateral action enforce the clause, so construed. We have here a classic conspiracy in restraint of trade: joint, collaborative action by dealers, the appellee associations, and General Motors to eliminate a class of competitors by terminating business dealings between them and a minority of Chevrolet dealers and to deprive franchised dealers of their freedom to deal through discounters if they so choose. Against this fact of unlawful combination, the "location clause" is of no avail. . . .

The District Court decided otherwise. It concluded that the described events did not add up to a combination or conspiracy violative of the antitrust laws. . . .

The trial court attempted to justify its conclusion on the following reasoning: That each defendant and alleged co-conspirator acted to promote its own self-interest; that General Motors, as well as the defendant associations and their members, has a lawful interest in securing compliance with the "location clause" and in thus protecting the franchise system of distributing automobiles—business arrangements which the court deemed lawful and proper; and that in seeking to vindicate these interests the defendants and their alleged co-conspirators entered into no "agreements" among themselves, although they may have engaged in "parallel action."

These factors do not justify the result reached. It is of no consequence, for purposes of determining whether there has been a combination or conspiracy under §1 of the Sherman Act, that each party acted in its own lawful interest. . . . [I]t has long been settled that explicit agreement is not a necessary part of a Sherman Act conspiracy—certainly not where, as here, joint and collaborative action was pervasive in the initiation, execution, and fulfillment of the plan. *United States* v. *Parke, Davis & Co., supra,* at 43; *United States* v. *Bausch & Lomb Optical Co.,* 321 U.S. 707, 722–723; *Federal Trade Comm'n* v. *Beech-Nut Packing Co.,* 257 U.S. 441, 455.

Neither individual dealers nor the associations acted independently or separately. The dealers collaborated, through the associations and otherwise, among themselves and with General Motors, both to enlist the aid of General Motors and to enforce the dealers' promises to forsake the discounters. The associations explicitly entered into a joint venture to assist General Motors in policing the dealers' promises, and their joint proffer of aid was accepted and utilized by General Motors.

As Parke Davis had done, General Motors sought to elicit from all the dealers' agreements, substantially interrelated and interdependent, that none of them would do business with the discounters. These agreements were hammered out in meetings between nonconforming dealers and officials of General Motors' Chevrolet Division, and in telephone conversations with other dealers. It was acknowledged from the beginning that substantial unanimity would be essential if the agreements were to be forthcoming. And once the agreements were secured, General Motors both solicited and employed the assistance of its alleged co-conspirators in helping to police them. What resulted was a fabric interwoven by many strands of joint action to eliminate the discounters from participation in the market, to inhibit the free choice of franchised dealers to select their own methods of trade and to provide multilateral surveillance and enforcement. This process for achieving and enforcing the desired objective can by no stretch of the imagination be described as "unilateral" or merely "parallel." . . .

There can be no doubt that the effect of the combination or conspiracy here was to restrain trade and commerce within the meaning of the Sherman Act. Elimination, by joint collaborative action, of discounters from access to the market is a *per se* violation of the Act.

. . . This [is] . . . not new doctrine, for it [has] . . . long been recognized that "there are certain agreements or practices which because of their pernicious effect on competition and lack of any redeeming virtue are conclusively presumed to be unreasonable and therefore illegal without elaborate inquiry as to the precise harm they have caused or the business excuse for their use," and that group boycotts are of this character. *Northern Pac. R. Co.* v. *United States*, 356 U.S. 1, 5. See also *Fashion Originators' Guild of America, Inc.* v. *Federal Trade Comm'n*, 312 U.S. 457, and *Eastern States Retail Lumber Dealers' Assn.* v. *United States*, 234 U.S. 600, 613–614, neither of which involved price-fixing.

The principle of these cases is that where businessmen concert their actions in order to deprive others of access to merchandise which the latter wish to sell to the public, we need not inquire into the economic motivation underlying their conduct. . . . Exclusion of traders from the market by means of combination or conspiracy is so inconsistent with the free-market principles embodied in the Sherman Act that it is not to be saved by reference to the need for preserving the collaborators' profit margins or their system for distributing automobiles, any more than by reference to the allegedly tortious conduct against which a combination or conspiracy may be directed—as in *Fashion Originators' Guild of America, Inc.* v. *Federal Trade Comm'n, supra*, at 468.

We note, moreover, that inherent in the success of the combination in this case was a substantial restraint upon price competition—a goal unlawful *per se* when sought to be effected by combination or conspiracy. *E.g., United States* v. *Parke, Davis & Co.*, 362 U.S. 29, 47; *United States* v. *Socony-Vacuum Oil Co.*, 310 U.S. 150, 223. And the *per se* rule applies even when the effect upon prices is indirect. *Simpson* v. *Union Oil Co.*, 377 U.S. 13, 16–22; *Socony-Vacuum Oil Co., supra*.

There is in the record ample evidence that one of the purposes behind the concerted effort to eliminate sales of new Chevrolet cars by discounters was to protect franchised dealers from real or apparent price competition. The discounters advertised price savings. . . . Some purchasers found and others believed that discount prices were lower than those available through the franchised dealers. . . . Certainly, complaints about price competition were prominent in the letters and telegrams with which the individual dealers and salesmen bombarded General Motors in November 1960. . . . And although the District Court found to the contrary, there is evidence in the record that General Motors itself was not unconcerned about the effect of discount sales upon general price levels.[4]

The protection of price competition from conspiratorial restraint is an object of special solicitude under the antitrust laws. We cannot respect that solicitude by closing our eyes to the effect upon price competition of the removal from the market, by combination or conspiracy, of a class of traders. Nor do we propose to construe the Sherman Act to prohibit conspiracies to fix prices at which competitors may sell, but to allow conspiracies or combinations to put competitors out of business entirely.

Accordingly, we reverse and remand to the United States District Court for the Southern District of California in order that it may fashion appropriate equitable relief. . . .

It is so ordered.

United States v. Arnold, Schwinn & Co.

388 U.S. 365 (1967)

Mr. Justice Fortas delivered the opinion of the Court.

The United States brought this appeal to review the judgment of the District Court in a civil antitrust case alleging violations of §1 of the Sherman Act. . . . The complaint charged a continuing conspiracy since 1952 between defendants and other alleged co-conspirators involving price fixing, allocation of exclusive territories to wholesalers and jobbers, and confinement of merchandise to franchised dealers. Named as defendants were Arnold, Schwinn & Company ("Schwinn"), the Schwinn Cycle Distributors Association ("SCDA"), and B. F. Goodrich Company ("B. F. Goodrich").[1] . . .

Appellee Schwinn is a family-owned business which for many years has been engaged in the manufacture and sale of bicycles and some limited bicycle parts and accessories. Appellee SCDA is an association of dis-

---

[4] In an inter-office memorandum, circulated among General Motors officials immediately prior to formulation of corporate policy *vis-à-vis* the discounters, it was stated that "It would appear that one of the real hazards of condoning this type of operation is that discounted prices are freely quoted to a large portion of the public." Moreover, we note that some discounters advertised that they would finance new-car purchases at an interest rate of 5½%, a rate substantially lower than that available at franchised Chevrolet dealers through G.M.A.C., a subsidiary of General Motors Corporation. . . . Finally, it is conceded that General Motors is intensely concerned that each of its dealers has an adequate "profit opportunity" . . . , a concern which necessarily involves consideration of the price realized by dealers.

[1] B. F. Goodrich negotiated a consent decree with the Government prior to trial, and dropped out of the case.

tributors handling Schwinn bicycles and other products. The challenged marketing program was instituted in 1952. In 1951 Schwinn had the largest single share of the United States bicycle market—22.5%. In 1961 Schwinn's share of market had fallen to 12.8% although its dollar and unit sales had risen substantially. In the same period, a competitor, Murray Ohio Manufacturing Company, which is now the leading United States bicycle producer, increased its market share from 11.6% in 1951 to 22.8% in 1961. Murray sells primarily to Sears, Roebuck & Company and other mass merchandisers. By 1962 there were nine bicycle producers in the Nation, operating 11 plants. Imports of bicycles amounted to 29.7% of sales in 1961. . . .

Schwinn sells its products primarily to or through 22 wholesale distributors, with sales to the public being made by a large number of retailers. In addition, it sells about 11% of its total to B. F. Goodrich for resale in B. F. Goodrich retail or franchised stores. There are about 5,000 to 6,000 retail dealers in the United States which are bicycle specialty shops, generally also providing servicing. About 84% of Schwinn's sales are through such specialized dealers. Schwinn sells only under the Schwinn label, never under private label, while about 64% of all bicycles are sold under private label. Distributors and retailers handling Schwinn bicycles are not restricted to the handling of that brand. They may and ordinarily do sell a variety of brands.

The United States does not contend that there is in this case any restraint on interbrand competition, nor does it attempt to sustain its charge by reference to the market for bicycles as a whole. Instead, it invites us to confine our attention to the intrabrand effect of the contested restrictions. It urges us to declare that the method of distribution of a single brand of bicycles, amounting to less than one-seventh of the market, constitutes an unreasonable restraint of trade or commerce among the several States.

Schwinn's principal methods of selling its bicycles are as follows: (1) sales to distributors, primarily cycle distributors, B. F. Goodrich and hardware jobbers; (2) sales to retailers by means of consignment or agency arrangements with distributors; and (3) sales to retailers under the so-called Schwinn Plan which involves direct shipment by Schwinn to the retailer with Schwinn invoicing the dealers, extending credit, and paying a commission to the distributor taking the order. . . . During the 1952–1962 period, as the District Court found, "well over half of the bicycles sold by Schwinn have been sold direct to the retail dealer (not to a cycle distributor) by means of Schwinn Plan sales and consignment and agency sales." Less than half were sold to distributors.

After World War II, Schwinn had begun studying and revamping its distribution pattern. As of 1951–1952, it had reduced its mailing list from about 15,000 retail outlets to about 5,500. It instituted the practice of franchising approved retail outlets. The franchise did not prevent the

retailer from handling other brands, but it did require the retailer to promote Schwinn bicycles and to give them at least equal prominence with
competing brands. The number of franchised dealers in any area was
limited, and a retailer was franchised only as to a designated location or
locations. Each franchised dealer was to purchase only from or through
the distributor authorized to serve that particular area. He was authorized
to sell only to consumers, and not to unfranchised retailers. . . .

Schwinn assigned specific territories to each of its 22 wholesale cycle
distributors. These distributors were instructed to sell only to franchised
Schwinn accounts and only in their respective territories which were
specifically described and allocated on an exclusive basis. The District Court
found "that certain cycle distributors have in fact not competed with each
other . . . and that in so doing they have conspired with Schwinn to unreasonably restrain competition contrary to the provisions of Section 1
of the Sherman Act." The court, however, restricted this finding and its
consequent order to transactions in which the distributor *purchased* the
bicycles from Schwinn for resale, as distinguished from sales by the distributor as agent or consignee of Schwinn or on the Schwinn Plan. The
United States urges that this Court should require revision of the decree
in this respect to forbid territorial exclusivity regardless of the technical
form by which the products are transferred from Schwinn to the retailer
or consumer. . . .

We come, then, to the legal issues in this case. We are here confronted
with challenged vertical restrictions as to territory and dealers. The
source of the restrictions is the manufacturer. These are not horizontal
restraints, in which the actors are distributors with or without the manufacturer's participation. We have held in such a case, where the purpose
was to prevent the distribution of automobiles to or by "discounters," that
a "classic conspiracy in restraint of trade" results. . . . Nor is this a case
of territorial or dealer restrictions accompanied by price fixing, for here
the issue of unlawful price fixing was tendered, litigated, decided against
the appellant, and appellant has not appealed. If it were otherwise—if
there were here a finding that the restrictions were part of a scheme
involving unlawful price fixing, the result would be a *per se* violation of the
Sherman Act. . . . The Government does not contend that a *per se* violation of the Sherman Act is presented by the practices which are involved
in this appeal. . . . Accordingly, we are remitted to an appraisal of the
market impact of these practices.

In *White Motor Co.* v. *United States*, 372 U.S. 253 (1963), this Court
refused to affirm summary judgment against the manufacturer even though
there were not only vertical restrictions as to territory and customer selection but also unlawful price fixing. The Court held that there was no
showing that the price fixing was "an integral part of the whole distribution system" and accordingly it declined to outlaw the system because
of the possibility that a trial laying bare "the economic and business stuff

out of which these arrangements emerge" might demonstrate their reasonableness. *Id.*, at 263. So here we must look to the specifics of the challenged practices and their impact upon the marketplace in order to make a judgment as to whether the restraint is or is not "reasonable" in the special sense in which §1 of the Sherman Act must be read for purposes of this type of inquiry. . . .

We first observe that the facts of this case do not come within the specific illustrations which the Court in *White Motor* articulated as possible factors relevant to a showing that the challenged vertical restraint is sheltered by the rule of reason because it is not anticompetitive. Schwinn was not a newcomer, seeking to break into or stay in the bicycle business. It was not a "failing company." On the contrary, at the initiation of these practices, it was the leading bicycle producer in the Nation. Schwinn contends, however, and the trial court found, that the reasons which induced it to adopt the challenged distribution program were to enable it and the small, independent merchants that made up its chain of distribution to compete more effectively in the marketplace. Schwinn sought a better way of distributing its product: a method which would promote sales, increase stability of its distributor and dealer outlets, and augment profits. But this argument, appealing as it is, is not enough to avoid the Sherman Act proscription; because, in a sense, every restrictive practice is designed to augment the profit and competitive position of its participants. Price fixing does so, for example, and so may a well-calculated division of territories. . . . The antitrust outcome does not turn merely on the presence of sound business reason or motive. Here, for example, if the test of reasonableness were merely whether Schwinn's restrictive distribution program and practices were adopted "for good business reasons" and not merely to injure competitors, or if the answer turned upon whether it was indeed "good business practice," we should not quarrel with Schwinn's eloquent submission or the finding of the trial court. But our inquiry cannot stop at that point. Our inquiry is whether, assuming nonpredatory motives and business purposes and the incentive of profit and volume considerations, the effect upon competition in the marketplace is substantially adverse. The promotion of self-interest alone does not invoke the rule of reason to immunize otherwise illegal conduct. It is only if the conduct is not unlawful in its impact in the marketplace or if the self-interest coincides with the statutory concern with the preservation and promotion of competition that protection is achieved. . . .

On this basis, restraints as to territory or customers, vertical or horizontal, are unlawful if they are "ancillary to the price-fixing" (*White Motor Co.* v. *United States, supra*, at 260) or if the price fixing is "an integral part of the whole distribution system." . . . [*United States* v. *Bausch & Lomb Optical Co.*, 321 U.S. 707 (1944) at 720.] In those situations, it is needless to inquire further into competitive effects because it is established doctrine that, unless permitted by statute, the fixing of prices at which others may sell is anticompetitive, and the unlawfulness of the price fixing infects the distribution restrictions. . . . At the other extreme, a manufacturer of a product other and equivalent brands of which are readily available in the market may select his customers, and for this purpose he may "franchise" certain dealers to whom, alone, he will sell his goods. Cf. *United States* v. *Colgate & Co.*, 250 U.S. 300 (1919). If the restraint stops at that point—if nothing more is involved than vertical "confinement" of the manufacturer's own sales of the merchandise to selected dealers, and if competitive products are readily available to others, the restriction, on these facts alone, would not violate the Sherman Act. It is within these boundary lines that we must analyze the present case.

The District Court here enjoined appellees from limiting the territory within which any wholesaler or jobber may sell any Schwinn product which it has purchased. It held that these are agreements to divide territory and, as such, are *per se* violations of §1 of the Sherman Act. The court made clear that it confined its order to transactions in which the distributor *purchases* from Schwinn. As to consignment, agency and Schwinn Plan transactions, the court held that, in these instances, "Schwinn has a right to allocate its agents or salesmen to a particular territory." The court also held that the franchising of retailers was reasonable in view of the competitive problem presented by "giant" bicycle retailers such as Sears and Ward and by other mass merchandisers, and it declined to enjoin appellees' practices with respect to confinement of sale by distributors or Schwinn to franchised retailers, or to forbid Schwinn and its distributors from continuing to prohibit franchised retailers from selling to discount houses or other unfranchised retailers for resale to the public.

As noted above, appellees have not appealed from the District Court's order, and, accordingly, we have before us only the Government's pleas: (1) that the decree should not be confined to *sale* transactions between Schwinn and wholesalers but should reach territorial restrictions upon distributors whether they are incident to sale and resale transactions or to consignment, agency or Schwinn-Plan relationship between Schwinn and the distributors; (2) that agreements requiring distributors to limit their distribution to only such retailers as are franchised should be enjoined; and (3) that arrangements preventing franchised retailers from supplying non-franchised retailers, including discount stores, should also be forbidden.

As to point (2), the Government argues that it is illogical and inconsistent to forbid territorial limitations on resales by distributors where the distributor owns the goods, having bought them from Schwinn, and, at the same time, to exonerate arrangements which require distributors to confine resales of the goods they have bought to "franchised" retailers. It argues that requiring distributors, once they have purchased the product, to confine sales to franchised retailers is indistinguishable in law and principle from the division of territory which the decree condemns. Both, the Government argues, are in the nature of restraints upon alienation which are beyond the power of the manufacturer to impose upon its vendees and which, since the nature of the transaction includes an agreement, combination or understanding, are violations of §1 of the Sherman Act. . . . We agree, and upon remand, the decree should be revised to enjoin any limitation upon the freedom of distributors to dispose of the Schwinn products, which they have bought from Schwinn, where and to whomever they choose. The principle is, of course, equally applicable to sales to retailers, and the decree should similarly enjoin the making of any sales to retailers upon any condition, agreement or understanding limiting the retailer's freedom as to where and to whom it will resell the products.

The appellant vigorously argues that, since this remedy is confined to situations where the distributor and retailer acquire title to the bicycles, it will provide only partial relief; that to prevent the allocation of territories and confinement to franchised retail dealers, the decree can and should be enlarged to forbid these practices, however effected—whether by sale and resale or by agency, consignment, or the Schwinn Plan. But we are dealing here with a vertical restraint embodying the unilateral program of a single manufacturer . . . raising the fundamental question of the degree to which a manufacturer may not only select the customers to whom he will sell, but also allocate territories for resale and confine access to his product to selected, or franchised, retailers. We conclude that the proper application of §1 of the Sherman Act to this problem requires differentiation between the situation where the manufacturer parts with title, dominion, or risk with respect to the article, and where he completely retains ownership and risk of loss.

As the District Court held, where a manufacturer *sells* products to his distributor subject to territorial restrictions upon resale, a *per se* violation of the Sherman Act results. And, as we have held, the same principle applies to restrictions of outlets with which the distributors may deal and to restraints upon retailers to whom the goods are sold. . . . On the other hand, as indicated in *White Motor*, we are not prepared to introduce the inflexibility which a *per se* rule might bring if it were applied to prohibit all vertical restrictions of territory and all franchising, in the sense of designating specified distributors and retailers as the chosen instruments through which the manufacturer, retaining ownership of the goods, will distribute them to the public. Such a rule might severely hamper smaller enterprises resorting to reasonable methods of meeting the competition of giants and of merchandising through independent dealers, and it might sharply accelerate the trend towards vertical integration of the distribution process. . . .

The Government does not here contend for a *per se* rule as to agency, consignment, or Schwinn-Plan transactions even though these may be used—as they are here—to implement a scheme of confining distribution outlets as in this case. Where the manufacturer retains title, dominion, and risk with respect to the product and the position and function of the dealer in question are, in fact, indistinguishable from those of an agent or sales-man of the manufacture, it is only if the impact of the confinement is "unreasonably" restrictive of competition that a violation of §1 re-sults from such confinement, unencumbered by culpable price fixing. . . . As the District Court found, Schwinn adopted the challenged distribution programs in a competitive situation dominated by mass merchandisers which command access to large-scale advertising and promotion, choice of retail outlets, both owned and franchised, and adequate sources of sup-ply. It is not claimed that Schwinn's practices or other circumstances resulted in an inadequate competitive situation with respect to the bicycle market; and there is nothing in this record . . . to lead us to conclude that Schwinn's program exceeded the limits reasonably necessary to meet the competitive problems posed by its more powerful competitors. In these circumstances, the rule of reason is satisfied.

We do not suggest that the unilateral adoption by a single manufacturer of an agency or consignment pattern and the Schwinn type of restrictive distribution system would be justified in any and all circumstances by the presence of the competition of mass merchandisers and by the demon-strated need of the franchise system to meet that competition. But cer-tainly, in such circumstances, the vertically imposed distribution restraints —*absent* price fixing and in the presence of adequate sources of alternative products to meet the needs of the unfranchised—may not be held to be *per se* violations of the Sherman Act. . . .

. . . Critical in this . . . [case] are the facts: (1) that other competitive bicycles are available to distributors and retailers in the marketplace, and there is no showing that they are not in all respects reasonably inter-changeable as articles of competitive commerce with the Schwinn product;[2] (2) that Schwinn distributors and retailers handle other brands of bicycles as well as Schwinn's; (3) in the present posture of the case we cannot rule that the vertical restraints are unreasonable because of their intermixture with price fixing; and (4) we cannot disagree with the findings of the trial court that competition made necessary the challenged program; that it was justified by, and went no further than required by, competitive pressures; and that its net effect is to preserve and not to damage competition in the bicycle market. Application of the rule of reason here cannot be confined to intrabrand competition. When we look to the product market as a whole, we cannot conclude that Schwinn's franchise system with respect to products as to which it retains ownership and risk constitutes an unreasonable restraint of trade. . . .

Accordingly, the judgment of the District Court is reversed and the cause remanded for the entry of a decree in accordance with this question.

It is so ordered.

[2] We do not regard Schwinn's claim of product excellence as establishing the contrary.

MR. JUSTICE CLARK and MR. JUSTICE WHITE took no part in the decision of this case.

MR. JUSTICE STEWART, whom MR. JUSTICE HARLAN joins, concurring in part and dissenting in part.

I agree with the Court's basic determination that Schwinn's marketing system is, under the rule of reason, entirely consonant with the antitrust laws. But I cannot understand how that marketing system becomes *per se* unreasonable and illegal in those instances where it is effectuated through sales to wholesalers and dealers. . . .

Schwinn's selective distribution policy may be said to embody restraints on trade. As such, it is subject to antitrust scrutiny, but the scrutiny does not stop with the label "restraint." The words written by Mr. Justice Brandeis for a unanimous Court in *Chicago Board of Trade* v. *United States,* 246 U. S. 231, 238, bear repeating:

Every agreement concerning trade, every regulation of trade, restrains. To bind, to restrain, is of their very essence. The true test of legality is whether the restraint imposed is such as merely regulates and perhaps thereby promotes competition or whether it is such as may suppress or even destroy competition. To determine that question the court must ordinarily consider the facts peculiar to the business to which the restraint is applied; its condition before and after the restraint was imposed; the nature of the restraint and its effect, actual or probable. The history of the restraint, the evil believed to exist, the reason for adopting the particular remedy, the purpose or end sought to be attained, are all relevant facts.

. . . It is worth emphasizing that the justifications for Schwinn's franchising policy rest not only on the facts of this particular record, but on larger issues of social and economic policy. This Court has recognized Congress' concern with the disappearance of the small independent merchant in the face of competition from vertically integrated giants. . . . This trend in many cases reflects the inexorable economic realities of modern marketing. But franchising promises to provide the independent merchant with the means to become an efficient and effective competitor of large integrated firms. Through various forms of franchising, the manufacturer is assured qualified and effective outlets for his products, and the franchisee enjoys backing in the form of know-how and financial assistance. These franchise arrangements also make significant social and economic contributions of importance to the whole society. . . .

Indiscriminate invalidation of franchising arrangements would eliminate their creative contributions to competition and force "suppliers to abandon franchising and integrate forward to the detriment of small business. In other words, we may inadvertently compel concentration" by misguided zealousness.[3] . . .

[3] Wilson, "Some Problems Relative to Franchise Arrangements," 11 *Antitrust Bull.* 473, 488. It should be noted that since the start of this litigation, Schwinn has taken over 30% of the wholesaling of its products by vertical integration.

For these reasons I completely agree with the Court's basic approach to this case. . . . It upholds the legality of the Schwinn Plan, which is the heart of Schwinn's marketing system, now accounting for 75% of the distribution of Schwinn's products. It also upholds the legality of Schwinn's agency and consignment arrangements.

But the Court inexplicably turns its back on the values of competition by independent merchants and the flexible wisdom of the rule of reason when dealing with distribution effected through sales to wholesalers. In Schwinn's particular marketing system, this mode of distribution plays a subsidiary role, serving to meet "fill-in" orders by dealers, whose basic stock is obtained through the Schwinn Plan. Without considering its function, purpose or effect, the Court declares this aspect of Schwinn's program to be *per se* invalid. It likewise applies the same automatic rule of illegality to strike down Schwinn's policy of ensuring that franchised dealers do not resell to unfranchised retailers and thus subvert the whole distributional scheme.

Despite the Government's concession that the rule of reason applies to all aspects of Schwinn's distribution system, the Court nevertheless reaches out to adopt a potent *per se* rule. No previous antitrust decision of this Court justifies this action. Instead, it completely repudiates the only case in point, *White Motor*. . . . The Court today is unable to give any reasons why, only four years later, this precedent should be overruled. . . . And I am completely at a loss to fathom how the Court can adopt its *per se* rule concerning distributional sales and yet uphold identical restrictions in Schwinn's marketing scheme when distribution takes the form of consignment or Schwinn Plan deliveries. It does not demonstrate that these restrictions are in their actual operation somehow more anticompetitive or less justifiable merely because the contractual relations between Schwinn and its jobbers and dealers bear the label "sale" rather than "agency" or "consignment." Such irrelevant formulae are false guides to sound adjudication in the antitrust field. . . .

The Court advances two justifications for its new *per se* rule. I do not find either persuasive. First, the Court correctly observes that the District Court invalidated territorial limitations on the resale activities of Schwinn's wholesalers. . . . But the Court completely overlooks the fact that the territorial limitations invalidated by the District Court were the product of a horizontal conspiracy between the wholesalers. . . . In striking down this horizontal division of markets between competing distributors, the District Court was simply following familiar precedent. . . . By contrast, the restrictions involved in the franchising methods now before us are quite different in nature, as the Court points out elsewhere in its opinion. . . . As the Court also emphasizes, the legal principles applicable to horizontal and vertical restrictions are quite different.[4] Thus, applying the rule

---

[4] One difference between a horizontal conspiracy and vertical restraints imposed by the manufacturer is that there is often serious question whether the latter conduct involves the "contract, combination . . . or conspiracy" required by §1 of the

of reason to the vertical restraints now in issue is not at all "illogical and inconsistent" with *per se* invalidation of the wholesalers' horizontal division of markets.

The Court's second justification for its new *per se* doctrine is the "ancient rule against restraints on alienation." . . . But it is hardly the practice of this Court to embrace a rule of law merely on grounds of its antiquity. Moreover, the common-law doctrine of restraints on alienation is not nearly so rigid as the Court implies. The original rule concerned itself with arbitrary and severe restrictions on alienation, such as total prohibition of resale. As early as 1711 it was recognized that only *unreasonable* restraints should be proscribed, and that partial restrictions could be justified when ancillary to a legitimate business purpose and not unduly anticompetitive in effect. . . .

Centuries ago, it could perhaps be assumed that a manufacturer had no legitimate interest in what happened to his products once he had sold them to a middleman and they had started on their way down the channel of distribution. But this assumption no longer holds true in a day of sophisticated marketing policies, mass advertising, and vertically integrated manufacturer-distributors. Restrictions like those involved in a franchising program should accordingly be able to claim justification under the ancillary restraints doctrine. . . .

. . . Moreover, the Court's answer makes everything turn on whether the arrangement between a manufacturer and his distributor is denominated a "sale" or "agency." Such a rule ignores and conceals the "economic and business stuff out of which" a sound answer should be fashioned. *White Motor Co.* v. *United States, supra,* at 263. The Court has emphasized in the past that these differences in form often do not represent "differences in substance." *Simpson* v. *Union Oil Co.,* 377 U.S. 13, 22. Draftsmen may cast business arrangements in different legal molds for purposes of commercial law, but these arrangements may operate identically in terms of economic function and competitive effect. It is the latter factors which are the concern of the antitrust laws. The record does not show that the purposes of Schwinn's franchising program and the competitive consequences of its implementation differed, depending on whether Schwinn sold its products to wholesalers or resorted to the agency, consignment, or Schwinn Plan methods of distribution. And there is no reason generally to suppose that variations in the formal legal packaging of franchising programs produce differences in their actual impact in the marketplace. Our experience is to the contrary. As stated in *United States* v. *Masonite Corp.,* 316 U.S. 265, 278, 280:

Sherman Act. . . . The District Judge in this case refused to find that the relevant conduct of Schwinn and its distributors amounted to a "contract," "combination" or "conspiracy." Instead, he stated that "the Schwinn franchising program was conceived, hatched and born into life . . . in the minds of the Schwinn officials," and agreed that "the action was unilateral in nature." . . .

[T]his Court has quite consistently refused to allow the form into which the parties chose to cast the transaction to govern.

. . . . .

So far as the Sherman Act is concerned, the result must turn not on the skill with which counsel has manipulated the concepts of 'sale' and 'agency' but on the significance of the business practices in terms of restraint of trade.

. . . . .

In view of the commendably careful and realistic approach the Court has taken an analyzing the basic structure of Schwinn's marketing program, it is particularly disappointing to see the Court balk at the label "sale," and turn from reasoned response to a wooden and irrelevant formula.

Tripoli Company, Inc. v. *Wella Corporation*

425 F.2d 932 (3d Cir. 1970),
cert. denied 400 U.S. 831 (1970)

GIBBONS, Circuit Judge.

. . . . .

Tripoli is a wholesale distributor of beauty and barber supplies to professional beauticians and barbers. Wella is the manufacturer of a line of cosmetics, some fifty in number, including hair dyes and tints, permanent waves, hair conditioners, setting lotions and many similar products. Tripoli was for over thirty years, until the summer of 1967, a wholesale distributor for Wella. About that time Wella learned that Tripoli was engaged not only in wholesale distribution to the trade, but also, under the trade style "The Beauty Cage" in retail sales to consumers. Wella then stopped selling to Tripoli, and this lawsuit followed.

Tripoli's complaint sought an injunction "to require (Wella) to resume sales to plaintiff under standard commercial terms" as well as damages suffered "by reason of the violation by (Wella) of the Clayton and Robinson-Patman Acts." . . . [T]he only factual allegation . . . is the seventh paragraph:

> After approximately thirty years of the above described business relationship, defendant has refused to sell its products to plaintiff on the ground that plaintiff has from time to time *charged its customers a price lower than that which defendant recommended as the resale price in the relevant market area.* (italics added).

. . . Wella's answer asserted that the true reason for termination was not resale price maintenance, but rather, the resale to retail customers of Wella products intended for the professional trade. Wella went further;

it denied that it recommended resale prices to Tripoli, and alleged that Tripoli was free to sell Wella products at any price it chose.

[Judge Gibbons then reviewed the evidence as to the existence of a resale price maintenance agreement in order to show that the allegation had been effectively abandoned by Tripoli and hence was not an issue in this proceeding.]

But while it abandoned the price maintenance charge, Tripoli did not abandon the fray. Instead, it adopted Wella's theory of the reason for cancellation. Relying on *United States* v. *Arnold, Schwinn & Co.*, 388 U.S. 365 . . . (1967), Tripoli contended that Wella's policy of restricting resale of its professional beauty care products to professional beauticians and barbers, after title to those products passed to a wholesaler, is a per se violation of [Section 1 of] the Sherman Anti-trust Act. . . .

It is clear that not all restraints in a system of distribution fall into the per se category. *United States* v. *Arnold, Schwinn & Co., supra. White Motor Co.* v. *United States*, 372 U.S. 253 . . . (1963). Those condemned in *Schwinn* as per se violations were post-sale restrictions on the territory in which or the retailers to whom a wholesaler could resell. That case does not, as plaintiff proposes, establish as a per se violation every attempt by a manufacturer to restrict the persons to whom a wholesaler may resell any product whatsoever, title to which has left the manufacturer. Rather, *Schwinn* must be read, as must all antitrust cases, in its factual context. That context is a restraint on the territories in which and retailers to whom a wholesale purchaser may resell a bicycle, a product so simple in use that most ultimate consumers are children. No considerations other than marketing and competition were advanced in *Schwinn* as justifications for the restraint. In that context the Supreme Court held:

Under the Sherman Act, it is unreasonable *without more* for a manufacturer to seek to restrict and confine areas or persons with whom an article may be traded after the manufacturer has parted with dominion over it. . . .

United States v. *Arnold, Schwinn & Co., supra*, at 379 . . . (italics added).

Here there is more, and the restraints are of a different order. Tripoli does not charge that it or any other Wella distributor is confined, in reselling, to a specific territory. Nor does Tripoli charge that it or any other Wella distributor is confined to reselling to "franchised" beauty or barber shops. The restraint is on a wholesale distributor's reselling products intended for professional application to non-professional retail end users. This restraint must be tested not by a per se rule but by the standard of reasonableness. . . .[1] By that standard Wella made a convincing demonstra-

---

[1] We are aware that in *United States* v. *Glaxo Group Ltd.*, 302 F. Supp. 1 (D.D.C. 1969), a district court read *Schwinn* as imposing a per se rule with respect to every post-sale restraint on alienation regardless of market context or purpose. We are not

tion . . . that in view of the nature of its products, the restraint in the market setting was not only reasonable but appropriate in the public interest. Tripoli, in response, came forward with nothing significant.

We consider first the nature of the products. Of some fifty, all but two are packaged in a manner intended for resale to the professional trade. The two products intended for sale to retail customers are hair conditioners, which have the effect of softening hair to make it more manageable. These are sold, through separate channels of distribution, to drug and grocery retailers. Wella's president testified on deposition (and that testimony is uncontradicted) that the chemical formulation of the two hair conditioners sold to retail channels is different from that sold to the professional trade; that the suggested method of application is different; and that the two products are not used for the same purpose. It is also undisputed that the hair conditioners intended for professional use are marketed in boxes containing a supply of smaller units for individual application, with the appropriate instructions and warnings furnished with the box; while the hair conditioners intended for retail sale are individually packaged and labeled, with appropriate instructions and warnings furnished with each application.

Except for the two hair conditioners sold through retail channels of distribution, all other Wella products are sold through wholesalers who resell to the professional beauty and barber trade, and each of those products is packaged with a label:

For sale to professionals only; sale to any other person is prohibited.

In addition, many of the products are sold with a label containing a warning:

CAUTION: This product contains ingredients which may cause skin irritation on certain individuals and a preliminary test according to accompanying directions should first be made. This product must not be used for dyeing the eyelashes or eyebrows—to do so may cause blindness.

The latter label is required on many of Wella's products by Section 601(a) of the Federal Food, Drug, & Cosmetic Act of 1938. . . .

Some Wella products are sold with an instruction sheet containing an instruction:

---

convinced, however, that the Supreme Court intended, for example, that an automobile manufacturer using wholesale intermediate sellers must permit distribution of automobiles through beauty parlors or barber shops rather than through dealers offering appropriate pre-sale and post-sale service. Other examples can be imagined. We do not believe that in the age of "consumerism" the Supreme Court intended so drastic a reduction of the areas in which a manufacturer may exercise responsibility to the consumer as is suggested in *Glaxo*. The restraint in *Glaxo*, moreover, operates in quite a different market context, since the patents there involved provide protection from inter-brand competition and the addition of the restraint had the added effect of limiting intra-brand competition. Neither situation is present in the instant case.

HYPERSENSITIVITY AND THE PATCH TEST

It is a well-known fact that some individuals are allergic to certain foods, drugs or cosmetics including hair coloring. Such persons are considered supersensitive or predisposed. To ascertain whether a person is predisposed to COLOR CHARM, the following standard patch test must be made before each application of COLOR CHARM:

Such an instruction is required for many Wella products by the Color Additive Regulations issued by the Federal Food and Drug Administration. . . .

It is undisputed that misuse of many of Wella's products can cause dangerous adverse effects such as blindness, burning or irritation of the scalp or brittleness of the hair. . . .

Pennsylvania has established a system of licensing for beauticians and for barbers. To obtain a license as a beautician one must pass an examination. . . . Wella has imposed on its wholesale distributors a requirement that their sales of its professional products line be restricted to persons in the licensed category. It states that its motive is the same as that of the licensing authorities, the protection of the public against injury.

It may well be that Wella is not as much interested in protecting the public from harm as in protecting itself from potential product liability. . . . But whichever motive is dominant, either furnishes a sufficient lawful main purpose, to which the restriction on resale of potentially dangerous products is reasonably ancillary. Even tie-in agreements designed to protect against warranty claims have been held valid. E.g., *Susser* v. *Carvel Corp.*, 332 F. 2d 505, 517 (2d. Cir.) *cert. granted*, 379 U.S. 885 . . . (1964), *petition for cert. dismissed*, 381 U.S. 125 . . . (1965). . . . Resale restrictions imposed for the same purpose have also been sustained. . . .

There is no allegation here of any attempt to shelter Wella's products from intra-brand competition among wholesalers calling on the same trade, nor has there been any showing that Wella's products have, by the restraint imposed, been sheltered from competition with other brands. On the contrary, the record discloses that Wella's distributors to the professional trade compete in the same territory, and that Tripoli itself has always handled competing brands. It is difficult to imagine, therefore, a circumstance in which the restriction on resale to the professional trade could have a meaningful anti-competitive effect. None is suggested in the record. . . .

Summarizing, Tripoli first charged a termination for resale price maintenance, but abandoned that contention and relied on the licensed user restraint as a per se violation. It did nothing to rebut Wella's showing that the licensed user restraint was reasonably ancillary to Wella's lawful purpose of protecting the public from injury and itself from liability. . . .

The judgment of the district court will be affirmed.

Siegel v. *Chicken Delight, Inc.*

311 F. Supp. 847 (N.D. Cal. 1970)

GEORGE B. HARRIS, Chief Judge.

This matter is before the Court on plaintiffs' motion for a directed verdict following the close of defendants' case and the submission of the evidence. . . .

The issues, simply stated, are: (1) Are the defendants' standard contract and practices requiring the purchase of various packaging items, cookers and fryers, and certain mix preparations for food a tying agreement in violation of Section 1 of the Sherman Act? (2) If so, have the plaintiffs been injured by the said violation?

Tying arrangements, by definition agreements in which the seller offers two separate items for sale but will not sell the first item (or tying item) unless the buyer agrees to purchase the second item (or tied item), have uniformly been treated harshly by the United States Supreme Court. . . . The instant case is conceptually an illustration of the classical tie. Defense counsel argues that this case involves a single product, "the Chicken Delight System," thus attempting to come within the single product ruling of *Times-Picayune Publishing Co.* v. *United States*, 345 U.S. 594 . . . (1953), wherein the traditional statement of the *per se* rule against tying arrangements was first enunciated by Mr. Justice Clark.

However, the case of *Susser* v. *Carvel Corp.*, 332 F. 2d 505 (2nd Cir., 1964), which is factually most akin to this litigation, clearly holds contra. Both the majority and the dissent in Susser recognize that a trademark license which is granted on the condition that the licensee purchase other products can clearly be a "tying item" within the meaning of the above cases. This Court is in full accord with such a finding. In the economic context of present franchising trends, it is clear that a franchise license is marketable separate and apart from the various products which the franchisees are required to purchase from and through the franchisor.

In the case at bar, it is manifest that the license to use the Chicken Delight name, trademark and method of operations was a tying item in the traditional sense. The tied items were the required paper packaging products, the cookers and fryers and the food preparation mixes. Thus, for purposes of the Sherman Act, this Court finds as a matter of law that a tying agreement exists.

With respect to the essential ingredient of market control, the cases dictate but one conclusion—that as a matter of law Chicken Delight's admittedly unique, registered trademark combined with its power to impose the tie-in demonstrates the existence of sufficient market power to bring the case within the Sherman Act. A review of *Northern Pacific Ry. Co.* v. *United States*, 356 U.S. 1 . . . (1957); *United States* v. *Loew's, Inc.*,

371 U.S. 38 . . . (1962); *Fortner Enterprises* v. *United States Steel*, 394 U.S. 495 . . . (1969) and *Advanced Business Systems & Supply Co.* v. *SMC Corp.*, 415 F. 2d 55 (4th Cir., 1969) demands this result. To enmesh the jury in the rubric of market power in light of the clear guidelines laid down in the above cases should be unnecessary. This Court clearly may and does rule upon this question as a matter of law.

[Chief Judge Harris then proceeded to review the above cases, concluding, among other things, that ". . . this Court is of the opinion that any distinction between the Sherman Act and Clayton Act with regard to the question of market power is wholly artificial."]

. . . . .

For purposes of the Sherman Act, the effect on interstate commerce need merely be said to be "not insubstantial." *International Salt Co.* v. *United States*, 332 U.S. 392, 396 . . . (1947). This test is fulfilled if the dollar amount is not *de minimis* or not "paltry." *Fortner Enterprises* v. *United States Steel*, 394 U.S. 495, 501–502 . . . (1969). In the present case (millions of dollars being involved), the dollar amount cannot be said to be *de minimis*. Thus, as a matter of law, this Court finds that the interstate commerce affected is "not insubstantial." A *per se* violation of the Sherman Act is therefore found to exist.

When a *per se* violation of the Sherman Act exists, the areas of justification for a tie-in are indeed narrow. . . . In this litigation, defendants propound four so-called justifications for the tie-in of the various required products. They are: (1) Quality control for protection of trademark good will; (2) New business justification; (3) A convenient accounting device for compensation of the trademark license; and (4) Franchisor's assurance of initial equipment and a continuing source of supply of essential items.

In the factual structure and posture of this case, the Court rules as a matter of law that the latter two asserted justifications cannot and do not justify so onerous an anti-competitive device as the tie-in agreement herein condemned.

Use of a tie-in cannot be justified as an accounting device for compensation for a trademark license. The defendants cite no relevant authority for such a proposition. In fact, such a justification is contrary to the uncontradicted evidence in this case, which evidence shows that the defendants charged no franchise fee or continuing royalty. Furthermore, an accounting method which specified a percentage of gross from the franchisees is just as convenient and has none of the anti-competitive effects of a tie-in.

Defendants' fourth attempted justification insists that they had a legal duty to assure franchisees of initial equipment and continuing supplies of other essential items. The admissions and the evidence are replete that defendants' alleged obligations could easily have been fulfilled without tying the purchase of those items to a trademark license. Defendants, like most franchisors, could have designated manufacturers and distributors who are available throughout the United States and anxious to do business as those sources of supply. This Court rules as a matter of law that such a justification is not available or defensive to the *per se* tying arrangement in this case.

In *United States* v. *Jerrold Electronics Corp.*, 187 F. Supp. 545, 559 (E.D.Pa., 1960), aff'd per curiam 365 U.S. 567 . . . (1961), the Supreme Court recognized the so-called new business justification. In *Jerrold* the sole restraint approved by the Court was the tie-in of an engineering service contract for highly complex equipment, during the early stages of a business whose technology was advanced and unproven. As technological knowledge became more widespread and definitive, the Court indicated that the restraint could no longer be justified. This defense can certainly be held, as a matter of law, not to apply to the case at bar. The undisputed facts are that defendants started their business in 1952 and, for the period 1963 through 1969 and into 1970 (the period relevant to this litigation), the purchase requirements, although expanded in the number of products required, prevailed unchanged.

The defendants further assert that the tie-in of the paper products, the dip and spice mixes and the cookers and fryers can be justified as necessary quality control to protect the good will of their trademark. Heavy reliance is placed upon the opinion of Mr. Justice Friendly in the *Susser* case, supra. The Court agrees that this defense has sufficient vitality, as a factual consideration, to reach the jury as to the dip and spice mixes and as to the cookers and fryers. However, the Court rules as a matter of law that there can be no justification for the tie-in of the paper products.

The guiding language on the issue of quality control justification was stated by Mr. Justice Frankfurter in *Standard Oil Co. of Cal. and Standard Stations* v. *United States*, 337 U.S. 293, 305–306 . . . (1948).

. . . The only situation . . . in which the protection of good will may necessitate the use of tying clauses is where specifications for a substitute would be so detailed that they could not practically be supplied. (emphasis supplied)

This language is fatal to defendants' contention as to quality control justification for the tied paper products.

Defendants' showing on paper packaging is nothing more than a recitation of the need for distinctive packaging to be used uniformly by all franchisees in identifying the hot foods. This was not contested. However, the admissions in evidence clearly demonstrate that the tied packaging was easily specifiable. In fact, the only specifications required were printing and color. Moreover, defendants have admitted that any competent manufacturer of like products could consistently and satisfactorily manufacture the packaging products if defendants furnished specifications. Those suppliers could have sold to the franchisees through normal channels of distribution. As a matter of law, therefore, this paper products tie-in cannot be justified on any grounds within the contemplation of acceptable authority.

The *Susser* case, on the other hand, does indicate that where quality of food is a consideration the quality control defense is relevant to the issue of justification of a tie-in. In this regard, Mr. Justice Friendly stated:

Although instances of impossibility of control through specification may indeed be rare in cases involving the proper functioning of mechanical elements of a machine * * * such cases are scarcely relevant to the problem of controlling something so insusceptible of precise verbalization as the desired texture and taste of an ice cream cone or sundae; that Carvel was able to specify this to its source of supply, whose product it regularly checked, does not show that administration could be confided to 400 dealers. 332 F. 2d at 520.

Such considerations are relevant to the asserted defense of Chicken Delight. The dip and spice mixes are alleged to be *secret* and to impart a unique and distinctive flavor to the final products. Likewise, the cooker is alleged to be unique and to prepare the food in a special manner. Contradictory testimony has been offered on this aspect of the litigation. As such, a question of fact exists for the jury to determine. . . .

To summarize, the Court finds as a matter of law that there is an unlawful tie-in arrangement; that sufficient market control exists; that a "not insubstantial" amount of interstate commerce is affected; that no justification exists with respect to the continuity of supply of paper products; that neither the alleged justifications of convenient accounting device nor continuing source of supply are defenses in this litigation; [and] that the new business justification is clearly inapplicable to this case. . . .

The Court rules that the jury may consider the asserted quality control justification as to the dip and spice mixes and cookers and fryers under appropriate instructions.

To the extent consistent with the above decision and opinion, plaintiffs' motion for directed verdict must be, and the same is hereby, granted.

Defendants' motion for directed verdict must be and the same is hereby denied.

PART V

Antitrust and Regulation

Chapter
13

DOES REGULATION
MAKE A DIFFERENCE?

The cases presented in this chapter serve two purposes. First, they supplement the recent merger decisions set forth in Chapter 5, and are of interest as merger cases alone. Second, they demonstrate a relatively new development in antitrust—attempts to reconcile the methods used by regulators with those favored by antitrust enforcement officials.

Parker v. *Brown*

338 U. S. 341 (1943)

MR. CHIEF JUSTICE STONE delivered the opinion of the Court.

The questions for our consideration are whether the marketing program adopted for the 1940 raisin crop under the California Agricultural Prorate Act is rendered invalid (1) by the Sherman Act, or (2) by the Agricultural Marketing Agreement Act of 1937, as amended, . . . or (3) by the Commerce Clause of the Constitution.[1]

Appellee, a producer and packer of raisins in California brought this suit in the district court to enjoin appellants—the State Director of Agriculture, Raisin Proration Zone No. 1, the members of the State Agricultural Prorate Advisory Commission and of the Program Committee for Zone No. 1, and others charged by the statute with the administration of the Prorate Act—from enforcing, as to appellee, a program for marketing the 1940 crop of raisins produced in "Raisin Proration Zone No. 1." . . .

As appears from the evidence and from the findings of the district court, almost all of the raisins consumed in the United States, and nearly one-half of the world crop, are produced in Raisin Proration Zone No. 1. Between 90 and 95 per cent of the raisins grown in California are ultimately shipped in interstate or foreign commerce. . . .

The California Agricultural Prorate Act authorizes the establishment, through action of state officials, of programs for the marketing of agri-

[1] We include here only that portion of the opinion relating to (1). IMS.

cultural commodities produced in the state, so as to restrict competition among the growers and maintain prices in the distribution of their commodities to packers. The declared purpose of the Act is to "conserve the agricultural wealth of the State" and to "prevent economic waste in the marketing of agricultural products" of the state. . . .

Upon the petition of ten producers for the establishment of a prorate marketing plan for any commodity within a defined production zone. . . , and after a public hearing . . . , and after making prescribed economic findings . . . showing that the institution of a program for the proposed zone will prevent agricultural waste and conserve agricultural wealth of the state without permitting unreasonable profits to producers, the Commission is authorized to grant the petition. The Director, with the approval of the Commission, is then required to select a program committee from among nominees chosen by the qualified producers within the zone, to which he may add not more than two handlers or packers who receive the regulated commodity from producers for marketing. . . .

The program committee is required . . . to formulate a proration marketing program for the commodity produced in the zone, which the Commission is authorized to approve after a public hearing and a "finding that the program is reasonably calculated to carry out the objectives of the Act." The Commission may, if so advised, modify the program and approve it as modified. If the proposed program, as approved by the Commission, is consented to by 65 per cent in number of producers in the zone owning 51 per cent of the acreage devoted to production of the regulated crop, the Director is required to declare the program instituted. . . .

Authority to administer the program, subject to the approval of the Director of Agriculture, is conferred on the program committee. . . . Section 22.5 declares that it shall be a misdemeanor . . . for any producer to sell or any handler to receive or possess without proper authority any commodity for which a proration program has been instituted. . . . Section 25 imposes a civil liability of $500 "for each and every violation" of any provision of a proration program.

The seasonal proration marketing program for raisins, with which we are now concerned, became effective on September 7, 1940. This provided that the program committee should classify raisins as "standard," "substandard," and "inferior"; "inferior" raisins are those which are unfit for human consumption, as defined in the Federal Food, Drug and Cosmetric Act . . . . The committee is required to establish receiving stations within the zone to which every producer must deliver all raisins which he desires to market. The raisins are graded at these stations. All inferior raisins are to be placed in the "inferior raisin pool," to be disposed of by the committee "only for assured by-product and other diversion purposes." All substandard raisins, and at least 20 per cent of the total standard and substandard raisins produced, must be placed in a "surplus pool." Raisins in this pool may also be disposed of only for "assured by-product and other diversion purposes," except that under certain circumstances the program committee may transfer standard raisins from the surplus pool to the stabilization pool. Fifty per cent of the crop must be placed in a "stabilization pool."

Under the program the producer is permitted to sell the remaining 30 per cent of his standard raisins, denominated "free tonnage," through ordinary commercial channels, subject to the requirement that he obtain a "secondary certificate" authorizing such marketing and pay a certificate fee of $2.50 for each ton covered by the certificate. Certification is stated to be a device for controlling "the time and volume of movement" of free tonnage into such ordinary commercial channels. Raisins in the stabilization pool are to be disposed of by the committee "in such manner as to obtain stability in the market and to dispose of such raisins," but no raisins (other than those subject to special lending or pooling arrangements of the Federal Government) can be sold by the committee at less than the prevailing market price for raisins of the same variety and grade on the date of sale. . . .

Appellee's bill of complaint challenges the validity of the proration program as in violation of the Commerce Clause and the Sherman Act; in support of the decree of the district court he also urges that it conflicts with and is superseded by the Federal Agricultural Marketing Agreement Act of 1937. The complaint alleges that he is engaged within the marketing zone both in producing and in purchasing and packing raisins for sale and shipment interstate; that before the adoption of the program he had entered into contracts for the sale of 1940 crop raisins; that, unless enjoined, appellants will enforce the program against appellee by criminal prosecutions and will prevent him from marketing his 1940 crop, from fulfilling his sales contracts, and from purchasing for sale and selling in interstate commerce raisins of that crop. . . .

Validity of the Prorate Program under the Sherman Act.

Section 1 of the Sherman Act, 15 U.S.C. §1, makes unlawful "every contract, combination . . . or conspiracy, in restraint of trade or commerce among the several States." And §2, 15 U.S.C. §2, makes it unlawful to "monopolize, or attempt to monopolize, or combine or conspire with any other person or persons, to monopolize any part of the trade or commerce among the several States." We may assume for present purposes that the California prorate program would violate the Sherman Act if it were organized and made effective solely by virtue of a contract, combination or conspiracy of private persons, individual or corporate. . . .

But it is plain that the prorate program here was never intended to operate by force of individual agreement or combination. It derived its authority and its efficacy from the legislative command of the state and was not intended to operate or become effective without that command. We find nothing in the language of the Sherman Act or in its history which suggests that its purpose was to restrain a state or its officers or agents from activities directed by its legislature. In a dual system of government in which, under the Constitution, the states are sovereign, save only as Congress may constitutionally subtract from their authority, an unexpressed purpose to nullify a state's control over its officers and agents is not lightly to be attributed to Congress.

The Sherman Act makes no mention of the state as such, and gives no hint that it was intended to restrain state action or official action directed by a state. The Act is applicable to "persons" including corporations . . . , and it authorizes suits under it by persons and corporations. . . .

There is no suggestion of a purpose to restrain state action in the Act's legislative history. The sponsor of the bill which was ultimately enacted as the Sherman Act declared that it prevented only "business combinations." . . . That its purpose was to suppress combinations to restrain competition and attempts to monopolize by individuals and corporations, abundantly appears from its legislative history. . . .

True, a state does not give immunity to those who violate the Sherman Act by authorizing them to violate it, or by declaring that their action is lawful, . . . and we have no question of the state or its municipality becoming a participant in a private agreement or combination by others for restraint of trade. . . . Here the state command to the Commission and to the program committee of the California Prorate Act is not rendered unlawful by the Sherman Act since, in view of the latter's words and history, it must be taken to be a prohibition of individual and not state action. It is the state which has created the machinery for establishing the prorate program. Although the organization of a prorate zone is proposed by producers, and a prorate program, approved by the Commission, must also be approved by referendum of producers, it is the state, acting through the Commission, which adopts the program and which enforces it with penal sanctions, in the execution of a governmental policy. The prerequisite approval of the program upon referendum by a prescribed number of producers is not the imposition by them of their will upon the minority by force of agreement or combination which the Sherman Act prohibits. The state itself exercises its legislative authority in making the regulation and in prescribing the conditions of its application. The required vote on the referendum is one of these conditions. . . .

The state in adopting and enforcing the prorate program made no contract or agreement and entered into no conspiracy in restraint of trade or to establish monopoly but, as sovereign, imposed the restraint as an act of government which the Sherman Act did not undertake to prohibit. . . .

Reversed.

.   .   .   .   .

Note: In two recent cases, *Washington Gas Light Co.* v. *Virginia Electric and Power Co.*, 438 F. 2d 248 (4th Cir. 1971) and *Gas Light Co. of*

Columbus v. *Georgia Power Co.*, 440 F.2d 1135 (5th Cir. 1971), the courts have held that promotional practices of electric utilities which have been approved (either expressly or tacitly) by state regulatory commissions are entitled to antitrust immunity under the *Parker* rule. The former has been settled out of court; the latter is currently before the Supreme Court on appeal.

United States v. *Philadelphia National Bank*

374 U.S. 321 (1963)

Mr. Justice Brennan delivered the opinion of the Court.

The United States, appellant here, brought this civil action . . . to enjoin a proposed merger of The Philadelphia National Bank (PNB) and Girard Trust Corn Exchange Bank (Girard), appellees here. The complaint charged violations of Section 1 of the Sherman Act, . . . and Section 7 of the Clayton Act. . . . From a judgment for appellees after trial . . . the United States appealed to this Court. . . . We reverse the judgment of the District Court. We hold that the merger of appellees is forbidden by Section 7 of the Clayton Act and so must be enjoined; we need not, and therefore do not, reach the further question of alleged violation of Section 1 of the Sherman Act.

I. The Facts and Proceedings Below

A. *The Background: Commercial Banking in the United States*

Because this is the first case which has required this Court to consider the application of the antitrust laws to the commercial banking industry, and because aspects of the industry and of the degree of governmental regulation of it will recur throughout our discussion, we deem it appropriate to begin with a brief background description.[1]

Commercial banking in this country is primarily unit banking. That is, control of commercial banking is diffused throughout a very large number of independent, local banks—13,460 of them in 1960—rather than concentrated in a handful of nationwide banks, as, for example, in England and Germany. There are, to be sure, in addition to the independent banks, some 10,000 branch banks; but branching, which is controlled largely by state law—and prohibited altogether by some States—enables a bank to extend itself only to state lines and often not that far. It is also the case, of course, that many banks place loans and solicit deposits outside their home area. But with these qualifications, it remains true that ours is essentially a decentralized system of community banks. Recent years, however,

---

[1] The discussion in this portion of the opinion draws upon undisputed evidence of record in the case, supplemented by pertinent reference materials. (The interested reader is referred to the footnotes in the original decision for a lengthy reading list). IMS.

have witnessed a definite trend toward concentration. Thus, during the decade ending in 1960 the number of commercial banks in the United States declined by 714, despite the chartering of 887 new banks and a very substantial increase in the Nation's credit needs during the period. Of the 1,601 independent banks which thus disappeared, 1,503, with combined total resources of well over $25,000,000,000, disappeared as the result of mergers.

Commercial banks are unique among financial institutions in that they alone are permitted by law to accept demand deposits. This distinctive power gives commercial banking a key role in the national economy. For banks do not merely deal in, but are actually a source of, money and credit; when a bank makes a loan by crediting the borrower's demand deposit account, it augments the Nation's credit supply.[2] Furthermore, the power to accept demand deposits makes banks the intermediaries in most financial transactions (since transfers of substantial moneys are almost always by check rather than by cash) and, concomitantly, the repositories of very substantial individual and corporate funds. The banks' use of these funds is conditioned by the fact that their working capital consists very largely of demand deposits, which makes liquidity the guiding principle of bank lending and investing policies; thus it is that banks are the chief source of the country's short-term business credit.

Banking operations are varied and complex; "commercial banking" describes a congeries of services and credit devices. But among them the creation of additional money and credit, the management of the checking-account system, and the furnishing of short-term business loans would appear to be the most important. For the proper discharge of these functions is indispensable to a healthy national economy, as the role of bank failures in depression periods attests. It is therefore not surprising that commercial banking in the United States is subject to a variety of governmental controls, state and federal. Federal regulation is the more extensive, and our focus will be upon it. It extends not only to the national banks, *i.e.*, banks chartered under federal law and supervised by the Comptroller of the Currency. . . . For many state banks . . . as well as virtually all the national banks . . . are members of the Federal Reserve System (FRS), and more than 95% of all banks . . . are insured by the Federal Deposit Insurance Corporation (FDIC). State member and nonmember insured banks are subject to a federal regulatory scheme almost as elaborate as that which governs the national banks. . . .

But perhaps the most effective weapon of federal regulation of banking is the broad visitatorial power of federal bank examiners. Whenever the agencies deem it necessary, they may order "a thorough examination of all the affairs of the bank," whether it be a member of the FRS or a non-

---

[2] Such creation is not, to be sure, pure sleight of hand. A bank may not make a loan without adequate reserves. Nevertheless, the element of bank money creation is real. *E.g.*, Samuelson, *Economics* (5th ed. 1961), 331–343.

member insured bank. . . . Such examinations are frequent and intensive. In addition, the banks are required to furnish detailed periodic reports of their operations to the supervisory agencies. . . . In this way the agencies maintain virtually a day-to-day surveillance of the American banking system. . . .

Federal supervision of banking has been called "[p]robably the outstanding example in the federal government of regulation of an entire industry through methods of supervision. . . . The system may be one of the most successful [systems of economic regulation], if not the most successful." . . . To the efficacy of this system we may owe, in part, the virtual disappearance of bank failures from the American economic scene.

B. *The Proposed Merger of PNB and Girard*

The Philadelphia National Bank and Girard Trust Corn Exchange Bank are, respectively, the second and third largest of the 42 commercial banks with head offices in the Philadelphia metropolitan area, which consists of the City of Philadelphia and its three contiguous counties in Pennsylvania. The home county of both banks is the city itself; Pennsylvania law, however, permits branching into the counties contiguous to the home county, . . . and both banks have offices throughout the four-county area. PNB, a national bank, has assets of over $1,000,000,000, making it (as of 1959) the twenty-first largest bank in the Nation. Girard, a state bank, is a member of the FRS and is insured by the FDIC; it has assets of about $750,000,000. Were the proposed merger to be consummated, the resulting bank would be the largest in the four-county area, with (approximately) 36% of the area banks' total assets, 36% of deposits, and 34% of net loans. It and the second largest (First Pennsylvania Bank and Trust Company, now the largest) would have between them 59% of the total assets, 58% of deposits, and 58% of the net loans, while after the merger the four largest banks in the area would have 78% of total assets, 77% of deposits, and 78% of net loans.

The present size of both PNB and Girard is in part the result of mergers. Indeed, the trend toward concentration is noticeable in the Philadelphia area generally, in which the number of commercial banks has declined from 108 in 1947 to the present 42. Since 1950, PNB has acquired nine formerly independent banks and Girard six; and these acquisitions have accounted for 59% and 85% of the respective banks' asset growth during the period, 63% and 91% of their deposit growth, and 12% and 37% of their loan growth. During this period, the seven largest banks in the area increased their combined share of the area's total commercial bank resources from about 61% to about 90%.

In November 1960 the boards of directors of the two banks approved a proposed agreement for their consolidation under the PNB charter. . . . Such a consolidation is authorized, subject to the approval of the Comptroller of the Currency. . . . But under the Bank Merger Act of

1960 . . . the Comptroller may not give his approval until he has received reports from the other two banking agencies and the Attorney General respecting the probable effects of the proposed transaction on competition. All three reports advised that the proposed merger would have substantial anticompetitive effects in the Philadelphia metropolitan area. However, on February 24, 1961, the Comptroller approved the merger. No opinion was rendered at that time. But as required . . . , the Comptroller explained the basis for his decision to approve the merger in a statement to be included in his annual report to Congress. As to effect upon competition, he reasoned that "[s]ince there will remain an adequate number of alternative sources of banking service in Philadelphia, and in view of the beneficial effects of this consolidation upon international and national competition it was concluded that the over-all effect upon competition would not be unfavorable." He also stated that the consolidated bank "would be far better able to serve the convenience and needs of its community by being of material assistance to its city and state in their efforts to attract new industry and to retain existing industry." The day after the Comptroller approved the merger, the United States commenced the present action. No steps have been taken to consummate the merger pending the outcome of this litigation.

. . . . .

II. THE APPLICABILITY OF SECTION 7 OF THE CLAYTON ACT TO BANK MERGERS

A. *The Original Section and the 1950 Amendment*

. . . . .

Fourth. It is settled law that "[i]mmunity from the antitrust laws is not lightly implied." . . . This canon of construction, which reflects the felt indispensable role of antitrust policy in the maintenance of a free economy, is controlling here. For there is no indication in the legislative history to the 1950 amendment of Section 7 that Congress wished to confer a special dispensation upon the banking industry; if Congress had so wished, moreover, surely it would have exempted the industry from the stock-acquisition as well as the assets-acquisition provision.

Of course, our construction of the amended Section 7 is not foreclosed because, after the passage of the amendment, some members of Congress, and for a time the Justice Department, voiced the view that bank mergers were still beyond the reach of the section. "[T]he views of a subsequent Congress form a hazardous basis for inferring the intent of an earlier one." . . . This holds true even though misunderstanding of the scope of Section 7 may have played some part in the passage of the Bank Merger Act of 1960. . . . The design fashioned in the Bank Merger Act was predicated upon uncertainty as to the scope of Section 7, and we do no violence to that design by dispelling the uncertainty.

B.   *The Effect of the Bank Merger Act of 1960*

Appellees contended below that the Bank Merger Act, by directing the banking agencies to consider competitive factors before approving mergers . . . immunizes approved mergers from challenge under the federal antitrust laws. We think the District Court was correct in rejecting this contention. No express immunity is conferred by the Act.[3] Repeals of the antitrust laws by implication from a regulatory statute are strongly disfavored, and have only been found in cases of plain repugnancy between the antitrust and regulatory provisions. . . .

In the *California [El Paso]* case . . . the Court held that the FPC's approval of a merger did not confer immunity from Section 7 of the Clayton Act, even though, as in the instant case, the agency had taken the competitive factor into account in passing upon the merger application. . . . We think *California* is controlling here. Although the Comptroller was required to consider effect upon competition in passing upon appellees' merger application, he was not required to give this factor any particular weight; he was not even required to (and did not) hold a hearing before approving the application; and there is no specific provision for judicial review of his decision. . . .

Nor did Congress, in passing the Bank Merger Act, embrace the view that federal regulation of banking is so comprehensive that enforcement of the antitrust laws would be either unnecessary, in light of the completeness of the regulatory structure, or disruptive of that structure. On the contrary, the legislative history of the Act seems clearly to refute any suggestion that applicability of the antitrust laws was to be affected. Both the House and Senate Committee Reports stated that the Act would not affect in any way the applicability of the antitrust laws to bank acquisitions. . . . Moreover, bank regulation is in most respects less complete than public utility regulation, to which interstate rail and air carriers, among others, are subject. Rate regulation in the banking industry is limited and largely indirect . . . ; banks are under no duty not to discriminate in their services; and though the location of bank offices is regulated, banks may do business—place loans and solicit deposits—where they please. The fact that the banking agencies maintain a close surveillance of the industry with a view toward preventing unsound practices that might impair liquidity or lead to insolvency does not make federal banking regulation allpervasive, although it does minimize the hazards of intense competition. Indeed, that there are so many direct public controls over unsound com-

---

[3] Contrast this with the express exemption provisions of, *e.g.*, the Federal Aviation Act . . . ; Federal Communications Act . . . ; Interstate Commerce Act . . . ; Shipping Act . . . ; Webb-Pomerene Act . . . ; and the Clayton Act itself. . . .

petitive practices in the industry refutes the argument that private controls of competition are necessary in the public interest and ought therefore to be immune from scrutiny under the antitrust laws. Cf. Kaysen and Turner, *Antitrust Policy* (1959), 206. . . .

It should be unnecessary to add that in holding as we do that the Bank Merger Act of 1960 does not preclude application of Section 7 of the Clayton Act to bank mergers, we deprive the later statute of none of its intended force. Congress plainly did not intend the 1960 Act to extinguish other sources of federal restraint of bank acquisitions having anticompetitive effects. . . .

III.   The Lawfulness of the Proposed Merger
under Section 7

The statutory test is whether the effect of the merger "may be substantially to lessen competition" "in any line of commerce in any section of the country." We analyzed the test in detail in *Brown Shoe Co.* v. *United States,* . . . and that analysis need not be repeated or extended here, for the instant case presents only a straightforward problem of application to particular facts.

We have no difficulty in determining the "line of commerce" (relevant product or services market) and "section of the country" (relevant geographical market) in which to appraise the probable competitive effects of appellees' proposed merger. We agree with the District Court that the cluster of products (various kinds of credit) and services (such as checking accounts and trust administration) denoted by the term "commercial banking," . . . composes a distinct line of commerce. Some commercial banking products or services are so distinctive that they are entirely free of effective competition from products or services of other financial institutions; the checking account is in this category. Others enjoy such cost advantages as to be insulated within a broad range from substitutes furnished by other institutions. For example, commercial banks compete with small-loan companies in the personal-loan market; but the small-loan companies' rates are invariably much higher than the banks', in part, it seems, because the companies' working capital consists in substantial part of bank loans.[4] Finally, there are banking facilities which, although in

---

[4] Cf. *United States* v. *Aluminum Co. of America,* 148 F. 2d 416, 425 (C. A. 2d Cir. 1945). In the instant case, unlike *Aluminum Co.,* there is virtually no time lag between the banks' furnishing competing financial institutions (small-loan companies, for example) with the raw material, *i.e.,* money, and the institutions' selling the finished product, *i.e.,* loans; hence the instant case, compared with *Aluminum Co.* in this respect, is *a fortiori.* As one banker testified quite frankly in the instant case in response to the question: "Do you feel that you are in substantial competition with these institutions [personal-finance and sales-finance companies] that you lend . . . such money to for loans that you want to make?"—"Oh, no, we definitely do not. If we did, we would stop making the loans to them." (R. 298.) The reason for the competitive disadvantage of most lending institutions *vis-à-vis* banks is that only banks obtain the bulk of their working capital without having to pay interest or

terms of cost and price they are freely competitive with the facilities provided by other financial institutions, nevertheless enjoy a settled consumer preference, insulating them, to a marked degree, from competition; this seems to be the case with savings deposits. In sum, it is clear that commercial banking is a market "sufficiently inclusive to be meaningful in terms of trade realities." *Crown Zellerbach Corp.* v. *Federal Trade Comm'n,* 296 F. 2d 800, 811 (C.A. 9th Cir. 1961).

We part company with the District Court on the determination of the appropriate "section of the country." The proper question to be asked in this case is not where the parties to the merger do business or even where they compete, but where, within the area of competitive overlap, the effect of the merger on competition will be direct and immediate. See Bock, *Mergers and Markets* (1960), 42. This depends upon "the geographic structure of supplier-consumer relations." Kaysen and Turner, *Antitrust Policy* (1959), 102. In banking, as in most service industries, convenience of location is essential to effective competition. Individuals and corporations typically confer the bulk of their patronage on banks in their local community; they find it impractical to conduct their banking business at a distance. . . . The factor of inconvenience localizes banking competition as effectively as high transportation costs in other industries. . . . Therefore, since, as we recently said in a related context, the "area of effective competition in the known line of commerce must be charted by careful selection of the market area in which the seller operates, *and to which the purchaser can practicably turn for supplies,*" *Tampa Elec. Co.* v. *Nashville Coal Co.,* 365 U.S. 320, 327 (emphasis supplied); see *Standard Oil Co.* v. *United States,* 337 U.S. 293, 299 and 300, n. 5, the four-county area in which appellees' offices are located would seem to be the relevant geographical market. Cf. *Brown Shoe Co., supra,* at 338–339. In fact, the vast bulk of appellees' business originates in the four-county area.[5] Theoretically, we should be concerned with the possibility that bank offices on the perimeter of the area may be in effective competition with bank offices within; actually, this seems to be a factor of little significance.[6]

We recognize that the area in which appellees have their offices does

---

comparable charges thereon, by virtue of their unique power to accept demand deposits. The critical area of short-term commercial credit . . . appears to be one in which banks have little effective competition, save in the case of very large companies which can meet their financing needs from retained earnings or from issuing securities or paper.

[5] The figures for PNB and Girard respectively are: 54% and 63% of the dollar volume of their commercial and industrial loans originate in the four-county area; 75% and 70%, personal loans; 74% and 84%, real estate loans; 41% and 62%, lines of credit; 94% and 72%, personal trusts; 81% and 94%, time and savings deposits; 56% and 77%, demand deposits; 93% and 87%, demand deposits of individuals. Actually, these figures may be too low. . . .

[6] Appellees suggest not that bank offices skirting the four-county area provide meaningful alternatives to bank customers within the area, but that such alternatives are provided by large banks, from New York and elsewhere, which solicit business in

not delineate with perfect accuracy an appropriate "section of the country" in which to appraise the effect of the merger upon competition. Large borrowers and large depositors, the record shows, may find it practical to do a large part of their banking business outside their home community; very small borrowers and depositors may, as a practical matter, be confined to bank offices in their immediate neighborhood; and customers of intermediate size, it would appear, deal with banks within an area intermediate between these extremes. . . . [See notes 5 and 6, *supra.*] So also, some banking services are evidently more local in nature than others. But that in banking the relevant geographical market is a function of each separate customer's economic scale means simply that a workable compromise must be found: some fair intermediate delineation which avoids the indefensible extremes of drawing the market either so expansively as to make the effect of the merger upon competition seem insignificant, because only the very largest bank customers are taken into account in defining the market, or so narrowly as to place appellees in different markets, because only the smallest customers are considered. We think that the four-county Philadelphia metropolitan area, which state law apparently recognizes as a meaningful banking community in allowing Philadelphia banks to branch within it, and which would seem roughly to delineate the area in which bank customers that are neither very large nor very small find it practical to do their banking business, is a more appropriate "section of the country" in which to appraise the instant merger than any larger or smaller or different area. Cf. Hale and Hale, *Market Power: Size and Shape Under the Sherman Act* (1958), 119. We are helped to this conclusion by the fact that the three federal banking agencies regard the area in which banks have their offices as an "area of effective competition." . . .

Having determined the relevant market, we come to the ultimate question under Section 7: whether the effect of the merger "may be substantially to lessen competition" in the relevant market. Clearly, this is not the kind

---

the Philadelphia area. There is no evidence of the amount of business done in the area by banks with offices outside the area; it may be that such figures are unobtainable. In any event, it would seem from the local orientation of banking insofar as smaller customers are concerned . . . that competition from outside the area would only be important to the larger borrowers and depositors. If so, the four-county area remains a valid geographical market in which to assess the anticompetitive effect of the proposed merger upon the banking facilities available to the smaller customer—a perfectly good "line of commerce," in light of Congress' evident concern, in enacting the 1950 amendments to Section 7, with preserving small business. See *Brown Shoe Co., supra,* at 315–316. As a practical matter the small businessman can only satisfy his credit needs at local banks. To be sure, there is still some artificiality in deeming the four-county area the relevant "section of the country" so far as businessmen located near the perimeter are concerned. But such fuzziness would seem inherent in any attempt to delineate the relevant geographical market. Note, 52 *Col. L. Rev.* 766, 778–779, n. 77 (1952). And it is notable that outside the four-county area, appellees' business rapidly thins out. Thus, the other six counties of the Delaware Valley account for only 2% of appellees' combined individual demand deposits; 4%, demand deposits of partnerships and corporations; 7%, loans; 2%, savings deposits; 4%, business time deposits.

of question which is susceptible of a ready and precise answer in most cases. It requires not merely an appraisal of the immediate impact of the merger upon competition, but a prediction of its impact upon competitive conditions in the future; this is what is meant when it is said that the amended Section 7 was intended to arrest anticompetitive tendencies in their "incipiency." See *Brown Shoe Co.* . . . Such a prediction is sound only if it is based upon a firm understanding of the structure of the relevant market; yet the relevant economic data are both complex and elusive. . . . And unless businessmen can assess the legal consequences of a merger with some confidence, sound business planning is retarded. . . . So also, we must be alert to the danger of subverting congressional intent by permitting a too-broad economic investigation. . . . And so in any case in which it is possible, without doing violence to the congressional objective embodied in Section 7, to simplify the test of illegality, the courts ought to do so in the interest of sound and practical judicial administration. . . . This is such a case.

We noted in *Brown Shoe Co.* . . . that "[t]he dominant theme pervading congressional consideration of the 1950 amendments [to Section 7] was a fear of what was considered to be a rising tide of economic concentration in the American economy." This intense congressional concern with the trend toward concentration warrants dispensing, in certain cases, with elaborate proof of market structure, market behavior, or probable anticompetitive effects. Specifically, we think that a merger which produces a firm controlling an undue percentage share of the relevant market, and results in a significant increase in the concentration of firms in that market, is so inherently likely to lessen competition substantially that it must be enjoined in the absence of evidence clearly showing that the merger is not likely to have such anticompetitive effects. . . .

Such a test lightens the burden of proving illegality only with respect to mergers whose size makes them inherently suspect in light of Congress' design in Section 7 to prevent undue concentration. Furthermore, the test is fully consonant with economic theory. That "[c]ompetition is likely to be greatest when there are many sellers, none of which has any significant market share,"[7] is common ground among most economists, and was undoubtedly a premise of congressional reasoning about the antimerger statute.

The merger of appellees will result in a single bank's controlling at least 30% of the commercial banking business in the four-county Philadelphia metropolitan area.[8] Without attempting to specify the smallest market share which would still be considered to threaten undue concentra-

---

[7] Comment, "Substantially to Lessen Competition . . .": "Current Problems of Horizontal Mergers," 68 *Yale L. J.* 1627, 1638–1639 (1959). . . .

[8] . . . We note three factors that cause us to shade the percentages given earlier in this opinion, in seeking to calculate market share. (1) The percentages took no account of banks which do business in the four-county area but have no offices

tion, we are clear that 30% presents that threat.[9] Further, whereas presently the two largest banks in the area (First Pennsylvania and PNB) control between them approximately 44% of the area's commercial banking business, the two largest after the merger (PNB-Girard and First Pennsylvania) will control 59%. Plainly, we think, this increase of more than 33% in concentration must be regarded as significant.

Our conclusion that these percentages raise an inference that the effect of the contemplated merger of appellees may be substantially to lessen competition is not an arbitrary one, although neither the terms of Section 7 nor the legislative history suggests that any particular percentage share was deemed critical. . . .

There is nothing in the record of this case to rebut the inherently anticompetitive tendency manifested by these percentages. There was, to be sure, testimony by bank officers to the effect that competition among banks in Philadelphia was vigorous and would continue to be vigorous after the merger. We think, however, that the District Court's reliance on such evidence was misplaced. This lay evidence on so complex an economic-legal problem as the substantiality of the effect of this merger upon competition was entitled to little weight, in view of the witnesses' failure to give concrete reasons for their conclusions.[10]

---

there; however, this seems to be a factor of little importance, at least insofar as smaller customers are concerned, see note [6], *supra.* (2) The percentages took no account of banks which have offices in the four-county area but not their home offices there; however, there seem to be only two such offices and appellees in this Court make no reference to this omission. (3) There are no percentages for the amount of business of banks located in the area, other than appellees, which originates in the area. Appellees contend that since most of the 40 other banks are smaller, they do a more concentratedly local business than appellees, and hence account for a relatively larger proportion of such business. If so, we doubt much correction is needed. The five largest banks in the four-county area at present control some 78% of the area banks' assets. Thus, even if the small banks have a somewhat different pattern of business, it is difficult to see how that would substantially diminish the appellees' share of the local banking business.

No evidence was introduced as to the quantitative significance of these three factors, and appellees do not contend that as a practical matter such evidence could have been obtained. Under the circumstances, we think a downward correction of the percentages to 30% produces a conservative estimate of appellees' market share.

9 Kaysen and Turner, *supra,* . . . suggest that 20% should be the line of prima facie unlawfulness; Stigler suggests that any acquisition by a firm controlling 20% of the market after the merger is presumptively unlawful; Markham mentions 25%. Bok's principal test is increase in market concentration, and he suggests a figure of 7% or 8%. . . . We intimate no view on the validity of such tests for we have no need to consider percentages smaller than those in the case at bar, but we note that such tests are more rigorous than is required to dispose of the instant case. Needless to say, the fact that a merger results in a less-than-30% market share, or in a less substantial increase in concentration than in the instant case, does not raise an inference that the merger is *not* violative of Section 7. See, *e.g., Brown Shoe Co.* . . . .

10 The fact that some of the bank officers who testified represented small banks in competition with appellees does not substantially enhance the probative value of their testimony. The test of a competitive market is not only whether small competitors flourish but also whether consumers are well served. . . . In an oligopolistic market,

Of equally little value, we think, are the assurances offered by appellees' witnesses that customers dissatisfied with the services of the resulting bank may readily turn to the 40 other banks in the Philadelphia area. In every case short of outright monopoly, the disgruntled customer has alternatives; even in tightly oligopolistic markets, there may be small firms operating. A fundamental purpose of amending Section 7 was to arrest the trend toward concentration, the *tendency* to monopoly, before the consumer's alternatives disappeared through merger, and that purpose would be ill-served if the law stayed its hand until 10, or 20, or 30 more Philadelphia banks were absorbed. This is not a fanciful eventuality, in view of the strong trend toward mergers evident in the area . . . and we might note also that entry of new competitors into the banking field is far from easy.[11]

So also, we reject the position that commercial banking, because it is subject to a high degree of governmental regulation, or because it deals in the intangibles of credit and services rather than in the manufacture or sale of tangible commodities, is somehow immune from the anticompetitive effects of undue concentration. Competition among banks exists at every level—price, variety of credit arrangements, convenience of location, attractiveness of physical surroundings, credit information, investment advice, service charges, personal accommodations, advertising, miscellaneous special and extra services—and it is keen; on this appellees' own witnesses were emphatic. There is no reason to think that concentration is less inimical to the free play of competition in banking than in other service industries. On the contrary, it is in all probability more inimical. For example, banks compete to fill the credit needs of businessmen. Small businessmen especially are, as a practical matter, confined to their locality for the satisfaction of their credit needs. . . . If the number of banks in the locality is reduced, the vigor of competition for filling the marginal small business borrower's needs is likely to diminish. At the same time, his concomitantly greater difficulty in obtaining credit is likely to put him at a disadvantage *vis-à-vis* larger businesses with which he competes. In this fashion, concentration in banking accelerates concentration generally.

We turn now to three affirmative justifications which appellees offer for the proposed merger. The first is that only through mergers can banks follow their customers to the suburbs and retain their business. This justification does not seem particularly related to the instant merger, but in any event it has no merit. There is an alternative to the merger route:

---

small companies may be perfectly content to follow the high prices set by the dominant firms, yet the market may be profoundly anticompetitive.

[11] Entry is, of course, wholly a matter of governmental grace. . . . In the 10-year period ending in 1961, only one new bank opened in the Philadelphia four-county area. That was in 1951. At the end of 10 years, the new bank controlled only one-third of 1% of the area's deposits.

the opening of new branches in the areas to which the customers have moved—so-called *de novo* branching. Appellees do not contend that they are unable to expand thus, by opening new offices rather than acquiring existing ones, and surely one premise of an antimerger statute such as Section 7 is that corporate growth by internal expansion is socially preferable to growth by acquisition.

Second, it is suggested that the increased lending limit of the resulting bank will enable it to compete with the large out-of-state banks, particularly the New York banks, for very large loans. We reject this application of the concept of "countervailing power." Cf. *Kiefer-Stewart Co.* v. *Joseph E. Seagram & Sons*, 340 U.S. 211. If anticompetitive effects in one market could be justified by procompetitive consequences in another, the logical upshot would be that every firm in an industry could, without violating Section 7, embark on a series of mergers that would make it in the end as large as the industry leader. For if all the commercial banks in the Philadelphia area merged into one, it would be smaller than the largest bank in New York City. This is not a case, plainly, where two small firms in a market propose to merge in order to be able to compete more successfully with the leading firms in that market. Nor is it a case in which lack of adequate banking facilities is causing hardships to individuals or businesses in the community. The present two largest banks in Philadelphia have lending limits of $8,000,000 each. The only businesses located in the Philadelphia area which find such limits inadequate are large enough readily to obtain bank credit in other cities.

This brings us to appellees' final contention, that Philadelphia needs a bank larger than it now has in order to bring business to the area and stimulate its economic development. . . . We are clear, however, that a merger the effect of which "may be substantially to lessen competition" is not saved because, on some ultimate reckoning of social or economic debits and credits, it may be deemed beneficial. A value choice of such magnitude is beyond the ordinary limits of judicial competence, and in any event has been made for us already, by Congress when it enacted the amended Section 7. Congress determined to preserve our traditionally competitive economy. It therefore proscribed anticompetitive mergers, the benign and the malignant alike, fully aware, we must assume, that some price might have to be paid.

In holding as we do that the merger of appellees would violate Section 7 and must therefore be enjoined, we reject appellees' pervasive suggestion that application of the procompetitive policy of Section 7 to the banking industry will have dire, although unspecified, consequences for the national economy. Concededly, PNB and Girard are healthy and strong; they are not undercapitalized or overloaned; they have no management problems; the Philadelphia area is not overbanked; ruinous competition is not in the offing. Section 7 does not mandate cutthroat competition in the banking industry, and does not exclude defenses based on dangers to liquidity or solvency, if to avert them a merger is necessary. It does require, however, that the forces of competition be allowed to operate within the broad framework of governmental regulation of the industry. The fact that banking is a highly regulated industry critical to the Nation's welfare makes the play of competition not less important but more so. At the price of some repetition, we note that if the businessman is denied credit because his banking alternatives have been eliminated by mergers, the whole edifice of an entrepreneurial system is threatened; if the costs of banking services and credit are allowed to become excessive by the absence of competitive pressures, virtually all costs, in our credit economy, will be affected; and unless competition is allowed to fulfill its role as an economic regulator in the banking industry, the result may well be even more governmental regulation. Subject to narrow qualifications, it is surely the case that competition is our fundamental national economic policy, offering as it does the only alternative to the cartelization or governmental regimentation of large portions of the economy. . . . There is no warrant for declining to enforce it in the instant case.

The judgment of the District Court is reversed and the case remanded with direction to enter judgment enjoining the proposed merger.

It is so ordered.

MR. JUSTICE WHITE took no part in the consideration or decision of this case.

MR. JUSTICE HARLAN, whom MR. JUSTICE STEWART joins, dissenting.

I suspect that no one will be more surprised than the Government to find that the Clayton Act has carried the day for its case in this Court.

In response to an apparently accelerating trend toward concentration in the commercial banking system in this country, a trend which existing laws were evidently ill-suited to control, numerous bills were introduced in Congress from 1955 to 1960. During this period, the Department of Justice and the federal banking agencies advocated divergent methods of dealing with the competitive aspects of bank mergers, the former urging the extension of Section 7 of the Clayton Act to cover such mergers and the latter supporting a regulatory scheme under which the effect of a bank merger on competition would be only one of the factors to be considered in determining whether the merger would be in the public interest. The Justice Department's proposals were repeatedly rejected by Congress, and the regulatory approach of the banking agencies was adopted in the Bank Merger Act of 1960. . . .

Sweeping aside the "design fashioned in the Bank Merger Act" as "predicated upon uncertainty as to the scope of Section 7" of the Clayton Act . . . , the Court today holds Section 7 to be applicable to bank mergers and concludes that it has been violated in this case. I respectfully submit that this holding, which sanctions a remedy regarded by Congress as inimical to the best interests of the banking industry and the public, and which will in large measure serve to frustrate the objectives of the Bank Merger Act, finds no justification in either the terms of the 1950 amendment of the Clayton Act or the history of the statute.

I

The key to this case is found in the special position occupied by commercial banking in the economy of this country. With respect to both the nature of the operations performed and the degree of governmental supervision involved, it is fundamentally different from ordinary manufacturing and mercantile businesses.

The unique powers of commercial banks to accept demand deposits, provide checking account services, and lend against fractional reserves permit the banking system as a whole to create a supply of "money," a function which is indispensable to the maintenance of the structure of our national economy. . . .

Deposit banking operations affect not only the volume of money and credit, but also the value of the dollar and the stability of the currency system. In this field, considerations other than simply the preservation of competition are relevant. Moreover, commercial banks are entrusted with the safekeeping of large amounts of funds belonging to individuals and corporations. Unlike the ordinary investor, these depositors do not regard their funds as subject to a risk of loss and, at least in the case of demand depositors, they do not receive a return for taking such a risk. A bank failure is a community disaster; its impact first strikes the bank's depositors most heavily, and then spreads throughout the economic life of the community. Safety and soundness of banking practices are thus critical factors in any banking system.

The extensive blanket of state and federal regulation of commercial banking, much of which is aimed at limiting competition, reflects these factors. Since the Court's opinion describes, at some length, aspects of the supervision exercised by the federal banking agencies . . . , I do no more here than point out that, in my opinion, such regulation evidences a plain design grounded on solid economic considerations to deal with banking as a specialized field.

This view is confirmed by the Bank Merger Act of 1960 and its history. . . .

Indeed the inapplicability to bank mergers of Section 7 of the Clayton Act, even after it was amended in 1950, was, for a time, an explicit premise on which the Department of Justice performed its antitrust duties. . . .

The inapplicability of Section 7 to bank mergers was also an explicit basis on which Congress acted in passing the Bank Merger Act of 1960. . . .

But instead of extending the scope of Section 7 to cover bank mergers, as numerous proposed amendments to that section were designed to accomplish, Congress made the deliberate policy judgment that "it is impossible to subject bank mergers to the simple rule of section 7 of the Clayton Act. Under that act, a merger would be barred if it might tend substantially to lessen competition, regardless of the effects on the public interest." . . . Because of the peculiar nature of the commercial banking industry, its crucial role in the economy, and its intimate connection with the fiscal and monetary operations of the Government, Congress rejected the notion that the general economic and business premises of the Clayton Act should be the only considerations applicable to this field. Unrestricted bank competition was thought to have been a major cause of the panic of 1907 and of the bank failures of the 1930's, and was regarded as a highly undesirable condition to impose on banks in the future. . . .

Thus the Committee on Banking and Currency recommended "continuance of the existing exemption from section 1 of the Clayton Act." . . . Congress accepted this recommendation; it decided to handle the problem of concentration in commercial banking "through banking laws, specially framed to fit the particular needs of the field. . . ." . . . As finally enacted in 1960, the Bank Merger Act embodies the regulatory approach advocated by the banking agencies, vesting in them responsibility for its administration and placing the scheme within the framework of existing banking laws. . . .

The congressional purpose clearly emerges from the terms of the statute and from the committee reports, hearings, and floor debates on the bills. Time and again it was repeated that effect on competition was *not to be the controlling factor* in determining whether to approve a bank merger, that a merger could be approved as being in the public interest even though it would cause a substantial lessening of competition. . . . [I]t was the congressional intention to place the responsibility for approval squarely on the banking agencies; the report of the Attorney General on the competitive aspects of a merger was to be advisory only. And there was deliberately omitted any attempt to specify or restrict the kinds of circumstances in which the agencies might properly determine that a proposed merger would be in the public interest notwithstanding its adverse effect on competition.

What Congress has chosen to do about mergers and their effect on competition in the highly specialized field of commercial banking could not be more "crystal clear." . . . But in the face of overwhelming evidence to the contrary, the Court, with perfect equanimity, finds "uncertainty" in the foundations of the Bank Merger Act . . . and on this premise puts it aside as irrelevant to the task of construing the scope of Section 7 of the Clayton Act.

I am unable to conceive of a more inappropriate case in which to overturn the considered opinion of all concerned as to the reach of prior legislation. For 10 years everyone—the department responsible for antitrust law enforcement, the banking industry, the Congress, and the bar—proceeded on the assumption that the 1950 amendment of the Clayton

Act did not affect bank mergers. This assumption provided a major impetus to the enactment of remedial legislation, and Congress, when it finally settled on what it thought was the solution to the problem at hand, emphatically rejected the remedy now brought to life by the Court.

The result is, of course, that the Bank Merger Act is almost completely nullified; its enactment turns out to have been an exorbitant waste of congressional time and energy. As the present case illustrates, the Attorney General's report to the designated banking agency is no longer truly advisory, for if the agency's decision is not satisfactory a Section 7 suit may be commenced immediately. The bank merger's legality will then be judged solely from its competitive aspects, unencumbered by any considerations peculiar to banking.[12] And if such a suit were deemed to lie after a bank merger has been consummated, there would then be introduced into this field, for the first time to any significant extent, the threat of divestiture of assets and all the complexities and disruption attendant upon the use of that sanction. The only vestige of the Bank Merger Act which remains is that the banking agencies will have an initial veto.

This frustration of a manifest congressional design is, in my view, a most unwarranted intrusion upon the legislative domain. I submit that *whatever* may have been the congressional purpose in 1950, Congress has now so plainly pronounced its current judgment that bank mergers are not within the reach of Section 7 that this Court is duty bound to effectuate its choice.

But I need not rest on this proposition, for, as will now be shown, there is nothing in the 1950 amendment to Section 7 or its legislative history to support the conclusion that Congress even then intended to subject bank mergers to this provision of the Clayton Act.

II

. . . . .

The legislative history of the 1950 amendment also unquestionably negates any inference that Congress intended to reach bank mergers. It is true that the purpose was "to plug a loophole" in Section 7. . . . But simply to state this broad proposition does not answer the precise questions presented here: what was the nature of the loophole sought to be closed; what were the means chosen to close it?

The answer to the latter question is unmistakably indicated by the relationship between the 1950 amendment and previous judicial decisions. . . .

. . . [T]he legislative history demonstrates that it was the asset-acquisi-

---

[12] Indeed the Court has erected a simple yardstick in order to alleviate the agony of analyzing economic data—control of 30% of a commercial banking market is prohibited. . . .

tion provision that was designed to plug the loophole created by *Thatcher, Swift,* and *Arrow.* . . .

I do not mean to suggest, of course, that Section 7 of the Clayton Act is thereby rendered applicable only to ordinary commercial and industrial corporations and not to firms in any "regulated" sector of the economy. . . . Rather, the absence of any mention of banks in the legislative history of the 1950 amendment, viewed in light of the prior congressional treatment of banking as a distinctive area with special characteristics and needs, compels the conclusion that bank mergers were simply not then regarded as part of the loophole to be plugged.

This conclusion is confirmed by a number of additional considerations. It was not until *after* the passage of the 1950 amendment of Section 7 that Representative Celler, its co-sponsor, requested the staff of the Antitrust Subcommittee of the House Committee on the Judiciary "to prepare a report indicating the concentration existing in our banking system." . . . It is also worth noting that in 1956 Representative Celler himself introduced another amendment to Section 7, explaining that "all the bill [H. R. 5948] does is plug a loophole in the present law dealing with bank mergers. . . . This loophole exists because section 7 of the Clayton Act prohibits bank mergers . . . only if such mergers are accomplished by stock acquisition." . . . The amendment passed the House but was defeated in the Senate.

For all these reasons, I think the conclusion is inescapable that Section 7 of the Clayton Act does not apply to the PNB-Girard merger. The Court's contrary conclusion seems to me little better than a *tour de force.*[13]

Memorandum of MR. JUSTICE GOLDBERG.

I agree fully with my Brother HARLAN that Section 7 of the Clayton Act has no application to bank mergers of the type involved here, and I therefore join in the conclusions expressed in his opinion on that point. However, while I thus dissent from the Court's holding with respect to the applicability of the Clayton Act to this merger, I wish to make clear that I do not necessarily dissent from its judgment invalidating the merger. To do so would require me to conclude in addition that on the record as it stands the government has failed to prove a violation of the Sherman Act, which is fully applicable to the commercial banking business. In my opinion there is a substantial Sherman Act issue in this case, but since the Court does not reach it and since my views relative thereto would be superfluous in light of today's disposition of the case, I express no ultimate conclusion concerning it. . . .

Note: In the case of *United States* v. *Phillipsburg National Bank and Trust Co.,* 399 U.S. 350 (1970), the principles set forth above were

---

[13] Since the Court does not reach the Sherman Act aspect of this case, it would serve no useful purpose for me to do so.

emphatically reaffirmed. Indeed, in a lengthy dissent, Justice Harlan declared that "[a]fter today's opinion the legality of every merger of two directly competing banks—no matter how small—is placed in doubt . . . ." (Id. at p. 374.)

United States v. El Paso Natural Gas Co.

376 U.S. 651 (1964)

Opinion of the Court by MR. JUSTICE DOUGLAS, announced by MR. JUSTICE CLARK.

This is a civil suit charging a violation of Section 7 of the Clayton Act, by reason of the acquisition of the stock and assets of Pacific Northwest Pipeline Corp. (Pacific Northwest) by El Paso Natural Gas Co. (El Paso). The District Court dismissed the complaint after trial, making findings of fact and conclusions of law, but not writing an opinion. The case is here on direct appeal. . . .

The ultimate issue revolves around the question whether the acquisition substantially lessened competition in the sale of natural gas in California—a market of which El Paso was the sole out-of-state supplier at the time of the acquisition.[1]

In 1954, Pacific Northwest received the approval of the Federal Power Commission to construct and operate a pipeline from the San Juan Basin, New Mexico, to the State of Washington, to supply gas to the then unserved Pacific Northwest area. Later it was authorized to receive large quantities of Canadian gas and to enlarge its system for that purpose. In addition, Pacific Northwest acquired Rocky Mountain reservoirs along its route. . . . By 1958 one-half of its natural gas sales were of gas from Canada.

In 1954 Pacific Northwest entered into two gas exchange contracts with El Paso. . . .

An executive of Pacific Northwest called these agreements a "treaty" to "solve the major problems which have been confronting us." A letter from Pacific Northwest to its stockholders stated:

This tri-party deal will benefit all concerned. It will give Westcoast[2] what they have been fighting for—a pipeline. It will mean that Pacific will expand its facilities, be a larger company, will protect its market from future competition by a Canadian pipeline and it caused the dismissal of the law suit of Westcoast against Pacific's present certificate. *It means that El Paso's California market will be protected against future competition*, and further it results in all parties *now working together for a common end rather than fighting each other.* (Italics added.)

---

[1] In 1956, El Paso supplied more than 50% of all gas consumed in the State, the remainder coming from intrastate sources.

[2] Westcoast Transmission Co., Ltd., a Canadian pipeline. IMS.

El Paso, however, could not get Commission approval to build the pipeline. . . . Consequently, a new agreement on that aspect was negotiated in 1955. . . . Pacific Northwest, still obligated to take 300 million cubic feet per day from Westcoast, disposed of the balance in its own market areas.

Prior to these 1954 and 1955 agreements Pacific Northwest had tried to enter the rapidly expanding California market. It prepared plans regarding the transportation of Canadian gas to California, where it was to be distributed by Pacific Gas & Electric (PGE). That effort—suspended when the 1954 agreements were made—was renewed when the new agreement with El Paso was made in 1955; and the negotiation of the 1955 contract with El Paso was conceived by Pacific Northwest as the occasion for "lifting of all restrictions on the growth of Pacific." In 1956 it indeed engaged in negotiations for the sale of natural gas to Southern California Edison Co. (Edison). The latter, largest industrial user of natural gas in Southern California, used El Paso gas, purchased through a distributor. It had, however, a low priority from that distributor, being on an "interruptible" basis, *i.e.*, subject to interruption during periods of peak demand for domestic uses. Edison wanted a firm contract and, upon being advised that it was El Paso's policy to sell only to distributors, started negotiations with Pacific Northwest in May 1956. The idea was for Pacific Northwest to deliver to Edison at a point on the California-Oregon border 300 million cubic feet of Canadian gas a day. In July 1956 they reached a tentative agreement. Edison thereupon tried to develop within California an integrated system for distributing Canadian gas supplied by Pacific Northwest to itself and others. El Paso decided to fight the plan to the last ditch, and succeeded in getting (through a distributor) a contract for Edison's needs. Edison's tentative agreement with Pacific Northwest was terminated. Before Edison terminated that agreement with Pacific Northwest, Edison had reached an agreement with El Paso for firm deliveries of gas; and while the original El Paso offer was 40¢ per Mcf, the price dropped to 38¢ per Mcf, then to 34¢ and finally to 30¢. Thereafter, and while the merger negotiations were pending, Pacific Northwest renewed its efforts to get its gas into California.

El Paso had been interested in acquiring Pacific Northwest since 1954. The first offer from El Paso was in December 1955—an offer Pacific Northwest rejected. Negotiations were resumed by El Paso in the summer of 1956, while Pacific Northwest was trying to obtain a California outlet. The exchange of El Paso shares for Pacific shares was accepted by Pacific Northwest's directors in November 1956, and by May 1957 El Paso had acquired 99.8% of Pacific Northwest's outstanding stock. In July 1957 the Department of Justice filed its suit charging that the acquisition violated Section 7 of the Clayton Act. In August 1957 El Paso applied to the Federal Power Commission for permission to acquire the assets of Pacific Northwest. On December 23, 1959, the Commission approved and the merger was effected on December 31, 1959. In 1962 we set aside the Commission's order, holding that it should not have acted until the District Court has passed on the Clayton Act issues. . . . Meanwhile (in October 1960) the United States amended its complaint so as to include the asset acquisition in the charged violation of the Clayton Act. . . . On review of the record—which is composed largely of undisputed evidence—we conclude that "the effect of such acquisition may be substantially to lessen competition" within the meaning of Section 7 of the Clayton Act.

There can be no doubt that the production, transportation, and sale of natural gas is a "line of commerce" within the meaning of Section 7. There can also be no doubt that California is a "section of the country" as that phrase is used in Section 7. The sole question, therefore, is whether on undisputed facts the acquisition had a sufficient tendency to lessen competition or is saved by the findings that Pacific Northwest, as an independent entity, could not have obtained a contract from the California distributors, could not have received the gas supplies or financing for a pipeline project to California, or could not have put together a project acceptable to the regulatory agencies. Those findings are irrelevant.

As we said in *Brown Shoe Co.* v. *United States* . . . : "Congress used the words '*may be* substantially to lessen competition' (emphasis supplied), to indicate that its concern was with probabilities, not certainties. Statutes existed for dealing with clear-cut menaces to competition; no statute was sought for dealing with ephemeral possibilities. Mergers with a probable anticompetitive effect were to be proscribed by this Act." See also *United States* v. *Philadelphia National Bank.* . . .

Pacific Northwest, though it had no pipeline into California, is shown by this record to have been a substantial factor in the California market at the time it was acquired by El Paso. At that time El Paso was the only actual supplier of out-of-state gas to the vast California market, *a market that expands at an estimated annual rate of 200 million cubic feet per day.* At that time Pacific Northwest was the only other important interstate pipeline west of the Rocky Mountains. Though young, it was prospering and appeared strong enough to warrant a "treaty" with El Paso that protected El Paso's California markets.

Edison's search for a firm supply of natural gas in California, when it had El Paso gas only on an "interruptible" basis, illustrates what effect Pacific Northwest had merely as a potential competitor in the California market. Edison took its problem to Pacific Northwest and, as we have seen, a tentative agreement was reached for Edison to obtain Pacific Northwest gas. El Paso responded, offering Edison a firm supply of gas and substantial price concessions. We would have to wear blinders not to see that the mere efforts of Pacific Northwest to get into the California market, though unsuccessful, had a powerful influence on El Paso's business attitudes within the State. We repeat that one purpose of Section

7 was "to arrest the trend toward concentration, the *tendency* to monopoly, before the consumer's alternatives disappeared through merger. . . ." *United States* v. *Philadelphia National Bank.* . . .

This is not a field where merchants are in a continuous daily struggle to hold old customers and to win new ones over from their rivals. In this regulated industry a natural gas company (unless it has excess capacity) must compete for, enter into, and then obtain Commission approval of sale contracts in advance of constructing the pipeline facilities. In the natural gas industry pipelines are very expensive; and to be justified they need long-term contracts for sale of the gas that will travel them. Those transactions with distributors are few in number. For example, in California there are only two significant wholesale purchasers—Pacific Gas & Electric in the north and the Southern Companies in the south. Once the Commission grants authorization to construct facilities or to transport gas in interstate commerce, once the distributing contracts are made, a particular market is withdrawn from competition. *The competition then is for the new increments of demand that may emerge with an expanding population and with an expanding industrial or household use of gas.*

The effect on competition in a particular market through acquisition of another company is determined by the nature or extent of that market and by the nearness of the absorbed company to it, that company's eagerness to enter that market, its resourcefulness, and so on. Pacific Northwest's position as a competitive factor in California was not disproved by the fact that it had never sold gas there. Nor is it conclusive that Pacific Northwest's attempt to sell to Edison failed. That might be weighty if a market presently saturated showed signs of petering out. But it is irrelevant in a market like California, where incremental needs are booming. That is underscored in the case by a memorandum dated October 18, 1956, which summarized a meeting at which terms of the acquisition were negotiated. It recited that Pacific Northwest had substantially concluded additional contracts for Canadian gas and that "Pacific plans on selling this additional volume of gas to the California market. . . ." On November 5, 1956, just three days prior to approval by the directors of Pacific Northwest of the stock exchange, it made a firm offer to PGE to supply up to 350 million cubic feet a day for 20 years. Even after that approval and before the actual exchange, the chief executive of Pacific Northwest, writing November 22, 1956, said: "I do not think for the present moment we should confuse the sale of gas from our system to California with El Paso taking part of the gas through their present system to California. Reason for this should the El Paso-Pacific deal collapse we would have nothing of substance with California."

Pacific Northwest had proximity to the California market. . . . Moreover, it had enormous reserves. . . . Had Pacific Northwest remained independent, there can be no doubt it would have sought to exploit its formidable geographical position *vis-à-vis* California. No one knows what success it would have had. We do know, however, that two interstate pipelines in addition to El Paso now serve California—one of the newcomers being Pacific Gas Transmission Co., bringing down Canadian gas. So we know that opportunities would have existed for Pacific Northwest had it remained independent.

Unsuccessful bidders are no less competitors than the successful one. The presence of two or more suppliers gives buyers a choice. Pacific Northwest was no feeble, failing company;[3] nor was it inexperienced and lacking in resourcefulness. It was one of two major interstate pipelines serving the trans-Rocky Mountain States; it had raised $250 million for its pipeline that extended 2,500 miles through rugged terrain. It had adequate reserves and managerial skill. It was so strong and militant that it was viewed with concern, and coveted, by El Paso. If El Paso can absorb Pacific Northwest without violating Section 7 of the Clayton Act, that section has no meaning in the natural gas field. For normally there is no competition—once the lines are built and the long-term contracts negotiated—except as respects the incremental needs.

Since appellees have been on notice of the antitrust charge from almost the beginning—indeed before El Paso sought Commission approval of the merger—we not only reverse the judgment below but direct the District Court to order divestiture without delay.[4]

Reversed.

MR. JUSTICE WHITE took no part in the consideration or decision of this case.

MR. JUSTICE HARLAN, concurring in part and dissenting in part.

I

. . . For reasons given in the Court's opinion, I agree that a violation of Section 7 of the Clayton Act has been established, and that the District Court erred in deciding otherwise. . . .

. . . This case affords another example of the unsatisfactoriness of the existing bifurcated system of antitrust and other regulation in various fields. In this case, the Federal Power Commission had indicated its approval of this merger as being in the public interest. The Department of Justice, however, considered the merger to be violative of the antitrust laws and, for that reason alone, against the public interest. This Court, under the present scheme of things has no choice on this record[5] but to sustain the position of the Department of Justice, as indeed it has felt constrained to do, albeit in my view with less justification, in other recent

---

[3] Cf. *International Shoe Co.* v. *Federal Trade Comm'n*, 280 U.S. 291.

[4] Cf. *Wisconsin* v. *Illinois*, 281 U.S. 179, 197.

[5] This Court has not had the benefit of an *amicus* brief from the Federal Power Commission.

cases involving dual regulation. Cf. *United States* v. *Philadelphia National Bank* . . . ; *United States* v. *First National Bank & Trust Co.*, decided today, . . . and my dissenting opinions in those cases. It would be unrealistic not to recognize that this state of affairs has the effect of placing the Department of Justice in the driver's seat even though Congress has lodged primary regulatory authority elsewhere.

It does seem to me that the time has come when this duplicative and, I venture to say, anachronistic system of dual regulation should be re-examined. Had the subtle and necessarily speculative questions involved in assessing the short-term and long-term effects of this merger been subject to appraisal by a single agency, under congressionally established standards marking the relationship between the different and often competing objectives of the antitrust laws and those governing the regulation of "interstate" natural gas, who can say that this case might not have called for a different outcome? . . .

Note: The *El Paso* case provides a graphic example of the problems involved in framing a workable divestiture decree. Despite nearly fifteen years of litigation, including four decisions by the Supreme Court, El Paso has yet to divest itself of Pacific Northwest.

Seaboard Air Line Railroad Co. v. *United States*

382 U.S. 154 (1965)

PER CURIAM. Atlantic Coast Line Railroad Company and Seaboard Air Line Railroad Company filed with the Interstate Commerce Commission an application for authority to merge. In the administrative proceedings, the applicants contended that the merger would enable them to lower operating costs, improve service, and eliminate duplicate facilities; other carriers opposed the merger on the ground that it would have adverse competitive effects; and the Department of Justice contended that the merger would create a rail monopoly in central and western Florida.

The Commission approved the merger, subject to routing and gateway conditions to protect competing railroads. It recognized that the merger would eliminate competition and create a rail monopoly in parts of Florida. But it found that the merged lines carried only a small part of the total traffic in the area involved; that ample rail competition would remain therein; and that the reduction in competition would "have no appreciably injurious effect upon shippers and communities." . . . In addition, the Commission noted that the need to preserve intramodal rail competition had diminished, due to the fact that railroads were increasingly losing traffic to truck, water, and other modes of competition.

A three-judge District Court set aside the order and remanded the case to the Commission for further proceedings. It concluded that the Commission's analysis of the competitive effects of the merger was fatally defective because the Commission had not determined whether the merger violated §7 of the Clayton Act . . . by reference to the relevant product and geographic markets. By thus disposing of the case, the District Court did not reach the ultimate question whether the merger would be consistent with the public interest despite the foreseeable injury to competition.

We believe that the District Court erred in its interpretation of the directions this Court set forth in *McLean Trucking Co.* v. *United States*, 321 U.S. 67 (1944), and *Minneapolis & St. Louis R. Co.* v. *United States*, 361 U.S. 173 (1959). As we said in *Minneapolis*, at 186:

> Although §5(11) does not authorize the Commission to "ignore" the antitrust laws, *McLean Trucking Co.* v. *United States*, 321 U. S. 67, 80, there can be "little doubt that the Commission is not to measure proposals for [acquisitions] by the standards of the antitrust laws." 321 U. S., at 85–86. The problem is one of accommodation of §5(2) and the antitrust legislation. The Commission remains obligated to "estimate the scope and appraise the effects of the curtailment of competition which will result from the proposed [acquisition] and consider them along with the advantages of improved service [and other matters in the public interest] to determine whether the [acquisition] will assist in effectuating the overall transportation policy." 321 U. S., at 87.

The same criteria should be applied here to the proposed merger. It matters not that the merger might otherwise violate the antitrust laws; the Commission has been authorized by the Congress to approve the merger of railroads if it makes adequate findings in accordance with the criteria quoted above that such a merger would be "consistent with the public interest." 54 Stat. 906, 49 U. S. C. Section 5 (2) (b) (1964 ed.).

Whether the Commission has confined itself within the statutory limits upon its discretion and has based its findings on substantial evidence are questions for the trial court in the first instance, *United States* v. *Great Northern R. Co.*, 343 U.S. 562, 578 (1952), and we indicate no opinion on the same. We therefore vacate the judgment of the District Court and remand the case to it for a full review of the administrative order and findings pursuant to the standards enunciated by this Court.

Vacated and remanded.

Thill Securities Corporation v. *The New York Stock Exchange*

433 F. 2d 264 (1970),
cert. denied, 401 U.S. 994 (1971)

CAMPBELL, District Judge.

The basic question presented here is whether stock-brokers who are members of the New York Stock Exchange should continue to enjoy their self-acquired freedom from competition by stock-brokers who are not members. Using the vehicle of Stock Exchange rules, members seem effectively to have negated the congressionally mandated principle of competition as it would otherwise apply to them.

The New York Stock Exchange ("Exchange") is the largest organized securities market in the United States. Its dominance of the securities industry is a well known and commonly accepted commercial and historical fact. It transacts well over 70 per-cent of the dollar value of all stock transactions on exchanges in the United States. . . . Its policies and practices have an ever increasing effect on our economy.

By the Exchange's Constitution, its membership is limited to 1366 members. In 1969 a membership sold for the record price of $515,000. . . .

The Exchange is governed by a 33 man Board, consisting of 29 members elected by the membership and a president and 3 governors who are to represent the public view and who are elected by the Board. The economic power of the Exchange and its members extends well beyond the operations of the Exchange itself. . . .

In many respects the Exchange has been delegated governmental authority. Its counsel describes it as a "unique self regulator." Under the Securities Exchange Act of 1934 (15 U.S.C. §78a . . .) it may adopt its own constitution and rules, and discipline violations thereof. The Securities Exchange Commission ("SEC") has the power, however, to order changes in Exchange rules respecting a number of subjects, set forth in section 19(b) of the Act.[1] 15 U.S.C. §78s(b). Except for the limited review authority of the SEC, the Exchange's economic power in the securities field appears complete and absolute.

Plaintiff Thill Securities Corporation, ("Thill") is a licensed securities dealer-broker, registered with the Securities and Exchange Commission, and a member in good standing of the National Association of Securities Dealers, Inc., but is not a member of the New York Stock Exchange. . . . In its complaint Thill charges the Exchange with substantial anti-competitive conduct in violation of the antitrust laws of the United States. Sherman Antitrust Act, §1 and §2 . . . and Clayton Act, §4. . . . Specifically, Thill charges that the Exchange has engaged in an unlawful and unreasonable combination and conspiracy in restraint of interstate trade and commerce and has unlawfully and unreasonably monopolized the securities market in the United States by among other things adopting, subscribing and adhering to a rule which prohibits any member of the Exchange from sharing any commission earned from the purchase or sale of securities with a non-member, even though the non-member may have furnished the order; and by discriminately discouraging customers and prospective customers of Thill and other non-members from doing business with non-members.

[1] There appears to be considerable doubt that the SEC has power to alter, amend or supplement Exchange rules dealing with any subject not specifically enumerated in section 19(b). See, Bicks, "Antitrust And The New York Stock Exchange," 21 *Bus. Lawy.* 129, 137 n. 42 (1965).

Thill alleges that as a proximate result of the unlawful and monopolistic rules and practices of the Exchange, it and other non-members of the Exchange are totally deprived of commissions or other fair compensation on transactions which they have initiated and serviced. It further alleges that the intended, necessary and actual effect of this unlawful conduct is to restrain trade by preventing any competition by and between members of the Exchange and non-member securities dealers and brokers. Thill alleges to have suffered damages in the amount of seven million dollars, for which it seeks treble damages ($21,000,000) under the antitrust laws. It also seeks a declaratory judgment that the Exchange's prohibition against sharing of commissions constitutes a violation of the antitrust laws; and an injunction prohibiting the Exchange from enforcing the prohibition. Subsequent to the filing of this action, Thill Securities Corporation went out of business.

The defendant Exchange does not contest the anti-competitive effects of its rule prohibiting the sharing of commissions—sometimes referred to as the antirebate rule. At oral argument its counsel admitted, as is obvious, that the conduct complained of would constitute a violation of the antitrust laws, were those statutes applicable to the activities of the Exchange in this case. Its position is that the Sherman Act does not apply to the rule of the Exchange prohibiting the sharing of commissions by members with non-members. It contends that this broad immunity is enjoyed by virtue of the Securities Exchange Act of 1934 . . . which authorizes registered national securities exchanges to adopt rules in respect to the "fixing of reasonable rates of commission" subject to review and revision by the Securities Exchange Commission under section 19(b) of the Act. . . . It also contends that the SEC has and is exercising exclusive review jurisdiction over such rules of the Exchange, and that its conduct is thus immune from antitrust liability. This immunity, in its view, extends beyond the "fixing of reasonable rates of commission" and includes rules relating to the "sharing" of commissions, because the prohibition against sharing of commission with non-member broker dealers is an integral part of the "fixing of reasonable rates."

The district court essentially agreed with the position taken by the Exchange. . . .

In our consideration of the issues presented in this appeal we must begin with the teachings of the Supreme Court in *Silver* v. *New York Stock Exchange*, 373 U.S. 341 . . . (1963). . . . [T]he Supreme Court soundly rejected any notion that the Exchange enjoyed blanket immunity from the enforcement of the antitrust laws simply because its activities were to a certain extent subject to the regulatory provisions of the Securities Exchange Act. On the contrary, the Court concluded that the proper approach is an *analysis* which reconciles the operation of both statutory schemes (the antitrust laws and the Securities Exchange Act) with one another rather than holding one completely ousted. In undertaking the analysis to attempt to reconcile the two statutes, courts were admonished that repeal or ouster of antitrust laws is not favored. . . .

Despite these admonitions the Exchange argues, as the court below concluded, that the antitrust court's analysis ends once it is determined that the conduct complained of, here the antirebate rule, is subject to potential review by the SEC under section 19(b).

. . . We disagree. . . . In our view, *Silver* teaches that a reconciliation of the two statutory schemes is not foreclosed simply because the Securities Act and the review jurisdiction of the SEC may touch upon the activity challenged under the antitrust laws. As the Court in *Silver* pointed out, the New York Stock Exchange's constitution and rules are permeated with instances of regulation of member relationships with non-members. . . . That general power to adopt rules relating to the relations of its members with non-members, however, does not in and of itself place the application of such rules outside the reach of the antitrust laws. Rather it is at this point that the analysis of reconciliation really begins.

Before the investing public of the United States may be deprived of the benefit of competition through the vehicle of Exchange rules, it must be established that the Exchange's exemption from the antitrust laws is necessary to discharge its responsibilities under the Securities Exchange Act. See Baxter, "NYSE Fixed Commission Rates: A Private Cartel Goes Public," 22 *Stan L. Rev.* 675, 689 (1970); Nerenberg, "Applicability of the Antitrust Laws to the Securities Field," 16 *West. Res. L. Rev.* 131 (1964); Johnson, "Application Of Antitrust Laws To The Securities Industry," 20 *S.W.L.J.* 536 (1966); "Comments of the United States Department of Justice, filed before the Securities Exchange Commission Inquiry into New York Stock Exchange Proposals to Permit Public Ownership of Member Corporations," *SEC release No. 8717*. In short, its exemption must be based on a showing of true necessity. As applicable here, it must be established that subjecting the antirebate rule to antitrust attack will frustrate the purpose of the Securities Exchange Act or make it substantially ineffective. . . .

In the record before us there is no evidence, save for the allegations of plaintiff, as to the effects of the anti-competitive conduct complained of; there is no evidence as to the extent to which the challenged rule is subject to actual review by the SEC; there is no evidence as to what in the regulatory scheme "performs the antitrust function"; and, most notably, there is no evidence as to why the antirebate rule must be preserved as "necessary to make the Securities Exchange Act work." In sum, this record falls woefully short of the meticulous analysis called for in *Silver*. . . .

As we observed above, there is no evidence in the record that the SEC is exercising actual and adequate review jurisdiction under the Act. Furthermore, even the fact that the SEC may be exercising its proper supervisory power over the rules of the Exchange does not in and of itself cloak the Exchange with antitrust immunity for its conduct relating to those rules.

Of course it is not disputed that in exercising its review power under section 19(b), the SEC, like other regulatory agencies, may weigh and consider antitrust factors. . . .

But, that fact does not vest the Commission with primary responsibility for the enforcement of competition as mandated by Congress in the antitrust laws. . . . [The] cases, particularly the *Philadelphia National Bank* case, squarely reject the Exchange's contention that the court's inquiry must end once it is established that its rules were adopted pursuant to its duty of self regulation under the 1934 Act and are subject to SEC review. . . .

In our view the facts here are much stronger in favor of application of the antitrust laws than were those in the *Philadelphia Bank* case. In reviewing the rules of the Exchange the SEC is not required to consider their effect upon competition. On the contrary, its history in reviewing rules adopted by the Exchange indicates a reluctance to do so. It has been suggested that the SEC has never, "forcibly altered an Exchange's commission rate structure, and there is little to indicate that it has even thoroughly investigated proposed rate revisions". Note: Monopolies—Immunity From Antitrust Liability—Minimum Commission Rates Of Stock Exchanges, 19 *Case Wes. Res. L. Rev.* 167, 173 (1967). . . . [T]he underlying data used by the SEC in reviewing each of the five rate increases since 1934 have been essentially those supplied by the Exchange, and have been very limited in scope and content. . . .

Legal writers have also been critical of the SEC's passive supervision of the Exchange. One has described the SEC as a "tame watchdog," as a result of which "self-regulation has come to mean, at least to the industry and particularly to the New York Stock Exchange, that the SEC will observe a rather passive role, leaving the industry to govern itself in its own wisdom." Jennings, Self-Regulation in the Securities Industry; The Role of the Securities and Exchange Commission, 29 *Law and Contemp. Prob.* 663, 664–5 (1964). See also, Note: Antitrust And The Stock Exchange, Minimum Commission or Free Competition, 18 *Stan. L. Rev.* 213 (1965).

Parenthetically, and by way of expressing our agreement with the Supreme Court's policy of strictly limiting all antitrust exemptions in deference to regulatory bodies, we also note that the history of United States regulatory agencies in general seems usually to record an ever growing absence of the spirit required for vigorous enforcement of the antitrust laws. Rather, it seems to demonstrate that shortly following the establishment of administrative procedures the regulatory agency usually becomes dominated by the industry which it was created to regulate.

Perhaps Congress had this possibility in mind when it strictly limited the powers of the regulatory agencies to enforce the antitrust laws. . . .

In remanding this cause to the district court where this inquiry may be pursued, we think it appropriate to note certain observations that have occurred to us in reviewing the record and in considering the arguments of both parties in this complex case.

Most important, before a court may abdicate its jurisdiction on the antitrust issue the defendant must establish its anticompetitive conduct as justified because it is necessary for the operation of the Securities Act.

We . . . offer the further suggestion that it seems particularly appropriate in a case of this nature for the court to invite the participation, by way of expert testimony and legal argument, of the government agencies so vitally interested in the issues before the court—the SEC and the Department of Justice.

We make the further observation, without prejudging the issue, that it is difficult to conceive how the Exchange can on remand argue that the antirebate rule is "necessary to make the Act work" when its members have gone to imaginative extremes to circumvent the rule when it serves their private economic purposes to do so. It appears from all we can read on the subject that the rule is honored much more in its breach than in its observance, as through various devices, member firms routinely share commissions or the equivalent with favored non-member brokers. . . .

It is also important to note that other national stock exchanges manage to make the Act work without need of the antirebate rule.

Finally, and apart from the antirebate rule, the complaint below raised additional issues which were not considered by the district court when it granted defendant's motion for summary judgment. Specifically, Thill alleges that the Exchange has engaged in unfair advertising practices aimed at undermining public confidence in the competence and reliability of non-member broker-dealers. It also alleges that members, through the benefit of the antirebate rule, pirate customers of non-members by assuring them that they can operate less costly than non-members because the non-member must tack on some commission for his services. Such allegations of predatory practices in such a vital industry clearly require more than summary dismissal and should be fully considered on remand.

Accordingly, the cause is reversed and remanded to the district court for full proceedings consistent with the conclusions herein.

[Chief Judge Swygert concurred.]

Pell, Circuit Judge (concurring in part and dissenting in part).

While I concur in the majority's determination to remand this cause for further proceedings, I find it necessary . . . to dissent [in part]. . . .

I . . . must respectfully question the majority's observation regarding lack of diligence on the part of regulatory agencies enforcing antitrust laws and succumbing to the domination of the industry which they were created to regulate. If it be a fact that there is an apparent lack of diligence this may consciously have been a result reached in balancing diverse public interests. However that may be, I do not have any basis in fact on which to concur in the observation. . . .

PART VI

Legal Monopolies and Antitrust

Chapter 14

PATENTS—THE RIGHT AND ITS LIMITS

Our patent laws are predicated upon the assumption that progress in the sciences and in the useful arts will best be promoted by granting to the inventor a legal monopoly of his discovery. Thus, in a sense, the patent laws may be viewed as exceptions to our antitrust policy of preserving competition. In another sense, however, the patent laws appear as instruments which are designed to accelerate technological progress by granting short-term monopoly privileges as offsets to the risks involved in introducing a new product or process; i.e., they may stimulate competition in the long-run, Schumpeterian sense of that word. In any event, conflict between the patent and antitrust laws has arisen only when the holder of the patent right is deemed to overstep the bounds of his lawful monopoly in an attempt to suppress competition. This may occur when, as in the *Hartford-Empire* case, patent cross-licensing is used, not to promote competition by making technological information more widely available in the industry, but to monopolize an entire industry. A patentee may also violate the antitrust laws when, as in the *International Salt* case, he uses the patent monopoly as a lever to gain dominance in another and totally different market.

Current trends appear to favor giving antitrust criteria greater weight than the standards of the patent statutes whenever the two conflict with one another. Thus, while the *General Electric* case held that a patentee could attach terms and conditions to the grant of a patent license, that right has since been significantly diluted. In *Hartford-Empire*, for example, the Supreme Court appeared to say that what a single patentee could do, two or more patentees, acting through a cross-licensing agreement, could not. Further, in *Lear* v. *Adkins*, the Court struck down a provision in a licensing agreement whereby a licensee agreed not to challenge the validity of the patent so licensed.

These cases provide at least a partial understanding of the varied and complex public policy issues involved in antitrust suits of this type. In addition, the *Hartford-Empire* case illustrates perhaps more clearly than any other in this general area the problem of framing an adequate decree

—one which prevents future antitrust violations without unnecessarily impinging on the patent right.

United States v. General Electric Company

272 U.S. 476 (1926)

Mr. Chief Justice Taft delivered the opinion of the Court.

This is a bill in equity brought by the United States in the District Court for the Northern District of Ohio to enjoin the General Electric Company, the Westinghouse Electric and Manufacturing Company, and the Westinghouse Lamp Company from further violation of the Anti-Trust Act of July 2, 1890. . . . The bill made two charges, one that the General Electric Company in its business of making and selling incandescent electric lights had devised and was carrying out a plan for their distribution throughout the United States by a number of so-called agents, exceeding 21,000, to restrain interstate trade in such lamps and to exercise a monopoly of the sale thereof; and, second, that it was achieving the same illegal purpose through a contract of license with the defendants, the Westinghouse Electric and Manufacturing Company and the Westinghouse Lamp Company.[1] . . .

The second question in the case involves the validity of a license granted March 1, 1912, by the Electric Company to the Westinghouse Company to make, use and sell lamps under the patents owned by the former. It was charged that the license in effect provided that the Westinghouse Company would follow prices and terms of sales from time to time fixed by the Electric Company and observed by it, and that the Westinghouse Company would, with regard to lamps manufactured by it under the license, adopt and maintain the same conditions of sale as observed by the Electric Company in the distribution of lamps manufactured by it. . . .

The Electric Company is the owner of . . . patents . . . [which] cover completely the making of the modern electric lights with the tungsten filaments, and secure to the Electric Company the monopoly of their making, using and vending.

The total business in electric lights for the year 1921 was $68,300,000, and the relative percentages of business done by the companies were, Electric 69 percent, Westinghouse, 16 percent, other licensees, 8 percent, and manufacturers not licensed, 7 percent.

. . . . .

. . . Had the Electric Company, as the owner of the patents entirely controlling the manufacture, use and sale of the tungsten incandescent

---

[1] For present purposes we focus upon the second of the two charges; the first raises issues that are peripheral to the subject of this chapter. IMS.

lamps, in its license to the Westinghouse Company, the right to impose the condition that its sales should be at prices fixed by the licensor and subject to change according to its discretion? . . .

The owner of a patent may assign it to another and convey, (1) the exclusive right to make, use and vend the invention throughout the United States, or, (2) an undivided part or share of that exclusive right, or (3) the exclusive right under the patent within and through a specific part of the United States. But any assignment or transfer short of one of these is a license, giving the licensee no title in the patent and no right to sue at law in his own name for an infringement. . . . Conveying less than title to the patent, or part of it, the patentee may grant a license to make, use and vend articles under the specifications of his patent for any royalty or upon any condition the performance of which is reasonably within the reward which the patentee by the grant of the patent is entitled to secure. It is well settled, . . . that where a patentee makes the patented article and sells it, he can exercise no future control over what the purchaser may wish to do with the article after his purchase. It has passed beyond the scope of the patentee's rights. . . . But the question is a different one which arises when we consider what a patentee who grants a license to one to make and vend the patented article may do in limiting the licensee in the exercise of the right to sell. The patentee may make and grant a license to another to make and use the patented articles, but withhold his right to sell them. The licensee in such a case acquires an interest in the articles made. He owns the material of them and may use them. But if he sells them, he infringes the right of the patentee, and may be held for damages and enjoined. If the patentee goes further, and licenses the selling of the articles, may he limit the selling by limiting the method of sale and the price? We think he may do so, provided the conditions of sale are normally and reasonably adapted to secure pecuniary reward for the patentee's monopoly. One of the valuable elements of the exclusive right of a patentee is to acquire profit by the price at which the article is sold. The higher the price, the greater the profit, unless it is prohibitory. When the patentee licenses another to make and vend, and retains the right to continue to make and vend on his own account, the price at which his licensee will sell will necessarily affect the price at which he can sell his own patented goods. It would seem entirely reasonable that he should say to the licensee, "Yes, you may make and sell articles under my patent, but not so as to destroy the profit that I wish to obtain by making them and selling them myself." He does not thereby sell outright to the licensee the articles the latter may make and sell, or vest absolute ownership in them. He restricts the property and interest the licensee has in the goods he makes and proposes to sell.

[Mr. Justice Taft then reviewed several earlier cases, including those which involved the setting of prices of unpatented materials used in conjunction with a patented article. He concluded that they were not relevant to the present case since "[the] price at which a patented article sells is certainly a circumstance having a more direct relation, and is more germane to the rights of the patentee, than the unpatented material with which the patented article may be used. Indeed, . . . price fixing is usually the essence of that which secures proper reward to the patentee."]

Nor do we think that the decisions of this Court holding restrictions as to price of patented articles invalid, apply to a contract of license like the one in this case. . . . These cases really are only instances of the application of the principle of *Adams* v. *Burke*, 17 Wall. 453, 456, . . . that a patentee may not attach to the article made by him, or with his consent, a condition running with the article in the hands of purchasers, limiting the price at which one who becomes its owner for full consideration shall part with it. They do not consider or condemn a restriction put by a patentee upon his licenses as to the prices at which the latter shall sell articles which he makes and only can make legally under the license. . . .

For the reasons given, we sustain the validity of the license granted by the Electric Company to the Westinghouse Company. The decree of the District Court dismissing the bill is

Affirmed.

Hartford-Empire Company v. United States

323 U.S. 386 (1945)

MR. JUSTICE ROBERTS delivered the opinion of the Court.

These are appeals from a decree awarding an injunction against violations of Sections 1 and 2 of the Sherman Act, as amended, and Section 3 of the Clayton Act. Two questions are presented. Were violations proved? If so, are the provisions of the decree right?

The complaint named as defendants . . . the leaders in automatic glassmaking machinery and in the glassware industry. The charge is that all the defendants agreed, conspired, and combined to monopolize, and did monopolize and restrain interstate and foreign commerce by acquiring patents covering the manufacture of glassmaking machinery, and by excluding others from a fair opportunity freely to engage in commerce in such machinery and in the manufacture and distribution of glass products. The gravamen of the case is that the defendants have cooperated in obtaining and licensing patents covering glassmaking machinery, have limited and restricted the use of the patented machinery by a network of agreements, and have maintained prices for unpatented glassware. . . .

In 1919 the Glass Container Association of America was formed. . . . The court below, on sufficient evidence, has found that the association, through its statistical committee, assigned production quotas to its members and that they and Hartford were zealous in seeing that these were observed.

In summary, the situation brought about in the glass industry, and existing in 1938, was this: Hartford, with the technical and financial aid of others in the conspiracy, had acquired, by issue to it or assignment from the owners, more than 600 patents. These, with over 100 Corning controlled patents, over 60 Owens patents, over 70 Hazel patents, and some 12 Lynch patents, had been, by cross-licensing agreements, merged into a pool which effectually controlled the industry. This control was exercised to allot production in Corning's field[1] to Corning, and that in restricted classes within the general container field to Owens, Hazel, Thatcher, Ball, and such other smaller manufacturers as the group agreed should be licensed. The result was that 94% of the glass containers manufactured in this country on feeders and formers were made on machinery licensed under the pooled patents.

The District Court found that invention of glassmaking machinery had been discouraged, that competition in the manufacture and sale or licensing of such machinery had been suppressed, and that the system of restricted licensing had been employed to suppress competition in the manufacture of unpatented glassware and to maintain prices of the manufactured product. The findings are full and adequate and are supported by evidence, much of it contemporary writings of corporate defendants or their officers and agents. . . .

We affirm the District Court's findings and conclusions that the corporate appellants combined in violation of the Sherman Act, that Hartford and Lynch contracted in violation of the Clayton Act, and that the individual appellants with exceptions to be noted participated in the violations in their capacities as officers and directors of the corporations. . . .

I. Little need be said concerning the legal principles which vindicate the District Court's findings and conclusions. . . .

. . . It is clear that, by cooperative arrangements and binding agreements, the appellant corporations, over a period of years, regulated and suppressed competition in the use of glassmaking machinery and employed their joint patent position to allocate fields of manufacture and to maintain prices of unpatented glassware.

The explanations offered by the appellants are unconvincing. It is said, on behalf of Hartford, that its business, in its inception, was lawful and within the patent laws; and that, in order to protect its legitimate interests as holder of patents for automatic glass machinery, it was justified in buying up and fencing off improvement patents, the grant of which, while leaving the fundamental inventions untouched, would hamper their use unless tribute were paid to the owners of the so-called improvements which, of themselves, had only a nuisance value.

The explanation fails to account for the offensive and defensive alliance

[1] The pressed and blown glass, or noncontainer field. IMS.

of patent owners with its concomitant stifling of initiative, invention, and competition.

Nor can Owens' contention prevail that it long ago abandoned any cooperation with the other corporate defendants and has been free of any trammel to unrestricted competition either in the machinery or glass field. Owens remained active in the association. It remained dominant in the suction field. It continued in close touch with Hartford and with other large manufacturers of glassware who were parties to the conspiracy. The District Court was justified in finding that the mere cancellation of the written word was not enough, in the light of subsequent conduct, to acquit Owens of further participation in the conspiracy. . . .

II. The Government sought the dissolution of Hartford. The court, however, decided that a continuance of certain of Hartford's activities would be of advantage to the glass industry and denied, for the time being, that form of relief. The court was of opinion, however, that the long series of transactions and the persistent manifestations of a purpose to violate the antitrust statutes required the entry of a decree which would preclude the resumption of unlawful practices. It was faced, therefore, with the difficult problem of awarding an injunction which would insure the desired end without imposing punishments or other sanctions for past misconduct, a problem especially difficult in view of the status and relationship of the parties.

At the trial the Government stated that in this suit it was not attacking the validity of any patent or claiming any patent had been awarded an improper priority.

At the time of the District Court's decision, Hartford had reduced the royalties of all its licensees to its then schedule of standard royalties so that all stood on an equal basis so far as license fees were concerned. Government counsel did not assert, or attempt to prove, that these royalties were not reasonable in amount.

Owens, as respects suction invention licenses, had removed all restrictive clauses; Hartford had done the same with respect to all its glass machinery licenses and so had Hartford and Lynch with respect to forming machine licenses. . . .

The association had ceased to allot quotas amongst the glass manufacturers or to furnish advance information or make recommendations to its members. The licensing system of Hartford remained that of leasing machinery built for it embodying the patented inventions. Rentals consisted of standard royalties on production. Under this system Hartford rendered a service in the repair, maintenance, and protection of the machines, which is valuable, if not essential, to the users. This was the status with which the court had to deal.

The applicable principals are not doubtful. The Sherman Act provides criminal penalties for its violation, and authorizes the recovery of a penal sum in addition to damages in a civil suit by one injured by violation. It also authorizes an injunction to prevent continuing violations by those acting contrary to its proscriptions. The present suit is in the last named category and we may not impose penalties in the guise of preventing future violations. This is not to say that a decree need deal only with the exact type of acts found to have been committed or that the court should not, in framing its decree, resolve all doubts in favor of the Government, or may not prohibit acts which in another setting would be unobjectionable. But, even so, the court may not create, as to the defendants, new duties, prescription of which is the function of Congress, or place the defendants, for the future, "in a different class than other people," as the Government has suggested. The decree must not be "so vague as to put the whole conduct of the defendants' business at the peril of a summons for contempt"; enjoin "all possible breaches of the law"; or cause the defendants hereafter not "to be under the protection of the law of the land." With these principles in mind we proceed to examine the terms of the decree entered. . . .

The court appointed a receiver for Hartford *pendente lite*. By paragraphs 10 to 20 of the final decree it continued him in office and gave directions as to his administration of Hartford's affairs, including certain actions to be taken to effectuate features of the decree affecting Hartford's business and licenses, which will later be described, and meantime to continue the receipt of royalties under existing licenses, these to be repaid to the licensees on the decree becoming final. . . .

. . . [T]he receivership and the impounding of funds were not necessary to the prescription of appropriate relief. The receivership should be wound up and the business returned to Hartford. The royalties paid to the receiver by Hartford's lessees may, unless the District Court finds that Hartford has, since the entry of the receivership decree, violated the antitrust laws, or acted contrary to the terms of the final decree as modified by this opinion, be paid over to Hartford. . . .

Paragraphs 21, 22, and 23 . . . forbid any disposition or transfer of possession of such machinery by any means other than an outright sale, and require Hartford to offer in writing to sell each of the present lessees all the machinery now under lease to such lessee at a reasonable price. . . .

All of the appellants attack these provisions. . . .

. . . The Government replies that the injunction is intended only to prevent them from again setting up a patent pool and monopolizing the patented inventions. . . . But the decree as entered requires that each of the defendants must hereafter forever abstain from leasing a patented machine, no matter what the date of the invention, and compels each of them if he desires to distribute patented machinery to sell the machine which embodies the patent to everyone who applies, at a price to be fixed by the court. The injunction as drawn is not directed at any combination, agreement or conspiracy. It binds every defendant forever irrespective of his connection with any other or of the independence of his action. . . .

[Paragraph 24 requires defendants to license all present and future patents on a royalty-free basis.]

Since the provisions of paragraphs 21 to 24 inclusive, in effect confiscate considerable portions of the appellants' property, we think they go beyond what is required to dissolve the combination and prevent future combinations of like character. It is to be borne in mind that the Government has not, in this litigation, attacked the validity of any patent or the priority ascribed to any by the Patent Office, nor has it attacked, as excessive or unreasonable, the standard royalties heretofore exacted by Hartford. Hartford has reduced all of its royalties to a uniform scale and has waived and abolished and agreed to waive and abolish all restrictions and limitations in its outstanding leases so that every licensee shall be at liberty to use the machinery for the manufacture of any kind or quantity of glassware comprehended within the decree. Moreover, if licenses or assignments by any one of the corporate defendants to any other still contain any offensive provision, such provision can, by appropriate injunction, be cancelled, so that the owner of each patent will have unrestricted freedom to use and to license, and every licensee equally with every other will be free of restriction as to the use of the leased or licensed machinery, method or process, or the articles manufactured thereon or thereunder.

It is suggested that there is not confiscation since Hartford might, with the later consent of the court, sell its patents. Under the decree as entered below nothing can be obtained by Hartford for the use of its patents and we cannot speculate as to what might be the ultimate adjustments made by the trial court in the decree.

If, as suggested, some of Hartford's patents were improperly obtained, or if some of them were awarded a priority to which the invention was not entitled, avenues are open to the Government to raise these questions and to have the patents cancelled. But if, as we must assume on this record, a defendant owns valid patents, it is difficult to say that, however much in the past such defendant has abused the rights thereby conferred, it must now dedicate them to the public.

That a patent is property, protected against appropriation both by individuals and by government, has long been settled. In recognition of this quality of a patent the courts, in enjoining violations of the Sherman Act arising from the use of patent licenses, agreements, and leases, have abstained from action which amounted to a forfeiture of the patents. . . .

Since paragraphs 21 to 24(*a*) inclusive are to be eliminated, this paragraph, which is ancillary to them, should also be deleted from the decree, but in view of the nature of the conspiracy found, an injunction should go against the further prosecution of all infringement suits pending at the date this suit was brought. Hartford and the other corporate defendants mentioned in paragraph 24 should be required to lease or license glass making machinery of the classes each now manufactures to any who may desire to take licenses, (under patents on such machinery or on improvements, methods or processes applicable thereto), at standard royalties and without discrimination or restriction, and if at the time of entry of the decree there are any alleged infringers who are willing to take such licenses they should be released, and the patent owner deprived of all damages and profits which it might have claimed for past infringement. The decree should, however, be without prejudice to the future institution of any suit or suits for asserted infringements against persons refusing to take licenses under any of the presently licensed inventions arising out of their use after the date of the decree. The decree should not forbid any defendant from seeking recovery for infringement, occurring after the date of the final decree, of patents not covering feeders, formers, stackers, lehrs, or processes or methods applicable to any of them.

Paragraph 27 cancels all outstanding agreements between corporate appellants. . . .

In view of what we have already said about these earlier paragraphs, the license agreements as modified by the parties and in accordance with the views here expressed, should be allowed to stand. . . .

Paragraph 28 orders cancellation of all Hartford machinery leases now outstanding and requires that each lessee be offered a new license (without royalty, pursuant to paragraph 24) and offered the right to purchase all of the machinery now held under lease (as required by paragraph 23). In view of what has been said this provision should not stand.

Paragraph 29 enjoins the insertion or enforcement of any provision in any agreement heretofore or hereafter made by any of the appellants which (*a*) directly or indirectly limits or restricts (1) the type or kind of product, whether glassware or any other, which can be produced on machines or equipment or by processes embodying inventions licensed under patents or patent applications, (2) the use of the product so produced, (3) the character, weight, color, capacity, or composition of the product, (4) the quantity, (5) the market, either as to territory or customers in or to which the product may be sold or distributed, (6) the price or terms of sale or other disposition of the product, or (7) the use of the machinery or equipment distributed or the inventions licensed in connection with any other machinery or equipment, or the use of it in any specified plant or locality; (*b*) authorizes termination of the license for unauthorized use; (*c*) provides that the licensee shall not contest the validity of any patent or patents of the licensor; (*d*) provides that improvements by the licensee on machinery leased and sold shall become the property of the lessor; (*e*) provides that rights to improvements and inventions covering licensed machinery or processes or methods shall become the exclusive property of the lessor or vendor; or (*f*) grants to any licensee a preferential position by lower rates of royalty, by different provisions of licensing, leasing, or sale, by exclusive licensing, rebate, discounts or requiring a share in net or gross income, or by any other means.

The paragraph now covers every kind of invention and every patent, present or future, in any field if owned or controlled or distributed by an appellant.

The injunction will stop all inventions or acquirement of patents in any field by any appellant unless for its own use in its business, for it sets such limitations upon the reward of a patent as to make it practically worthless except for use by the owner. It is unlimited in time. It is not limited to any joint action or conspiracy violative of the antitrust laws; it covers inventions in every conceivable field.

The Government now agrees that this injunction should be limited to glassmaking machinery and glassware as defined in paragraph 1 of the decree of the District Court. . . .

Paragraph 31 requires court approval of "any agreement between any of the defendants" and "of any license agreement made pursuant to this judgment." This is too sweeping. The provision is without limit of time and not terminable upon fulfilment of any condition. . . . This paragraph, if retained, should be restricted in application to lease or license agreements and agreements respecting patents and trade practices, production and trade relations.

By paragraph 33 each of the individual defendants is enjoined from "holding, controlling, directly or indirectly, or through corporations, agents, trustees, representatives, or nominees, any of the issued and outstanding capital stock, bonds, or other evidences of indebtedness of more than one corporation engaged either in the manufacture and sale of glassware or in the manufacture or distribution of machinery used in the manufacture of glassware or in both. . . ." . . . The purpose of dealing with stock ownership is to prevent aggregation of control to the end of establishing a monopoly or stifling competition. The ownership of a few, or even a few hundred, shares of stock of a glass manufacturing company not in competition with the company of which a defendant happens to be a director or officer can have no tendency towards such a result. . . .

Moreover, the injunction is against ownership of bonds of any such company. It is difficult to see how such ownership in any reasonable amount by any of the individuals in question could tend towards a violation of the Sherman Act. . . .

The decree should be modified to prohibit acquisition of stocks or bonds of any corporate appellant by any other such appellant, and to prohibit only the acquisition of a measure of control through ownership of stocks or bonds or otherwise, by any individual in a company competing with that with which he is officially connected or a subsidiary or affiliate of such competing company. . . .

Paragraphs 37 to 39 are directed at the Glass Container Association. . . .

The injunctions entered in paragraphs 37 to 39, inclusive, compel the association to abolish its statistical committee and to refrain from establishing any committee with similar functions. . . .

We think the injunction as respects the association, while leaving it in existence, practically destroys its functioning, even as an innocent trade association for what have been held lawful ends. The association has undoubtedly been an important instrument of restraint and monopoly. It may be made such again, and detection and prevention and punishment for such resumption of violations of law may be difficult if not impossible. In the light of the record, we think it better to order its dissolution, and to provide that the corporate defendants be restrained for a period of five years from forming or joining any such trade association. . . .

Paragraph 52 deals with the problem of suppressed or unworked patents. Much is said in the opinion below, and in the briefs, about the practice of the appellants in applying for patents to "block off" or "fence in" competing inventions. In the cooperative effort of certain of the appellants to obtain dominance in the field of patented glassmaking machinery, many patents were applied for to prevent others from obtaining patents on improvements which might, to some extent, limit the return in the way of royalty on original or fundamental inventions. The decree should restrain agreements and combinations with this object. But it is another matter to restrain every defendant, for the indefinite future, from attempting to patent improvements of machines or processes previously patented and then owned by such defendant. This paragraph is, in our judgment, too broad. In effect it prohibits several of the corporate defendants from applying for patents covering their own inventions in the art of glassmaking. For reasons elsewhere elaborated it cannot be sustained. . . .

A patent owner is not in the position of a quasi-trustee for the public or under any obligation to see that the public acquires the free right to use the invention. He has no obligation either to use it or to grant its use to others. If he discloses the invention in his application so that it will come into the public domain at the end of the 17-year period of exclusive right he has fulfilled the only obligation imposed by the statute. . . .

[The judgment of the District Court was reversed in part and affirmed in part, and the decree was vacated and remanded. Justices Douglas, Murphy and Jackson took no part in the consideration or decision of the case. Justices Black and Rutledge each separately dissented in part.]

International Salt Co., Inc. v. *United States*

332 U.S. 392 (1947)

MR. JUSTICE JACKSON delivered the opinion of the Court.

The Government brought this civil action to enjoin the International Salt Company, appellant here, from carrying out provisions of the leases of its patented machines to the effect that lessees would use therein only

International's salt products. The restriction is alleged to violate Section 1 of the Sherman Act, and Section 3 of the Clayton Act. . . .

It was established . . . that the International Salt Company is engaged in interstate commerce in salt, of which it is the country's largest producer for industrial uses. It also owns patents on two machines for utilization of salt products. . . . The principal distribution of each of these machines is under leases which, among other things, require the lessees to purchase from appellant all unpatented salt and salt tablets consumed in the leased machines. . . .

. . . In 1944, appellant sold approximately 119,000 tons of salt, for about $500,000, for use in these machines.

The appellant's patents confer a limited monopoly of the invention they reward. From them appellant derives a right to restrain others from making, vending or using the patented machines. But the patents confer no right to restrain use of, or trade in, unpatented salt. By contracting to close this market for salt against competition, International has engaged in a restraint of trade for which its patents afford no immunity from the antitrust laws. . . .

Appellant contends, however, that summary judgment was unauthorized because it precluded trial of alleged issues of fact as to whether the restraint was unreasonable within the Sherman Act or substantially lessened competition or tended to create a monopoly in salt within the Clayton Act. We think the admitted facts left no genuine issue. Not only is price-fixing unreasonable, *per se*, *United States* v. *Socony-Vacuum Oil Co.* . . . ; *United States* v. *Trenton Potteries Co.* . . . , but also it is unreasonable, *per se*, to foreclose competitors from any substantial market. . . . The volume of business affected by these contracts cannot be said to be insignificant or insubstantial and the tendency of the arrangement to accomplishment of monopoly seems obvious. Under the law, agreements are forbidden which "tend to create a monopoly," and it is immaterial that the tendency is a creeping one rather than one that proceeds at full gallop; nor does the law await arrival at the goal before condemning the direction of the movement. . . .

Appellant also urges that since under the leases it remained under an obligation to repair and maintain the machines, it was reasonable to confine their use to its own salt because its high quality assured satisfactory functioning and low maintenance cost. . . .

Of course, a lessor may impose on a lessee reasonable restrictions designed in good faith to minimize maintenance burdens and to assure satisfactory operation. . . . But it is not pleaded, nor is it argued, that the machine is allergic to salt of equal quality produced by anyone except International. If others cannot produce salt equal to reasonable specifications for machine use, it is one thing; but it is admitted that, at times, at least, competitors do offer such a product. They are, however, shut out of the market by a provision that limits it, not in terms of quality, but in terms of a particular vendor. Rules for use of leased machinery must not be disguised restraints of free competition, though they may set reasonable standards which all suppliers must meet. . . .

Judgment affirmed.

[Mr. Justice Frankfurter, joined by Mr. Justice Reed and Mr. Justice Burton, dissented in part.]

Lear, Inc. v. Adkins

395 U.S. 653 (1969)

MR. JUSTICE HARLAN delivered the opinion of the Court.

In January of 1952, John Adkins, an inventor and mechanical engineer, was hired by Lear, Incorporated, for the purpose of solving a vexing problem the company had encountered in its efforts to develop a gyroscope which would meet the increasingly demanding requirements of the aviation industry. The gyroscope is an essential component of the navigational system in all aircraft, enabling the pilot to learn the direction and attitude of his airplane. With the development of the faster airplanes of the 1950's, more accurate gyroscopes were needed, and the gyro industry consequently was casting about for new techniques which would satisfy this need in an economical fashion. Shortly after Adkins was hired, he developed a method of construction at the company's California facilities which improved gyroscope accuracy at a low cost. Lear almost immediately incorporated Adkins' improvements into its production process to its substantial advantage.

The question that remains unsettled in this case, after eight years of litigation in the California courts, is whether Adkins will receive compensation for Lear's use of those improvements which the inventor has subsequently patented. At every stage of this lawsuit, Lear has sought to prove that, despite the grant of a patent by the Patent Office, none of Adkins' improvements were sufficiently novel to warrant the award of a monopoly under the standards delineated in the governing federal statutes. . . . In response, the inventor has argued that, since Lear has entered into a licensing agreement with Adkins, it was obliged to pay the agreed royalties regardless of the validity of the underlying patent.

The Supreme Court of California unanimously vindicated the inventor's position. While the court recognized that generally a manufacturer is free to challenge the validity of an inventor's patent, it held that "one of the oldest doctrines in the field of patent law establishes that so long as a licensee is operating under a license agreement he is estopped to deny the validity of his licensor's patent in a suit for royalties under the agreement. The theory underlying this doctrine is that a licensee should not be permitted to enjoy the benefit afforded by the agreement while simultaneously urging that the patent which forms the basis of the agreement is void." 67 Cal. 2d 882, 891, 435 P. 2d 321, 325–326 (1967).

Almost 20 years ago, in its last consideration of the doctrine, this Court also invoked an estoppel to deny a licensee the right to prove that his licensor was demanding royalties for the use of an idea which was in reality a part of the public domain. *Automatic Radio Manufacturing Co.* v. *Hazeltine Research, Inc.*, 339 U.S. 827, 836 (1950). We granted certiorari in the present case, 391 U.S. 912, to reconsider the validity of the *Hazeltine* rule in the light of our recent decisions emphasizing the strong federal policy favoring free competition in ideas which do not merit patent protection. . . .

I

. . . On February 4, 1954, Adkins filed an application with the Patent Office in an effort to gain federal protection for his [gyroscope] improvements. At about the same time, he entered into a lengthy period of negotiations with Lear in an effort to conclude a licensing agreement which would clearly establish the amount of royalties that would be paid.

These negotiations finally bore fruit on September 15, 1955, when the parties approved a complex 17-page contract which carefully delineated the conditions upon which Lear promised to pay royalties for Adkins' improvements. . . .

The progress of Adkins' effort to obtain a patent followed the typical pattern. In his initial application, the inventor made the ambitious claim that his entire method of constructing gyroscopes was sufficiently novel to merit protection. The Patent Office, however, rejected this initial claim, as well as two subsequent amendments, which progressively narrowed the scope of the invention sought to be protected. Finally, Adkins narrowed his claim drastically to assert only that the design of the apparatus used to achieve gyroscope accuracy was novel. In response, the Office issued its 1960 patent, granting a 17-year monopoly on this more modest claim.

During the long period in which Adkins was attempting to convince the Patent Office of the novelty of his ideas, however, Lear had become convinced that Adkins would never receive a patent on his invention and that it should not continue to pay substantial royalties on ideas which had not contributed substantially to the development of the art of gyroscopy. In 1957, after Adkins' patent application had been rejected twice, Lear announced that it had searched the Patent Office's files and had found a patent which it believed had fully anticipated Adkins' discovery. As a result, the company stated that it would no longer pay royalties on the large number of gyroscopes it was producing at its plant in Grand Rapids, Michigan (the Michigan gyros). Payments were continued on the smaller number of gyros produced at the company's California plant (the California gyros) for two more years until they too were terminated on April 8, 1959. . . .

II

Since the California Supreme Court's construction of the 1955 licensing agreement is solely a matter of state law, the only issue open to us is raised by the court's reliance upon the doctrine of estoppel to bar Lear from proving that Adkins' ideas were dedicated to the common welfare by federal law. . . .

. . . . .

III

The uncertain status of licensee estoppel in the case law is a product of judicial efforts to accommodate the competing demands of the common law of contracts and the federal law of patents. On the one hand, the law of contracts forbids a purchaser to repudiate his promises simply because he later becomes dissatisfied with the bargain he has made. On the other hand, federal law requires that all ideas in general circulation be dedicated to the common good unless they are protected by a valid patent. . . . When faced with this basic conflict in policy, both this Court and courts throughout the land have naturally sought to develop an intermediate position which somehow would remain responsive to the radically different concerns of the two different worlds of contract and patent. The result has been a failure. Rather than creative compromise, there has been a chaos of conflicting case law, proceeding on inconsistent premises. . . .

A

It will simplify matters greatly if we first consider the most typical situation in which patent licenses are negotiated. In contrast to the present case, most manufacturers obtain a license after a patent has issued. Since the Patent Office makes an inventor's ideas public when it issues its grant of a limited monopoly, a potential licensee has access to the inventor's ideas even if he does not enter into an agreement with the patent owner. Consequently, a manufacturer gains only two benefits if he chooses to enter a licensing agreement after the patent has issued. First, by accepting a license and paying royalties for a time, the licensee may have avoided the necessity of defending an expensive infringement action during the period when he may be least able to afford one. Second, the existence of an unchallenged patent may deter others from attempting to compete with the licensee.[1]

Under ordinary contract principles the mere fact that some benefit is received is enough to require the enforcement of the contract, regardless of the validity of the underlying patent. Nevertheless, if one tests this result by the standard of good-faith commercial dealing, it seems far from

---

[1] Of course, the value of this second benefit may depend upon whether the licensee has obtained exclusive or nonexclusive rights to the use of the patent. Even in the case of nonexclusive licenses, however, competition is limited to the extent that the royalty charged by the patentee serves as a barrier to entry.

satisfactory. For the simple contract approach entirely ignores the position of the licensor who is seeking to invoke the court's assistance on his behalf. Consider, for example, the equities of the licensor who has obtained his patent through a fraud on the Patent Office. It is difficult to perceive why good faith requires that courts should permit him to recover royalties despite his licensee's attempts to show that the patent is invalid. . . .

Even in the more typical cases, not involving conscious wrongdoing, the licensor's equities are far from compelling. A patent, in the last analysis, simply represents a legal conclusion reached by the Patent Office. Moreover, the legal conclusion is predicated on factors as to which reasonable men can differ widely. Yet the Patent Office is often obliged to reach its decision in an *ex parte* proceeding, without the aid of the arguments which could be advanced by parties interested in proving patent invalidity. Consequently, it does not seem to us to be unfair to require a patentee to defend the Patent Office's judgment when his licensee places the question in issue, especially since the licensor's case is buttressed by the presumption of validity which attaches to his patent. Thus, although licensee estoppel may be consistent with the letter of contractual docrine, we cannot say that it is compelled by the spirit of contract law, which seeks to balance the claims of promisor and promisee in accord with the requirements of good faith.

Surely the equities of the licensor do not weigh very heavily when they are balanced against the important public interest in permitting full and free competition in the use of ideas which are in reality a part of the public domain. Licensees may often be the only individuals with enough economic incentive to challenge the patentability of an inventor's discovery. If they are muzzled, the public may continually be required to pay tribute to would-be monopolists without need or justification. We think it plain that the technical requirements of contract doctrine must give way before the demands of the public interest in the typical situation involving the negotiation of a license after a patent has issued.

We are satisfied that *Automatic Radio Manufacturing Co.* v. *Hazeltine Research, Inc., supra*, itself the product of a clouded history, should no longer be regarded as sound law with respect to its "estoppel" holding, and that holding is now overruled. . . .

．　．　．　．　．

IV

．　．　．　．　．

The judgment of the Supreme Court of California is vacated and the case is remanded to that court for further proceedings not inconsistent with this opinion.

It is so ordered.

Index of Cases

INDEX OF CASES

Addyston Pipe & Steel Co. v. United States, 175 U.S. 211 (1899) . . . 64
Adkins; *see* Lear, Inc. v.
Allis-Chalmers Mfg. Co. v. White Consol. Industries, Inc., 414 F.2d 506
   (3d Cir. 1969), *cert. denied*, 396 U.S. 1009 (1970) 198
Aluminum Co. of America; *see* United States v.
American Can Co.; *see* United States v.
American Tobacco Co. v. United States, 328 U.S. 781 (1946) 104
Appalachian Coals, Inc. v. United States, 288 U.S. 344 (1933) 67
Arnold, Schwinn & Co.; *see* United States v.
Automobile Manufacturers Assn.; *see* United States v.

The Bendix Corp.; *see* Federal Trade Commission:
Borden Co.; *see* Federal Trade Commission v.
Brown; *see* Parker v.
Brown Shoe Co. v. United States, 370 U.S. 294 (1962) 128

Carvel Corp.; *see* Susser v.
Cement Institute; *see* Federal Trade Commission v.
Chas. Pfizer & Co.; *see* United States v.
Chicken Delight, Inc.; *see* Siegel v.
Consolidated Foods Corp.; *see* Federal Trade Commission v.
Container Corp. of America; *see* United States v.
Continental Baking Co.; *see* Utah Pie Co. v.
Continental Can Co.; *see* United States v.

E. I. duPont de Nemours & Co.; *see* United States v.
El Paso Natural Gas Co.; *see* United States v.

Federal Trade Commission: The Bendix Corp., Docket No. 8739 (1970),
   1970 Trade Cases ¶19, 288 181
Federal Trade Commission v. Borden Co., 383 U.S. 637 (1966), *reconsid-*
ered, 391 F.2d 175 (5th Cir. 1967) 260
Federal Trade Commission v. Cement Institute, 333 U.S. 683 (1948) . . 88
Federal Trade Commission v. Consolidated Foods Corp., 380 U.S. 592
   (1965) 193
Federal Trade Commission v. Morton Salt Co., 334 U.S. 37 (1948) . . . 247
Federal Trade Commission v. Procter & Gamble Co., 386 U.S. 568 (1967) 168
Federal Trade Commission v. Standard Oil Co. (of Indiana), 355 U.S. 396
   (1958) 256
Fortner Enterprises, Inc. v. United States Steel Corp., 394 U.S. 495 (1969) 306

General Electric Co.; *see* United States v.

Grinnell Corp.; *see* United States v.

Hartford Empire Co. v. United States, 323 U.S. 386 (1945) 408

International Salt Co. v. United States, 332 U.S. 392 (1947) 415
International Tel. & Tel. Corp.; *see* United States v.

Jerrold Electronics Corp.; *see* United States v.

Lear, Inc. v. Adkins, 395 U.S. 653 (1969) 417
Ling-Temco-Vought, Inc.; *see* United States v.
Loew's Inc.; *see* United States v.

Magrane-Houston Co.; *see* Standard Fashion Co. v.
Morton Salt Co.; *see* Federal Trade Commission v.

Nashville Coal Co.; *see* Tampa Electric Co. v.
New York Stock Exchange; *see* Thill Securities Corp. v.
Northern Pacific Ry. v. United States, 356 U.S. 1 (1958) 282

Paramount Film Distributing Corp.; *see* Theatre Enterprises, Inc. v.
Parker v. Brown, 338 U.S. 341 (1943) 369
Penn-Olin Chemical Co.; *see* United States v.
Philadelphia Nat'l Bank; *see* United States v.
Procter & Gamble Co.; *see* Federal Trade Commission v.

Seaboard Air Line R.R. v. United States, 382 U.S. 154 (1965) (*per curiam*)   395
Siegel v. Chicken Delight, Inc., 311 F. Supp. 847 (N.D. Cal. 1970) . . . 363
Socony-Vacuum Oil Co.; *see* United States v.
Standard Fashion Co. v. Magrane-Houston Co., 258 U.S. 346 (1922) . . 318
Standard Oil Co. of California (and Standard Stations, Inc.) v. United
States, 337 U.S. 293 (1949) 320
Standard Oil Co. (of Indiana) v. Federal Trade Commission, 340 U.S. 231
(1951) 252
Standard Oil Co. (of Indiana); *see* Federal Trade Commission v.
Standard Oil Co. of New Jersey v. United States, 221 U.S. 1 (1911) . .   9
Susser v. Carvel Corp., 332 F.2d 505 (2d Cir. 1964), *cert. granted*, 379 U.S.
885 (1964), *cert. dismissed as improvidently granted*, 381 U.S. 125 (1965)   332

Tag Manufacturers Institute v. Federal Trade Commission, 174 F.2d 452
(1st Cir. 1949) 96
Tampa Electric Co. v. Nashville Coal Co., 365 U.S. 320 (1961) 325
Terminal Railroad Association of St. Louis; *see* United States v.
Thatcher Manufacturing Company v. Federal Trade Commission, 272 U.S.
554 (1926) 127
Theatre Enterprises, Inc. v. Paramount Film Distributing Corp., 346 U.S.
537 (1954) 113
Thill Securities Corp. v. New York Stock Exchange, 433 F.2d 264 (7th Cir.
1970), *cert. denied*, 401 U.S. 994 (1971) 396

Trenton Potteries Co.; *see* United States v.
Triangle Conduit & Cable Co. v. Federal Trade Commission, 168 F.2d 175
(7th Cir. 1948), *aff'd sub nom.*, Clayton Mark & Co. v. FTC, 336 U.S. 956
(1949)   111
Tripoli Co. Inc. v. Wella Corp., 425 F.2d 932 (3d Cir. 1970), *cert. denied*,
400 U.S. 831 (1970) 359

United Shoe Machinery Corp.; *see* United States v.
United States v. Aluminum Co. of America, 148 F.2d 416 (2d Cir. 1945) .   25
United States v. American Can Co., 87 F. Supp. 18 (N.D. Cal. 1949) . . . 276
United States v. Arnold, Schwinn & Co., 388 U.S. 365 (1967) 349
United States v. Automobile Manufacturers Assn., 307 F. Supp. 617, (C.D.
Cal. 1969), 1969 Trade Cases ¶72,907, *appeals dismissed and aff'd*, 397
U.S. 248 (1970) 100
United States v. Chas. Pfizer & Co., 426 F.2d 32 (2d Cir. 1970) 115
United States v. Container Corp. of America, 393 U.S. 333 (1969) . . . 78
United States v. Continental Can Co., 378 U.S. 441 (1964) 143
United States v. E. I. duPont de Nemours & Co., 351 U.S. 377 (1956) . . 41
United States v. El Paso Natural Gas Co., 376 U.S. 651 (1964) 390
United States v. General Electric Co., 272 U.S. 476 (1926) 406
United States v. General Motors Corp., 384 U.S. 127 (1966) 343
United States v. Grinnell Corporation, 384 U.S. 563 (1966) 54
United States v. International Tel. & Tel. Corp., 324 F. Supp. 19 (D. Conn.
1970) 209
United States v. Jerrold Electronics Corp., 187 F. Supp. 545 (E.D. Pa.
1960), *aff'd per curiam*, 365 U.S. 567 (1961) 286
United States v. Ling-Temco-Vought, Inc., 1970 Trade Cases ¶73,105
(W.D. Pa. 1970) 223
United States v. Loew's, Inc., 371 U.S. 38 (1962) 298
United States, Northern Pacific Ry. v., 356 U.S. 1 (1958) 282
United States v. Penn Olin Chemical Co., 378 U.S. 158 (1964) 232
United States v. Philadelphia National Bank, 374 U.S. 321 (1963) . . . 373
United States v. Socony-Vacuum Oil Co., 310 U.S. 150 (1940) 72
United States v. Terminal Railroad Association of St. Louis, 224 U.S. 383
(1912) 226
United States v. Trenton Potteries, 273 U.S. 392 (1927) 65
United States v. United Shoe Machinery Corp., 110 F. Supp. 295 (D. Mass.
1953), *aff'd*, 347 U.S. 521 (1954) 33
United States v. United States Steel Corp., 251 U.S. 417 (1920) 16
United States v. Von's Grocery Co., 384 U.S. 270 (1966) 157
United States Steel Corp.; *see* Fortner Enterprises, Inc. v.
United States Steel Corp.; *see* United States v.
Utah Pie Co. v. Continental Baking Co., 386 U.S. 685 (1967) 267

Von's Grocery Co.; *see* United States v.

Wella Corporation; *see* Tripoli Co., Inc. v.
White Consol. Industries, Inc.; *see* Allis-Chalmers Mfg. Co. v.